Contents

AFRICAN WRITERS

AFRICAN WRITERS

C. BRIAN COX

Editor

VOLUME II

CHARLES SCRIBNER'S SONS
Macmillan Library Reference USA
Simon & Schuster Macmillan
NEW YORK

Simon & Schuster Prentice Hall International
LONDON MEXICO CITY NEW DELHI SINGAPORE SYDNEY TORONTO

Charles Scribner's Sons
An Imprint of Simon & Schuster Macmillan
1633 Broadway
New York, NY 10019

LIBRARY OF CONGRESS CATALOGING-IN-PUBLICATION DATA

African writers / C. Brian Cox, editor.
p. cm.
Includes bibliographical references and index.
ISBN 0-684-19651-4 (set : alk. paper). — ISBN 0-684-19771-5 (v. 1: alk. paper). — ISBN 0-684-19772-3 (v. 2 : alk. paper)
1. African literature—Bio-bibliography—Dictionaries.
2. Authors, African—Biography—Dictionaries. 3. African literature—Dictionaries.
PL8010.A453 1997
896—dc20
[B] 96-16128
CIP

1 3 5 7 9 11 13 15 17 19 20 18 16 14 12 10 8 6 4 2

PRINTED IN THE UNITED STATES OF AMERICA

The paper used in this publication meets the minimum requirements
of the American National Standard for Information Sciences—
Permanence of Paper for Printed Library Materials, ANSI Z39.48–1984.

Najīb Maḥfūẓ

1911–

ROGER ALLEN

THE EGYPTIAN NOVELIST Najīb Maḥfūẓ (Naguib Mahfouz) was awarded the Nobel Prize in literature in 1988. With that gesture the Nobel committee not only recognized the life and work of a remarkable Egyptian writer but also drew the attention of western readers to Arabic fiction, with which they had for the most part been unfamiliar and unconcerned (with the possible exceptions of *The Arabian Nights* and the sentimental fiction of Jubrān Khalīl Jubrān). Maḥfūẓ's career coincides with and indeed represents the complete integration of the novel genre into contemporary Arabic cultural life. The reception of his works by a larger international audience after the award of the Nobel Prize has provided yet another interesting example of the modes of reception in the west for exemplars of nonwestern literary traditions.

THE MODERN ARABIC NOVEL

The earliest examples of the novel in modern Arabic literature date back to the middle of the nineteenth century. They can thus be placed within the context of a process of change known in Arabic as *al-nahḍah* (the revival). In the earliest stages in the development of the novel genre, some writers chose to revive earlier narrative types, especially the *maqāmah*, a short, picaresque tale that made use of all the elaborations of traditional Arabic prose style while sardonically commenting on the foibles of contemporary society and its mores. Muḥammad al-Muwayliḥī (1858–1930), in particular, used this "classical" narrative type to criticize the state of Egyptian society under British occupation at the end of the nineteenth century and thus presents one precedent for the emergence of a novelistic tradition.

However, far more popular in both content and style were romantic, philosophical, and historical narratives imported into the Arabic-speaking region, beginning in the mid nineteenth century. With the rapid expansion of the press in Egypt—still the favored medium for initial publication of works of fiction—a number of authors (many of them publishers of newspapers) published in serial form historical and romantic adventure novels that soon developed a small but eager reading public for fiction. In 1911, the year of Maḥfūẓ's birth, an Egyptian intellectual studying in France, Muḥammad Ḥusayn Haykal, was writing *Zaynab*, a novel about rural life in Egypt and the oppressive impact on young people of traditional attitudes toward marriage.

This period of early developments in fiction coincided with Maḥfūẓ's youth and adolescence. In reminiscing about his childhood reading preferences, he has cited the works of many important literary pioneers: the highly moralistic *Al-Naẓarāt* (Essays) of Muṣṭafā Luṭfī al-Manfalūṭī (1876–1924), whose style was regarded as a model of a new quest for clarity; *Al-Ayyām* by Ṭāhā Ḥusayn (1889–1973), a remarkable third-person autobiographical narrative; and the writings of Ibrāhīm al-Māzinī (1890–1949), Tawfīq al-Ḥakīm (1898?–1987), Maḥmūd Ṭāhir Lāshīn (1894–1954), and Maḥmūd Taymūr (1894–1973), each of whom contributed to the development of different facets of the novel genre during the 1930s, the period that marked the beginnings of Maḥfūẓ's career as a writer.

THE CAREER OF AN EGYPTIAN NOVELIST AND CIVIL SERVANT

Maḥfūẓ was born in al-Jamāliyyah, a quarter in the old part of Cairo, on 10 December 1911, although his birth was not registered until the following day, leading many, including himself, to cite 11 December as his date of birth. He was the youngest child in the family by a number of years; thus, despite the presence of older brothers and sisters, he essentially grew up in his parents' house as an only child.

When Maḥfūẓ was six years old, his father, a civil servant, moved the family to the more prosperous suburb of al-ʿAbbāsiyyah. His childhood was filled with contentment; references to youthful escapades, teenage friends, and ephemeral love affairs in such fictional works as *Al-Marāyā* (1972; *Mirrors*) and *Qushtumur* (1988; the title refers to the name of a cafe) seem more than a little autobiographical in their affectionately close attention to detail. Maḥfūẓ has commented on the extent to which the intellectual and emotional crises of Kamāl, the protagonist in *Qaṣr al-Shawq* (1957; *Palace of Desire*), the second book of his Cairo trilogy, reflect his own at a similar age. He began to read extensively, adding translated adventure novels and the incipient fiction of the early generation of modern Arab litterateurs to the required "classical" readings that were part of the school curriculum.

Maḥfūẓ was only eight years old during the 1919 revolution in Egypt, but the event affected him greatly. It figures prominently in the first book of the trilogy, *Bayn al-Qaṣrayn* (1956; *Palace Walk*), and the leader of the revolution, Saʿd Zaghlūl, is a political figure for whom Maḥfūẓ had enormous respect. The reverence for "the leader of the nation" contained in ʿĀmir Wajdī's musings in *Mīrāmār* (1967; *Miramar*) reflects the author's own political affections. However, while Maḥfūẓ has not been shy about expressing his opinions on political matters, in particular since accepting an invitation in the early 1970s to write a weekly column for the Cairo newspaper *Al-Ahrām*, he has generally preferred to concentrate on what might be termed "intellectual politics." Even as a teenager, he admired the courageous stand of Ṭāhā Ḥusayn, one of the giants of twentieth-century Arab thought, who used his book *Fī al-shiʿr al-jāhilī* (1926; On pre-Islamic poetry) not only to question the authenticity of the earliest corpus of Arabic literary creativity but also to suggest a more "scientific" approach to the study of all texts, including the Qurʾān. In the ensuing fracas Ṭāhā Ḥusayn was taken to court and deprived of his university post, but not before his gesture had made the significance of new modes of scholarly analysis clear to a younger generation of Egyptian students.

After secondary school Maḥfūẓ went to Cairo University to study philosophy. He seems to have done extremely well, since he was invited to continue toward a graduate degree after his graduation in 1934, and he began work on a master's thesis. However, he had begun writing articles on philosophical topics soon after his matriculation at the university in 1930. In view of his later intellectual concerns, the titles of these essays are instructive: "Death and Rebirth of Beliefs" (published in *Al-Majallah al-jadīdah*, October 1930); "Plato and His Philosophy" (*Al-Maʿrifah*, November 1931); "The Meaning of Philosophy" (*Al-Jihād*, August 1934); and "Society and Human Development" (*Al-Majallah al-jadīdah*, November 1934). But philosophy was not Maḥfūẓ's only concern during his undergraduate days. In a further reflection of his interest in the intellectual issues of the time—in this case the so-called Pharaonism movement, which sought to link Egypt's quest for independence with the glories of its ancient history—Maḥfūẓ undertook an Arabic translation of a popular English monograph, *Ancient Egypt*, by James Baikie. These varied interests were fostered by Salāmah Mūsā, the editor of *Al-Majallah al-jadīdah* (The new review) and a renowned Copt intellectual with strong socialist leanings, who encouraged the young Maḥfūẓ to publish not only his philosophical writings but also his initial attempts at fiction.

During the 1930s Maḥfūẓ also published a number of short stories in journals. Some were inspired by the theme of ancient Egypt, like "Yaqzat al-mūmiyāʾ" (The mummy awakes); others responded to current events, such as "Badhlat al-asīr" (The prisoner of war's uniform), which was inspired by the fighting in Abyssinia in 1936; still others had a more philosophical bent, such as "Hams al-junūn" (The whisper of madness). This last story provided the title for a collection of stories that has generally been regarded as Maḥfūẓ's first published book of fiction, even though its exact date of publication is problematic. During this decade, Maḥfūẓ's interest in writing novels increased considerably, and he began systematically to read as much western fiction as possible, including most of the major writers in the Anglo-American, French, Russian, and Scandinavian traditions. His particular favorites included Fyodor Dostoyevsky, Thomas Mann, Franz Kafka, and Albert Camus.

For a number of reasons 1939 proved to be a significant year for Maḥfūẓ. He began his civil-service career, which lasted until his retirement in 1971. His first novel, *ʿAbath al-aqdār* (1939; Mockery of the fates), which is set in ancient Egypt, was published. Most important, the onset of World War II gradually drew Egypt into the conflict that would transform the map of the Middle East and alter forever previous patterns of world hegemony. Indeed, political and societal turmoil in Egypt was great enough that, after the publication of two more novels set in ancient Egypt, Maḥfūẓ abandoned a project to write a series of such works and turned his attention to the portrayal of contemporary Egyptian society. Through a series of novels set in the older quarters of Cairo, he set the standard by which the social-realist novel in Arabic would be judged and, through a continuous process of honing and developing his craft as a writer of fiction, laid the technical groundwork for the emergence of a vigorous tradition of the novel during the postrevolutionary decades of the 1950s and 1960s. The culmination of this series of novels was al-Thulāthiyya (Trilogy), a massive undertaking of both research and writing that was completed just before the 1952 Egyptian revolution, one of the major transforming events in modern Middle Eastern history.

Maḥfūẓ's efforts to publish the trilogy coincided with the initial years of the Egyptian revolution, a period of political uncertainty, enormous change, and huge expectations. The emergence of ʿAbd al-Nāṣir (Nasser) as a national leader occurred at the same time as the establishment of a new type of global politics, particularly the beginning of the cold war between the Soviet Union and the United States. Through negotiations over the building of the Aswan Dam and the supply of arms from Czechoslovakia, ʿAbd al-Nāṣir was among the first nonwestern political leaders to exploit the situation. The failure of the Tripartite Invasion of the Suez Canal in 1956 after the nationalization of the canal served to confirm ʿAbd al-Nāṣir's status as an Arab leader of major stature. At this time (1956–1957), Maḥfūẓ, who had been concentrating on writing scenarios for films as part of his position in the Ministry of Culture, finally saw his trilogy published.

The Arab world in general and Egyptians in particular, riding the crest of a wave of independence and exploring new local and international political roles, found their struggles for political rights during previous decades, their confrontations with the cultural and military might of the west, and their aspirations for a better future reflected in the pages of the trilogy. The three volumes were filled with authentic characters from all walks of life, detailed descriptions of Cairene homes, streets, stores, and markets, and graphic accounts of intellectual debates, love affairs, and political demonstrations. Maḥfūẓ was awarded the State Encouragement Prize for Literature in 1957, and his work was warmly received throughout the Arab world.

In the final volume of the trilogy, *Al-Sukkariyyah* (1957; *Sugar Street*), the two grandsons of the family are in prison: one for being a member of the Communist Party, the other for belonging to the Muslim Brotherhood. Such divisions in Egyptian society, temporarily set aside during the initial euphoria over the success of the revolution and the expulsion of the royal family, soon resurfaced. Large numbers of Communist Party and Muslim Brotherhood members were jailed as the leaders of the revolution set out to establish and implement their political priorities and goals and, with help from the Soviet Union, construct the agencies and networks needed to maintain them. As many creative writers were to discover, this political structure included an increasingly elaborate censorship and surveillance system.

During this period of uncertainty, when the trilogy was being received with such acclaim, Maḥfūẓ's next work of fiction returned to a topic that had long been the focus of his intellectual interests: the confrontation of religion and science in the modern world. *Awlād ḥāratinā* (1967; *Children of the Alley* or *Children of Gebelawi*), an allegorical work that combines an analysis of this theme with the role of violence in societal transformation, was first published in the newspaper *Al-Ahrām* in 1959. It was a perplexing work for uncertain political times: those readers in search of the detailed realism of Maḥfūẓ's previous novels were disappointed by its nonspecificity of time and place; the religious authorities who detected allegorical representations of God and Islamic prophets were outraged. Beyond its unique context and method, *Children of the Alley* was a transitional work that led into a decade of immense productivity for Maḥfūẓ.

The 1960s were a troubled period for Egypt, for its young revolution, and for people like Maḥfūẓ who supported the basic principles and goals of the revolution while being deeply disturbed by the methods adopted to maintain and develop them. In a series of increasingly symbolic and critical novels that begins with *Al-Liṣṣ wa-al-kilāb* (1961; *The Thief and the Dogs*), Maḥfūẓ charts the developing unease of the middle class, particularly the intellectuals, with the course of the revolution. Official disapproval of *Thartharah fawq al-Nīl* (1966; *Adrift on the Nile*) was so pronounced that Maḥfūẓ narrowly avoided imprisonment, a fate met by many of his fellow writers during these years. The novel that followed it, *Miramar*, provided a yet more explicit condemnation of the course of Egyptian history in the 1950s and 1960s.

The June 1967 war between Egypt and Israel was a brutal confirmation of what Maḥfūẓ and other writers had been suggesting for some time: in the words of the Egyptian critic Faruq ʿAbd al-Qādir, it was "a defeat of systems, organizations, structures, ideas, and leaders." This event marks a watershed in modern Arab history and consequently in Maḥfūẓ's writing career. His immediate response to the disaster was a series of cryptic, highly symbolic, and often cyclical stories; they are now included in the collections *Taḥta al-miẓallah* (1967; Under the shelter), *Ḥikāyah bi-lā bidāyah wa-lā-nihāyah* (1971; Story with no beginning or end), and *Shahr al-ʿasal* (1971; Honeymoon). These stories participated in the process of retrospection and self-criticism that followed *al-naksah* (the setback), as the 1967 war was termed. With ʿAbd al-Nāṣir's death in 1970 and Anwar al-Sādāt's ascendancy to the presidency, recrimination was added to the list of reactive activities, as protégés of the former president tried to outdo each other in their exposés of the practices and foibles of the previous regime.

Maḥfūẓ retired from the civil service in 1971. To supplement his pension and his relatively small income from the publication of his fiction, he accepted a position as weekly columnist for *Al-Ahrām*, joining Tawfīq al-Ḥakīm, the illustrious playwright, and Yūsuf Idrīs (1927–1991), one of the Arab world's finest short-story writers, in contributing to the newspaper.

At this time, he established an almost unbreakable daily routine, one that journalists had to learn to deal with when he won the Nobel Prize in 1988. It began with an early morning walk to his favorite café, the Ali Baba on Tahrir Square in central Cairo, where he would peruse the day's newspapers. After a walk back to his apartment in Aguza, he would eat lunch and take a nap before writing for two or three hours. On Thursday and Friday evenings, friends and admirers would gather at a selected café; one evening would be for his more personal acquaintances—the so-called *ḥarāfīsh,* or riffraff—the other a more public event. Summer months would always be spent in his beloved Alexandria, where he maintained a similar routine.

Links between literature and the political process have always been close within the Arab world, and no more so than in the postrevolutionary period, when most regimes considered the country's writers of literature to be co-opted to the cause of change and growth, regardless of the methods used and the success of the resulting social situation. In most countries in the region, the strictest modes of censorship constituted the norm, and writers who chose to express their opposition to official governmental policies were imprisoned, exiled, or silenced through various modes. While Maḥfūẓ faced this situation during much of his career, his wide reputation as a novelist rendered him somewhat immune to the worst consequences of a frank expression of opinion.

In discussing conditions during the 1960s—certainly the grimmest period in modern Egyptian history—Maḥfūẓ and his colleagues acknowledge the practical uses of symbolism as an obscurantist device alongside its more obvious aesthetic functions, but his later works are more blunt and unequivocal in their critical focus on societal ills. The changes that took place in Egyptian society during the Sādāt presidency provided much material for him, and for that reason his output during the period tended to reflect the interests and concerns of a local, Egyptian reading public rather than that of the Arab world as a whole. The policy of "opening up" the Egyptian economy, *infitāh*—which allowed the Egyptian entrepreneurial class to amass considerable wealth while food became more expensive, the urban atmosphere more polluted, Cairo hopelessly overcrowded, and housing unaffordable for the younger generation—distressed Maḥfūẓ. Such crushing social problems became regular topics of his novels. But in spite of such expressed opposition to Sādāt's domestic policies, Maḥfūẓ did not join the chorus of intellectuals who condemned Sādāt's decision to visit Jerusalem and thereafter sign the Camp David peace accords in 1979. This silence earned Maḥfūẓ the opprobrium of many of his fellow writers in Egypt and, more generally, throughout the Arab world, an attitude reflected in the mixed reception that greeted the announcement of the Nobel Prize in 1988.

Maḥfūẓ's Nobel Prize came as a reward to an Arab author for devoting much of his career to the establishment of the novel as a genre that reflects and changes contemporary Arab societies. As is often the case, particularly for nonwestern writers, it was awarded at the close of a distinguished career. Thereafter, Maḥfūẓ found his normal routine and the intense privacy he enjoyed with his wife and two daughters severely disrupted by an overwhelming number of television specials and interviews. His eyesight was never particularly good, and his hearing had also begun to deteriorate. Following surgery in London for a severe heart condition (one of his extremely rare excursions outside Egypt), he cut back on his activities, though he published *Qushtumur* in 1988, a wistful retrospective about growing up in al-ʿAbbāsiyyah.

In October 1994 the tranquil routines of Maḥfūẓ's latter days were savagely interrupted when, on the anniversary of the announcement of the Nobel Prize in 1988, he became the first target of what one of the popular Islamic movements in Egypt intended to be a campaign of kidnappings. The attempt failed, but in the process Maḥfūẓ was stabbed in the neck. Fortunately, his apartment lay directly opposite the police hospital, where he immediately underwent the prolonged operation that saved his life. Since that time, his life has been radically transformed, but his indomitable spirit shows itself in his determination to continue expressing himself even if that now involves dictation to others.

FICTION IN THE PREREVOLUTIONARY PERIOD

Given the close connection between the rise of national consciousness among the Arab peoples and the development of the novel and the societal role of the novelist, on the one hand, and Maḥfūẓ's own intense concern with the larger philosophical issues confronting modern humanity, on the other, it is hardly surprising that his career as a novelist can be conveniently divided into phases that reflect the course of modern Egyptian history. The major divide in both is represented by the determining events of the Egyptian revolution of 1952. Even within those two historical periods, it is possible to further divide his output. In the prerevolutionary epoch—essentially, between the two world wars—there are the novels of the Pharaonism period and then the series of novels about the Cairene quarters culminating in the trilogy. In the postrevolutionary era, there are the novels of the 1960s and—after the debacle of the June 1967 war—those of the Sādāt and Husni Mubārak years, the 1970s and 1980s.

Pharaonic Novels

The three historical novels set in ancient Egypt, *ʿAbath al-aqdār* (1939), *Rādūbīs* (1943), and *Kifāḥ Tība* (1944; Struggle at Thebes), are generally regarded by critics as the initial novelistic efforts of a young writer experimenting with the technical aspects of a complex fictional genre while exploiting his interest in his country's earliest history against the backdrop of its continuing search for identity and political independence. Some attempts have been made to link the story of *Rādūbīs*, which is about a young pharaoh who becomes enamored of a glamorous courtesan, with the antics of the young King Fārūq (Farouk), but, from a long-term perspective, these novels can be seen as addressing the intellectual concerns of the 1930s.

Cairene Novels

With the beginning of World War II, the fragile institutions of liberal democracy that had been created in Egypt after World War I and the almost continuous confrontations with British authority were bound to be the sources of tension. Foreign troops were prominently visible throughout the country, and political corruption was rampant. In February 1942, any pretense to the subtleties of diplomacy on the part of the British authorities was thrust aside: the British ambassador utterly humiliated the king of Egypt by moving tanks to positions outside the royal palace and demanding the installation of a pro-British Wafdist government. Such a context, with all its social, political, and cultural ramifications, would provide rich material for any novelist, and Maḥfūẓ felt compelled to take the challenge. In a series of works published in the late 1940s and early 1950s he portrayed the lives of Egyptians in the older quarters of Cairo as they tried to eke out a living under such conditions. In so doing, he created a yardstick for Arabic social-realist fiction that was to serve Arab writers well in the post-revolutionary era of the 1950s and beyond.

In both *Khān al-Khalīlī* (1945; the title is a place-name), probably the first in the series, and *Al-Qāhirah al-jadīdah* (1946; Modern Cairo), Maḥfūẓ establishes his model. The settings are in these older parts of Cairo, although work and quests for a better life and entertainment take certain characters to more modern districts. For the protagonists, life is a continual struggle, and in attempts to improve their lots they constantly confront the privilege and corruption of the aristocracy and the overriding authority of the British occupying forces. There seems no escape from poverty and social oppression, particularly in the most famous novel in the series, *Zuqāq al-Midaqq* (1947; *Midaq Alley*). The novel lovingly details a microcosm of Egyptian society. Here Maḥfūẓ relishes his developing skill at establishing utterly authentic spatial backgrounds and peopling them with memorable characters. Some of these characters could well be taken from medieval Arabic prose narratives, such as Zayṭah, who specializes in making beggars appear misshapen (the traditional craft known as *musha*ʿʿ*ib*). The relationships among these characters are masterfully handled, particularly in the ever-so-polite but utterly duplicitous encounters between the mother of the beautiful Ḥamīdah and Mrs. ʿAfīfī, the marriage arranger. As the novel comes to an end, Ḥamīdah has been seduced into becoming a prostitute for British soldiers, and her erstwhile beloved, ʿAbbās the barber, who works at a British barracks, is crushed to death in a bar as he confronts her with the consequences of her decision. The message for the Egyptian readership during the postwar political turmoil of the late 1940s could not have been clearer.

A similar fate befalls Nafīsah, the daughter of the family that is the principal focus of *Bidāyah wa-nihāyah* (1949; *The Beginning and the End*). While the eldest son, Ḥasan, earns money as a drug dealer and thug, his two younger brothers aspire to a better life, one as an army officer, the other as a school teacher. It is Ḥasanayn, the military cadet, who is summoned to the police station to pick up his sister, who has been arrested for prostitution, and he forces her to jump to her death in the Nile. Contemplating the horror of what he has done, he follows her.

Cairo Trilogy

Maḥfūẓ has stated that the research and writing involved in producing his monumental fifteen-hundred-page trilogy. *Bayn al-Qaṣrayn* (1956; *Palace Walk*), *Qaṣr al-Shawq* (1957; *Palace of Desire*), and *Al-Sukkariyyah* (1957; *Sugar Street*)—all three titles referring to streets and districts in old Cairo and thus best left untranslated—took five years to complete before the revolution of 1952. Picking up on and greatly elaborating the family-saga framework of *The Beginning and the End*, the trilogy expands the temporal dimension of the previous novels to incorporate the entire interwar period in Egyptian history (1917–1944) and to trace larger-scale events through the careers, relationships, and crises of the ʿAbd al-Jawwād family. Discussing the genre of the novel, Georg Lukacs wrote in *The Theory of the Novel* (1920), "We might almost say that the entire inner action of the novel is nothing but a struggle against the power of time" (1971 trans., p. 122); the remark certainly applies to Maḥfūẓ's portrait of Egypt and one of its families.

Each of the three novels is set in a different quarter of the city. The first volume, *Bayn al-Qaṣrayn*, begins shortly before the end of World War I. The members of the family are introduced and the intricate web of relationships carefully revealed. The father emerges as a complex and somewhat tyrannical figure, willing to confine his wife, Amīnah, to the home while he philanders with a woman of low virtue. One of the crises in the first volume occurs when, at her son's suggestion, Amīnah disobeys her husband's strict injunction and visits a mosque. When she is involved in a traffic accident and her husband discovers what she has done, he throws her out of the house. It requires the passage of time and the intercession of children and friends to persuade the husband to allow her back into the family home. At the conclusion of the first volume, the eldest son of the family is killed in the 1919 rebellion.

In the second volume, *Qaṣr al-Shawq*, the second son, Kamāl, goes to a teachers college, where he is introduced to Darwinism and modern scientific thought. He clashes bitterly with his father over questions of traditional beliefs and modern values. By the third volume, *Al-Sukkariyyah*, secular university education is available to members of the younger generation and men and women mingle freely within that context.

In assessing the significance of the trilogy and of all of Maḥfūẓ's social-realist novels before the revolution, we need to consider two temporal frameworks: the period immediately following their publication and 1988, when Maḥfūẓ won the Nobel Prize. In the heady days immediately preceding the establishment of the United Arab Republic between Egypt and Syria in 1958, the publication of this huge work captured the historical moment. Egyptians read, probably for the first time in a work of Arabic fiction, a minutely detailed reflection of their recent political and social life, accurate not only in its portrayal of place and time but also in its representation of trends and attitudes through the members and generations of the ʿAbd al-Jawwād family. In these three novels Maḥfūẓ can be seen as following the lead of European novelists, giving the revolution a societal agenda by considerably detailing the miseries of immediate past history. Furthermore, given that the 1950s were to witness revolutions and political and social change in other Arab countries as well, it is hardly surprising that the trilogy was read throughout the Arab world and soon acknowledged as a masterpiece of Arabic fiction. Not only were Maḥfūẓ's previous writings now studied with increased scrutiny, but great works were expected of him.

The second historical moment is the awarding of the Nobel Prize in 1988. In the chronology of Maḥfūẓ's career, the publication of the trilogy marks the midpoint for a writer who was constantly concerned with the development of novelistic technique and the adaptability of the genre as a vehicle and expression of the process of change. While the Nobel committee and, after 1988, readers of the French and English translations of the trilogy have been fascinated by Maḥfūẓ's skill in crafting an elaborate portrait of a family and society in a very different cultural tradition, the trilogy, from a technical perspective, is a transitional work. In other words, it is only one stage, albeit a major one, in a progression of novels that have helped to establish a contemporary Arabic genre of the novel, in all its necessary variety. By definition, this is a continuing process.

In a real sense the burden of popularity thrust on this work in particular after the awarding of the Nobel Prize has been unfortunate. To use the trilogy as a basis for terming Maḥfūẓ, as some writers have done, "the Dickens/Balzac of Cairo" is to emphasize the temporal disjuncture between the era of those two great European novelists (nineteenth century) and that of Maḥfūẓ. Furthermore—and in the larger context of the Arabic novel, more significant—to judge Maḥfūẓ solely by the trilogy does not take into account the evolution of his career from the date of publication of the three novels to the awarding of the Nobel Prize. It is therefore important for western readers of his translated novels to be aware that, while the trilogy fulfills a colossally important historical role in the development of modern Arabic fiction, Maḥfūẓ himself is among those who would consider some of his later works as more developed and successful exercises in fiction.

FICTION IN THE POSTREVOLUTIONARY PERIOD

Children of the Alley

A two-year gap separates the publication of the final volume of the trilogy, *Al-Sukkariyyah*, and the appearance of Maḥfūẓ's next work of fiction, *The Children of the Alley*, in the newspaper *Al-Ahrām* in 1959. The serialized novel was an instant source of controversy, and it was banned from further publication (a book version of the text was published in Beirut in 1967). This work also returned to haunt its author in 1988. During the furor over Salman Rushdie's novel *The Satanic Verses* (1988), Maḥfūẓ, a newly prominent Muslim writer of fiction, defended Rushdie's rights as an author. Twenty-nine years after its publication in book form, *Children of the Alley* was reinvoked as a sign of Maḥfūẓ's own disrespect for Islam. Shaykh ʿUmar ʿAbd al-Raḥmān, a well-known popular Islamic preacher, issued a death sentence against Maḥfūẓ, who felt constrained to term the work his "illegitimate child."

The source of this controversy is a heavily allegorial work tracing humanity's religious heritage against the background of frequent political upheaval and violence. The novel carries even further the experiments in technique that Maḥfūẓ was attempting while composing the trilogy. Whereas in previous novels the action is set in particular parts of the city that are depicted in great detail, the title *Awlād ḥāratinā*, which translates literally as "Children of Our Quarter" or "Children of Our Alley," presents the reader with the entity that has a heavy symbolic resonance in a number of subsequent works, the "quarter" or "alley." The title of the first English translation, *Children of Gebelawi*, thus misses the symbolic function of the "quarter" to which Maḥfūẓ attaches so much importance in this and other works. Outside the quarter of this novel is a large house, where a powerfully symbolic figure named Jabalawi (Gebelawi in Egyptian dialectal pronunciation) presides.

The work is divided into five sections, each named after a "leader," evoking key figures in the history of the great monotheistic religions. For example, the first, named Adham, is not far removed from Adam, and the second, named Jabal ("mountain"), is a reference to Moses. The last leader is named ʿArafah (from the verb meaning "to know" and therefore *scientia*); it is he who kills Jabalawi, and at the conclusion of the novel the reader is left to assume that science has supplanted religion in the minds of the residents of the quarter. As ʿArafah himself, echoing Friedrich Nietzsche, succinctly puts it: "God be praised, Jabalawi is dead!" While *The Children of the Alley* is a major step forward in Maḥfūẓ's search for vehicles through which to express his intellectual concerns and one that has been a continuing cause célèbre in terms of its topic and its reception at the hands of the religious establishment, it is only a limited success as a work of fiction, due in no small part to the inconsistent allegorical layering of the story.

Novels of the 1960s

Between 1961 and 1967 Maḥfūẓ published six novels, as well as two collections of short stories. That this astonishing outpouring of activity coincided with some of the darkest years in modern Egyptian history, characterized by an oppressive level of governmental control over society and a great deal of disillusion among the intellectual community after the heady days of the late 1950s, is no accident. Maḥfūẓ's reading of such authors as Kafka and Camus, coupled with his increased awareness of the inefficiency of the techniques of naturalism, led him to abandon the mode of the externalized omniscient narrator painting a generously detailed portrait of time, place, and character and to enter the private world of the individual's mind to assess the true extent of his or her alienation from society and its institutions. Henceforth the depiction of the spatial dimension is more terse and allusive, as can be seen in this passage from *Al-Summān wa-al-kharīf* (1962; *Autumn Quail*):

> Everything around seemed to promise a deathlike repose. Grief-stricken people are apt to welcome any kind of sedative, even if it is poison. This small, furnished flat showed that civilization was not entirely devoid of a little mercy at times. There was the sea stretching away into the distance till it sank over the horizon; from the mildness of October it derived a certain wisdom and tenderness.
>
> (p. 66)

Maḥfūẓ also increasingly uses internal monologue to reveal emotions and motivations.

The first of these novels to be published was *The Thief and the Dogs*, in which a released prisoner, Saʿīd Mahrān, seeks revenge on his wife and her lover for framing him but succeeds instead only in killing innocent bystanders. Spurned in his attempts to get help from his former supporters, he finds temporary shelter with the prostitute Nūr but is eventually cornered in a cemetery. Here, already, the themes of "fair-weather socialism" and opportunism are raised. These themes are seen from the side opposing the revolution in *Autumn Quail*, which explores the downfall of a senior governmental official from the prerevolutionary period. His rejection of new political and social realities is finally jolted by the Tripartite Invasion of the Suez Canal in 1956.

Disillusion with the course of the revolution reaches its acme in the two final novels in this series, published in 1966 and 1967. In *Adrift on the Nile*, a group of cultural intellectuals meet on a houseboat in the evening and, against a backdrop of drugs and sex, explore the meaninglessness of their roles in society. In *Miramar*, Maḥfūẓ takes his readers into an Alexandria boardinghouse, which serves as a microcosm of Egyptian society, where a group of disparate characters from different classes and generations gather, talk, fight, and flirt; the frequent focus of these interactions is a lovely peasant girl, Zahra, whose trustful simplicity and determination to succeed make her an obvious symbol of Egypt. The main event of the novel, however, is the suicide of Sirḥān al-Buḥayrī, a senior figure in the Arab Socialist Union, whose plans to improve his lifestyle by robbing a truck loaded with fabric ends in failure. The corruption of the public sector, the alienation of the older generation from the process of revolution, the continued exploitation of the poor — all these factors combine in *Miramar* to produce Maḥfūẓ's crushing view of the course of his country's revolution immediately before the event that would radically transform the Middle East, Egypt's 1967 war with Israel.

Arab writers of fiction reacted to this tragedy in a variety of ways: anger, silence, exile. Maḥfūẓ's immediate reaction took the form of lengthy, often cyclical, short stories. When he turned his attention to longer narratives again, it was to produce yet another unusual work, *Mirrors*, in which the narrator, through a retrospect on his life and career, surveys the recent history of Egypt and its people. Many subjects in these vignettes comment with extreme frankness about politics, including the Egyptian revolution, international relations, and the continuing dilemma of the Palestinians' struggle with Israel.

Maḥfūẓ continued his retrospective mode even more directly in one of his most notorious works, *Al-Karnak* (1974), which was made into a highly successful and exploitative film. The major topic is the secret police's brutal suppression of political debate, especially among the younger generation, during the dark days of the 1960s; the images of mental and physical torture in *Al-Karnak* are among the most harrowing scenes in Maḥfūẓ's entire oeuvre. Duing this phase of his career (the 1970s), Maḥfūẓ was not shy about expressing his extreme disquiet over the ever-widening economic gap between the haves and have-nots in his homeland, which serves as a major theme in his personal favorite among his novels, *Malḥamat al-ḥarāfīsh* (1977; *The Harafish*), yet another work that follows the life, loves, and dislikes of the inhabitants of a particular quarter over several generations. At one point in this period, Maḥfūẓ's increasing frankness was sufficient to lead the regime to remove him from the rolls of the Writers' Union, thus officially preventing his publication. He was, however, in the best possible company: al-Ḥakīm, Idrīs, and the literary critic Luwīs ʿAwaḍ met the same fate. It was to everyone's great relief when this unwise political gesture was canceled shortly afterward.

Novels of the 1970s and 1980s

Maḥfūẓ's fiction during the 1970s and 1980s presents the literary critic with something of a dilemma. A survey of his writing up to the fateful year of 1967 shows that, in an almost two-decade-long stream of creativity, he not only laid the foundation for a fully developed tradition of realistic fiction in Arabic but also proceeded to expand his experiment into new, more allusive directions. This prolific output and the way his works reflected the problems and aspirations of incipient revolutionary Arab societies as a whole earned him the respect and critical admiration of the intelligentsia throughout the region. While this role was recognized in the Nobel committee's citation of 1988, there was no mention of any work published after 1967, and the announcement concentrated heavily on that monument of Arabic fiction completed in 1952, the trilogy.

Such a critical imbalance is, of course, the direct result of the relative availability of Maḥfūẓ's pre- and post-1967 novels in translation; furthermore, the relatively diminished interest of western translators in the post-1967 novels reflected a similar sentiment among critics in the Arab world. It seems fair to suggest that, during the 1970s and 1980s, a younger generation of Arab novelists—most of them freely acknowledging their debt to "the master"—further expanded the tradition of the novel for which he had provided the groundwork. Beyond that, Maḥfūẓ's considerable output during the same period tended to reflect a set of more local, intrinsically Egyptian concerns and, from a technical perspective, to be "retrospective." Examples of his interest in Egyptian issues include *Amām al-ʿarsh* (1983; Before the throne), in which a succession of Egyptian rulers from Pharaonic times through Sādāt is summoned to appear before a committee and questioned about their policies, and *Yawm qutila al-zaʿīm* (1985; The day the leader was killed), in which the tribulations of an English family, especially the inability of members of the younger generation to find housing, are explored. When one of the characters describes "the leader" as "just a lousy actor, that's all. . . . He goes around saying 'My friend Begin, my friend Kissinger.' Let me tell you, the uniform belongs to Hitler; the routine is sheer Charlie Chaplin" (p. 47), one senses that the voice of the narrator is conveying a heavy burden of authorial ire.

Within the context of narrative technique and retrospect, one may point to *Al-Bāqī min al-zaman sāʿah* (1982; One hour left), which, in much abbreviated form, replicates the trilogy's concern with the life of a single family during a period of history—in this case the 1960s and 1970s, with the 1973 war with Israel, known in Egypt as the October Crossing, as the novel's focal point. One may also point to *Ḥadīth al-ṣabāḥ wa-al-masā'* (1987; Morning and evening conversation), which replicates the alphabetical listing found in the earlier *Mirrors* by providing an updated series of Egyptian vignettes.

Two of the most interesting works from this period invoke the earlier tradition of Arabic narrative. In *Layālī alf laylah* (1982; *Arabian Nights and Days*), Maḥfūẓ introduces many of the major figures from *The Arabian Nights*: King Shahrayār, Maʿrūf the Cobbler, Sindbād, and Aladdin. In *Riḥlat ibn Faṭṭūmah* (1983; *The Journey of Ibn Fattouma*), he utilizes the life journey of the title character—an adaptation of the fourteenth-century traveler Ibn Baṭṭūṭah—to explore various systems of authority and the role of religious belief in the quest for fulfillment and bliss.

As we survey Maḥfūẓ's total oeuvre and take account of its impact, we almost inevitably conclude that the topics and technique of his works written in the 1970s and 1980s have reduced the breadth of effect that his earlier works enjoyed and demanded. Yet Maḥfūẓ still qualifies as the founder of the mature tradition of the novel in Arabic and the forger of new paths in two distinct historical phases of that prolonged developmental process.

CONCLUSION

In summarizing Maḥfūẓ's achievement, it is useful to note that his educational background differs from that of many other modern Arabic fiction writers in that his primary focus of academic interest was philosophy. The question "What is madness?" opens the title story of his first collection, *Hams al-junūn* (1939; The whisper of madness). Following the patterns of development within the western fictional tradition, he has chosen to focus primarily on the life and problems of Egypt's urban middle class and in particular the intellectuals and bureaucrats. Whereas other modern Arab novelists have been motivated by political and literary concerns to venture outside the modern metropolis and portray the harsh realities of life among the rural peasantry, Maḥfūẓ has consistently set his works in the city and among the class he knows best. But alongside these characteristic issues Maḥfūẓ has also shown a continuing interest in such questions as the nature of madness, the alienation of contemporary humanity and the search for consolation, and the role of religion in modern societies in which humanistic values predominate.

Maḥfūẓ's writing style is a direct reflection of his personality: from the outset it has served as an instrument of precision and, along with changes and developments in fictional technique, it too has adapted. Given the predominance of urban issues and especially the civil-servant class in his writings, there is a happy link between the depiction of the routine and familiar and a style that prefers concision to elaboration. Yet Maḥfūẓ can write passages of truly poetic beauty, as in the opening lines of *Miramar*: "Alexandria. At last, Alexandria, Lady of the Dew. Bloom of white nimbus. Bosom of radiance, wet with sky-water. Core of nostalgia steeped in honey and tears" (p. 1).

However, Maḥfūẓ's combination of topic and style differs from that of some other writers of fiction: for example, the image-filled descriptions of Palestinian novelist Jabrā Ibrāhīm Jabrā, the replications of the traditional storyteller found in some novels by Saudi Arabian author ʿAbd al-Raḥmān Munīf, and, perhaps most important, the wayward and creative stylistic brilliance of fellow Egyptian Idrīs. The way in which Maḥfūẓ adapted his writing style to match changes in narrative technique can best be illustrated by contrasting the quotation from *Miramar* with a passage from the earlier *Midaq Alley*:

> However, there are two stores—that of ʿAmm Kāmil, the confectioner, to the right of the

alley's entrance, and the barber's saloon on the left. They both stay open till shortly after sunset. ʿAmm Kāmil has the habit—actually he regards it more as a right—of putting a chair right by the front of his store and taking a nap with a fly-whisk in his lap. The only thing that will wake him up is either a yell from a customer or else ʿAbbās the barber's teasing.

(p. 6)

As Maḥfūẓ's writing style has become more allusive and sardonic, his novels have become repositories of jokes and one-liners for which Egyptians are justly famous, a national trait that his acquaintances know him to possess in abundance. A few examples follow:

> People keep asking me why the theater is flourishing these days. The answer is that we've all become actors!
>
> (*Mirrors*, p. 88)

> For him philosophy starts with Ibn Rushd [Averroes] and now it's finishing with Ibn Kalb (son of a bitch)!
>
> (*Mirrors*, p. 164)

> Just look at these streets, right in the middle of the city! They're filthy. Any day now, flies are going to start demanding their citizen's rights!
>
> (*Mirrors*, p. 172)

> I'm much better than they are. I'm completely liberated! I'm affiliated with a previous age, one before all this fuss about religion and proper behavior.
>
> (*Afrāḥ al-qubbah*, 1981; trans. as *Wedding Song*, 1984, p. 71)

The narrative craft of Maḥfūẓ developed at a particular point in the history of modern Arabic fiction; his writings reflect the aspirations and frustrations of the Arab world during one of the most crucial and exciting periods in that troubled region's modern history. In a vast outpouring of painstakingly crafted creativity, he has portrayed the society that he knows best, the Egyptian bureaucratic middle class, in its encounter with crushing internal and external forces. He has addressed himself, often at personal risk, to the controversies of the day and to larger philosophical questions. In his hands the historical moment (or rather, considering the length of his career and the bulk of his contribution, multiple historical moments) and the novel genre were impeccably linked. The Arabic novel is the continuing beneficiary of that fact.

Selected Bibliography

ARTICLES AND TRANSLATIONS

Miṣr al-qadīmah. Cairo: Maktabat Miṣr, 1932. Trans. of *Ancient Egypt* by James Baikie.

Ḥawla al-dīn wa-al-dīmugrātiyyah. Cairo: Maktabat Miṣr, 1989. Collection of articles.

SHORT-STORY COLLECTIONS AND FICTIONAL PIECES

Hams al-junūn. Cairo: Maktabat Miṣr, 1939.

Dunyā Allāh. Cairo: Maktabat Miṣr, 1962.

Bayt sayyiʾ al-sum ʿah. Cairo: Maktabat Miṣr, 1965.

Taḥta al-miẓallah. Cairo: Maktabat Miṣr, 1967.

Khamārat al-qiṭṭ al-aswad. Cairo: Maktabat Miṣr, 1969.

Ḥikayah bi-lā bidāyah wa-lā-nihāyah. Cairo: Maktabat Miṣr, 1971.

Shahr al-ʿasal. Cairo: Maktabat Miṣr, 1971.

Al-Marayā. Cairo: Maktabat Miṣr, 1972.

Al-Jarīmah. Cairo: Maktabat Miṣr, 1973.

Ḥikāyāt ḥāratinā. Cairo: Maktabat Miṣr, 1975.

Al-Ḥubb fawq haḍbat al-haram. Cairo: Maktabat Miṣr, 1979.

Al-Shayṭān yaʿiz. Cairo: Maktabat Miṣr, 1979.

ʿAṣr al-ḥubb. Cairo: Maktabat Miṣr, 1980.

Ra'aytu fī-mā yarā al-naʾim. Cairo: Maktabat Miṣr, 1982.

Amām al-ʿarsh. Cairo: Maktabat Miṣr, 1983.

Al-Tanẓīm al-sirrī. Cairo: Maktabat Miṣr, 1984.

Ṣabāḥ al-ward. Cairo: Maktabat Miṣr, 1987.

Al-Fajr al-kadhib. Cairo: Maktabat Miṣr, 1989.

NOVELS

ʿAbath al-aqdār. Cairo: Maktabat Miṣr, 1939.

Rādūbīs. Cairo: Maktabat Miṣr, 1943.

Kifāḥ Tība. Cairo: Maktabat Miṣr, 1944.

Khān al-Khalīlī. Cairo: Maktabat Miṣr, c. 1945.

Al-Qāhirah al-jadīdah. Cairo: Maktabat Miṣr, c. 1946.

Zuqāq al-Midaqq. Cairo: Maktabat Miṣr, 1947.
Al-Sarāb. Cairo: Maktabat Miṣr, c. 1948.
Bidāyah wa-nihāyah. Cairo: Maktabat Miṣr, 1949.
Bayn al-Qaṣrayn. Cairo: Maktabat Miṣr, 1956.
Qaṣr al-Shawq. Cairo: Maktabat Miṣr, 1957.
Al-Sukkariyyah. Cairo: Maktabat Miṣr, 1957.
Al-Liṣṣ wa-al-kilāb. Cairo: Maktabat Miṣr, 1961.
Al-Summān wa-al-kharīf. Cairo: Maktabat Miṣr, 1962.
Al-Ṭarīq. Cairo: Maktabat Miṣr, 1964.
Al-Shaḥḥādh. Cairo: Maktabat Miṣr, 1965.
Thartharah fawq al-Nīl. Cairo: Maktabat Miṣr, 1966.
Awlād ḥāratinā. Beirut: Dar al-Ādāb, 1967. First publ. in the newspaper *Al-Ahrām*, Cairo, 1959.
Mīrāmār. Cairo: Maktabat Miṣr, 1967.
Al-Ḥubb taḥt al-maṭar. Cairo: Maktabat Miṣr, 1973.
Al-Karnak. Cairo: Maktabat Miṣr, 1974.
Qalb al-layl. Cairo: Maktabat Miṣr, 1975.
Ḥaḍrat al-muḥtaram. Cairo: Maktabat Miṣr, 1977.
Malḥamat al-ḥarāfīsh. Cairo: Maktabat Miṣr, 1977.
Afrāḥ al-qubbah. Cairo: Maktabat Miṣr, 1981.
Al-Bāqī min al-zaman sāʿah. Cairo: Maktabat Miṣr, 1982.
Layālī alf laylah. Cairo: Maktabat Miṣr, 1982.
Riḥlat ibn Faṭṭūmah. Cairo: Maktabat Miṣr, 1983.
Al-ʿĀʾish fī al-ḥaqīqah. Cairo: Maktabat Miṣr, 1985.
Yawm qutila al-zaʿīm. Cairo: Maktabat Miṣr, 1985.
Ḥadīth al-ṣabāḥ wa-al-masāʾ. Cairo: Maktabat Miṣr, 1987.
Qushtumur. Cairo: Maktabat Miṣr, 1988.

TRANSLATIONS OF SHORT STORIES AND FICTIONAL PIECES

God's World. Trans. by Akef Abadir and Roger Allen. Minneapolis: Bibliotheca Islamica, 1974.
Mirrors. Trans. by Roger Allen. Minneapolis: Bibliotheca Islamica, 1977.
The Time and the Place. Trans. by Denys Johnson-Davies. New York: Doubleday, 1991.

TRANSLATIONS IN COLLECTIONS

"Zaabalawi." Trans. by Denys Johnson-Davies. In *Modern Arabic Short Stories*. Oxford, U.K.: Oxford University Press, 1967.
"The Mosque in the Narrow Lane" and "Hanzal and the Policeman." In Mahmoud Manzalaoui, ed., *Arabic Writing Today: The Short Story*. Cairo: American Research Center in Egypt, 1968.
"The Tavern of the Black Cat." Trans. by A. F. Cassis. In *Contemporary Literature in Translation* 19 (summer/fall 1974). Short story.
"The Chase." Trans. by Roger Allen. In *Mundus Artium* 10 (1977). Play.
"The Conjurer Made Off with the Dish." Trans. by Denys Johnson-Davies. In *Egyptian Short Stories*. London: Heinemann Educational Books, 1978.
"Harassment." Trans. by Judith Rosenhouse. In *Journal of Arabic Literature* 9 (1978); play.
"Investigation." Trans. by Roger Allen. In *Edebiyat* 3 (1978). Short story.
"An Old Photograph." Trans. by Roger Allen. In *Nimrod* 24 (spring/summer 1981). Short story.
"A Man and a Shadow," "Under the Bus Shelter," and "The Time and the Place." In Ceza Kassem and Malek Hashem, eds., *Flights of Fantasy: Arabic Short Stories*. Cairo: Elias Modern, 1985.
"The Mummy Awakes." Trans. by Roger Allen. In Alamgir Hashmi, ed., *The Worlds of Muslim Imagination*. Islamabad, Pakistan: Gulmohar, 1986. Short story.

TRANSLATIONS OF NOVELS

Midaq Alley. Trans. by Trevor Le Gassick. Beirut: Khayat, 1966; Washington, D.C.: Three Continents, 1974.
Miramar. Trans. by Fatma Moussa-Mahmoud. London: Heinemann Educational Books, 1978.
Children of Gebelawi. Trans. by Phillip Stewart. Washington, D.C.: Three Continents, 1981.
Al-Karnak. Trans. by Saad al-Gabalawy. In *Three Contemporary Egyptian Novels*. Fredericton, Canada: York, 1984.
The Thief and the Dogs. Trans. by Trevor Le Gassick and Mustafa Badawi. Cairo: American University in Cairo Press, 1984.
Wedding Song. Trans. by Olive E. Kenny. Cairo: American University in Cairo Press, 1984.
Autumn Quail. Trans. by Roger Allen. Cairo: American University in Cairo Press, 1985.
The Beginning and the End. Trans. by Ramses Hanna Awad. Cairo: American University of Cairo Press, 1985.
The Search. Trans. by Mohamed Islam. Cairo: American University in Cairo Press, 1985.

The Beggar. Trans. by Kristin Walker Henry and Nariman Khales Naili al-Warrah. Cairo: American University in Cairo Press, 1986.

Respected Sir. Trans. by Rasheed El-Enany. London: Quartet, 1986.

Fountain and Tomb. Trans. by Soad Sobhy, Essam Fattouh, and James Kenneson. Washington, D.C: Three Continents, 1988.

Palace Walk. Trans. by William Maynard Hutchins and Olive E. Kenny. New York: Doubleday, 1990.

Palace of Desire. Trans. by William Maynard Hutchins, Lorne M. Kenny, and Olive E. Kenny. New York: Doubleday, 1991.

The Journey of Ibn Fattouma. Trans. by Denys Johnson-Davies. New York: Doubleday, 1992.

Sugar Street. Trans. by William Maynard Hutchins and Angele Botros Samaan. New York: Doubleday, 1992.

Adrift on the Nile. Trans. by Frances Liardet. New York: Doubleday, 1993.

The Harafish. Trans. by Catherine Cobham. New York: Doubleday, 1994.

Arabian Nights and Days. Trans. by Denys Johnson-Davies. New York: Doubleday, 1995.

Children of the Alley. Trans. by Peter Theroux. New York: Doubleday, 1996.

CRITICAL STUDIES

Abu-Haidar, Jareer. "*Awlad haratina* by Najib Mahfuz: An Event in the Arab World." In *Journal of Arabic Literature* 16 (1985).

Allen, Roger. "Najib Mahfuz in World Literature." In *The Arabic Novel Since 1950: Critical Essays, Interviews, and Bibliography.* Cambridge, Mass.: Dar al-Mahjar, 1992.

———. "The Impact of the Translated Text: The Case of Najib Mahfuz's Novels, with Special Emphasis on the Trilogy." In *Edebiyat,* 4, no. 1 (1993).

———. "Najib Mahfuz and the Arabic Novel: The Historical Context." In Michael Beard and Adnan Haydar, eds., *Naguib Mahfouz: From Regional Fame to Global Recognition.* Syracuse, N.Y.: Syracuse University Press, 1993.

———. *The Arabic Novel: An Historical and Critical Introduction.* 2nd ed. Syracuse, N.Y.: Syracuse University Press, 1995.

———, ed. *Modern Arabic Literature.* New York: Ungar, 1987.

Beard, Michael, and Adnan Haydar, eds. *Naguib Mahfouz: From Regional Fame to Global Recognition.* Syracuse, N.Y.: Syracuse University Press, 1993.

El-Enany, Rasheed. *Naguib Mahfouz: The Pursuit of Meaning.* London: Routledge, 1993.

Jad, ʿAli B. *Form and Technique in the Egyptian Novel, 1912–1971.* London: Ithaca, 1983.

Kilpatrick, Hilary. *The Modern Egyptian Novel: A Study in Social Criticism.* London: Ithaca, 1974.

Le Gassick, Trevor. "The Trilogy of Najib Mahfuz." In *Middle East Forum* 39, no. 2 (1963).

———. "An Analysis of *Al-Hubb taht al-matar* (Love in the rain): A Novel by Najib Mahfuz." In R. C. Ostle, ed., *Studies in Modern Arabic Literature.* Warminster, U.K.: Aris & Phillips, 1975.

———, ed. *Critical Perspectives on Naguib Mahfouz.* Washington, D.C.: Three Continents, 1991.

Mahmoud, Mohamed. "The Unchanging Hero in a Changing World: Najib Mahfuz's *Al-Liss wa ʾl-kilab.*" In *Journal of Arabic Literature* 15 (1984). Repr. in Trevor Le Gassick, ed., *Critical Perspectives on Naguib Mahfouz.* Washington, D.C.: Three Continents, 1991.

Mikhail, Mona. *Studies in the Short Fiction of Mahfouz and Idris.* New York: New York University Press, 1992.

Milson, Menahem. "Nagib Mahfuz and the Quest for Meaning." In *Arabica* 17 (1970).

———. "An Allegory on the Social and Cultural Crisis in Egypt: *ʾWalid al-ʿAna* by Najib Mahfuz." In *International Journal of Middle East Studies* 3 (1972).

———. "Reality, Allegory, and Myth in the Work of Najib Mahfuz." In *Asian and African Studies* 11 (fall 1976).

Peled, Mattityahu. *Religion, My Own: The Literary Works of Najīb Maḥfūẓ.* New Brunswick, N.J.: Transaction Books, 1983.

Sakkut, Hamdi. *The Egyptian Novel and Its Main Trends from 1913 to 1952.* Cairo: American University in Cairo Press, 1971.

———. "Najib Mahfuz's Short Stories." In R. C. Ostle, ed., *Studies in Modern Arabic Literature.* Warminster, U.K.: Aris & Phillips, 1975.

Somekh, Sasson. *The Changing Rhythm: A Study of Najib Mahfuz's Novels.* Leiden: E. J. Brill, 1973.

———. "'Zaʿbalawi'—Author, Theme, and Technique." In *Journal of Arabic Literature* 1 (1970).

Albert Memmi

1920–

GUY DUGAS

TRANSLATED BY JOHN FLETCHER

ALBERT MEMMI'S work is best approached in light of European colonization as experienced by an indigenous Jewish population in an Islamic country. When Memmi was born in Tunis toward the end of 1920, Tunisia was a French protectorate in which colonial rule was firmly established. The population of the country was mixed, cosmopolitan, and strongly hierarchized. The French "protectors" enjoyed the greatest advantages and were the most feared, respected, and envied members of society. The Italians and Maltese were less affluent but accorded a number of minor privileges to which they clung proudly and jealously. At the bottom of the social pyramid were the indigenous people, the most deprived and cruelly exploited segment of the population. There were two distinct elements among the indigenes. The majority by far were the Muslim Arabs, who had a secure base in their own language and religion. The Jewish minority consisted of approximately fifty thousand people—about the same number as French colonists—who were proud of their ancient traditions and links with Phoenicians and Berbers that dated back thousands of years.

In two of his novels, *Le Scorpion; ou, La Confession imaginaire* (1969; *The Scorpion*) and *Le Désert; ou, La Vie et les aventures de Jubaïr Quali El-Mammi* (1977; The desert), Memmi takes pride in tracing the history of his family back to such far-off times: "It pleases me to imagine that some of my ancestors were there to welcome Queen Dido's companions, when they took refuge on our shores, or the men who founded Phoenician trading posts" (*The Scorpion*, p. 17).

Unlike some contemporary historians, however, Memmi refuses to paint a rosy picture of relations between Arabs and Jews in Islamic countries. While Jewish folk memory cherishes the recollection of laudable feelings of solidarity and mutual understanding, it also bears the scars of contempt, discrimination, and persecution. In Tunisia, for instance, the Samuel Sfez (Batou) affair has left an indelible mark on Jewish minds and is related in Memmi's *La Terre intérieure* (1976; The interior land). In June 1857, Sfez, a Jew, got into an argument with a Muslim and was sentenced to death, despite appeals for clemency from several foreign consulates.

In 1881, under the pretext of subduing disturbances on the Tunisian-Algerian frontier, France obliged the bey to accept the status of protectorate. The arrival of the French seems to have improved the situation of the Jewish minority somewhat. At the same time, however, colonization provoked unease in and even destabilized the Jewish community. Because it flattered their vanity and served their policy aims in the Maghreb (North Africa), the French encouraged the Jews to emulate them, but full assimilation was out of the question, as it would have undermined French cultural and political authority.

Jewish youths in particular were exposed to the full impact of western civilization. They eagerly took up offers of admission to the republic's schools and to schools established by the Alliance Israélite Universelle (an organization founded in Paris in 1860 with the aim of educating the Jewish community both in the Yiddish tradition and in French modernity) and were keen to breathe the new air of freedom and modernity wafting across the Mediterranean Sea. Although less systematically than in Algeria, ever increasing numbers of Jews took French citizenship. Nevertheless, because most Jews remained deeply embedded in the traditional way of life of Muslim Arab society, the habits and customs of the vast majority changed very little.

So it was with the Memmi family. They were almost illiterate artisans and lived if not quite in the Hara, the squalid Jewish ghetto in Tunis, then in its immediate vicinity. This is the sociohistorical trajectory of Memmi's multifaceted career, from the Tunis Hara to the French university. In this context, Memmi emerged as a prophet of decolonization, theorist of dependency, and chronicler of lacerating divisions.

LIFE AND POLITICAL PHILOSOPHY

Memmi was born on 15 December 1920, the eldest of eight children of Marguerite Sarfati and François Memmi. His father was a saddler, and his uncle a tailor. The parents fostered an atmosphere of wisdom and piety in the family: in 1924 Memmi went to rabbinical school, and in 1927 to the school of the Alliance Israélite Universelle in the rue Malta Srira in Tunis. Sometimes he helped in his father's workshop, where he listened avidly to the stories told by an old family friend, an Italian workman named Joseph. In 1932, Memmi had the good fortune to be offered an unsecured loan by the Jewish community that enabled him to enroll at the French lycée in Tunis.

Between 1933 and 1938, he attended French secondary school and took an active part in local Jewish youth groups. This dual allegiance to mutually antagonistic organizations constituted a painful apprenticeship in the art of being Jewish and different. On graduation in 1939 from the Lycée Carnot, the most important French secondary school in Tunisia, he was awarded the honor prize in philosophy. This success made him decide to study philosophy at university. As his brother Georges Memmi, also a novelist, put it in *Qui se souvient du Café Rubens?* (1984; Who remembers the Rubens Café?): "The eldest son embarked upon university studies which my father realized to his great disappointment would lead neither to leather-work nor to saddlery as a career. . . . Every day father would conjure up for us the sad spectacle of the shop left empty after his death. To make himself heard he would cough so hard he ran out of breath."

Memmi spent the academic year 1941–1942 as a first-year philosophy student at the University of Algiers and began publishing short articles and novellas in some of the newspapers of the Jewish community. In 1943, as a result of the anti-Semitic laws of Philippe Pétain's Vichy government that were enforced in France and Algeria, he was expelled from college and suffered the painful experience of incarceration in a forced labor camp in eastern Tunisia. In 1945 he returned to Algiers and traveled widely in the Mediterranean basin. In 1946 he moved to Paris to continue his philosophical studies at the Sorbonne, where his professors were Daniel Lagache and Georges Gurvitch. Gurvitch was particularly influential because he steered Memmi toward sociology and appointed him teaching assistant.

Because Memmi's scholarship from the Tunisian government did not provide enough money to live on, he gave private lessons in philosophy and French to make ends meet. He also wrote for *Hillel*, the journal of the French Association of Jewish Students, and for Edmond Charlot, Albert Camus's publisher in Algeria. During this period of black despair caused by poverty and solitude, he embarked on his first novel, *La Statue de sel* (1953; *The Pillar of Salt*), in order to make sense of his existence. On 24 December 1946 he married a "blond, blue-eyed Frenchwoman," Marie-Germaine Dubach, who came from a devout Catholic Alsatian family. The symbolic promises and actual difficulties of this mixed, albeit long-lasting, marriage provided the theme of his second novel, *Agar* (1955; *Strangers*). In 1951, Memmi and his wife returned to Tunisia, where he took a post as a philosophy teacher at the Lycée Carnot.

In 1952 he founded and headed the Educational Psychology Center in Tunis. Although the human drama he encountered in his work caused him sleepless nights, it provided him with a valuable collection of materials on group interaction, racism, and mixed marriages, among other topics. In March 1953 *The Pillar of Salt* was published; it won the Carthage Prize in Tunisia, and in Paris the following year it carried off the Fénéon Prize. The novel's success catapulted Memmi into the first rank of young French Maghrebian writers; and its prestige was further enhanced in 1955 when Camus agreed to write a preface for the second edition. Memmi published in the *Revue FSJU*, the review of Fond Social Juif Unifié, an article titled "Our Ghetto," which advocated the demolition of the Jewish area of Tunis and set him on a collision course with the Jewish community, a confrontation exacerbated by his harsh depiction of Tunisian Jewry in his first two novels.

Meanwhile nationalist pressures were increasing in Tunisia, which was accorded internal autonomy in 1954. Sensing that they would have no place in an independent Tunisia, whatever might be said to the contrary, the Jews emigrated en masse to Israel and France. Writing a regular arts column in the nationalist daily *L'Action*, Memmi advocated full independence provided that the rights of minorities were respected. In 1955 *Strangers* (first titled *The Way to the World*) was published. Although it was a finalist for the Goncourt Prize, the most important literary prize in France, it left many of its readers confused. It seemed to refute mixed marriage as a solution to the individual problems of identity and acculturation.

Tunisia attained full independence in 1956. The following year Habib Bourguiba, head of the newly independent Tunisian government, abolished the bey and declared the republic. Despite the government's continued appointment of Jewish ministers, the community's exodus proceeded apace. For personal as much as for political reasons, Memmi and his wife in their turn decided to leave for good and to settle in Paris. In his essay *Portrait du colonisé, précédé d'un portrait du colonisateur* (1957; *The Colonizer and the Colonized*), Memmi lays out the psychosociological background of colonial oppression and demonstrates the formation of the strange duo of oppressor and oppressed in its shadow. By asserting that decolonization would not come about through class struggle, as the French Left, including the writer-philosopher Jean-Paul Sartre, proclaimed in these days, but instead through the sort of nationalist agitation he had seen at work in Tunisia, Memmi alienated the French political establishment. His argument is strengthened by the fact that the solution he proposed ran counter to his own personal interest and the interest of his community, the Jewish and French minorities in decolonized Tunisia.

In 1957 Memmi was appointed associate professor at two institutions: the French Business School and the National School of Social Science in Paris. Between 1957 and 1960 he collaborated with Gurvitch on numerous studies of the sociology of literature. He also spoke with Camus for the last time. Camus was cold and distant, probably because he took umbrage at an article included in *The Colonizer and the Colonized* titled "Le Colonisateur de bonne volonté" (The well-meaning colonialist), which Camus took to be a portrait of himself. Camus died in a car accident in 1960 before the misunderstanding could be patched up.

Memmi also offended the Jewish community with his "depiction of the Jewish condition today" in the essay *Portrait d'un Juif* (1962; Portrait of a Jew), based on his own self-portrait. In 1963 he visited Israel for the first time, describing himself as a "left-wing Zionist," a supporter of the Jewish national movement and the state of Israel who was seeking "justice for [his] own people without causing injustice to others." He drew attention to the situation within Israel of Sephardic Jews and to the lack of interest shown to the Palestinian question. These articles were later collected in *Juifs et Arabes* (1974; *Jews and Arabs*).

In 1964 Memmi published an essay interpreting Sigmund Freud's works in relation to Freud's Jewish roots and through this and other works became recognized as an authority on the sociology of Jewry. He also wrote an introduction to an anthology of French Maghrebian writing, and his interest in Francophone writers, and in Maghrebian authors of whatever origin, continued throughout his career.

Memmi's attention then turned to racism; while the study *Le Racisme: Description, définition, traitement* (1982; Racism) was the eventual fruit of his prolonged meditation on the subject, he published several books in the 1960s linking racism, colonialism, and anti-Semitism. He contributed an introduction to the French translation of James Baldwin's *The Fire Next Time* (1963) and to other works by or about African Americans. In these texts he drew parallels between the conditions of Jews, African Americans, and colonized peoples, for all were classifiable as oppressed minorities. In 1966 he embarked on a lecture tour of the United States, which enabled him to study the African-American community firsthand. In the essay *L'Homme dominé* (1968; *Dominated Man: Notes Toward a Portrait*), he added women, proletarians, and domestic servants to the list of oppressed minorities. In every instance, he argued controversially, the relationship between overlord and underling was one of complex mutual dependency.

In his book *La Libération du Juif* (1966; *The Liberation of the Jew*), he argues that the foundation of the state of Israel was a solution to a national problem comparable to the solutions arrived at by other oppressed minorities' liberation movements, and as such constituted the only outcome possible to the "misfortune of being a Jew." This book upset many different groups, including Zionists, who did not appreciate being called unfortunate, and anti-Zionists, who resented Memmi's parallel between Jewish aspirations to statehood and other independence struggles.

This spate of sociological writing led to Memmi's appointment as professor of sociology at the University of Paris X, Nanterre, and as visiting professor and teaching fellow at the University of Seattle in 1970. He returned to writing novels with *The Scorpion* (1969), in which the narrative voice is doubled and shared between two brothers who are at once very close and very different. The novel also entertains a project for writing under different colors, a theory of literature and of writing technique that Memmi expanded and developed in a later essay, *L'Écriture colorée; ou, Je vous aime en rouge: Essai sur une dimension nouvelle de l'écriture, la couleur* (1986; Writing in color; or, I love you in red: Essay on a new dimension of writing, color).

Between 1971 and 1973 the Arab-Israeli conflict worsened, and Memmi felt the need to add his voice as an "Arab Jew" to the thorny dialogue by taking part in the Jerusalem Zionist Congress in the 1970s. In his address to the congress, he confirmed his support for the state of Israel but also stated his reservations about its Palestinian policy. On 24 November 1974, he shared a platform with Colonel Muʿammar Muḥammad al-Gadhafi of Libya at an important colloquium in Paris, at which Memmi prophesied that one day the Israelis would agree to sit down with representatives of the Palestine Liberation Organization in face-to-face talks. His collection of essays *Jews and Arabs*, which deals with this issue, appeared in the same year.

When Memmi visited Canada in 1975, many Quebecers assured him that they recognized themselves in the portrait Memmi painted in *The Colonizer and the Colonized.* He also gave several interviews on the fundamentals of his political philosophy and his practice as a writer, especially the close links between art and life. As vice president of the International Association of Poets, Playwrights, Editors, Essayists, and Novelists (PEN) in France between 1977 and 1980, Memmi advocated the release of the Moroccan poet Abdellatif Laâbi and other dissidents from jail.

In 1977 Memmi published *Le Désert*, a semihistorical novel that attributes to an explicitly Jewish protagonist the life and adventures of one of the leading figures of the Muslim world, the great philosopher and historian Ibn-Khaldūn. The award of the Italian Simba Prize in 1978 recognized Memmi's services to Africa; in the same year he was elected to the French Overseas Academy of Sciences. In 1979 Memmi published *La Dépendance: Esquisse pour un portrait du dépendant* (*Dependence: A Sketch for a Portrait of the Dependent*), in which he extends the analysis of dualistic relationships from the connection between domination and subjection to the relation between provision and dependency. In this text Memmi sets out to define the concepts of "provision" and "provider," with God as the "supreme provider."

Over the next couple of years, as medical and educational circles began to take a strong interest in theories of dependency, Memmi was frequently invited to write articles and give lectures on the subject both in France and abroad. When the Center for Study and Research into Dependency (CRED) was set up in Paris in 1980, he was invited to run it. In 1982 he published *Le Racisme*, an essay that confirmed that Memmi had embarked on developing a philosophy of human relations, with his portrait of the universal "oppressed person" as a starting point.

In April 1982, a film based on *The Pillar of Salt* was shown during the first International Festival of Jewish Culture, held at Vincennes, France. In 1985 Memmi was invited to contribute to a distinguished series titled *Ce que je crois* (My credo), which gave him the opportunity to set out his beliefs on a number of topics close to his heart; and his poems were collected under the title *Le Mirliton du ciel* (1985; Heaven's doggerel). This volume was reissued with several new poems and short texts in 1990, and Memmi's journalism was collected under the titles *Bonheurs: 52 semaines* (1992; Happiness: 52 weeks), and *Ah quel bonheur!* (1995; Oh what happiness!).

In 1987 he retired from his chair at the University of Paris X. To mark both this occasion and the thirtieth anniversary of the publication of *The Colonizer and the Colonized*, three separate colloquia were held in his honor, and the proceedings were subsequently published. In 1988, with all his earlier novels available in paperback editions, Memmi published *Le Pharaon: Roman* (The pharaoh), in which the protagonist, once again doubled as in *The Scorpion*, is caught up in the troubles of postcolonial Tunisia. In this novel Memmi touches on the issue of the relation between the history of the Tunisian Jewish community and the history of Tunisia itself.

The emergence of Islamic fundamentalism and the publicizing of acts of defiance toward the secular state gave rise in both France and Arab countries to much public discussion, in which Memmi became involved in his capacity as vice president of the French Association for Secular Republicanism. In 1993, to protect himself against what he saw as the danger of "straying into smugness and into acts of complicity," Memmi set out his convictions in *À contre-courants* (Against the tide), a philosophical dictionary made up of sixty entries, in which he summed up his political attitude in the following terms: "We are witnessing the return in insolent strength of fascism and fundamentalism. Against such demons there is only one untainted banner for us to march under, and that is the banner of secular humanism."

FICTIONAL WORKS

Memmi's fiction moves from pure autobiography to complex games with autobiography. Given the transparency and openness of his novels, and his adherence to historical facts and chronology, it is tempting to view them as painstaking attempts to seize hold of and master a diffuse sense of identity and a problematic existence. These works reflect a passionate search for identity that in its ardor is close to the author's own.

The Pillar of Salt

In *The Pillar of Salt* (1953), the Jewish hero Mordecai is bathed in the warmth of family life. Protected by the ghetto wall, he lives securely under the firm authority of a strictly hierarchized community. At first he feels at ease among his people, shielded from the upheavals of the outside world by what Memmi describes in *Le Mirliton du ciel* as "tender, warm, exasperating, irreplaceable family love." But as he necessarily opens up to the world, first by going to a French school, he learns through other people's perceptions of him to recognize the differences, starting with his family name, that set him apart from those around him.

Little by little, Mordecai discovers that his native culture, inbred conditioning, basic way of life, and humble ghetto dialect have all created a gulf between himself and the world he strives to enter. At the same time his cultural development, his aspirations, and the things he guiltily finds fascinating cut him off irremediably from the milieu of his birth. Although Mordecai willingly rejects his origins, they prevent him from being accepted by the group he longs to join. At the end of the novel, realizing that he cannot be a member of either world, and after resisting the impulse to kill himself, he chooses to run away to a life of adventure.

Strangers

Although the anonymous protagonist of Memmi's second novel, *Strangers* (1955), is presented not as a philosophy student but as a doctor, the book is clearly intended as a sequel to *The Pillar of Salt.* Convinced that the way to secure a place in the world to which he aspires is through a mixed marriage, the hero marries a Christian, a "blond Frenchwoman with blue eyes." When he brings her home, the attitude of his mother and of the Jewish community toward his foreign spouse rankles him on several occasions. At the same time, however, he cannot stop himself from springing fiercely to the defense of his family when his wife questions the Jewish values with which he claims to disagree. This nonsensical behavior puts him in a most awkward position: having rejected both his traditional family and his modern, western way of life he finds himself obliged to give in to one side or the other.

The outline of Memmi's life suggests that these first two novels are autobiographical, and he has frequently pointed out the links between his life and work. But it would be simplistic to reduce Memmi's work to such an interpretation, for he is fully conscious both of the impossibility of conducting a search for self-identity only through writing and of the playful impulses that all creative artists harbor within them. As he puts it in *Ce que je crois*: "I have never really known how to make myself out. I've tried, I really have, but for some reason it was never very satisfactory. Identity is and remains a pretty doubtful business" (p. 24).

The Scorpion

Memmi's third novel, *The Scorpion* (1969), opens with the disappearance of Emile, a writer obsessed with the search for self. His brother, Marcel, a well-known ophthalmologist and a more down-to-earth personality, is asked to sort out Emile's affairs. The novel synthesizes the story of a quest for a lost unity and the confrontation between reality and people's perception of it. Whereas Memmi's first two novels are rigorously organized, the structure of *The Scorpion* seems dispersed, even disjointed.

The novel's use of multiple narrative voices and an appropriate writing style for each character conveys differing perceptions of reality. Likewise, doubled or multiplied characters offer several potentialities within the protagonist; Emile and Marcel may be considered as two sides of the same character. Such devices reveal a fragmented self patiently attempting to re-create itself through a network of correspondence, vague signs, and subtle analogies.

There are many questions for Marcel in the manuscripts, rough drafts, and other documents Emile has accumulated. He wonders whether he will recognize the world in which he himself grew up, whether reality can have the same meaning for the two brothers, and what, if anything, the brothers have in common. The technique of doubling has two advantages: it introduces an element of humor lacking in the earlier novels, and it subverts the strongly unified narrative that is often a feature of autobiographical fiction. For example, in *Strangers*, in which all the characters appear to be seen from the narrator's point of view, it is difficult to consider the story as anything other than autobiography.

An icon at the heart of the story, much discussed by the two narrators, plays a particularly important part in subverting the autobiographical genre. Emile, who is extremely preoccupied with his ethnic origins, attaches much importance to a medal depicting Numidian horsemen on which the name MEMMI has been engraved. He claims delightedly that it represents convincing proof of the secular roots of the Jewish community in North Africa, and on the basis of it he elaborates a theory that he considers unassailable. He calls it "our family history" and stresses that exactness is the sole guarantee of truth against the wilder flights of the imagination.

Unfortunately for Emile, his brother immediately queries this rigorous construction point by point and calls it "mistaken," "pure fantasy," and even "madness." Disagreement over interpretation of the past occurs again in response to a photograph taken of their mother flanked by her two sisters. As all three are dressed in traditional bedouin costume, Emile characterizes the photo as "typical of our mother," of her origins and condition, whereas Marcel reveals once again that it is a trick:

> Now what's this all about? It's a fine photograph, all right, but it's just more showing off. I know about that picture too, and I've been told the story of it any number of times. The only true thing in it was our mother's beauty—the beauty of a wild doll, compared with the mediocre plainness of her sisters—and perhaps Imilio, who was in her womb, because the fact is she is pregnant, which explains the water-jug (to hide her stomach). The photograph, taken in Bedouin clothing, was the whim of a pregnant woman.
>
> (p. 142)

Le Désert

In *Le Désert* (1977), Memmi turned to the historical novel. Set in a largely imaginary fourteenth century, it relates the life and adventures of Memmi's ancestor Jubaïr Quali El-Mammi. While the genealogical quest remains important—this time the impulse to reconstruct imaginatively a Semitic family tree takes precedence over concentrating on one or two generations—his fourth novel plays games with history that verge on pure spoof.

Any quest for identity presupposes a painful confrontation with the self—the veritable "wrestling with the angel" that is the theme of *The Pillar of Salt* and *Strangers*. But because introspection entails probing others by whom the self is necessarily defined, it also makes it possible to define what the self represents to the other. Since, for Memmi, apprehension of the world logically stems from the attempt to understand oneself, the individual must strive to achieve something that is far from easy: a synthesis between the self and the world. That synthesis consists of the reconquest of the "realm of the within," which inevitably leads to "the putting of humankind to the test" (*Le Désert*, p. 22). In this novel as in the earlier ones, Memmi's characters pursue the twin aims of "cultivating the most acute awareness of themselves and of their place in the world" (*The Scorpion*, p. 206).

Le Pharaon

The hero of Memmi's fifth novel, *Le Pharaon* (1988), is Armand Gozlan, a Tunisian Jewish professor known as "The Pharaoh," who lives through the period of national independence that was simultaneously so exciting and so disappointing for the local Jewish community. Against the background of this communal drama is played out the personal tragedy of the professor and one of his students, with whom he falls in love. Their affair is doomed not only because she is much younger than he but also because she is a rich heiress from an old colonial family.

Another character in the novel, which features several characters from earlier books, is the author Benillouche, who is described as "the only decent writer in the country" and as the exact opposite of Gozlan. Benillouche is a Zionist activist, whereas Gozlan plunges into the independence struggle shoulder-to-shoulder with Tunisian Muslims and dreamed in his youth of the "fabulous project" of compiling a "new Bible." This was intended to be "a book for the whole of humanity" and was to have included not only the great religious texts but also Epictetus' *Manual* and Jean-Jacques Rousseau's *Social Contract*.

Disillusioned with writing and resigned to the fact that the Jews will not have a place in the new Tunisian state, Gozlan refuses the Zionist solution and chooses instead to leave the country and retreat into his ivory tower. This decision recalls the denouement of Memmi's first novel, in which the protagonist's name is, interestingly enough, Benillouche. However, Gozlan does not leave for a new country such as Argentina, Benillouche's destination in *Pillar of Salt*. He leaves for Paris in order to join the intellectual community.

After writing two desperate, cathartic autobiographical novels, Memmi refreshed his creative methods in *The Scorpion*, *Le Désert*, and *Le Pharaon* by exploiting the imaginative possibilities of the autobiographical conventions he had previously respected.

ESSAYS

Memmi is not only a novelist; he has also published sociological, philosophical, and literary essays. The ideas developed in these works fall into three broad categories: the relationship between domination and subjection; the relationship between dependency and provision; and the problems of philosophical writing.

Domination and Subjection

Heading the first category is the essay Memmi wrote after temporarily abandoning fiction in 1956, preferring for a while to render his personal experience in a form different from autobiographical fiction. *The Colonizer and the Colonized* was published in 1957 at the height of the Algerian war and was a great success. Its originality lay in the fact that in establishing the notion of the "duo," or couple, it rejected Marxist theories of colonialism propounded by Sartre and the French West Indian psychoanalyst Frantz Fanon. These theories, fashionable at the time, argued that national liberation movements were but one aspect of the wider, essentially antagonistic class struggle.

Memmi's view was that, on the contrary, the colonizer and the colonized were indissolubly linked within a system that took the shape of a pyramid of petty tyranny. Within that pyramidal structure, the oppressor and the oppressed enjoy small advantages, minor privileges that result in each participant dominating someone else: "Everyone is the oppressed of someone else and, at the same time, the oppressor of someone else" is how Memmi pithily expresses it in *The Colonizer and the Colonized* (p. 46).

Other essays about the relation between domination and subjection are *Portrait of a Jew* (1962), *The Liberation of a Jew* (1966), and *Dominated Man* (1968). In *Portrait of a Jew*, Memmi seeks to "depict the Jewish condition today" on the basis of his own experience and to analyze the "misfortune of being Jewish." Feeling that this account was overly pessimistic, he gives a more upbeat diagnosis in *The Liberation of the Jew*.

These reflections on the Jewish condition and on the colonial situation fed directly into his next book, *Dominated Man*, in which he examines a wider range of human relationships. Misogyny, or hatred of women, for instance, is based on the same notion of "minor privilege" that underpins colonialism as are the unequal relations between master and servant, white and black, and so on. The duo formed by colonizer and colonized can readily, Memmi argues, be replicated in other pairings: white and black, man and woman, Jew and non-Jew. All these duos are similar but not identical to one another. They generate a network of dynamic correlations, of complex and ambiguous relationships, in which the most obvious emotion is the largely justified one of resentment, even hatred, over differences of condition that are all too real. At the same time less negative sentiments can be entertained: the longing to assimilate or resemble the other, on the one side, and paternalism, even genuine affection, on the other.

It follows from this argument that before any attempt is made to secure one's freedom, a careful study has to be undertaken in order to find out what specific form of domination is involved: "The liberation of the oppressed can only be effected in respect of the specific oppression concerned" (*The Liberation of the Jew*, pp. 238–239). As a result "no effective liberation can be proposed unless and until the specificity of the condition of each has been grasped" (*L'Homme dominé*, p. 117).

Dependency and Provision

From these different analyses, surveys carried out with his students, and personal experience in a clinical environment recorded in the introduction to *Dependence*, Memmi deduces that these relations of domination and subjection, which arise out of aggression and conflict, exist side by side with relations of dependency and provision. These are born of natural and cultural desires and needs. In *À contre-courants* Memmi defines dependency as "a more or less willingly accepted constraining relationship with a real or ideal being, object, group, or institution, the relationship in question involving the satisfaction of a need or a desire."

Thus the duo of dominator and dominated coexists with that of provider and dependent, thereby preserving the dialectic of the active and passive subject. All individuals can find themselves at one moment dependents, at another providers; but providers can be either individuals (living or imaginary, God being the absolute provider) or things (for example, alcohol or tobacco). This philosophy, however, is not as pessimistic as it might at first seem. If dependency and provision raise the question of individual freedom, they are also intimately bound up, in the realms of art and love, with positive notions of pleasure and creation. The problem for Memmi is not so much whether one can avoid dependency as how one can live with it. Any form of dependency can, after all, be altered or substituted for any other, so that it is perfectly possible, Memmi argues in *À contre-courants*, to "envisage an optimistic philosophy developing out of the notions of dependency and provision."

Among all the possible duos, one stands at the nexus of dependency and provision: the couple that is formed by a man and a woman, be they lovers or spouses. After studying woman as a particularly oppressed being in *Dominated Man*, Memmi stresses in *Ce que je crois* "that marvel of nature, the male-female couple"—the source of both sexual pleasure, which he regrets denigrating in some of his novels, and personal fulfillment—as one of the most effective instruments for procuring happiness, but also an enclosed space of dominance. In other words, "with its enthusiasms and its sufferings, its moments of delirious happiness or unhappiness, the couple is the most fertile source of discoveries about the nature of being" (*Ce que je crois*, pp. 222–223).

In the essays *Dependence* (1979) and *Le Racisme* (1982) Memmi moves increasingly in the direction of a large-scale sociological theory of oppression. He analyzes notions like racism, which he categorizes as the symbol and epitome of all oppression, as not only "dimensions of the individual and collective psyche" but also concepts for the "understanding of beings, groups, and their various behaviors and habits." It is hardly surprising, given the breadth of Memmi's thought, that the later essays increasingly took the form of fragmented writings, the brief, theoretical utterances of a wide-ranging pedagogical mind. This was particularly true of the definitions Memmi contributed to various dictionaries and encyclopedias, his occasional journalism, and the fragmented *À contre-courants.*

Problems of Philosophical Writing

Memmi's taste for the fragmentary can also be seen in his fiction, particularly in the short texts collected in *Le Mirliton du ciel*, but it is particularly true of the nonfiction written while he was devoting himself to university teaching. Indeed, Memmi has scant esteem for pure philosophy. He eschews all dogmatism and particularly what he calls "the temptations of abstraction," preferring instead the fragmentary but proximate representation of life as it is lived. In his opinion "the philosopher contemplates life from too great a distance; the fragile system that he constructs as a result cannot cope with the complexities of life" (*Bonheurs*, p. 129).

Memmi's essays reject the impenetrability of much philosophical writing. Instead, they are designed like preliminary sketches or puzzles that deepen and progressively widen the insight that serves as their starting point, systematically conceptualizing all the while on the basis of actual experience or field research. Memmi clearly envisages his work as a developing opus, with each book slotted deliberately and necessarily into the next, for as he explains in *The Liberation of the Jew*:

> I have told how, at a crucial period in my life, I felt compelled to come to grips with these problems, and I set myself to this enormous and urgent task. And so, although at first I had no intention of doing so, I described in succession the life of a North African, the story of a mixed marriage, the portrait of the colonized, then that of a Jew. Perhaps I will never get to the end of this inexhaustible inventory.
>
> (p. 167)

Despite the contradictions that exemplify the life of Memmi—a Tunisian Jew who married a Frenchwoman from a practicing

Christian family, a child of the ghetto who became a French writer and university teacher (with the success in achieving intimacy with French language and culture that implies), and a North African intellectual who drew upon his personal experience to create a continually renewed body of work—there is no contradiction between the essayist and the novelist. Memmi's work explores a few remarkably consistent themes from a dazzling variety of angles.

Selected Bibliography

NOVELS

La Statue de sel. Paris: Corréa, 1953.
Agar. Paris: Corréa Buchet-Chastel, 1955.
Le Scorpion; ou, La Confession imaginaire. Paris: Gallimard, 1969.
Le Désert; ou, La Vie et les aventures de Jubaïr Quali El-Mammi. Paris: Gallimard, 1977.
Le Pharaon: Roman. Paris: Julliard, 1988.

ESSAYS, POETRY, JOURNALISM

Portrait du colonisé, précéde d'un portrait du colonisateur. Paris: Corréa, 1957.
Portrait d'un Juif. Paris: Gallimard, 1962.
La Libération du Juif. Paris: Gallimard, 1966.
L'Homme dominé. Paris: Gallimard, 1968.
Juifs et Arabes. Paris: Gallimard, 1974.
La Dépendance: Esquisse pour un portrait du dépendant. Paris: Gallimard, 1979.
Le Racisme: Description, définition, traitement. Paris: Gallimard, 1982.
Ce que je crois. Paris: Grasset, 1985.
L'Écriture colorée; ou, Je vous aime en rouge: Essai sur une dimension nouvelle de l'écriture, la couleur. Paris: Périple, 1986.
Le Mirliton du ciel. Paris: Lahabè, 1985. Rev. ed. Paris: Julliard, 1990.
Bonheurs: 52 semaines. Paris: Arléa, 1992.
À contre-courants. Paris: Nouvel Objet, 1993.
Ah quel bonheur! Paris: Arléa, 1995.
Le Juif et l'autre. Paris: De Bartillist, 1995.

INTERVIEWS

La Terre intérieure. Paris: Gallimard, 1976.

TRANSLATIONS

The Pillar of Salt. Trans. by Edouard Roditi. New York: Orion, 1955. Rev. ed. Boston: Beacon, 1992.
Strangers. Trans. by Brian Rhys. New York: Orion, 1960.
Portrait of a Jew. Trans. by Elisabeth Abbott. New York: Orion, 1962. Rev. ed. New York: Viking, 1971.
The Colonizer and the Colonized. Trans. by Howard Greenfeld. New York: Orion, 1965. Expanded ed. with intro. by Jean-Paul Sartre. afterword by Susan G. Miller. Boston: Beacon, 1992.
The Liberation of the Jew. Trans. by Judy Hyun. New York: Orion, 1966. Rev. ed. New York: Viking, 1973.
Dominated Man: Notes Toward a Portrait. Trans. by Eleanor Levieux. Boston: Beacon, 1968.
The Scorpion. Trans. by Eleanor Levieux. New York: Orion, 1971.
Jews and Arabs. Trans. by Eleanor Levieux. Chicago: J. P. O'Hara, 1975.
Dependence: A Sketch for a Portrait of the Dependent. Trans. by Philip A. Facey. Boston: Beacon, 1984.

CRITICAL STUDIES

Dugas, Guy. *Albert Memmi, écrivain de la déchirure.* Sherbrooke, Canada: Éditions Naaman, 1984.
Elbaz, Robert. *Le Discours maghrébin: Dynamique textuelle chez Albert Memmi.* Longueil, Canada: Le Préambule, 1988.
Guérin, Jeanyves, ed. *Albert Memmi, écrivain et sociologue: Actes du colloque de Paris X-Nanterre, 15 et 16 mai 1988.* Paris: L'Harmattan, 1990.
Roumani, Judith. *Albert Memmi.* Philadelphia: Celfan, 1987.

Thomas Mokopu Mofolo

1876–1948

DANIEL P. KUNENE

WHEN THOMAS Mokopu Mofolo was born on 22 December 1876 in Khojane, Lesotho, this southern African country had not only shrunk to a minute size as a result of continuous onslaughts by the Boers from the Orange River Sovereignty, but it had also become a protectorate (in reality, a colony) of Britain. French missionaries had arrived in Lesotho in 1833, and Mofolo's parents, Abner and Aleta, had been converted to Christianity. Mofolo's Christianization thus began at home and continued through the church, secular schools, and the Bible School at Morija.

Although the church aimed its message directly at its targets, the school was the most successful Christianizing instrument. In addition to giving students the power to read the Bible, it also used subtler means—insinuating the Christian message into the content of all its subjects, including literature, history, geography, and the sciences. Farsighted missionaries such as Dr. James Stewart of Lovedale argued vehemently for missions to spend money on establishing schools. In his *Dawn in the Dark Continent* (1903), Stewart maintained that "if missionary education communicated no other power than ability to read the Bible, it would still justify itself" (p. 180).

Mofolo was born into a traditional Sesotho culture. While the missionaries had made significant progress in their attempts to Christianize the Basotho people, the majority of the Basotho continued to live according to traditional values and beliefs. The influence of this pervasive culture must have remained with the young Mofolo even as he attended the elementary school at Qomoqomong in the Quthing District run by the Reverend Frederic Ellenberger and then studied from 1894 to 1896 at the Bible School. From there he went to train as a teacher at the Morija Training School. This education was not free, and after completing only one year of his three-year course, Mofolo had to quit school and find work with the intention of saving money and resuming his training later. G. H. Franz quotes Mofolo's description of what happened next:

> I lacked money for school fees, and wrote and told Mr. Dyke that I was not coming back to school in 1898. During that week I went to the Maloti to bring down horses to take me to work amongst the White People. At dawn I set out to go to work, but when I passed the post office I found a letter from Mr. Dyke which prevented my going and ordered me back to school permitting me to complete my studies "on credit."
>
> I turned back at once and went home to tell my parents of the change in plans.
>
> (p. 168)

Not only did Mofolo obtain his teacher training at Morija, but several times, starting in the late 1890s, he was employed by the Morija Sesuto Book Depot, which was to become a major publishing house for Basotho authors. Indeed by this time Azariel M. Sekese's *Buka ya pokello ya mekgwa ya Basotho, le maele le ditshomo* (1893), a collection of Basotho customs, proverbs, and folktales, had been published there. Then, in 1900, the Anglo-Boer War of 1899–1902 interrupted the work of the Depot as well as the printing office, and Mofolo went to Leloaleng Technical School to learn carpentry.

After teaching at Bensonvale Institution in the Cape Province, and then in Maseru, the capital of Lesotho, he was called back to Morija to become secretary to the Reverend Alfred Casalis and also to proofread for the publishing house. This work quickened his latent talent as a writer, and according to Albert Gérard he was encouraged "to do some writing of his own by several missionaries" (1971, p. 109), specifically Casalis, Sam Duby, and the Reverend Edouard Jacottet.

Among the intellectually challenging activities taking place at Morija at that time was publication of the newspaper *Leselinyana la Lesotho* (The little light of Lesotho), which was established in 1863 by the Reverend Adolphe Mabille. This newspaper stimulated popular interest in reading and writing and became a vehicle for many literary efforts by Christianized Basotho. To be able to interpret marks on a paper and decipher the words of a message was nothing short of a miracle or witchcraft; to be able to make those marks oneself was a newfound power; to see one's own writing in print in a newspaper was a tremendous thrill and source of pride. As a vehicle for accelerating the Christianizing process, therefore, *Leselinyana* had tremendous potential, which the missionaries fully exploited.

The primary reason for establishing this newspaper, however, was to challenge, and in the process discredit, many customs and practices of the Basotho. Mabille states this as his purpose in a December 1863 letter to his parents accompanying a copy of "the first number of my newspaper" (in the Morija Archives). The paper published protracted debates, mostly favoring the missionaries, on such questions as *lebollo* (circumcision), bride-price, or *bohadi* (passing of cattle, prior to marriage, from the parents of the groom to the parents of the bride), the Basotho's knowledge, or lack thereof, of God prior to the arrival of the missionaries, and so on. As early as the 1 October 1864 issue, *Leselinyana* unleashed a vicious attack on the custom of circumcision as having no value whatsoever and being "a disgraceful game in which big men deceive their children with lies" (quoted in Kunene, 1989, p. 51). This attack becomes worse when it takes the form of a series of rhetorical questions: "What is taught at the circumcision lodge besides lies, theft, fornication and conceit? Who among the circumcised ever come out of these knowing how to make grass basins or grain storage baskets, or how to tailor blankets, or to thatch houses, or to love and obey his parents, or to honour his Creator?" (quoted in Kunene, 1989, p. 51).

When, therefore, Mofolo begins his first book, *Moeti oa bochabela* (1907; *The Traveller of the East*), with words that depict the Basotho as savages, his intention is deliberate and self-conscious. He states that the Basotho of the premissionary days, in which his story is set, were living in deep, pitch-black darkness and ate each other like animals of the veld. At the same time, Mofolo conveys a sense of the enormous reservoir of Basotho traditional values. The struggle between these opposing values—that is, between tradition and change—characterizes Mofolo's work throughout his career.

MOETI

Moeti was first published as a volume in September 1907 after bimonthly installments had run in *Leselinyana* beginning in January of that year. The missionaries received the book with much excitement, and a long introduction-cum-review by the Reverend Hermann Dieterlen accompanies its first announcement in *Leselinyana* and strongly urges the Basotho to buy it. Dieterlen says: "Today there has come into existence a book which ought to be publicised and bought and read by each and every one who calls himself a Mosotho or who loves the Basotho and their traditions. Its name is *Moeti oa Bochabela.* Its writer is Thomas Mofolo who works at the Book depot at Morija."

The opposition of tradition and change is accomplished in this book through the contrast of darkness and light and other compatible images: night versus day; beasthood versus humanity; people, who are controlled by greed, lust for power, sexual promiscuity, and failure to impose self-restraint and are inherently evil, versus nature (animals, vegetation, sun, moon, stars), which is above moral judgment; ugliness versus beauty; wrong versus right; war and strife versus peace and security; and, ultimately, black people and their values versus white people and their values. To represent these oppositions artistically, Mofolo creates the characters Phakoane, who represents evil, and Fekisi, who represents good.

As the novel begins, Mofolo presents a corrupt society which engages in all manner of evil: excessive indulgence in carnal pleasures; drunkenness; gross injustice; rampant killings and murders of innocent people; and constant wars motivated by nothing more than sheer savagery and love of violence and destruction. One day there is a total eclipse of the sun—the darkness is deeper than the darkness of night—which is interpreted as a manifestation of divine wrath occasioned by man's sinfulness. As a consequence of this event and its interpretation, the evil Phakoane, who has killed his wife while he was drunk, is driven to insanity and runs bleary-eyed, shouting and screaming for forgiveness. Eventually he falls down and dies. Mofolo describes a spectacular death scene:

> [Phakoane] threw himself repeatedly on the ground complaining that something was gnawing him inside. He perspired profusely. At last the people saw his fingers getting blistered and blackened, oozing liquid like roasting meat. The same thing happened to his feet and his heels. You could feel pity for him, poor man. At last he died, and his face had a most frightening appearance; it was distorted and very strained, and it had gone very black and ugly, just like the face of a murderer. When they wrapped him in a cowhide to go and bury him, the corpse's mouth opened wide, and its facial muscles tightened like someone feeling excruciating pain. The people threw it down and ran away, and only buried it the next day. Even then, it looked so frightening that they buried it in a great hurry and ran away, since they felt so afraid.
>
> (*Moeti*, pp. 29–30)

The eclipse also precipitates the hero Fekisi's departure in search of God and a society that obeys the laws of God. As darkness descends in the middle of the day, order gives way to chaos because the normal rhythm of life is disrupted. People and animals alike are thrown into a state of utter confusion:

> The cattle bellowed. They scattered in flight and fell down the slopes. . . . The animals ran away, colliding with people since they did not know where they were going. Over there in the village, a person who was outside would try to find his house but would walk into a rock. He would try to feel his way towards his house but would collide with another person, or with a dog, or some other object. Dogs screamed and howled.
>
> (p. 27)

This is a symbolic representation of the society that Fekisi wants to escape, a society that has no future and collides with all kinds of obstacles because it lacks light. Fekisi fervently believes the sun to be God's eye, a messenger who daily reports what he has seen when he returns to his master at sunset.

Through its eclipse, the sun has demonstrated its displeasure at the people's sinful lives. Anticipating the imminent destruction of his society, Fekisi (whose thoughts are portrayed as voices, visions, and dreams) decides to start his journey out of darkness toward light.

How does Fekisi know where to go when he leaves his village? On the night following the eclipse, he has a dream in which he sees, far away in the east, a place that fits the image of Ntswanatsatsi (or Ntsoanatsatsi) as described by the elders of his community when he had asked them where God lives. Ntswanatsatsi, they told him, "is toward the east where there is a dense growth of reeds growing in a great pool of water, where there is a great fountain bubbling, where the sun comes out." And, they continued, that is why the Basotho say "a child comes out of a deep pool," which, in a nutshell, is the Basotho story of the origin of humankind (p. 19).

In his dream Fekisi sees a silhouette floating in space toward the place he knows must be Ntswanatsatsi. A white Christ figure, it is covered in transparent mist; its hair is so long that it sweeps the ground and Fekisi cannot see where it ends. The face of the apparition, even though seen only in silhouette, is so beautiful that its radiance makes Fekisi weep.

Whether Mofolo intends it or not, the image represents a beautiful marriage between Eden and Ntswanatsatsi, symbols of two religions that on the surface are incompatible. Yet early in the book, Mofolo in fact concedes that the Basotho of premissionary days were conscious of the existence of a supreme being higher in authority than the ancestral spirits: "The ancient Basotho ... believed that there was a living God who had created all things. They believed that God rejected all evil. They said that God hated witchcraft and things like that" (pp. 2–3).

He also states that Basotho dirges sung at funerals show that they believed that life continued after death. As part of their burial rites, he says, they put seeds and implements in the hands of the deceased, who was addressed "as if he/she was hearing them" and was asked to beg for rain and an abundance of crops from the higher God. The funeral songs express a longing for that place:

> O, if only I too could be taken to heaven!
> Why do I lack wings? For else I too would go
>   there!
> If there was a string hanging down
> I would hold on to it
> And climb up to my people in that
> place of peace.
>
> (p. 3)

Despite the implications of the pitch-black darkness in the opening sentences of the novel, Mofolo works to contradict assertions that the Basotho were ignorant of God before the missionaries arrived: "songs like these show that right there in the midst of so much darkness a little knowledge of God was still to be found" (p. 3).

That Fekisi travels eastward emphasizes the novel's metaphor of light. The sun is Fekisi's constant guide, and every morning when it rises and "hits him on the forehead" he knows that he is still on the right course. By the time he reaches the sea, Ntswanatsatsi has faded out of the picture.

The sea presents a challenge different from the other barriers he has thus far confronted, such as forests, rivers, deserts, and mountains: it is a wilderness of sand and endless water; it is hard to walk in the sand; it is impossible to maintain the eastward direction with the water barring his way; the seawater is salty and undrinkable. He succumbs to exhaustion and frustration and falls down unconscious. At this point Mofolo makes reference to the arrival of three French missionaries in Lesotho, as he introduces three white elephant hunters who work to revive Fekisi. Here Mofolo reverses the historical order of the missionary project: Fekisi goes out to meet his saviors, and they take him overseas. This artistic manipulation merely serves the story's original intent, that Fekisi exile himself from his people and his homeland.

As he sails with them, thus happily continuing his eastward journey, the white men divest Fekisi of everything that represents his culture, including his language and myths. Fekisi's sea passage therefore represents both cleansing (by water) and separation (the space between his old world and the new one to which he is being transported), both of which are quintessential metaphors for rites of passage. In this new world, he finds the kind of society he has yearned for, and in the novel's second spectacular death scene, he finds God.

Death is the final judgment in which evil is punished and good rewarded. Fekisi has reached a place that seems to answer his notion of a righteous society and stays at the house of the local minister, but he is not yet sure if this is the end of his journey. Not long after his arrival, there is an important church service to which he is invited and in which several ministers officiate. Toward the end of the service, the presiding minister calls on the congregation to come and kneel before the altar for blessings. As wave after wave of the congregation comes forward, the minister's eyes meet those of Fekisi, who is kneeling but whose head is not bowed like those of the rest of the congregation.

Fekisi is "looking intently at the wall on the eastern side of the building, above the altar," with "a great longing in his eyes, and his hands folded on his chest." While the minister intones some words from the Bible, "Fekisi got up quickly and took two steps forward. His eyes were intense and sharp as arrows, gazing fixedly at the spot above the altar, like someone who saw an omen on that spot.... His face was transformed and was bright, and it shone with an amazing glory, like the face of a newborn child" (pp. 73–74).

A mist, at first thin but then becoming dense, flows down from the ceiling and creeps down the wall to the spot where Fekisi is gazing. The ministers flee from the platform in fear. Fekisi stares even harder, as if his eyes will pop out of his face. He sees the silhouette he has seen in a dream in Lesotho, which is exceedingly beautiful with "eyes, [that] were full of truth and love and compassion." It is "the Son of Man in person" with three men on either side of him. "Fekisi ran forward with his arms stretched out, and he threw himself on the altar shouting: 'Hail, my Jesus! I have longed for you. Oh, that I may go with you home to the Lord.'" This incident is followed by voices coming out of the mist, saying: "Open the doors for him and let him enter, for he loved the Son of Man in hard times and in good times" (pp. 73–74). His face, after he dies, is full of joy and peace.

Moeti begins with deep darkness and concludes with a blaze of celestial light as Fekisi is admitted into heaven. The lives of Fekisi and Phakoane, and their deaths, are twin metaphors that reinforce the contrasting images of darkness and light. Mofolo exploits the visual impact of these vividly portrayed pictures of the two men as they die: Phakoane's appearance evokes revulsion, disgust, and fear, while Fekisi's calls forth a sense of peace, serenity, and reassurance.

Death is such a powerful force in this work because it was a powerful weapon from the pulpit. The fear of death was exploited by missionaries to convert people to Christianity by promising a beautiful, glorious life in heaven with God to those who lived a good, Christian life, and eternal burning in hell for those who lived a life of evil and corruption, with their torturer, the devil, as a constant companion. A comparison of the two death scenes illustrates these sharply contrasting fates of people's souls after death. It is clear from the distortion of Phakoane's features after his death and during his burial that the devil has already begun his job. No one wants to die like that. Fekisi's death is projected as the crowning glory of a life dedicated to the pursuit of goodness and the search for the vital force, or God.

The novel's didactic intent seems overtly to reinforce the missionaries' condemnation of many Basotho customs, which explains their enthusiastic reception of this book. And many critics were glad to read the evils of which Mofolo wrote as fact, not fiction. G. H. Franz, for example, considered the book as "painting a vivid picture of the early life of the Basotho, and showing up all the evils in lurid colours" (p. 174). In reference to Fekisi's description of a murder plot—in which he intervenes and saves the intended victim—in a village of the Batlokoa in the early stages of his journey, Franz concludes that Fekisi "soon finds that people of other Bantu races are no better than his own people." In fact, Alice Werner found it necessary to sound a note of caution, remarking that "one finds that native converts, flushed with the joy of enlightenment and progress, are apt to exaggerate the evils of their former state and overlook its better features; they want, like most young and enthusiastic reformers, to scrap the past wholesale" (1925, p. 431).

A more careful reading nonetheless reveals that, while overtly and enthusiastically advocating the new culture, Mofolo parenthetically articulates the Basotho myth of origin. It is an important parenthesis because this myth constitutes a strong countermotif that, for at least the early part of the story, runs parallel to the Bible's Eden myth. Examined this way, *Moeti* ceases to be "pure mission stuff" (p. 101), as Janheinz Jahn characterizes it, and reveals itself as a complex statement on the contradictions and ambiguities of change.

PITSENG

These contradictions and ambiguities persist in Mofolo's second novel, *Pitseng*, published in 1910. Mofolo wrote *Pitseng* within the context of a concatenation of auspicious events signaling the political awakening of the Basotho. In 1907 Mofolo helped found the highly nationalistic political organization Kopano ea Tsoelopele (Union for Progress). The Kopano's first president, Cranmer 'Matsa Sebeta, was a long-standing critic of white-dominated institutions in Lesotho, starting with the Paris Evangelical Missionary Society (PEMS) itself. Sebeta rejected the PEMS schools and established his own in 1886. He resigned from the missionary church in 1899 to join the recently established African Methodist Episcopal Church (A.M.E.) also known as the Ethiopian Church. A.M.E. was totally black-controlled and was formed by blacks who were disgruntled with the Wesleyan Methodist Church's white monopoly of power within the church hierarchy.

These nationalistic stirrings were further reinforced by the founding, in 1904, of the black-owned newspaper, *Naledi ea Lesotho* (The Star of Lesotho). This newspaper and its successor, *Mochochonono*, are described by Les and Donna Switzer in *The Black Press in South Africa and Lesotho* (1979) as the "only known publications independent of the missionary societies, the British colonial government and other white individuals and institutions, and even the monarchy, in Lesotho during this period" (p. 51).

In *Pitseng*, Mofolo the conservative and Mofolo the progressive are still struggling for a balance. He criticizes the way missionaries and whites in general have undermined admirable Basotho customs in matters of love, courtship, and marriage. There are striking parallels between the criticisms he levels at the whites and some of the demands of the Kopano. At the same time, the people of Pitseng (like Fekisi's people in *Moeti*) are described as living in darkness until the arrival of the novel's hero, the Christian "Mr. Katse."

The man who sets the action in motion in this book remains nameless throughout the story, except for the nickname he is given by his students. They call him Mr. Katse (Mr. Cat) because of his cap made from the skin of a wild cat. When Mofolo introduces him on his journey to revive the church and school in Pitseng, he is only "a certain young man." He is undertaking this journey on orders from his seniors, the white missionaries, to preach and teach in Pitseng. From that point on, he is known as *mmoledi* (preacher). That Mofolo expects the reader readily to accept the namelessness of this character suggests a carryover from the oral tradition, where actors in the stories are often nameless or identified by their characteristics, the functions they fulfill in the story, or their familial relationships.

Mr. Katse's dearest wish is that his two students Alfred Phakoe and Aria Sebaka will discover each other and marry, which in fact happens toward the end of the story but not before they have been buffeted by various temptations to join in the self-indulgence, sometimes amounting to recklessness, of the youth around them. Their marriage is the culmination of long and difficult journeys, which they undertake as a response to Mr. Katse's remarkable sermon on the elusive nature of true love.

Aria's impressionable young mind makes her imagine a world in which young lovers and married couples love each other with the wonderful love articulated in the sermon: she "was very impressed by the lives of the inhabitants of that land, and she wished that the same would happen in Lesotho. She for her part would try to live like them even though she was still but a little girl" (p. 36). In Alfred, the sermon sparks skepticism and resolve: "Alfred wondered whether such love really existed. . . . Thereupon he resolved to try with all the strength in his heart and soul, to be like the virgin who was said to have been betrothed to Jesus" (p. 36). Indeed Alfred's search turns into something of a saga: he travels to various parts of southern Africa and observes the love, courtship, and marriage customs of different peoples, yet he finds none that answers to the stringent qualities described by Mr. Katse.

After Mr. Katse dies, Alfred is appointed to his position by the people of Pitseng, who find him the most suitable and natural successor to his late mentor. This appointment is crowned by his marriage to Aria. The Pitseng that Alfred takes over is different from the one Katse stepped into at the beginning of his career. At that time Pitseng was spiritually impoverished despite its wealth of pastures, arable land, and wild game, a veritable paradise of pristine innocence and nature's bounty. People observed "old Sesotho customs" rather than the modern ways; sent their children to circumcision lodges, not schools, because there were none; and drank to excess. But Katse worked hard to change this situation; therefore, Alfred inherits a Pitseng where great numbers of erstwhile nonbelievers have been converted, largely because Mr. Katse was generous, compassionate, and selfless as he applied his Christian principles to serve the needs of people.

The book ends with a highly lyrical, romantic description of the bride and groom, bridesmaids and best men, wedding service, and general festivities in the village. On the afternoon of this clear and beautiful spring day, the young couple and their entourage take a long, slow stroll in the fields splashed with wildflowers, and flocks of birds fly this way and that as if to greet them. It is a poetic conclusion, akin to a hymn to nature, in which Mofolo's descriptive powers are at their best.

With the two young people's curiosity and resolve as a pretext, Mofolo uses this novel to give vivid pictures of Christianized and westernized Basotho youth engaging in ephemeral and promiscuous relationships, and he observes ruefully: "Courtship has become a plaything. This beautiful thing that belongs to mature young men and young women seeking to establish their homes, and which is the vehicle whereby to consummate their youth, has today become a plaything and a mockery" (p. 25).

Several times in this story, Mofolo engages in long excursuses to describe in detail the Basotho's approved way of pursuing courtship and marriage. Love and sex are only meaningful and acceptable in the context of marriage. The entire process is subject to parental, extended family, and ultimately societal scrutiny and approval. The individual finds fulfillment within these forms of socially sanctioned behavior.

The arrival of the whites disrupted this idyllic situation and indirectly but strongly moved the Basotho youth toward a more individual-oriented mode of behavior that made parental and other societal controls obsolete. In two lengthy digressions, Mofolo extols the virtues of the old system and roundly condemns the new white values:

> This is exactly where the heathens are telling the truth when they say that these evil things come from the whites, and have entered into Lesotho through the Christian converts, because this habit whereby a young man and his girl friend make their own decision about marriage began with the converts. This spirit has completely destroyed the youth of Lesotho.
>
> (p. 26)

A reader deduces that the unconverted Basotho who continued to live in their traditional style were vocal about what they saw as a destructive trend. The irony here is that Mofolo, to judge by this book and *Moeti*, would still like to see these "heathens" converted to Christianity, as Mr. Katse does so successfully in Pitseng Valley.

The other instance in which Mofolo rejects white influences is expressed in terms of images of darkness and light, similar to those projected so strongly in *Moeti*. This time, however, definitions are marked by oxymora, in which darkness and light coexist:

> The modern days are said to be days of light, of wisdom, of progress, while the olden days, the days of the *difaqane*, are said to have been days of darkness, of foolishness, and ignorance. But in this matter of marriage we have found that to many people those days of old were days of wisdom, and not darkness and ignorance, and it is the modern days that are days of darkness and ignorance, and not of wisdom and light.
>
> (p. 128)

Mofolo consciously and vehemently advocates a cultural tolerance that recognizes the good of both cultures and rejects the bad. He clearly and unequivocally rejects white cultural chauvinism.

The assertion that the days of the *difaqane* were days of light is a dramatic reversal of the position Mofolo holds so strongly at the beginning of *Moeti*. The word *difaqane* (a Sothoization of the Zulu *imfecane*) was first used to describe Shaka's (in Sotho, Chaka's) wars, which set many nations in flight and destroyed their villages and crops. In *Moeti*, Mofolo applies the *difaqane* metaphor to the Basotho of Fekisi's time, describing people as no better than animals who eat each other. He tells of surprise raids and attacks that separated families. But the positive things about Basotho culture, which Mofolo ignores in his first novel in order to dramatize the evil he perceives, suddenly surface in *Pitseng*, and we are shown some light in the darkness of the *difaqane*. Mofolo mourns the passing of those days. Noting that the young men and women of Lesotho at the turn of the century were indulging in promiscuous relationships, he says, "The Lesotho of old is finished, it is finished together with its beautiful ways, because it was a frightfully shameful thing for a person to do something like that in the olden days" (p. 34).

But those were also the days when the *bohadi* custom was observed, a custom with which Mofolo vehemently disagrees. He suggests that many parents who force their daughters to marry men they don't love are interested more in obtaining a large *bohadi* than in their daughters' happiness. He likens the *bohadi* custom to a sale, an argument also used by the missionaries in condemning what came to be known as "cattle" marriages. According to Mofolo, *bohadi* has become a mercenary transaction and has lost its original meaning and dignity.

Mofolo, then, strives for mutual accommodation between the old and the new. Despite his criticism of Pitseng before Katse arrives, he warns against unthinkingly casting aside all Sesotho customs in the belief that they are bad and accepting wholesale all of the European ways on the assumption that they are good.

CHAKA

In writing *Chaka* (1925), Mofolo undertook to bring together biography, history, and fiction. Each of these genres makes its own demands on the writer, and most importantly, the end result must be a coherent story. Mofolo recognized the importance of history and fiction and strove to make the marriage work. Choosing Chaka, king of the Zulus in the early part of the nineteenth century, as his biographical subject, he attempted to enter the psyche of his protagonist to find out why he did the things he did as he grew up and, particularly, after he became king—in other words, how he saw the world and himself in it. Research to verify certain facts, imaginative creativity, and descriptions of the power of witchcraft and other supernatural manifestations all play important roles and are fully exploited by Mofolo in order to achieve his two main aims: to be truthful to history and tell a good story.

Mofolo's reply to the Reverend S. M. Malale, who challenged him on a point of historical accuracy, affirms the need for integrity in both representing reality and allowing the artist freedom to create unfettered by the demands of factual accuracy—to represent truth as both fact and fiction. In *Leselinyana* of 10 August 1928, he concedes to Malale that he may indeed have made an error in representing the facts the way he did in the episode in question and goes on to say:

> I believe that errors of this kind are very many in the book *Chaka*; but I am not very concerned about them because I am not writing history, I am writing a tale. Or I should rather say I am writing what actually happened, but to which a great deal has been added, and from which a great deal has been removed, so that much has been left out, and much has been written that did not actually happen, with the aim solely of fulfilling my purpose in writing this book.

To coalesce history and fiction so that they reinforce each other in order to produce the kind of powerful story that *Chaka* is, Mofolo boldly creates motives where the historian can only make tentative speculations. For instance, some ambiguity surrounds the circumstances of the historical Chaka's life: Was he born out of wedlock? How did that come about? Mofolo's answer to the first question corroborates history, but for motivation—that is, in answer to the question "why?"—he allows his imagination free rein by letting Senzangakhona, who lacks a son and heir from his first three wives, act contrary to custom by having sexual intercourse with Nandi, the young woman he has chosen to be his next wife. On learning that Nandi is at least two months into her pregnancy, Senzangakhona makes quick preparations to marry her. She gives birth to a boy, which fulfills Senzangakhona's wish but also creates a potentially explosive situation because conception of the heir goes contrary to societal norms. This well-chosen motif leads naturally into the motif of the jealous co-wives.

Mofolo also addresses another ambiguous historical issue: Did Senzangakhona chase Nandi out of his household back to her birth home? If so, why? Again history corroborates Mofolo's answer to the first question. The motivation, on the other hand, is purely fictional. The senior wives, who have given birth to sons of their own since the birth of Chaka and are driven by jealousy and ambition for one of them to replace Chaka as Senzangakhona's successor, threaten to expose Nandi's premarital pregnancy and involve her and Senzangakhona in a scandal and political embarrassment. When they demand the expulsion of Nandi and Chaka, Senzangakhona, who contrary to historical explanations still loves both of them, feels too threatened to resist their demands.

Mofolo deftly juggles the old and the new, seeking to harmonize them. As a result, the narrator recognizes the good and the bad in the Zulu society that provides the sociocultural context for *Chaka.* He castigates the evil in Chaka as the evil of one individual in an otherwise normal society of polygamous marriages, belief in witchcraft, worship of ancestral spirits, and other cultural traits that would have earned harsh criticism in *Moeti.* The society itself is peaceful until Chaka arrives. According to the narrator, "the sufferings which were occasioned by the *difaqane* were unknown in the olden days when the people were still settled upon the land. The nations were living in peace, each one in its own original territory where it had been from the day that Nkulunkulu, the Great-Great One, caused the people to emerge from a bed of reeds" (p. 4).

The Zulu worldview is fully accepted. When Nandi engages a traditional doctor to strengthen Chaka with her powerful charms and magical skills, there is nothing but approval from the narrator. But he also expresses misgivings that the blessings Chaka receives to enable him to meet the challenges facing him are mixed with the danger that his soul is about to be corrupted. The doctor endows him with powers to ensure that "even if his attackers should surround him in a large group, they will never defeat him, but instead he will scatter them with ease. He will kill rather than be killed" (p. 14).

The narrator finds it gratifying to know that because of his newfound powers, Chaka, when confronted by his erstwhile persecutors, his fellow herdboys, "would give them terrible gaping wounds with his blows, till they fled," and that "soon all the herdboys gave up fighting him, and he became their leader" (p. 15). The narrator also explains how, up to that time, Chaka "had never been the one to provoke a fight, and he was not quarrelsome, but now these medicines spurred him on and he even went to the pastures in defiance of his grandmother's orders" (p. 15), that is, to provoke a fight. Ominous signs indicate that the new Chaka will love war and go out of his way to be the aggressor. In fact, in the last two paragraphs of the second chapter, Chaka has "an uncontrollable desire to fight" (p. 14), dreams about the glories of war and conquest, and sees himself putting to flight hordes of enemy warriors. Yet the narrator suspends judgment and continues to believe that Chaka is capable of human compassion and kindness. After all, he uses his powers to kill a lion and thereby relieves the village from continuous harassment and saves a man from being mauled by the lion. He also saves a girl by killing a hyena that has her in its jaws.

Nonetheless, warning signs occur, even early in the story. A serpentine monster with two tongues, which suggest duplicity, emerges out of a dark, mysterious pool and implicitly demands that Chaka accept it by locking his eyes into its own. A voice booming out of the deep, after promising Chaka conquest over people and nature, cautions him to "go by the right path" (p. 24). It is not surprising when, later in the story, Isanusi tells Chaka: "the great king who once visited you at the river is a person who loves war; if you do not spill blood, he will not be pleased with you" (p. 45).

Isanusi, the diviner, is the incarnation of evil. His duplicity, which he uses throughout to lure Chaka and trap him into compromising situations, is reflected, at their first encounter in the wilderness, by his face, which changes at the blinking of an eye from deepest hatred and guile to deepest love and compassion. Chaka is being warned to be wary of this man and to reject him before it is too late. But Chaka, the innocent victim of hatred and persecution, rejected by his father, and ready to grab any straw, falls easy prey to Isanusi's guiles.

Mofolo's vigilant narrator, who observes this encounter with increasing alarm, gives up all hope when Chaka accepts the medicine described by Isanusi as "extremely evil, but... also extremely good" (p. 43). The diviner, who describes this as "a medicine associated with the spilling of blood, with killing," commands Chaka to "Choose!" whether or not he will accept it (p. 43). Without hesitation, Chaka replies, "I want it," and the narrator proclaims that "now the final link has been cut, Chaka has deliberately chosen death instead of life" (p. 43).

Throughout the novel, Mofolo underscores the importance of personal responsibility for the moral choices one makes in life. Chaka confronts many of these choices: to accept or not to accept the double-tongued serpentine monster of the deep pool; to accept or not to accept the double-faced Isanusi; to welcome or reject the medicine that requires the continuous spilling of blood for its efficacy; to determine who is "the best loved one" he has to sacrifice; to kill or reprieve "the best loved one" and consequently become or not become the greatest king ever known.

The river scene where Chaka meets the deep-pool monster constitutes a choice in its own way: The monster slides out of the pool toward him as he stands near the bank. When it sticks out its tongues, Chaka shuts his eyes out of fear and the monster withdraws. Not feeling it touch him, Chaka opens his eyes again and sees the eyes of the monster still gazing straight into his own eyes—but the monster is about to disappear under the water with its tongues withdrawn. The monster obviously interprets Chaka's shutting his eyes as rejection. Realizing this, Chaka

> looked direct into the pupils of its eyes, and it too looked at him in a like manner. They stared at each other, the snake in its own abode and the man come there to provoke it. . . .
>
> At last the snake came out of the water again. . . . He stared at it till it reached the point where it had been when he shut his eyes. It stuck out its tongues and wrapped them around his neck, and they crossed at the back of his head and came to join again in front.
>
> (p. 23)

If Chaka intends to reject the monster, all he needs to do is keep his eyes shut. But he opens them and purposefully locks his gaze with that of the monster.

A similar staring contest occurs later between Chaka and Isanusi. In their early exploratory exchanges, before Chaka knows who this stranger is, Isanusi says, " 'You must look straight into my eyes as I talk to you,' and they looked at each other" (p. 38). Once again, Chaka makes a choice.

In all the choices that Chaka has to make, however, Isanusi's role is to suggest, to plant an idea in Chaka's mind and watch it grow. Isanusi stays in the background while goading Chaka toward the choice he wants him to make. With carefully chosen words, he guides, prompts, insinuates, and cues, but never states explicitly. The way he guides Chaka toward recognizing him when they first meet is a case in point. He is determined that his identity should be first articulated by Chaka; when Chaka is too slow to recognize him, he resorts to an ultimatum. With some irritation he says: "If even now you still don't know who I am, or if you have now changed your mind, you must tell me so that I may pass on and go where they are waiting for me" (p. 40).

At last the message gets through to Chaka, and, almost insane with joy, he asks, "Tell me, is it you who are supposed to complete . . ." and then chokes with emotion (p. 40). In response, Isanusi simply nods his head.

Isanusi's role is to confirm that Chaka's decision is correct but never to enunciate it himself. When, at their first meeting, Chaka responds to a question by explaining that all he wants is his father's kingship restored to him, Isanusi says: "I understand. All you want is your father's kingship, beyond that there is nothing you want, not even a kingship that surpasses that of your father. That is what you are saying, is that not so? (p. 41). Thus, without actually saying so, he insinuates that there are greater things for which to strive. Chaka immediately takes the cue and responds enthusiastically that, if there is a greater kingship than his father's, of course he wants it.

But the most painful choice that Chaka has to make is that between a kingship higher even than that of Dingiswayo, the most powerful king of the time, and someone he loves more than anyone else in the world. In order to obtain this ultimate kingship, Chaka's armies have to be fortified with medicines mixed with the blood of this most beloved one. Who *is* the best-loved one? Isanusi knows (it is Noliwa, who is Chaka's betrothed and Dingiswayo's sister), but once again he stands aside and watches as Chaka's mind surveys the field: His mother? His brothers? No, none of these: "But among these whom you have mentioned there is none whom you love with the love I have just described, that one you have left out. Please think of that one, and then tell us your truest wish" (p. 101).

The moment Chaka utters Noliwa's name which he does with the same casual air as the other names he has already suggested, Isanusi interrupts him with "Very well!" (p. 101). Once again Chaka has "chosen" rather than been told; Isanusi simply confirms.

Will Chaka sacrifice Noliwa for greater kingship or spare her and be satisfied with the power he already has? Although Chaka agrees without hesitation to sacrifice Noliwa, Isanusi is firm about preventing a hasty decision and gives him a year (reduced to nine months at Chaka's insistence) to weigh the situation. At the conclusion of this period, Chaka has not wavered. As Chaka is on the point of making his fateful decision, Isanusi indicates that this step will take them to the point of no return where things will be outside Isanusi's control and he will be unable to undo what he has done. At that point, Isanusi suggests, other forces, greater and more terrible than he, will take over. Or, perhaps more to the point, the beast that will possess Chaka will grow into an uncontrollable monster, defying even its own creator. He pleads with Chaka not to make this decision too hastily, and to give it more thought, because "it is necessary that a person should understand what he is doing while there is still time, so that he should not afterwards regret when regret is of no further use" (p. 123).

Isanusi seems genuinely afraid of the evil power he is about to unleash. For one brief sentence, he lets his mind wander away from the present and from Chaka and half-musingly contemplates the human condition generally as he warns that "a person" should be aware of the consequences of his or her actions. Then his mind returns, and he resumes his dialogue with Chaka.

Early on in the story, as he was hiding from his pursuers in the forest and contemplated his life thus far, Chaka had concluded that there is no justice or fairness in the world: "he realized that here on earth people live by might only, and not by right; ... and he decided that, from that day on, he would do just as he pleased, and that, whether a person was guilty or not, he would simply kill him if he so wished, for that is the law of man" (p. 35). When they meet in the wilderness not long thereafter, Isanusi says to Chaka, in language that is remarkably similar to Chaka's own, "I believe that you have, in a small way, seen the affairs of this world, that people live by favouritism and bias, by hatred and by strength; and now you too must part with mercy from this very day, because mercy devours its owner" (p. 41). Mofolo thus creates Isanusi as an incarnation of Chaka's ambition and as a confirmer of what Chaka already is. From the beginning, Chaka is responsible for his choices. The pretense that Isanusi guides him is merely an artistic ploy.

Mofolo succeeds remarkably well in integrating history, biography, and fiction in this story. Yet sometimes he vacillates between historian and artist, unable to decide which he wants to be. A good example of this uncertainty is the scene where Chaka returns, at early dawn, from a vigil at his father's grave on the day that he is to be installed as successor. It is clear from the summary that follows this scene that Mofolo is relying, for the details of this information, on informants who are identified as "those who saw him" (p. 83). What they say does not stand up to the rigorous logic Mofolo applies to it, so it cannot properly be called history; yet, Mofolo is unwilling to suspend disbelief and rely totally on his creativity.

Despite his doubts, Mofolo, in his dual role as author and narrator, will not discredit his informants. He therefore uncritically restates what they have said. In this scene, we are told that "those who saw him when he entered the village say that Chaka ... came riding on a horse with a smooth shining coat, led by ... a young maiden who surpassed all the maidens of the world in beauty" (p. 83). Mofolo queries the major elements of this statement: there were no horses in Natal Province at that time, he asserts, and "even the two which Dingiswayo had brought ... from the Colony had already died" (p. 83). As regards the maiden, some people suggest that she was Noliwa, but Mofolo argues that Noliwa has not yet arrived. Furthermore, whatever her identity, Mofolo asks "where did she vanish" (p. 84), since she was never seen again after that? "Yet," he concludes, "in spite of all that, those who saw Chaka say he came riding a horse, of that they have no doubt whatsoever" (p. 84).

Letters written to *Leselinyana* by the Basotho who had read *Chaka* reveal that many of them could not identify the boundary between history and fiction and appealed to Mofolo to identify the genre. This confusion suggests that the marriage between factual and fictional representation has been successfully consummated, thus creating anxiety in the reader and making him or her participate in the quest for balance.

CONCLUSION

It is a marvel that, in only three short novels and just a few years, Mofolo went through a process of internal conflict in which he desperately sought to come to terms with the new order of missionaries, a capitalist economy based largely on the mining industry and its demand for migrant labor, a religion that preached self-denial and suffering as necessary for the reward of everlasting life after death, where poverty resulting from the new capitalism could easily be accepted by its victim as the suffering so prescribed. It was a religion marked also by a deep sense of sin and guilt and the need to endure the terrible consequences of one's sins. Mofolo's agonizing evaluation of the benefits and disadvantages of this new order took him through the stages of what on the surface looks like wholesale and unquestioning acceptance in *Moeti* (which is nonetheless marked by a fundamental, though largely unconscious, respect for the beliefs of the Basotho) to querying some of the new values by direct authorial intervention in *Pitseng* and to an upsurge of admiration for the values of black people in *Chaka*, where Christian moral judgments are not overt, but implied. In *Chaka*, therefore, Mofolo has come full circle, and his admiration of traditional African values grows naturally and effortlessly.

Why, after such an auspicious beginning—the three novels plus an unpublished manuscript in the four years from 1906 to 1909—did Mofolo suddenly fall silent? Some well-motivated speculation points to a soured relationship with the missionaries on account of their veto power over works they did not approve. *Chaka* was the object of heated debate between those who saw it as encouraging belief in witchcraft, and therefore not to be published, and those who appreciated its literary value and insisted that it be published. It was finally published in 1925. In addition, around 1908 Mofolo presented a manuscript, identified by the French translation of its title, "L'Ange déchu" (The fallen angel), which was rejected, apparently with some words of reprimand to the author for engaging in trivial or irrelevant subjects.

Faced with the problems of contractual agreements that might not be understood by the writers they served, missionary publishers preferred to purchase manuscripts outright, which often resulted in misunderstanding and suspicion, especially if the book happened to be popular and sell well. Jacques Zurcher, a Swiss missionary in Lesotho who first met Mofolo in 1922, has expressed his conviction that the lack of continuous financial reward to authors was why Mofolo stopped writing (personal correspondence with the present writer, 1979). Mofolo had personal problems as well, including a departure from Morija, a series of unsuccessful business ventures that ended in protracted litigations and penury, and declining health after he suffered a stroke and temporarily lost his ability of speech in 1941 — all of which resulted in frustration and cynicism. Mofolo died on 8 September 1948.

Selected Bibliography

All quotations from Mofolo's work are translations into English from the original Sesotho by the present writer.

NOVELS

Moeti oa bochabela. Morija, Basutoland: Sesuto Book Depot, 1907, 1968.

Pitseng. Morija, Basutoland: Sesuto Book Depot, 1910, 1970.

Chaka. Morija, Basutoland: Sesuto Book Depot, 1925, 1957.

TRANSLATIONS

Chaka: An Historical Romance. Trans. by Frederick Hugh Dutton. London: Oxford University Press, 1931.

The Traveller of the East. Trans. by Harry Ashton. London: Society of Promoting Christian Knowledge, 1934.

Chaka the Zulu. Trans. by Frederick Hugh Dutton. London: Oxford University Press, 1949.

Chaka. Trans. by Daniel P. Kunene. London: Heinemann, 1981; with an introduction by the translator.

CRITICAL STUDIES

Ambrose David. "The Leribe Collection"; a personal collection comprising discarded British colonial government files and other documents, salvaged from Major Bell's Tower in Leribe in 1978–1979 and stored in the National University of Lesotho library.

Attwell, David. "Mofolo's *Chaka* and the Bambata Rebellion." In *Research in African Literatures* 18 (spring 1987).

Beuchat, P. D. "Literary Composition." In James Walton, ed., *The Teaching of Southern Sotho: Report of a Conference held at the Lerotholi Technical School on 27–30 June 1960.* Maseru, Basutoland: 1961.

———. *Do the Bantu Have a Literature?* Johannesburg, South Africa: Institute for the Study of Man in Africa, 1962.

Damane, Mosebi. *Marath'a lilepe: A puo ea Sesotha.* Morija, Basutoland: Sesuto Book Depot, 1960.

Dathorne O. R. "Thomas Mofolo and the Sotho Hero." In *New African* 5 (1966).

Decaunes, Luc. "Une épopée bantoue." In *Présence africaine* 5 (1948).

Doke, Clement M. "Scripture Translation into Bantu Languages." In *African Studies* 17, no. 2 (1958).

Ellenberger, Victor. *A Century of Mission Work in Basutoland (1833–1933).* Trans. from the French by Edmond M. Ellenberger. Morija, Basutoland: Sesuto Book Depot, 1938.

Franz, G. H. "The Literature of Lesotho (Basutoland)." In *Bantu Studies* 4 (1930).

Gérard, Albert. "An African Tragedy of Hubris: Thomas Mofolo's *Chaka.*" In Brom Weber, ed., *Sense and Sensibility in Twentieth-Century Writing: A Gathering in Memory of William Van O'Connor.* Carbondale: Southern Illinois Press, 1970.

———. *Four African Literatures: Xhosa, Sotho, Zulu, Amharic.* Berkeley: University of California Press, 1971.

———. "Rereading *Chaka.*" In *English in Africa* 13 (May 1986).

Gollock, Georgina Anne. "*The Traveller of the East*, by Thomas Mofolo." In *Africa* 7 (1934).

Guma, Samson Mbizo. "Southern Sotho Literature Today." In *Africa Digest* 15 (1968).

Jabavu, Davidson Don Tengo. Review of *Chaka.* In *South African Outlook* 62 (1932).

Jacottet, Edouard. *The Morija Printing Office and Book Depot: An Historical Survey.* Morija, Basutoland: 1912.

Jahn, Janheinz. *Neo-African Literature: A History of Black Writing.* Trans. from German by Oliver Coburn and Ursula Lehrburger. New York: Grove Press, 1968.

Kunene, Daniel P. *The Works of Thomas Mofolo.* Los Angeles: African Studies Center, University of California, 1967.

———. "The Imagery of Darkness and Light in Thomas Mofolo's *Moeti oa bochabela.*" In Alastair Niven, ed., *The Commonwealth Writer Overseas: Themes of Exile and Expatriation.* Brussells: Didier, 1976.

———. "Shaka in the Literature of Southern Africa." In Donald Burness, ed., *Shaka, King of the Zulus, in African Literature.* Washington, D.C.: Three Continents Press, 1976.

———. "The Chaka Controversy: New Light on the Role of the Missionaries." In Kofi Anyidoho, Abioseh M. Porter, Daniel Racine, and Janice Spleth, eds., *Interdisciplinary Dimensions of African Literature.* Washington, D.C.: Three Continents Press, 1985.

———. "Ntsoanatsatsi/Eden: Superimposed Images in Thomas Mofolo's *Moeti oa bochabela.*" In *English in Africa* 13 (May 1986).

———. *Thomas Mofolo and the Emergence of Written Sesotho Prose.* Johannesburg, South Africa: Ravan Press, 1989.

Kunene, Daniel P., and Randal A. Kirsch. *The Beginning of South African Vernacular Literature: A Historical Study.* Los Angeles: University of California, for the Literature Committee of the African Studies Association, 1967.

Lazarus, Neil. "The Logic of Equivocation in Thomas Mofolo's *Chaka.*" In *English in Africa* 13 (May 1986).

Lenake, Johnny M. "A Brief Survey of Modern Literature in South African Bantu Languages: Southern Sotho." In *Limi* 6 (June 1968).

Letele, G. L. "Some Recent Literary Publications in Languages of the Sotho Group." In *African Studies* 3 (1944).

Livre d'or de la mission de Lessouto. Paris: Maison de Missions Evangélique, 1912.

M. L. "Chaka: Fidélité et infidélité chez les paiëns." In *Le Monde nonchrétiene* 1 (1947).

Malaba, Mbongeni. "The Legacy of Thomas Mofolo's *Chaka.*" In *English in Africa* 13 (May 1986).

Mangoaela, Zakia D. "Thomas Mofolo — Writer." In *Basutoland Witness* 4 (April–June 1951).

Mohapeloa, M. D. *Letlole la lithoko tsa Sesotho.* Johannesburg, South Africa: Afrikaanse Pers-Boekhandel, 1950.

Moloi, Alosi S. "The Germination of Southern Sotho Poetry." In *Limi* 8 (June 1969).

Mphahlele, Ezekiel. *The African Image.* London: Faber & Faber, 1962; new and rev. ed., 1974.

Norton, W. A. "Sesuto Praises of the Chiefs." In *South African Journal of Science* 18 (1921–1922).

Smith, Edwin. Review of *Chaka.* In *Africa* 4 (1931).

Wauthier, Claude. *The Literature and Thought of Modern Africa.* Trans. from the French by Shirley Kay. London: Pall Mall, 1966.

Werner Alice. "A Mosuto Novelist." In *International Review of Missions* 14 (1925).

———. "Some Native Writers in South Africa." In *Journal of the African Society* 30 (1931).

Es'kia Mphahlele

1919–

PETER N. THUYNSMA

ES'KIA MPHAHLELE published under the name Ezekiel Mphahlele prior to 1979, but the name change upon returning to South Africa from a twenty-year exile did nothing to suppress an unusually heavy dependence on personal experience, a strong folk sensitivity, and a constant wrangling over the condition of exile. It is not only exile on alien soil that dominates his work, but also exile on ancestral soil. These features characterize his personality and his writing, and out of this vortex he has created two autobiographies, three novels, more than twenty-five short stories, two verse plays, and a number of poems. Add to these two edited anthologies, essay collections, individual essays, public addresses, awards, and a Nobel Prize nomination in literature in 1969, and what emerges is a dean of African letters.

As a young reader Mphahlele seized upon the maxim that a story had to be well told, which became the credo that drove his work. This belief is reflected in his critical criteria and his creative writing. He views life as framed experience, ordered and patterned into a story. This may not be an extraordinary trait in a writer, but as Mphahlele's mainstay it is of major critical consequence.

Personal experience, whether real or imagined, formed his creative impulse. Its simplicities and complexities determine the lives of his characters and become microcosms of the South African experience and of the more specific black South African experience. He treats his critical and creative work as a forum in which to examine himself and feel experience spinning around him and dancing past. As Ursula Barnett argues, his writing "is less successful when he cannot feel an incident as real, or identify with a situation emotionally" (p. 54). He is, in fact, in a constant discourse with the experiences of his own life.

BIOGRAPHY

A basic familiarity with Mphahlele's background is imperative to understanding the fabric and texture of his writing, to touching the "felt thought" so characteristic of an African writer. His is a story of a goatherd, office clerk, teacher, acclaimed academic, and award-winning writer. Little is private about his life, which has moved from his native South Africa, to exile abroad, and back home again. His poetry is intensely personal, and his large body of fiction is almost an extension of his own life. Even his criticism betrays his restless consciousness in exile, which continues after his return to home soil.

Mphahlele was born in Marabastad, outside Pretoria, on 17 December 1919, but was soon taken to live with his paternal grandmother in rural northern Transvaal near Pietersburg, at the village of Maupaneng. These were less than happy childhood years under the tyrannical grandmother, and his first autobiography, *Down Second Avenue* (1959), records her harshness alongside images of fearsome, towering mountains. It is a period of fear, loss, bewilderment, displacement, and, to a minor extent, alienation. But during these years he also developed a sense of storytelling and of the need to shape experience:

> Looking back to those first fifteen years of my life—as much of it as I can remember—I cannot help thinking that it was time wasted. I had nobody to shape them into a definite pattern. Searching through the confused threads of that pattern a few things keep imposing themselves on my whole judgement. My grandmother; the mountain; the tropical darkness which glowworms seemed to try in vain to scatter; long black tropical snakes; the brutal Leshoana river carrying... cattle, boulders; world of torrential rains; the solid shimmering heat beating down on yearning earth; the romantic picture of a woman with a child on her back and an earthen pot on her head, silhouetted against the mirage.
>
> (p. 18)

He had also learned how to make it through each day, how to survive, which was a valuable lesson, for when the country boy returned to Pretoria, a tough ghetto life lay in wait. Some of the early obstacles came at school, for in the fifth grade he was told he was "backward": "The principal said I was backward. My aunt said I was backward. So said everybody. Mother didn't know. I had no choice but to acknowledge it" (p. 47). Despite it all, there emerged a boy who ferociously consumed anything he could learn. His determination resulted in a teachers' certificate from Adams College, Natal, in 1940 and a matriculation by correspondence studies two years later while he worked as a teacher and shorthand typist at the Ezenzeleni Institute for the Blind in Roodepoort, west of the Johannesburg city center. He went on to teach English and Afrikaans at Orlando High School in what is today Soweto until he was banned from teaching in 1952 for campaigning against the Bantu Education Act. From 1952 to 1953 he returned to Ezenzeleni as secretary, and in 1954 he entered his first brief exile in what was then Basutoland as a teacher in Maseru.

Academic honors began when a bachelor of arts degree was awarded him in 1949. A bachelor of arts with honors degree followed in 1955 and a master's degree with distinction in 1956, both in English literature. All three degrees were awarded by the University of South Africa, and studies were conducted via correspondence. His master's was the first cum laude degree to be awarded to a black South African, and the official policy of apartheid obliged the University of South Africa to arrange a separate graduation ceremony. Mphahlele received his doctorate in 1968 from the University of Denver and an honorary doctorate in Humane Letters from the University of Pennsylvania in 1982. An equivalent tribute came from the University of Colorado in 1994. Similar honors were accorded him in South Africa when he received honorary doctorates in literature from the University of Natal in 1983 and Rhodes University in 1986. In the same year he received the Ordre des Palmes medal from the French government in recognition of his contribution to French language and culture.

Ghetto life in South Africa could hardly anticipate such academic accolades. Among the scant career options available after he was barred from teaching in 1952 was a post as a journalist, and his love for writing was strong enough to make him join the staff of *Drum* magazine in Johannesburg in 1955. In his short stay with this magazine, he held the posts of political reporter, copy editor, and fiction editor. Discontented with his role as a journalist and deeply disillusioned by the South African situation, he resolved in 1957 to leave for a life in exile, which led him to Nigeria, France, Zambia, and two sojourns in the United States. Twenty years later he returned to his native South Africa.

Spatially, Mphahlele's career is a map of Africa and the world. Yet against such a broad and colorful canvas, his creative involvement with the African experience has been restricted to specific themes. His work shows a keen awareness of the strength of black women. He often depicts the ambivalence of the African personality caught between a rural and urban sensibility. His human landscape inevitably eclipses physical setting, and the white-black encounter dominates his themes. Mphahlele thrives on the communal point of view as he comes to grips with his milieu and Pan-African worldview. He is always engaged in some form of self-definition, which he locates in cultural imperatives. As he addresses the African experience, he is determined to write about something in depth and not merely describe it.

AUTOBIOGRAPHY

Down Second Avenue

The autobiography *Down Second Avenue* provides a splendid introduction to the panorama of Mphahlele's writing. Begun in South Africa, it was completed in the early days of his twenty-year exile, which began in Nigeria in 1957. Driven by a contemplative tempo, *Down Second Avenue* is more an autobiographical essay than a novel, yet its narrative is poetic enough to involve the reader in its world. Incidents are picked from memory with ease and care, and each is precisely suited to the overall purpose of the work: to articulate an existence and comb it for meaning.

The work is a poignant record of the development of a personality within the dynamics of African culture, showing how the African is inseparable from his or her past, which is also a rehearsal of the future. *Down Second Avenue* serves as a theater in which Mphahlele confirms his identity; a feature not uncommon to other autobiographies by black South Africans. Coming as it does after exercises in short stories, it is a logical extension of shorter narratives around a common theme. By basing the work on experience, Mphahlele makes it an exciting and realistic venture with credible characterization. African-American models by James Baldwin and Richard Wright, as well as early slave narratives, provide similar examples. There are, for instance, remarkable structural similarities with Wright's *Black Boy* (1945), although Mphahlele did not read Wright's autobiography until after *Down Second Avenue* had been published.

Mphahlele clearly enjoyed the romance of reconstructing his life and shaping the lives of those who helped him grow. He often identifies with an incident in the most emotional of terms, yet with careful authority over possible lapses into sentimentality. A device he uses to combat such lapses is the interlude. At five crucial junctures, Mphahlele pauses for introspection. Here he is intensely personal and even confessional. In each interlude he adopts a near stream-of-consciousness mode and works his way through a crisis. The first reflects on poverty and the slums. The second comes immediately after lively accounts of a street gang and street wisdom, of Rebone, Ma-Lebona, and Ma-Bottles — each a figure in a raw ghetto world. Their depressing details get the better of him, and in the interlude he wishes he had the luck of the biblical Moses. Ironically his renegade father's name was Moses — the father who scalded his mother with steaming curry and who walked out on the family. In this interlude, Mphahlele emotionally recounts, feels, and assesses his youth: "No use trying to put the pieces together. Pieces of my life. They are a jumble. My father's image keeps coming back only to fade. I can't think of him but as a harsh, brutal, cold person. Like his mother. And that brutal limp of his. The smell of the paraffin from the stove and the smell of boiling potatoes and curry" (pp. 74–75). Eight chapters later, he documents his mother's death and steps out of the narrative into the third interlude. Here he also mourns the passing of Marabastad: the ghetto was razed under the government's forced removal policies.

Marriage and religion enter the narrative. Adulthood and its responsibilities in black South Africa begin to assert a stranglehold, and his career forces him into the fourth interlude, which marks his six-month-long exile in Basutoland. Here the style is crisper, much more controlled and academic. With this change, the narrative quality alters dramatically. A severity enters, and the adult explores the few options his environment offers. As white South Africa begins to suffocate him, his antiwhite sentiment grows and gives way to violent protest:

> The main weakness in South African writers is that they are hyper-conscious of the race problem in their country. They are so obsessed with the subject of race and colour that when they set about writing creatively they imagine that the plot they are going to devise, the characters they are going to create and the setting they are going to exploit, must subserve an important message or important discovery they think they have made in race relations.
>
> (pp. 195–196)

In the final interlude, he struggles with the decision to leave South Africa for a life of exile. A fully mature mind speaks, depressed but not in despair. Mphahlele contemplates present-day Soweto. His own place in the scheme is that of "life thrown into a barbed-wire tangle; the longer it is made to stay there the more it is entangling itself and hurting itself; and the more it is hurting itself the more impotent it is becoming, and the more it is failing to save itself; so much the longer it will remain in the coils, degraded" (p. 204).

These five interludes are invaluable punctuation devices. They reveal much of Mphahlele's development and provide an ingenious inner frame for the work. They do not, however, reveal the vibrancy of the work itself.

Down Second Avenue has a brilliant cast of characters. Like their dialogue, however sparse, the characters are earthy and colloquial. They speak in the idiom of their ghetto and mother tongues, and most are, like the venerable Aunt Dora, trying to come to terms with reality. Others stumble through Mphahlele's memory, like the sentimental view of an unreachable girlfriend, Rebone. Aunt Dora and Mphahlele's mother, Eva, share the limelight as the most admirably dominating women in the author's life and have an inescapable presence: Aunt Dora's comes through physical assertion, Eva's through a quiet, more subtle aura. For Aunt Dora, "the past never seemed to hold any romantic memories; she never spoke about the future; she simply grappled with the present" (p. 107).

And grapple she does. She is volatile, active, and protective; she loves life, intimidates at least one of Mphahlele's teachers, and beats up an Indian shopkeeper. Yet she is implicitly obedient to her passive husband. Eva is the epitome of motherly tenderness and stands in sharp contrast to Mphahlele's menacing father. Mphahlele portrays his mother romantically and sentimentally. She remained, in life, a major influence on her son and his private symbol for Africa's resilience and tenderness.

Afrika My Music

Mphahlele emerges as a natural and sensitive hero in *Down Second Avenue*, but not in *Afrika My Music: An Autobiography 1957–1983* (1984). Within the conventions of the memoir, the later work is a broad and colorful mural of the people who have been part of his life, and much less emphasis is given to his inner self. With bold strokes, he sketches a literary history of which he is an integral part. In robust style, he raids his past to rationalize his decisions. But it is not a straightforward memoir. It is a review of a man sparring with his reader's suspected judgments of how he has managed his whirlwind life. There are no interludes to grant him respite here; this time authorial commentary is his choice of form.

In *Afrika My Music*, Mphahlele examines how, as an author and exile, he has represented his people. He winces as he recounts the placelessness of exile and its tyranny of time. Exile failed to give him a commitment to a locality, and he remembers tugging at the moorings of Nigeria, France, Kenya, Zambia, and twice at those that tied him to the American piers.

The narrative structure of *Afrika My Music* is particularly striking. Its opening image is of a mature man recalling the ironies of the most recent events in his life. Then, in a series of concentric circles, he spreads out internationally and returns. But he does not return to the porch of his Lebowakgomo home in South Africa; rather, he returns to a new porch (or perch) having gathered mountain flora from nearby mountains for his rock garden. Ironically, the mountains he has looted are the same fearsome, towering hills that tormented him in those childhood nights as a goatherd in *Down Second Avenue*.

This book leads everywhere before it returns to the porch of the Lebowa region and mirrors a life that is content and reconciled; he had moved away from his birthplace and returned after twenty years. Unlike *Down Second Avenue*, with its accounts of ghetto life, *Afrika My Music* represents the Mphahlele who has written himself out of the ghetto. But having achieved this, he feels no more free from the tyranny of color that dominates South African life.

Afrika My Music, though a personal celebration, is an energetic sweep across a human landscape that is disrupted only by such historical events as the shooting of black demonstrators at Sharpeville in 1960. Ironies elevate this memoir into an art form, particularly when the narrative deals with the condition of exile. For the first time, his wife, Rebecca, is unveiled as "unsinkable Rebecca," and when he touches on their role as parents, he reveals their anguish over their elder son's delinquency. Here we get a glimpse into the trepidations that may have led to the father-son subtheme in his first novel, *The Wanderers* (1971).

The title, *Afrika My Music*, while as metaphorical as *Down Second Avenue*, is less easily defined. It is the work's alternative title—the original "Round Trip to Liberty" was dropped—yet it embraces the work without restricting it. Here is a syncopated record that hints at several cathartic and traumatic moments, which ground the work to a number of significant halts in its composition, ostensibly because for Mphahlele this was not a mere record of events. Consequently, a certain patchiness betrays the long journey from Wayne, Pennsylvania, where it was begun, to Lebowakgomo. As in *Down Second Avenue*, there is a large measure of the "I am us" formula, so typical of Mphahlele, so utterly humanist.

In the many cameos of fellow exiles, Mphahlele reveals how well he could listen to another's music and drama as he attended to the fiber of another's character, concerns, and interests. In the end he is a man at peace with himself, a man who has reconciled his beliefs and commitments but who remains disturbed by the inequalities in his land. He yearns for human dignity, and success for him means something different from fame: "It isn't fame you want in my line of work, it is having your shadow noticed... to have a presence" (p. 22).

FICTION

The Wanderers

The Wanderers (1971) marks Mphahlele's first attempt at novel-length fiction. Completed in

1968, the manuscript was submitted as a dissertation for a doctorate in the creative writing program at the University of Denver, where he also taught. The African Studies Center at the University of California, Los Angeles, awarded the unpublished novel its first prize, naming it the best African novel for 1968–1969. At the same time, Mphahlele was elected to the Phi Beta Kappa honorary society and nominated for the Nobel Prize in literature. In ten years of exile, he had become a senior and distinguished academic. Through his work as director of the African program with the Paris-based Congress for Cultural Freedom (later renamed the International Association for Cultural Freedom), his activities throughout the continent placed him at the center of a burgeoning literature. He organized conferences and workshops on education, writing, the arts, and the press. He was instrumental in establishing Chemchemi Creative Center in Kenya and the Mbari Club in Nigeria. In the early 1960s he also boldly challenged the emergent romanticism in the literary movement of Négritude and became its chief dissident.

In fiction as in autobiography, Mphahlele uses personal experience. He also bears witness to his own conscience. *The Wanderers* leans heavily on the autobiographical as it confronts the thoughts and events through which Mphahlele lived. Here is, on one level, the sequel to *Down Second Avenue* and the bridge between it and *Afrika My Music*. Here too he wrestles with the distinction between autobiographical fiction and fictional autobiography.

Book One is a thin outline of Mphahlele's early adulthood as described in *Down Second Avenue*. Timi Tabane has been banned from teaching and is forced to become a journalist, without a real liking for his job, for *Bongo* magazine. He becomes too deeply and personally involved in investigating the disappearance of a man into a labor-farm system. When the story is eventually published in *Bongo*, it leads to several reforms, and Timi emerges a hero. His impersonation of a laborer drives home the frustrations he feels as a black South African. The abduction case only deepens his ambivalence about whether or not to leave South Africa: to "stay and pit my heroism against the machine and bear the consequences if I remained alive; or stay and shrivel up with bitterness; or face up to my cowardice, reason with it and leave" (p. 59). When he decides to leave, his application for a passport is refused, so he crosses the border illegally.

Book Two is narrated by the editor of *Bongo*, Steven Cartwright. He, too, faces a personal crisis. He is a man with a liberal conscience, yet he cannot escape from his whiteness. He despises the white government and falls in love with Naledi, whose husband's disappearance Timi has investigated. Their circumstances—she as a black woman, he as a white man—however, make a union in South Africa difficult. This second book is a drawn-out account of several related events. It is a dense and labored narrative from Cartwright's sickbed.

Book Three has no specific narrator and jumps ahead two years into the fictional West Africa country of Iboyoru, where Timi Tabane has a teaching post. His family joins him some time later in Iboyoru. When Iboyoru suffers a military coup d'état, Steven Cartwright, now a journalist based in England, comes out to report. He has not only resolved to leave South Africa, but also married Naledi. However, the chief feature of Book Three is Mphahlele's focus on Timi's son, Felang. This is an unadulterated recounting of Mphahlele's painful relationship with his own eldest son, Anthony.

Timi resumes his role as character-narrator in Book Four with the Tabane family living in Lao-Kiku, which represents the Kenya of Mphahlele's wanderings. Timi's relationship with Felang continues to deteriorate to the point that the boy jettisons his family. Timi transfers his disillusionment with Iboyoru to Lao-Kiku and to Africa itself. The relentlessness of his African exile is compounded by Felang's death.

In *Afrika My Music*, Mphahlele says of fiction: "In fiction, as in drama, you work with diversities, conflict, and you need an intimate familiarity with the world you depict. You need a locale, its smell, its taste, its texture.... In the process of composition, you are tied to the place that contains the experience" (p. 168). In this comment, Mphahlele expresses his commitment to the lessons gained from his own experience and perhaps justifies his weaving a rather thin plot into a novel of such substantial length. Minute details abound; the experience of the narrative is the very texture of its protest aesthetic.

Despite the novel's somber, if not morbid, story line, there are also moments of humor that surpass even those of Aunt Dora's fight with Abdool in *Down Second Avenue*. But the humorous incidents are almost callously juxtaposed with tragic circumstances. Mphahlele's portrayal of a township funeral in Book One appropriately illustrates the sardonic humor. The funeral sequence in the novel goes beyond its apparent absurdity to become an example of African humanism and ghetto poverty. Timi says:

> "I haven't the time to go about looking for Kabinde and paying him twenty shillings to say a few words over a corpse when not even its wife cares."
>
> Of course I had *some* time. But I just did not see that the costly coffins, hearses and bus convoys that went down Nadia Street to the cemetery gave a corpse greater dignity than this one had in a crude but acceptable coffin. Once a small group passed, all solemnly rigged up for a funeral. It turned out that the coffin was full of liquor.
>
> (p. 46)

The sardonic situation is compounded by the fact that liquor was contraband in black possession during apartheid years. Following the arrangements Timi makes is a description of himself; his wife, Karabo; his mother-in-law, the widow; the not-too-sober driver; and the coffin precariously perched on a horse-drawn cart: "Karabo and I sat at the back, our legs dangling. The driver stopped several times to greet friends and chat a little" (p. 46).

Timi, a little uneasy, has his embarrassment confirmed when one of his journalist colleagues spots them and retorts, "What's this ...a one-man bus boycott?" The irony of the funeral arises from abandoning traditional rites: the quality of the man's burial is determined by his financial circumstances at death. This sense of absurdity is a defense that black South African writers have adopted to combat a debilitating atmosphere and to proclaim life over idea. And so they, and Mphahlele in particular, are almost jesuitical in resisting despair.

Chirundu

The influence of his African exile is also evident in Mphahlele's second novel. *Chirundu* (1979) was born out of his attempt in 1968 to reestablish African residence in Zambia, which lasted a mere twenty-one months. This more determined venture into fiction concerns bigamy charges filed against a cabinet minister in an independent central African country. This work also marks Mphahlele's dissatisfaction with the limited themes of many younger writers, especially those in South Africa. In *Chirundu* he explores the resonance of African mythology, and in so doing he presents a fresh variation of a common theme: the confrontation between a traditional African sensibility and a western one.

By revealing much of the story's conclusion early on Mphahlele takes on the challenge of sustaining the reader's interest. At the outset, he describes Chimba Chirundu's fall from power. The process begins with his demotion from minister of internal affairs to minister of transport and public works. The novel gives us an intimate view of personal, political, and moral corruption in which we are made to examine our own attitudes toward polygamy in Africa, African education as part of the colonial inheritance, and missionary-imported religion. Three strains of action are involved: Chimba's relationships with his two wives, Tirenje and Monde; his nephew Moyo's rise within the ranks of organized labor; and a portrait of a group of South African refugees. The three strains are drawn together by complex structural patterning similar to the expansive episodic structures of oral narratives and praise speech.

Mphahlele constructs the past through elaborate flashbacks that are inextricably bound to the present. He sets traditional rural Africa against the chaos of the urban present. Chirundu and Tirenje were married under Bemba law, but Chirundu also insisted on registering their marriage under a British colonial ordinance. After independence, Chirundu's power and status lead him to take a mistress, Monde. The affair becomes serious, and to head off speculation and rumor Chirundu decides to marry Monde. Tirenje, after heartrending attempts to repair their marriage, feels that she has no alternative but to file bigamy charges in a modern court of law. Chirundu knows he cannot contest the charges, but he wishes to challenge the law by breaking it.

Similarly, gloom and defeat surround the narrative of the refugees. Chirundu's nephew, Moyo, however, is a symbol of hope. He values the order of the old world and learns that it must be projected. However transparent a symbol he may be, he is the hope set against the disillusionment of newfound power and the exile of refugees. His foundation is solidly laid but without any guarantees for the future. As a faint but glimmering hope, Moyo is perhaps all Mphahlele can muster when he considers independent Africa's dismal political record.

In their writings, black South Africans have addressed the dynamics of the present but are largely consumed by bitterness and anger and have little time to employ indigenous cultural elements beyond diction and idiom. Mphahlele is acutely aware of this absence of resonance and invests Moyo with a substantial cultural foundation. The boy's confidence stems directly from his faith in his ancestors. Through the governing motif of *nsato* the python, king of reptiles, Mphahlele achieves another mythological dimension. The python becomes a versatile and dramatic symbol of power, which Mphahlele uses to illustrate sexual power when Chirundu embraces Tirenje in happier years and unbridled power when he is *nsato*, "gone mad because he is full of himself" (p. 81).

Not only are there strong parallels with Mphahlele's Zambian sojourn (the bigamy case is based on an actual incident), but also autobiographical incidents. Local and refugee characters are often based on real people, and Mphahlele frequently uses them as mouthpieces. Studs Letanka, for example, longs to return to South Africa to teach, as Mphahlele had desired. An even more notable instance of Mphahlele speaking directly through a character is in Chirundu's anti-Christian invective, which makes him the victim and symbol of modern Africa's decadence. In this way, *Chirundu* becomes an uncompromising indictment of the abuse and hypocrisy of newfound power.

Clearly a dramatic departure from the essentially South African setting of his earlier work, *Chirundu* is not without its weaknesses. The story is drawn from a rather mundane situation and unfolds less organically than *Down Second Avenue*. But meticulous attention to characterization, overall thematic value, and beautifully lyrical prose go a long way toward making up for its weaknesses. Tirenje, for example, is warm and unforgettable, compassionate and loyal. She is undoubtedly a symbol of Africa's strength and another manifestation of Mphahlele's admiration for the power of the black woman. Overall, however, the narrative seems forced; the multiple shifts in time and persona develop a choppiness that reflects the author's condition of exile. He finds himself alienated and rootless, free to be no one and free to be impotent. Exile has made him excessively sensitive and observant, and so he prefers a kaleidoscopic view.

SHORT FICTION

Mphahlele's consummate strength lies in his short fiction. It launched his career as a writer at the age of twenty when he retold a folktale at Adams College. He maintains that he began writing and continued to write for the sheer joy of it, but also admits that reading his early work is somewhat embarrassing with its "clumsy, heavy and awkward idiom" (Couzens, *A Conversation with Es'kia Mphahlele*). Despite his repudiating the style in his first collection, *Man Must Live, and Other Stories* (1946), this anthology carries a thematic title that has developed into a major element in his work; Mphahlele regards as a central statement and as the basis of action that the individual must survive. Yet Mphahlele can be eminently forgiving toward the means of survival within the tyranny of place that was South Africa.

Stories of Survival

In *Man Must Live, and Other Stories* vague characters move through weak plots, but these stories represent Mphahlele's first steps in using literature to come to terms with his own life. It is as if he used literary exercises to confirm his responsibilities and commitments. These stories display the strengths that hostile environments extract to ensure survival. Zungu of the title story is a portrait of tenacity. Knowing how to live is paramount to a man whose physical size alone makes him stand out in crowds of people. But Zungu's brashness and bluster hide a deep uncertainty about himself. He eventually chooses a wife who, along with her children, comes to belittle him constantly. He takes to drinking heavily and slowly begins to disintegrate until his desperation drives him to set his house on fire. By sheer chance he remembers his code that "man must live" and rushes out on fire. He is taught the true reality of the life he must live.

Stilted language and a reliance on personal history pervade the other stories. The melodrama of "Tomorrow You Shall Reap" is particularly overbearing, but Mphahlele's use of fiction in this story is striking. The mother of the story's narrator kills herself after her husband abandons the family. The boy is allowed to explore these circumstances in the face of a love affair of his own. Prophetically, he says:

> Yet, I told myself not to think of it. I must think of a new life at a boarding school. I must not pity myself even if the circumstances seem to justify self-pity. I must try to run away from my conscious self and dope myself with romantic ideas and ambitions so that I should feel the pain of blunt reality.
>
> (p. 50)

As early as 1946, Mphahlele had begun to explore the meaning of raw experience in fiction. Whatever the incentive, be it autobiography, hearsay, or a newspaper item, he scours an incident for its dramatic quality and associations.

Two major anthologies followed *Man Must Live. The Living and Dead, and Other Stories* was published in Nigeria in 1961. Six years later *In Corner B* was published in Nairobi. Selected contents of both volumes (plus another story) have since been anthologized in *The Unbroken Song: Selected Writings of Es'kia Mphahlele* (1981). *The Unbroken Song* includes a broad spectrum of Mphahlele's short fiction that grew from the South African setting. In many stories the exiled self confirms its responsibility to home soil. All his moods are on display here, including guilt, and each mood reveals his struggle to find his bearings in exile.

"The Living and the Dead" shows Stoffel Visser, a character who is frantically defensive, suspicious of every black person, and distrustful of anyone else around him. Although circumstances in the story challenge his attitudes, even to the point of releasing some hidden compassion, these are short-circuited and he only reconfirms his distrust. He reminds himself of his whiteness first, then of his limited humanity. Like Zungu, his code of survival must hold true. Here, as in most of his writing, Mphahlele makes no effort to create a multidimensional character; he is not interested in Visser the man, only in Visser's relation to blacks. Constructing multifaceted characters need not be the concern of a short story, and so Visser's limitation could be a matter of convention; yet that Mphahlele casts most, if not all, of his white characters in a stereotypical mold also has thematic significance. At its most basic level, the South African racial environment breeds Visser's distrust and Mphahlele's relative ignorance of whites. Consequently, part of the stories' meaning lies in the limited vision and function that Mphahlele is able to afford these characters.

"Man Must Live," "The Living and the Dead," "The Leaves Were Falling," and "Tomorrow You Shall Reap" demonstrate the same aspects of the moral dilemma that the black-white encounter entails. Incidents of actual conflict are inevitable, and in "Dinner at Eight" one is struck by the almost casual tone and quiet relentlessness with which the story develops. The white character, Miss Pringle, is a representative character: an extreme paternalist who loves to have blacks hover around her. Mphahlele locates her sexual frustration in her transparent defiance of the system. The sexual undertones, however, are never realized. After refusing several invitations to dinner, Mzondi kills her with his crutch—his symbol of police brutality and the lessening of his manhood.

"The Suitcase" is another tale in which dreams die. Here the irony is couched in an event. Timi finds an apparently forgotten suitcase on a bus and fantasizes about its contents. When policemen arrest him on suspicion of theft, he avidly maintains ownership, but when he and the police discover the contents—a dead baby—Timi tries to disown his newly claimed property. Suspense is maintained throughout and illustrates Mphahlele's basic theory that purpose determines form. There is a definite ironic point to which he directs his tale and from which he eliminates incidental information. He needs a portrait only of Timi's fantasies concerning a tangible object; he does not need to establish Timi as a character, as he would have to do in a novel.

"Mrs. Plum"

All the stories in *The Unbroken Song* have appeared elsewhere. All have received positive critical acknowledgment, but few have provoked as much comment as "Mrs. Plum," in which character and plot are meticulously patterned in a story that approaches the length of a novella, but with the techniques of an excellent short story. "Mrs. Plum" is Mphahlele's finest short story.

Mrs. Plum's paternalism has more substance than Miss Pringle's in "Dinner at Eight." Mrs. Plum's domestic helper, Karabo, has an apparent simplemindedness that provides all the motivation for her employer's concern. Karabo is made to eat food that is foreign to her at the family table with a knife and fork. She is treated well and paid regularly, yet there is no real attempt made to understand her. She is no more than a target for Mrs. Plum's patronizing intentions. Bewildered at first, Karabo develops in the course of events. Because she is the narrator, her learning process is also ours. She is always an intelligent observer, even without the lessons she learns from other domestic servants in the neighborhood. Karabo teaches herself and soon learns that, despite Mrs. Plum's liberal gestures, the racial code does not allow either her or Mrs. Plum to regard each other as individuals.

This racial code is the testing ground as Mphahlele weaves complications into the plot: Mrs. Plum's daughter Kate falls in love with a black physician; Karabo fancies him too, but blacks who are invited to the Plum residence tend to treat Karabo as inferior. Mrs. Plum's affection for her dogs, Monty and Malan, borders on the immoral; she hoses down a police raiding party with Karabo's aid, refuses to pay the fine, and is jailed for fourteen days. Karabo, despite her surface simplicity, is sincere, cheerful, and consistent, and she demonstrates a firm grasp of situations; above all she knows her limitations. To her Mrs. Plum is a human being, albeit an eccentric one. Mrs. Plum's relationship with her dogs marks her neurosis and sterility. Nevertheless, if Karabo senses Mrs. Plum's concerns for blacks, she also senses abstract codes informing her actions.

Mrs. Plum reflects the white liberal's dilemma, and her position is untenable and unenviable. Mphahlele's abhorrence of domestic animals is also fully exploited here, and the implications are thoroughly racial, since domestic servants are often treated worse than household pets. Ultimately, he demonstrates how seriously he regards his responsibility as a writer: no matter how narrow or focused his vision, he means to explore the dynamics of the South African worldview. His need to tell a story is irrepressible. In "Panel on South African Fiction and Autobiography" (1976) he maintains, "I write because it is a compulsive act. I believe people write because it is a compulsive cultural act" (p. 20).

CRITICAL SCHOLARSHIP

Mphahlele is as highly regarded as a literary and cultural commentator as he is a creative writer. His master of arts degree in 1956 was awarded cum laude, and his thesis was published in 1962 as *The African Image.* His candid approach to examining the many facets of race gives the work remarkable authority. The relaxed exploration is also a formal version of his search for a definition of self. He does not aim at absolute objectivity, but represents instead the options and attitudes that determine possible choices. In the process he mirrors an image of the black man and the personality behind the image. His view of the francophone African philosophy of Négritude has provoked important debates and led to major redefinitions. In essence, he confronted an aspect of black pride and pronounced it inadequate.

In *The African Image* he is free of the demands of fiction, but does not cut loose from his characteristic stance: he insists on the personal dimension. Here is yet another search for his true communal value, for the validity of his black personality.

Voices in the Whirlwind and Other Essays appeared in 1972 during his second residence in Colorado. The title essay, the first of six essays in the collection, works out a personal definition of poetry and its meaning. His approach is that of a teacher, and he discusses some of his classroom techniques in teaching poetry. His premise is that poetry is a state of mind, and he goes on to view African and African-American poetry in relation to western thought through Christopher Caudwell's, Laurence Lerner's, and I. A. Richards' respective theories of literary function and aesthetics. The fourth essay, "Implications of Color Identity in Pan-Africanism," is the only one that is first published in this collection. In it he looks at the possibilities for unifying blacks and again touches on Négritude. But any optimism that this collection of essays may engender is more or less smothered in the closing lines of the last essay, "Censorship in South Africa," which captures the depths of his disillusionment with the South African social fabric: "While the Bantu writer is afraid of the written law of censorship, because he is naturally afraid of arrest, detention, and banning, the Afrikaner writer is afraid of both the written law and the sanctions of the tribe, which operate deep down in the subconscious" (p. 215). Along with the pieces included in these two collections, Mphahlele has published is a vast number of critical essays in major journals. Most were penned in exile, which remains a prominent theme. His critical work also includes countless lectures and extensive journalism.

POETRY

In an early poem, "Exile in Nigeria 1960," written after three years in exile, Mphahlele is stung by guilt: Why was he fortunate enough to bask in freedom in Nigeria? He turns to poetry to explore his ambivalence. What emerges is one of the clearest examples of Mphahlele the artist using the form as vehicle to express the cumulative experiences of his culture. He works at finding relevant metaphors and symbols from his background, and his imagery captures the reality and the anguish.

> My claws have poison
> only let me lie down a while,
> bide my time,
> rub my neck and whiskers,
> file my claws and remember.
> (in *The Unbroken Song*, p. 270)

He resolves to use his freedom to serve the people he has left behind, but this leads him to the near-obsessive wrestlings of his twenty-year exile. Exile begins with the harrowing harmattan that sweeps across northern Nigeria:

> Northern wind
> all I know
> is that you numb and jolt me
> lash the water off my flesh
> and fill me with a sense of insufficiency,
> vague longings and forlorn moments and
> brittle promises—maddening!
> ("Exile in Nigeria 1960,"
> in *The Unbroken Song*, p. 265)

His poetic imagery refines free verse into visual prosody allowing ready access to a factual and concrete realism. Cultural images become ideas: always the associations, always the tug of the south. Sometimes when placelessness threatens more acutely, it provokes an angry outburst, but more often he entertains a remote hope:

> somewhere a woman gives the world an artist:
> a child who sings and dances,
> dreams and weaves a poem round the universe
> plunging down the womb.
> ("Somewhere," in *The Unbroken Song*,
> pp. 278–279)

The "cult of youth," as Mphahlele often called it, held frightening implications for him as a United States resident. He feared growing old in a culture that he felt shunned the elderly, whereas growing old for an African should be noble. This fear compounded the discomfort of exile, and in the latter parts of the twenty years he yearned to know his burial place. Thus his declaration in a letter to Guy Butler that he wanted "to lay my shadow on ancestral soil" is hardly surprising; *Afrika My Music* confirms this desire.

He acknowledges that he was unable to draw nourishment from the worlds of his exile and is firm in his resolve to begin again, despite the existing odds:

> I've tunnelled through
> back again
> beneath pounding footsteps of five decades
> bearing down on me,
> because I must step forward
> and be counted with the rest
> whose lives derive their meaning from
> the tyranny of place
> here on this killing ground,
> here where the ancestors forever
> keep their vigil.
> ("A Prayer," in *The Unbroken Song*, p. 307)

In "A Prayer," as elsewhere, there is no time for refined metrics: always the diagrammatic structure, the vibrant vocabulary of protest. He regards it as imperative to register his encounter with history as realistically as he can, no matter how private it may be.

CONCLUSION

Es'kia Mphahlele's career as a writer and teacher has spanned a global tapestry of experiences—both geographically and spiritually. Mphahlele the young writer was part of the firestorm of the 1960s in the company of Chinua Achebe, Wole Soyinka, Ngũgĩ wa Thiong'o, and others. They burst onto the international literary scene with an enviable energy and engaged each other and the mainstream literati in all manner of themes. Mphahlele the firebrand lashed out at Négritude for its simplistic reduction of the African personality. He championed African culture and the African's invigoration of the inherited English idiom. But this energy often drew its inspiration from exile and captured the pain of those years where he and his wife adapted to their new cultural environments, while their children adopted the exile worlds. His novels explore those tensions while his poetry and short fiction rub the abrasive textures.

His retirement into rural South Africa marks a strong contrast to the turbulent years of his youth. As a young man he chafed under the strictures of a fledgling apartheid era that denied him the freedoms he required as a creative writer. Twenty years of exile failed to douse his fiery determination to return, and he did so in 1978. In 1994, he cast his first vote and saw the dawn of human dignity on his ancestral soil.

His later writings turned from fiction to social commentary in newspapers and magazines. He focused his pen on community development and founded the Council for Black Education and Research in Soweto and a host of reading clubs in Lebowa. He chaired the University of Venda's council in the early years out of Bantustan apartheid and served on several community boards. In 1994, he and his wife celebrated fifty years of marriage, only a few miles from the now less fearful mountain of his childhood. There the mighty waters of *Down Second Avenue*'s Leshoana River have long dried up; the little schoolhouse where he was pronounced "backward" sports a new fence and newer classrooms.

The whirlwind brought him full circle and left him time to ponder fresh themes and sketch the plots of a new literature in a new land—a new era that he helped found.

Selected Bibliography

BIBLIOGRAPHY

Woeber, Cathrine, and John Read, comps. *Es'kia Mphahlele: A Bibliography*. Grahamstown, South Africa: National English Literary Museum, 1989.

COLLECTED WORKS

Man Must Live, and Other Stories. Cape Town, South Africa: African Bookman, 1946.

The Living and Dead, and Other Stories. Ibadan, Nigeria: Ministry of Education, 1961.

In Corner B and Other Stories. Nairobi, Kenya: East African Publishing House, 1967, 1972.

The Unbroken Song: Selected Writings of Es'kia Mphahlele. Johannesburg, South Africa: Ravan Press, 1981.

Renewal Time. Columbia, La.: Readers International, 1988.

SELECTED WORKS

Down Second Avenue. London: Faber & Faber, 1959, 1985.

The African Image. London: Faber & Faber, 1962. Rev. ed., New York: Praeger, 1974.

The Wanderers. New York: Macmillan, 1971. Repr. Cape Town, South Africa: David Philip, 1984.

Voices in the Whirlwind and Other Essays. New York: Hill & Wang; London: Macmillan, 1972.

"The Return of Motalane." In *Greenfield Review* 5, nos. 3/4 (1976–1977).

Chirundu. Johannesburg, South Africa: Ravan Press, 1979, 1994.

"Oganda's Journey." In *Staffrider* 2, no. 3 (1979). Dramatization of a story by Grace Ogot.

Afrika My Music: An Autobiography, 1957–1983. Johannesburg, South Africa: Ravan Press, 1984.

Father Come Home. Johannesburg, South Africa: Ravan Press, 1984.

INTRODUCTIONS

Emergency. By Richard Rive. New York: Collier, 1970.

Climbié. By Bernard Dadié. London: Heinemann Educational Books, 1971.

Night of My Blood. By Kofi Awoonor. Garden City, N.Y.: Doubleday, 1971.

No Sweetness Here. By Ama Ata Aidoo. Garden City, N.Y.: Doubleday, 1972.

ESSAYS

"The Syllabus and the Child." In *The Good Shepherd* (November 1952).

"African Teachers." In *Fighting Talk* (October 1955).

"Blackest Magic!" In *Drum* (September 1956).

[Naledi, pseud.]. "South African Fiction: The Non-White Character." In *Fighting Talk* 11, no. 8 (1957).

"Négritude: A Phase." In *New African* 2, no. 5 (1963). Repr. with modifications as "A Reply." In Gerald Moore, ed., *African Literature and the Universities.* Ibadan, Nigeria: Ibadan University Press, 1965.

"African City People." In *East Africa Journal* 1, no. 3 (1964).

"African Literature." In Lalage Bown and Michael Crowder, eds., *The Proceedings of the First International Congress of Africanists, Accra 11–18 December 1962.* Evanston, Ill.: Northwestern University Press, 1964.

"The Fabric of African Cultures." In *Foreign Affairs* 22 (July 1964). Repr. in *Voices in the Whirlwind.* New York: Hill & Wang, 1972.

"The Language of African Literature." In *Harvard Educational Review* 34 (spring 1964).

"An African Writer Looks at Israel." In *Jewish Quarterly* 13, no. 3 (1965).

A Guide to Creative Writing: A Short Guide to Short-Story and Novel Writing. Nairobi, Kenya: East African Literature Bureau, 1966.

"African Literature for Beginners." In *Africa Today* 14, no. 1 (1967).

"African Literature: What Traditions?" In *Denver Quarterly* 2 (summer 1967).

"African Literature and Propaganda." In *Jewel of Africa* 1, no. 4–5 (1968).

"Realism and Romanticism in African Literature." In *Africa Today* 15, no. 4 (1968).

"African Literature—A Dialogue of the Two Selves." In *Horizon* 11, no. 10 (1969).

"Censorship in South Africa." In *Censorship Today* 2 (August–September 1969). Repr. in *Voices in the Whirlwind.* New York: Hill & Wang, 1972.

"Black Literature at the University of Denver." In *Research in African Literatures* 3, no. 1 (1972).

"Variations on a Theme: Race and Color." In *Présence africaine* 83 (1972).

"From the Black American World." In *Okike* 4 (1973).

"The Tyranny of Place." In *New Letters* 40, no. 1 (1973).

"The Voice of Prophecy in African Poetry." In *Umoja* 1, no. 2 (1973).

"Why I Teach My Discipline." In *Denver Quarterly* 8, no. 1 (1973).

"From the Black American World, II." In *Okike* 5 (1974).

"The Function of Literature at the Present Time: The Ethnic Imperative." In *Transition* 45 (1974). Repr. in *Denver Quarterly* 9, no. 4 (1975).

"South African Black Writing 1972–1973." In *Ba Shiru* 5, no. 2 (1974).

"Notes from the Black American World, III." In *Okike* 8 (1975).

"The African Critic Today: Toward a Definition." In Houston A. Baker, Jr., ed., *Reading Black: Essays in the Criticism of African, Caribbean, and Black American Literature.* Ithaca, N.Y.: Cornell University African Studies and Research Center, 1976.

"Homage to L. S. Senghor." In *Présence africaine* 99–100 (1976).

"Notes from the Black American World: Images of Africa in Afro-American Literature." In *Okike* 11 (1976).

"Panel on South African Fiction and Autobiography." In *Issue* 6, no. 1 (1976).

"Higher Education in South Africa." In *The International Encyclopedia of Higher Education.* Vol. 8. Boston: Northeastern University Press, 1977.

"South Africa: Two Communities and the Struggle for a Birthright." In *Journal of African Studies* 4, no. 1 (1977).

"A South African Exile's Return: Back to Ancestral Ground." In *First World* 1, no. 3 (1977).

"Exile, the Tyranny of Place, and the Literary Compromise." In *UNISA English Studies* 17, no. 1 (1979).

"Education: Towards a Humanistic Ideology." In *Report on the Conference on Educational Priorities in a Developing State, University of the North, 9–11 January 1979.* Pretoria, South Africa: De Jager-Haum, 1980.

"Landmarks of Literary History in South Africa." In *The Voice of the Black Writer in Africa.* Johannesburg, South Africa: University of the Witwatersrand Press, 1980.

"The Tyranny of Place and Aesthetics: The South African Case." In *English Academy Review* (1981). Repr. in Charles Malan, ed., *Race and Literature/Ras en literatuur.* Pinetown, South Africa: Owen Burgess, 1987.

"Africa in Exile." In *Daedalus* (spring 1982).

"African Literature and the Social Experience in Process." Typescript of inaugural lecture given at the University of the Witwatersrand, 25 October 1983.

"Literature: A Necessity or a Public Nuisance—An African View." Sol Plaatje Anniversary Lecture. Mafikeng: University of Bophuthatswana (9 September 1983). Repr. in *Classic* 3, no. 1 (1984).

"South African Literature vs. the Political Morality." In *AUETSA Papers* (1983). Repr. in *English Academy Review* (1983).

"My Experience as a Writer." In M. J. Daymond, J. U. Jacobs, and Margaret Lenta, eds., *Momentum: On Recent South African Writing.* Pietermaritzburg, South Africa: University of Natal Press, 1984.

"Prometheus in Chains: The Fate of English in South Africa." In *English Academy Review* 2 (1984).

"Images of Africa." In *South African Outlook* 117 (1986). Repr. in *The Capricorn Papers* 6 (1986).

Poetry and Humanism: Oral Beginnings. Johannesburg, South Africa: Witwatersrand University Press for the Institute for the Study of Man in Africa, 1986. Twenty-second Raymond Dart lecture.

"Foreword." In *Echoes of African Art.* Comp. and intro. by Matsemela Manaka. Johannesburg, South Africa: Skotaville Press, 1987.

REVIEWS AND EDITIONS

Conference of African Writers of English Expression. 7 vols. Kampala, Uganda: Makere College, 1962.

Modern African Stories. With Ellis Ayitey Komey. London: Faber & Faber, 1964, 1977.

African Writing Today. Harmondsworth, U.K.: Penguin, 1967.

"A Disarming Reticence." Review of *The Jail Diary of Albie Sachs.* In *New African* 7, no. 2 (1968).

Thought, Ideology, and Literature in Africa. Denver, Colo.: University of Denver, 1970.

The Voice of the Black Writer in Africa. With Tim Couzens. Johannesburg, South Africa: University of the Witwatersrand Press, 1980.

INTERVIEWS

Couzens, Tim. *A Conversation with Es'kia Mphahlele.* Johannesburg, South Africa: Witswatersrand University CTV Videotape, 1983.

Couzens, Tim, Norman Hodge, and Kate Turlington. "Looking In: Interviews with Es'kia Mphahlele." In *English Academy Review* 4 (1987).

Hossmann, Irmelin. "Ezekiel Mphahlele ou la hantise de la vie communautaire." In *Afrique* 44 (1965).

Howlett, Muriel. "Outlook: African Viewpoint." BBC General Overseas Service (11 and 13 July 1962). Tape 7 1/2 TBU 164461.

Manganyi, N. C. "Looking In: In Search of Es'kia Mphahlele." In *Looking Through the Keyhole.* Johannesburg, South Africa: Ravan Press, 1981.

Nkosi, Lewis, and Richard Rive. "Modern African Writers: The Black Writer in Exile." In *Negro Digest* 14, no. 2 (1964).

"Un panorama de la littérature africaine de langue anglais: Entretien avec l'écrivain Ezekiel Mphahlele." In *Afrique* 20 (1963).

Schreeve, Gavin. "A Rebel and His Roots." In *Guardian* (7 May 1979).

CRITICAL STUDIES

Barnett, Ursula A. *Ezekiel Mphahlele.* Boston: Twayne, 1976. This was the first extensive biography of Mphahlele, but was done mostly through correspondence and so suffers from certain inaccuracies.

Christie, Sarah, Geoffrey Hutchings, and Don Maclennan. "Ezekiel Mphahlele: *Down Second Avenue* (1959)." In *Perspectives on South African Fiction.* Johannesburg, South Africa: Ad. Donker, 1980.

Hodge, Norman. "Dogs, Africans, and Liberals: The World of Mphahlele's Mrs. Plum." In *English in Africa* 8 (March 1981).

———. "'The Way I Looked at Life Then': Es'kia Mphahlele's *Man Must Live and Other Stories.*" In *English in Africa* 13 (October 1986). See this number for other articles on Mphahlele.

Manganyi, N. Chabani. *Exiles and Homecomings: A Biography of Es'kia Mphahlele.* Johannesburg, South Africa: Ravan Press, 1982.

Matute, Ana M. "The International Symposium on the Short Story: Part Three." In *Kenyon Review* 31 (1969).

Thuynsma, Peter N., ed. *Footprints Along the Way: A Tribute to Es'kia Mphahlele.* Braamfontein, South Africa: Skotaville Publishers; Yeoville, South Africa: Justified Press, 1989.

Meja Mwangi

1948–

J. ROGER KURTZ

MEJA MWANGI belongs to the second generation of Kenyan creative writers in English. He began his prolific writing career in the 1970s, a decade after his better-known compatriots Ngũgĩ wa Thiong'o and Grace Ogot had started publishing their works. When he burst onto the scene with the award-winning *Kill Me Quick* (1973), Mwangi was hailed as a rising star on the East African literary scene who was helping to disprove Taban lo Liyong's oft-cited claim in "East Africa, O East Africa / I Lament Thy Literary Barrenness" (*Transition* 4, no. 2, 1965) that East Africa was a literary desert. Mwangi has established himself as one of Kenya's most prolific writers, publishing eleven novels in seventeen years in addition to writing short stories and children's books and working on film projects. His works have received awards in Kenya and abroad and have been translated into six languages; two of his novels have been made into films.

If there is a single writer whose work represents the entire range of Kenyan narrative fiction in the mid 1990s, it is Mwangi. Practically all Kenyan—indeed, one might even say African—writing shares a general thematic preoccupation with the interaction of tradition and modernity in African society. African writers have examined this interaction from a number of angles: the disintegration of traditional ways of life after the arrival of Europeans in the colonial era; the disequilibrium caused by European formal education; the torment of the "been-to" upon reentering African society after studying or working in the west; the influence of missionaries; and in the postcolonial setting, the development of a new African political and economic elite and the dilemmas of life in the modern African city.

While Mwangi has touched on all of these concerns, one might divide his work into three major categories. The first comprises his Mau Mau novels. The armed resistance to British colonialism in Kenya, which came to be known as the Mau Mau revolt and reached its height in the 1950s, was a formative experience for many Kenyans, especially those from the Kikuyu (or Gĩkũyũ) ethnic group to which Mwangi belongs. Like other Kikuyu writers, he found material for his early novels in the Mau Mau experience, which resulted in *Carcase for Hounds* (1974) and *Taste of Death* (1975). The thrillers that he began to write in the late 1970s and 1980s form a second category of texts that has put him at the heart of a raging debate among Kenyan literary critics over the merits of popular literature. The third category of his writing consists of novels set in the city. Mwangi's urban trilogy—*Kill Me Quick*, *Going Down River Road* (1976), and *The Cockroach Dance* (1979)—is compelling and innovative as it deals with what is arguably the most pressing contemporary social problem in Kenya: the effects of the rapid urbanization that the country has experienced since independence in 1963. Critical acclaim for Mwangi's writing has come predominantly from these tales of city life.

DEVELOPMENT AS A WRITER

Mwangi was born in Nanyuki, in Kenya's Central Province, on 27 December 1948. He no longer uses his given name, David Dominic Mwangi, preferring instead to go by the childhood nickname given by his mother. Although not a major city, Nanyuki is an important center in a region that was part of the so-called white highlands, an area set aside by the colonial administration exclusively for settlement by European farmers during the colonial era when Mwangi was born. The region features fertile farmland and an excellent climate. As part of the colonization of Kenya, the resident Kikuyu and Masai populations were either forced off this land onto "native reserves" or permitted to remain as squatters and laborers on the new ranches owned by whites.

Because expropriation of land by British settlers was most blatant in this part of the colony, and land is important to the Kikuyu tradition, Central Province was the most active area of armed resistance to the colonial authorities. The Land and Freedom Army, also known by the enigmatic name of Mau Mau, effectively used its base in the forests of Central Province to become a powerful force in the movement toward independence. In some of the same ways that the Vietnam War was a watershed in the U.S. consciousness, the Mau Mau struggle was a defining and divisive experience for the colony, and later the nation, of Kenya. In the 1950s, as resistance fighters in increasing numbers took to the forests of Mount Kenya or the Aberdare mountain range—both areas near Mwangi's home in Nanyuki—the colonial administration declared a state of emergency, restricting movement in the area, resettling people into more easily controlled "villages," and using Kenyan Home Guard soldiers to combat what the administration termed a terrorist movement.

Given its historical and social significance, the Mau Mau experience had a powerful impact on the imaginations of Kenyan, and particularly Kikuyu, writers. Mwangi experienced what is known as "the Emergency" as a child, living in the area of main conflict, and turned fifteen two weeks after Kenya achieved political independence. Both the promises of political independence and the troubled time leading up to that point were central to his consciousness.

The 1970s, when Mwangi was entering his twenties and beginning to publish, was a time of disillusionment with the unfulfilled hopes of independence in East Africa and a time of crisis for Nairobi, Kenya's capital. What might be considered a genre of "disillusionment literature" developed that vigorously criticized the new African political and economic elite, which appeared to have betrayed the nation by using education and positions of privilege for personal rather than collective gain. The term *neocolonialism* was coined to describe a situation in which only a few of the faces in the power structure changed, leaving unjust colonial structures firmly in place. The disillusioned intellectual—typically someone who had once been optimistic about the potential for national development and the intellectual's role in that process, only to become embittered by neocolonial realities—surfaced as an important character in Kenyan writing.

Around 1970 Mwangi moved to Nairobi to continue his education. In addition to the climate of political disillusionment, the city's population quickly outgrew the capacity of its infrastructure. Although rapid growth has characterized Nairobi throughout its history, in the decade after independence the growth reached unprecedented heights, particularly after restrictions on African immigration to the city were dropped. By the early 1970s housing, employment, and transportation facilities were under more strain than ever. Slums, always a feature of Nairobi's geography, were growing at alarming rates. The government responded with a number of autocratic measures reminiscent of colonial-era tactics, lending credence to charges that Kenya's social system was neocolonial. Established as a depot and later an administrative center for the Uganda railway at the end of the nineteenth century, Nairobi became the capital of British East Africa in 1907. Historically, Nairobi had been designed for white people, and the colonial government adopted almost without changes the South African model of racial segregation in housing and business. Pass laws were issued to restrict immigration, for example, and vagrancy acts allowed the government to return unwanted immigrants to the countryside. In the late 1960s, when the postindependence relaxation of immigration restrictions greatly increased the city's population, the government reinstated some of the colonial-era vagrancy laws; President Jomo Kenyatta urged Nairobi residents who had no jobs to "go back to the land." These measures had relatively limited impact, and Nairobi continued to grow rapidly.

While in Nairobi, Mwangi was unable to gain admission to the University of Nairobi, so he is unusual among Kenyan writers in that he was not part of the university community, the traditional source of creative writers and artists in postcolonial East Africa. He completed his ordinary-level exams at Nanyuki secondary school and his advanced-level training at Kenyatta College near Nairobi. Mwangi applied for but was denied admission to the journalism and television-broadcasting programs at the University of Nairobi. He instead embarked on a career of practical experience in the film industry. Mwangi worked and traveled throughout East Africa as a sound engineer with the French Broadcasting Corporation and later joined the staff at the British Council in Nairobi as a film librarian. While at the British Council, he wrote his first novel, *Carcase for Hounds.*

The influence of film on Mwangi's writing cannot be overemphasized. As a child in Nanyuki, he regularly attended the open-air films offered by the mobile movie theaters that came through town mostly showing Hollywood productions. After he moved to Nairobi in 1970, he had a chance to see British and American films on a regular basis. Later, his connections with French television and with the British Council led to jobs on a number of major films shot in Kenya. Mwangi was location manager for *Shadow on the Sun* (1988), casting director for *The Kitchen Toto* (1987), and assistant director for the Hollywood films *Out of Africa* (1985), *Gorillas in the Mist* (1988), and *White Mischief* (1988). A decidedly cinematic vision subsequently developed in his writing, along with a narrative style reminiscent of fast-moving popular film. Mwangi's characters, like many Kenyans of Mwangi's generation and younger, are conversant in tough-guy American slang; they reflect the alienation and individualism most obvious in urban postcolonial Kenya. Not surprisingly, two of Mwangi's novels have been associated with films: *Carcase for Hounds* was made into *Cry Freedom*, and *The Bushtrackers* (1979), which originated as a screenplay collaboration with the American journalist Gary Strieker, was published to coincide with the film's release.

THE MAU MAU NOVELS AND CHILDREN'S STORIES

Although *Carcase for Hounds* was the first novel that Mwangi wrote, it was the second to be published and the second to be filmed. It has much in common with Mwangi's other novel about Mau Mau, *Taste of Death.* Both feature fast-paced action and snappy dialogue. Each uses an omniscient narrator who presents the perspective of both the Mau Mau fighters and the white government forces opposing them. Both personalize the conflict by setting up an individual Mau Mau leader against an opposing colonial military commander. The film version of *Carcase for Hounds*, a Nigerian production directed by Ola Balogun under the title *Cry Freedom*, is a fairly loose adaptation of Mwangi's original story. The setting is generically African, not specific to Kenya, and Balogun added romantic entanglements that are not in Mwangi's original.

Reflections by historians and fiction writers on the effects of Mau Mau and the accompanying state of emergency, so divisive for Kenya as both a colony and a republic, led to debates over historical accuracy versus revisionism. Colonial writers like Robert Ruark and Elspeth Huxley portrayed the Land and Freedom Army atavistically—that is, they saw the army as an unfortunate throwback to a savage past—and Kenyan writers, including Mwangi, have been accused of unwittingly accepting and perpetuating that negative image. Because the national bourgeoisie and the political elite that emerged after independence are not the same people who fought the Mau Mau wars, the argument goes, that history had to be rewritten to downplay the heroism of the guerrilla fighters and to emphasize instead the role of Jomo Kenyatta and other postindependence political leaders. Thus, according to David Maughan-Brown, Mwangi, like Charles Mangua in *A Tail in the Mouth* (1972) and Godwin Wachira in *Ordeal in the Forest* (1968), participates in "criminalizing" the movement through his representation of Mau Mau in *Carcase for Hounds* and *Taste of Death* ("Four Sons of One Father," 1985, p. 186).

If Mwangi's adult novels are open to this charge, his children's stories, in which Mau Mau figures significantly, are not. When he began writing for children, Mwangi chose the setting that he knew best from his childhood: Nanyuki of the 1950s. *Jimi the Dog* (1990) and *Little White Man* (1990) both deal with the adventures of young Kariuki, the son of a cook in the house of the settler farmer Bwana Ruin. While *Jimi the Dog* focuses on how Kariuki gets and raises a puppy, it also addresses issues of social injustice under colonialism. *Little White Man* deals more seriously and in depth with the armed resistance. "I am not certain," Kariuki begins, "when I first heard the word *mau-mau*" (p. 1). Mau Mau becomes an integral part of young Kariuki's experience. His friendship and adventures with Nigel, the son of a settler farmer, involve the boys in encounters with freedom fighters in the nearby forest. When Nigel is captured, Kariuki goes to find his friend, only to discover that his brother, Hari, is among the rebels. In a sobering conclusion, Hari is killed by government soldiers after arranging for the release of the two boys. *Little White Man* transcends the genre of the children's story because all of the characters are more complex and nuanced than the relatively caricatured representations in Mwangi's Mau Mau novels for adults, *Taste of Death* and *Carcase for Hounds*.

CHRONICLING THE URBAN POOR

In the three years before the appearance of Mwangi's *Kill Me Quick* in 1973, a number of Kenyan authors published novels dealing with life in the city, which subsequently became a distinctive theme in Kenyan writing. Earlier fiction had focused on conflicts surrounding the integration of western and traditional ways of life or on issues of nation building in the postcolonial era. A veritable explosion of novels that dealt exclusively with the vagaries of city life began in 1970 with Leonard Kibera's *Voices in the Dark*. Other writers in this vein included Charles Mangua (*Son of Woman*, 1972), George Kamau Muruah (*Never Forgive Father*, 1972), Mike Mwaura (*The Renegade*, 1972), and Mwangi Ruheni (*What a Life!*, 1972). Mwangi was thus neither the first nor the only writer to treat the urban setting in depth, but his urban novels remain the paradigmatic and in many ways the most interesting examples of the urban genre from Kenya.

Urbanization may be the single most significant social phenomenon in postcolonial Kenya. Although East Africa is by global standards relatively underurbanized, the rate of urban growth in the region has been extremely high; Nairobi, the region's major city, has manifested the accompanying problems. The disparities of segregation by class and race during the colonial era remained in the postcolonial years. The most obvious signs of these problems were the impoverished shantytowns and slums — Mathare Valley being the most infamous, though not the largest — that filled the marginal spaces within and between the more affluent suburbs and the modern downtown.

Mwangi's urban novels offer a riveting account of the constant struggle for survival that marks life in Nairobi's poorest sectors. *Kill Me Quick*, *Going Down River Road*, and *The Cockroach Dance* re-create landscapes of stinking back alleys and ramshackle dwellings and the severe social problems that accompany them — inadequate housing and jobs, nonexistent waste-removal services, corrupt officials, alcoholism, thievery, and juvenile delinquency. Mwangi's vivid descriptions of Nairobi's underbelly resemble what has been described as the "excremental vision" of the Ghanaian writer Ayi Kwei Armah: filth, grime, and foul odors fill the text.

The urban setting of these novels converts many of Mwangi's narrative weaknesses into strengths. The individualism that is so tiring in the popular fiction and the Mau Mau novels is no longer a cliché but a fitting response to the tough urban setting. The inconsistency of tone and perspective is less problematic because city life itself is inconsistent. The portrayal of women, deeply problematic in his popular novels, becomes less objectionable if not yet laudable. Women are portrayed as sex objects, but then everyone and everything is objectified and prostituted in this dehumanized urban setting. Mwangi's tales demonstrate the disruption of traditional structures, including family roles and gender relations, by the urban social milieu.

The main characters in these novels exemplify what Angus Calder has appropriately dubbed the "Mwangian Man," an intelligent, usually well educated, individual whose inability to find a job that uses his skills, or sometimes any job at all, leads him to ever greater cynicism, disillusionment, and despair. Meja in *Kill Me Quick*, Ben in *Going Down River Road*, and Dusman Gonzaga in *The Cockroach Dance* are, despite their differences, classic examples of the Mwangian Man; while Moshesh in *The Return of Shaka* and the young Juda Pesa in *Striving for the Wind* represent a later, if incomplete, return of the Mwangian Man. This character, above all else, has invested Mwangi's writings with their critical edge.

Kill Me Quick

The problem of street children, or the "parking boys" as they are sometimes known, occupies *Kill Me Quick* (1973), the novel that put Mwangi on the East African literary map. The novel is also at least partially autobiographical; Mwangi wrote *Kill Me Quick* after graduating from secondary school and discovering that he and his friends could not find jobs. *Kill Me Quick* is a first-person narrative in the picaresque tradition. Its protagonists, the adolescent dropouts Meja and Maina, whose names play on the Swahili phonetic rendering of "major" and "minor," represent one of the pressing social problems in Nairobi: the growing number of orphaned or destitute boys (and, beginning in the late 1980s, girls as well) who roam Nairobi's streets, surviving through handouts and their wits. In *Kill Me Quick* delinquency leads to involvement with street gangs and more serious crimes; in the end Maina is convicted of murder and is likely to hang, while Meja languishes in prison. *Kill Me Quick* won Mwangi the 1974 Kenyatta Award for Literature, a significant achievement for a first novel.

Going Down River Road

Going Down River Road (1976) solidified Mwangi's literary reputation, winning him the Kenyatta Award for a second time in 1977. It is the Nairobi novel par excellence. More deliberately and ultimately more successfully than in *Kill Me Quick*, Mwangi re-creates Nairobi's backyard, the peripheral areas such as Eastleigh and Mathare Valley that house the disenfranchised and the powerless as well as the River Road area where Nairobi's inexpensive bars are located. Again, a socially marginal character is the protagonist. Ben is a construction worker on a new addition to Nairobi's growing skyline, the twenty-four-story, ironically named Development House. When the novel opens, Ben has just moved in with Wini, a prostitute and secretary with a son simply known as Baby. The tone (or more accurately, the smell) of the entire novel is established in the novel's memorable opening lines:

> Baby should not have drunk coffee. He urinated all of it during the night and now the smell lay thick and throat-catching, overcoming even the perfume of his mother's bed across the room. In the bed Ben lay with the boy's mother curled in his large arms, warm and soft and fast asleep. But Ben was not asleep anymore. The pungent baby urine stink had awakened him long before his usual waking up time.
>
> (p. 2)

When Wini deserts them both for a wealthy white man, Ben in a moment of compassion that he occasionally regrets continues to care for Baby. Evicted from Wini's Eastleigh apartment, they take the downwardly mobile step of moving in with Ben's work buddy, Ocholla, in a shantytown shack along the Nairobi River. Eastleigh, a section of Nairobi known for its Somali and Ethiopian refugee populations, at least had solid buildings, but the Nairobi River slum houses an even more destitute population. The impoverished residents of this type of illegal settlement are in no position to consider the impossible tasks of acquiring building permits or meeting construction codes when they set up their shacks. The inhabitants are at the mercy of city council extortionists who provide no basic services and burn down the tenants' shacks when they cannot pay "tax" money. But Mwangi shows that even in Nairobi Valley, life is not as bad as it could be. Perhaps the lowest rung on the Nairobi social ladder is represented by Mathare Valley, "the only place in the city where they may keep chickens or perish" (p. 100). In a brilliant passage, Ben passes along the lip of Mathare Valley aboard a city bus on his way to Kariobangi to pick up another supply of *bhang* (marijuana), which he uses to bribe his foreman in order to be assigned more desirable tasks:

> From up here the shanty town appears just as a rubbish heap of paper, scrap iron, dust and smoke. Appearances are deceptive. Down there live enough construction labourers, unlicensed fruit peddlars and illicit liquor brewers to cause concern to the whole city police. It can be nightmarish hunting for vagrants down there. Almost everyone is a vagrant, that is including women and children. And they drink [*chang'aa*] and smoke *bhang*, two things that cannot stand the sight of a policeman. A few coppers have got themselves knocked cold by unknown assailants down there. Coppers find it easier to follow behind the City Council constabulary who have the right to raze the place down any day in the interest of public health. In the resulting smoke and chaos the policemen descend into the forbidden valley, make a few desperate arrests, then scramble out before the place regenerates into solid, obstinate, granite resistance to law and order.
>
> (p. 140)

Mwangi excels in this vivid portrayal of Nairobi's marginal spaces. Morning finds Ben on the roads and paths leading to the city center, along with crowds of other workers who cannot afford bus fare. No other Kenyan writer has so effectively captured this Sisyphus-like morning ritual that Mwangi describes as an "endless routine trudge, the tramp of the damned at the Persian wheel" (p. 6).

As Mwangi shows, Nairobi is replete with contradictions. Development House, for example, is located on Haile Selassie Avenue at the edge of the financial and business district and next to the site of a new eight-hundred-bed tourist hotel. Workers like Ben and Ocholla, who are constructing the building, live in Nairobi's poorest areas; apart from their temporary, low-paying jobs, they are unlikely to benefit from Development House. Mwangi uses the construction of the new building to structure the novel's action: in the first chapter Development House is four stories high; it grows to seven stories by Chapter 7, thirteen by Chapter 11, and its final elevation of twenty-four stories by Chapter 20. By contrast, River Road is an area of bars, nightclubs, and cheap hotels frequented by the working classes of Nairobi. Here Ben and Ocholla drink the illegal brews *chang'aa* and *karara*, find prostitutes, and pick fights.

Going Down River Road ends on an ambivalent but predominantly somber note. Mwangi maintains a tentative but fragile hope for the future, as Ben convinces Baby to return to school after a bout of delinquency. Meanwhile, Development House has been completed and the workers are out of a job; but construction of another big building is about to begin. Ocholla's large, hungry family has unexpectedly joined him from their rural home, where the crops have failed and life is hard. Ocholla tells Ben that he and Baby will have to move out. They argue, but as Ocholla runs out of a bar and heads down River Road, Ben chases him as the novel closes: "Ocholla!" Ben hollers hoarsely. "Wait for me; don't leave me here alone. Buddy!" (p. 215).

The Cockroach Dance

In many ways, *The Cockroach Dance* (1979) is a perfected remake of *Going Down River Road*. Again, Mwangi has created a buddy story, this time featuring Dusman Gonzaga and Toto, two roommates in Dacca House. Dusman tries to convince himself that this unsightly address on smelly, undesirable Grogan Road is only temporary, but when thieves take the wheels from his broken-down Triumph Herald car, Dusman's last symbol of freedom and possible escape is destroyed. Grogan Road is literally and symbolically adjacent to River Road. The excremental ambience—the bars and brothels, the thieves and cockroaches that operate with equal impunity, the streets filled with drunks, beggars, and survivors—creates a landscape similar to those in Mwangi's earlier urban novels. Even some of the key images reappear. Compare Dusman's discovery of "a hungry cockroach gnawing at the plastic nozzle of a can of the most reputable insect decimator on the market" (*The Cockroach Dance*, p. 189) to Ben's explanation that "You cannot kill them.... You find them playing with the insecticide container, trying to eat the plastic lid" (*Going Down River Road*, p. 20).

Mwangi again portrays vividly the "tramp of the damned" in Nairobi's underbelly. His preferred metaphor in *The Cockroach Dance*, however, is an embittered version of Shakespeare's notion of life as a drama, rather than the Sisyphus-like image that appeared in *Going Down River Road*. Dusman observes: "The events that take place daily on these same streets leave you with a dry acid taste in your mouth. Real life dramas, written by an eccentric old bastard, having no apparent beginning or end, no winners, only losers and choreographed by a sadistic bitch-goddess" (p. 43).

In *The Cockroach Dance*, Mwangi is as creative as ever, and his humor is as gut-wrenching as his sensory descriptions. Dusman is relatively fortunate for a resident of

Grogan Road; he at least has an education and a job. Unfortunately, he belongs to that class of young Nairobians who are overqualified and underemployed. He manifests his frustrations with his dead-end job through fantasies about the parking meters it is his duty to read: "Dusman Gonzaga had dreamed ... he had become a parking meter magnate. He had installed miniature meters on the dirty kitchen table for the roaches that came in hordes to forage for crumbs. He had invented special ones with split-second electronic timing devices for the mice and rats out by the garbage cans" (p. 3). Dusman even invents meters for the vagrants and beggars of downtown Nairobi.

As the novel progresses, cockroaches emerge as the predominant metaphor for Nairobi's derelict populations. *The Cockroach Dance* is, in effect, the story of how Dusman changes his attitude toward these "milling masses" who "sweat sticky, black pitch" (p. 57). His stance is at first reactionary: "Give them a job, force them to work, or take them out and let the army use them as dummies for target practice" (p. 58). But a week of sick leave gives Dusman time to reflect on his experience on Grogan Road and its living conditions. Slowly but surely, he begins to identify with the masses, beginning with "the faceless ones" who inhabit Dacca House. Dusman becomes obsessed with cockroaches, to the point of ordering them in a restaurant. By the end, he is a tentative revolutionary, who concludes that "the wretched of the earth," like tenacious cockroaches that survive despite the odds, "will in the long run, prize something out of the tight claws of the not so wretched" (p. 157). Dusman leads the Dacca House tenants, the faceless ones that he once despised, in a rent strike that is unresolved as the novel closes.

This growth in social awareness is the most important difference between *Going Down River Road* and *The Cockroach Dance*. In *The Cockroach Dance*, Mwangi presents a broader historical and social vision than in his earlier work. Nairobi's structure did not arise overnight; it developed over time, with roots in the colonial era, as *Going Down River Road* and *The Cockroach Dance*, two major narrative interventions on the history and development of Grogan Road, testify.

Mwangi's characters are more vivid and memorable than ever in *The Cockroach Dance*. Their Swahili names make clear that many of them are deliberate caricatures. For example, the residents of Dacca House include the family of Sukuma Wiki, a vegetable peddler. *Sukuma wiki,* a green vegetable similar to kale, is commonly eaten with the staple *ugali*. The common view of *sukuma wiki* as a budget stretcher is evidenced by its name, which means "to push the week." In a comic extension, Sukuma's wife is named Vuta, whose full name translates to "pull the week." Chupa na Debe ("bottles and cans") is modeled after real Nairobi residents who eke out a living by collecting and reselling bottles and cans. Mganga ("doctor") is the resident witch doctor, whose dubious treatments Dusman carefully avoids. Then there is the Bathroom Man with his wife and child. Dusman's change in attitude toward this family, who lives in a bathroom, is a measure of his changing reaction to the rest of the faceless masses. He finally stops directing his indignation at the family and focuses instead on the real culprit, the landlord Tumbo Kubwa ("big belly").

Short Stories

The urban setting has been Mwangi's most successful. The five short stories that he has published also deal with urban themes. "An Incident in the Park" (1988), for instance, is about mob justice, an all-too-common occurrence in Nairobi. A vegetable hawker, running from the police who are demanding his license, is accosted by a lunchtime crowd in downtown Uhuru Park and stoned to death. In choosing Uhuru Park as his setting, Mwangi has identified yet another important space in Nairobi's urban landscape, an area where the unemployed sleep the day away. Only the lunchtime rush of workers hurrying from their government offices downtown and back disrupts the quiet of the park. The incident Mwangi describes in this story neatly summarizes the issues of alienation and poverty that inform all of his urban texts.

The other short stories also present vignettes of urban life. Ben, the construction worker from *Going Down River Road*, wanders through Nairobi bars in "Like Manna from Heaven" (1974) and meets a sympathetic prostitute in "No Credit: Terms Strictly Cash!" (1976). "I Say Tham" (1975) is reminiscent of *Kill Me Quick*, featuring a shoeshine boy who picks up chronic tuberculosis in prison. In "Coming Back" (1975), the protagonist, who lives in Nairobi, visits his rural home community and discovers that a former girlfriend has died in a car accident.

POPULAR FICTION

The first generation of East African writers, indeed African writers in general in the independence era, worked from an implicit consensus that a writer's task was one of involvement in and commitment to nation building and social improvement. To be an artist was to be an activist. The creation of "committed literature," or *littérature engagée*, was the unquestioned task of the writer. While there may have been disagreements about specific ideological positions, as in the Négritude debate, no one questioned that the writer's primary duty was to improve society. Not coincidentally, writers from this era emerged from the major regional educational institutions—Makerere University in Kampala, Uganda, the University of Dar es Salaam in Tanzania, and the University of Nairobi—since these were the centers of debate about social direction in East Africa.

Beginning in 1970, however, a new generation of writers emerged in Kenya who created texts that critics classified under the generally pejorative category of "popular literature." These popular texts stand in stark contrast to the committed writing that dominated in the previous generation and provoked one of the most heated critical debates surrounding Kenyan and East African writing in the decades following their initial appearance. The popular texts include a plethora of detective, adventure, crime, and romance tales; they are characterized by shallow characters, simple plots, and fast action. Unlike committed writing, the popular novels are generally acknowledged to be potboilers; some, like Charles Mangua's *Son of Woman* (1972), often designated the first of this genre from Kenya, were specifically created for novel-writing competitions sponsored by publishing firms. Critics frequently cite western popular writers, most notably James Hadley Chase, Agatha Christie, Ian Fleming, and Robert Ludlum, as well as popular Hollywood films, as models for this genre.

Both local and international critics vilified these Kenyan popular texts. They deemed them amoral, pornographic, trivial, and a bad influence on young people. In *The Season of Harvest: Some Notes on East African Literature*, a leading Kenyan critic, Chris Wanjala, led the charge: "There is a case of literature in Kenya which is a trashy and scabrous imitation of brothel and low life especially yarned for the low-brow reader in this country. It portrays the depraved scenes of sex, the dilemma of the prostitute and the cancer of unemployment" (pp. 135–136). Other observers, unable to pass up the opportunity of extending Taban lo Liyong's metaphor, suggested that with this explosion in popular literature, the East African literary desert might now be blooming, but in a harvest of weeds.

Despite criticism, these texts, as their name implies, proved immensely popular. After the success of *Son of Woman*, Kenyan publishing houses in the 1970s began special series to facilitate publication of these types of books.

Beginning in the late 1970s, Mwangi also began to write texts that qualified as popular literature. To many of his admirers, these books were disappointing, lacking the critical edge that had marked his earlier works, especially his urban novels. Mwangi's response to this criticism has been sanguine: he has argued that at this point in Kenya's literary history, it is simply important to provide texts that people will read; since people buy and read popular texts, these are the sort that should be made available. "My only mistake," he has said, "was that I didn't use a pseudonym for my popular novels, and use my own name for the rest. That way I would have avoided all this criticism (personal communication, 1993). Mwangi did use a pseudonym —David Duchi—for one of his adventure texts, *Assassins on Safari* (1983), but plans with the Longman publishing company for a whole series under this name never materialized.

Mwangi's writing style suits the popular genre. His cinematic vision comes to the fore in the popular novels, which feature spitfire action and frantically paced dialogue. If disappointing when compared with his more serious works, these texts are certainly among the best written of their genre from Kenya. Mwangi usually takes an event from modern Kenyan or African history or politics as his point of departure: *The Bushtrackers* (1979) involves poachers in Kenyan game parks; *Bread of Sorrow* (1987) features freedom fighters and diamond smugglers in southern Africa; civil war and famine in the Horn of Africa are found in *Weapon of Hunger* (1989); the South African liberation struggle is portrayed in *The Return of Shaka* (1989); and *Striving for the Wind* (1990) involves land-tenure issues in postcolonial Kenya.

Mwangi's foray into the popular genre began with *The Bushtrackers*, which began as a collaboration with the American television journalist Gary Strieker. Film and novel were coordinated to debut together; Strieker created the screenplay, and Mwangi wrote the novel. The story treats one of the better-advertised problems of Kenya in the late 1970s, the decimation of wildlife by poachers. Frank Burkell, a white Englishman, and the Kikuyu Johnny Kimathi are park rangers working together in Tsavo Game Park. Johnny retires from this dangerous profession upon marrying and opens a shop on Nairobi's Grogan Road. When the U.S.-based Mafia steps up its ivory-smuggling operations and even breaks into Johnny's store and home because of his refusal to pay "protection" money, Johnny becomes angry. He teams up with Frank once again, and amid exciting chase scenes, exploding cars, and fancy shooting, the buddies successfully eliminate the poaching threat and Grogan Road's extortionists in one fell swoop.

Assassins on Safari involves the Kenyan tourist industry and foreign operatives. Kanja, a police reservist turned freelance bodyguard, becomes embroiled in a plan by German mercenaries to assassinate the U.S. secretary of state during a visit to Kenya's Amboseli Game Park. By foiling the plot, Kanja strikes a blow for Kenyan pride and national sovereignty, proving that the Kenyan police are capable of enforcing the law in their own country. "For the sake of Commissioner Omari and all the other men in our security service who had been made to stand back like little boys and watch the Americans," Kanja concludes, "I was glad I had blundered onto the stage and stolen the show" (p. 163).

Bread of Sorrow features blackmail, exploding airplanes, gunrunning for South Africa's African National Congrress (ANC), diamonds in the mouth of a corpse, Mozambique Liberation Front (FRELIMO) guerrillas, Rastafarians, and spectacular scenery. The action moves from London, to Johannesburg, to Mozambique, to Nanyuki, and finally to Msimbati, a small island off the Tanzanian coast. On this island lives Colonel Bridges, an eccentric white man based on the historical figure Leslie Rogers, who, after retiring from the East African colonial service, settled on a small Tanzanian island, designed his own flag, and declared himself sultan and his island an independent country. Much of the novel is about how the politically conservative South African Peter Jones comes to side with the ANC.

Weapon of Hunger alludes to the situation in Ethiopia in the mid 1980s. The fictional nation of Borku is experiencing a drought and famine, which are exacerbated by a civil war in the separatist region of Arakan, a clear reference to Eritrea, which achieved independence in 1993. Jack Rivers, an American rock star who has raised money for famine relief in the region (an allusion to the Band Aid fund-raising and relief efforts of 1985–1986), is concerned that the food supplies are not reaching the famine-struck areas. He organizes a crew of unemployed musicians and makes a daredevil attempt to drive a convoy of one hundred trucks full of food through the desert, spurning government resistance and scorning rebels and bandits.

Of all the Kenyan popular novels, Mwangi's thrillers are among the most creative and most consistently well written. They nevertheless demonstrate the weaknesses of many of his novels in other genres. The same inconsistency of detail that Angus Calder, among others, has criticized in Mwangi's novels about Mau Mau arises in his popular texts: plots tend to hinge on far-fetched events, and the fast-paced action and snappy dialogue, usually a plus, at times become so clipped as to strain credulity. Mwangi also has a penchant for technical detail: if a character drives a car or flies an airplane, we are sure to be informed precisely what type of car or plane is involved; if a gun is loaded or fired, he states its caliber and describes the precise sound it makes. Although usually effective, this technique misfires when these details are clearly inaccurate or impossibly far-fetched. As in his other works, the portrayal of women in Mwangi's thrillers is generally abominable. Almost every female character serves as an object of male sexual desires. When their usefulness is over, women are discarded unceremoniously or even brutally. Like cars and guns, they have little importance except as signifiers of male potency and control.

Mwangi's novels of the late 1980s and early 1990s, *The Return of Shaka* (1989) and *Striving for the Wind* (1990), occupy ambiguous positions in relation to the rest of his popular works. While they read like popular novels, both endeavor to address serious issues. By this time, he had clearly demonstrated his ability to write a thriller; however, he also wanted to be considered a serious writer, a sentiment he had expressed at the end of the 1970s. As he explained in an interview with Bernth Lindfors:

> The popular writing can't go on. I mean, one can only write so much on a certain subject before the readers tire and eventually return to the more serious literature. The excitement caused by the emerging popular writing should soon settle down. There is a great future for serious writing here. . . . I like to develop a serious story in prose.
> (1980, pp. 76, 79)

Mwangi had in fact already produced serious works in his urban trilogy. But he did not abandon altogether the popular style that had served him so well; *Bread of Sorrow* and *Weapon of Hunger* were published several years after his conversation with Lindfors. This tension between writing styles produced the ambiguities of *The Return of Shaka* and *Striving for the Wind*, which are hybrids of the popular and the serious. While they display many of the same characteristics as Mwangi's thrillers, these novels deal in a much more complex way with contemporary African social issues. At the same time that they draw on some of the tropes of popular writing, they also contain a critical commentary on the genre.

In *The Return of Shaka*, he takes as his subject the situation of African students in the United States, with whom he became acquainted during a term with the International Writing Program at the University of Iowa in

1975–1976. As he explains: "When I was in the U.S., I met a lot of East Africans in my travels through San Francisco, Washington and Chicago. As we talked, I realized that there was a great need to tell their sad story. I hope to go back and learn more about this situation before finishing this novel" (Lindfors, p. 76). Mwangi did not in fact return to the United States but manages to tell this "sad story." Moshesh, the son and heir of the traditional leader in a fictional country reminiscent of South Africa, is studying in the United States and plans with a number of his compatriots, also students or professors at U.S. schools, for an armed invasion to liberate his homeland. Backed by generous finances from the father of Moshesh's American girlfriend, the group hires weapons and a crack group of mercenaries, who are hanging out in Alabama pool halls. Everything falls apart in the end, however, and it becomes clear that the whole plan was a grand delusion. The anticlimactic conclusion of *The Return of Shaka* contains two serious critiques: on the one hand, of those African students abroad who compensate for feelings of guilt or failure by inventing elaborate fantasies about who they are and what they will do for their homeland; on the other, of the texts that support those fantasies, namely the popular genre in which Mwangi himself participated.

Striving for the Wind, another ambiguous text, is Mwangi's most impressive novel after his urban trilogy. While the prose is still snappy and the action fast paced, the story carries a serious message. The novel is set in Mwangi's home area in rural Central Province and concerns the issue of postcolonial land tenure. Baba Pesa (literally, "father of money") is a greedy landowner in the former white highlands who is intent on capturing the remaining parcel of land in his area, which is owned by the poor Baba Baru ("father of dirt"). Pesa's intelligent but disillusioned son, Juda, provides critical commentary. In the end Baru and Pesa are forced to cooperate and help each other with their harvests, and Pesa rediscovers the cultural and spiritual values of the land, rather than seeing it merely as a source of income. The power of Pesa (money) over Baru (dirt) is weakened. *Striving for the Wind* received honorable mention for the Commonwealth Award in 1991.

NEW DIRECTIONS IN THE 1990s

Mwangi came of age as a writer just as Kenya was entering a brief golden age of postcolonial fiction: the 1970s saw more Kenyan titles from more Kenyan-based publishers than any decade before or later—after the 1970s the number of publications declined precipitously. Particularly with the dramatic deterioration of the Kenyan economy in the 1990s, publishers tended to stick to school texts, which were sure moneymakers. Mwangi's frustration with the mixed critical reception of his later works coincided with this decline, which affected all Kenyan writers. The perceived disjuncture between his popular adventure texts and his serious urban novels was a common criticism of his later writing; while *Going Down River Road* and *The Cockroach Dance* are generally acknowledged to be his best works, they are inescapably similar to each other. Mwangi, it seems, needed a new angle. As Calder argues, his writing lacks a social vision and a sense of audience; furthermore, Calder suggests, it is characterized by "the unselfconscious deployment of the techniques of 'popular' fiction, which is a source of both weakness and of strength" (p. 177).

The Return of Shaka and *Striving for the Wind* represent an attempt both to find that new angle and to create a blend of popular and serious styles. Also at this time Mwangi began publishing children's stories, a project that, as he explains, resulted from his frustration with the critical reception of his works. In addition, the children's stories extend his earlier interests. When he was growing up in Nanyuki, Mwangi wrote and illustrated stories to entertain his brother. He has explained his interest in writing for children in terms similar to those used to justify his popular fiction: as an outgrowth of his desire to get people interested in reading. There is simply not enough written for children from a Kenyan or African perspective, Mwangi has argued in personal communication. His children's stories have been his most successful works. *Little White Man* was Mwangi's best-selling book; it has been translated into Dutch, French, and German, and the German-language edition enjoyed international exposure after it received the Deutscher Jugendliteratur Preis in 1992.

Mwangi had always been unusual among Kenyan writers in that he did not emerge from the university community. Apart from a brief stint as a participant in the International Writing Program at the University of Iowa, Mwangi's studies included only two years at Kenyatta University College. Consequently, when he was awarded a scholarship to pursue a bachelor's degree in English at Leeds University in 1990 he accepted it, partly as a way to remedy what he considered a gap in his experience and partly as an opportunity to take a break from writing.

Mwangi's dissatisfaction with the critical response to his work continued to push him toward an interest in film. Even though Kenya has served as the location for a large number of North American and British films, the local film industry is practically nonexistent. Funding constraints and bureaucratic restrictions have effectively stifled local initiatives in this direction; East Africa, no longer a literary desert, may still be characterized as a cinematic one, particularly when its endeavors are compared with developments in West African film. With his wealth of experience in the logistical aspects of film, his decidedly cinematic vision, and his previous forays into this field, Mwangi—who has done so much to help Kenya's literary desert bloom—is as well suited as anyone to alter the landscape in Kenyan film. Given his record as one of the most innovative and wide-ranging of contemporary Kenyan writers, it would be fitting for him to break new ground in this medium as well.

Selected Bibliography

NOVELS

Kill Me Quick. Nairobi, Kenya: Heinemann Educational, 1973.

Carcase for Hounds. Nairobi, Kenya: Heinemann, 1974.

Taste of Death. Nairobi, Kenya: East African Publishing House, 1975.

Going Down River Road. Nairobi, Kenya: Heinemann, 1976.

The Bushtrackers. Nairobi, Kenya: Longman, 1979. Based on the screenplay by Gary Strieker.

The Cockroach Dance. Nairobi, Kenya: Longman, 1979.

[David Duchi, pseud.] *Assassins on Safari.* Nairobi, Kenya: Longman, 1983.

Bread of Sorrow. Nairobi, Kenya: Longman, 1987.

The Return of Shaka. Nairobi, Kenya: Longman, 1989.

Weapon of Hunger. Nairobi, Kenya: Longman, 1989.

Striving for the Wind. Nairobi, Kenya: Heinemann, 1990.

SHORT FICTION

"Like Manna from Heaven." In *Joe Magazine* (Nairobi) (November 1974).

"Coming Back." In *Joe Magazine* (Nairobi) (September 1975).

"I Say Tham." In *The Daily Iowan* (Iowa City) (21 November 1975).

"No Credit: Terms Strictly Cash!" In *Joe Magazine* (Nairobi) (June 1976).

"An Incident in the Park." In Valerie Kibera, ed., *An Anthology of East African Short Stories.* Essex, U.K.: Longman, 1988.

CHILDREN'S STORIES

Jimi the Dog. Nairobi, Kenya: Longman, 1990.

Little White Man. Nairobi, Kenya: Longman, 1990.

The Hunter's Dream. London: Macmillan, 1993.

INTERVIEWS

"Audience, Language, and Form in Committed East African Writing: An Open Discussion with Meja Mwangi." In *Komparatistische Hefte* 3 (1981).

Brauer, Dieter, and R. Stroebinger, eds. *African Writers on the Air.* Cologne, Germany: Deutsche Welle, 1984.

Lindfors, Bernth. "Meja Mwangi: Interview." In *Kunapipi* 1, no. 2 (1979). Repr. in *Mazungumzo: Interviews with East African Writers, Publishers, Editors, and Scholars.* Papers in International Studies, African Series, 41. Athens, Ohio: University Center for International Studies, Africa Program, Ohio University, 1980.

Nichols, Lee. "Meja Mwangi." In *Conversations with African Writers: Interviews with Twenty-six African Authors.* Washington D.C.: Voice of America, 1981.

CRITICAL STUDIES

Adeeko, Adeleke. "Two Writers on a Plundered Economy: A Study of Style and Vision in Selected Works of Ngũgĩ and Mwangi." Master's thesis, University of Ife, Nigeria, 1985.

Bardolph, Jacqueline. "Le Roman de langue anglaise en Afrique de l'Est, 1964–1976." Ph.D. diss., University of Caen, France, 1981.

———. "Visions de Nairobi dans la littérature d'Afrique de l'Est." In René Richards, ed., *Les Images de la ville dans les littératures africaines.* Montpellier, France: Centre d'Études et de Recherches sur les Pays d'Afrique Noire Anglophone. Dossier CERPANA, 3, 1983. Proceedings of a conference held at Montpellier, October 1982.

———. "La Littérature du Kenya: Resistance, conscience nationale, et littérature." In *Notre librairie* 85 (1986).

Barrett, Lindsay. "Liberation War Is Brought to Screen." In *West Africa* (20 April 1981).

Calder, Angus. "Meja Mwangi's Novels." In G. D. Killam, ed., *The Writing of East and Central Africa.* London: Heinemann, 1984.

Chakava, Henry. *Notes on Meja Mwangi's* Kill Me Quick. Nairobi: Heinemann Educational, 1976.

Colmer, Rosemary. "The Development of the Sub-Saharan Black African Novel in English." Ph.D. diss., Macquarie University, Australia, 1980.

Dorsey, David. "Didactic Form of the Novel: With Evidence from Meja Mwangi and Others." In Kofi Anyidoho, Abioseh M. Porter, Daniel Racine, and Janice Spleth, eds., *Interdisciplinary Dimensions of African Literature.* Washington, D.C.: Three Continents, 1985.

Gakwandi, Shatlo A. "The Novel in East Africa." In Samuel Omo Asein and Albert Olu Ashaolu, eds., *Studies in the African Novel.* Ibadan, Nigeria: Ibadan University Press, 1986.

Gerard, Albert S. *European-Language Writing in Sub-Saharan Africa.* Budapest, Hungary: Akademiai Kiado, 1986.

Gikandi, Simon. "The Growth of the East African Novel." In G. D. Killam, ed., *The Writing of East and Central Africa.* London: Heinemann, 1984.

Imfeld, Al, and Gerd Meuer. "Meja Mwangi: Life Among the Slum Dwellers." In *Afrika* 21, no. 5 (1980).

"Kenya: Meja Mwangi." In *Lotus* (Cairo) 40–41 (1979).

Knight, Elizabeth. "Mirror of Reality: The Novels of Meja Mwangi." In *African Literature Today* 13 (1983).

Maughan-Brown, David. "Four Sons of One Father: A Comparison of Ngũgĩ's Earliest Novels with Works by Mwangi, Mangua, and Wachira." In *Research in African Literatures* 16 (summer 1985).

———. *Land, Freedom and Fiction: History and Ideology in Kenya.* London: Zed, 1985.

Mbong, Johannes Ngole. "The Presentation of Women in the African Novel." Master's thesis, Fourah Bay College, University of Sierra Leone, 1981.

"Meja Mwangi." In Ulrich Eckhardt, ed., *Horizonte-Magazin 79.* Berlin: Berliner Festspiele GmbH, 1979.

Nazareth, Peter. "Bringing the Whole Mountain Down." In *Afriscope* 6 (April 1976).

Oriaku, Remigius Onyejekwe. "Protest and Revolution in the Kenyan Novel: The Examples of Ngũgĩ wa Thiong'o and Meja Mwangi." Master's thesis, University of Ibadan, Nigeria, 1982.

Palmer, Eustace. "Two Views of Urban Life: Meja Mwangi, *Going Down River Road*; Nuruddin Farah, *A Naked Needle.*" In *African Literature Today* 9 (1978).

———. *The Growth of the African Novel.* London: Heinemann, 1979.

———. "Meja Mwangi's *The Cockroach Dance.*" In *Fourah Bay Studies in Language and Literature* 2 (1981).

Parasuram, A. N. *Guide to Meja Mwangi*: Kill Me Quick. Madras, India: Minerva, 1977.

Taiwo, Oladele. "Language and Theme in Three African Novels." In *Literary Half-Yearly* 22, no. 1 (1981).

Teyie, J. A. O. "Meja Mwangi: The Urbanization of a Writer. Analysis of *Kill Me Quick*, *Going Down River Road*, and *The Cockroach Dance*." Master's thesis, University of Nairobi, Kenya, 1982.

Tsuchiya, Satoru. "Modern East African Literature: From *Uhuru* to *Harambee*." In *World Literature Today* 52 (fall 1978). Repr. in *Afriscope* 8, no. 4 (1978).

Wanjala, Chris. *The Season of Harvest: Some Notes on East African Literature.* Nairobi: Kenya Literature Bureau, 1978.

Agostinho Neto

1922–1979

PHYLLIS A. PERES

ANTÓNIO AGOSTINHO NETO, Angola's most celebrated poet and native son, was born on 17 September 1922 in Kaxikane, a Kimbundu village in the Icolo e Bengo region located approximately forty miles (sixty-four kilometers) from the Angolan capital of Luanda. Neto's parents, Maria da Silva Neto and Agostinho Pedro Neto, were teachers; his father was a Methodist pastor as well. Following graduation from high school in Luanda, Neto took a job with the Health Service in Luanda in 1944 and became involved in cultural and political activities. He participated in the Movimento dos Novos Intelectuais (Movement of New Intellectuals) in the late 1940s, a period when Angolan cultural identity was undergoing rapid transformation.

In Portugal's African colonies, especially in Angola, the literary-cultural movements that emerged in the late 1940s and early 1950s were initially concerned with the negation of Portuguese colonial identity. However, cultural entities such as the musical group Ngola Ritmos, the Movement of New Intellectuals, the literary-arts journal *Mensagem* (published in Luanda, 1951–1952), and other manifestations of growing nationalist sentiments moved beyond the negation of colonial identity to vindicating and redefining Angolan identity. That various persons linked to these and subsequent movements—such as Neto, António Jacinto, Mário António, Viriato da Cruz, and José Luandino Vieira, to cite just a few—would play significant roles in the Angolan liberation struggle of 1961–1975, as well as in postindependence society, underscores the profound relationship between cultural and political independence. Perhaps no figure is more representative of that relationship than Neto.

POLITICAL LIFE

While working for the Health Service, Neto decided to become a physician; he was able to save enough money to go to Portugal in 1947 and begin his studies, first at the medical school at the University of Coimbra and then at the University of Lisbon. After two years he received a scholarship from the American Methodist Church.

Like other African students in Lisbon, Neto immersed himself in political and cultural activities. Upon his arrival in Lisbon, he became one of the leading figures in the Casa dos Estudantes do Império (Overseas Students House), the center for cultural activities for African students in Portugal. In 1951, he spent three months in the prison at Caxias, a suburb of Lisbon, for collecting signatures on a petitition to be sent to the International World Peace Conference in Stockholm, Sweden.

Following his release from Caxias, Neto became involved in the Movement for the Democratic Unity of Youth as the representative from the Portuguese colonies in Africa. He was arrested in February 1955 for participating in an alliance of workers, peasants, and students. Imprisoned at Caxias from February 1955 to June 1957, Neto, already an acclaimed poet, became the object of an international campaign pressuring the fascist Portuguese New State to release him. Those who participated in the effort to free Neto included the French intellectuals Jean-Paul Sartre and Simone de Beauvoir, the Cuban poet Nicolás Guillén, and the Mexican muralist Diego Rivera. During his imprisonment Neto remained politically active and wrote numerous poems. Following his release, he completed his medical studies and married Maria Eugénia da Silva in 1958. They had two daughters and a son.

Neto returned to Angola in 1959 and assumed a leadership role in the Movimento Popular para a Libertação de Angola (Popular Movement for the Liberation of Angola, or MPLA), which had been formed when several nationalist movements joined forces in December 1956. The period 1957–1960 was marked by intense Portuguese police activity against nationalist leaders and activists, many of whom were already in exile at MPLA external headquarters in Conakry, Guinea. Mass arrests and trials of MPLA militants took place in Angola in 1959.

Neto was arrested on 8 July 1960, at his medical practice in Luanda. A peaceful protest in Kaxikane, Neto's birthplace, turned into a massacre when demonstrators were met with police violence; thirty people were killed and over two hundred wounded. Neto was sent to the Cape Verde Islands, also a colony of Portugal, where he was allowed to practice medicine under police surveillance. He was made honorary president of the MPLA while in exile, and he was still on the islands when MPLA forces began the long liberation struggle with an attack on prisons in Luanda on 4 February 1961. Neto was arrested again in Cape Verde and sent to Lisbon's Aljube Prison on 17 October 1961.

A second international campaign was waged for his release, this time with the added efforts of the MPLA, which called for solidarity with its honorary president and all Angolan political prisoners. The New State regime bowed to pressure once again, and in March 1962 placed Neto under restricted residence in Portugal—he could leave his house but not Lisbon. He escaped, and with his family traveled to MPLA external headquarters in Léopoldville, Belgian Congo (now Kinshasa, Zaire). Neto was elected president of the MPLA at the movement's first national conference in December 1962. He remained president throughout the protracted liberation struggle; on 11 November 1975 he declared Angola's independence on behalf of the MPLA–Workers' Party. Neto was sworn in as Angola's first president, a position he held until his death from cancer in Moscow on 10 September 1979.

THE POET OF *SACRED HOPE*

Throughout his years of intense political activity, Neto was linked to several literary-cultural groups, both in Angola and in Portugal. After his early association with the Movement of New Intellectuals in Angola, he continued his cultural activities while studying medicine in Portugal. In 1950, in Coimbra, he organized the series *Momento—antologia de literatura e arte* (Moment—anthology of literature and art) in collaboration with fellow Angolans Lúcio Lara and Orlando de Albuquerque. During the 1950s, Neto's poetry appeared mainly in such Angolan and Portuguese journals and anthologies as *Momento*, *Mensagem* (published in Luanda), *Mensagem* (published by the Casa dos Estudantes do Império), *Cultura*, *Poesia negra de expressão portuguesa*, *Antologia de poesia negra de expressão portuguesa*, and *Estudos ultramarinos*. However, it was not until after the outbreak of the nationalist struggle in Angola that Neto's poetry began to be widely translated. In 1963 he published *Con occhi asciutti* in Italy; this collection appeared in Portugal in 1974 as *Sagrada esperança*. English translations of some of Neto's poems appeared in *Modern Poetry from Africa* (1963), edited by Gerald Moore and Ulli Beier, as well as in Ezekiel Mphahlele's *African Writing Today* (1967). The English translation of *Sagrada esperança*, *Sacred Hope*, was published in 1974.

Sacred Hope contains poems from the period 1945–1960, including some written during Neto's detentions in Portugal, Luanda, and Cape Verde. The collection reflects transitions in Neto's poetic work as well as in Angolan poetry, most notably a shift from the renunciation of colonial identity to an affirmation of *angolanidade* (Angolanness). Some might see this shift as evidence that the Angolan poetry of this period was circumstantial; however, more than being merely a manifestation of growing nationalism, Angolan poetry was above all a rejection of acculturated identity and a rooting of the collective Angolan self.

Not surprisingly, Neto's poems from the 1940s are marked by a deep anticolonial stance, often expressed in descriptions of night, darkness, fear, and death. "Partida para o contrato" ("Departure for Forced Labor") is a critique of the contract-labor system enforced in colonial Africa, by which Angolan workers were sent to plantations on the island of São Tomé. Neto does not write of the horrors or abuses of the contract system; rather, he focuses on the woman whom Manuel, an Angolan worker, leaves behind:

> Não há luz
> não há norte na alma da mulher
>
> Negrura
> Só negrura...
> (*Sagrada esperança*, p. 36)

> There is no light
> no bearing in the woman's soul
>
> Blackness
> Only blackness...
> (*Sacred Hope*, p. 42)

"Departure for Forced Labor" dates from 1945, but even in this early poem of darkness and negation, Neto poses the question "Até quando?" ("Until when?"), which would resonate throughout Angolan poetry in the 1950s.

In "Crueldade" ("Cruelty"), the *musseque*—the shantytown neighborhood of Angolan blacks—of Sambizanga is hardened into night as the colonial police arrest participants at a neighborhood dance. The dark silence of Sambizanga is contrasted to the lights and cruel laughter of the European sections of Luanda; the white laughter trivializes the arrests of black *musseque* dwellers as a banality of everyday life in colonial Luanda. The Sambizanga residents need not question the arrests, for they already know the answers.

Darkness also permeates "Noite" ("Night") as the poet wanders and falls through the dark neighborhoods of slaves with unknown, unlit streets:

> Onde as vontades se diluíram
> e os homens se confundiram
> com as coisas
> (*Sagrada esperança*, p. 56)

> Where wills are diluted
> and men become like
> things
> (*Sacred Hope*, p. 58)

As in Neto's other poems, this is not a romantic elaboration of darkness and despair but rather the depiction of worlds, without light or life, in which African humanity has been enslaved to European colonial dreams. Creating irony, Neto turns around any romantic vision of "noite," since the poem is not about shades of night—it is about the darkness of colonization.

While poems like "Night" portray the silence and darkness as a result of colonial domination, other poems of *Sacred Hope* give voice to Angolan resistance and determination. For example, "Contratados" ("Contract Workers") counters the darkness and despair of "Departure for Forced Labor." The contract workers in the former poem are no less desperate or displaced, for Neto stresses that they are "Cheios de injustiças / caladas no imo das suas almas" (*Sagrada esperança*, p. 65); "Filled with injustice / silent in their innermost souls" (*Sacred Hope*, p. 67). Rather, even with their fearful hearts and faraway looks, still they sing—not yet songs of protest, but voices of life not willing to be drowned in colonial conditions.

Similarly, "Aspiração" ("Aspiration"), written in 1949, begins with a mournful song that follows the African diaspora to the Congo, to Georgia, and to Amazonas. The song becomes at once personalized and universalized in the diaspora, and is played on the *quissange* (an Angolan stringed instrument) as well as a guitar or saxophone. More important, the song is also accompanied by a desire to be "transformado em força / inspirando as consciências desesperadas" (*Sagrada esperança*, p. 69); "transformed into a Force / inspiring desperate consciousness" (*Sacred Hope*, p. 70). "Aspiration," like other poems of the 1950s, registers resistance to the colonial power and African identification. That this identity is based on the African diaspora throughout the world recognizes the spirit of Angola's independence movement beyond the confines of simple nationalism or simplistic negation of colonial identity. Neto stresses the importance of identifying with African peoples throughout the diaspora in their struggle to attain freedom and human rights.

This sense of awakening and resistance prevails throughout *Sacred Hope*, for the volume is purposefully framed with poems of hope and struggle. The first poem in this anthology, "Adeus à hora da largada" ("Farewell at the Hour of Parting"), describes a hopeful departure in search of life and light. In a sweeping stanza of social realism, the poem depicts contemporary colonial Angola—the naked children in the villages, the contract workers on the coffee estates, the black men filled with fear and drunk with rage—and it also looks to the future of a liberated Angola:

> Amanhã
> entoaremos hinos à liberdade
> quando comemorarmos
> a data da abolição desta escravatura
> (*Sagrada esperança*, p. 36)

> Tomorrow
> we shall sing anthems to freedom
> when we commemorate
> the day of the abolition of this slavery
> (*Sacred Hope*, p. 40)

Angolan poetry of the 1950s searches for national identity in the everyday lives of Angolans as they struggle to survive in colonial society. "Farewell at the Hour of Parting" sets the tone for these stories of survival, which are present in many of the volume's poems. "Quitandeira" ("Marketwoman") is one such poetic story, that of a fruit vendor whose own voice mixes with that of the poet. As she sells her oranges, the *quitandeira* tells of the deaths of her children as contract workers, her search for solace in alcohol and religion, and the poetry of her own body. Her story also plays against contemporary colonization in Luanda, as traditional neighborhoods of the city become paved and built to accommodate the massive wave of post–World War II Portuguese settlers. The *quitandeira*'s life appears to belong to the processes of colonialism, and even the poetic voice claims that

> A quitandeira
> que vende fruta
> vende-se
> (*Sagrada esperança*, p. 49)

> The marketwoman
> who sells fruit
> sells herself
> (*Sacred Hope*, p. 53)

However, in a turnabout, the *quitandeira* reclaims her life through the articulation of her story, so that even in the process of selling herself, the possibility of repossessing herself remains.

This poetic identification of *angolanidade* with the masses of African people marks Neto's poetry as well as that of other Angolan writers of the Generation of 1950, who included Viriato da Cruz, Mário António, and António Jacinto. It entailed not only a negation of colonial identity but also a deep questioning of all processes of colonial assimilation. This questioning, as well as the parallel quest to define an Angolan national community, forms the thematic basis for Neto's poem "Mussunda amigo" ("Friend Mussunda"). Mussunda, which literally means someone who was born feet first, is a common name in Kimbundu, a Bantu language of Angola. In this poem the name is endowed with a cultural significance and does not refer to a specific individual. This is reinforced through the use of Kimbundu in the poem as a means of asserting cultural identity between two childhood friends who have grown apart; this distance is evident in the placement of subject pronouns in the poem. The *eu* (I) of the poetic voice stands apart from the *tu* (you), and the whole of the poem is an attempt to reestablish the solidarity of the two friends. Ironically, the verses are insufficient, for the very act of writing emphasizes the colonial process of selective acculturation: "E escrevo versos que não entendes / compreendes a minha angústia?" (*Sagrada esperança*, p. 80); "And I write poems you cannot follow / Do you understand my anguish?" (*Sacred Hope*, p. 83). The solidarity is reestablished through the use of the Kimbundu language, shared memory, and a collective vision of the future; the poem ends with the joining of the disparate subjects and an affirmation of communal identity: "Nós somos"; "We are."

The importance of shared culture forms the basis of many of Neto's poems, particularly those written on the eve of the outbreak of armed struggle. "Noites de cárcere" ("Prison Nights"), written while the poet was jailed in Luanda in 1960, voices a solidarity not of suffering but of resistance. The poem begins outside the prison, with a short journey through the surrounding neighborhoods and *musseques* in a land "empobrecida de tudo pelo medo / e enriquecida pela certeza" (*Sagrada esperança*, p. 115); "impoverished of all by fear / and enriched by certainty" (*Sacred Hope*, p. 122). The fear is born of colonialism, and the certainty is that of national liberation. Here the prison nights are moonlit and shielded from the darkness, even in the face of torture, madness, and hatred. These moonlit nights belong to the drums mourning a corpse and to a weary, wakeful prisoner whose heart beats, not like a drum but like a time bomb.

Neto's poem centers on this prisoner and the nocturnal noises of pain and madness from torture conducted in the other cells. But more important, the poem stresses that the prisoner is not alone, even in the isolated cell. The use of the plural possessive pronoun—"nosso sangue nosso espírito"; "our blood, our spirit"—underscores the collectivity of the struggle at all levels. When the poet claims, "É nossa! É nossa!" ("It is ours! It is ours!"), he refers to both land and nation. "Prison Nights," like "Friend Mussunda," contains lines, in Kimbundu as creolized by Portuguese, extolling solidarity and liberation through a shared culture of resistance.

Other poems that date from Neto's imprisonment in 1960 are similarly adamant in their exaltation of national freedom. Two such celebrated works are "O içar da bandeira" ("The Hoisting of the Flag") and "Havemos de voltar" ("We Shall Return"). The first poem, dedicated to the heroes of the Angolan people, contains a condensed history of colonial resistance from Queen Ginga (1581–1663), who united several tribal groups in an armed campaign against the Portuguese, to contemporary nationalists. Neto refers to Ngola Ritmos, the musical group; the Liga Africana (a progressive group from the 1920s) and its protonationalist newspaper, *Farolim*; as well as to individual MPLA militants, many of whom were also in prison. "The Hoisting of the Flag" foretells the poet's return to an Angola in the midst of a revolution, with thousands of friends perished, but "para sempre vitoriosos na sua morte pela vida" (*Sagrada esperança*, p. 121); "forever victorious in your death for life" (*Sacred Hope*, p. 128). He returns to a land filled with both hope and certainty, and to a collective raising of the flag of independence.

"We Shall Return," quite possibly Neto's best-known poem in Angola, was written in Aljube Prison in Lisbon in 1961. It, too, celebrates the return to Angola, but not just of the poet. The collective *nós* (we) is evident in the *havemos* of the poem's title, as well as in the repetition of that phrase in every verse. Present as well is the expediency of that collective return and a profound love for the Angolan land, people, and culture:

A frescura da mulemba
às nossas tradições
aos ritmos e às fogueiras
havemos de voltar
(*Sagrada esperança*, p. 130)

To the shade of the *mulemba*
to our traditions
to the rhythms and bonfires
we shall return
(*Sacred Hope*, p. 134)

This deeply moving poem, written in imposed exile and in a prison cell, claims Angolan nationhood with a collective voice of reconciliation and certainty.

Written in 1953, Neto's no less certain "O caminho das estrelas" ("The Pathway to the Stars") lit up the dark nights of colonialism with a tracing of the road to freedom. Here the pathway follows the graceful curve of the gazelle's neck, the harmony of drumbeats, and clear African rhythms. "The Pathway to the Stars," like so many of Neto's other poems, overtly presents one of his joyous paradoxes. Because the collective voices of freedom so clearly drum liberation to a strong African beat, the pathway to the stars always leads along the gazelle's neck "para a harmonia do mundo" ("for harmony in the world"). Rooted in Angola and the search for *angolanidade*, Neto's poetry of *Sacred Hope* claims a collective life force that moves beyond a single nation's struggle for liberation to a diasporic celebration of freedom.

"NÁUSEA"

Neto wrote several short stories, but only one was ever published. "Náusea" first appeared in 1952 in *Mensagem*, the literary-cultural journal issued by the Associação dos Naturais de Angola in Luanda. It also was anthologized in 1960 in *Contistas Angolanas*.

"Náusea" centers on the transformation of Luanda into a city of Portuguese settlers beginning in the 1940s. One of the primary programs of the Portuguese New State and its longtime prime minister, António Salazar, was the development of the African colonies — especially Angola and Mozambique — as areas of economic exploitation and European settlement. "Náusea" focuses on the Europeanization of both the city of Luanda and the *ilha* (island) of Luanda, as well as the demographic and socioeconomic implications for Africans such as João, the story's central character. Neto employs a prolonged interior monologue that allows João, an old man who had moved from the *ilha* to the city in his youth, to comment directly on the transformations and their impact on Angolans. His character is balanced by his nephew, who does not have a generational vision and therefore is incapable of comprehending João's profound horror at the changes that have taken place.

The other central character of "Náusea" is Kalunga, the personification of the sea, which is both friend and enemy to João. Raised in a family of fishermen, João views the sea as part of his community and the *ilha* as his true home. He goes to the Ilha de Luanda to relax, relive his childhood, and escape from the miserable conditions of the city's *musseques.* The sea is also an enemy, though, in a historical sense: it has brought boats, automobiles, roads, and even zippers—in short, European civilization. It has also been the pathway for the colonization of Africa and the exploitation of Africans as well as for the departure of millions of human beings during the Atlantic slave trade and contemporary programs of forced labor.

Written before 1952, "Náusea" shares many thematic features with Neto's early poetry. The title refers to the profound anguish of the colonized character in João, who is disgusted at his own helplessness in the face of domination. His nausea is misinterpreted as a physical sickness by his nephew, who still believes in the trappings of colonialism and does not see what lies beyond the material wealth—and beyond his reach. João's anguish does not envision the hope of Neto's later poetry but rather lingers painfully by the sea, Kalunga, which has meant both survival and destruction.

CONCLUSION: WRITING AN ANGOLAN LITERATURE

The Generation of 1950, of which Neto was very much a part, was primarily concerned with the revalidation of African identity within an increasingly Europeanized colonial society. To call their poetry "Angolan" meant a renunciation of colonial identity and, more important, an articulation of a nation. Angola was born of colonialism at the Berlin Conference of 1884–1885, at which Africa was carved up among the European powers. In this search for Angolan identity within a territory fourteen times the size of Portugal, the Generation of 1950 sought to define a "nationalizable" culture.

As part of this articulation of an Angolan culture, Neto and other poets writing in the 1950s were engaged in the creation of an Angolan literature. One of the salient features of this literature was that it could not be termed "colonial." Some features of this literature are articulated in Neto's poetry: the identification with the African common people in Angola, the repeated allusions to shared cultural history and memory, the collectivity of prenationalist and nationalist struggle, and the use of Kimbundu, one of the several major Bantu languages spoken in Angola.

The identification with common people, so evident in Neto's "Marketwoman" and "Friend Mussunda," negates colonial programs of assimilation that sought to create a subclass of "black Portuguese." To become *assimilado* (assimilated) in Portuguese Africa meant not only an acceptance of Portuguese language, customs, education, and religion but also a negation of African identity. While seeking to reestablish that identity, Neto's poetry always recognizes the pitfalls of assimilation. Thus, Mussunda is not able to read the verses that celebrate his commitment to the struggle; likewise, the *quitandeira* mocks the poets who have appropriated her identity in their verse. What is essential, however, is that within the poetic articulation of "nation," those colonial barriers can be crossed, if not torn down. Ultimately "Friend Mussunda" affirms *angolanidade* across class lines and celebrates collective identity.

The use of Kimbundu serves important functions in Neto's poetry. First, it establishes an immediate African identity. This shared language also evokes a collective memory that is echoed in the emerging culture of the liberation struggle. Thus, in "Prison Nights," the use of a creolized Kimbundu in the prison underscores the solidarity within the vision of the end of colonization.

This shared identity is further enforced in Neto's poetry through a rooting within Angola. Poems such as "We Shall Return" celebrate Angolan topography and traditions. Like so many poems of the Generation of 1950, Neto's works identify with Angola in the descriptions of flora, fauna, and land that actively evoke a nativism untouched by colonial domination. In this manner, Neto's poetry participates in the foundation of an Angolan literature that turns against acculturated discourse in a search for a vision of Angola.

As the eminent Angolan poet of his time, Neto wrote a vision of Angola that moves from the negation of colonial identity to the affirmation of *angolanidade* and solidarity within the nationalist struggle. Neto's poems detail the darkness, pain, and death of colonial practices and domination. But these poems are also a joyous celebration of Angolan national identity and territory. For example, "Farewell at the Hour of Parting" searches for the light and life beyond colonialism. Furthermore, Neto's poetry, so deeply rooted in the emerging Angolan nation, details continuing exploitation, suffering, joy, and hope in other areas of Africa and the diaspora. This particular vision of universality makes Neto one of the founding poets not only of Angolan literature but also of emergent African poetry.

Selected Bibliography

COLLECTIONS

Colectânea de Poemas. Lisbon, Portugal: Casa dos Estudantes do Imperio, 1961.

Sagrada esperança. Ed. by Marga Holness. Lisbon, Portugal: Sá da Costa, 1974. Luanda, Angola: União dos Escritores Angolanos, 1979, 1985.

Ainda o meu sonho. Luanda, Angola: União dos Escritores Angolanos, 1980. Political speeches on national culture.

ANTHOLOGIES INCLUDING NETO'S WORK

Poesia negra de expressão portuguesa. Ed. by Francisco Tenreiro and Mário de Andrade. Lisbon, Portugal: Livraria Escolar Editora, 1953. Repr. Linda-a-Velha, Portugal: Editora África, 1982.

Antologia de poesia negra de expressão portuguesa. Ed. by Mário de Andrade. Paris: P. J. Oswald, 1958. Trans. by Jean Todriani and André Joucla-Ruau as *La Poésie africaine d'expression portugaise.* Paris: P. J. Oswald, 1958, 1969.

Estudos ultramarinos (Lisbon), no. 3 (1959).

Mákua—antologia poetica. Sá da Bandeira, Angola: Imbondeiro, 1963.

Modern Poetry from Africa. Ed. by Gerald Moore and Ulli Beier. Baltimore, Md.: Penguin, 1963.

African Writing Today. Ed. by Ezekiel Mphahlele. Harmondsworth, U.K.: Penguin, 1967.

When Bullets Begin to Flower. Ed. by Margaret Dickinson. Nairobi, Kenya: East Africa Publishing House, 1972.

The Word Is Here: Poetry from Modern Africa. Ed. by Keorapetse Kgositsile. Garden City, N.Y.: Anchor Books, 1973.

Literatura africana de expressão portuguesa. Ed. by Mário de Andrade. Lisbon, Portugal: Sá da Costa, 1975.

No reino de Caliban. Ed. by Manuel Ferreira. Lisbon, Portugal: Seara Nova, 1976.

SHORT STORY

"Náusea." In *Mensagem* (Lisbon) (October 1952). Also in *Contistas angolanos.* Lisbon, Portugal: Casa dos Estudantes do Imperio, 1960.

TRANSLATIONS

Messages to Companions in the Struggle. Richmond, Canada: Liberation Support Movement Information Center, 1972. Political speeches.

Sacred Hope. Trans. by Marga Holness. Dar es Salaam: Tanzania Publishing House, 1974. Repr. London: Journeyman/UNESCO, 1988.

CRITICAL STUDIES

António, Mário. "Agostinho Neto: Nascimento de um poema." In *Angolé: Artes & letras* 2, no. 6 (1987).

Burness, Donald. *Fire: Six Writers from Angola, Mozambique, and Cape Verde.* Washington, D.C.: Three Continents, 1977.

———. "Agostinho Neto and the Poetry of Combat." In Donald Burness, ed., *Critical Perspec-*

tives on Lusophone Literature from Africa. Washington, D.C.: Three Continents, 1981.

Chalendar, Gerard. "Para uma nova abordagem a poetica de Neto." In *Angolé: Artes & letras* 2, no. 6 (1987).

Davidson, Basil. "British Tribute to Antonio Agostinho Neto." In *People's Power in Mozambique, Angola & Guinea-Bissau* 14 (1979).

Enekwe, Ossie Onuora. "The Legacy of Antonio Agostinho Neto." In *Okike*, no. 18 (June 1981).

Ferreira, Manuel. "A renuncia impossível de Agostinho Neto." In *Jornal de letras, artes & ideias* (7–13 September 1987).

Hamilton, Russell. *Voices from an Empire.* Minneapolis: University of Minnesota Press, 1975.

———. *Literatura africana, literatura necessária.* Vol. 1, *Angola.* Lisbon, Portugal: Edições 70, 1981.

———. "Agostinho Neto: A poesia do paradoxo e o paradoxo da poesia." In *Angolé: Artes & letras* 1, no. 3 (1986).

Holness, Marga. "The Poetry of Agostinho Neto." *Afriscope* 5, no. 5 (1975).

Kandjimbo, Luís. "A dimensão actual e histórico-literária de Agostinho Neto." In *Estudos portugueses e africanos* 16 (July/December 1990).

Martinho, Fernando. "The Poetry of Agostinho Neto." In *World Literature Today* 53 (winter 1979).

———. "O negro americano e a América na poesia de Agostinho Neto." In *África* (Lisbon) 2 (1980).

Moser, Gerald. "A língua em poética de Agostinho Neto e Amílcar Cabral." In *Angolé: Artes & letras* 2, no. 5 (1987).

Pallister, Janis L. "Agostinho Neto: Pure Poetic Discourse and Mobilization Rhetoric." *Studies in Twentieth Century Literature* 15 (winter 1991).

Soremekun, Fola. "Angolan Populist Poetry in Historical Context." In *Ufahmu* 16, no. 1 (1987–1988).

Ngũgĩ wa Thiong'o

1938–

ROBERT CANCEL

NGŨGĨ WA THIONG'O was neither the first nor the last African writer to be imprisoned by his own government. Yet his period of imprisonment in many ways embodies his growth as a writer and activist, with all the powerful ideas and contradictory associations that characterize his entire career. Jailed partly because of his virulent denunciation of the stifling of Kenyan arts, drama, and language as a result of western cultural imperialism, Ngũgĩ was "happy . . . for a prison reunion with Voltaire; Balzac; Molière; Zola; Flaubert; Tolstoy; Chekhov; Gorky; Sembène Ousmane; Shakespeare; Bertrand Russell; [and] Claude McKay" in his cell (p. 132). Ngũgĩ's account of this experience and the activities that led to his arrest in *Detained: A Writer's Prison Diary* (1981) offers a way to understand his worldview as well as learn the details of his incarceration from 31 December 1977 to 12 December 1978.

At the time of his detention, Ngũgĩ was in the middle of a critical period in his artistic work. In 1976 he had been approached by his neighbors in Limuru, a rural district north of Nairobi, and asked to use his talents to help them better their lives. At this point, Ngũgĩ was by far East Africa's best-known novelist, having recently completed his fourth and most controversial novel, *Petals of Blood* (1977). He and his neighbors cofounded the Kamĩrĩĩthũ Community Educational and Cultural Centre. They designed and staffed a successful adult literacy program. Later that year, in a process involving the collaboration of writers, peasants, and workers, Ngũgĩ, his colleague Ngũgĩ wa Mĩrĩĩ, and their neighbors produced a play in the Gĩkũyũ (or Kikuyu) language, *Ngaahika ndeenda* (1980; *I Will Marry When I Want*). Casting the play, building the stage, creating props and sets, and composing dialogue and songs were worked out on the basis of an initial outline and with the cooperative interaction of the people of Limuru, who became involved through the Kamĩrĩĩthũ Centre.

The play was immensely successful; it attracted large crowds to its dress rehearsals in September and opened to a paying audience on 2 October at the center's two-thousand-seat outdoor theater. Busloads of people arrived for each performance, excited to hear the play performed in Gĩkũyũ and enthusiastic for its activist message. By 16 November, however, the Kiambu District commissioner withdrew the license for performances, citing "public security" reasons. Ngũgĩ was soon arrested, his house searched, and books confiscated; he was detained without trial for nearly a year. The arrest culminated the Kenyan government's growing resentment of his vitriolic attacks on the Jomo Kenyatta administration's policies on economics, politics, and culture. Ngũgĩ labeled the regime neocolonial, greedy, and determined to retain power at the expense of the suffering masses of Kenya. Although he had maintained his outspoken stance for nearly a decade, the decision to use Gĩkũyũ as an artistic medium of protest seemed the final straw that brought on Ngũgĩ's detention.

Ngũgĩ rose to prominence in a way that was both common and unusual among African writers—common in that he moved through a colonial education system that weeded out all but a few students, unusual in that he came from the peasant and working class of Kenyans. He attended school at the time of the uprising of the Land and Freedom Army, known most commonly as "Mau Mau," in central Kenya of the 1950s. The rebellion led the British government in 1952 to declare a state of emergency, often referred to as "the Emergency," that officially lasted until 1960, at least two to four years after any significant guerrilla activity. Ngũgĩ closely identified with these significant historical events and used them as both background and center for his literature.

UPBRINGING

Ngũgĩ wa Thiong'o was born James Ngũgĩ on 5 January 1938 at Kamĩrĩĩthũ, Limuru, in Kiambu District in central Kenya. His mother, Wanjiku wa Ngũgĩ, was Thiong'o wa Nduucu's third of four wives. Ngũgĩ was the fifth of his mother's six children. The Thiong'o family was large, consisting of some twenty-seven children. They lived on land owned by a Kenyan elder of the Church of Scotland Mission (CSM). Ngũgĩ has said of his early life: "My parents were not Christians. But at the same time they did not practice much of the Gĩkũyũ forms of worship. My father was skeptical of religious and magical practices that went with rites of passages and rhythms of the seasons. He believed in land and hard work" (Sicherman, 1990, p. 18). Thiong'o wa Nduucu labored in fields owned by others to support the family. In 1948 Ngũgĩ's parents separated, and he and his siblings lived with his mother, Wanjiku.

Ngũgĩ attended a CSM school in Limuru from 1947 to 1948, and then enrolled in Maanguuu Karing'a, an independent school, in 1948. The curriculum was a combination of standard European subjects, traditional Gĩkũyũ values, and the history of the Gĩkũyũ land. In 1954 Maanguuu became a government school; the same year, Ngũgĩ, while beginning his avid reading of Robert Louis Stevenson's adventure writing, underwent the Gĩkũyũ rites of initiation into manhood. Against the backdrop of these multicultural influences, the military stage of the peasant-led Mau Mau uprising peaked in violent intensity. In the midst of the Emergency, Ngũgĩ won a seat at Alliance High School, the country's most prestigious secondary school, which was mostly staffed by British educators. On his first trip home from Alliance, he found that his village had been destroyed and the villagers were in the process of being relocated. These events had been orchestrated by the colonial government to destroy bases of supply or support for the guerrilla fighters living in the Aberdares and Kakamega forests.

Ngũgĩ's own family was involved in the uprising. His brother Wallace Mwangi was a guerrilla for several years, and, because of her son's involvement in the struggle, Wanjiku was once arrested and tortured by the authorities. One of his stepbrothers, who was deaf and mute, was shot by Home Guard soldiers—black Kenyans who served the settler governments as a militia and counter-insurgent entity—when he did not hear their orders to stop. Ngũgĩ has described events such as that of "my cousin, Gichini wa Ngũgĩ, just escaping the hangman's rope because he had been caught with live bullets; uncles and other villagers murdered because they had taken the oath" (*Secret Lives*, 1976, p. xii). The "oath" is a portion of the Gĩkũyũ male initiation ceremony that was adopted by the early fighters of the Land and Freedom Army as a pledge to honor Gĩkũyũ customs and to defend them in the face of outside enemies. Colonial officials felt this oath was a kind of magical binding to savagery and tried to get captives first to admit to having taken the oath and then to renounce it.

This period was formative for Ngũgĩ in many ways. He was reaching unprecedented heights in his educational pursuits, since few people from Limuru had made it so far through the colonial system, but at the same time his home and people were directly engaged in a bloody anticolonial struggle. In an article on his schoolboy reading of the adventure series featuring Biggles, a dashing young British pilot, Ngũgĩ emphasizes the strange juxtapositions of this period in his life:

> So in reading Biggles in the years 1955 and 1956, I was involved in a drama of contradictions. Biggles, the flying ace and squadron leader of the Royal Air Force, could have been dropping bombs on my own brother in the forests of Mount Kenya. . . . He would have been pitted against my own brother who, amidst all the fighting in the forest, still found time to send messages to me to cling to education no matter what happened to him. In the forests they, who were so imbued with Kenya nationalist patriotism, had celebrated my being accepted in the same Alliance High School where I was to meet Biggles, an imaginary character so imbued with a sense of British patriotism.
>
> (*Moving the Centre*, 1993, pp. 138–139)

The exploration of these contradictions informs many of Ngũgĩ's earlier works, and the rejection, perhaps the repudiation, of such contradictions spurs his later critical and literary efforts.

At Alliance High School, Ngũgĩ continued his voracious reading of European writers that began in primary school. The Kenyan colonial school system followed the model of other British colonies, using popular and canonical literary works to bolster the image and culture of the empire, thereby building "good" citizens and creating colonized subjects. In Alliance's library Ngũgĩ read such works as Leo Tolstoy's trilogy of *Childhood, Boyhood,* and *Youth,* which directly spurred him to write his first published piece, "I Try Witchcraft," which appeared in the high school magazine. Years later, Ngũgĩ told how a teacher at Alliance added a sentence to the opening of the story to provide it with a moral: "Christianity is without doubt the greatest civilising influence" (Sicherman, 1990, p. viii).

In his writings from the late 1960s to the late 1970s, Ngũgĩ reflected on his early education with some bitterness. Scholars of his writing and ideas tend to point to this period as marking a change in his philosophy. Ngũgĩ indeed felt he had somehow not done enough for the nationalist cause during the Emergency or immediately afterward. But an incident from his Alliance days suggests that, even at the age when education was considered of paramount importance, Ngũgĩ displayed a skill for both debating ideas and arriving at the contradictory core of the educational experience:

> One of my earliest experiences at that school, in 1955, was taking part in a debate on a motion that Western education had done more harm than good. Although I was new in the school, I remember quite vividly standing up and trembling with anger, and saying that Western education could not be equated with the land taken from the peasants by the British. And I remember holding up a fountain pen and giving the example of someone who comes and takes away food from your mouth and then gives you a fountain pen instead. I asked the audience: Can you eat a fountain pen? Can you clothe yourself with a fountain pen or shelter yourself with it?. . . There was, though, a period when I became rather too serious a Christian, waking up

> for prayers at five o'clock in the mornings. This may have cut the wings off my social concerns.
> (Sicherman, pp. 20–21)

This portrait of the elite school, its activities linked to both the intellect and religion, is a clear reflection of the colonial era as well as the British education system of the time. As a student, Ngũgĩ excelled within that system, serving for a time as a dormitory prefect and finishing second in the entire school in the 1959 Cambridge exam, a set of standardized tests administered throughout the British colonies.

EARLY WRITINGS

After briefly working as a primary-school teacher in Gatundu, Ngũgĩ began his studies at Makerere University in Kampala, Uganda, in 1959. At that time Makerere was the first university college in East Africa, and its structure and curriculum were modeled after the University of London. The faculty was mostly British, and the standards, considering the stringent qualifications needed for admission to the university, were very high. He found a diverse and well-stocked library at Makerere that included the nascent contemporary literatures of Africa and the Caribbean. His first fiction piece was published in the university's literary magazine, *Penpoint*, in 1960. During this period he wrote short plays, which are collected in *This Time Tomorrow* (1970), and more short stories, which are collected in *Secret Lives*. Ngũgĩ took an increasingly central role in the campus's cultural activities as a writer, editor, and organizer. At the end of 1961 the manuscript of his first novel, "The Black Messiah," which was revised and published as *The River Between* (1965), won first prize in a contest sponsored by the East African Literature Bureau, and in 1962 his short play *The Rebels* (1961) was produced for Ugandan radio. In November 1962 his full-length play *The Black Hermit* (1963) was performed at the Uganda National Theatre as part of Uganda's independence celebrations.

From May 1961 to May 1962, Ngũgĩ was a regular columnist for the *Sunday Post* and, from June 1962 to August 1964, for the *Daily Nation* and *Sunday Nation*. He wrote on various topics, from current political developments to reviews of theater and literature. These articles reflect his youthful engagement with many spheres of national life; however, he later repudiated these forms of expression and opinion as naive and politically dishonest.

Ngũgĩ's drama and short-story writing focused on several themes during his years at Makerere. His first published short story was "The Fig Tree," which appears as "Mugumo" in *Secret Lives*. The earliest stories are set in rural villages and treat the lives of peasants, often women, in the contexts of love, loss, and striving. "Mugumo" focuses on a young bride, Mukami, who is alienated from her older husband by an unexplained distance in their marriage. As she flees the household of cruel elder wives and a violent husband, Mukami finds herself in the wilderness near the sacred *mũgumo* tree, the altar of Murungu, the Gĩkũyũ creator god. As a storm lashes the area, Mukami falls unconscious at the base of the tree. She awakens transformed:

> "I must go home. Go back to my husband and my people." It was a new Mukami, humble yet full of hope who said this. . . . Blood thawed in her veins and oh! She felt warm—so very warm, happy and light. Her soul danced and her womb answered. And then she knew—knew that she was pregnant, had been pregnant for some time.
> (*Secret Lives*, pp. 7–8)

"Mugumo," as well as a similar Ngũgĩ story of the same period, "And the Rain Came Down!" which also appears in *Secret Lives*, depicts a rural wife's seemingly desperate life, which is transformed by contact with the land, the elements, and the Gĩkũyũ gods through some kind of trial. The endings of both stories are positive and life affirming. The link between the characters and the land—in all its traditional meanings—is vital. Ngũgĩ has acknowledged an early stylistic debt to D. H. Lawrence, a comparison also made by Jonathan Karaira, the student editor to whom he showed his first story at Makerere. His link to Lawrence was more than stylistic when it came to portraying the thoughts of women and men and the effect of the environment or setting on their perceptions. In these early stories and plays Ngũgĩ also developed themes related to events of the Emergency and focused on the toll in human lives of the violent struggle and its aftermath.

THE RIVER BETWEEN

Although *Weep Not, Child* (1964) was published first, *The River Between* (1965) was the first novel that Ngũgĩ wrote. *The River Between* was a revision of his prizewinning manuscript, "The Black Messiah." This earlier title, like those of several other works, reveals much about the book's focus and Ngũgĩ's early ambivalence toward Christianity and the Bible. The novel is a highly schematic story of events set in the 1930s and 1940s in rural Kenya that focuses on the conflict between Christian and traditional beliefs.

The events are set among Gĩkũyũ people living on two adjoining ridges, Kameno and Makuyu, which are divided by the Honia River. The people of Kameno follow the dictates of their land-based religion, which are mythically provided by their creator, Murungu. A line of prophets followed the earliest ancestors and guided the people in their actions. Makuyu, led by the convert and cleric Joshua, became a center for Christian practices. The novel's main character, Waiyaki, is a charismatic young man, descended from Kameno's line of prophets, who is sent to the mission school to learn the ways of the colonialists in order to understand and resist their claims to the land. Inevitably, Waiyaki becomes a person of two distinct worlds and must find for himself and his people a creative path between them.

Ngũgĩ drew heavily on events and conditions in Kenya in the 1930s and 1940s for this novel. The CSM in the Gĩkũyũ areas strongly opposed the long-standing practice of female initiation, in particular the excising of genitalia, and issued an edict forbidding Christians to take part in or even associate with those who participated in the ceremony. In part this stance was due to the belief that the practice was dangerous and "barbaric." Later, the government kept circumcised girls out of schools. However, many local Gĩkũyũ saw the opposition as another attempt by the church and colonial government to break the unity and identity of the people. Resistance to the edict was widespread and at times violent. The issue was highly politicized, as nationalist groups like the Kikuyu Central Association stood against the government while Christian clerics and government-appointed chiefs supported the restrictions. The church eventually demanded that Christians completely dissociate themselves from relatives, neighbors, and friends who practiced such rites. Similarly, mission schools would not accept students who underwent or advocated the initiation procedure.

One immediate and dramatic consequence of this conflict was the creation of independent Gĩkũyũ schools as education systems parallel to those of the missions. Two organizations founded these schools: Kikuyu Karing'a Education Association (KKEA) and Kikuyu Independent Schools Association (KISA). Although funding was inadequate and much was left to the creativity of the associations and teachers, these independent schools became the primary source of formal education for Gĩkũyũ children. By 1936 in Central Province, there were forty-four independent schools and one government school. Gĩkũyũ educated in the KISA and KKEA systems were generally aware of the inequities of colonial relations and focused on the need for land and labor reform.

In *The River Between*, Waiyaki is caught up in these developments on several levels. He is the first son of Chege, a descendant of Mugo wa Kibiro, the great seer who prophesied the coming of white strangers to the land of the Gĩkũyũ. Chege feels his son might be the prophesied leader who is supposed to move the people out from under the weight of oppression: "Salvation shall come from the hills. From the blood that flows in me, I say from the same tree, a son shall rise. And his duty shall be to lead and save the people" (p. 20). Awed and somewhat frightened by his father's revelations, Waiyaki attends the mission school at Siriana and falls in love with learning and the worlds it opens to him.

Waiyaki is moved to action by dramatic events during his late adolescence. Although he is one of the best students at the mission secondary school at Siriana, he comes home to take part in the initiation into adulthood of *rika,* or his age-group. The young women of the ridge are also undergoing initiation at the same time. Among them, in direct defiance of all her father stands for, is Muthoni, the daughter of the cleric Joshua. When her wound does not heal and she dies from infections, the rift between the Christians and followers of the traditional religion becomes all but irreparable. Church members are forbidden to undergo initiation or to allow their relatives to. Circumcised students are not allowed in the mission schools. For their part, the non-Christians renounce the church and its schools and start their own institutions. One of the best and brightest, Waiyaki is selected to head the local independent school. His fellow teachers are his friends Kinuthia and Kamau.

For all his intelligence and leadership qualities, Waiyaki is torn by indecision and a tragic sense of the divisions within his society. He is haunted by Muthoni's dying visions of uniting her Christian beliefs with the Gĩkũyũ worldview. Furthermore, Waiyaki fears that the schism between Christians and the followers of Murungu will cause a chaos that will ultimately ruin the society and lead to the loss of its land and identity to the white settlers and their government. This fear is played out against the development of a militant antigovernment, anti-Christian movement known as the Kiama. Once Waiyaki falls in love with Nyambura, Muthoni's sister and Joshua's daughter, the stage is set for a confrontation between the warring Gĩkũyũ constituencies.

In the face of the mounting conflict, Waiyaki finds himself directed to the voices of the past, which visit him in prophetic fashion. He comes to see himself as the savior long ago foretold by the great seers of his lineage. His vision is a syncretic one, like Muthoni's, in which the best elements of both traditions are combined. In this respect Waiyaki personifies a protagonist Ngũgĩ uses in varying contexts in most of his novels: the character who is torn between cultures, who strives for a synthesis between the things brought by the west and the things indigenous to Kenya. In Ngũgĩ's first two novels, this protagonist ends up broken and defeated.

The zealotry in the novel recalls the lines from William Butler Yeats's poem "The Second Coming" (1920), from which Chinua Achebe took the title of his first novel, *Things Fall Apart* (1958), and, more significant, creates an intertextual echo of that novel: "The best lack all conviction, while the worst / Are full of passionate intensity." Kamau's father, Kabonyi, is at base an opportunist who fears Waiyaki's strength and popularity because he wants power for himself and his son. Conversely, Waiyaki agonizes over his beliefs and direction, trying to steer clear of conflicts that he considers divisive: "What had he to do now? How could he organize people into a political organization when they were so torn with strife and disunity? Now he knew what he would preach if he ever got another chance:

education for unity. Unity for political freedom" (p. 143). As the novel ends, Kabonyi has convinced everyone that Waiyaki has betrayed them, and Waiyaki will not save himself by denying his love for Nyambura. They are led away to an unstated but implied death.

WEEP NOT, CHILD

In his second novel, *Weep Not, Child* (1964), Ngũgĩ again used historical events as the context of his story. Njoroge comes from a polygamous family in central Kenya. His father, Ngotho, is the farm manager for a white settler named Howlands. The political crisis that culminates in the Emergency of the 1950s has severe consequences for Ngotho and his family.

Njoroge, like Waiyaki in *The River Between*, is a bright student who progresses steadily and successfully through the education system. From the beginning, Njoroge's progress at school is set against the major issue that occupies his father and brothers, the land. At a gathering early in the novel, they recount the origin myth, whereby Murungu gave the land to the first man and woman, Gĩkũyũ and Mumbi. They also remember the prophecy of Mugo wa Kibiro, who foresaw the arrival of the whites. Ngotho recalls serving the British during the East African campaign of World War I, during which he built roads and cleared forests for the infrastructure of the war:

> The war ended. We were all tired. We came home worn out but very ready for whatever the British might give us as a reward. But, more than this, we wanted to go back to the soil and court it to yield, to create, not to destroy. But Ng'o! The land was gone. My father and many others had been moved from our ancestral lands.
>
> (p. 29)

Ngotho became a *muhoi*, a tenant living on someone else's land and paying rent in labor, crops, or money. One of Njoroge's elder brothers, Boro, had fought in World War II and come home bitter over his experience and the death of his brother Mwangi in that war.

Again, Ngũgĩ's young protagonist finds himself in a romantic relationship that bridges a bitter gap among Gĩkũyũ people. Mwihaki, whom Njoroge has known since early childhood, is a beautiful young woman who has always loved him. She is also the daughter of Jacobo, the wealthy man who owns the land Ngotho lives on and who collaborates with the colonial forces, as a "chief," during the Emergency. As events spiral down to their tragic conclusion, Boro, who has joined the Mau Mau insurgents in the forest, kills Jacobo. When Ngotho hears of Jacobo's death, he knows his son was the killer, and he offers himself to the authorities by confessing to the murder. After Ngotho dies from torture by the authorities, represented by his old employer, Howlands, Boro seeks out the white settler and kills him as well. In the end, Njoroge is tortured by the authorities, expelled from Siriana secondary school for supposed Mau Mau activities, and soon dismissed from the only employment he could find to support the family, working as a clerk at an Indian shop.

The novel is a portrait of a society under duress, caused by the loss of land, livelihood, pride, and the subsequent militant reaction to these conditions. As in *The River Between*, the young protagonist of *Weep Not, Child* is caught in a violent vortex of events that spells the end of his aspirations and conviction that education can solve the problems of his people. More than in his first novel, Ngũgĩ explores in *Weep Not, Child* the interior fears and thoughts of at least four major characters. The development of several voices creates a textured, nuanced presentation of a crucial period during which so many people underwent profound changes in an escalating, violent clash of cultures.

NGŨGĨ AT LEEDS AND AS UNIVERSITY TEACHER

Ngũgĩ graduated Makerere University with an upper second honors degree in arts with Joseph Conrad as his subject. Under a scholarship from the British Council, he began studies at Leeds University in England in September 1964. He so impressed his instructors that after the first term he was admitted to a two-year master of arts research program. He studied Caribbean literature, with a special focus on his dissertation topic: "A Study of the Theme of Alienation in the Fiction of the West Indies with Particular Reference to the Novels of George Lamming." He never received the master's degree because he did not make the revisions to his thesis recommended by his mentors. He did, however, become active in university life and read voraciously in Caribbean literatures and the revolutionary writings of the Martinican psychoanalyst and social philosopher Frantz Fanon and the early Marxist theorists: Karl Marx, Friedrich Engels, and V. I. Lenin. While Fanon clearly had a formative effect on Ngũgĩ's thinking, he later suggested that Fanon's ideas—including his call to develop a true contemporary "national culture" to replace what the Europeans had labeled as inferior or savage beliefs, and his suggestions that violence was a cathartic element in achieving liberation from colonization—were romantic and needed to be counterbalanced by Marxist-Leninist economic theories. While at Leeds, his first two novels were published, and he won several literary prizes. In 1966 he completed the manuscript for *A Grain of Wheat* (1967), and he returned to Kenya in 1967.

By October 1967 Ngũgĩ was appointed special lecturer in English at the University of Nairobi and became the first black African member of the department. In September 1968 he and two fellow lecturers, Taban lo Liyong and Henry Owuor-Anyumba, wrote a proposal for the abolition of the Department of English. They promulgated the idea that African universities and curricula needed to emphasize the literature of their own cultures in English and vernacular languages, written and oral, to foster appropriate social and cultural visions. The focus on national literature could then widen to include other African literatures, then literatures of the Caribbean and African-American diaspora, then other third-world literatures, and, finally, European literature, including English. The proposal sent out a strong message on how these scholars perceived the goals of an African university and national culture. Within a year and a half, the proposal was adopted and the Department of Literature was born.

In 1969, before the department was established, Ngũgĩ resigned from the University of Nairobi over issues of academic freedom and took the time to travel and lecture on various topics. He served for one year as a visiting fellow in creative writing at Makerere University, spent 1970–1971 as a visiting associate professor at Northwestern University in Chicago, and began writing *Petals of Blood* (1977). In August 1971 Ngũgĩ returned to the University of Nairobi, and by April 1973 he succeeded Andrew Gurr as acting head of the Department of Literature.

A GRAIN OF WHEAT

Written mainly during Ngũgĩ's time at Leeds University, *A Grain of Wheat* (1967) is widely considered to be his most successful novel. He had honed the skills that were less evenly displayed in his first two books. His interest in Christian ideology and the messages of the Bible combined with a growing facility to portray different but sympathetic characters. Using the historical era from the Emergency (1952–1960) to Kenya's first independence celebration (1963), Ngũgĩ orchestrates a meditation on the nature of heroism in historical and personal perspectives. Furthermore, for the first time he used the complex structure of fragmenting time in the progression of narrative events. The book begins in the present, several days before the first Uhuru ("freedom" in Swahili) celebration, then moves characters back and forth, in a series of personal ruminations, to the days before and during the fierce struggle against the colonial government. In the process Ngũgĩ not only examines the dynamics of political struggle and its personal toll, but also looks presciently to the problems of the postcolonial era.

There are no fewer than eight major characters in the novel, and the narrative voice constantly shifts among them. Initially, Ngũgĩ focuses on the inability of neighbors and relatives to communicate. Mugo, the reclusive "hero" of the struggle, suffers from depression and a lack of resolve in the conduct of his life. He refuses to be a speaker at the Uhuru celebration and wants only to be left alone. His neighbors in the village of Thabai include Gikonyo and Mumbi, the husband and wife who, in their private interactions, seem angrily estranged. Gikonyo several times attempts to speak to his wife but at the last minute decides against it. Two former Mau Mau fighters, General Russia and Koinandu, are helping to organize the celebrations, which they see as a retribution for the betrayal of their late leader, Kihika, the guerrilla general. From another quarter, John Thompson, district officer and former Home Guard commander, is to leave Kenya soon, and, in a scene that parallels the earlier one between Gikonyo and Mumbi, he cannot communicate his feelings to his wife. Karanja, the colonial messenger, frets over his fate after the changes in government.

The second section of the novel recounts the events that brought the characters to their present states of mind. The chaotic developments of the Emergency are depicted from the perspectives of actors outside the events and of those directly taking part in them. What emerges is a poignant story of people swept up in a historical whirlwind. Where earlier Ngũgĩ had splashed widely spaced paints onto the canvas of his novels, here he paints a multitextured yet carefully integrated representation of a period and a people. Heroism is exposed as something that feeds myth, legend, and song but also something that is often removed from the truth of actual actions and intentions.

Among its revelations, the narrative describes Mugo's involuntary ascension to the status of hero of the struggle. A private person who was abused by his relatives after being orphaned, Mugo wants only to till his land. As the struggle reaches its early period of confrontation, he is pulled into action by Kihika, who imagines a certain closeness to their relationship. Mugo's reticence and somber nature are mistaken for strength and quiet resolve as Kihika confides his numerous plans. Thinking he will be drawn into something he wants no part of, something he fears will endanger his life and those of his neighbors, Mugo informs on Kihika. Kihika is portrayed as a politically aware young man who from early on is infused, in some ways obsessed, with a messianic vision of leading his people out of colonial bondage. To this end, he has carefully read and annotated a Bible, choosing passages that focus on sacrifice and struggle in a just cause. The title of the novel comes from several passages that connote the importance of sacrifice in the renewal of life, and underlined sections from Kihika's Bible are the epigraphs to two parts of the novel.

Kihika's sister, Mumbi, is first seen as the young woman who falls in love with and is romanced by the young carpenter Gikonyo. When the Emergency takes him away and later results in his arrest and imprisonment in a series of detention camps, Mumbi is left with Gikonyo's mother to eke out a living in the tumultuous days of the struggle, which is characterized by the Home Guard's repressive activities. The village is destroyed, and the people are relocated in the government's effort to cut supply lines and contact with the guerrillas. When Gikonyo finally, after years of silence, confesses his Gĩkũyũ male initiation oath and is set free, he hungers only for the comfort of his home and wife. He is consequently shocked to find Mumbi with a child who cannot possibly be his. From that point, his interests turn to business and making money, and he neither tries to find out who the child's father is nor shares his wife's bed. The truth is that, after suffering so long and rebuffing the colonial messenger Karanja's advances, Mumbi succumbed to Karanja only after the news that Gikonyo was alive and would soon be released pushed her into near delirium.

Karanja feels the weight of his actions differently. He was a member of the despised Home Guard, and during the struggle he was given a great deal of power after he informed on many of the oath takers in his village and performed his duties in a self-serving capacity. He fears the coming of African self-rule and regrets the departure of his white protectors. Finally, John Thompson is revealed as a failed liberal who came to Africa with a vision of educating "the African" and allowing him to be the equal of the European. Over the years, his work as a civil servant leads to cynicism and hatred toward the local people. During the Emergency he serves as a military commander and eventually captures Kihika with Mugo's help. He ends up commandant of the notorious detention camp at Rira, where he oversees a massacre of inmates that shocks the world into censuring the British and settler governments and pushing for independence.

Many of the characters and events in the novel are taken from the struggles of the Land and Freedom Army. Of the principal characters, Kihika recalls the best-known Mau Mau leader, Dedan Kĩmathĩ, who led similarly daring and successful raids on the colonial forces and who was also betrayed, captured, and hanged by the government. Indeed, Ngũgĩ keeps the characters of the novel in parallel to many historical figures, such as Harry Thuku, Chief Waiyaki, and Jomo Kenyatta. The massacre at Rira closely approximates the events at Hola camp, where the beating deaths of inmates made news all over the world and contributed to accelerating negotiations for independence. The names Mugo, Gikonyo, and Mumbi are linked to the historical and mythological figures Mugo wa Kibiro, the seer, and Gĩkũyũ and Mumbi, the primal ancestors.

These evocations come into focus in the third section of the book, when Uhuru day arrives and the planned events take some surprising turns. As the speeches wind down, the former guerrillas are about to accuse Karanja as Kihika's betrayer when Mugo walks slowly to the stand and explains, in his halting yet riveting manner, that it is he who turned in the rebel leader. The sky clouds over and it begins to storm as Mugo plods from the celebration back to his home. Everything is thrown into doubt. The man who everyone saw as one of the greatest heroes of the struggle has just confessed to being a traitor. The crowd disperses in the downpour, and only a handful of celebrants are left to slaughter the sacrificial ram that was to be the central event of the ceremonies.

The scene focuses the novel's exploration of the struggle and its heroes throughout history. Mugo had been seen in the long line of Gĩkũyũ heroes who opposed colonialism from its outset: Chief Waiyaki, Harry Thuku, Jomo Kenyatta, and Kihika. The two elders who have lived through the struggle since its inception, Warui and Wambui, are left to rethink all they had believed about heroism. They are forced to examine the problem of setting one's hopes in an individual leader. Sacrifice takes on a new dimension as all must admit to Mugo's bravery in keeping another man from being accused of the crime he himself had committed. In the end, as his thoughts turn to starting a new life, Gikonyo envisions carving a gift for Mumbi that would depict a husband, child, and pregnant wife. For her part, Mumbi has made it clear that her life with Gikonyo must be negotiated, altered from the way things had been. The independence era must be built, in other words, on creative new models and true commitment.

HOMECOMING

After *A Grain of Wheat*, Ngũgĩ took some years before writing his next novel. His critical essays were collected and published in 1972 under the title *Homecoming: Essays on African and Caribbean Literature, Culture, and Politics*. These essays reveal the development of a new critical consciousness regarding the relation between literature and society. In the author's note to the collection, Ngũgĩ warns of the "professional friends and interpreters of the African" who extol the virtues of certain areas and groups to the rest of the western world: "We must never succumb to the poisonous and divisive flattery of our enemies. We must find for ourselves what are the most enduring links between us and all our brothers scattered over the world. We can then build on these links, build a socialist black power" (p. xix). The collection is a skilled examination of issues of national culture and the literary responses of African and Caribbean writers to colonialism and post-independence problems.

On national culture, Ngũgĩ emphasizes the importance of a relevant local and global vision that negates the claims made in *The Tempest* by Prospero—seen by postcolonial scholars as the archetypal colonizer—in favor of creating "a revolutionary culture which is not narrowly defined by the implications of tribal traditions or national boundaries but looks outward to Pan-Africa and the Third World, and the needs of Man" (p. 19). He also declares that the time is ripe for someone "with intellectual honesty" to "write the true history of Mau Mau as a cultural, political and economic expression of the aspirations of the African peasant masses, putting it in its revolutionary context" (pp. 29–30). When independence was achieved, the Kenyan government played down the significance of the mostly peasant uprising that attempted to win back the precious land lost to colonial expansionist policies. As the years passed, the government began to recognize the contributions of that seminal nationalist struggle. However, by the 1970s, in order to curtail opposition to the government, the authorities once again threw Mau Mau, or rather its use as a symbol of nationalist and liberation initiatives, into a dubious or even seditious official valuation.

During the same period, at the Fifth Annual Assembly of Presbyterian Churches of East Africa in Nairobi, Ngũgĩ gave a talk entitled "Church, Culture, and Politics" (in *Homecoming*), in which he pointed out the essential collusion between the Christian evangelical mission and colonial expansion in Kenya. His remarks so angered one elderly cleric that the listener stood up and pointed out Ngũgĩ's inextricable tie to Christianity in his very name. After brief consideration, he changed his name from James Ngũgĩ to Ngũgĩ wa Thiong'o. He also began the writing and speaking that formed the theoretical and rhetorical basis of his next collection of critical essays, *Writers in Politics* (1981).

PETALS OF BLOOD

Even though *Petals of Blood* (1977) was by far Ngũgĩ's most direct attack on the inequities and hypocrisy of the postindependence era in Kenya, the novel was officially launched by the Kenyan government, which sent Vice President Mwai Kibaki to affirm its commitment to free speech. As in his previous works, many of the events in the novel are based on social and historical realities. The plot revolves around the murder of three prominent men—Chui, Kimeria, and Mzigo—in the town of Ilmorog in north-central Kenya. The four primary suspects are rounded up and questioned by the police. Ngũgĩ uses this structure to explore the lives of the four protagonists and, by extension, the lives of the people around them. As in *A Grain of Wheat*, he moves the action back and forth in time, with the characters' shifting perspectives weaving a stark and dispirited vision of postcolonial life.

The four protagonists are Munira, a schoolteacher and headmaster; Abdulla, a shopkeeper and former freedom fighter; Karega, who is expelled from school and becomes a union organizer; and Wanja, a "bar girl." Their lives intersect in the village of Ilmorog just before the developments that lead to the construction and growth of New Ilmorog. This transition from sleepy rural village to dynamic provincial town enables Ngũgĩ to explore the personal and institutional corruption that leads the characters to their fateful implication in the murders.

Ngũgĩ moves from an evocative realism to a more schematized imagery of characters and events. The novel spans a good deal of time and distance. In the first few chapters Ilmorog is described in the third-person narrative voice that dominates the novel. It is a voice that at times lapses into a "we," suggesting a speaker and audience of Ilmorog residents. When Munira arrives during the dry season, Ngũgĩ records his initial impression of the dilapidated school buildings in the following way:

> Godfrey Munira, a thin dustcloud trailing behind him, first rode a metal horse through Ilmorog to the door of a moss-grown two-roomed house in what was once a schoolyard. ... Unhurriedly, he clipped loose the trouser bottoms, beat them a little with his hands—a symbolic gesture, since the dust stubbornly clung to them and to his shoes—before moving back a few steps to re-survey the door, the falling-apart walls and the sun rotted roof.... Was it any wonder that teachers ran away at first glance?
>
> (p. 5)

The same voice depicts the skepticism the wary village residents feel toward the new teacher, wondering if "he was a little crazed." But Munira, for his own complex reasons, finds purpose and a bit of peace in the resuscitation of the failed educational mission in this dusty rural village. He essentially has fled the outside world of family and responsibility to create for himself a place where he is needed and eventually lauded.

Throughout the early part of the novel, the main characters arrive at Ilmorog seeking to deny or negate personal histories. Wanja has come to stay with her aunt, running from the fast city life and the erosion of her self-respect. Karega is a disillusioned student, fleeing the politics of the nation's best-known secondary school, Siriana; he and other student leaders have been expelled for what the school authorities, shying away from any kind of social activism and striving for a false sense of academic neutrality, labeled as "political" activities. Abdulla, a wary former guerrilla, has recently arrived at Ilmorog and set up a small bar and restaurant. As the characters' past and present lives are examined in a series of personal flashbacks and conversations in present time, Kenya's history from the 1940s to the mid 1970s is surveyed in only vaguely disguised form.

The elements of colonial and postindependence education are examined on several levels. Munira's education at Siriana is at first a marvelous, eye-opening experience. As time goes on, however, he becomes disillusioned with the elitist school and its underlying racism. He, along with several other student leaders, including the charismatic Chui, are expelled for leading a strike to redress several inequities. When Karega arrives at Ilmorog, he too recounts the events that led to his own expulsion from Siriana. The issues and actors strongly parallel Munira's experience, thereby suggesting the lack of real change between the colonial and postindependence periods. Munira eventually comes to disdain "politics" and takes a narrow approach to the education of his students. The relevance of education and the ways in which the system has stifled creativity and critical inquiry are at the core of the novel's themes of protest.

In the character of Abdulla, Ngũgĩ returns to the question of the Mau Mau freedom fighters and their disenfranchisement at independence. The young men who took no part in the struggle, who stayed in school or were involved with commerce, came to the fore in the new government of the nation. They became wealthy and turned the system to their advantage, while the peasants who fought in the rebellion went unrewarded for their sacrifice. Most of those who took part in the struggle became part of the growing numbers who had their land and livelihood appropriated by the wealthy minority in the new government. The taking of land and the alienation of its rightful owners reestablished in the independence era the practices of the white colonial settlers in the time before Uhuru. Abdulla was among the most active fighters in the movement. He vividly describes that participation during the long march that the group of villagers makes from Ilmorog to the capital to present their desperate, drought-spawned grievances to the government. Abdulla, hobbling on his one leg and inspiring the walkers, spends the periods of rest discussing the struggle and rekindling patriotic spirit by singing the songs of that era. Ngũgĩ employs the image of the march in a way similar to Sembène Ousmane in *Les Bouts de bois de Dieu* (1960; *God's Bits of Wood*), in which women and children march from Thies to Dakar to support the railway strike of 1947–1948. As in Sembène's novel, history provides a prime source of material for Ngũgĩ's fictional texture.

In the character of Wanja, Ngũgĩ examines the plight of a rural young woman who attempts to live a productive life and is pushed onto a path of prostitution and degradation. While writing the novel, Ngũgĩ had become concerned with the plight of women in Kenya. In Wanja he makes clear that unchecked power relations between the sexes pose serious impediments to the economic and educational advancement of women. Wanja, once spurned in a love affair with the older, wealthy Kimeria, is left with few options, most of which point to a life of subjugation to and dependence on men.

The student-activist turned unionist, Karega, is another figure in an evolving set of characters that began with Waiyaki in *The River Between*. After his expulsion from Siriana, his life is thrown into disorder. Karega moves through the kinds of jobs that so many young dropouts must take in order to survive. Inevitably, they are reduced to working as hustlers and vendors on the roadside, trying to sell curios or food to passing tourists and eventually turning to crime. Part of the condemnation of postcolonial Kenya is tied to its dependence on foreign capital in the form of investment and tourism. Karega finally discovers the pursuit that will give focus to his talents and energy, as he is caught up in the struggles of workers in the developing industries of New Ilmorog. The situation is reminiscent of that in Ngũgĩ's hometown of Limuru, which is near a Bata shoe factory and similar local industries that depend on low-paid workers for their profits.

NGAAHIKA NDEENDA

As *Petals of Blood* made its way out of the printers and into bookstores and libraries, eliciting immediate responses, Ngũgĩ was engaged in the production of *Ngaahika ndeenda* (1980; *I Will Marry When I Want*). While the true impact of the play lies in its development, staging, and reception by a Gĩkũyũ-speaking community, the plot itself explores two common areas of concern for Ngũgĩ. On the one hand, the play is about the machinations of a wealthy man, Ahab Kĩoi wa Kanoru, to gain the small parcel of land owned by an honest and well-liked farm laborer, Kĩgũũnda. Among the ploys used to move the peasant into irreversible debt is the demand that he remarry his wife of many years in an expensive Christian ceremony. At the same time, Kĩgũũnda's daughter, Gathoni, is courted by

Kĩoi's son, John Mũhũũni. She disobeys her parents and runs off on a vacation with the wealthy suitor, thinking they will marry. This thought spurs Kĩgũũnda and his wife to make a commitment to the expensive ceremony. In the end Gathoni becomes pregnant and is abandoned by the son of Kĩoi, and her father is left landless by the great debt he has incurred. Capitalist greed and its collusion with Christianity are linked with the tenuous and powerless position of young women in contemporary society. Stylistically, this well-worn theme is dramatically fleshed out by the many songs that serve as chorus and commentary for the play's events. In these dramaturgical activities the close links to Gĩkũyũ oral culture and history are forged with the desperate conditions of peasants and workers. The play celebrates their consciousness of and resistance to those conditions in powerful cultural expression.

WRITERS IN POLITICS

Ngũgĩ's public talks, newspaper articles, and critical essays of this period became more strident and polemical in their description of Kenya's problems and the need for fundamental, radical changes. Many of these pieces were collected in the 1981 publication *Writers in Politics.* While most of the entries were written before Ngũgĩ's 1977–1978 detention, several were written later and provide perspectives that set the others in a near-prescient framework. Specific charges and complaints form the substance of the essays, and in the later pieces these are hammered across in a discourse that is at once angry and prescriptive. In these later essays, Ngũgĩ emphasizes the crucial importance of writing in African languages and the necessity for African intellectuals and educated artists to cooperate with and learn from the peasants and workers of their societies.

In one of his most effective predetention pieces, "J. M.—A Writer's Tribute," Ngũgĩ rails against the disappearance and assassination of J. M. Kariũki, the opposition member of parliament who wrote the historical memoir *Mau Mau Detainee* (1963):

> Who betrayed J. M. Kariũki? Who killed him? I felt the truth pain, the truth hurt. For it was we, we who have kept silent and propped up an unjust oppressive system, because we were eating a bit of the fruits. So we kept quiet when Gama Pinto was killed, when Mboya was murdered; when Kũng'ũ Karumba disappeared. We kept quiet saying this was not really our *shauri* [affair, business]. . . . This generation will never keep silent again. Not even if they have to pay with their blood.
>
> (p. 85)

The suggestion of personal guilt or culpability is more specifically developed in other parts of the collection. The discourse is based on Ngũgĩ's feelings about his earlier writings and activities as a student and independence-era writer:

> My colonial university education at Makerere had blinded me to the true nature of colonialism and imperialism. It had turned me into a parrot and an animated puppet mouthing out phrases prepared for me in European textbooks.
>
> ("J. M.—A Writer's Tribute," p. 83)

> I myself can remember writing in 1962 how I looked forward to the day when all the preoccupation of African writers with colonial problems and politics would be over and we would all sit back and poke sophisticated irony at one another and laugh at ourselves whatever that was supposed to mean: we would then indulge in the luxury of comedies of social manners (what a philistine hollow bourgeois idea!) or explore the anguished world of lonely individuals abstracted from time and actual circumstances.
>
> ("Writers in Politics," p. 78)

Ngũgĩ's impression of himself as a young, privileged member of an educated African colonial bourgeoisie rankled and spurred him on to a revision of his personal and public persona. The change of names was only the first step in reinventing himself for the struggle to which he was committed.

WRITINGS IN GĨKŨYŨ

After his release from detention, Ngũgĩ, like Wole Soyinka before him, turned out several publications in rapid succession. Aside from *Writers in Politics* and *Detained: A Writer's Prison Diary* (1981), he published a Gĩkũyũ-language novel written in prison. His prison diary details the writing of this book and also contains a collage of different kinds of writing, including letters he wrote while incarcerated, texts of government and newspaper statements, official documents on his dismissal from his position as head of department at the University of Nairobi, and similar texts that frame his account of the period spent in detention. The situation of living in detention paralleled Soyinka's time in prison during the Nigerian civil war (1967–1970). Although Ngũgĩ had complained in *Homecoming* of Soyinka's artistic self-indulgence, Ngũgĩ at one point in his detention received and was ironically comforted by a copy of Soyinka's prison diary, *The Man Died* (1972). The commentary on African writers and their vulnerability as opposition voices is clear, even voices so diametrically different in styles and approaches as those of Ngũgĩ and Soyinka.

During his detention throughout most of 1978, Ngũgĩ expanded his efforts to write in the Gĩkũyũ language. The play *I Will Marry When I Want* had convinced him of the necessity of reaching the peasants and workers of his immediate community in their own language. It seems clear that, despite his attacks on the Kenyatta government in *Petals of Blood*, it was the popularity of his theatrical efforts that was the direct cause of Ngũgĩ's incarceration. He was determined that his next novel would be in Gĩkũyũ and thereby resurrected the title of a book he had started in English several years earlier. Ngũgĩ also chose to employ several of the commonly known images of his culture's oral tradition, what he terms "orature," in the depiction of this strongly allegorical plot.

Caitaani mũtharaba-inĩ (1980; *Devil on the Cross*) was begun while Ngũgĩ was in detention, where he used the familiar tactics of the imprisoned writer: writing on toilet paper and hiding his work from the guards. Eventually his writing was confiscated. Ngũgĩ had to reach back for the language he was born into and convert it into a literary language. He had to devise new imagery and translate the vocabulary of contemporary European concepts. The story focuses on a grotesque gathering in rural Kenya, in which "thieves and robbers" come together to contest the title of the greatest criminal. Along the way, several people are swept into the activities, and their development is the core of the novel.

Again, Ngũgĩ uses the device of exploring individual histories. He constructs several venues in which stories can be shared among characters. The most effective tableau is set on a *matatu*, or small bus, that carries the protagonists to the contest. In this commonly known vehicle of transport, which is intended for peasants and workers rather than the wealthy, Ngũgĩ has discovered a dynamic metaphor. Furthermore, as the passengers pass the time telling their stories, class and economic conditions are reflected in both the personal visions and the activities of the *matatu* driver and several of the wheeler-dealers on the bus. Another powerful image in the novel is a stock character of Gĩkũyũ oral traditions, the *marimũ*, a cannibalistic ogre who has a mouth both in the front and the back of its head. It serves as a model of greedy consumption and corruption, mirroring Ngũgĩ's view of his country's ruling classes.

The main character in the novel is Warĩinga, a secretary in Nairobi who has lost her job because she spurned her boss's sexual advances, the latest in a long line of oppressive and hopeless situations in her life. Like Wanja in *Petals of Blood*, Warĩinga is induced to leave school by a love affair with a wealthy older man who abandons her when she becomes pregnant. After a related series of setbacks, she decides to return to her hometown, Ilmorog. She passes through the crucible of the meeting at the cave, which constitutes most of the novel's action, where the thieves and robbers contest the title. Near the book's conclusion, Warĩĩnga has undergone a dramatic transformation. She has become, in many ways, Ngũgĩ's ideal revolutionary woman. Rejecting the ready-made roles for women, Warĩĩnga attends a polytechnical institute and becomes a skilled automobile mechanic. She works in a garage that shares the profits among the worker-owners, studies martial arts, and dresses in a style that rejects western ideas of beauty and highlights the natural, African elements of her body and mind. Furthermore, she is about to wed her intellectual student-suitor, Gatuĩria.

Gatuĩria is another of Ngũgĩ's intellectual, liberal characters. A brilliant student of music, he would like to create a truly revolutionary oratorio that tells the history of his nation. The piece combines instrumentation and musical styles of both Africa and the west. Intended as a wedding present for Warĩĩnga, the two-hundred-page score is a complex rendering of sounds and themes from the land and its people. As is the case with similar protagonists in Ngũgĩ's work, Gatuĩria is eventually sobered by the weight of corruption and injustice in his environment, and his efforts are turned to mockery, as he fails to understand the depth and degree of his and his family's complicity in crimes against the masses. The novel ends with this startling realization, as Warĩĩnga uses a gun to kill the "Rich Old Man from Ngorika" who was responsible for her initial degradation.

Published in 1980 in Nairobi, *Devil on the Cross* sold well in its original Gĩkũyũ version. Ngũgĩ was gratified by its popularity, as it rapidly went through several printings. He was particularly pleased to note the book's reception in rural areas, where literate people were designated to read the Gĩkũyũ text to their nonliterate neighbors.

Since the government had not reinstated him as a professor in the Department of Literature, Ngũgĩ was involved with efforts to get his job back. By November 1981, he returned to work with the Kamĩrĩĩthũ Community Education and Cultural Centre, fashioning a new Gĩkũyũ-language play, *Maitu njugira* (Mother, sing for me), a drama set in Kenya in the 1930s. The play employed the same techniques of staging and communal development of dramatic elements that characterized the production of *I Will Marry When I Want.* The plot follows highly symbolic events in settler-dominated Kenya with characters' names taken from various eras of nationalist activity—such as Kang'ethe and Kariũki, who are based on the historical figures of Joseph Kang'ethe and J. M. Kariũki—to emphasize the timeless necessity for courage, unity, and struggle. Songs and traditional dances, often modified to suit contemporary issues and images, filled the production with communal participation and commentary.

Although the government reneged on an agreement to exhibit the play at the National Theatre, nearly fifteen thousand people viewed its public "rehearsals" at the University of Nairobi before these too were prohibited. In March 1982, the Kamĩrĩĩthũ Community Education and Cultural Centre was deregistered as an organization by the government, and the open-air theater in Kamĩrĩĩthũ was torn down by troops and police. Later that year, while in London to publicize the English version of *Devil on the Cross*, Ngũgĩ heard that he would be arrested on his return to Kenya and opted to become an exile. During his first year in London, he wrote *Matigari ma njirũũngi* (*Matigari*), which in 1986 was published in Gĩkũyũ in Kenya and sold strongly. Within months, the government heard rumors of a man named Matigari roaming the countryside stirring up the people with thoughts of truth and justice:

"There were orders for his immediate arrest, but the police discovered that Matigari was only a fictional character in a book of the same name. In February 1987, the police raided all the bookshops and seized every copy of the novel" (*Matigari*, 1989, p. viii).

Ngũgĩ's second novel in Gĩkũyũ treats the return in the 1980s of a freedom fighter who has been living in the forests since the Emergency. Matigari turns out to be a magical specter, who, as he visits the current society and meets people, becomes progressively saddened, shocked, and eventually angry. Ngũgĩ draws on the structures of oral narrative and epic, as the main character moves through a series of trials and interactions in a repetitive framework of action and dialogue. In *Devil on the Cross* he had attempted a broad synthesis of satire, tragedy, and activism in a format that drew on oral traditions combined with literary models. In *Matigari* he chose a purer form of approximating the oral heroic narrative. Matigari is both warrior and trickster, a youthful fighter and wise elder. He is a catalyst for the young people of his home to rise up against the oppressive system that confounds their hopes of a better life.

Stylistically, the English translation of *Matigari* reads more smoothly and effectively than *Devil on the Cross*, the translation of *Caitaani mũtharaba-inĩ*. It is difficult to judge whether this is a matter of the translator (Wangũi wa Goro for the former and Ngũgĩ for the latter) or whether the mythological, epic format is perhaps easier to approximate in English. In either case, the structure and focus of *Matigari* are less strained than those of *Devil on the Cross*. The focus in *Matigari* is on a single unifying hero, who garners support and is joined by the boy Mũriũki and the young woman Gũthera. As the characters move through the disturbing world of neocolonial Kenya, they draw strength from Matigari's physical prowess and magical skills, the two types of power often exhibited by African epic heroes: he merges the talents of the physically prodigious Shaka and Liyongo and the shape-changing sorcerers Mwindo and Sunjata. He further combines these powers with the more mundane ideology and weaponry of the contemporary guerrilla fighter: "Just wait till the night falls. I will get my AK47 from under the *mũgumo* tree, Matigari said to himself, and then they will see me truly armed to the teeth" (p. 153).

The imagery of the *mũgumo* tree suggests the circle, or rather the spiral, of Ngũgĩ's writing. In his earliest short stories the same tree is a source of comfort and magical renewal for his protagonists. In the postcolonial world, the tree becomes an icon for the link between past mythological power and contemporary revolutionary struggle. The earlier biblical images of sacrifice and ambiguous justice are supplanted by Gĩkũyũ, and more broadly African, militant ties of magic and revolutionary bullets. Matigari and Gũthera disappear while crossing the river toward the forest and its impenetrable staging base and shelter. A hail of government bullets supposedly cuts them down, but the bodies are never recovered, allowing for the continuation of their lives in myth and song. As the boy Mũriũki gazes over the river looking for the two protagonists, he

> recalled the night of the workers' strike. And suddenly he seemed to hear the workers' voices, the voices of the peasants, the voices of the students and of other patriots of all the different nationalities of the land, singing in harmony:
>
> Victory shall be ours!
> Victory shall be ours!
>
> (p. 175)

In 1986 Ngũgĩ published *Decolonising the Mind: The Politics of Language in African Literature*, by far his most successful and popular collection of theoretical writing. The essays are closely reasoned, well-written arguments about the contested question of African-language writing and national culture. Ngũgĩ combines careful scholarship with personal experience in evocative juxtapositions of theory and real life that make a strong case for writing in local languages and the power of communal theater to spur the liberation of the culture and mind of the neocolonial subject. Among the powerful images of colonial cultural suppression he evokes is one from his childhood:

> Thus one of the most humiliating experiences was to be caught speaking Gĩkũyũ in the vicinity of the school. The culprit was given corporal punishment—three to five strokes of the cane on bare buttocks—or was made to carry a metal plate around the neck with inscriptions such as I AM STUPID or I AM A DONKEY. Sometimes the culprits were fined money they could hardly afford.
>
> (p. 11)

By the end of the 1980s Ngũgĩ's theoretical writing and status as political exile coincided with developing theories of postcolonial discourse. He was a visiting professor at Yale University, where he shared ideas with colleagues and students that were distillations of poststructuralist and New Historicist theories. One offshoot of these interactions was his 1993 publication, *Moving the Centre: The Struggle for Cultural Freedoms.* The essays are varied and rich in their allusions and references to issues of culture, pluralism, colonial writing and its influence on the colonized, and the goals for a unified and united Africa. He travels several avenues to investigate his most relevant concerns. These include writing about a common global culture, discussions of the colonial-era European writings of Isak Dinesen (Karen Blixen), and the Biggles adventure books for boys. In many ways, the essays suggest a broader depth of scholarly field than any of his previous collections. The basic ideas are, as always, the ones Ngũgĩ began with: the negative effects of exploitation on the colonized, the alienation of people from their land and the fruits of their labor, the importance of cultural activity in the liberation process, and specific examples of how greed, betrayal, and racism characterize the history of the imperial impulse.

Selected Bibliography

NOVELS AND SHORT STORIES

Weep Not, Child. London: Heinemann, 1964.
The River Between. London: Heinemann, 1965.
A Grain of Wheat. London: Heinemann, 1967.
Secret Lives. London: Heinemann, 1976.
Petals of Blood. London: Heinemann, 1977.
Caitaani mũtharaba-inĩ. Nairobi, Kenya: Heinemann, 1980.
Matigari ma njirũũngi. Nairobi, Kenya: Heinemann, 1986.

CHILDREN'S BOOKS

Njamba Nene na mbaathi i mathagu. Nairobi, Kenya: Heinemann, 1982.
Bathitoora ya Njamba Nene. Nairobi, Kenya: Heinemann, 1984.
Njamba Nene na chibu king'ang'i. Nairobi, Kenya: Heinemann, 1986.

PLAYS

The Rebels. In *Penpoint* (October 1961).
The Black Hermit. Kampala, Uganda: Makerere University Press, 1963.
This Time Tomorrow. Nairobi, Kenya: East Africa Literature Bureau, 1970.
The Trial of Dedan Kĩmathi. With Mĩcere Mũgo. London: Heinemann, 1976.
Ngaahika ndeenda. With Ngũgĩ wa Mĩriĩ. Nairobi, Kenya: Heinemann, 1980.

LITERARY CRITICISM AND COMMENTARY

Homecoming: Essays on African and Caribbean Literature, Culture, and Politics. London: Heinemann, 1972.
Detained: A Writer's Prison Diary. Exeter, N.H.: Heinemann, 1981.
Writers in Politics. London: Heinemann, 1981.
Barrel of a Pen: Resistance to Oppression in Neo-Colonial Kenya. Trenton, N.J.: Africa World, 1986.
Decolonising the Mind: The Politics of Language in African Literature. Nairobi, Kenya: Heinemann, 1986.
Moving the Centre: The Struggle for Cultural Freedoms. Nairobi, Kenya: East African Educational Publishers, 1993.

TRANSLATIONS

Devil on the Cross. Trans. by Ngũgĩ wa Thiong'o. London: Heinemann, 1982.

I Will Marry When I Want. With Ngũgĩ wa Mĩriĩ. Trans. by Ngũgĩ wa Thiong'o and Ngũgĩ wa Mĩriĩ. London: Heinemann, 1982.

Njamba Nene and the Flying Bus. Trans. by Wangũi wa Goro. Nairobi, Kenya: Heinemann, 1986.

Njamba Nene's New Pistol. Trans. by Wangũi wa Goro. Nairobi, Kenya: Heinemann, 1986.

Njamba Nene and the Cruel Chief. Trans. by Wangũi wa Goro. Nairobi, Kenya: Heinemann, 1988.

Matigari. Trans. by Wangũi wa Goro. Oxford, U.K.: Heinemann, 1989.

CRITICAL STUDIES

Bardolph, Jacqueline. "Ngũgĩ wa Thiong'o's *A Grain of Wheat* and *Petals of Blood* as Readings of Conrad's *Under Western Eyes* and *Victory.*" In *Conradian* 12 (May 1987).

Björkman, Ingrid. *Mother, Sing for Me: People's Theatre in Kenya.* London: Zed, 1989.

Cancel, Robert. "Literary Criticism as Social Philippic and Personal Exorcism: Ngũgĩ wa Thiong'o's Critical Writings." In *World Literature Today* 59 (winter 1985).

Cook, David, and Michael Okenimkpe. *Ngũgĩ wa Thiong'o: An Explanation of His Writing.* London: Heinemann, 1983.

Crehan, Stewart. "The Politics of the Signifier: Ngũgĩ wa Thiong'o's *Petals of Blood.*" In *World Literature Written in English* 26 (spring 1986).

Harrow, Kenneth. "Ngũgĩ wa Thiong'o's *A Grain of Wheat*: Season of Irony." In *Research in African Literatures* 16 (summer 1985).

Jeyifo, Biodun. "Writing for the Masses." In *Guardian* (Lagos) (23 October 1986).

Killam, G. D. *An Introduction to the Writings of Ngũgĩ.* London: Heinemann, 1980.

Killam, G. D., ed. *Critical Perspectives on Ngũgĩ wa Thiong'o.* Washington, D.C.: Three Continents, 1984.

Levin, Tobe. "Women as Scapegoats of Culture and Cult: An Activist's View of Female Circumcision in Ngũgĩ's *The River Between.*" In Carol Boyce Davies and Anne Adams Graves, eds., *Ngambika: Studies of Women in African Literature.* Trenton, N.J.: Africa World Press, 1986.

Lindfors, Bernth. "Ngũgĩ wa Thiong'o's Early Journalism." In *World Literature Written in English* 20 (spring 1981).

Magel, E. A. "Symbolism and Regeneration in Ngũgĩ wa Thiong'o and Mĩcere Mũgo's *The Trial of Dedan Kĩmathi.*" In *Canadian Journal of African Studies* 17, no. 2 (1983).

Nama, Charles. "Daughters of Moombi: Ngũgĩ's Heroines and Traditional Gĩkũyũ Aesthetics." In Carol Boyce Davies and Anne Adams Graves, eds., *Ngambika: Studies of Women in African Literature.* Trenton, N.J.: Africa World Press, 1986.

Ogunjimi, Bayo. "Language, Oral Tradition, and Social Vision in Ngũgĩ's *Devil on the Cross.*" In *Ufahamu* 14, no. 1 (1984).

Robson, Clifford B. *Ngũgĩ wa Thiong'o.* London: Macmillan, 1979.

Sicherman, Carol. *Ngũgĩ wa Thiong'o: A Bibliography of Primary and Secondary Sources, 1957–1987.* New York: Zell, 1989.

———. ed. *Ngũgĩ wa Thiong'o, the Making of a Rebel: A Sourcebook in Kenyan Literature and Resistance.* New York: Zell, 1990.

Tanure Ojaide
1948–

G. D. KILLAM

TANURE OJAIDE was born in 1948 in Okpara, a small town in the Western Region of Nigeria. He attended St. George's College in Obinomba and the Federal Government College in Warri. He received a bachelor of arts degree in English from the University of Ibadan, Nigeria, in 1971, and then went to study in the United States, where, at Syracuse University, he received a master of arts degree in creative writing in 1979 and a doctorate in English in 1981. He has since taught African literature and creative writing in Nigeria at the University of Maiduguri and in the United States.

Ojaide published his first collection of poems, *Children of Iroko*, in 1973. His second, *Labyrinths of the Delta* (1986), won the Commonwealth poetry competition for the African region in 1987. In 1988 he was awarded the All-Africa Okigbo Prize for Poetry for *The Eagle's Vision* (1987). His next two poetry collections are *The Endless Song* (1989) and *The Fate of Vultures and Other Poems* (1990). The manuscript for *The Fate of Vultures* won the Association of Nigerian Authors poetry award in 1988, and its title poem brought Ojaide the 1988 British Broadcasting Corporation's Arts and Africa poetry award. Ojaide published another collection of poetry, *The Blood of Peace*, in 1991.

Ojaide's poetry can be situated within what the critic Funso Aiyejina calls the "alter/native tradition" in recent Nigerian poetry. In his essay "Recent Nigerian Poetry in English: An Alter-Native Tradition," Aiyejina describes Ojaide as a "new traditionalist" (p. 124), a public poet whose sympathies and concerns are with the downtrodden masses of Nigeria. He makes his appeal to them, and on their behalf, by employing a poetic style derived from indigenous roots, and characterized by direct statement. Free of idiosyncratic language and arcane imagery, Ojaide's poetry instead relies on parable and on references to traditional ritual adjusted to contemporary purposes.

Ojaide is one of many post–civil war Nigerian poets who saw the hopes that began in 1960 with Nigeria's independence come to an end in the civil war (1967–1970). Moreover, the self-servingness and abnegation of successive political leaders seemed to bear out the betrayal of hope for a democratic society. Ojaide's published peers include Pol Ndu, Ossie Enekwe, Obiora Udechukwu, Dubem Okafor, Catherine Acholonu, Mamman Vatsa, Odia Ofeimum, Niyi Osundare, Harry Garuba, and Femi Fatoba. Ojaide defines the poetry of his generation in a 1989 essay, "The Changing Voice of History: Contemporary African

Poetry," in which he identifies two trends in African, principally Nigerian, poetry. He calls them the "old" and the "new," and in so doing is concerned with both thematic and technical preoccupations. He writes that there has been "a gradual parting of the ways between those poets directly influenced by western, especially English, modernist poets and the younger poets who are highly influenced by traditional African poetic techniques and are preoccupied with socio-economic matters and contemporary political issues" (p. 108). Ojaide admits that there is a danger of oversimplifying the difference between the earlier and the contemporary poets. He admits, as well, that the " 'new poetry' is a development from" and a "reaction against the old" (p. 109) and that he himself owes a debt to the "older" poets, especially Christopher Okigbo. He says, further, that "as the older poets of the age have changed in their pre-occupations and techniques some of the qualities of the younger poets abound in the old. . . . Conversely, some of the qualities of the old abound in the new" (pp. 109–110).

Nevertheless, Ojaide distinguishes certain basic differences between the two generations of poets, differences that provide a context for discussing his poetry. The older poets were concerned with the conflict between indigenous and alien cultures; the younger poets are concerned with problems relating to socioeconomic issues in contemporary culture. The older poets, heavily influenced by western modernism, produced poetry that was idiosyncratic, difficult, and obscure; the younger poets, because of their populist political commitments, cultivate a poetry that is unpretentious, clear, and simple. The concern of the older poets was to universalize their poetic experience. The younger poets are concerned with the local, the particular, and the pragmatic. The older poets stood aloof from society, believing that their art would be diminished through contact with the populace. They were suspicious of society, which they felt was antagonistic to them. However much they sought through their work to recommend a just society by contending with political powers, they believed that poetry was a private preoccupation and occupation, and that they had to live in solitude to achieve the introspective life which, through contemplation, allowed them to convert personal experience into myth. The poetry of Wole Soyinka and Okigbo is seen as typical of the product of this generation of poets.

Ojaide acknowledges that the influence of Okigbo was particularly strong on his first volume, *Children of Iroko*. He says that these poems show the poet-artist as a kind of exile in society. The poems, therefore, tend to be private in nature and to be ambiguous, obscure, and difficult in their quasi-philosophical attempts to universalize personal experience. This early collection is marked by Ojaide's attempt to create myth out of personal experience, and it reveals an overall cynicism about human potential, typical of the artist who dissociates from an inadequate society. In the poem "Exile," for example, the poet-artist is presented as a man apart who "might be born a prince in some archaic/forest kingdom" (p. 23). His gift, embodied in his sensitivity to language, might be "bruised by the abused claws of bad language" (p. 23). He finds support for his stance in the experience of Aleksandr Solzhenitsyn, the Russian dissident writer and winner of the 1970 Nobel Prize in literature. Solzhenitsyn, "like a candle . . . burning in the wind" (p. 44), set his integrity and honesty as spokesman for the people against political corruption in the state. For this he is

> Abandoned in the heritage of agonising
> Creativity, his anguish of the exile
> In his land — another foetus of hatred.
>
> (p. 44)

Ojaide's early poems share another quality with the so-called older poets, another mark of what he calls his respect for "the innate talents of the literary elders." This quality could be described as a deliberate vagueness, ambiguity, and obscurity, a creation of systems of personal symbols to convey meaning, and a paucity of direct statement.

CHILDREN OF IROKO

Children of Iroko (1973) embodies a poetic that Ojaide had to explore in order to set aside. The collection contains thirty-one poems and is in many ways an apprentice volume, but in its subject matter and themes, its poetic sources and use of language, its various tones and moods, and its use of imagery, it points the way to the secure voice of subsequent volumes.

The populist tone of the poems is established at the outset:

> TIGERS OWN the homes,
> Where shall the goats sleep;
> Where shall the travelling virgins sleep
> In a village of lust?
>
> ...
>
> Recruits fight the war,
> The world congratulates
> And remembers the generals.

Ojaide's satiric treatment, his irony, and his anger are directed at the army, at political leaders, at academics—at anyone whom power corrupts:

> Who pays examination papers as dowry
> Who donates an undeserved "A" to his Mistress
> The scorpions bitterest venom confuse the don's brow
> Sango's strongest bolt smashes the don's brains.

Although the volume includes poems concerned with abstract issues such as injustice and inequality (for instance, "Message of Lust"), these concerns are often expressed in finite language that specifically considers the poor, underprivileged, and disenfranchised, as in "They Are Crying." Some poems deal with specific events in Nigeria: the civil war; the death of a fellow student in a demonstration at Ibadan; political events in Burundi; the war in Vietnam. The literary importance of *Children of Iroko* resides, therefore, not so much in its talented emulation of the attitudes and techniques of the older poets, but rather in verses of direct expression that reveal the poet seeking his own voice, poems that anticipate the clarity of vision and presentation of the later volumes.

LABYRINTHS OF THE DELTA

Labyrinths of the Delta (1986) appeared thirteen years after *Children of Iroko* and marked a complete break from the earlier poetry. Ojaide's second volume concentrated on public, political, and social themes and demonstrated that he had developed an authentic, personal poetic voice to give expression to such themes. The wide gap between the privileged few and the disenfranchised masses, created by the cynical abnegation of leadership in Nigeria in league with international finance capitalism, became Ojaide's subject, as it did for all of the poets of his generation. Ojaide says in "The Changing Voice of History": "There came a shift from the cultural and the political to socio-economic matters as economic hardships began to tell excruciatingly on the African populace. The influence of the times is in this regard responsible for the younger writers' pre-occupation with socio-economic problems of their environment" (p. 113).

In *Labyrinths of the Delta*, Ojaide continued to draw his material from the past, from oral tradition, but he revivified it through his personal vision and talent, making it contemporary—active and influential. His principal concern was with an unsatisfactory historical present. He incorporated into his vision what was useful in the past, and by doing so he produced a vision of a more sufficient future. For Ojaide, as for most Nigerian writers of the independence and post–civil war periods, "the past" conjured a conception of homogeneous communities with an agreed-upon social order embodied in rituals. From Chinua Achebe on, Nigerian writers (and writers from other parts of Africa) were feeling the obligation to reconstitute society by showing what was valuable before the advent of colonial rule and foreign political and cultural domination, thus to provide a means of promoting a more satisfactory and comprehensive future. The poetry became rooted in the present because it is conditions in the present that prompt the poet to write.

Ojaide's poetry was now marked by solidarity with the poor and exploited. He drew attention to coincident experiences of blacks in other parts of the world in, for example, "To a Black Student" and "At the United Nations Gallery," and to the social problems of other dispossessed races in "Visit to American Indians." But his principal concern was with the consequences to ordinary Nigerians of the politics of corruption, exploitation, and oppression and the maladministration of those in power.

Labyrinths of the Delta has two major parts and two central preoccupations. Part One is called "The Sentence," "sentence" being used in the sense in which human beings are condemned, by the fact of their humanity, to an arduous journey through life. The poet is thus condemned to be a part of and a witness to this process. He will record the dangers to confront and overcome, and the rewards for waging the battle: "I have to slay / the serpents to wear celestial jewels" ("Jewels," p. 1). Part Two, "The Struggle to Be Free," specifically asks how contemporary Nigerians can break out of the social, political, and moral imprisonment that they are experiencing. Within these two major parts of the volume are five sections in which, when examined according to their implied chronology, Ojaide presents a logical historical sequence moving from the precolonial through the colonial past to the present. The lesson he draws from the past is that it had its tyrants, just as the present does—here represented in "Labyrinths of the Delta" by the figure of the tyrant Ogiso, who "castrated the manly among us" and "choked flaming faggots into men's throats" (p. 23). Strength to combat the tyrant is sought through the invocation of the sea goddess, the "Water Bride," who reunites the people with their ancestors and provides the cohesiveness through which the people combat and destroy the tyrant, thus bringing an era of idyllic peace.

This peace is shattered by the advent of colonialism, of the "conquistadors" who introduced the exploitation and commercialization of nature and instituted, with the force of the gun behind them, a foreign religion that fragmented the spiritual and social autonomy of the society.

> Conquistadors drove gunboats from the
> Atlantic,
> Crossed the air, destroyed the foetuses
> spawning in wombs,
> And opened up the land into whitelaced shrines.
> They drove stakes into the labyrinths of the
> Delta, fearing
> They would wander into cannibalistic snares.
> Then flashing gold at our faces, broke our love
> ("Labyrinths of the Delta," pp. 25–26)

Anarchy replaces cohesion. In "The Hunters," the colonialists infect Africans with the "bastardy in their ways," corrupt them with "luxuries" by disguising "their wolfish desires / in brightly draped missions" (p. 28). The result is that Africans are reduced to the level of animals—"where there's been no hyena, a cobra thrives"—where Africans betray Africans—"we stab ourselves with imported swords" ("Africa Now," p. 32). Contemplation of the past can provide the possibility of regeneration in the present:

> But we shall not forget
> Our father's names
> . . .
> And we shall go back to them
> Through the same door
> Still elephants in our hearts.
> ("Revealing the Secret," p. 41)

Ojaide the artist—fulfilling his traditional role—becomes the agent of possible regeneration through his vision, his courage, his unassailable integrity, and his willingness to sacrifice himself in the service of his people.

The central portion of *Labyrinths of the Delta* is concerned with describing and exemplifying the ideal contemporary artist. To those qualities associated with the artist's traditional role, the ideal—perhaps, in the context of contemporary Nigeria, idealized—artist-poet disdains material possessions, for it is seeking these that has corrupted leaders. Accordingly, Ojaide stands with the impoverished, free of material possessions, convinced of his personal integrity, fearless in challenging corrupt leaders, and knowing that his contemporary role has historical precedents understood by the people he speaks to and for. In "I Sing of Love," for example, Ojaide reminds the people of the latent power they possess: "I sing," says the poet, "of the hidden spirit in our midst" (p. 78). In "Calls," the poet

> ... goes afar with his songs to find the stranger
> who will recover what has been stolen from
> the land;
> he is the wind, his heart the sea that feeds it;
> his voice creates a path for the warrior to move
> his faith to the remote souls of the land.
> (p. 63)

The poet's role is spiritual, inspirational, and insistent, as in "It Sounds More Clearly":

> But the heralds of salvation are with us,
> they mime their message in the street;
> no one denies this terrible vision:
> the earth translates the steps of these strangers
> into a loud call—each year it sounds more
> clearly;
> the dawn arrives misted in choral mufmufs.
> (p. 97)

The poems in *Labyrinths of the Delta* are simple statements, sometimes lyrical, sometimes in prosody approaching prose, of firm belief. The poet, the confident visionary, sums up his life and gives expression to the desires and will of the people, the poems reflecting the poet's emotions in contemplating his subject matter. "When Your God Is a Pander" is Ojaide's denunciation of contemporary Nigerian political and administrative leadership: a leader should represent the people, should foster their well-being and protect them, but in fact, according to Ojaide, the typical Nigerian leader is "gone out of the threshold," a man consumed by greed, "an unleashed wolf with a human mask," a man with "a hundred hearts in one body." He is quick to invoke "the mystique of his crown," to make possible and to justify his self-servingness, his acquisitiveness, and his vindictiveness (p. 2).

The one exception to this generalized condemnation is found in "The Death of the Warrior," in which Ojaide laments the death of General Murtala Mohammed, the Nigerian head of state who was assassinated in 1976. Ojaide, like other Nigerian writers, sees Mohammed as a symbol of responsible, benevolent, and, in personal terms, disinterested leadership. "The Death of the Warrior" implies the qualities of the ideal leader. It is one poem in contrast to many that enumerate the opposite qualities. "Wanted: Disrespect," "When We Have to Fly," "Chicho," "Indirect Song," "Antithesis," and "Africa Now" all deal with political leadership, and all expose tyranny, exploitation, and oppression supported by violence used to suppress voices of opposition and secure privilege. In writing about these conditions, the poet exposes himself to the dangers he denounces:

> It's only indirect songs
> We must sing aloud
> To escape the fiery eyes
> of power. Lest a mighty staff
> Knock out our brains,
> And the Chief toast peace with our skulls.
> ("Indirect Song," p. 33)

"To the Bull" is a bestiary poem that allegorizes the successive regimes in Nigerian politics since independence in 1960. Various animals, symbolic of various leaders, are shown as practicing duplicity and chicanery to dupe the people—the jackal promised peace "but threw us into war"; the deer betrayed the people at the battle front; the tortoise "sold us / to build his own shell." In "Waiting," all of the possible agents for reinstituting justice—the police, religious leaders (the priests and imams), the army, the youth, the democratic processes themselves—are found wanting. The result is social anarchy. This state of affairs is summed up in "It Sounds More Clearly":

> The laid-off, like stray rabid dogs,
> threaten the city that bred them;
> the hungry with steel fangs fight over the
> remnants
> of the sumptuous tables of the rich;
> the uninsured labourers at the chemical factory
> baptise their sinecure managers with
> carcinogenic fumes...
>
> (p. 97)

The poems in the volume resonate with images of "kicking," "hanging," "clubbing," "bruises," "crutches," "stretchers," all of which attest to the tyranny of the rulers. Contrasted with the power brokers and powermongers are the exploited, tyrannized masses, those who through their labor—paradoxically, those with "invisible hands"—"lend their skills to keep things together" and "make the egoist / fatten his image and stomach." Ironically, "Only the very day they are needed / are they remembered" ("Conscripted Sweat," p. 34). These are the people from whom the powermongers

> extract oil from my wet soil,
> prospect for iron in my bones,
> and level my forest for timber.
> Then they heap barrels on my back,
> strap billets on my shoulders,
> and tie hardwood to my sides.
>
> ("We Are Many," p. 72)

"Ughelli" presents a more personalized and more angry portrait of the heartless and ruthless dispossession of such people. Ughelli, a town in the oil belt of the Niger Delta, is personified to portray the rape of the natural environment:

> To see her dry-skinned when her oil rejuvenates
> hags
> to leave her in darkness when her fuel lights the
> universe
> to starve her despite all her produce
> to let her dehydrate before the wells bored into
> her heart
> to have her naked despite her innate industry
> to keep her without roads when her sweat tars
> the outside world...
>
> (p. 74)

In "The New Warriors," Ojaide repudiates his connection with the oppressor—rejects his corrupting gifts, pits his "blood against / the rabid bite of asinine representatives," prefers "penury" to gifts from "benevolent slavers." He "bathed / with the same soap of the populace, / ate the same bread with the rest of the street." He "shared in the agonies of the forgotten; / they have given their blood to anaemic neighbours / to survive untold crises" (p. 4).

At the same time Ojaide recognizes that he must wage his fight with tact and cunning, understanding the danger of overplaying his hand—as in "When We Have to Fly" and "Indirect Song." Yet even though he recognizes that the process of reform will be slow and that it implicitly requires caution, an overriding and all-encompassing optimism shapes and informs the poems in the latter section of the collection:

> I sing with a full throat of my mother, my land,
> I sing of the hidden spirit in our midst,
> I sing of the redeemer in the womb of time,
> I sing of the revolution incubating in the heart,
> I sing of the pain before delivery.
>
> ("I Sing of Love," p. 78)

And the poems look forward with certainty to success:

> That day of salvation comes, it comes
> draped in national colours;
> it steps over shrines of dead gods, it comes
> in the crescendo of possessing curses and
> prayers.
>
> ("It Sounds More Clearly," p. 97)

THE EAGLE'S VISION

Ojaide continues and concentrates his exposure of the corruption of the politician and the political processes in *The Eagle's Vision* (1987), developing and elaborating the persona of the politician from images established in *Labyrinths of the Delta.* In this third collection the politician is presented as a figure who uses the product of the people's labors to acquire a position of power and wealth, then repudiates the workers once his personal quest is achieved:

> Once in the palace, those with knowledge of
> love
> forgot what they knew; they always forgot
> what would make us wear endless smiles.
> They ordered the helpless to prop their iron
> roofs;
> they made state armchairs of sacred trees—
> they saw themselves as a different tribe
> and displayed their decorated weapons
> everywhere.
> ("The Whirlwind," p. 43)

Images drawn from nature—the owl, the nightbird, the snake, "the beast draped as idol"—are associated with the "witch" and the "robber." The latter, in turn, are equated with portrayals of leaders dehumanized by a solitary greed.

What distinguishes this volume from its predecessors are poems that describe the difficulty of sustaining the quest and poems that examine a lack of unanimity in the citizenry for whom he speaks—even among the literary community, an exploration which in turn reveals a degree of confusion in the poet's own mind:

> We who had the secret of metamorphosis—
> birds of war, so invisible to the enemy,
> especially when threatened by the big ones—
> confused the word with indulgences.
>
> ...
>
> We are no longer whole; in the cleavage
> prowls the beast, the nightmare of our time.
> ("The Chase," p. 39)

But the poet's confidence returns:

> ... despite the misery the stone imposes on our
> tongues,
> despite the travesties of night in children's fears,
> despite the hardness of the soil on our souls,
> life grows anew, patient in its awakening.
> ("New Life," p. 53)

THE ENDLESS SONG

In Ojaide's fourth volume, *The Endless Song*, the mood of doubt and uncertainty that characterizes *The Eagle's Vision* is replaced by a muted confidence in the power of poetry while at the same time the poet recognizes that he may or may not succeed in his quest. He is still a man of the people, and his quest and purposes are certain:

> From the scaffold of pain we keep watch over
> them,
> from the perilous precipice of misery we keep
> watch over them,
> from the exposed post of lowliness, cold and
> clammy,
> from the slums of existence we keep watch over
> them.
> ("We Keep Watch over Them," p. 5)

Yet his task is a daunting one:

> The leopard that haunts us will die,
> maybe in our lifetime, maybe not;
> time plies the ambush with an invisible hand.
> Let's not dance because we won the mock-
> battle...
> ("The Vision," p. 3)

At its highest point the poet's mood is one of supreme confidence—and this is the prevailing mood of the volume:

> I am now the calabash of their wishes, the crop
> they planted in the wilderness of their desperate
> minds.
> It will take me revolutions to grow above
> normal size, it
> takes a crossbreeding of genes to surpass
> seasonal crops,

it takes the power of the elephant to survive
being haled
into the fashionable company of the stunted
chiefs.
I have to supplant known habits with secret
guides
to live safely in the strange landscape of fate.
("Ploughing the Wilderness," p. 15)

Except for the four "Songs for Ita" (personal love lyrics, which are generally rare if not altogether absent in Nigerian poetry), the containing metaphor in the volume is the questioning poet seeking the experience of his people, to which he gives expression:

Nomadic at heart, I moved
from desiccated plains towards darkening
horizons;
I had to dip my tongue in mirages
and salivate in honeyed desires.
("Desert Rain," p. 33)

The quest produces an "endless song," as the poet begins "to tie the loose ends of history" and ends with a caution:

Do not sing your praise-name before the
contest,
lest you bare your tactics and in the end cry of
folly—

...

Never speak disparagingly of the condemned in
your judgement;
you are yourself sentenced to the human
concession from birth,
It baffles, how we erect pyramids for the dead
who need only a pit.
("Fatalities," p. 57)

As in the earlier volumes, Ojaide draws on oral tradition both to suggest the cyclical patterns of history and, more important, to reveal how a sense of justice will inevitably assert itself through collective action. And he sustains his belief in the capacity of human beings to endure and prevail through poems dedicated to poets like himself—Pablo Neruda, Osip Mandelstam, Boris Pasternak, Tchicaya U Tam'si, Emmanuel Milingo, and Jorge Luis Borges—that convey and sustain his self-appointed role of poet-as-conscience and inspiration to his people.

THE FATE OF VULTURES

The confident self-assurance of *The Endless Song* (which reveals a middle ground between the almost unrestrained optimism of *Labyrinths of the Delta* and the prevailing doubt of *The Eagle's Vision*) is sustained in *The Fate of Vultures and Other Poems* (1990). The themes Ojaide treats here are familiar: the relationship, in various moods, between the poet and society; the corruption of contemporary leadership and the abuses of power; political and economic mismanagement; religious strife. What sets this volume off from the earlier books is its introspective nature. While sustaining his role as spokesman, Ojaide acknowledges the need to distance himself from the masses and to restrain his attack on the enemy:

Stop them

lest your enemies think you are too weak
you hurl a stone mountain at them
and you become a murderer

lest your friends call you hard-hearted
you lavish all you have on them
and you become a pauper

...

before they devour you
for their own reasons your own fears
stop them with an instant "No".
("No," p. 43)

Having achieved this useful personal space, the poet can still sing for the dispossessed, now with a confidence bred of maturity:

Now that I am forty
I will not abandon my road
I will wield the matchet [*sic*]
against adversaries;
with it I fan myself
when secure in dreams.

Whatever I hold firmly
can talk back to me
and do my bidding.
Whatever I plant in my heart
will grow out
now that I am forty.
("Now That I Am Forty,"
p. 98)

CONCLUSION

Ojaide's poetry is essentially lyrical, and even when it has the surface quality of prose, the imagery and the ellipsis—characteristic of traditional African imagery, rhythm, and music—sustain it. It traces a poetic development that moves from celebration through doubt to confident maturity. Coincident with this is Ojaide's domestication of the English language to express his African experience. He has, having cleared his own poetic space, produced a politically motivated and accessible body of poetry. Ojaide employs his resources to interrogate the sociopolitical situation of Nigeria in particular, and of African nations in general.

Selected Bibliography

POETRY

Children of Iroko. Greenfield Center, N.Y.: Greenfield Review Press, 1973.

Labyrinths of the Delta. Greenfield Center, N.Y.: Greenfield Review Press, 1986.

The Eagle's Vision. Detroit, Mich.: Lotus Press, 1987.

The Endless Song. Lagos, Nigeria: Malthouse Press, 1989.

The Fate of Vultures and Other Poems. Lagos, Nigeria: Malthouse Press, 1990.

The Blood of Peace and Other Poems. Oxford, U.K., and Portsmouth, N.H.: Heinemann, 1991.

CRITICISM

"The Changing Voice of History: Contemporary African Poetry." In *Geneva-Africa* 27, no. 1 (1989).

The Poetry of Wole Soyinka. Lagos, Nigeria: Malthouse Press, 1994.

"New Trends in Modern African Poetry." In *Research in African Literature* 26, no. 1 (1995).

CRITICAL STUDIES

Aiyejina, Funso. "Recent Nigerian Poetry in English: An Alter-Native Tradition." In Yemi Ogunyemi, ed., *Perspectives on Nigerian Literature: 1700 to the Present.* Vol. 1. Lagos, Nigeria: Guardian Books, 1988.

Bamikunle, Adermi. "Literature as a Historical Process: A Study of Ojaide's *Labyrinths of the Delta.*" In Chidi Ikonne, Emelia Oko, and Peter Onwudinjo, eds., *African Literature and African Historical Experiences.* Ibadan, Nigeria: Heinemann, 1991.

———. "The Stable and the Changing in Nigerian Poetry." In *World Literature Written in English* 32 (1992).

Knipp, Thomas. "Frank Chipasula's *Whispers in the Wings* and Tanure Ojaide's *The Blood of Peace.*" In *Callaloo* 16 (1993).

Sallah, Tijan M. "*The Eagle's Vision*: The Poetry of Tanure Ojaide." In *Research in African Literature* 26, no. 1 (1995).

Gabriel Okara

1921–

CHANTAL ZABUS

ALTHOUGH GABRIEL OKARA'S literary output is much slimmer than the production of his Nigerian contemporaries, he rightfully can be considered the doyen of Nigerian letters. He is one of the earliest practicing modern African poets, and although he is a most unorthodox novelist, the growth of the African novel cannot be fully understood without considering his one and only novel, *The Voice* (1964).

Okara did not train at the pioneering University College of Ibadan (now University of Ibadan) like many of his peers: Chinua Achebe, Elechi Amadi, Flora Nwapa, John Munonye, Nkem Nwankwo, Wole Soyinka, John Pepper Clark, Mabel Segun, and Christopher Okigbo. In the 1940s and early 1950s, while poets like Michael Dei-Anang, Raphael E. G. Armattoe, and Dennis Osadebay were dutifully imitating the English Lake poets and early modernists, Okara had begun to emancipate himself from the ascendancy of British letters. Although his poetry inevitably shows the influence of foreign diction, he remains a self-made, self-taught writer and a freewheeling, fiercely independent person endowed with both an intense religious or mystic sentiment and a serene mastery of the word.

BIOGRAPHY

Gabriel Imomotimi Gbaingbain Okara was born 24 April 1921 at Bumoundi in Yenogoa Local Government Area of Rivers State in the Ijọ (or Ijaw) country of the Niger Delta in Nigeria. His parents were Samson G. Okara, a businessman, and Martha Olodiama, both members of the Ekpetinma clan. A Christian, he was educated at St. Peter's and Proctor's Memorial School (1926–1935) and at the Government College of Umuaḥia (1935–1940). He resumed his education during World War II at Yaba Higher College (now Yaba College of Technology), where a classmate was the writer T. Moloforunso Aluko. He developed into a fine teacher and a visual artist under the aegis of the renowned sculptor Ben Enwonwu, before the war took him to Gambia, where he worked for British Airways (1941–1944).

Upon returning to Nigeria, Okara took up bookbinding, journalism, and occasional writing. He received the first prize in the British Council's 1952 short-story competition for his piece "The Iconoclast." In 1953 he was awarded the silver cup for the best entry in poetry ("The Call of the River Nun") at the

Nigerian Festival of Arts. His parallel journalistic career was crowned in 1959 by a certificate in comparative journalism from the Medill School of Journalism at Northwestern University in Evanston, Illinois.

In 1964, Okara became a part-time lecturer in English at the University of Nigeria at Enugu, where in 1950 he had started a branch of the Government Press. That same year also saw the publication of his novel, *The Voice*, which captures the disillusionment following the independence of Nigeria from Great Britain on 1 October 1960 (Nigeria became a republic on 1 October 1963).

The postindependence years were far from smooth. Since 1964, Okara had been head of the Eastern (primarily Igbo) Region Government Information Office. On 30 May 1967, the Eastern Region seceded, proclaiming itself the Republic of Biafra. On 6 July, Nigeria's federal government declared war on the republic. From 1967 to 1969 Okara served as director of the Cultural Affairs Division of the Biafran Ministry of Information. After steadily losing ground in the bloody civil war, the Igbo secessionists, led by Chukwuemeka Odumegwu Ojukwu, capitulated on 12 January 1970. Okara then became principal secretary to the governor of Rivers State, a state that was founded partly to allow such minorities of the Eastern Region as the Ijọ and the Ikwerre to escape Igbo hegemony.

From 1973 to 1975, Okara was general manager of the Rivers State Broadcasting Corporation, which ran the first and only FM radio station in black Africa. Upon retirement in 1975, he spent about ten months as commissioner of information and broadcasting; between 1977 and 1983, he was writer-in-residence for the Rivers State Council on Arts and Culture. He received the Commonwealth Poetry Prize in 1979 for "The Fisherman's Invocation," which gave its title to the sole collection of his poetry. He also was awarded an honorary doctorate by the University of Port Harcourt in Rivers State in 1982.

Okara's lectures on poetry, as well as on Ijọ and African culture to students at all levels, were part of his ongoing efforts to involve Nigerians in the cultural and literary upsurge occurring in the postcolonial Nigerian nation-state. In the 1980s, his target audience became the children and teenagers of Nigeria, and in the 1990s he published folktales and myths that have enriched Nigerian and African children's literature.

Okara was a founding member of the Nigerian English Studies Association and of the Association of Nigerian Authors (another prominent member of which is Nobel Prize winner Wole Soyinka). He has been married and divorced three times, and has two children. In the mid 1990s, well into his seventies, he was still lecturing and traveling. He also was contemplating writing a magnum opus titled "The Rise and Fall of Tortoise," the folk hero of West African lore.

POETRY: HIS RIVER'S COMPLEX COURSE

Although they are extensively anthologized, Okara's extant poems were collected in a slim volume, *The Fisherman's Invocation*, in 1978, a quarter of a century after he received his first poetry prize for "The Call of the River Nun" in 1953. The collection contains thirty-three poems reaped from anthologies and periodicals. Hundreds of others, however, along with short stories, reportedly have been lost, due mainly to Okara's carelessness (at first possibly due to an ill-defined sense of authorship) but also to his numerous moves from Enugu to Aba and from Umuahia to Owerri during the Nigerian civil war. Three poems were irredeemably lost: "The Gambler," "I've Killed the Year That Killed Me," and "Leave Us Alone to Heal Our Wounds," a war poem that, Theophilus Vincent says, was set to music and performed. "Metaphor of a War," "River Nun-2," and "The Dancer" were poems published in the September 1982 issue of *Okike*.

Okara was closely connected with the Mbari Writers and Artists Club, the moving spirit behind which was the German scholar Ulli Beier, and with the magazine *Black Orpheus*, in which Okara published both his poems and short stories, including a trial chapter from *The Voice*. *Black Orpheus* was the main organ of dissemination not only for African literary criticism but also, and more importantly, for the works of such diverse poets as Christopher Okigbo (1932–1967), who was killed during the federal army's seizure of the university town of Nsukka, and John Pepper Clark.

Okara and Clark share the same mental landscape or "mindscape," traversed by the many inlets and rivulets of the West African seacoast and, more particularly, by the mass of creeks around the mouth of the Niger Delta. Yet both of them, to varying degrees, waded in other currents; they were influenced by the European modernist school of T. S. Eliot, William Butler Yeats, and the Irish priest-poet Gerard Manley Hopkins.

Possibly because he was for the most part self-taught, Okara was less inclined to academic exercises than was Clark, whose "Ibadan Dawn" is purportedly modeled after Hopkins' "Pied Beauty" and distinctly echoes "The Windhover" and "Hurrahing in Harvest." Another poem by Clark is titled "Variations on Hopkins on Theme of Child Wonder," which, in Emeka Okeke-Ezigbo's opinion, returns a leaden echo to Hopkins' "Spring and Fall." Hopkins, with Ezra Pound and T. S. Eliot, had so many Nigerian imitators that the Nigerian troika of Afrocentric critics—Chinweizu, Jemie Onwuchekwa, and Ichechukwu Madubuike—denounced "the Hopkins Disease" in *Toward the Decolonization of African Literature*.

The Fisherman's Invocation was joint winner of the prestigious Commonwealth Poetry Prize in 1979, along with the New Zealand poet Brian Turner's *Ladders of Rain*. The prize is the only thing these two poets could ever share; Kirsten Holst Petersen saw the two collections as "heterogeneous worlds yoked violently together" (p. 155). The joint prize not only forced the British Commonwealth umbrella to stretch further afield but also obviously put Okara's name on the literary map, well beyond the confines of Nigerian or West African literature.

The tone that predominates in *The Fisherman's Invocation* is one of gentleness, as when one meets Okara in person, combined with an overwhelming sadness, as he moves effortlessly and economically among private, public, and cosmic levels. His use of nature may come in part from his reading in the English Romantic poets, especially William Wordsworth. (Wordsworth's poem "Spring" is reputed to have spurred Okara to write poetry.) But such familiar bearings are quickly shaken by unusual and at times violent imagery and a beat reminiscent of oral traditional songs. Although Okara's prosody is yet to be analyzed, his sonorous verse undeniably has some of the "sprung rhythm" quality of Hopkins' verse, which went so far as to foreground the "speech framed to be heard" at the expense of meaning.

The structure of most of Okara's poems is characterized by a "fearful symmetry." Like much Romantic poetry, a typical Okara poem is composed of two premises: first, a statement, a narrative piece, or a description, a contrastive juxtaposition of opposing symbols; second, the illustration or the application of an independent moral coda to demonstrate the universality of the initial statement and, as in music, to bring a natural conclusion to the poetic movement. Conjunctions such as *yet* and *but* indicate the shift from the first to the second premise, as in the second part of "Freedom Day"; the last two lines of "Cancerous Growth"; and the last three lines of "Christmas 1971," a poem conceived just after the end of the Biafran War:

> But love and peace will sprout skywards like a sapling
> straight and strong from land
> dripping with water from Pilate's hands.
> (*The Fisherman's Invocation*, p. 51)

As Ayo Mamudo observes, some of these moral accretions are not always appropriate, as in "Suddenly the Air Cracks." When Okara senses that he is lapsing into didacticism, that is, the manners of a teacher, he resorts to the dramatic mode, where he has, as in the ancient Greek chorus, two or several "voices" acting diverse parts. The concept of warring "teaching voices," as he calls them, is taken up again in *The Voice*, which is an extension of the dramatic mode and reads as an allegory. Okara appears throughout the collection as unfailingly Christian, as he "weakly genuflect[s] / to the calling Angelus bells" (p. 40) in "Expendable Name" or admires "Our Lady's Cathedral," the late-medieval "Frauenkirche" (misspelled "Fanvenkirche") in Munich, which, to him, embodies the absolute "twin-towered faith" (p. 35).

Invocations and Other Calls

The title poem, "The Fisherman's Invocation," is Okara's most ambitious poetic work because, while adopting a deliberately non-political slant, it reflects through indigenous imagery the tribulations of nation-building as well as the traumas that befall the self. It was written before Nigeria's independence in 1960 but was not published until 1963 (in *Black Orpheus*, no. 13, pp. 34–43). As an "invocation," the poem appropriately comes first in the volume and thus guards the entrance to the collection. It suggests both the call upon God in prayer, as used by the preacher before the sermon, and the preacher's ascription of praise to God at the end of a sermon.

"The Fisherman's Invocation" inevitably recalls the parables of Christ in the Gospels, and as a parable typifying spiritual relations, it prefigures *The Voice*. The poem is a dialogue between two voices: the teaching voice of the Fisherman paddling the canoe and the hesitant learning voice of the initiate. In "one teaching moment" (p. 3), the teacher orders his doubtful pupil to cast a net "to the back of the canoe" to secure the day's catch. The simple act of fishing in the Niger Delta creeks and of hauling the net from a canoe with "the Back / caught in the meshes of Today" soon becomes a large metaphor for the communal, ancestral past, with its potent deities and fearful masquerades resisting, like the counter-current of the water; yet caught, fishlike, by the tugging strength of the present. Interestingly, what Okara calls "the Front" (as opposed to "the Back") signifies both the present and the future, as if it were a translation of the imperfect tense in some sub-Saharan African languages (and Arabic), thereby setting the poem against a nonwestern conception of time. To his fearful companion's nightmarish vision of the past as a desert or a dried-up well, the Fisherman insists that the past may turn out to be a fertile, feminine body, an archetypal mother not to be defiled:

> There's water from a river
> flowing from the bottom of the Back
> of the womb.
> (p. 5)

The Fisherman briefly becomes a cosmic hunter, for the teacher's "invocation" is to

> stalk the Back in the forest
> stalk the Back in the heavens
> stalk it in the earth
> stalk it in your umbilical cord
> (p. 5)

which entails looking for the past in one's origin and development as a human being. The mention of the "umbilical cord" is not fortuitous, for, in Ijọ belief, it is buried at birth in the native soil and thereby forces its owner to return to it at the moment of death, as the protagonist is compelled to do in *The Voice*. But the Fisherman's pupil is frightened, "caught in grim / teeth of trap of Today" (p. 6). This triggers the Fisherman's lament that if the ancestral voices (those "prophesying war," as in Samuel Taylor Coleridge's "Kubla Khan") cannot be retrieved, the Front will be "a still-birth Front," a stillborn child.

The "Invocation" proper follows, as the pupil—Man—is mesmerized by the oathlike repetitions ("You are seeing" is repeated six times). Under hypnosis, the initiate experiences the first birth pangs and comes to see and hear, as if in a trance: "I can hear, I can hear the Front / coming gently coming painfully coming." Meanwhile, the Fisherman invokes the soothing moon that acts as a midwife, the sun, and the drums before the Front is born from Man's "ruptured inside" (p. 9), where it had been incubating as in Jupiter's thigh. The birth described in the poem recalls the Ijọ creation myth of man giving birth in a gush of bubbling water, "coming with sound of river / rushing over a fall subduing / barriers of height and stone" (p. 8); then as "a ball of fire / searing through my being" (p. 9).

A strange baptismal rite ensues, when the Child-Front is blessed with the Gods' "mystic touch" (p. 9). Man has engendered a child who is half-formed, "not yet human" (p. 10). To his anxious, skeptical questioning about whether the child is a monster, the Fisherman asks him, in a long homily, to be patient and let the sun finish its course. In the fourth part of the poem, "Birth Dance of the Child-Front," Man rejoices, singing and dancing to the beating drums.

The last part of the "Invocation" has overtones of Shakespeare's *The Tempest*—"the celebration is now ended" (p. 15)—amid echoes of Yeats's "Second Coming" and other "Annunciation" poems in which, curiously, women do not give birth or conceive through intercourse with a male. The poem ends, however, with a blissful vision of the newborn Child-Front gluttonously feeding from the "measureless breasts of the Back" and contentedly "sleeping with breasts in his mouth" (p. 15), as one might imagine the god-child Dionysus fed by a group of bacchantes. The child and, by the same token, newly independent Nigeria, had good prospects for growth.

Although the poems were written in such diverse places as Germany (Munich, 1963) and Nigeria (Umuahia, 1968; Ogwa, 1969; and Port Harcourt, 1970) over a decade, the central icon is, not surprisingly, the riverbank, inspired by the Niger Delta. Okara's river has mythical dimensions; Robert Fraser sees it as a curve inscribed by history that "meanders between the heritage of the past and the challenge of the future" (p. 193), between the Back and the Child-Front.

The much anthologized prizewinning poem "The Call of the River Nun" (first published in the first issue of *Black Orpheus* in 1957) takes up the "found'ring canoe" of "The Fisherman's Invocation" as it goes "down / its inevitable course" (p. 16) until its fragile shell is broken by the crested waves. The image of the upturned canoe prefigures the end of *The Voice*, where the boat in which the two outcasts are tied back to back is "drawn into a whirlpool. It spun round and round and was slowly drawn into the core and finally disappeared" (*Voice*, p. 127). The vengeful river of life and history also evokes Matthew Arnold's "life's stream" in "In Utrumque Paratus" and Alfred, Lord Tennyson's flood "from out our bourne of Time and Place" in "Crossing the Bar." More pointedly, one can imagine a sinuous, tortured mindscape caused by the "final call" of the River Nun as it is flowing from source to sea, enlarging its flow the way Okara is enlarging his theme. The poem also borrows freely from Wordsworth's "Lines Written in Early Spring" and "Valedictory Sonnet to the River Duddon." But it is imbued not so much with the mood of bidding farewell as with that of nostalgia. Indeed, when Okara conceived the poem, he was away from his Ijọ native country, and the Udi Hills surrounding the city of Enugu (in

Anambra State), where he was working, must have seemed the very antithesis of the familiar riverbanks.

Amid images of navigation such as the canoe, the stars, and the pilot, the poet is dispossessed, and his poor means do not enable him to answer the call:

> Shall my pilot be
> my inborn stars to that
> final call to Thee
> O my river's complex course?
> (p. 17)

The calling to "Thee," to the "incomprehensible God" (p. 17), is reminiscent of George Herbert's rebellion and final submission to God in "The Collar."

"One Night at Victoria Beach" describes the white-robed Aladuras, a revivalist Christian sect, praying on Lagos Beach. Their impassioned, but empty, fanatical prayers are counterpointed as in a cinematic shot-countershot with the fishermen's casting of cowries (little shells used as money) in an effort to conjure up the "Babalawo," the priest of the Yoruba god Ifa, and one catches furtive glimpses of lovers and palm-wine drinkers. These other fishermen, the dead ones, "long dead with bones rolling / nibbled clean by nibbling fishes" conjure up the dead men's "bones . . . picked clean and the clean bones gone" in the Welsh poet Dylan Thomas' "And Death Shall Have No Dominion." Allegedly, Thomas' influence (as in "Before I Knocked") can also be detected in the first lines of Okara's "Were I to Choose":

> When Adam broke the stone
> and red streams raged down to
> gather in the womb,
> an angel calmed the storm
> (p. 21)

Some critics have also perceived Blakean and Yeatsian overtones. At the end of the poem, Okara is left to contemplate the discrepancy between the two belief systems. He is here not so much pathetically left on the beach, as Fraser suggests, "in his trouser turn-ups" (p. 198), as about to surrender to the bewitching call of the prayer and to genuflect in the sand before the wind kills his budding prayer.

In the same religious vein, the unfinished poem "The Revolt of the Gods" (1969) recalls Percy Bysshe Shelley's twelve-canto poem "The Revolt of Islam," written a century and a half earlier. Yet, in its structure, this verse drama in three brief scenes is probably closer to *Prometheus Unbound*, a lyrical drama in four acts, and the equally unfinished *Hellas*. But, of course, even in a finished form, a long poem by Okara would never approximate the length of Shelley's longer poems. Part One of "The Revolt of the Gods" consists of an exchange between the diverse Gods of the Pantheon, who commiserate their helplessness while being capriciously "driven / hither and thither" by the wind and forced to survive "in the twilight of life and death" (p. 58) by Man's whimsical theology. The Old God feebly brandishes his only weapons, the obsolete "lightning and thunder" (p. 59), whereas the Young God, with the insightful directness and impetuousness of his youth, sees the frailty behind Man's self-bestowed grandeur. Eavesdropping on a conversation among four slightly inebriated mortals confirms the Gods' powerlessness in the face of such insolent camaraderie.

Between the Drum and the Concerto

Okara's concern with the clash between cultural insiders and outsiders has been said to derive from the ideological posturing of the French Négritude movement. This movement started with Antillean and African intellectuals in Paris in the 1930s, who looked back to a prelapsarian, untouched Africa before it was colonized by the European powers, and therefore subscribed to a Manichaean or dualist view of Africa and the west. Okara is preoccupied with the modern, westernized African individual who is at an inevitable crossroads between two cultures or, more positively, on the verge of embracing an emergent, syncretic neo-African culture.

"The Snowflakes Sail Gently Down" illustrates such a conflict. It starts with the same recollection in tranquillity that permeates some of the Romantic poems such as Coleridge's "Frost at Midnight," but has the additional feeling of alienation that the poet experiences during his stay in a bleak, wintry America. The site is Northwestern University in 1959. The poet soon falls into a "dead sleep" induced by the snow falling and the overheated room. What might at first be construed as nightmarish, Gothic ravens or what Kenneth L. Goodwin calls "the black birds of Western depredation" (p. 145)—"black / birds flying in my inside"—are actually African nesting birds "hatching on oil palms bearing suns / for fruits" (p. 30). These birds, representing a black Africa glistening with fertility, are artfully silhouetted against the snowy backcloth of a mournful America, the archetypal place of usury and unlawful appropriation, where the sun is a fraudulent coin that does not pay off.

This light-and-shade, or chiaroscuro, effect that one might find in a painting is taken a step further in "Spirit of the Wind," in which the white storks are at first "white specks in the silent sky"; then the essence of the stork is seen as "caged / in Singed Hair and Dark Skin" (p. 22) in the earthbound poet's buoyant black prison of the self.

Of all the poems about culture conflict, "Piano and Drums" is the most famous. The poet laments the eroding of traditional ways and is

> lost in the morning mist
> of an age at a riverside keep
> wandering in the mystic rhythm
> of jungle drums and the concerto.
> (p. 20)

But the jungle drums are here beating as they would in British colonial films such as Zoltan Korda's *Sanders of the River* (1935), complete with predatory, ready-to-pounce panthers, snarling leopards, and "hunters crouch[ing] with spears poised." They are sharply contrasted to the plaintive, tearful wail of a piano solo, which Okara told Robert Fraser he identified as "Rachmaninov First" (p. 194).

The "telegraphing" drums have less immediacy than the mystic drum in the poem of that title, which beats in the poet's "inside" so loud that the once tenderly smiling lover turns into an oracular priestess, with "feet and leaves growing on her head / and smoke issuing from her nose," and her lovely mouth becomes a gaping "cavity belching darkness" (p. 27). The lover's keen desire is frustrated by rejection; his call or invocation is met by a demonic, unresponsive woman.

Poems of Love and War

The young Okara's amorous fire is "smouldering" in his middle-aged phase in "To Paveba," as in Shakespeare's Sonnet 73 or Thomas Hardy's "I Look into My Glass." The fire can be revived by "young fingers" that, because of his almost ascetic vow not to yield to love, have to be "shyly push[ed] aside" (p. 33). Yet in "To a Star," he will "break [his] vow" of chastity "to the rhythm of the ageing drums" (p. 55). "Silent Girl," about the requited love of a "sweet silent girl" (p. 44), is the weakest of his love poems, possibly because the dynamics of reciprocity is missing and the ideological thrust stifles the poem. Many of these poems express a weary sense of growing old, of "the dead weight of years" ("To Paveba"), of being grounded on "trembly feet" ("Celestial Song"); the poet is in his early forties, no longer at "the close of one and thirty," as in "Were I to Choose."

Okara has much of the romantic visionary, and the meaning of his "love poems" often eddies out beyond the apparent naive lyricism. Some affectedly refined aspects of his craft have made him liable to charges of preciosity. But he is very capable, as in his wartime poems written from the Biafran civilian's point of view, of conjuring up the "gruesome glee" of bombing during the civil war and the resulting "stacked" bodies in the morgue, as in "Suddenly the Air Cracks" and "Cross on the Moon"; or the leprous fingers trying to pluck from the sky the plane "Flying over the Sahara"; or the wounds festering in the streets of Port Harcourt in "The Glowering Rat."

And there is no affectation in his reproachful address to the warmongers in "Expendable Name" and "Come, Come and Listen"; or in his celebration of the mercy flights to Biafra in "Rain Lullaby"; or in his hurtful response to "today's wanton massacre" (p. 41) presumably the Igbo massacre by the Northern Hausa on 13 December 1968, in "Cancerous Growth." He is also able to dwell without any artificiality on the emotional superiority of the rural naif whose fiery passion slowly thaws the icy cynicism of the alienated, westernized town dweller in "You Laughed and Laughed and Laughed." Some poems are imbued with a nostalgia for the genuine laughter of childhood, for the poet has learned to become insincere, a positioning that prefigures a projected novel, tentatively titled "The Making of a Cynic."

THE VOICE

If Okara was recognized early as a poet, he was a late starter as a novelist (he was forty-four when *The Voice* was published), except that he never thought of himself as a novelist. Indeed, *The Voice* (1964) is what Arthur Ravenscroft calls "a poetic novel" (p. 4). As such, it is the novelistic exploration or continuation of some of the themes articulated in Okara's poetry: Africa versus the west and the spiritual losses resulting from the encroachment of materialism. In the poem "Once Upon a Time," Okara laments: "Now they shake hands without hearts / While their left hands search / my empty pockets" (*The Fisherman's Invocation*, p. 18). The moral dissolution he here alludes to could be that of the people of Amatu in *The Voice*, where the Christian Trinity has been ousted by "the shadow-devouring trinity of gold, iron, concrete" (*Voice*, p. 89).

The notion of "voice," of the "spirit urging within" (in "Spirit of the Wind") becomes an overwhelming concept. The main protagonist is called Okolo, which means "the voice" in Ịjọ. The voices luring the "madman" in the poem "Adhiambo" (p. 32) echo the voices calling upon Okolo to search for "it." "It" is the purposely nameless object of quest, for naming is a divisive process and a name is "expendable" or likely to be destroyed, as the poet makes clear in "Expendable Name." The goal of the quest is syncretic and common "to Christians, Moslems, Animists" alike (p. 112). Also, the dialogue between the First, Second, and Third messengers in the first scene of *The Voice* is an expansion of the dramatic mode used in some of the poems. This technique of juxtaposition that consists in playing off character against character finds its stylistic corollary in the novel's short, dramatic sentences strung together without any transition. Thematically, the silencing of the "voice" within the messengers prefigures the silencing of Okolo's dissenting voice as it drowns in the silent, unmoved river.

The "voice" is not always the redeeming spoken word. Voicelessness or silence is often synonymous with honesty, as the silence of Okolo and the sixteen-year-old girl (whom he is accused of abusing while protecting her from the storm) is sharply contrasted with the shrill, accusatory voice of the girl's mother and, more generally, with the harsh, loud voices of depredation. One other way in which the theme of corruption is woven into the linguistic fabric of the novel is through the metaphors Okolo uses; their lush humanity and ripeness are in direct contrast to the stark materialism of the people of Amatu.

Though not overtly Christian, Okolo has been compared to William Langland's fourteenth-century visionary character Piers Plowman because of Okolo's hallucinatory wandering through the corrupt city of Sologa (probably to be taken as Lagos). Okolo's personal odyssey also suggests John Bunyan's seventeenth-century allegorical piece *The Pilgrim's Progress* as well as the Passion of Christ, for it is strewn with echoes from the Bible—particularly, as Emmanuel Obiechina has pointed out, Mark 16:14, Luke 24:48–49, and the opening of St. John's Gospel—"In the beginning was the Word, and the Word was with God, and the Word was God."

Like *Fragments* (1970), by the Ghanaian Ayi Kwei Armah, *The Voice* starts with the return to the native land of a "been-to," someone who has "been to" Europe or the United States for higher education. He is jolted by the corruption, the materialism, and the moral bankruptcy in his people. Although *The Voice* is, in its parabolic approach, close to later Ghanaian novels such as Kofi Awoonor's *This Earth, My Brother*... (1971) or Armah's *The Beautyful Ones Are Not Yet Born* (1968), the novel shares with the more "realistic" West African novels like those of Chinua Achebe a disillusionment with the leaders' promises of the "coming thing." Okolo is "no longer at ease" (after T. S. Eliot's phrase, which Achebe used as a title for a novel in 1960).

Okolo diligently starts a cleansing campaign of the Federation of Nigeria, if only "by basketfuls" (p. 50), but his message is left unheeded. He is ostracized by his own people, threatened to be confined in an asylum, then, in the last phase of his martyrdom, set adrift down the river, bound back to back to another outcast, the alleged witch Tuere. Okolo and Tuere, the twin symbols of an irretrievable past, will be mourned only by Ukule, the crippled custodian of Okolo's words. Tuere's words to Ukule—"tell our story and tend our spoken words" (p. 127)—may be said to echo Christ's parting words to the apostles after his resurrection. But what is significant here is that the purveyors of Okolo's words are a cripple and a woman, both emblematic of the dispossessed, the minorities, and, more largely, what the Martinican psychiatrist and ideologist Frantz Fanon has called "the wretched of the earth."

Unlike the protagonist in Armah's *Fragments,* whose quest ends in the demented realization of the ubiquity of materialism, Okolo's quest ends in self-sacrifice and death. Okolo is both a prophet and a heretic, a Christ or a Hamlet precariously straddling alienation and commitment. He is someone whose words reek of prophecy and the "courage to speak up," as Okara told Bernth Lindfors in an interview (pp. 42–43). Okolo's "straight words" at first ring hollow when weighed against the "crooked words" of the brutal autocrat Izongo and the elder Abadi, who holds master's and doctoral degrees and uses his "big book learning" (p. 45) for devious political ends. Izongo is undoubtedly the precursor of Achebe's "a man of the people" (in the novel of that title, 1966) and the panoply of corrupt authorities teeming in Nigerian novels. Abadi is like those African political leaders who pose as socialist revolutionaries and denounce imperialism while being conservative and reactionary at heart.

Although Okara objected to being paired with T. Moloforunso Aluko solely on the criterion of age, *The Voice* is, like Aluko's work, imbued with pessimism about post-colonial Nigeria. Nevertheless, because it is an extended parable, a prophetic allegory, and thus a far cry from political pamphleteering, references to the actual Nigerian situation may go undetected. As Okara put it in an interview, those in government were not threatened by such a denunciation of corruption because they "were too busy pocketing their loot to read between the lines of a novel they hardly had heard of" (interview by Zabus, p. 111).

Okara's "teaching voice" intimates that Okolo's straight words ultimately will triumph over the crooked words of corrupt politics, imported ideology, and, presumably, the British word order—that is, the logocentric or self-referential relation between word and referent in the English language.

Linguistic Experimentation in *The Voice*

What sustains the linguistic experimentation in *The Voice* is the metaphorical fight between the ideology of "the straight word" and that of "the crooked word." The "straight words" in *The Voice* are supposed to be said in Ijọ, whereas the "crooked words" of political propaganda are said, for the most part, in English (except when Izongo uses the idioms of the people to get their votes). How, then, does Okara differentiate between the English Okolo uses to speak Ijọ and the English with which he addresses the white man? What signals the shift from one register to another by the same speaker? Okolo's main medium is an English informed with Ijọ thought patterns, word order, and concepts. This accounts for the novel's quaint, pseudo-naive language that consciously achieves what Amos Tutuola, a decade earlier, had stumbled upon with the botched Yoruba-informed English of *The Palm-Wine Drinkard and His Dead Palm-Wine Tapster in the Deads' Town* (1952). Okara's experimentation with English rests on an ideological positioning that he defined thus:

> As a writer who believes in the utilization of African ideas, African philosophy and African folk-lore and imagery to the fullest extent possible, I am of the opinion the only way to use them effectively is to translate them almost literally from the African language native to the writer into whatever European language he is using as his medium of expression.
>
> ("African Speech," p. 15)

This method has enabled him to "translate . . . literally" or transliterate the English "he is timid" from its Ijọ equivalent "he has no chest" or "he has no shadow." When such lexical and semantic innovations (affecting the "words" and the "meaning" of a language, respectively) are extended to syntax or sentence construction, the result may be both stilted and alluring, as in "Who are you people be?" (p. 26) or "everybody surface-water-things tell" (p. 34). The postponement of the verb, of the negative, or both can be traced to Ijọ syntactical patterns. Here are two examples (Zabus, *African Palimpsest*, p. 124), with (1) the Ijọ original and (2) its transliteration:

> "To every person's said thing listen not" (p. 7)
> (1) *Kịmị gbá yémọ́ sẹ̀ pòù kụ́mọ̣*
> (2) Man say things all listen not;
>
> "He always of change speaks" (p. 66)
> (1) *Yémọ́ dèímịnị̀ bárá sèrìmọ́sẹ̀ èrí ẹ̀rẹ̀mịnị̀*
> (2) things changing how always he (is) speaking.

The double and triple coinages, words strung together and hyphenated, also can be traced to Ijọ. For instance, "surface-water-things" (p. 34) is derived from the Ijọ *ọ̀gọ̀nọ̀ bènì yèámọ̀* (literally, up-water-things); "coming-in people" (p. 27) from *sụ́ọ́ bómịnị́ kịmịamọ́* (comes-in-people); "wrong-doing-filled inside" (p. 31) from *búlóù sè kịrịghà-yè-mịẹ̀n* (inside all wrong-thing-do); "a fear-and-surprise-mixed voice" (p. 66) from *yé ọ̀wẹ̀ị má tàmàmáa mọ̀ gụ̀ánìmì ókólo* (thing fear and surprise with mixed voice) (Zabus, *African Palimpsest*, p. 125).

"Inside," one of Okara's most innovative concepts in *The Voice*, not only harks back to the Ijọ *biri*, meaning "the inner hall of a man's integrity wherein he judges and is judged" (Fraser, p. 190) and connoting "soul" or "spirit" (Ravenscroft, p. 16). It also derives from Hopkins' concept of "inscape," which "stands for any kind of formed or focused view, any pattern discerned in the natural world. . . . [ranging] from sense-perceived pattern to inner form" (p. 171). According to Vincent, Okara conceived of it as "the invisible shape of things"—or, as he put it in an interview, "the essence of man, tree or mountain" (Zabus, p. 103). "Inscape" itself was derived from the medieval philosopher John

Duns Scotus' notion of "thisness," the peculiar integral form that, he believed, inhabited every distinctive individual body: "a *haecceitas*, or thisness, as well as a generic *quidditas*, or whatness" (Warren, p. 170).

The double and triple coinages that abound in *The Voice* and were already observable in Okara's poetry may be traced not only to Ijọ but also to the influence of Hopkins, who himself had, according to Emeka Okeke-Ezigbo, "studied Welsh poetry, where the devices of alliteration, internal rhyme, and assonance constitute the system known as *cynghanedd*" (p. 121). Possibly Ijọ is in the English text the way Latin or Anglo-Saxon was in Hopkins' poetry. Yet, of course, whereas Latin and Old English are extinct, Ijọ is alive and thriving as the fourth registered language in Nigeria after Yoruba, Hausa, and Igbo (excepting the official language, English, and Arabic).

These coinages may in fact reflect an earlier and "purer" English in that they obliquely refer to the way Old English or Anglo-Saxon might have developed without the Roman conquest, presumably by compounding. For instance, according to Richard C. Trench, "redemption" might have been called "again-buying" (Warren, p. 174). According to another theory, put forth by William Barnes, which argues that the Old English stock is still capable of extension by compounding, we should be saying "sunprint" or "flameprint" instead of "photograph"; "inwoning" and "outwoning" instead of "subjective" and "objective" (Warren, pp. 174–175). These theories from Trench and Barnes had a tremendous impact on Hopkins' compounding method. Some of the movements and organizations in which Hopkins participated and with which he wrestled—such as fin-de-siècle linguistic renovation, England, and the Roman Catholic Church—are the same ones with which Okara had to come to terms almost a century later, and in an equally colonized context. But the similarity ends there. Ironically, whereas Hopkins probably indulged in compounding in an attempt to restore to the English language some alleged Anglo-Saxon impetus it had once possessed, Okara's not-so-hidden agenda is to bend English to suit his poetic disposition and his Ijọ temperament. This enterprise is also likely to enrich English, and it points to the double-edged subversiveness of linguistic experimentation within the larger project of decolonizing language.

Although Okara has been described as a "natural poet," he has also been called, and not necessarily by his detractors, the most artificial of all West African novelists. Both his art and his artifice are permeated with indigenous rhetoric such as rules of address; proverbs; the hyperbolic statements characteristic of the *copia* ("flow" or "abundance" in Latin) of oral narrative and, incidentally, of drum language; the formulaic content (to help recall) of oral performance; the ample use of eulogies or praise-names, such as "*unless-you-provoke-me!*" and "*he-who-keeps-my-head-under-water*" (*Voice*, pp. 98–99), meant to extol heroes in epic poetry.

Inherent in Ijọ (and most sub-Saharan African languages) is reification, the conversion of a person or an abstract concept into a "thing" or, as Emmanuel Ngara puts it, the "concretization of insubstantial things [as in] 'two chunks of darkness'" (p. 46). Okolo's confusion of mind is therefore given the quality of "thingness" and is likened to a "room with chairs, cushions, papers scattered all over the floor by thieves" (*Voice*, p. 76).

Word repetition is a recurrent device in some of Okara's poems—for instance, "drooping" in "Metaphor of a War" (in "Three Poems," in *Okike*, September 1982) and variations of "dance" in "The Dancer" (also in "Three Poems") and of "press" in "Silent Girl." In *The Voice*, repetition in "Izongo laughed a laugh" (p. 35), "the black black night" (p. 76), and "the cold cold floor" (p. 27) harks back to most West African languages, as well as to pidgin and creole variants. But when Okara writes about the "frustrated eyes, ground-looking eyes, harlots' eyes, nothing-looking eyes, hot eyes, cold eyes . . . " (p. 80), he is doing more than just using the inner resources of the Ijọ language; he is resorting to a highly developed feature in traditional oral narrative that is always accompanied by the storyteller's voice modulations, tonal punnings, facial contortions, and flamboyant gestures.

More particularly, Okara is using epistrophe by ending sentences or clauses with the same word; and anaphora by repeating the word or phrase in successive clauses, as in "Okolo ran. Okolo ran." Such a reiterative technique, derived in part from the use of repetition in the Bible, is also used in the black church sermon and in jazz improvisation. Generally, such discourse (musical or verbal) draws attention to its repetition and exploits repetition as a structural and rhythmic principle.

Linguistic Experimentation in the African Context

Such a degree of language experimentation as Okara's has to be set against various rhetorics worldwide but also in the larger context of the debate that originated at the first conference of African writers held at Makerere University in Kampala, Uganda, in June 1962—which, to Kenyan writer Ngũgĩ wa Thiong'o's astonishment, did not feature the greatest living Africans writing in Swahili (Shaaban Robert) and Yoruba (D. O. Fagunwa) (p. 6). Indeed, the conference concerned the African writer's use of English as a literary medium.

Recalling the occasion, Okara distinguishes three schools of thought: the neometropolitans, who hold that an African writer should write in the former colonizer's language and even surpass it; the rejectionists, who, like Ngũgĩ, said farewell to English to embrace Gĩkũyũ (or Kikuyu) and KiSwahili, arguing that by rejecting the European languages, they were eradicating cultural imperialism from the continent of Africa; and the evolutionists/experimenters, who are engaged in "the continuing quest, through experimentation, for a mode of employing the English language, which we have appropriated, to give full expression to our culture" ("Towards the Evolution," p. 16). Okara proclaims that he and Chinua Achebe belong to the third school, because of their attempts to "emulsify English with the patterns, modes and idioms of African speech until it becomes so attenuated that it bears little resemblance to the original" (p. 17).

John Pepper Clark has talked about the experiment as "a kind of blood transfusion, reviving the English language by the living adaptable properties of some African language" (p. 37); yet he urges transfusion as opposed to a surgical transplantation like Okara's. Conversely, Ngũgĩ has taken Achebe, Tutuola, and Okara to task for injecting "black blood" into the foreign language's rusty joints (p. 7). Of Okara, he says: "Why not make literary monuments in our own languages? Why in other words should Okara not sweat it out to create Ijaw, which he acknowledges to have depths of philosophy and a wide range of ideas and experiences" (p. 8).

At first considered as being in a line of development from Tutuola's books, *The Voice* entered a phase of mixed reception. Emmanuel Ngara deemed it a stylistic dead end that does not hold "a great promise for the future" (p. 57). Even Chinweizu, the virulent "Afrocentric" critic, deemed *The Voice* a failure, whereas the structuralist critic Sunday Anozie saw it as "the Swan song of the Period of Romanticism" (1970, p. 12).

The "post-Romantic" period proved Anozie right, for parabolic approaches to the Nigerian novel since the mid 1960s have been few and far between. Writers have been eschewing private visions like Okara's and moving toward embracing politics along more realistic lines. *The Voice* is now perceived not only as the messianic vision of "an older generation" (the realistic counterpart being Aluko's urban fiction) but also as an unprecedented attempt at revamping colonial attitudes toward the dominant language.

TWICE-TOLD TALES

For Achebe's notion of "the novelist as teacher," one could substitute "the poet as teacher" or, more accurately in the case of Okara, "the storyteller as teacher." Okara is a natural oral performer, and although the itinerant storytellers of yore are no more, he has taken it upon himself to tell stories, especially those that translate Ijọ myths and legends, as in "Ogboinba," the Ijọ creation myth (1958). When he was commissioned by the government, later in his career, to write books for children, he gleefully took up the offer because, he said in an interview, "the thought of writing for children has always been with me" (interview by Zabus, p. 101). The "folk tale for children," as *Little Snake and Little Frog* is subtitled, came out in 1982, the same year as *Juju Island: Fiction for Teenagers*, which was followed by *Christmas Twins & Tonye and the King Fish.*

The story that most appeals to Okara, and that he most often tells the children when he goes back to his native village, is the story of Tortoise, an ancient-looking living fossil who, because of his weakness and slow demeanor, was "invested with intelligence, wisdom and tricks which Man has thought out as weapons to get out of tight situations" (interview by Zabus, p. 108). The tale of Tortoise is, of course, part of the corpus of southern Nigerian (principally Igbo, Efik, Ijọ, and Yoruba) mythical tales and legends, and the wily Tortoise pops up in many proverbs. Yet what concerns Okara most is the sequel to the tale: after using Tortoise to try out his ideas of survival without physical force, Man "returned him [Tortoise] to his pristine state as an ordinary animal" (interview by Zabus, p. 109). In a larger context, Okara identifies the "Tortoise stage" in the history of humankind as "the period when Man has settled in farming groups. They had more leisure perhaps to be able to talk about their wars and things like that, as we tell stories in the evening" (interview by Zabus, p. 107).

These tales should not be confused with the early short stories Okara wrote for *Black Orpheus*, such as "The Crooks," which opposes the town dwellers' cunning to that of scruffy-looking rustics who turn out to be as much crooks as the Lagos rogues. Unlike these stories meant for an adult readership, Okara's tales are part of Nigerian juvenilia, along with Cyprian Ekwensi's *The Drummer Boy* (1960), *The Passport of Mallam Ilia* (1960), and *An African Night's Entertainment* (1962); Onuora Nzekwu and Michael Crowder's *Eze Goes to School* (1963); and Nkem Nwankwo's *Tales out of School* (1964). The collection that comes closest to Okara's production for young people is *Twilight and the Tortoise* (1963), by Yoruba writer Kunle Akinsemoyin, which features Tortoise as a thinker but also, as is often the case in tales explaining the origins of things, as a cunning thief who once was outwitted and, out of shame, has been hiding his face ever since.

Okara told such tales in English on television and in Ijọ in the village. He is therefore participating in two types of orality: a primary orality in that, during village storytelling sessions, he tells a story as it was told when oral culture was untouched by western-oriented writing or print, thereby preserving an oral economy of thought and indirectly teaching the children ways of acquiring, formulating, storing, and retrieving knowledge; and a secondary orality, the electronic orality of present-day Nigeria's technological culture, as it is implemented by telephone, radio, and, most important, television.

Whatever means Okara uses to convey his stories, the "voice" during a storytelling session in the village or on television is a "teaching voice" like that of the Fisherman in his "Invocation." And it teaches the "Child-

Front" of postindependence Nigeria about both the past and the future. Okara's voice will carry beyond the "waves" of radio-television and the Niger Delta. It is a voice that, unlike Okolo's voice, will not be committed to the silence of the river.

Selected Bibliography

POETRY

"The Mystic Drum." In Gerald Moore and Ulli Beier, eds., *Modern Poetry from Africa.* Harmondsworth, U.K.: Penguin, 1963.

The Fisherman's Invocation. London: Heinemann Educational Books, 1978; Benin City, Nigeria: Ethiope, 1978.

"Three Poems." In *Okike,* no. 22 (September 1982).

Ten poems in *Black Orpheus* 5, no. 1 (1983).

NOVEL

The Voice. London: André Deutsch, 1964; London: Heinemann Education Books, 1969, 1970; New York: Africana, 1970, 1986.

SHORT STORIES AND ESSAYS

"Ogboinba: Ijaw Creation Myth." In *Black Orpheus,* no. 2 (January 1958).

"The Crooks." In *Black Orpheus,* no. 8 (1960).

"African Speech, English Words." In *Transition* 3 (1963). Repr. in G. D. Killam, *African Writers on African Writing.* Evanston, Ill.: Northwestern University Press, 1973.

"Tubi." In *Flamingo* 4, no. 1 (1964).

"Poetry and Oral English." In *Journal of the Nigerian English Studies Association* 8 (May 1976).

"Towards the Evolution of an African Language for African Literature." In *Kunapipi* 12, no. 2 (1990).

CHILDREN'S LITERATURE

Juju Island: Fiction for Teenagers. Port Harcourt, Nigeria: Macmillan, 1982. Repr. as *An Adventure to Juju Island.* Lagos, Nigeria: Heinemann Educational Books, 1992.

Little Snake and Little Frog: Folk Tale for Children. Port Harcourt, Nigeria: Macmillan, 1982. Repr. Lagos, Nigeria: Heinemann Educational Books, 1992.

Christmas Twins & Tonye and the King Fish. Port Harcourt, Nigeria: Macmillan, n.d.

INTERVIEWS

Lindfors, Bernth, ed. *Dem-Say: Interviews with Eight Nigerian Writers.* Austin, Tex.: African and Afro-American Studies and Research Center, 1974.

Wren, Robert, "Interview of Gabriel Okara." In *African Literature Association Bulletin* 17 (summer 1991).

Zabus, Chantal. "Of Tortoise, Man, and Languages." In Holger G. Ehling, ed., *Critical Approaches to* Anthills of the Savannah. No. 8 of the Matatu series. Amsterdam, Netherlands, and Atlanta, Ga.: Rodopi, 1991.

CRITICAL STUDIES

Anozie, Sunday O. "The Theme of Alienation and Commitment in Okara's *The Voice.*" In *Bulletin of the Association for African Literature in English,* no. 3 (1965).

———. "The Problem of Communication in Two West African Novels." In *Conch* 2, no. 1 (1970).

Asein, Samuel O. "The Significance of Gabriel Okara as Poet." In *New Literature Review* 11 (November 1982).

Ashaolu, Albert Olu. "A Voice in the Wilderness: The Predicament of the Social Reformer in Okara's *The Voice.*" In *International Fiction Review* 6 (summer 1978).

Beckmann, Susan. "Gabriel Okara: *The Fisherman's Invocation.*" In *World Literature Written in English* 20 (fall 1981). A review.

Booth, James. *Writers and Politics in Nigeria.* New York: Africana, 1981.

Burness, Donald. "Stylistic Innovations and the Rhythm of African Life in Okara's *The Voice.*" In *Journal of the New African Literature and the Arts,* no. 13–14 (1972).

Chinweizu, Jemie Onwuchekwa, and Ihechukwu Madubuike. *Toward the Decolonization of Afri-*

can Literature. Enugu, Nigeria: Fourth Dimension Publishers, 1980; Washington, D.C.: Howard University Press, 1983.

Clark, John Pepper. *The Example of Shakespeare.* London: Longman, 1970.

Echeruo, Michael J. C. "Gabriel Okara at Seventy: A Poet and His Seasons." In *African Literature Association Bulletin* 17 (summer 1991). Repr. in *World Literature Today* 66 (summer 1992).

Egudu, Romanus N. "A Study of Five of Gabriel Okara's Poems." In *Okike*, no. 13 (1978).

Fraser, Robert. *West African Poetry: A Critical History.* Cambridge, U.K.: Cambridge University Press, 1986.

Gingell, S. A. "His River's Complex Course: Reflections on Past, Present, and Future in the Poetry of Gabriel Okara." In *World Literature Written in English* 23, no. 2 (spring 1984).

Goodwin, Kenneth L. "Gabriel Okara." In his *Understanding African Poetry: A Study of Ten Poets.* London: Heinemann, 1982.

Iyasere, Solomon O. "Oral Tradition in the Criticism of African Literature." In *Journal of Modern African Studies* 14, no. 2 (1976).

———. "Narrative Techniques in Okara's *The Voice.*" In *African Literature Today* 12 (1982).

Killam, G. D. *African Writers on African Writing.* Evanston, Ill.: Northwestern University Press, 1973.

King, Bruce. "The Poetry of Gabriel Okara." In *Chandrabhàgà* 2 (1978).

———, ed. *Introduction to Nigerian Literature.* New York: Africana, 1972.

Kirpal, Viney. "The Structure of the Modern Nigerian Novel and the National Consciousness." In *Modern Fiction Studies* 34 (spring 1988).

Lindfors, Bernth. "Gabriel Okara: The Poet as Novelist." In *Pan-African Journal* 4 (fall 1971).

Macmillan, M. "Language and Change." In *Journal of Commonwealth Literature* no. 1 (September 1965). A review.

Maduakor, Obi. "Gabriel Okara: Poet of the Mystic Inside." In *World Literature Today* 61 (winter 1987).

Mamudu, Ayo. "Okara's Poetic Landscape." In *Commonwealth: Essays and Studies* 10 (fall 1987).

Moore, Gerald. "Dirges of the Delta." In *Afriscope* 10, no. 11 (1980).

———, ed. *African Literature and the Universities.* Ibadan, Nigeria: Ibadan University Press, 1965.

Ngara, Emmanuel. *Stylistic Criticism and the African Novel: A Study of the Language, Art, and Content of African Fiction.* London: Heinemann, 1982.

Ngũgĩ wa Thiong'o. "The Language of African Literature." In his *Decolonising the Mind: The Politics of Language in African Literature.* London: James Currey, 1986; Portsmouth, N.H.: Heinemann, 1986.

Obiechina, Emmanuel N. "Art and Artifice in Okara's *The Voice.*" In *Okike* 1 (September 1972).

———. "Language." In his *Culture, Tradition, and Society in the West African Novel.* Cambridge, U.K.: Cambridge University Press, 1975.

Okeke-Ezigbo, Emeka. "The 'Sharp and Sided Hail': Hopkins and His Nigerian Imitators and Detractors." In Richard F. Giles, ed., *Hopkins Among Poets: Studies in Modern Response to Gerard Manley Hopkins.* Hamilton, Canada: International Hopkins Association, 1985.

Okpaku, Joseph, ed. *New African Literature and the Arts.* Vol. 1. New York: Crowell, 1970.

Palmer, Eustace. *An Introduction to the African Novel.* London: Heinemann, 1972; New York: Africana, 1972.

Petersen, Kirsten Holst. "Heterogeneous Worlds Yoked Violently Together: The Commonwealth Poetry Prize." In *Kunapipi* 1, no. 2 (1979).

Ravenscroft, Arthur. "Introduction." In Okara's *The Voice.* London: Heinemann Educational Books, 1969, 1970; New York: Africana, 1970, 1986.

Roscoe, Adrian A. "Okara's Unheeded Voice: Explication and Defense." In *Busara* 2, no. 1 (1969).

———. *Mother Is Gold: A Study in West African Literature.* Cambridge, U.K.: Cambridge University Press, 1971.

Scott, Patrick. "The Older Generation: T. M. Aluko and Gabriel Okara." In Albert S. Gérard, ed., *European-Language Writing in Sub-Saharan Africa.* Vol. 2. Budapest, Hungary: Akadémiai Kiadó, 1986.

———. "Gabriel Okara's *The Voice*: The Non-Ijo Reader and the Pragmatics of Translingualism." In *Research in African Literatures* 21 (fall 1990).

Senanu, K. E., and Theophilus Vincent, eds. *A Selection of African Poetry.* London: Longman, 1976.

Taiwo, Oladele. *Culture and the Nigerian Novel.* New York: St. Martin's Press, 1976.

Vincent, Theophilus. "Introduction." In Okara's *The Fisherman's Invocation.* London: Heinemann Educational Books, 1978; Benin City, Nigeria: Ethiope, 1978.

Warren, Austin. "Instress of Inscape." In Geoffrey H. Hartman, ed., *Hopkins: A Collection of Critical Essays.* Englewood Cliffs, N.J.: Prentice-Hall, 1966.

Webb, Hugh. "Allegory: Okara's *The Voice.*" In *English in Africa* 5 (September 1978).

Williams, Katherine. "Decolonizing the Word: Language, Culture, and Self in the Works of Ngũgĩ wa Thiong'o and Gabriel Okara." In *Research in African Literatures* 22 (winter 1991).

Wright, Derek. "Ritual and Reality in Four African Novelists." In *Literary Criterion* 21, no. 3 (1986).

———. "Ritual and Reality in the Novels of Wole Soyinka, Gabriel Okara, and Kofi Awoonor." In *Kunapipi* 9, no. 1 (1987).

Wright, Edgar, ed. *The Critical Evaluation of African Literature.* London: Heinemann, 1973.

Zabus, Chantal. "Gabriel Okara." In Hans Bertens, Theo D'Haen, Joris Duytschaver, and Richard Todd, eds. *Post-War Literatures in English.* Alphen, Netherlands: Samson, 1989.

———. "Under the Palimpsest and Beyond: The 'Original' in the West African Europhone Novel." In Geoffrey V. Davis and Hena Maes-Jelinek, eds., *Crisis and Creativity in the New Literatures in English.* Amsterdam, Netherlands: Rodopi, 1989.

———. "Linguistic Guerilla in the Maghrebian and West African Europhone Novel." In *Africana Journal* 15 (1990). Repr. in Clarisse Zimra, Jonathan Ngate, and Kenneth Harrow, eds., *Criss-Crossing Boundaries in African Literatures.* 1986 annual selected papers of the African Literature Association. Washington, D.C.: Three Continents Press, 1991.

———. *The African Palimpsest: Indigenization of Language in the West African Europhone Novel.* Amsterdam, Netherlands, and Atlanta, Ga.: Rodopi, 1991.

Christopher Okigbo
1932–1967

FUNSO AIYEJINA

CHRISTOPHER Ifeanyichukwu Okigbo was born 16 August 1932 in Ojoto, a small forest village some ten miles from Onitsha—the legendary home of the Onitsha market literature—located on the eastern bank of the Niger River in the Eastern Region of Nigeria. Like most educated Igbo families at that time, Okigbo's family had converted to Catholicism. (The Igbo, or Ibo, are one of three major ethnic groups in Nigeria, the other two being the Yoruba and the Hausa.) His father, James I. Okigbo, taught at several primary schools within the heartland of the Igbo area as well as at Asaba, on the western bank of the Niger; his mother was Anna Onugwalobi. The fourth of five children, Okigbo received his primary education at Umolobia Catholic School, where his father taught. As a teacher's son, he experienced both the westernized life of the mission compound where he lived and the vibrant rituals and festivals of the village.

Okigbo was, by most accounts, precocious and hyperactive, and something of a truant, preferring outdoor activities to schoolwork. Nonetheless, he excelled in both sports and academic work, in 1945 passing the competitive examination to enter Government College, Umuahia, then the most prestigious secondary school in Eastern Nigeria.

At Umuahia, where he was a classmate of Vincent Chukwuemeka Ike and two years behind Chinua Achebe, both of whom went on to become novelists, Okigbo was a compulsive reader. He developed an interest in music, mathematics, literature, and Latin, and also became an outstanding athlete, excelling in soccer and cricket. He passed the Cambridge standardized high school exams with distinctions in most of his favorite subjects. Of the fourteen students from his class who took the university entrance examination in March 1950, he was one of the ten to pass and be admitted to the University College, Ibadan, then the only university in Nigeria. (It is now the University of Ibadan.)

In 1951, Okigbo entered Ibadan to study medicine. Like Achebe before him, he changed his discipline after the first year, opting to major in classics. He graduated in 1956 with a bachelor of arts and third-class honors in Latin after repeating a year, having missed part of his degree examination in 1955 because he was more interested in pursuing an absorbing interest, most likely romantic, out of town. While at Ibadan, he continued to distinguish himself in sports and in music. He accompanied the dramatist Wole Soyinka on the piano in his first public appearance as a singer.

After graduating, Okigbo worked briefly for the Nigerian Tobacco Company and the United Africa Company, as private secretary to the federal minister of research and information in Lagos (1956–1958); as a teacher at Fiditi Grammar (Secondary) School, Fiditi (1958–1960), and as the acting university librarian at the University of Nigeria, Nsukka (October 1960–1962). Getting the job at Nsukka is an example of Okigbo's daring spirit. When he announced that he was going to interview for the job, a friend and professional librarian is reported to have been scandalized. Reminded that he had no background in librarianship, Okigbo announced that he had bought a book on the subject and was going to read it during the journey to the interview. He read the book and got the job.

At Nsukka, Okigbo was part of a new university in a newly (1960) independent country. He found Nsukka's idyllic rural setting, the availability of books, and the presence of writers and critics at the university ideal for his development as a poet. There were regular debates and discussions about the craft of poetry. Away from the university, Okigbo interacted with the local people, absorbing their festivals, folklore, and philosophy. He showed particular interest in the music and poetry of the masquerade cult. His subsequent affirmation of poetry as a ritual conforms with the ritual role of the poetry he experienced as a young boy in his home village of Ojoto and as an adult living at Nsukka with its vibrant poetic culture. His "Lament of the Lavender Mist," one of the "Four Canzones" (1962; *Collected Poems*, 1986), betrays the influence of the kind of poetry and music to which he was exposed at Nsukka.

In 1962, Okigbo left Nsukka to join Cambridge University Press at Ibadan as their West African representative. While Nsukka had provided Okigbo with the ideal environment for developing intellectually as a poet, Ibadan, as the political hub of Western Nigeria, provided him with the opportunity to experience an atmosphere that was politically as well as creatively charged. In the words of O. R. Dathorne, Ibadan in the early 1960s was

> alive and exciting; everybody was there. Ulli Beier was very much the godfather of some very ungodly wards. So much was beginning to happen. Wole Soyinka after being launched by Mbari had his MSS accepted by the Oxford Press. Then Andre Deutsch had encouraged him to complete *The Interpreters.* J. P. Clark was writing his early verse and was shortly to go to Princeton and return sooner than expected to write *America, Their America.* Demas Nwoko had begun his famous black Adam and Eve sculptures. Everybody fought with everyone else. In this environment I met Christopher Okigbo....
>
> ...When everyone did meet in Clark's flat just under mine, J. P. talked J. P., Okigbo talked Okigbo; Soyinka refrained, saying that it was a mutual admiration society. But everybody wrote.
>
> ("African Literature IV," p. 79)

While the writers wrote, the political temperature of independent Nigeria was rising dangerously, forcing the private Okigbo to begin to write more about public and political issues. Of the poems of this period, *Limits* (1964), *Distances* (1964), and *Path of Thunder* (1968) are undoubtedly his most public-spirited poems. Stylistically, the influence of Yoruba poetry, especially the *oriki* (praise poem), is evident in these poems. Many of the lines in "Lament of the Masks" (1965), a memorial poem to William Butler Yeats, echo lines from a traditional praise poem to the Timi of Ede.

Okigbo, an Igbo Catholic, married across ethnic and religious lines, just as he had made friends across those lines. In 1963, he married Safinat, daughter of the *attah* of Igbirra, a prominent Muslim king from Northern Nigeria. The marriage was unhappy, and they never lived together for any length of time. In 1966, he divorced his wife by means of a phone call. On the evidence of his dedication of *Labyrinths* (1971) to her and their daughter, Ibrahimat, Okigbo seemingly continued to adore her despite their inability to make the marriage work.

Okigbo was in the process of leaving Cambridge University Press to join an Italian contract financier in Lagos when the political turmoil in Nigeria came to a head in 1966. He was forced to join the exodus of the Igbo to Eastern Nigeria, away from the systematic slaughter unleashed on them in retaliation for the bungled coup d'état of 15 January 1966. Only non-Igbo political and military leaders had been executed in the coup, which was masterminded by a predominantly Igbo group of young military officers.

Back in Enugu, Okigbo teamed up with Chinua Achebe to set up a publishing house, Citadel Press, with the major aim of encouraging the production of children's literature. Following the declaration of independence by the Eastern Region as the new Republic of Biafra and the outbreak of war between Biafra and the federal government of Nigeria, Okigbo, without any military training, volunteered for the Biafran army and was commissioned as a major. In August 1967, during one of the first battles of the war, Okigbo was killed defending one of the approaches to Nsukka, the university town where his creative genius had blossomed.

Okigbo participated in most of the major literary ventures that helped to nurture the birth and development of African literature. Most Nigerian writers of his generation either collaborated with him to create an ideal literary climate or were beneficiaries of some of the structures he was instrumental in creating. At Nsukka, he was the moving spirit behind the formation of the short-lived African Authors Association; at Ibadan, he was an active member of Mbari, the writers' and artists' club whose magazine *Black Orpheus* was the medium in which many Nigerian and African writers were first published. Okigbo was also the West African editor of *Transition* (*Chin'daba*), which long functioned as the authoritative African journal of ideas.

Okigbo's generosity and hospitality knew no bounds. At both Nsukka and Ibadan, he kept an open house to which many aspiring writers flocked for inspiration and encouragement. "His vibrancy and heightened sense of life," affirms Achebe in his preface to *Don't Let Him Die,* "touched everyone he came into contact with." He had "a gift for fellowship" and was "greedy for friendship as indeed he was for all experience, for risk and danger.... He relished challenges and the more unusual or difficult the better" (1978, p. vii). Okigbo's most enduring memorial, however, is his multivocal, multilayered, and imagistic poetry, which continues to challenge critics and inspire poets.

EARLY POETRY AND PHILOSOPHY

Okigbo's poetry is autobiographical, religious, political, imagistic, and mythopoeic. He started his poetic career disdaining the practice of categorizing writers by race or region. He wanted to be a poet, not an African poet. In addition, he felt he was a poet's poet, refusing at the first Conference of African Writers of English Expression at Makerere University in Kampala, Uganda, in June 1962 to read his poems because the audience was made up of nonpoets. Okigbo envisioned poetry as a means for self-expression, for projecting the many moods of the inner self, and as a record of inner conflict within the context of the dynamics of rituals and myths. He embraced the "old classics" with the same passion he did the "new greats." He read and was influenced by Ovid, Catullus, Horace, Virgil, Tacitus, Aristophanes, Aeschylus, Sophocles, Aristotle, John Keats, Samuel Taylor Coleridge, Robert Browning, T. S. Eliot, Ezra Pound, and Allen Ginsberg of the Beat Generation in the United States.

In consonance with his notion of the purity of poetry, he rejected the first prize awarded to his *Limits* at the First Negro Festival of Arts held in Dakar, Senegal, in 1966. Unknown to Okigbo, the American writer Langston Hughes, who had been impressed by the quality of *Limits*, had submitted it for the poetry competition at the festival. Okigbo confided in a letter to Sunday Anozie, his literary biographer:

> I found the whole idea of a negro arts festival based on colour quite absurd. I did not enter any work either for the competition, and was most surprised when I heard a prize had been awarded to LIMITS. I have written to reject it.
> (1972, p. 21)

In the light of Okigbo's philosophy of poetry, he consciously borrowed from whatever sources appealed to him, regardless of time, region, or race. His style is therefore highly eclectic.

Although Okigbo started writing actively after graduating from Ibadan in 1956, it was not until 1958 that he realized that he had an abiding passion for poetry and that poetry would be the means by which he would perform his traditional religious obligations as the reincarnation of, and successor to, his maternal grandfather, the priest of Idoto, the river goddess of his home village. In a 1965 interview with Marjory Whitelaw, Okigbo revealed that his creative activity was one way of performing his priestly functions: "Every time I write a poem, I am in fact offering a sacrifice. My *Heavensgate* is in fact a huge sacrifice" (p. 36).

Okigbo's earliest poems, all included in *Collected Poems*, are "On the New Year" (1958–1959), "Moonglow" (1960), "Love Apart" (1962), and "Four Canzones" (1962). (The four canzones—lyric poems often set to music—are "Song of the Forest," "Debtor's Lane," "Lament of the Flutes," and "Lament of the Lavender Mist.") The major strain running through these apprentice poems is the poet's lament of his exile from his idyllic rural origins, and his unease at the clangor and "endless succession / of tempers and moods" of high society in urban centers like Lagos ("Debtor's Lane," p. 9; all page citations for Okigbo's poetry refer to *Collected Poems*). Okigbo's celebration of the "fruitful fields" ("Song of the Forest," p. 8) of the rural area echoes the Négritude philosophy, with its almost exclusive celebration of blackness, and anticipates his protagonist's ultimate return to Idoto, as village and as an indigenous philosophy, in his first major poem sequence—*Heavensgate* (1962)—and his subsequent poetry.

In addition to the theme of return to origin and tradition implicit in these early poems, they also signify the nature of Okigbo's poetics, especially as an eclectic stylist. They reveal his classical education, his African literary and philosophical heritage, and his range of reading of both the classical and the modern poetry. For example, "Song of the Forest" is based on the first verse of Virgil's First Eclogue, "Tityrus," and "Debtor's Lane" is suffused with echoes of T. S. Eliot's *The Hollow Men.* But, although the poems echo works by writers as diverse as Miguel Hernández, T. S. Eliot, and Virgil, the lyrical lament and liturgical strain that are hallmarks of Okigbo's mature poetry are already evident in the following lines from "Lament of the Lavender Mist":

> AND SHE took me to the river
> Believing me a child—
>   Spirit of the wind and the waves—
> offering me love in a
> Feeding bottle—
>   Kernels of the water of the sky—
> And she led me by the water
> Believing me a child—
>   Echoes of the waters of the beginning—
> But the outstretched love
> Dried as it reached me—
>   Shadows of the fires of the end.
> (p. 14)

Okigbo's choice of the instruments to which the canzones should be performed (drums; *ogene*, a hollow metal gong; and flutes) is evidence of his commitment to the African heritage and environment even while he borrowed freely from other cultures. This confirms his assertion to Robert Serumaga: "I belong, integrally, to my own society just as, I believe, I belong also integrally to some societies other than my own" (p. 144).

HEAVENSGATE: PORTRAIT OF THE POET AS A YOUNG BOY

Heavensgate is explicitly autobiographical. In this volume, Okigbo reveals the nature of his formal and informal education, recalls people from his childhood who had impacted on his consciousness, and commits himself as poet-priest to the services of mother Idoto, the river goddess as well as the village stream from which he drank and in which he washed as a child. According to Okigbo in the introduction to *Labyrinths*, the personage of this poem, who is like Orpheus, is about to begin a journey of self-discovery and self-realization, and must submit himself to the cleansing powers of the water spirit that nurtures all creation.

Heavensgate opens as the celebrant returns to source for purification; he is contrite and repentant as he pleads for acceptance:

> BEFORE YOU, mother Idoto,
>   naked I stand;
> before your watery presence,
>   a prodigal
>
> leaning on an oilbean,
> lost in your legend.
>
> Under your power wait I
>   on barefoot,
> watchman for the watchword
>   at *Heavensgate*;
>
> out of the depths my cry:
> give ear and hearken . . .
>   ("The Passage," p. 19)

The celebrant is humbled by the awe-inspiring power of Idoto, and his cry for help and acceptance, like that of David in Psalm 130, is out of the depth of his being. The conflation of traditional and foreign images and references in the poem is an indication of the cosmopolitan and eclectic psychological makeup of the poet-protagonist. As Okigbo was quick to affirm: "I do not feel that in fact as a Christian I have ever been uprooted from my own village gods. . . . I believe in fact all these gods are the same as the Christian God—that they are different aspects of the same power, the same force" (interview by Whitelaw, p. 30).

The rest of *Heavensgate* reveals the process by which Okigbo's cosmopolitan and holistic intelligence was created. Okigbo takes us back to the "dark waters of the beginning" and the introduction of light, by God, to give form to the formless. In "The Passage" the same light is also presented as a hint of the future destruction of the world by fire:

> Rays, violet and short, piercing the gloom,
> foreshadow the fire that is dreamed of.
>
> Rainbow on far side, arched like boa bent to
>   kill,
> foreshadows the rain that is dreamed of.
>   (p. 20)

Lines like the above derive their power from their suggestiveness and the multiplicity of meanings inherent in them. Although they clearly intimate the biblical story of the creation, the Flood, and the promise of Armageddon, they also recall African myths, especially those linking the rainbow and the boa. The rainbow is linked to the boa in Igbo mythology as a premonition of some mysterious event, especially death. Among the Yoruba, the rainbow is the sign that the boa has excreted; whoever gets a piece of the excrement will become wealthy. In Ghana, the rainbow is seen as the result of the communion between the sun and the moon. The density of meaning in Okigbo's poetry often derives from such multivalent images and references.

If Okigbo's poetry is multivalent and multivocal, it is probably because of the complexity of his task, which involves having to reconcile contrasting and antagonistic traditions. He has "to tell / the tangled-wood-tale" (the cross of Christianity) and to "mourn / a mother on a spray" (the dying African tradition). It is a situation as nebulous as the "Rain and sun in single combat" ("The Passage," p. 20).

In "Initiations," the second fragment of *Heavensgate*, Okigbo focuses attention on education, both formal and informal. The formal is represented by Christianity, envisioned in violent images ("SCAR OF the crucifix / over the breast, / by red blade inflicted. . . ."; p. 22) and concretized in the person of Kepkanly, the mythologized version of the drillmaster from Okigbo's school days. Okigbo's suspicion of Christian ethics, in part a consequence of the violence with which it was inflicted on him, is implied in his presentation of John the Baptist, the forerunner of Jesus Christ:

> so comes John the Baptist
> with bowl of salt water
> preaching the gambit:
> life without sin, without
>
> life; which accepted,
> way leads downward
> down orthocenter
> avoiding decisions.
> (p. 22)

While Kepkanly drills colonial ideas into the poet-protagonist and John the Baptist attempts to convert him into a nonthinking disciple, Jadum (a half-demented village minstrel) and Upandru (a village explainer and wisecracker) present him with an alternative philosophy—a traditional African philosophy:

> AND THIS from Jadum,
> . . .
> Do not wander in speargrass,
> After the lights,
> Probing lairs in stockings,
> To roast
> The viper alive, with dog lying
> Upsidedown in the crooked passage . . .
> Do not listen at keyholes,
> After the lights,
> To smell from other rooms,
> After the lights—
> . . .
> AND THIS from Upandru:
>
> Screen your bedchamber thoughts
> with sun-glasses,
> who could jump your eye,
> your mind-window,
>
> And I said:
> The prophet only the poet.
> And he said: Logistics.
> (Which is what poetry is) . . .
> (pp. 24–25)

In his contacts with Kepkanly and John the Baptist, the poet is treated as a mere receptacle. By contrast, he is an active participant in the informal educational process of the village. He can engage in banter with Upandru. Little wonder, then, that he ultimately opts to seek and embrace mother Idoto, the icon of the village tradition, in "Watermaid," the third fragment. The poet-protagonist's vigil pays off as mother Idoto appears to him in all her glory "with the armpit-dazzle of a lioness, / . . . wearing white light about her" (p. 27); she is escorted by the waves and crowned with moonlight. Yet this manifestation is very brief, leaving the poet-protagonist abandoned and disappointed, but determined to purify himself further to prepare for her future manifestations. The additional ritual cleansing in "Lustra," the fourth fragment of *Heavensgate*, pays off in "Newcomer," the fifth fragment, where there is a minor manifestation of mother Idoto in the guise of Georgette, the poet's niece, whose birth is celebrated in this final movement of the poem.

Essentially, *Heavensgate* presents poetry as a record of an intelligence engaged in a multipronged, multilayered, and cross-cultural spiritual quest. It is Okigbo's offering to the divine essence of Idoto, his muse-elect.

LIMITS: THE PERSONAL INTO THE PUBLIC

The protagonist's personal search for salvation and his desire to be accepted by mother Idoto that started in *Heavensgate* continue in "Siren Limits," the first part of *Limits*. But in the second part, "Fragments out of the Deluge," the search is no longer private and individualistic; the focus has widened to embrace a communal search for fulfillment.

"Siren Limits" opens with the image of a vociferous and confident protagonist (weaverbird, he-goat-on-heat) who waits, anticipating his acceptance by Idoto, the "Queen of the damp half light" (p. 39). The protagonist's confidence has been achieved through painstaking self-sacrifice. His dedication and struggle are presented within the context of Okigbo's anxiety to make his mark as an individual—he had successful older brothers—and as a poet striving to make an impact on his society:

> FOR HE WAS a shrub among the poplars,
> Needing more roots
> More sap to grow to sunlight,
> Thirsting for sunlight,
>
> A low growth among the forest.
>
> Into the soul
> The selves extended their branches,
> Into the moments of each living hour,
> Feeling for audience
>
> Straining thin among the echoes;
>
> And out of the solitude
> Voice and soul with selves unite,
> Riding the echoes,
> ...
> A green cloud above the forest.
> (p. 40)

Following his dialogue with the self, the poet-protagonist becomes empowered to talk with and about his society. He can now go forth with "eve-mist on shoulders," with "brand burning out at hand-end," and sing:

> ... tongue-tied,
> Without name or audience,
> Making harmony among the branches.
> ("Limits III," p. 41)

He is possessed and subdued by the hallucinatory influence of the armpit fragrance of the "oblong-headed lioness," against whom there is no shield ("Limits IV," p. 43).

"Fragments out of the Deluge" highlights the conflict between Christianity and traditional Africa. This fragment signals the sociopolitical dimension of Okigbo's poetic consciousness. Until this poem, his poetry had tended to focus on the individual and the search for self-realization. But in "Fragments out of the Deluge," Okigbo presents, in retrospect, some details about his protagonist and his milieu. He examines the collective rape of Africa and its "mysteries" by colonialism. This is his treatment of the theme of culture clash, which has been central to African literature since the colonial experience.

It is instructive to note that this sequence, which deals with the destruction of traditional African culture, opens with the metamorphosis of an Egyptian pharaoh into a fennel branch — a metaphor for resurrection or reincarnation. From Egyptian civilization, Okigbo moves on to the figure of Christ as Messiah, who, in spite of his miracles and parables ("seed wrapped in wonders"; p. 45), was rejected and crucified ("They cast him in mould of iron / And asked him to do a rock-drill—"; p. 45). But after rejecting and killing him, a cult developed around him ("And to the cross in the void came pilgrims; / Came, floating with burnt-out tapers"; p. 46). From among such pilgrims, men like Flannagan (a well-known Irish priest in Nigeria in the 1940s) set out for Africa to "*sow the fireseed among grasses*" (p. 46). The protagonist, now presented as a sunbird, sees this as the beginning of a larger tragedy—the tragedy of the near-total destruction of African culture predicted in "Limits VIII":

> 'A fleet of eagles,
> over the oilbean shadows,
> Holds the square
> under curse of their breath.
>
> ...
>
> Out of the solitude, the fleet,
> Out of the solitude,
> Intangible like silk thread of sunlight,
> The eagles ride low,
> Resplendent . . . resplendent;
>
> (p. 47)

The sentient and prophetic sunbird sings with the lyricism of the poet's childhood nurse, Eunice, but he is ignored. By "Limits X," the sunbird's prophecies are fulfilled: the eagles arrive and destroy the sunbird and the oil bean of tradition, looting all the treasures. In spite of this destruction, however, "Limits XI" returns to the promise of hope with which "Fragments out of the Deluge" opens. Okigbo affirms the possibility of dead gods growing out of their abandonment:

> And the gods lie unsung,
> Veiled only with mould,
> Behind the shrinehouse.
>
> Gods grow out,
> Abandoned;
> And so do they . . .
>
> (p. 50)

The ritual rebirth inherent in this image echoes the quality displayed by the buried pharaoh and the ignored Christ, whose influence spread beyond their original bases after their death. Consistent with the theme of ritual rebirth and regeneration with which *Limits* opens, Okigbo closes it with the image of the visionary sunbird killed in "Limits X" by the ravaging "fleet of eagles," now resurrected and singing "again / From the LIMITS of the dream" (p. 51)—but he is singing about the barbarity of humankind, a vision similar to that which Picasso captures in his *Guernica.*

SILENCES: IN THE EYE OF THE STORM

Silences continues Okigbo's foray into the public and the political realm started in "Fragments out of the Deluge," advancing his preoccupation from the colonial era to the contemporary. In the introduction to *Labyrinths*, Okigbo reveals that *Silences* was inspired by "the events of the day"—the first part, "Lament of the Silent Sisters" (1963), by the political crisis in Western Nigeria in 1962 and the 1960 assassination of the anti-imperialist Patrice Lumumba, the first prime minister in the Congo (now Zaire), by reactionary forces; the second part, "Lament of the Drums" (1965), by the imprisonment of Chief Obafemi Awolowo, the leader of the opposition in Nigeria, and the tragic death of his eldest son in an automobile accident.

Silences is, in essence, a dirge (song of lament) inspired by the tragedy of independent Africa. But, in presenting the tragedy of contemporary Africa, Okigbo turns to Gerard Manley Hopkins, Malcolm Cowley, Raja Ratnam, Stéphane Mallarmé, Rabindranath Tagore, Federico García Lorca, and his then unpublished poet-friend Peter Thomas for voices and images powerful enough to convey the magnitude and universal dimension of the tragedy. Because of the communal nature of the tragedy, Okigbo presents his lament within the dirge tradition of Africa with its call-and-response participatory structure.

The political chaos of Africa finds graphic expression in the image of a storm-tossed ship, with neither faith nor compass to guide it to safety:

> *Crier:* IS THERE . . . Is certainly there . . .
> For as in sea-fever globules of fresh
> anguish immense golden eggs empty
> of albumen sink into our balcony . . .
>
> How does one say NO in thunder . . .

For in breakers in sea-fever compass or
cross makes a difference: certainly
makes not an escape ladder . . .

Where is there for us an anchorage; . . .
("Lament of the Silent Sisters I," p. 55)

The prospect of an anchorage is dim when all around there are only scavengers waiting to feed on the carcass of Africa. "Lament of the Silent Sisters II" conveys the African tragedy in the context of Nigeria and Zaire, presenting Awolowo and Lumumba as archetypal heroes who have been victimized on account of their philosophies, leaving the poet to record the "sigh of our spirits" (p. 57) in "Lament of the Silent Sisters II" to "Lament of the Silent Sisters V."

"Lament of the Drums" particularizes and concentrates the tragedy of Africa in the figure of the imprisoned Awolowo. Okigbo invokes the long drums and cannons, which are traditionally employed in celebrating the apotheosis of ancestors, to speak out about the "Babylonian captivity" (p. 62) of Awolowo. He commemorates Awolowo's "*tears of grace*" and "*inviolable image*"; he casts him in the image of Palinurus, a helmsman, "alone in a hot prison," keeping the "dead sea awake with nightsong," unloved in his empty catacomb (p. 63). He admonishes the fishermen who "*rake the waves or chase their wake*," in the dark waters by the sea (Awolowo was imprisoned at Calabar, a coastal town in southeastern Nigeria), to "*Weave for him a shadow out of your laughter / For a dumb child to hide his nakedness* . . ." (p. 64). The dumb child here may be the grieving poet or any of the many disciples of Awolowo who were left speechless, both by his political travails and by the death of his son. The magnitude of the tragedy concretized in Awolowo is given lyrical and continental stress in "Lament of the Drums V":

FOR THE FAR *removed there is wailing:*

For the far removed;
For the Distant . . .

The wailing is for the fields of crop:

The drums' lament is:
They grow not . . .

The wailing is for the fields of men:

For the barren wedded ones;
For perishing children . . .

The wailing is for the Great River:

Her pot-bellied watchers
Despoil her . . .
(p. 66)

Although Okigbo's focus is Awolowo, he sees him mainly as a prototype of the larger tragedy of Africa and the victims of that tragedy. The lament is as much for Awolowo (the "far removed," the "Distant") as it is for the fields of crops and the men who are laid waste as a result of Africa's many wars, and for the "Great River" (the Niger or any one of Africa's rivers), which is being despoiled by its potbellied rulers.

DISTANCES: AN APOCALYPTIC VISION OF UTOPIA

Distances resumes the spiritual pursuit of a receding ideal that had been interrupted at the end of "Siren Limits" when the protagonist was rendered unconscious by the armpit fragrance of the oblong-headed lioness. Okigbo considered *Distances* a poem of homecoming, in both the spiritual and the psychic sense. The protagonist finds fulfillment in a form of psychic union with a supreme spirit who is both destructive and creative. In this poem, all of Okigbo's conflicting emotions and visions are ingathered for an implosive resolution in a phantasmagoria during which the protagonist is accepted into the cavernous bridal chamber of mother Idoto, thus fulfilling his desire for a spiritual fusion with his goddess.

Distances, Okigbo's most hauntingly beautiful poem sequence, operates at the level of the transcendental and the surreal. Inspired in part by the poet's actual experience of surgery under general anesthesia, *Distances* presents a questing protagonist in a state of possession, having been transported from flesh to phantom on a horizontal plane (operating table or altar). In the process of this psychic journey, the protagonist is paddled from reality to dream, from consciousness to unconsciousness, through a dark labyrinth to the birthday of earth, to the "other balcony" (p. 69) with its serene lights and redolent fountains bristling with signs, and finally to the inflorescent white chamber of the watermaid, into which he is invited. The protagonist, astonished into speechlessness ("perforated / mouth of a stranger: empty of meaning, / stones without juice—"; p. 75), accepts the invitation to fuse with his watermaid/muse/mother Idoto:

> and in the orangery of immense corridors,
> I wash my feet in your pure head, O maid,
>
> and walk along your feverish, solitary shores,
>
> seeking, among your variegated teeth,
> the tuberose of my putrescent laughter:
>
> I have fed out of the drum
> I have drunk out of the cymbal
>
> I have entered your bridal
> chamber; and lo,
>
> I am the sole witness to my homecoming.
> ("Distances VI," p. 76)

Between the protagonist's transformation from flesh to phantom and his acceptance into the bridal chamber of the watermaid, he confronts a number of obstacles, the most challenging being Death, who is presented as a dimension of the watermaid:

> DEATH LAY in ambush that evening in that
> island;
> voice sought its echo that evening in that island.
> And the eye lost its light,
> the light lost its shadow.
>
> . . .
>
> It was an evening without flesh or skeleton;
> an evening with no silver bells to its tale;
> without lanterns, an evening without buntings;
> and it was an evening without age or
> memory—
> ("Distances II," p. 70)

Within this context, Death, as the chief celebrant, reigns supreme "in a cloud of incense, / paring her fingernails" (p. 71) in the manner of the image of God in James Joyce's *Portrait of the Artist as a Young Man.* The protagonist envisions himself as one of the many ministrant-victims of Death:

> And in the freezing tuberoses of the white
> chamber, eyes that had lost their animal
> colour, havoc of eyes of incandescent rays,
> pinned me, cold, to the marble stretcher,
>
> until my eyes lost their blood
> and the blood lost its odour,
>
> . . .
>
> At her feet rolled their heads like cut fruits;
> about her fell
> their severed members, numerous as locusts.
>
> Like split wood left to dry, the dismembered
> joints of the ministrants piled high.
>
> She bathed her knees in the blood of attendants;
> her smock in entrails of ministrants . . .
> ("Distances II," pp. 70–71)

The carnage which Death wreaks on her ministrants recalls the behavior of Ogun, the Yoruba god of war and creativity, who, in a moment of manic exhilaration, decimated his own disciples. The protagonist survives the carnage to struggle on with other pilgrims in their attempt to attain the top of the stone steps and discover the secret word ("shibboleth") that will qualify them for entry into the bridal chamber.

The protagonist is one of an assortment of pilgrims who are grouped in units that recall the earlier equation of mankind to mathematical shapes in *Heavensgate.* In *Heavensgate,* Okigbo equates morons, fanatics, priests, popes, organizing secretaries, and party managers to the square; brothers, deacons, liberal politicians, selfish "selfseekers"—all who are good at doing nothing at all—to the rhombus; and the rest of mankind to the quadrangle. In *Distances,* he groups the pilgrims in accordance with their commitment to, and the stage attained in their search for acceptance into, the utopia represented by the watermaid. While prophets, martyrs, and lunatics struggle to attain the top of the stone steps of self-realization and union with the muse, the "dantini" (most likely a word Okigbo invented for "playboys") are cavorting in the clearing, the "dillettanti" (self-conscious patrons of the arts) are in the garden, and the "vendors princes negritude/ politicians" are lost in "the tall wood" (p. 72), unconcerned about the quest for illumination.

Daunting though the quest may be, the poet-protagonist struggles on with "SWEAT OVER hoof in ascending gestures" (p. 74). Each of his steps, "the step of the mule in the abyss," takes him toward the sanctuary in the molten bowels of the earth, as he searches

> for the music woven into the funerary rose
> the water in the tunnel its effervescent laughter
> the open laughter of grape or vine
> the question in the inkwell the answer on the monocle
> the unanswerable question in the tabernacle's silence—
>
> ("Distances V," p. 74)

The protagonist's quest is elemental, universal, and eternal; his religion is nameless; his "sigh is time's stillness, in the abyss . . . the stillness of the kiss . . ." (p. 74); and the fashion, when it is finally achieved, is implosive rather than explosive: "I am the sole witness to my homecoming." Here, then, as Okigbo affirms it in his introduction to *Labyrinths,* "The self that suffers, that experiences, ultimately finds fulfilment in a form of psychic union with the supreme spirit that is both destructive and creative. The process is one of sensual anaesthesia, of total liberation from all physical and emotional tension; the end result, a state of aesthetic grace" (reprinted in *Collected Poems,* p. xxiv).

PATH OF THUNDER: A FINAL TESTAMENT

In *Path of Thunder,* published posthumously in 1968, Okigbo continues his examination of Nigeria's political crisis, the subject matter of "Lament of the Drums." *Path of Thunder* can be divided into poems dealing with the situation in Nigeria immediately before the January 1966 coup d'état and poems dealing with the coup and its aftermath.

The pre-coup poems ("Elegy of the Wind" and "Come Thunder") capture the general state of anarchy that characterized Nigeria as a result of the constitutional crisis caused by the rigged federal election in 1964 and the rigged regional election in the West in 1965. The poet—"the sappling [*sic*] sprung from the bed of the old vegetation" who has shouldered his "way through a mass of ancient nights to chlorophyll" (p. 90)—laments the arson, the deaths, and the arrogance displayed by those who have aborted the happiness of the electorate; and warns of an impending revolution ("the thunder among the clouds"; p. 92). These poems present the public fulfillment of the protagonist's apocalyptic vision in "Distances II." The death that "lay in ambush that evening in that island" (p. 70) is manifested as death lying "in ambush along the corridors of power" (p. 92). As a result of the carnage, the protagonist—a "man of iron throat" who is set to "make broadcast with eunuch-horn of seven valves" (p. 90)—is disoriented. He is like a man leaning on a "withered branch,/A blind beggar leaning on a porch" (p. 90). His fate is like that of the "uncircumcised at the sight of the flaming razor" or that of "The bleeding phallus,/Dripping fresh from the carnage," crying out "for the medicinal leaf" (p. 91). Many had hoped that the January 1966 coup would be the medicinal leaf that would heal the nation's "bleeding phallus."

In the post-coup poems, Okigbo, employing the techniques of a fabulist, celebrates the hunters (soldiers) who have deployed thunder (guns and tanks) against the elephants (politicians) who had been ravaging the forest (nation). Although he is elated at the demise of the elephant class, the poet is quick to warn of the consequences of an impending betrayal of the people by the new hunter class: "But already the hunters are talking about pumpkins: / If they share the meat let them remember thunder" ("Hurrah for Thunder," p. 94).

By May 1966, it had become obvious that the generals who had sidelined the architects of the January coup and appropriated the reins of power were bent on creating an "iron dawn" (a military dictatorship) and taking the nation down an iron path paved with decrees and commandments. The eagles, which had held sway over the ritual oil bean, had now metamorphosed into robbers (soldiers and their political allies) descending "to strip us of our laughter, of our thunder" (p. 98). Against this background of continuing carnage, Okigbo affirms, in "Elegy for Alto," humanity's unending cycle of hope and disillusionment:

> THE GLIMPSE of a dream lies smouldering in a
> cave, together with the mortally wounded
> birds.
>
> . . .
>
> AN OLD STAR departs, leaves us here on the
> shore
> Gazing heavenward for a new star approaching;
> The new star appears, foreshadows its going
> Before a going and coming that goes on
> forever . . .
>
> (p. 99)

Path of Thunder is Okigbo's final testament. It represents a successful blend of theme and style, and of the personal and the public. It is an artistic triumph and an affirmation that Okigbo, the poet's poet, has become the people's poet. Its lyrical intensity, its incantatory nature, and its fabular construction are descended from traditional African folk poetry, especially the dirge form, which Okigbo seemed to have gradually grown to favor, even when writing about a subject as western as Yeats.

CONCLUSION

Okigbo has remained a source of inspiration and a challenge to other poets, especially African poets and those who appreciate the value of technical excellence and the possibility of articulating complex ideas and emotions through the medium of poetry. Romanus Egudu has aptly described Okigbo as the poet of Nigerian history. There is a sequence in his poetry that parallels an aspect of the history of Nigeria from precolonial times up to the eve of the Nigeria-Biafra war (which ended with Biafra's defeat in 1970). "Siren Limits" documents the destruction of African culture by colonialism, "Lament of the Drums" focuses on the postindependence constitutional crisis that culminated in the imprisonment of Awolowo, and *Path of Thunder* examines the breakdown of law and order after the January 1966 coup, which was designed to rescue the nation from the brink of political collapse but set in motion a more violent cycle of carnage. By electing Awolowo (a Yoruba), who was not a political darling of the Igbo people, as the heroic protagonist of "Lament of the Drums," Okigbo demonstrates his ideological courage and a refusal to be partisan unless a partisan position, like his support of the Biafran ideal, coincides with his apprehension of truth and justice.

But Okigbo is more than a poet of Nigerian history. He is as concerned with Nigeria as he is with Africa and humanity. "Lament of the Silent Sisters" is as much about Patrice Lumumba of the Congo as it is about humanity adrift with no rescue in sight. Although he has often been accused, by both readers and critics, of being abstruse and obscure, he has remained, according to Theophilus Vincent, "the best and most remarkable poet in African literature" (p. 31). Such high praise for Okigbo's poetry, argues Vincent, is a consequence of his successful mythmaking, the universal dimension of his themes, the lyricism of his poems, his evocation of Africa, and his multifaceted imagery.

Okigbo's poetry explores the various levels and dimensions of human experience: the personal and the public, the pure and the profane, the conscious and the unconscious. He crystallizes experiences into metaphors that express the complexity of the human condition. His poetry captures the ramifications of humanity's spiritual quest against the background of the complexity of contemporary Africa. He demonstrates that the conflicts engendered by the contact between Europe and Africa cannot be resolved by exorcising one in favor of the other. As he put it to Robert Serumaga in an interview:

> The truth, of course, is that the modern African is no longer a product of an entirely indigenous culture. The modern sensibility which the modern African poet is trying to express, is by its very nature complex, and it is a complex of values, some of which are indigenous, some of which are exotic, some of which are traditional, some of which are modern. Some of these values we are talking about are Christian, some are non-Christian, and I think that anybody who thinks it is possible to express consistently only one line of values, indigenous or exotic, is probably being artificial.
>
> (p. 144)

Okigbo is essentially the poet of the human condition. His poetry, although rooted in African time and space, always captures the spiritual struggle of the universal human being, the mental anguish to which the questing intelligence is inevitably subjected, and the unceasing cycle of hope and disillusionment that defines the pattern of human life. The abandoned protagonist may agonize about his loss and pain, but he must struggle on toward the summit. Okigbo's poetry is distinguished by an eeriness that is both challenging and rewarding. Because of the lyrical evocation of nature in his poetry and the multivocality of his imagery, there is also, even in his most arcane poems, an abundance of vision and a range of possibilities for interpretation. At his best, as Chinua Achebe affirms, he is "as visually clear as a fine crystal glass." The variety of the thirty-four memorial poems to Okigbo collected in *Don't Let Him Die* testifies to the power of his personality and the spread of the influence of his poetry, life, and death.

Selected Bibliography

BIBLIOGRAPHIES

Anafulu, Joseph C. "Christopher Okigbo, 1932–1967: A Bio-Bibliography." In *Research in African Literatures* 9 (1978).

Baldwin, Claudia A. "Christopher Okigbo." In her *Nigerian Literature: A Bibliography of Criticism, 1952–1976*. Boston: G. K. Hall, 1980.

Lindfors, Bernth. "Okigbo, Christopher." In his *Black African Literature in English: A Guide to Information Sources*. Detroit, Mich.: Gale, 1979.

Purcell, J. M. "Christopher Okigbo (1932–1967): Preliminary Checklist of His Books." In *Studies in Black Literature* 4, no. 2 (1973).

SEPARATE WORKS

"On the New Year." In *Horn* (Ibadan) (1958–1959).

"Moonglow." In *Fresh Buds* (Ibadan) (1960).

"Love Apart." In Frances Ademola, ed., *Reflections*. Lagos, Nigeria: African Universities Press, 1962.

"Four Canzones." In *Black Orpheus*, no. 1 (1962).

Heavensgate. Ibadan, Nigeria: Mbari, 1962.

"Lament of the Silent Sisters." In *Transition*, no. 8 (1963). Part One of *Silences*.

Limits. Ibadan, Nigeria: Mbari, 1964.

Lament of the Drums. Ibadan, Nigeria: Mbari, 1965. Part Two of *Silences*.

"Distances." In *Transition*, no. 16 (1964).
"Lament of the Drums." In *Transition*, no. 18 (1965); *Black Orpheus*, no. 17 (1965).
"Lament of the Masks: For W. B. Yeats, 1865–1939." In D. E. S. Maxwell and B. S. Bushrui, eds., *W. B. Yeats, 1865–1965: Centenary Essays*. Ibadan, Nigeria: Ibadan University Press, 1965.
"Path of Thunder." In *Black Orpheus* 2 (February 1968).

COLLECTED WORKS

Labyrinths; with Path of Thunder. London: Heinemann, 1971; New York: Africana, 1971. Contains *Heavensgate*, *Limits*, *Silences*, *Distances*, and *Path of Thunder*.
Christopher Okigbo: Collected Poems. London: Heinemann, 1986. Preface by Paul Theroux and intro. by Adewale Maja-Pearce. Includes "On the New Year," "Love Apart," "Moonglow," "Four Canzones," "Lament of the Masks," "Dance of the Painted Maidens," and *Labyrinths; with Path of Thunder.*

INTERVIEWS

Duerden, Dennis. Interview with Okigbo, London, August 1963. In Cosmo Pieterse and Dennis Duerden, eds., *African Writers Talking.* London: Heinemann, 1972; New York: Africana, 1972.
Nkosi, Lewis. Interview with Okigbo, Ibadan, Nigeria, August 1962. In Cosmo Pieterse and Dennis Duerden, eds., *African Writers Talking.* London: Heinemann, 1972; New York: Africana, 1972.
Serumaga, Robert. Interview with Okigbo, London, July 1965. In Cosmo Pieterse and Dennis Duerden, eds., *African Writers Talking.* London: Heinemann, 1972; New York: Africana, 1972. First published in *Cultural Events in Africa* 8, supp. (1965).
Whitelaw, Marjory. "Interview with Christopher Okigbo, 1965." In *Journal of Commonwealth Literature* 9 (July 1970).

CRITICAL STUDIES

Acholonu, Catherine. "Ogbanje: A Motif and a Theme in the Poetry of Christopher Okigbo." In *African Literature Today*, no. 16 (1988).
———. "From Rhetoric to Occultism: The Word as Music and Drama in Okigbo's *Labyrinths.*" In *African Literature Today*, no. 17 (1991).
Adedeji, Joel A. "A Dramatic Approach to Okigbo's *Limits.*" In *Conch* 3, no. 1 (1971).
Anozie, Sunday O. "Okigbo's *Heavensgate*: A Study of Art as Ritual." In *Ibadan* 15 (March 1963).
———. "Christopher Okigbo: A Creative Itinerary, 1957–1967." In *Présence africaine*, no. 64 (1967).
———. "A Structural Approach to Okigbo's 'Distances.'" In *Conch* 1 (March 1969).
———. "Poetry and Empirical Logic: A Correspondence Theory of Truth in Okigbo's *Laments.*" In *Conch* 2, no. 1 (1970).
———. *Christopher Okigbo: Creative Rhetoric.* New York: Africana, 1972.
Cartey, Wilfred G. *Whispers from a Continent: The Literature of Contemporary Black Africa.* New York: Random House, 1969; London: Heinemann, 1971.
Dathorne, O. R. "African Literature IV: Ritual and Ceremony in Okigbo's Poetry." In *Journal of Commonwealth Literature* 5 (July 1968).
———. "Okigbo Understood: A Study of Two Poems." In *African Literature Today* 1, no. 1 (1968).
———. "Christopher Okigbo: The Voice of Ritual." In his *African Literature in the Twentieth Century*. Minneapolis: University of Minnesota Press, 1975; London: Heinemann, 1976.
Echeruo, Michael J. C. "Traditional and Borrowed Elements in Nigerian Poetry." In *Nigeria Magazine* 89 (June 1986).
Egudu, Romanus N. "Okigbo Misrepresented: Edwin Thumboo on 'Love Apart.'" In *Présence africaine*, no. 76 (1970).
———. "Ezra Pound in African Poetry: Christopher Okigbo." In *Comparative Literature Studies* 8 (June 1971).
———. "Defence of Culture in the Poetry of Christopher Okigbo." In *African Literature Today*, no. 6 (1973).
———. "Okigbo's 'Distances': A Retreat from Christ to Idoto." In *Conch* 5, no. 1/2 (1973).
———. "African Literature and Social Problems." In *Canadian Journal of African Studies* 9, no. 3 (1975).
———. "Cultural Oppression: The Poetry of Christopher Okigbo." In his *Four Modern West African Poets*. New York: NOK, 1977.

———. "Christopher Okigbo and the Growth of Poetry." In Albert S. Gérard, ed., *European-Language Writing in Sub-Saharan Africa*. Vol. 2. Budapest, Hungary: Akadémiai Kiadó, 1986.

———. "Christopher Okigbo." In Yemi Ogunbiyi, ed., *Perspectives on Nigerian Literature*. Vol. 2. Lagos, Nigeria: Guardian Books, 1988.

Etherton, Michael J. "Christopher Okigbo and African Tradition: A Reply to Professor Ali A. Mazrui." In *Zuka* 2 (1968).

Gomwalk, Philemon Victor. "The Stages of Style and Thematic Pre-occupation in Okigbo's Poetry of *Labyrinths*." In *Kuka* (Zaria, Nigeria) (1978–1979).

Heywood, Annemarie. "The Ritual and the Plot: The Critic and Okigbo's *Labyrinths*." In *Research in African Literatures* 9 (spring 1978).

Ikiddeh, Ime. "Iron, Thunder and Elephants: A Study of Okigbo's *Path of Thunder*." In *New Horn* 1, no. 2 (1974).

Izevbaye, Dan S. "From Reality to Dream: The Poetry of Christopher Ikigbo." In Edgar Wright, ed., *The Critical Evaluation of African Literature*. London: Heinemann, 1973.

———. "Okigbo's Portrait of the Artist as a Sunbird: A Reading of *Heavensgate*." In *African Literature Today*, no. 6 (1973).

Leslie, Omolara. "The Poetry of Christopher Okigbo: Its Evolution and Significance." In *Ufahamu* 4, no. 1 (1973).

———. "Christopher Okigbo: The Development of a Poet." In *New Horn* 1, no. 2 (1974).

Lindfors, Bernth. "Okigbo as Jock." In *English in Africa* 6 (March 1979).

Mazrui, Ali Amin. "Abstract Verse and African Tradition." In *Zuka* 1 (1968).

———. "Meaning Versus Imagery in African Poetry." In *Présence africaine*, no. 66 (1968).

Moore, Gerald. "Vision and Fulfillment in West African Literature: The Poetry of Christopher Okigbo." In his *The Chosen Tongue: English Writing in the Tropical World.* New York: Harper & Row, 1970.

Ndu, Pol. "Mytho-Religious Roots of Modern Nigerian Poetry: Christopher Okigbo—*Heavensgate*." In *Greenfield Review* 5, no. 3/4 (1976/1977).

Nwoga, Donatus Ibe. "Okigbo's *Limits*: An Approach to Meaning." In *Journal of Commonwealth Literature* 7 (June 1972).

———. "Plagiarism and Authentic Creativity in West Africa." In *Research in African Literatures* 6 (spring 1975).

———. ed. *Critical Perspectives on Christopher Okigbo*. Washington, D.C.: Three Continents Press, 1984.

Ogundele, Wole. "From the Labyrinth to the Temple: The Structure of Okigbo's Religious Experience." In *Okike* 24 (June 1983).

Olaogun, Modupe. "Graphology and Meaning in the Poetry of Christopher Okigbo." In *African Literature Today*, no. 17 (1991).

Stanton, R. J. "Poet as Martyr: West Africa's Christopher Okigbo, and His *Labyrinths with Path of Thunder*." In *Studies in Black Literature* 7 (winter 1976).

Theroux, Paul. "Christopher Okigbo." In *Transition* 5, no. 22 (1965).

———. "Christopher Okigbo." In Bruce King, ed., *Introduction to Nigerian Literature*. New York: Africana, 1972.

Thomas, Peter. "The Water Maid and the Dancer: Figures of the Nigerian Muse." In *Literature East and West* 12 (March 1968).

———. "An Image Insists." In *Greenfield Review* 8, no. 1/2 (1980).

Thumboo, Edwin. "Dathorne's Okigbo: A Dissenting View." In *African Literature Today*, no. 3 (1969).

Udoeyop, Nyong J. "A Branch of Giant Fennel." In his *Three Nigerian Poets*. Ibadan, Nigeria: Ibadan University Press, 1973.

Vincent, Theophilus. "Okigbo's *Labyrinths*." In *Black Orpheus* 2, no. 7 (1972).

MEMORIALS

Achebe, Chinua, and Dubem Okafor, eds. *Don't Let Him Die: An Anthology of Memorial Poems for Christopher Okigbo (1932–1967)*. Enugu, Nigeria: Fourth Dimension, 1978. Preface by Achebe.

Mazrui, Ali Amin. *The Trial of Christopher Okigbo*. London: Heinemann, 1971.

Omotoso, Kole. "Christopher Okigbo: A Personal Portrait, 1932–1967." In *New Horn* 1, no. 2 (1974).

Povey, John. "Epitaph to Christopher Okigbo." In *Africa Today* 14, no. 6 (1967).

Thomas, Peter. "Ride Me Memories: A Memorial Tribute to Christopher Okigbo." In *African Arts* 1 (summer 1968).

Udechukwu, Obiora. *Homage to Christopher Okigbo: Catalogue*. Nsukka, Nigeria: Odunke, 1975.

ENTRIES IN BIOGRAPHICAL DICTIONARIES

Herdeck, Donald E., ed. *African Authors: A Companion to Black African Writing.* Washington, D.C.: Black Orpheus Press, 1973.

Jahin, Janheinz, Ulla Schild, and Almut Nordman. *Who's Who in African Literature.* Tübingen, Germany: H. Erdmann, 1972.

Walsh, William. "Christopher (Ifeanyichukwu) Okigbo." In James Vinson and D. L. Kirkpatrick, eds., *Contemporary Poets.* 2nd ed. London: St. James's Press, 1975.

Zell, Hans M., and Helene Silver, eds. *A Reader's Guide to African Literature.* New York: Africana, 1971.

Ben Okri

1959–

ATO QUAYSON

BEN OKRI'S novels and short stories exemplify two trends in modern African narrative: mimetic realism and a reworking of mythology. The careers of some of the best African novelists encompass a similar move from realism toward mythology. Chinua Achebe, Ngũgĩ wa Thiong'o, and Ayi Kwei Armah all began with realism and later experimented with forms of narrative that drew on nonrealist sources. Okri's writing balances these two tendencies and displays the strengths and weaknesses of both. Receiving the 1991 Booker Prize in England for *The Famished Road* confirmed him as a major new voice in African and world literature, put him in the same league with the most innovative African writers, and encouraged comparisons to such cosmopolitan postcolonial writers as Gabriel García Márquez and Salman Rushdie.

EARLY LIFE

Okri was born on 15 March 1959 in Minna, Nigeria, to Silver Oghekeneshineke Loloje Okri and Grace Okri, both members of the Urhobo ethnic group of southwestern Nigeria. At the time his father was a clerk with Nigerian Railways. After Nigerian independence in 1960, Silver Okri went to England to study for a law degree. Ben joined his parents in 1962 and went to John Donne Primary School at Peckham in London. This period was one of the most enjoyable of his childhood, when he had many friends and read a lot of comics. It was cut short, however, in 1966, when he had to return to Nigeria with his mother. So reluctant was he to depart from his friends in England that he had to be tricked by his mother into boarding the ship that was to take them home. Back in Nigeria, he attended school at Ibadan and Ikenne before going to Urhobo College at Warri for his secondary education. He seems to have been the youngest boy in his class of 1968, and by the end of his secondary education in 1972 he was just fourteen years old. After secondary school, he moved to Lagos, where he studied at home for his advanced levels and a diploma in journalism.

Two experiences during adolescence prompted Okri to begin writing. In 1976 his father returned from law studies in England with a collection of classics that included works by Charles Dickens, Mark Twain, and Aristotle, as well as Greek and Roman histories. Okri read the books voraciously and fed his imagination with a great range of ideas. During this period he also experienced the disappointment of being refused admission to any of the Nigerian universities. He filled his time writing short stories, poems, and articles of social criticism. The first of these articles, published in a newspaper in 1976, was about the inefficiency of rent tribunals in the ghettos of Lagos and the merciless rent increases randomly imposed by landlords. Many of his earliest short stories were based on articles of social criticism that had been rejected for publication by local newspapers and journals. His concern with the condition of the underclass and of slum dwellers never left him, and his work has continually focused on their predicament. Significantly, he spent this period of his adolescence in Ajengule, a slum district in Lagos, where his father took briefs for the poor. His home was a hive of activity, and he often heard the complaints that people filed with his father. In 1978, he left Nigeria for the University of Essex in England, where he was admitted to study philosophy and English. He stayed in England following his university studies.

His social ideals were formed by a combination of his growing awareness of the injustice in society, his disappointment at not being admitted for university education in Nigeria, and his passionate reading in the classics. During these formative years, he was simultaneously living in a world of beautiful ideas and in the harsh realities of the slums. His attempt to mediate the contradictions in these two realms of experience, the intellectual and the physical, gives his writing such experimental verve. Never fully satisfied with his own craft, he has always sought new idioms to express these disparities.

EARLY WORK: *FLOWERS AND SHADOWS* AND *THE LANDSCAPES WITHIN*

Okri's first novel, *Flowers and Shadows* (1980), was completed when he was a nineteen-year-old undergraduate at the University of Essex. It centers on the pernicious corruption of Jonan Okwe, a businessman, and the problematic legacy that he bequeaths his nineteen-year-old son, Jeffia. Jonan's dealings have cast long shadows, and there is a threat to his much-vaunted equanimity in the imminent visit of Sowho, his half brother who has been in jail because Jonan framed him. Mrs. Okwe, who has a series of premonitory nightmares, intuitively grasps the ominousness of Sowho's visit. With these inarticulate parental anxieties as a backdrop, the young Jeffia is gradually initiated into the harsh knowledge of his father's ruthless business practices by a series of coincidences. Driving home from a late-night party, he comes across a distraught nurse, Cynthia, and an injured man, Gbenga, by the roadside. Gbenga, a former employee of his father's has been mugged on the orders of Jonan Okwe; Jeffia is shocked when he recognizes the man's mutilated face. As a relationship develops between Cynthia and Jeffia, he is further unsettled by the discovery that Cynthia's father was also once employed by Jonan Okwe. Framed by Jeffia's father and put in jail for two years, Cynthia's father is at the edge of his sanity and an alcoholic.

After a mad car chase, Jonan and Sowho die at the end of the novel in a crash when Jonan suffers a heart attack behind the wheel. Jeffia is left to fend for his mother, and they have to move into a poorer area of Lagos. The overwhelming sense of tragedy in this novel is partly relieved by the promise offered in the relationship between Jeffia and Cynthia and by her father's overcoming his initial reservations and accepting the young man on his own terms.

Okri introduces *The Landscapes Within* (1981) with two complementary epigraphs—James Joyce's "Welcome, O life! I go to encounter for the millionth time the reality of experience and to forge in the smithy of my soul the uncreated conscience of my race," from *A Portrait of the Artist as a Young Man* (1916), and Achebe's "For whom is it well, for whom is it well? There is no one for whom it is well," from *Things Fall Apart* (1958)—that relate to the peculiar situation of the central character, Omovo, who is an artist. The novel traces Omovo's artistic impressions of social life and also explores his troubled relationships with his friends, father, and stepmother, as well as with Ifeyinwa, a young married woman with whom he has an illicit love affair. The general impression is of the young artist growing up in a state of personal anomie in reaction to the squalor of individual conditions and the corruption of society. The artist in Omovo attempts to establish a correlation between his consciousness and society. Yet his mind continually reverts to the image of green scum near the bathroom as the compound in which he lives. He even paints a "scumscape," which he entitles "Drift." Despite, or perhaps because of, its being seized by security forces in a frenzy of censorship at an art exhibition, and despite his painting other impressions of society in an attempt at an epiphanic resolution of contradictions within and without, the scumscape remains for Omovo the most potent symbol of the corrupt state of Nigerian society.

Some of the central themes to which Okri returns in later works are set out in these first two novels. The issue of corruption is handled with a moral fervor that derives from his early journalistic efforts at social criticism. In this focus on corruption he takes up some of the dominant concerns of the African novel from Achebe's *No Longer at Ease* (1960) to Ngũgĩ's *Petals of Blood* (1978). His difference is in centering on the family as a prism through which the contradictions in society are refracted. The tensions between father and son in his first two novels result as much from the absurd effects of a totally corrupting environment as from the faults of the parents. In *Flowers and Shadows,* Jonan is motivated to such ruthless corruption because his own father died poor and told him on his deathbed that poverty was a sin. Armed with this disconcerting knowledge and the desire to avoid his father's mistakes, Jonan sinks deeper and deeper into corrupt practices that bring him wealth but destroy his capacity for expressing love and tenderness toward his wife and son. In *The Landscapes Within*, the stress of living in the ghetto makes Omovo's father break out in mindless violence against his offspring to relieve his unresolved sense of failure and his inability to provide for their needs.

Even at this early stage, Okri demonstrates remarkable powers of narrative description, although his narrative occasionally lapses into the episodic. In *The Landscapes Within*, a descriptive density synchronizes with the portrayal of the artist's growing consciousness and slows down the pace of the narrative to enhance the anomie that governs the world of the novel. Perhaps the central weakness in these first two novels, however, lies not so much in the narrative technique as in the characterization of women. The women in these early novels are passive victims of men's desires and excesses. Both Jeffia's mother in *Flowers and Shadows* and Ifeyinwa in *The Landscapes Within* are long-suffering and passive. Only Cynthia is depicted as able to assert herself against the excesses of men. Yet even she is portrayed as dispensing care and healing to the weak men in her life, particularly her alcoholic father and the young and inexperienced Jeffia. She is thereby projected as symbolic of spiritual healing, a function that matches neatly with her occupation as nurse. The stereotype of the caring nurse undermines her stronger characteristics, which place her beyond the roles allotted to most women in the two novels, and makes her an object of men's fantasies. In *The Famished Road* and its sequel, *Songs of Enchantment*, the stereotype of the passive woman is exploded by the boisterous and assertive Madame Koto.

THE SHORT STORIES

Between the publication of Okri's second novel in 1981 and *The Famished Road* in 1991 stand ten years of experimentation. In this period he was a freelance broadcaster for BBC television's African department and poetry editor for *West Africa* magazine in

London. He published short stories in journals and newspapers including *New Statesman*, *Firebird*, *Paris Review*, and *PEN New Fiction*. In this period his writing also began to gain recognition. In 1984 he was awarded a grant by the British Arts Council, and in 1987 he won the Commonwealth writers' prize for Africa and the Aga Khan prize for fiction from the *Paris Review* for *Incidents at the Shrine*, his first collection of short stories. A year later, a second collection, *Stars of the New Curfew*, was published.

Most of the stories in *Incidents at the Shrine* (1986) have an urban setting and chart the contours of the African city from the perspective of its underclass, depicting it as a zone of predatoriness and incomprehensible contradictions. The thematic webwork of the stories depends for its effectiveness on the reader moving backward and forward within the collection. In "Masquerades" and "Converging City," Okri creates disconcerting but humorous assaults on the reader's sense of smell to convey the discomfort that marks the lives of the characters.

"Masquerades" hints at the disturbing double life of a latrine carrier. To combat the sense of worthlessness brought on by his occupation, he rehearses a playboy's role every night by soaking himself in expensive perfumes and going out with prostitutes from the dance halls. The story ends on a ruthless note when, in an act of revenge, his adversaries deposit a bucket full of excrement from the latrines in the middle of his room.

This discomfort brought on by stench echoes "Converging City," where the nature of the city's incomprehensibility is given an ironic twist when Agodi, a religious fanatic, is thrown by a wrestler onto the putrescent carcass of a cow by the side of a crowded city street. The stench attracts jubilant flies as well as the questioning eyes of the gathered crowd. Agodi's position in this scene epitomizes the social and economic discomfort from which he desperately seeks to flee. By the end of the story, the central character's efforts at reviving his ailing business are destroyed when his decrepit shop is robbed by thieves. In response, he turns tenaciously to his religion, but Okri underlines the financial motives behind his apparent spirituality. "He announced that in the forests of the city he had achieved blindness and had seen God. He declared that he was now a true prophet. God and money, he said, were inseparable. He founded a new church and had several business cards printed. His new signboards sprang up along the busy street" (p. 36). In the fierce struggle for survival in a city where predatory impulses run wild in manifestation of inhumanity and corruption, even religion takes on a desperate utilitarian inflection.

Other stories also tell of the religious proclivities born of despair with city life. In "The Dream-vendor's August" and "Incidents at the Shrine," Okri represents people turning to religion in times of crisis. In "The Dream-vendor's August," a tissue of beliefs that derives from cheap esoteric literature is the basis of Ajegunle Joe's sense of the spiritual realm. The rings on his fingers, for which he claims associations with Merlin, Master Eckhart, and Aladdin, the latter having "been found on the dead body of Isaac Newton" (pp. 114–115), serve to depict a confused state of beliefs originating in a sense of desperation with the destitution of city life. The spiritual chaos in this story functions as an ironic counterpart to the spiritual strengthening in "Incidents at the Shrine." In the latter story, Anderson, bewildered by a disturbing series of events beginning with his dismissal from work, returns to his village where, through a series of hallucinatory experiences, he is reinitiated into the spiritual heritage of his tribe. "Incidents at the Shrine" is also significant for the fusion of dreamlike processes with events in the real world. In this respect, it is formally linked with "A Hidden History," in which Okri explores the allegorical wasteland of an unnamed western city where apocalyptic images rooted in the physical environment of rubble and the concrete jungle mix with rats, green mists, and references to the life of a lunatic at a garbage dump, all to give an unsettling impression of decadence and destruction. These formal experiments recur in his short stories and appear in more mature form in *The Famished Road.*

The other stories in the collection are written in a pared-down style and refer to realities beyond the African city. The first story, "Laughter Beneath the Bridge," which is set during the Nigerian civil war of 1967–1970, explores the effects of war on an innocent girl and her male friend from the perspective of a young boy. The setting of an unnamed western city is again adopted for "Disparities," in which the reflections of a destitute man are interwoven with the heartrending knowledge that a senior Nigerian official has just "misplaced" a quarter of a million pounds in the back of a cab. "Crooked Prayer" is a touching exploration of marital strife caused by childlessness, viewed through the eyes of an innocent boy. The stories in this collection read like snapshots of city life in which the images alter their contours when set against each other.

In *Stars of the New Curfew* (1988) Okri returns to some of the concerns of the first collection. "In the Shadow of War" explores another aspect of the Nigerian civil war, this time from the perspective of a curious boy, and "In the City of Red Dust" tells of the humiliation endured by two friends who make ends meet by selling pints of their blood to the local hospital. More noteworthy, however, is that Okri here extends his range of experimentation and innovation with narrative form: four of the six stories in this collection interfuse the penumbral and surreal state of the spirit world with the real world.

"What the Tapster Saw" is perhaps the most radically experimental story as it recalls the folkloric resources of Amos Tutuola and other traditional storytellers. The opening, "there was once an excellent tapster" (p. 183), is a direct echo of the opening of folktales, and the narrative follows the adventures of this tapster. At the beginning, he falls from a palm tree and, much disturbed, goes to the shrine of Tabasco, a renowned medicine man, for spiritual assistance. Tabasco assures him that nothing is really wrong. The narrative then follows the tapster on a palm-wine-tapping trip into the forest, where he encounters spirit figures, such as three glass-eyed turtles (one of which has the face of Tabasco), a multicolored snake, and disembodied voices. He goes through a series of curious experiences: his body, for instance, is multiplied in form, and he sees strange visions of the future. He also experiences a cryptic esoteric dream of mythical figures that include "the famous blacksmith, who could turn water into metal; the notorious tortoise, with his simple madness for complex situations; and the witch-doctors, who did not have the key to mysteries" (p. 193). He finally wakes up in Tabasco's shrine to be told that he has been dead for seven days after falling from the palm tree. His experiences in the spirit realm were those of a dead person. This narrative twist suggests the extent to which the spirit world is subtly interwoven with the real world and the journey of the tapster is our own journey of discovery into the multifariousness of existence.

In most of the stories in which Okri suggests a link between the spiritual and the earthly, the narrative perspective shifts between the two worlds. A sense of unreality grows steadily upon the central characters until the esoteric realm invades the real world and recedes only to leave the real world no longer the same in the eyes of both the characters and the readers. This is the case particularly in "Worlds That Flourish" and in the title story. In "When the Lights Return," there is a nebulous, in-between quality to the setting of the tale because of the pervasive darkness brought on by the failing electricity supply and the spectral characteristics of Maria, with which her boyfriend, Ede, has to content. In "What the Tapster Saw," Okri complicates perspectives by setting the story within the world of folklore. The folklore markers in the narrative establish the spirit world as the dominant perspective. The experiments with narrative form in these two collections reflect a loss of faith in the adequacy of realism to capture the Nigerian condition. As Okri said in an interview with Jane Wilkinson, "I've come to realize you can't write about Nigeria truthfully without a sense of violence. To be serene is to lie. Relations in Nigeria are violent relations. It's the way it is, for historical and all sorts of other reasons" (p. 81). The coalescing of realism with nonrealist forms of narrative gives formal expression to Okri's uncanny intuitive grasp of the dislocations marking life in Nigeria.

THE FAMISHED ROAD AND *SONGS OF ENCHANTMENT*

The Famished Road (1991) represents the fruition of the experimentation initiated in the short stories. In this work Okri combines on an epic scale the variety of the spirit world with the humdrum grit of deprivation and dispossession in the ghetto.

The very first words of the novel establish an epic quality that is later replaced by the troubled events of ordinary existence: "In the beginning there was a river. The river became a road and the road branched out to the whole world. And because the road was once a river it was always hungry" (p. 3). The reference to a beginning beyond time is reminiscent of biblical creation narratives and of the creation myths of peoples all over the world. Drawing on the biblical implications of these first sentences, the first chapter paints an idyllic setting of pure dreams, the abode of *abiku*, who are children caught in the cycle of death and rebirth. Azaro is an *abiku* who refuses the enticements of the idyllic realm portrayed in the first chapter and comes to reside in the real world. He is born to poor parents living in a slum in a nameless African city. He is never completely free of the essential nature of *abiku*, however, and has the uncanny capacity of existing simultaneously in the real and spirit worlds.

The narrative traces life in the ghetto: Azaro's experiences of conviviality and despair in the compound where he lives, the effects of political campaigning on the lives of the hapless slum dwellers, and his father's pursuit of boxing ambitions to earn enough money to rid the world of hunger and injustice. It tells of Azaro's mother's struggles as she hawks wares in the market; it also tells of the assertiveness, entrepreneurship, and political affiliations of Madame Koto, the owner of a neighborhood palm-wine bar, who later takes a keen interest in Azaro. Traversing the plot of these simple events are numerous forays into the spirit world through the consciousness of Azaro.

The narrative digresses frequently from descriptions of real-world events into experiences of the spirit world. These digressions suggest that the two realms are in permanent intercourse. What makes this interaction possible is that Azaro is a child of two worlds and all events in the narrative are narrated by him. The nature of the spirit world is variable. Sometimes Azaro has to contend with his spirit companions who want to entice him back to the idyllic world from which he has departed. In an early encounter, they show him images that he can barely understand, images of "a prison, a woman covered with golden boils, a long road, pitiless sunlight, a flood, an earthquake, death" (p. 7). His inability to comprehend the significance of the world of spirits plagues him throughout the novel.

At times he has to contend with malevolent spirits who want to kidnap him to augment their power, and at other times he seems to drift into a no-man's-land of spirits where he is partly an observer of the wonders of the spirit world and partly a pursued object. Azaro also has the capacity of invading the consciousness of other characters and animals. Once, he gets entangled in his mother's dream.

At another time, he enters the consciousness of a duiker (a type of antelope) and is transported into strange spiritual realms of titanic encounters. In yet another instance, he sees into Madame Koto's corpulence and discovers she is pregnant with three *abiku* children struggling to be born. At every turn, he is alone in these spiritual encounters and in his perception of the subliminal spirit world beyond the real.

Yet the lack of comprehension that marks his esoteric encounters signals an important qualification of the mythopoeic potential Okri draws upon for this novel: Azaro lacks the titanic stature of folktale heroes. He is not assisted by magic or any spiritual forces, and his narrow escapes depend mainly on the sudden and arbitrary narrative shifts between the spirit and real worlds. Furthermore, though he is frequently pursued by malevolent spirits, there is no sense that these spirits fall into a clear moral scheme of good and evil. Okri avoids the simple heroism and morality of folktale and mythology in this novel to suggest that the spirit world is as chaotic and incomprehensible as the real world.

The language Okri uses to describe these spirit adventures is of a poetic quality unprecedented in the African novel. The suggestiveness of this passage gives an example:

> I ran through the night forests, where all forms are mutable, where all things exchange their identities, and where everything dances in an exultation of flame and wisdom. I ran till I came to the Atlantic, silver and blue under the night of forests. Birds flew in the aquamarine sky. Feathers gyrated on to the waves. The sky was full of dense white clouds moving like invading armies of mist and ghosts over the deep serene blue and under the regenerative stars.
>
> (p. 457)

The sense of an infinite potential for transformation is conjured in the shifting images of color, water, clouds, and birds. There is a simultaneous feeling of stillness and motion because we are encouraged to dwell on images while being aware of movement suggested in verbs like "exchange," "dance," and "gyrate." The effect is much like a surreal painting in its incongruity with the suggestion of suppressed activity in the contour of the images playing on the surface of the canvas. Even in *An African Elegy* (1992), a collection of poetry, Okri does not match the expressive power of *The Famished Road.* Except for poems in which he expresses deeply felt emotions, such as "You Walked Gently Towards Me" and "I Held You in the Square," and those in which he replicates some of the themes from his fiction, such as "Demolition Street: London, 83" and "Political Abiku," this collection of poetry is an anticlimax compared with the beauty of the prose of his award-winning novel. Perhaps it is best to view his poetry as an expression of unrealized poetic potential, which, ironically, finds voice in his prose.

In *Songs of Enchantment* (1993) Okri returns to prose. Written while he was a fellow commoner in creative arts at Trinity College, Cambridge, from September 1991 to August 1993, it reproduces the setting and characters of *The Famished Road.* Most of the events take place in the hallucinatory realm of dreams where forces of good and evil are pitted against each other. Azaro's prizefighting father has offended his tender but remote mother by flirting with a beggar girl, and the novel at first seems to promise an exploration of family strife and possible reconciliation. Other concerns take over, however, when Okri presents the violent repression unleashed by "The Party of the Rich" and "The Party of the Poor" on the neighborhood. The situation is exacerbated when Azaro's friend Ade and Ade's father are killed in brawls related to Madame Koto's car. The story takes on the tone of Greek tragedy when the political parties forbid burial of the dead bodies. Azaro's father heroically flouts the prohibition and buries the bodies, thus challenging the machinations of the forces of chaos. To complicate matters, the forces of evil coalesce around Madame Koto and a rising symbol of spiritual destruction, the Jackal-headed Masquerade. This development magnifies the role of Madame Koto and extends her desire for commercial success to encompass a desire for domination of the world.

Regrettably, this sequel calcifies into callow moralism in which the outcome of the battle between the forces of good and evil is obvious from the start. Unlike in *The Famished Road*, access to the spirit world is no longer limited to Azaro. All the major characters drift back and forth between the spirit world and the real world. Furthermore, the spiritual forces in this novel fall into clearly defined camps of good and evil. Since Okri tips the balance of the mythopoeic in favor of its inherent moral imperative, the narrative takes on a moral fervor that can have only one conclusion: the defeat of evil by good.

CONCLUSION

In developing an idiom that draws on mythology as well as realism, Okri poses new questions for his readers, questions that only acute attention to the diversity of existence can help us to answer. In his own way, he has refocused for African and postcolonial literature what virtual reality has done in the entertainment industry. It is a question of looking anew at the old and being prepared to luxuriate in the shock of rediscovery.

With *Astonishing the Gods* (1995), a haunting novel set on an enchanted island, Okri extends his experiments with mythological narratives and shows his masterful interfusion of dream and reality, of truth and the imagination. In certain respects, however, it is *Birds of Heaven* (1996) that offers the best point from which to attempt an overview of his work. *Birds of Heaven* is a small book in two parts, a brief essay titled "Beyond Words: A Secular Sermon" and a series of aphorisms. By means of the brief essay in the first part and the aphorisms in the second, Okri offers suggestive points of view on the relationship of words and stories to human problems. It is important, for instance, to remember that "a people are as healthy and confident as the stories they tell themselves. Sick story-tellers can make their nations sick. And sick nations make for sick story tellers" (p. 18). It is also important to keep in mind that "when we have made an experience or a chaos into a story we have transformed it, made sense of it, transmuted experience, domesticated the chaos" (p. 23). It is clear that Okri sees stories as a means by which a people create beneficial or dangerous modes of self-apprehension and that the stories that are lived by are important indices of the spiritual life of a people.

Birds of Heaven reveals Okri as a deeply humane writer. It is reasonable to infer that he believes in the possibility of good art to change the way people think about themselves and, thereby, the way in which they relate to other people. That he affirms this optimistic viewpoint while creating a fusion of mythical apprehensions within novelistic discourse shows a deep commitment not just to art, but to an art that challenges our ways of perceiving reality and forces us to understand the varying complexities that underly our existence.

Selected Bibliography

SELECTED WORKS

Flowers and Shadows. London: Longman Drumbeat, 1980.

The Landscapes Within. Burnt Mill, U.K.: Longman, 1981.

Incidents at the Shrine. London: Heinemann, 1986. Short stories.

Stars of the New Curfew. London: Secker and Warburg, 1988. Short stories.

The Famished Road. London: Jonathan Cape, 1991.

An African Elegy. London: Jonathan Cape, 1992. Poetry.

Songs of Enchantment. London: Jonathan Cape, 1993.

Astonishing the Gods. London: Phoenix, 1995.
Birds of Heaven. London: Phoenix, 1996.

ESSAYS

"Fear of Flying." In *West Africa* (3 November 1980).
"Journeys Through the Imagination." Review of *The Witch Herbalist of the Remote Town,* by Amos Tutuola. In *West Africa* (14 February 1983).
"How Reality Overwhelms Good Fiction." In *Guardian* (Manchester) (26 September 1985).
"Meditations on Othello." In *West Africa* (23 and 30 March 1987).
"Fresh Interpretations." Review of *The Literature Machine,* by Italo Calvino. In *West Africa* (25 January 1988).
"Redreaming the World." In *Guardian* (Manchester) (9 August 1990).

INTERVIEWS

Blishen, Edward. "ICA Guardian Conversations with Ben Okri." London: Institute of Contemporary Arts, 1988.
Iloegbunam, Chuks. "Conversation with Ben Okri." In *Guardian* (Lagos) (26 October 1983).
Ledger, Fiona. "Interview with Ben Okri About His Collection of Short Stories *Incidents at the Shrine.*" In *BBC Arts and Africa* 656 (1986).
Morris, Patricia. "The Tiger Pounces." In *African Concord* (Lagos) (30 October 1986). Okri discusses Wole Soyinka.
Sweetman, David. "Interview with Ben Okri About His First Novel *Flowers and Shadows.*" In *BBC Arts and Africa* 345 (1980).
Wilkinson, Jane. "Ben Okri." In Jane Wilkinson, ed., *Talking with African Writers: Interviews with African Poets, Playwrights, and Novelists.* London: Currey, 1992.

CRITICAL STUDIES

Ayer, Pico. "The Empire Writes Back." In *Time* (8 February 1993). General evaluation of contemporary postcolonial literature.
Bandele-Thomas, Biyi. "Ben Okri: A Literary Giant in His Own Right." In *Nigeria Home News* (London) (26 April–2 May 1990).
Barnacle, Hugo. "Village Life with Thugs, Dragons, and Unicorns." In *Independent* (London) (3 April 1993).
Cribb, T. J. "Transformations in the Fiction of Ben Okri." In Anna Rutherford, ed., *From Commonwealth to Post-Colonial.* Sydney: Dangaroo, 1992. Traces the different epistemologies in Okri's fiction from the early novels to the short stories.
Davies, Hunter. "Ben Okri's Green-Apple, Left-Handed Sort of Day." In *Independent* (London) (23 March 1993).
Fraser, Robert. "The Magic of the Jackals." Review of *Songs of Enchantment.* In *West Africa* (12 April 1993).
Garuba, Harry. "Ben Okri: Animist Realism and the Famished Genre." In *Guardian* (Lagos) (13 March 1993).
Gbadamosi, Gabriel. Review of *The Famished Road.* In *Wasafiri* 14 (autumn 1991).
Grant, Linda. "The Lonely Road from Twilight to Hard Sun." In *Observer* (London) (27 October 1991).
Griffiths, Lorraine. "Okri: Biography." In *Times* (London) (13 March 1993).
Howard, Philip. "There Is Wonder Here." In *Times* (London) (24 October 1991).
Jeyifo, Biodun. "The Voice of a Lost Generation: The Novels of Ben Okri." In *Guardian* (Lagos) (12 July 1986).
Maja-Pearce, Adewale. *A Mask Dancing: Nigerian Novelists of the Eighties.* London: Hans Zell Publishers, 1992.
Obi, Amanze. "The Triumph of Insignificance." In *Guardian* (Lagos) (10 November 1991).
Omotoso, Kole. "No Poor Relation." In *Guardian* (Manchester) (23 March 1993).
Onuekwusi, Jasper A. "Social Criticism in the Fiction of Young Nigerian Writers: Iyayi and Ben Okri." In Ernest Emenyonu, ed., *Literature and Society: Selected Essays on African Literature.* Oguta, Nigeria: Zim Pan-African Publishers, 1986.
Porter, Abioseh Michael. "Ben Okri's *The Landscapes Within*: A Metaphor for Personal and National Development." In *World Literature Written in English* 23 (fall 1988).
Quayson, Ato. "Esoteric Webworks as Nervous System: Reading the Fantastic in Ben Okri's Writing." In Abdulrazak Gurnah, ed., *Essays on African Writing 2.* London: Heinemann, 1995.

———. "Orality—(Theory)—Textuality: Tutuola, Okri and the Relationship of Literary Practice to Oral Traditions." In Stewart Brown, ed., *Pressures of the Text.* Birmingham, U.K.: Centre of West African Studies, 1995.

Richards, David. "'A History of Interruptions': Dislocated Mimesis in the Writings of Neil Bisoondath and Ben Okri." In Anna Rutherford, ed., *From Commonwealth to Post-Colonial.* Sydney, Australia: Dangaroo, 1992.

Taylor, D. Y. "Word Chains." In *Sunday Times* (London) (4 April 1993).

Taylor, Paul. "Dreams of a Boy on Earth." In *Independent* (London) (3 March 1993).

Tredell, Nicolas. "Uncertainties of the Poet." In *London Review of Books* (25 June 1992).

Winder, Robert. "The Road to Discovery." In *Independent* (London) (24 October 1991).

Wodall, James. "In the Land of Fighting Ghosts." In *Times* (London) (25 March 1993).

Kole Omotoso

1943–

UKO ATAI

BANKOLE AJIBABI OMOTOSO was born on 21 April 1943 in the southwestern town of Akure, in Ondo State, Nigeria. He was the second of three children of Yoruba parents, Gabriel Omotoso Falibuyan and Ajibabi Daramola Osukoti. (The Yoruba are one of the three major ethnic groups in Nigeria.) His father died when Omotoso was a boy, and he and his mother had to return to her own parents' house. This disruption of the child-parent relationship perhaps made Omotoso aware, at an early age, of the near defenselessness of the human being. What might have been a damaging sense of destitution, however, in his later life proved a source of creative impetus and energy. His writing and public comments are inspired by a deep concern for those he sees as the defenseless: whether an individual, a group of individuals, or even society as a whole. In his writings, Omotoso (himself a reggae enthusiast) exemplifies the refrain of a popular 1970s reggae song by the Jamaican-born, London-based artist Jimmy Cliff: "he who feels it knows it."

What the young Omotoso lost in terms of early parental love and nurturing, he made up for by growing up with his maternal grandparents. In a lively and large family atmosphere, the women and children would gather in the evenings and exchange stories, including traditional Yoruba tales about the wit and exploits of the tortoise and tales about "typical situations" that involved friends having a disagreement and trying to settle it. Omotoso's creative imagination was strongly influenced by the stories about the diminutive, defenseless tortoise, who nevertheless has the right to life like every other creature. From the stories about "typical situations" he learned narrative strategies that he later employed to great effect in his novels and short stories, where conflict creates the tension in the plot, and conflict resolution is achieved with compelling suspense.

The young Omotoso soon became adept at creating his own stories. Literary and narrative inventiveness, keen observation, and a sense of the social and political environment were the distinguishing features of stories he wrote during high school in his hometown, and then, from 1961 to 1963, at King's College, Lagos, where he became editor of the school's literary magazine. At the University of Ibadan, where he studied Arabic and French and received his bachelor's degree in 1968, he contributed to *Horizon*, the magazine of the English department. In 1974 Omotoso became literary editor for the Nigerian monthly magazine *Afriscope*. He found a forum for social commentaries and political anecdotes and articles in "A Writer's Diary," the column in the magazine *West Africa* that he began writing in 1976.

FICTION ABOUT NIGERIAN SOCIETY

In his fiction, Omotoso focuses on identifying the problems in Nigerian society and proposing solutions. The political history of Nigeria is as complex as its peoples are multicultural. Essentially a British creation, what is now Nigeria came into being in 1914. Thereafter, the story of Nigeria has been one of recurring waves of nationalist attempts at self-government, independence, and self-determination. Omotoso grew up during the 1940s and 1950s, a period of militant nationalism, a succession of constitutional conferences, labor unrest, strike actions, riots, and death by police bullets. This eventful period culminated in independence from Britain on 1 October 1960. With independence came the burning hope—nurtured and spread by nationalist leaders including Dr. Nnamdi Azikiwe, the Igbo leader; Chief Obafemi Awolowo, the Yoruba leader; Herbert Macaulay, the "father of Nigerian nationalism"; and Ernest Ikoli, the "dean of Nigerian journalists"—of a brighter, and more prosperous, future. According to Azikiwe, independence would give Nigerians the opportunity to walk "majestically with the other races of mankind" (quoted in James S. Coleman, *Nigeria: Background to Nationalism*, 1958, p. 410).

Although Omotoso lived his childhood and adolescence sharing the nationalists' dreams of peace, progress, and prosperity, as an adult and as a writer, he was forced to watch the systematic deferment of these dreams after independence. For decades after freedom from colonial rule, Nigeria was cursed by civil strife, including a civil war (1967–1970) and incessant military coups d'état. These events, together with undemocratic rule, political chicanery, and bureaucratic cynicism resulted in a steady decline in the quality of life in a nation that, because it is the most populous black nation on earth, is often looked upon as representative of the black race.

In his writings, Omotoso reacts to this social decadence with profound shock and anxiety, but not despair. That the dreams and hopes of independence could almost disappear and the sociocultural life of a nation so richly endowed with natural and human resources be mindlessly ruined seems unreal to him. To represent this unreal society—a society that is so grotesque as to be unbelievable, yet from which he draws inspiration and about which he writes—Omotoso creates a fiction full of social caricature that nonetheless seems highly realistic. The link he creates to mediate between the unreality of his society and the realism of his fiction is humor.

In his collection of short stories *Miracles and Other Stories* (1973), the detailed characters he creates, the gestures he gives them, and the social as well as psychological situations into which he places them exemplify his profound dissatisfaction with Nigerian society and his passionate embrace of a fictional alternative. The fictional alternative, laced with events from real life, seems more insulated and less threatening to live with. In the story "The Gamblers," for instance, Omotoso bases his portrayal of a group of con men and their atrocious scheming on his observations of the habitués of street corners and beer parlors, where such illegal activities are often conducted. An accumulation of details captures the gritty scene in high resolution:

> The apprentice swung open the back of the bus. Immediately a crowd of men heaved themselves inside, and found seats. A tall, black, clean-shaven man in *agbada*, *soro* and *eletiaja* sat next to the schoolboy....
>
> ... On the side where the young woman and the apprentice sat were four other men. One was a round-headed Hausaman. He wore a browning *agbada* and a pair of blue jeans. He carried a blue travelling bag in which were shaving materials, a two-edged dagger and a pack of cards....

> Next to him sat a man in *dansiki* and shorts. He had a wild look; blood-red eyes set in deep sockets. Under his narrowing nostrils a semicircular thicket of moustache grew fan-wise over his thick upper lips. His teeth were brown. He leaned forward from his seat expectantly and frighteningly. From time to time he took an anxious look at the Hausaman....
>
> ...The Hausaman drew out the cards and ran them against his right thumb. He picked out three cards—the Queen of Spades, the Queen of Hearts and what is locally called the joker....
>
> The schoolboy craned his neck.
>
> (1978 edition, pp. 28–31)

But if Omotoso's invented reality seems too difficult to bear, the story is also softened with relaxing pieces of harmless humor: "The apprentice wore khaki shorts with the seat threadbare, exposing his light skin. When asked why he did not mend the shorts or get another pair, he said that the shorts were ideal, being air-conditioned through the seat" (p. 26).

In his fiction, Omotoso transforms his anxiety about the disintegration of society into an attempt to revitalize society and give form to its decay and chaos. Because the fictional scenes that he creates are so immediate—seemingly real, but more lively and better organized than the depressing incoherence of real life—Omotoso makes the abnormality of Nigerian society comprehensible. Confronted with a social reality that is so decadent and chaotic it seems impossible to alter for the better, Omotoso creates a fictional reality, robust and well-ordered, that allows him to identify the problems in society and propose diagnoses, treatments, and cures. Omotoso intends these treatments and cures to be transferred to the ailing society. This, then, is the basis of his style: to juxtapose social and historical facts with invented, fictional characters and situations.

In his conception of reality and fiction, Omotoso asserts a materialist view, which emphasizes the reality in physical matter and, by extension, in social life. To the questions of what reality is and what realism is, he would most likely respond: reality is fundamentally social and historical, not imaginary or apparent; realism is an artistic attitude that involves great accuracy in the representation of social life, points out the undesirable aspects of social life, and suggests remedies. This attitude, in turn, requires that works of creativity be relevant to the life of society.

THE WRITER'S IDEAS AND VALUES

Literature, as a cultural front in the ongoing struggle for social and political progress, is inextricable from Omotoso's African experience. In a 1979 monograph titled *The Form of the African Novel*, he argues for a radical conception of the African novel:

> After political freedom was granted with West Minister [*sic*] type constitutions, national anthems and flags it was found that democracy was in for a rough time in the hands of these Africans. One after the other the army either took over political control or a so-called one man dictatorship is established....
>
> Little by little African countries have been forced to find alternative process of attaining development for their nation-states.
>
> In the same way, the type of novel which the African novelist inherited from Europe is far from being adequate for the reality which the African novelist has to deal with.
>
> (p. 71)

Consequently, since "disease, ignorance and poverty, defeat, loss of self consciousness and inability to cope with the demands of the new way of life" constitute social reality for the African peoples, it would be unthinkable and a sheer waste of effort for an African "novelist to mould deathless prose and compose timeless works of art" (p. 71). Rather, African art and literature should "partake of the process of radical social change" (p. 74).

While Omotoso dismisses the relevance of European literary models and urges the creation of a narrative form that both reflects and affects social process in Africa, his radicalism is marked by a profound sense of balance and social justice. Change, Omotoso believes, should come not through uninformed sloganeering or mindless revolutionary bloodshed, but through an objective investigation of the causes of society's problems and a reasoned and planned approach to solving them. In his plays, novels, short stories, and anecdotes, self-interrogation and investigation of what went wrong, where, how, and why are primary in defining and resolving human conflicts. Omotoso sees this approach as a creative mandate: "Writing continues to be my way of interrogating my history, my present and the future of Nigeria and Africa" (quoted from informal correspondence with this writer).

Omotoso is deeply concerned about human, especially African, self-development, self-perfection, and self-fulfillment. In a report for *West Africa* (7 March 1983), Hans Zell, publisher of the *Journal of Commonwealth Literature*, describes Omotoso as "a 'revolutionary' with a heart, and a soul, and, mercifully, a 'revolutionary' with a sense of humour!" (p. 607).

The variety of Omotoso's literary work indicates the tenacity with which he continuously seeks the idea of the dignity of the African person. He presents a refreshing reappraisal of the social, economic, political, and cultural effects of the contact between Europe and Africa in colonialism. He believes that if Africa was damaged by the encounter with Europe, Africa has to shoulder some of the blame. He also believes that succeeding generations of Africans, particularly the postcolonial educated and privileged elite, have the responsibility of righting the wrongs of that encounter and updating Africa's social, economic, political, and cultural agenda.

In his speech at the opening of the second International Book Fair of Radical Black and Third World Books in London in March 1983, Omotoso spelled out what is to be done in order to realize Africa's comprehensive historic agenda. Successful implementation of this agenda, according to Omotoso, depends on the "correct reading of our priorities" (reported in *West Africa* on 28 March 1983, p. 813). These priorities lie in the areas of politics, economics, and culture. Omotoso believes that in the political realm, Africans need to "debate the question of the Nation-State as bequeathed to us by the colonial heritage and decide how it works in the present global dispensation." Additionally, Africa needs to "resolve the contradiction of nationality in that Nation-State and ethnic grouping in that state." To improve the economic situation of Africa would require "as equal a distribution as possible of the available national resources by way of services to our people and the opening of opportunities." On the subject of culture, Omotoso urges Africans "to see the beauty and the limitless possibilities of the acceptance of our double inheritance—our folk traditional oral inheritance and the interaction with our colonial heritage."

Africans, he concludes, "are not a people of either-or as far as our cultural priorities are concerned." This cultural stance points the way forward for the African agenda through "the vanguard of our masses and our mass organisations contributing their creative genius and their spontaneity and the vanguard of our intellectual workers bringing their analysis and their prognostications under the direction and instruction of our mass organisations" (p. 813).

Over the years, Omotoso has drawn inspiration from Cheikh Anta Diop's intellectual and philosophical thoughts on the African "personality"—the cultural and historical legacy of Africans. Diop, a Senegalese professor of Egyptology at the University of Dakar's Institute for Fundamental Research in Black Africa—a man renowned as a historian, linguist, mathematician, anthropologist, physicist, and philosopher—has systematized and elaborated on the anteriority and remarkable continuity of African civilization and history.

As the cradle of humanity, both Africa and Africans have, in Diop's conclusion, given humankind its civilizing leaven and vitality. Therefore, it is the responsibility of succeeding generations of Africa's scholars and intellectuals to recapture their lost historical consciousness and, with the resilience and optimism inherent in the act of reclaiming, empower Africa's struggle for cultural emancipation.

In the light of Diop's theses about the African personality, Omotoso's concerns become understandable. Characters in his novels and short stories march or struggle on with amazing resilience, even unto death. In the short story "Miracles Take a Little Longer," from the collection *Miracles and Other Stories*, for example, Omotoso tells the story of a handsome, slim twelve-year-old boy from a poor rural family. His name is Lasisi, but his schoolmates call him "Lasti Brown." Even at his age, Lasisi is on his way to becoming a professional sprinter. Already armed with the tricks of the trade, "he ran gracefully, landing each time on his toes, getting new strength from the push such landing gave him" (p. 68). One morning, after having "gone to bed the evening before healthy," he wakes up paralyzed. The rest of the story describes the ordeal that Lasisi and his parents undergo. In spite of his paralysis, Lasisi often tells his small sister, Remi, some "tortoise story." But Remi herself is also stricken with paralysis and dies. Lasisi survives. He survives by sheer will, aided by the concern and care of his teacher and his doctor. In this story of human suffering and endurance, Omotoso's attitude comes through in the words of Lasisi's father: "Can we have the courage to go through all this again and again and again? What has being a man got to do with it? I am talking about human suffering" (p. 83). Even though Lasisi's parents have buried eight children, Lasisi, the promising star of the tracks, survives.

In innumerable sketches for television programs, Omotoso's humor, even when dire conditions confront his characters, speaks of hope, optimism, and continuity. In his plays, which reenact the stark, sociopolitical realities of society, this same resilience and resistance to despair are evident.

This sense of resilience and optimism characterizes the efforts of many revolutionaries in the ongoing struggle to recapture the soul and personality of Africa and Africans in the aftermath of colonialism. Amilcar Cabral, the leader of the independence movement for Guinea-Bissau, who was assassinated in 1973, and António Agostinho Neto, the first president of an independent Angola, who died in 1979, translated Diop's thoughts and findings about the soul and personality of Africa into action. Omotoso clearly endorses, in his column in *West Africa*, Cabral's and Neto's recapturing "their lost historical consciousness," their subsequent "correct reading" of Africa's priorities, and, ultimately, their "reasoned and planned" struggle to "right the wrongs" of the colonial encounter in their respective parts of Africa.

"JUST BEFORE DAWN"

Beginning in 1976, Omotoso covered an unending variety of social and political issues in his column, "A Writer's Diary," in *West Africa*. For example, in "Writing Wrongs for Children," he emphasizes that "not even children's writing and publishing could be detached from the political situation in Africa" (7 March 1983, p. 607); in "The Ideas of Ali Mazrui," Omotoso argues that, given the African condition, prominent African scholars cannot afford the luxury of so-called independent thinking because "no ideas in human history have been independent" (7 March 1983, p. 605); and in "Alexander Solzhenitsyn and the Third World" (15 August 1983), he regrets the Russian writer's inability to understand the nature and scope of the sociopolitical problems that militate against Africa's overall progress.

In "Looking the Sun in the Face," Omotoso assessed his place and that of other writers in contemporary Africa. He says of himself: "I must be one of the most fortunately placed writers in Nigeria. I span that nebulous area between the old and the new" (8 August 1983, p. 1823). Omotoso recognizes his position as one of transition, given Africa's efforts at moving from its colonial experience to postcolonial emancipation and selfhood. The pride in his statement comes from his sense of feeling honored by history; he is among those who will midwife the new Africa; he sees himself working constructively and optimistically in the period "just before dawn."

In most of these anecdotes, Omotoso addresses social and political issues, yet he maintains a passionate concern for human subjects and situations as well as aesthetic goals. In some of the columns—for example "Only a Joke?" (28 March 1983), he uses satire to juxtapose the normal and abnormal in African society.

NOVELS AND PLAYS

Omotoso wrote his first novel, *The Edifice* (1971), in 1969, while working toward his doctoral degree at the University of Edinburgh. The concerns that he elaborates in his later work are already present here: for example, the need for postcolonial Africans, as individuals and as members of society, to define themselves in order to achieve self-actualization in the future. In *The Edifice*, Dele, whose full Yoruba name, Bamidele, implies a plea to return home, goes to Britain to study and finds it difficult living in a culture that is Other and accepting the ways of a people who are Other. Nonetheless, he meets, falls in love with, and marries a white woman named Daisy. At the wedding, Dele feels that "those who came looked as if they were at a funeral ceremony. My funeral" (p. 92). Omotoso stages the wedding as an opportunity for the symbolic marriage of cultures. Confronted with such a momentous, overloaded event, however, Dele allows his sense of self to recede and resorts to asserting himself negatively through making excuses. Back home in Nigeria after his first marriage has collapsed, Dele marries another white woman, Susan.

Cast loosely in the mold of the stream-of-consciousness novel, *The Edifice* is divided into two parts, in which Dele dramatizes his memoirs, and an epilogue, narrated by Daisy. Omotoso returns to the stream-of-consciousness narrative strategy in his fifth novel, *Sacrifice* (1974). In *Sacrifice*, however, the narrated memoirs, which give *The Edifice* a racy, airy texture, become solidified, written "Notes." This change in technique may have been caused by Omotoso's searching for a narrative mode that would more immediately reflect the progressively decaying sociopolitical ethos in many African societies. The fictional mode he develops to capture this changing society might be termed *faction*—a portmanteau of *fact* and *fiction*—which he uses to good effect in *Just Before Dawn* (1988).

In *To Borrow a Wandering Leaf* (1978), Omotoso uses the "wandering leaf" as a metaphor of the alienated African administrators who occasionally make the ritual rounds of an impoverished countryside but have effectively distanced themselves from the lives of the people. In the epigraph to the novel, Omotoso states: "There is hope in the Earth of Aiyede. But hands must put the seed within to raise hope. This Earth cannot be fertile and also [impregnate] herself. There is need for organization." Unfortunately, as the story reveals, the whole country—unspecified but clearly Nigeria—remains "wasted by ten years of politics, ten years of planlessness" (p. 22).

In fact, the world that Omotoso so passionately reflects in his writing seems always under some imprecation. In his first play, *The Curse* (1976), he depicts the use and abuse of power. The sequel to the nightmare evoked by *The Curse* comes in another play, darkly titled *Shadows in the Horizon* (1977).

Omotoso has described his novel *Fella's Choice* (1974) as "a straightforward kind of spy story" (Lindfors, p. 54). The love for his country prompts Fella Dandogo to undertake the risky detective work of countering the anti-Nigerian activities of South Africa's Bureau for State Security. After reading the first paragraph of a volume that sets forth the philosophy of Force Headquarters, which has commissioned him, he is enthusiastic: "This was straight talking. This was fire-ball. At last somebody in Nigeria was using his black mahogany head" (p. 15). Gradually, logically, and systematically the details that motivate the espionage and its counteraction are assembled, analyzed, and integrated into the planning and execution of the successful action of this thriller.

After writing *Fella's Choice*, Omotoso declared, "I think I'll stick to realistic writing" (Lindfors, p. 54). In making this declaration, Omotoso recognizes two options in his fiction: a realistic and a nonrealistic approach. He decides that pointing obliquely to real social decay would not serve his commitment to helping to regenerate his society. He carries out his promise to write realistically in the conception and execution of *Just Before Dawn*. In lieu of a preface, Omotoso quotes a passage from Lerone Bennett, Jr.'s "The Road Not Taken," which originally appeared in *Ebony* magazine (August 1970). Bennett describes the creation of a nation as a series of decisions and choices. With this quote as his starting point, Omotoso announces his intention to take a realistic approach to the mostly factual material of this novel. Omotoso sees himself as a writer working just before the dawn in a new era of his country's social and political history; his novel is the culmination of extensive research that forms the basis for a depiction of Nigeria's quest of progress. The story is populated with a huge cast of real-life English and Nigerian characters, many of whom, along with their supporters, were still living and politically active at the time. Reporting the turns, twists, and high moments of Nigeria's quest, Omotoso maintains a high degree of objectivity. His sympathy for and identification with Nigeria in this blend of historical facts and imaginative fiction come through in the wit and humor that characterize this "faction."

CONCLUSION

Omotoso writes in a hurry, which somewhat accounts for the light, racy feel of his fiction. He is almost always certain about his narrative materials and the use to which he wishes to put them. With a full schedule of teaching and academic research responsibilities in Nigeria and abroad, creative work for stage and television, and professional responsibilities to the Association of Nigerian Authors and the African Writers' Association, time constraints often demand speed and brevity. But the reader must not take Omotoso in a hurry. He compensates for the raciness of his writing with a delicately fresh and judicious use of the English language. Although he is certainly not a poet, his ability to evoke a situation, mood, or character through detailed but uncluttered description gives poetic value and permanence to his work.

In addition, his work is also characterized by an abiding, deeply held sense of commitment to the restoration of the dignity of the African person. This project would certainly require a reappraisal of the ordering of the contemporary Nigerian society. The constant and ardent articulation of this commitment does not accord with the elite in postindependence Nigeria, the military. Consequently, Omotoso quietly left Nigeria with his family in early 1992 for the safety and freedom of postapartheid South Africa, where he teaches English at the University of Western Cape, outside of Cape Town. The first fruit of this migration to South Africa is his appropriately titled *Season of Migration to the South* (1994). Understandably, the book has not been made available in Nigeria.

Selected Bibliography

NOVELS

The Edifice. London: Heinemann, 1971.
The Combat. London: Heinemann, 1972.
Fella's Choice. Benin City, Nigeria: Ethiope, 1974.
Sacrifice. Ibadan, Nigeria: Onibonoje, 1974, 1978.
The Scales. Ibadan, Nigeria: Onibonoje, 1976.
To Borrow a Wandering Leaf. Akure, Nigeria: Fagbamigbe, 1978.
Memories of Our Recent Boom. Harlow, U.K.: Longman, 1982.
Just Before Dawn. Ibadan, Nigeria: Spectrum Books, 1988.

PLAYS

The Curse. Ibadan, Nigeria: New Horn Press, 1976.
Shadows in the Horizon: A Play About the Combustibility of Private Property. Ibadan, Nigeria: Sketch Publishing Co., 1977.

ARTICLES

"Literature and Society in Africa North of the Sahara." In *Seminar Ser.* 1, no. 2 (1976–1977).
"Looking the Sun in the Face." In *West Africa* (8 August 1983).
"Responses." In *West Africa* (18 July 1983).
"The Wages of To-Write." In *West Africa* (11 April 1983).
"Bitter Struggle Under the Sweet Talk." In *South* (London), no. 63 (January 1986).
"Getting Back to Africa." In *West Africa* (1 September 1986).

TRAVEL

All This Must Be Seen. Moscow: Progress Publishers, 1986.

SHORT STORIES

Miracles and Other Stories. Ibadan, Nigeria: Onibonoje, 1973, 1978.
Kingdom of Chance and Other Stories. Ibadan, Nigeria: Onibonoje, 1982.

ESSAYS

The Form of the African Novel. Akure, Nigeria: Fagbamigbe, 1979.
Discovering African Literature. Oxford, U.K.: Ikenga, 1982.
The Theatrical into Theatre. London: New Beacon, 1982.

INTERVIEWS

Adeniyi, Tola. "Writers' Search for Audience in Africa." In *Daily Times* (Lagos) (12 March 1974).
Ezughah, Dili. "Omotoso Banished into Creative Bliss." In *Guardian* (Lagos) (9 June 1986).
Kargbo, Kolosa. "Colonialism: The Writer's Blessing in Disguise?" In *Vanguard* (Lagos) (8 August 1985).
Lakoju, Tunde, and Duro Irojah. "Extract from an Interview with Dr. Kole Omotoso." In *Mirror* 2 (1975–1976).
Lindfors, Bernth. "Kole Omotoso Interviewed." In *Cultural Events in Africa* 103 (1973). Repr. in Lindfors, ed. *Dem-Say: Interviews with Eight Nigerian Writers.* Austin: African and Afro-American Studies and Research Center, University of Texas, 1974.
"Newsliners." In *Newswatch* (Lagos) (15 April 1985).
Tetteh-Lartey, Alex. "Interview with Kole Omotoso about *Fella's Choice* and *The Combat.*" In *BBC Arts and Africa* 74 (1975).
———. "Interview with Kole Omotoso About *Memories of Our Recent Boom* and About English as a Literary Language." In *BBC Arts and Africa* 433 (1982).
———. "Interview with Kole Omotoso About Nigerian Theatrical Activity, Especially at Universities." In *BBC Arts and Africa* 610 (1985).
Walder, Dennis. "Interview with Kole Omotoso." In *Transition* (Kampala, Uganda) 44 (1974).
Zell, Hans M. "Interview: Kole Omotoso." In *Africa Book Publishing Record* 2 (1976).

CRITICAL STUDIES

Balogun, F. Odun. "Populist Fiction: Omotoso's Novels." In *African Literature Today* 13 (1983).
Bozimo, Willy. "Dr. Omotoso: Novelist and Academician." In *Spear* (Lagos) (July 1976).

———. "The Literary World of Kole Omotoso." In *Spear* (Lagos) (September 1976).

Dash, Cheryl M. L. "An Introduction to the Prose Fiction of Kole Omotoso." In *World Literature Written in English* 16 (1977).

Dasylva, Ademola Omobewaji. "Art, Audience, and Society in Kole Omotoso's Fiction." Master's thesis, University of Ife, Nigeria, 1984.

Dohan, Oyado. "Kole Omotoso in Review." In *Indigo* (Lagos) 2, no. 3 (1975).

Nazareth, Peter. "The Tortoise Is an Animal, but He Is Also a Wise Creature." In *Umoja* (Dar es Salaam, Tanzania) 2, no. 2 (1975).

Ofeimun, Odia. "Kole Omotoso: The Novelist as Guerilla." In *Guardian* (Lagos) (22 November 1986).

Onoriose, Wilfred. "Kole Omotoso and the Nigerian Novel in the Seventies." Master's thesis, University of Ibadan, Nigeria, 1978.

Femi Osofisan

1946–

GARETH GRIFFITHS

THE NIGERIAN PLAYWRIGHT Femi Osofisan (Babafemi Adeyemi Osofisan) was born on 16 June 1946. He attended primary and secondary schools in Ilesha, Ile-Ife, and Erunwon, then furthered his education at Government College, Ibadan. He attended the University of Senegal, Dakar, in 1968, and then the University of Ibadan, where he received a bachelor's degree in French in 1969 and a doctorate in 1974. He also attended the University of Paris III between 1971 and 1973. In 1973 he became a member of the faculty at the University of Ibadan, in the theater arts department; he has also been a visiting professor at a number of universities in Africa, Europe, and the United States. His many academic and writing honors include visiting fellowships at Cambridge in 1986 and Cornell in 1992. He was a participant in the Iowa International Writer's Program in 1986, artist in residence at Napoule, France, in 1990, and guest writer at the Japan Foundation in 1991.

In addition to his academic career, Osofisan has been a productive journalist: he helped found a Lagos paper, the *Guardian*; was a columnist and editorial member of the *Daily Times* of Nigeria in 1990 and 1991; and served in an editorial capacity on the critical journals *Black Orpheus*, *Ibadan Journal of African and Comparative Literature*, and *Opon Ifa*. He won the Association of Nigerian Authors prize in 1983 and again in 1986. He has been president of the Association of Nigerian Authors and vice president for West Africa of the Pan-African Writer's Association. His talents also extend to translation, including a 1983 translation from the French of Alain Ricard's *Theatre and Nationalism: Wole Soyinka and LeRoi Jones*.

The author of some twenty stage plays as well as many television plays, a volume of poetry, several short stories, and two longer pieces of prose fiction, Osofisan is among the most prolific and influential of the new generation of Yoruba writers writing in English. (The Yoruba, predominant in the southwestern states of Nigeria, are one of the three major ethnic groups in Nigeria, the other two being the Igbo and the Hausa.) This new generation includes such writers as Kole Omotoso and Bode Sowande, who began writing in the 1970s and whose work challenged the work of the first generation of postindependence Nigerian writers, such as the Yoruba Wole Soyinka and the Igbo Chinua Achebe, by taking a more overtly political stand. Osofisan's plays have been widely produced in Nigeria; together with Omotoso and Sowande, he was instrumental in developing the style and form of the English-language drama initiated in Nigeria by Soyinka in the early 1960s, and in making contemporary Nigerian drama engage directly with the problems of bringing about social change and radical political action.

As a social and literary critic, Osofisan is usually categorized with other exponents of the so-called *bolekaja* (combat) criticism, such as Omotoso, Niyi Osundare, Biodun Jeyifo, and Odia Ofeimun. These young writers and critics opposed what they saw as the lack of commitment to social change in the first generation of Nigerian critics and writers. Nevertheless some, like Osofisan, continued to draw on the techniques and themes of the earlier writers, especially Soyinka, whose influence Osofisan acknowledged even as he disputed the social and political effects of what he perceived to be Soyinka's reification of mythic readings of culture and his tendency to idealize the role of the sacrificial hero in effecting social change. For Osofisan, Soyinka failed to engage with the forces of myth and history in a critical and interrogative way. Although Osofisan also turned to Yoruba history and mythology for his plots, he sought to radicalize these sources, often inverting their effect by turning them on their heads.

For example, in the 1979 play *Morountodun* (published in 1982), Osofisan reorders the traditional story of the legendary Yoruba princess Moremi so that at the end of his version the position of the rebellious peasants is endorsed. In Osofisan's retelling, the heroine Titubi parallels the heroine of the original story, Moremi, as she offers herself for capture in order to penetrate the secrets of the enemies of the state and discover their weak points. But, unlike Moremi, Titubi recants this role when she sees the poverty and misery of the people, and she uses her position to aid the rebels. The play turns the original myth, which celebrates the power of those who rule the community, into a celebration of those who oppose the rulers in the name of social justice. In many of Osofisan's other plays, from *Red Is the Freedom Road* (first produced in 1969 as *You Have Lost Your Fine Face*, revised in 1974 under the new title, and published in 1982) to *Esu and the Vagabond Minstrels* (first produced in 1984, revised in 1986, and published in 1991), the same process of subverting mythic and historic events and figures is a characteristic feature.

Despite his consciously radical intentions, however, Osofisan—like Soyinka before him—always resisted the more extreme demands of the "combat criticism" school. He continued to insist that artistic excellence was inseparable from social effectiveness. Perhaps for this reason, and despite his desire to speak to and for the common people of Nigeria, he has had greater success with an elite audience. For the mass audience to which he aspired, the challenging forms his work takes have sometimes proved a barrier. Osofisan later defended these choices by arguing for the need to expose a more radical social agenda to the emerging intellectual middle class in the universities and in the auditoriums of the national theater. Nevertheless, throughout his career he has struggled with the intractable problem of addressing the masses directly through his art.

THE EARLY PLAYS: POLITICAL RADICALISM AND THE STAGE

In the late 1960s and 1970s, younger writers like Osofisan wanted to see everyday problems of corruption and political incompetence become part of the subject of drama. They were also determined to take theater away from the campuses and larger towns and bring it more directly to the people. Despite these progressive concerns, they often drew upon historical and legendary material to effect their aim. They were aware of the appeal of this material to a broad audience, an appeal that had been exploited by the leaders of the popular commercial theater troupes that operated successfully in Nigeria in the 1950s and 1960s, led by figures such as Herbert Ogunde and Duro Ladipo.

Typical of the work of Osofisan in this period is *Red Is the Freedom Road*. The play is a good illustration of Osofisan's early style, even in the 1974 revised version. Using a deceptively simple style, Osofisan creates an absorbing story that can also be read as an allegory of contemporary politics and social conditions in Nigeria.

The action of *Red Is the Freedom Road* is set in the precolonial past. The royal prisoner Akanji leads a revolt against his master, persuading his fellow slaves to refuse their subjugated position. The bulk of the king's army is made up of former prisoners of war, and Akanji appeals to the pride in their past identities when he challenges them to revolt against the king. The story offers a representation, transposed into the past, of the hegemonic nature of colonial and neocolonial power, from which only an awakening of pride and the return to an independent self-image can release people. Since the army suppresses its own people, the parallel with the colonial and neocolonial elite is clear.

Osofisan weaves into the story a series of complex personal and moral choices. Akanji hides from his family the real reason for his agreeing to serve as the new army commander, that is, to gain the power he needs for a successful rebellion. To gain the king's confidence, he abuses and deceives his wife and inadvertently causes the death of his own mother. Akanji anguishes over the consequences that his secrecy has brought on his family, and the play explores the excruciating dramatic tensions of his suffering. This interweaving of themes of personal ethics and political action, characteristic of Osofisan's work at this time, prevents the plays from being merely polemical.

Despite Osofisan's strong political commitment, *Red Is the Freedom Road* acknowledges the complexities of the recent history of rebellions for "freedom" in Nigeria. The play uses two soldiers as commentators. Standing aside from the revolt, they cynically change sides according to the flow of events and comment sardonically on the disillusionment of many Nigerians with the promises of coups and revolutions to bring about freedom and change. The play also makes clear references to the events of the Nigerian civil war, fought from 1967 to 1970 between the Nigerian government and the secessionist republic of Biafra; to some extent Akanji can be seen to represent the victorious Federal leader, General Yakubu Gowon. Reference to Gowon seems especially evident in comments that the soldiers make about leaders who win wars only to fail to install an effective and just peacetime regime.

In *A Restless Run of Locusts*, produced in 1970 and published in 1975, Osofisan opted for a modern setting and a more overt portrait of the problems associated with contemporary political life. The "hero," Sanda, an opposition party candidate against the corrupt Chief Kuti, is drawn quickly into the miasma of politics when he decides to hide the truth about his brother's death on the orders of the leader of the opposition party. By putting the party's need to appear to have clean hands ahead of the need for justice that his own brother's death clearly demands, Sanda makes the fatal compromise that leads to his moral downfall. The scheme results in the suicide of Chief Kuti, who feels remorseful for his actions and their consequence. The suicide is an unlikely act on his part, given his character, and reveals a weakness in the plot of this early piece. Chief Kuti's death leads Sanda to realize the false path he has begun to tread. Sanda's attempt at atonement leads to his own death at the hands of his political allies. Chief Kuti's daughter Iyabo, has been Sanda's lover (against her father's will) and is pregnant with his child; she and Mrs. Kuti are left alone to raise the child and to mourn their dead. Despite some interesting moments, the play is a simple and melodramatic fable that ultimately fails to convince.

With *The Chattering and the Song*, first produced at the University of Ibadan in 1974 (published in 1977), Osofisan's mature dramaturgy begins to take shape. *The Chattering and the Song* weds European drama to traditional Yoruba forms. Ifa, one of the most important Yoruba sacred traditions and a recurring feature in Osofisan's drama, is integrated into the play as a central feature of the narrative. Ifa is the principal divination cult based on a long and complex body of Ifa wisdom preserved in the Yoruba oral tradition. Much of this wisdom has now been published as a corpus of texts. The practice of Ifa is centered on such divination shrines as the one at Ile-Ife but is widespread throughout the Yoruba community. The ritual is as important to Osofisan's work as Ogun, the Prometheus-like Yoruba god, is to Soyinka's. The Ifa divination corpus emphasizes the responsibility of human beings, and the moral choice facing them, who consult its text for readings. As such it is a central metaphorical element in Osofisan's work, which strongly emphasizes personal and social morality and the complex choices this morality frequently entails.

Centering on the relationships, personal and political, within a group of young Nigerian intellectuals, *The Chattering and the Song* traces the shifting alliances and betrayals of these radical students from a variety of social backgrounds. The plot begins with the shift in emotional and political allegiance of the young painter Yajin from her fiancé, Mokan, to the powerful, if morbid, radical Sontri. Sontri's courtship of Yajin, employing the riddling conventions of Ifa, dramatizes the overpowering sexual and intellectual attraction through potent animal metaphors: Yajin is compared to the doe covered by the stag, or to the willing prey of Sontri as the hunting eagle. Mokan, who pretends to be reconciled to the loss of Yajin, covertly joins the secret police. When Yajin stages an early radical play written by Sontri as part of their engagement feast, Mokan comes out of hiding and arrests Sontri.

The play-within-the-play allows a second level of action through which the political implications can be further developed. Sontri's play deals with the reign of the famous Yoruba king Alafin Abiodun, allowing Osofisan to present a revisionary reading of this high point of Yoruba culture. Osofisan emphasizes the tendency of even the most enlightened ruler to revert to arbitrary and brutal action when his entrenched authority is challenged.

In 1977 Osofisan produced *Who's Afraid of Solarin?* (published in 1978), the first play in which he rewrote an existing text in a Nigerian context. He repeated this technique in such works as *Midnight Hotel* (1982, published in 1986), based on *L'Hotel du libre échange* (1894; *Hotel Paradise*) by Georges Feydeau, the French master of the *boulevardier* farce, as well as in rewrites of "classic" African plays of the first generation of writers in English. Soyinka was the source for *No More the Wasted Breed* (produced and published in 1982), and the work of the Nigerian playwright and poet John Pepper Clark served as a basis for *Another Raft* (1987, published in 1988).

Who's Afraid of Solarin? reworks Nikolay Gogol's *The Inspector General*, finding a ready parallel between the corrupt officials in the regime of Olusẹgun Ọbasanjọ in the late 1970s and the corrupt, self-seeking, and inept bureaucrats of czarist Russia. The play celebrates the real-life figure of Dr. Tai Solarin, an official dedicated to fighting corruption and malpractice. When the corrupt local officials around the aptly named Chief T. D. Gbonmiaiyelobiojo—the name's Yoruba meaning is "lavish user of the water of life"—known as T. D. G., hear of an incognito visitor in their region, they immediately jump to the conclusion that he is the incorruptible Dr. Solarin.

Of course, the visitor is not Solarin or even an official at all; he is Isola, a small-time crook fleeing Lagos one step ahead of the police.

From Chief T. D. G.'s servant, Polycap, Isola learns of the officials' fear that he is Solarin and he recognizes a golden opportunity to exploit these fellow crooks' fear, gullibility, and corruption to the fullest.

The officials try to bribe the "incorruptible" Solarin, who proves surprisingly cooperative. Isola's real identity is ultimately revealed through his diary, in which he had recorded his opinions of them all before escaping in Chief T. D. G.'s car with the loot. The play ends with the announcement by two beggars (who have observed all of the action) that the real Dr. Tai Solarin has arrived. The audience understands that the genuine Solarin will have his work cut out for him.

The following year, in *Once Upon Four Robbers* (1978, published in 1982), Osofisan took the dramatic parallel between crooks and politicians a step farther. The play explores the premise that since corruption is so endemic to Nigeria, the armed robbers—also endemic to postindependence Nigerian life under the Gowon regime—are, paradoxically, the most honest men in the society, since their robbery is at least performed in the open, free from hypocrisy. At the end of the play, the audience is invited to choose between the robbers and the soldiers, who have joined the government as part of its law-and-order campaign to protect the property of the newly rich. Osofisan thus involves his theatergoers directly in the action; the play ends with the audience members being asked to indicate which side they support by means of a vote.

His next play, *Morountodun* (1979, published in 1982), a revision of a familiar Yoruba story, also ends with a direct, though less formal, appeal to the audience to exercise its judgment: "The real struggle, the real truth, is out there among you, on the street, in your home, in your daily living and dying" (p. 79). Both endings invite audience intervention in resolving the action, and this has led the Nigerian poet Niyi Osundare to compare Osofisan with Bertolt Brecht, whose dramaturgical use of audience intervention is Osofisan's likely model. Certainly until this time Osofisan had been the most consistently radical of the new playwrights, using his plays to speak uncompromisingly for a Marxist resolution of Nigeria's problems along class lines by inviting direct popular struggle. In this respect too he shows a clear debt to the Brechtian tradition of politically engaged theater.

RESPONSE TO THE SOCIAL AND POLITICAL DEVELOPMENTS OF THE 1980s

At the beginning of the 1980s, in *The Oriki of a Grasshopper* (1981, published in 1986), Osofisan sounds a more hesitant note. For the first time, he exhibits decreasing confidence in the ability of intellectuals to influence events, especially in the wake of the increased corruption following the Nigerian oil boom of the mid 1970s. In a 1982 article titled "Enter the Carthaginian Critic...?" he commented on the worsening situation in Nigeria: "It is not the writer who will correct [this]...situation. The writer can help diagnose and increase awareness; he can protest and move others to protest; he cannot cure or heal" (p. 40).

In the earlier *Once Upon Four Robbers*, the dominant note was anger: anger against the hypocrisy of the Gowon government and its callous disregard for human life as it protected the property of a newly affluent middle class spawned by the oil wealth; anger, too, at the self-destructive willingness of the poor to see "robbers" as their enemies and "soldiers" as their protectors. In *Once Upon Four Robbers* Osofisan calls attention to the firing squads who publicly executed those accused of armed robbery at Bar Beach, Lagos, and illustrates allegorically that the soldiers and their victims are members of the same alienated and disrupted families. But by 1981 anger was replaced in Osofisan's work by a sense of despair. The early attempts of Osofisan and other English-language playwrights of the new generation to move their radical concerns out into the community clearly had fallen on deaf ears. But *The Oriki of a Grasshopper*, as it dramatizes the plight of the contemporary intellectual in Nigeria, looks directly at how Nigeria's radical intellectuals—distanced by education and economic security from the masses on whose behalf they claim to speak—have a dangerously close relationship with the new generation of university-educated businessmen and politicians whose values they claim to oppose.

Set during a university production of Samuel Beckett's *Waiting for Godot* (the choice of this 1952 play symbolizing, perhaps, the apathetic mood of the Nigerian intelligentsia), *The Oriki of a Grasshopper* takes place in the aftermath of a student strike that has led to the arrest of a number of faculty members accused of supporting political subversion. Imaro, a theater studies lecturer, and his friend Claudius, now a wealthy businessman, are waiting for the third actor, the brother of Moni. Moni is a former student of Imaro's who is now his mistress. The brother fails to arrive, and it becomes clear that he has been arrested. Claudius confesses that Imaro would also have been arrested had it not been for Claudius' intervention with the authorities. Moni bitterly denounces Imaro, accusing him of betraying his friends and principles by accepting the businessman's protection. Imaro decides that since he appears compromised among the radicals, he may as well give up his work and enter business. Claudius illustrates the sycophantic role businessmen need to survive in modern Nigeria as he defends the behavior of the political flunkeys whom he has to deal with daily to succeed in business. He argues that people like Imaro are needed to continue the struggle against these values, in the hope that they will remind Nigerians of the possibility of an alternative way in "the future." Imaro seems to accept this, but for Moni, this is only further evidence that Imaro has become what she characterizes as the establishment's "token marxist" (p. 43).

Moni sees Imaro as a kind of sop for Claudius' conscience; he personifies a friendly but ineffective liberal and artistic enclave to which society can retreat for refreshment after the cut-throat struggle of corrupt business and politics. The ending of the play does not resolve this ambiguous portrait of the modern artist and intellectual. Although Moni agrees to help Imaro to dream his dream of freedom for the last time, by helping him in his planned protest against the government for the recent arrests, she makes it clear to him that she will leave afterwards before he traps her "in [his] failure" (p. 43). The play has a special poignancy since it seems to speak directly of Osofisan's own situation and that of Nigeria's literary intellectuals as a group during this period. By this time in his career Osofisan seems to acknowledge the failure of the intellectual left to provide anything more than a mere rhetoric of hope and change, in the face of the nation's seemingly intractable problems of corruption and a widespread social alienation.

TELEVISION AND THE POPULAR AUDIENCE

Perhaps seeking a wider, popular audience for his political message, in the early 1980s Osofisan turned more actively to writing short plays produced for television, which were later adapted for the stage. These television plays are uneven in achievement. For example, *The Inspector and the Hero* (1981, published in 1990) reverts to the direct polemic of the early work, presenting a worthy if melodramatic and rather wooden account of the ideal official who refuses to bow to corruption, even though he is tempted by the wife of one of the corrupt figures who reveals that she is an undercover agent herself and invites him to join her in the official "take." *Altine's Wrath* (1983, published in 1986) is another melodramatic account of the effect of corruption, this time involving the rebellion of Altine, a traditional, uneducated countrywoman (a so-called bush wife), when her husband, a corrupt official, threatens to leave her for his "modern," city-bred and western-educated mistress. The play reveals that Altine, apparently rendered dumb and submissive by her husband's physical and mental brutality, has in fact secretly educated herself and appropriated the ill-gotten wealth he had secreted away in her name. The play ends with Altine's death from accidental poisoning, a twist that obviates her triumph and seems only to undermine the moral of an already rather unbelievable fable.

Osofisan perhaps believed that television demanded a more popular style—simple, polemical, melodramatic—to communicate directly with the mass public drawn to the new medium. He had sought to write for this same mass public when he had brought the early plays to village and town venues in the late 1960s and early 1970s. Certainly he was correct in assuming that by the early 1980s television had become a highly effective way to reach the popular audience.

Despite the uneven quality of some of this work, others of these plays, such as *Fires Burn and Die Hard*, also written for television in 1981 and revised for staging in 1989 (published in 1990), are among the subtlest and most effective of Osofisan's plays. In *Fires Burn and Die Hard* the theme is once again corruption, but its presentation of the particular plight of Nigerian women gives this play a new and powerful dimension.

At the center of this story is the Market Women's Association, an actual organization regarded as one of the most effective potential means for women to exercise power in Nigerian society (as Nina Emma Mba argues in her innovative 1982 study, *Nigerian Women Mobilized: Women's Political Activity in Southern Nigeria, 1900–1965*). Osofisan shows that the patriarchal opposition to economic self-determination for women comes from both traditional leaders and those of the modern state. The play opens on the eve of the ceremonial opening of a new market, built at the substantial cost of fourteen million naira after the old market was destroyed by fire. Through sometimes illicit trading of smuggled goods and the economic independence this has given them, the ten thousand members of the Market Women's Association have created an alternative female economic and social power structure.

A deputation consisting of representatives of the state governor and the traditional ruler arrives to announce that divination has revealed that the old market was burned down deliberately. They demand expiation by sacrifice, and since the discovery of the culprit seems virtually impossible, they will allow one of the Market Women's leaders to accept punishment in the arsonist's stead. The punishment devised for the scapegoat figure has a strong element of sexual degradation: she must dance naked through the market distributing the ashes of the ritual purification. Temi, the association's treasurer, nonetheless begs to be allowed to perform the abasing ritual. In a long speech she describes how participating in the Market Women's movement has enabled her to achieve an identity and a sense of personal power apart from her husband. It has "freed [her] from drudgery, from always living like second-hand clothing in the wardrobe of [her] husband" (p. 91). The Alhaja, president of the Market Women's Association, refuses her offer; the Alhaja confesses that she herself burned down the market to prevent the discovery of contraband goods in her stall, goods that her modern, mission-educated son had threatened to reveal to the police.

The play presents a subtle portrait of the varying functions of money and of corruption in the power structures of Nigerian society. Osofisan analyzes how power operates not only in terms of simplistic ideas of absolute good and evil or of the competing virtues of traditional and modern life, but also in terms of the complex results of social change, especially of the shifting social roles of women in modern Nigeria. The audience is shown how the desire for financial independence and prosperity motivates these women to oppose a powerful complex of forces that otherwise limit and suppress women as they search for an empowered social role.

In contrast with the feisty Temi, who is anything but subservient to her husband, the Alhaja, despite her powerful role and economic success, remains bound to her traditional role as mother. The character of the Alhaja illustrates the continuing power of a patriarchal society to construct women's ideas of themselves and shows how women police themselves by conforming to idealized roles as wives, mothers, and daughters. In a traditional fashion, the Alhaja regards the birth of her son as the primary justification of her life as a woman and a mother, and she uses the money she has earned through trading to educate him. Osofisan shows how the Alhaja is sentimentally attached to her son and then is exploited and betrayed by him. As Osofisan has argued in earlier plays such as *The Oriki of a Grasshopper*, it is impossible to be successful in contemporary Nigerian business without being involved in bribery and other illegal activities. By betraying his mother to the authorities for trading in smuggled goods, the Alhaja's son advances himself in the eyes of those in power. The weakness of sentimentality in the armor of this strong woman has been created, ironically, by her own self-image as a woman and a mother. The multiple ironies here are reminiscent of those in other texts, such as Buchi Emecheta's novel *The Joys of Motherhood* (1979), that deal with similarly traditional attitudes and their tragic consequences for Nigerian women.

Osofisan's work for television may have begun as another attempt to reach out to a mass audience, but in practice it constituted a further appeal to the kind of middle-class audience he had first engaged at the campus theaters of the 1960s and 1970s; the Nigerian audience for television plays, especially those with radical content or form, remained small and elite. The mass television audience that had developed in Nigeria in the 1970s and 1980s was largely captured by the new soap operas, whether derived from the traditional Yoruba folk operas or from appropriations of western television forms such as the police crime show or the situation comedy. This popular audience did not respond strongly to plays such as *Fires Burn and Die Hard* or even *Altine's Wrath*, although the latter clearly seeks to provide the melodramatic themes and rapid plot twists demanded by viewers. In the late 1980s and early 1990s Osofisan increasingly returned to the campus stage and more openly embraced the role of educating and developing the consciousness of the intellectual elite. Given the perilous and precarious condition of the Nigerian intelligentsia in the early 1990s, Osofisan may well have chosen a less glamorous but equally necessary role in promoting the possibility of political change in Nigeria.

THE CONTINUING STRUGGLE AGAINST AUTHORITARIANISM

Osofisan responded to the international challenges of the late 1980s regarding the political effectiveness of Marxist class struggle with a series of new and sophisticated plays. These later works analyze the contemporary issues facing Nigeria in newly powerful and optimistic ways. The change from a relatively simple model of class struggle to a more complex analysis of the economic and political bases of the Nigerian struggle against authoritarianism informs these writings. Of note is Osofisan's rewriting of John Pepper Clark's famous allegory of Nigerian society, *The Raft*, in the play *Another Raft* (1987, published in 1988), along with such plays as *Twingle-Twangle, a Twynning Tayle* (1988), *Aringindin and the Nightwatchmen* (1989), and *Yungba-Yungba and the Dance Contest* (1990), all published in 1992.

In 1990, Osofisan also published a novel, *Cordelia*, his first since the short novel *Kolera Kolej* (1975). This outburst of creativity demonstrates that Osofisan continued to take an optimistic view of the future of Nigeria and a positive view of the role of the ordinary Nigerian in resisting corruption and authoritarian solutions to the nation's problems, which continued with each of the several failed civilian governments and the military coup that toppled it.

The most notable feature of the long, allegorical play that Osofisan constructs on the skeleton of Clark's play is that, unlike Clark, whose play does not emphasize the divisions in Nigerian society between the rich and poor, Osofisan represents Nigerians as coming from a wide range of social and economic backgrounds. The play provides a much more detailed account of the penetration of traditional culture by the corrupt values of modern, urban society, exposing the collusions between the old society and the new ideas. The play depicts the journey of a group of Nigerians on a raft to the neglected shrine of the water goddess, and the raft provides for an allegory in which "the fate of our nation... is at stake" (p. 4).

Osofisan presents Nigeria as a society that has turned its back on tradition without developing an alternative beyond selfish, individual aggrandizement. Even the traditional religious offices are now objects of secular status, exploited only for their prestige and economic value. The responsibilities traditionally associated with such offices are now neglected. The play also explores the history of Nigeria from slavery through white colonization to the present day. Each figure on the raft represents a specific group or class, including traditional rulers, modern businessmen, secular intellectuals, and the farmers and artisans whose labor and skill all depend upon. This long and complex text is resolved in a ritual song that celebrates the need for these diverse interests to come together if Nigeria is to survive. Class struggle is present, though it seems less emphasized than national unity: success comes to those

> who do not waste their energy away
> in endless conflicts and recriminations
> fighting their own brothers and sisters.
> (p. 84)

But the materialist basis of any real social change is acknowledged, and the play conveys the importance of political demystification. As one of the characters comments, in the task of achieving social reconciliation and progress "there is no goddess but our muscles!" (p. 85).

Another Raft is occasionally too heavily symbolic, and the allegory sometimes overpowers the action. A better balance is struck in later plays like *Aringindin and the Nightwatchmen* and *Yungba-Yungba and the Dance Contest*. The former successfully weds realistic social analysis with the heightened dramatic language and action that Osofisan favors. *Aringindin and the Nightwatchmen* examines the difficulty of achieving social security without handing over freedom in the process—extending the examination of the issue of freedom and law and order initiated in *Once Upon Four Robbers*. Aringindin, a soldier returned from war, offers to rid the local market of thieves and robbers by initiating a vigilante force of "nightwatchmen." He is opposed, at first, by the traditional ruler (the Baale), who emphasizes the need to retain the links with older social values; but the politician Kansillor (Councillor) supports him, and his offer is embraced after he and Kansillor engineer robberies by their own men to justify their takeover. Like many politicians before him, Kansillor learns too late that the strong-arm men he thinks will bring him to power are likely to overwhelm him, too, in the end. At the end of the play Aringindin, an enigmatic, silent, brutally effective character, is married off to Kansillor's daughter; her lover, the teacher Ayinde, had warned earlier of the dangers of authoritarian rule and been killed for his pains by Aringindin's thugs. The play powerfully dramatizes the dangers of authoritarianism, defusing the commonest arguments—for example, that it is necessary to ensure social security and economic growth—used to justify the despotic use of power. In this sense the play allegorizes the contemporary politics of Nigeria, but it does so in a realistic setting: the town market is a dramatically effective microcosm of the larger Nigerian society, yet it also stands on its own as a believable dramatic entity.

In a similar vein, *Yungba-Yungba and the Dance Contest* examines the pressures against democracy in contemporary Nigeria. The young daughters (from three families) who compete for the annual dance title bestowed by the water-goddess shrine discover that the priestess of the shrine will retain permanently the power that traditionally was passed to the new dance contest winner each year and thereby ensured that authority remained up-to-date. When the young dancers demand a return to this system, the priestess argues that only by holding on to power has she prevented the internecine warfare that characterized the families' relations in the past. The analogy with the military regimes of the 1980s (such as that of General Ibrahim Badamasi Babangida) and their reluctance to hand over power to civilian governments is clearly made. We can also hear an echo of contemporary politics in the cynical way in which the strife of the families is deliberately encouraged by the authorities in order to justify their retention of power.

Yungba-Yungba and the Dance Contest offers a sophisticated account of the function of art in society. Osofisan shows how art can be employed either as a means to expose social injustice by liberal critics or as a weapon to maintain the status quo by conservative forces. The inspired idea of using a traditional dance contest as an overall metaphor for the modern political process allows Osofisan to suggest that traditional art and custom may become a means of sidetracking social concerns. He tackled but had not unravelled this same issue in *The Oriki of a Grasshopper*, whose title also invokes the traditional art of the Yoruba praise-poem (*oriki*). But in *Yungba-Yungba and the Dance Contest* the art metaphor also becomes the basis of the action.

CONCLUSION

Osofisan's work throughout his career has emphasized the social responsibility of the playwright. He has sought in a number of ways to make the theater reflect the problems of Nigerian society and to make his plays a platform for exploring these social issues. His dramaturgy has been designed to emphasize open rather than closed dramatic structures. These open structures invite active analysis rather than simply offering fixed and definite answers; they have included audience participation and choice in addressing the issues raised by the action. In embracing the participatory and critical nature of theater as an art he has clearly been influenced by such European writers as Brecht, but he has also been aware of traditions within his own culture. For example, Osofisan often incorporates into his plays the important critical dimension of traditional divination rituals such as Ifa, which centers on questioning the future. Although Ifa, like all divination traditions, stresses the foreknowledge of the gods, it is not a fatalistic tradition in that it allows its devotees to participate in choosing the shape of their future by acquiring knowledge of their options. It also emphasizes the moral responsibility and retribution that accompany that choice, making Ifa especially meaningful as a central feature of Osofisan's creative vision.

Selected Bibliography

SELECTED WORKS

Kolera Kolej. Ibadan, Nigeria: New Horn Press, 1975. Novella.

A Restless Run of Locusts. Ibadan: Onibonoje Press, 1975. Drama.

The Chattering and the Song. Ibadan: New Horn Press, 1976. Drama.

Who's Afraid of Solarin? Ibadan: Scholars Press, 1978. Reiss. Ibadan: Heinemann, 1991. Drama.

Morountodun and Other Plays. Ibadan: Longman, 1982. Includes *Morountodun, No More the Wasted Breed, Red Is the Freedom Road.*

Once Upon Four Robbers. Ibadan: BIO, 1982. Reiss. Ibadan: Heinemann, 1991. Drama.

Altine's Wrath. In *Two One-Act Plays.* Ibadan: New Horn Press, 1986.

Beyond Translation: Tragic Paradigms and the Dramaturgy of Ola Rotimi and Wole Soyinka. Ile-Ife, Nigeria: Monographs in African Literature, 1986. Literary criticism.

Farewell to a Cannibal Rage. Ibadan: Evans Brothers, 1986. Drama.

Midnight Hotel. Ibadan: Evans Brothers, 1986. Drama.

[Okinbo Launko, pseud.] *Minted Coins.* Ibadan: Heinemann, 1986. Poetry.

The Orality of Prose: A Comparativist Look at the Works of Rabelais, Joyce, and Tutuola. Ile-Ife, Nigeria: Monographs in African Literature, 1986. Literary criticism.

The Oriki of a Grasshopper. In *Two One-Act Plays.* Ibadan: New Horn Press, 1986. Repr., with an intro. by Abiola Irele, in *The Oriki of a Grasshopper and Other Plays.* Washington, D.C.: Howard University Press, 1995. Drama.

Another Raft. Lagos: Malthouse Press, 1988. Drama.

Birthdays Are Not for Dying and Other Plays. Lagos: Malthouse Press, 1990. Includes *Fires Burn and Die Hard* and *The Inspector and the Hero.*

[Okinbo Launko, pseud.] *Cordelia.* Lagos: Malthouse Press, 1990. Novel.

Esu and the Vagabond Minstrels: A Fertility Rite for the Modern Stage. Ibadan: New Horn Press, 1991.

Aringindin and the Nightwatchmen. Ibadan: Heinemann, 1992. Drama.

Twingle-Twangle, a Twynning Tayle. Lagos. Longman, 1992. Drama.

Yungba-Yungba and the Dance Contest: A Parable for Our Time. Ibadan: Heinemann, 1992. Drama.

ARTICLES

"Tiger on Stage: Wole Soyinka and Nigerian Theatre." In Oyin Ogunba and Abiola Irele, eds., *Theatre in Africa.* Ibadan: Ibadan University Press, 1978.

"Enter the Carthaginian Critic...?" In *Okike,* no. 21 (July 1982).

"Ritual and the Revolutionay Theatre: The Humanistic Dilemma in Contemporary Nigerian Theatre." In *Okike,* no. 22 (September 1982).

"Do the Humanities Humanize? A Dramatist's Encounter with Anarchy in Nigeria." Public lecture presented in Ibadan, Nigeria, and repr. in French translation in *Politique africaine* (13 March 1984).

INTERVIEWS

Dunton, Chris. "Theatre as a Game." In *West Africa* (24 April 1989).

Enekwe, Ossie. Interview with Osofisan in *Greenfield Review* 8, nos. 1–2 (spring 1980).

CRITICAL STUDIES

Dunton, Chris. "Truth from Contraries: Form in the Work of Femi Osofisan." In *African Literature Today* 17 (1991).

———. *Make Man Talk True: Nigerian Drama in English Since 1970.* London: Hans Zell, 1992.

Hunwick, Una. "The Impact of Modern Theatre on the Nigerian Audience." In *Nigeria Magazine* 54, no. 3 (July–Sept. 1986).

Jeyifo, Biodun. *The Truthful Lie: Essays in a Sociology of African Drama.* London: New Beacon Books, 1985.

———. "Femi Osofisan as Literary Critic and Theorist." In Yemi Ogunbiyi, ed., *Perspectives on Nigerian Literature, 1700 to the Present.* Vol. 2. Lagos: Guardian Books, 1988.

Niyi Osundare

1947–

G. D. KILLAM

NIYI OSUNDARE was born in a Yoruba family in Ikere-Ekiti in Ondo State, Nigeria. He received his bachelor of arts with honors in English literature from the University of Ibadan, Nigeria, in 1972; his master of arts from the University of Leeds, England, in 1974; and his doctorate from York University, Toronto, in 1979. A university lecturer in English, he began teaching at the University of Ibadan in 1974. He was a Fulbright scholar and writer in residence at the University of Wisconsin in 1990–1991 and visiting associate professor of African and Caribbean literature at the University of New Orleans in 1991–1992. He then returned to the University of Ibadan.

Osundare had published eight volumes of poetry by the mid 1990s: *Songs of the Marketplace* (1983), *Village Voices* (1984), *A Nib in the Pond* (1986), *The Eye of the Earth* (1986), *Moonsongs* (1988), *Waiting Laughters* (1990), *Songs of the Season* (1990), and *Selected Poems* (1992). He published a critical commentary, *The Writer as Righter*, in 1986.

Osundare is also a freelance journalist, and his poetry column in the Lagos newspaper *Newswatch* has done much to popularize poetry in Nigeria. He has been honored with several literary awards, including the Association of Nigerian Authors poetry prize and the Commonwealth poetry prize, both in 1986 for *The Eye of the Earth*, and the Noma Award for *Waiting Laughters* in 1991.

POETRY FOR THE PEOPLE

The populist purposes of Osundare's poetry are plain in his first volume, *Songs of the Marketplace*. One of his mentors is the Chilean poet and diplomat Pablo Neruda, whose words he uses as the epigraph to the volume: "I made an unbreakable pledge to myself/That the people would find their voices in my song." In the first poem, "Poetry Is," he asserts his artistic purposes in conjunction with his populist theme of social obligation. According to Osundare, poetry is:

> not the esoteric whisper
> of an excluding tongue
> not a claptrap
> for a wondering audience
> not a learned quiz
> entombed in Grecoroman lore
>
> Poetry is
> a lifespring
> which gathers timbre
> the more throats it plucks
> harbinger of action
> the more minds it stirs

Poetry is
the hawker's ditty
the eloquence of the gong
the lyric of the marketplace
the luminous ray
on the grass's morning dew

Poetry is
what the soft wind
musics to the dancing leaf
what the sole tells the dusty path
what the bee hums to the alluring nectar
what rainfall croons to the lowering eaves

Poetry is
no oracle's kernel
for a sole philosopher's stone

Poetry
is
man
meaning
to
man.

(pp. 3–4)

The reference to "Grecoroman lore" is crucial to Osundare's poetic, for through it he repudiates the uses to which the pre–civil war generation of Nigerian poets, such as Wole Soyinka and Christopher Okigbo, put their postcolonial educational inheritance. These poets, according to Osundare, brought "the whole mechanistic apparatus of European poetry... the modernist pretensions... to African soil. That was why Soyinka was difficult. And Okigbo too. And this comes from the poetic practice and canons of people... who believe that poetry must be difficult" (*Vanguard*, Lagos, 10 February 1985, p. 4). In an essay entitled "Words of Iron, Sentences of Thunder: Soyinka's Prose Style" (in *African Literature Today*, no. 13, 1993), Osundare describes what for him makes Soyinka's work obscure. Through his criticism of Soyinka, Osundare reveals his ideas about the appropriate form and content of poetry. In an article in *West Africa*, he urges Soyinka "to find a middle ground between his journalistic and his creative styles of writing. He should work towards greater 'audience consciousness' and towards achieving a 'transparency which is simple but delicate'" (6 August 1984, p. 1579). The two poems Osundare wrote each week—"as a matter of policy and challenge"—in his popular Sunday column in the *Nigerian Tribune*, "Songs of the Season," are devoted to demonstrating that "verse journalism"—poetry for the general public in the popular presses—can

> convince the audience that poetry can be accessible, enjoyable and relevant at the same time. (A grandly ironical occupation in a culture whose very vein is lyrical and artistic!) In other words, my experimental verse journalism is part of an on-going attempt to rescue (Nigerian) poetry from the "labyrinths" and "crypts" of the frustrating obscurity into which it has been pushed by the Soyinkas and Okigbos.
> (in *World Literature Written in English* 29, 1989, p. 3)

For Osundare, "the greatest dilemma the Nigerian writer faces today is how to marry these two: the mass-oriented kind of literature and the so-called serious literature" (as reported by Sina Odugbemi, in *Vanguard*, Lagos, 10 February 1985, p. 4).

In "The Poet," from *A Nib in the Pond*, Osundare extends his populist theories about the function of poetry to include the role of the poet, who

is not a prophet,
God's hollow ventriloquist,
auguring past futures
in dated tongues
the poet's eyes are washed
in the common spring
though seeing beyond
the hazy horizon
of lowering skies

...

Who says the poet
should leave the muck
unraked?

in a land of choking mud
how can the poet
strut
clean
in feathered sandals
and
pretend to the world
he never smells?

(p. 10)

Although he eschews the obscurity and arcane language of the pre–civil war poets, Osundare has in common with his peers (including most of those of the first generation) a political dimension to his writing that makes it potentially revolutionary and transformative. Like the novelist Chinua Achebe in *Anthills of the Savannah* (1987), Osundare wrestles with the problem of making literature accessible and available to the masses and dissociating it from the socioeconomic processes that make it elitist. He does this by drawing on the oral tradition of his agrarian roots. In the stories, songs, and rituals of this tradition, as well as the forms, moods, and tones, he finds a model for making his verse accessible to the oppressed people in Nigerian society, who are victims of a self-serving political and economic leadership. Coincident with this search for an appropriate poetic model is his desire, which aligns him with such poetic peers as Tanure Ojaide, Odia Ofeimun, and Femi Fatoba, to revitalize poetry and prompt his audience to action.

Osundare's poetry combines the meditative with the rhetorical and displays a wide range of topics: European cultural influence and poetry as well as the abstractions of love, pride, humility, honesty, cowardice, misery, and corruption. His moods—lyrical, celebratory, ironical, satirical, humorous, bitter—are equally various as he exposes corruption in Nigerian society. Many of his poems are occasional, such as "Shout of the People (in Memory of Nigeria's Fifth Coup d'État)" from *Songs of the Season*; "Prisoners of Conscience (for Ngũgĩ wa Thiong'o)," "Soweto," and "For Bob Marley" from *Songs of the Marketplace*; and "Foreign Aid," "For Ngũgĩ wa Thiong'o," and "For the Sandinistas."

EARLY POEMS

Songs of the Marketplace

Osundare's first volume, *Songs of the Marketplace* (1983), is avowedly the work of an apprentice: "It contained all kinds of poems. Some of the poems I wrote when I was in high school. I just polished them up.... Inevitably that collection is eclectic" (interview by Ajibade, p. 44). Even so, in this volume Osundare displays the range of reflection and comment on popular issues that characterizes his later verse. For example, he ironically evokes the plunder of Africa during the colonial period in "On Seeing a Benin Mask in a British Museum," a poem he wrote for the art festival FESTAC 77:

Here stilted on plastic
A god deshrined
Uprooted from your past
Distanced from your present
Profaned sojourner in a strange land

Rescued from a smouldering shrine
By a victorianizing expedition
Traded in for an O.B.E.
Across the shores

...

Retain the tight dignity of those lips
Unspoken grief becomes a god
When all around are alien ears
Unable to crack the kernel of the riddle.

(pp. 39–40)

There are also angry occasional poems for people, such as "For Bob Marley" and "Prisoners of Conscience (for Ngũgĩ wa Thiong'o)," and for events, such as "Namibia Talks" and "Soweto." "Soweto" expresses anger at the South African government's brutal violence against black protesters in Sharpeville in 1960 and in Soweto in 1976, and it prophesies the end of apartheid in that country:

> First
>   SHARPEVILLE
> Now
>   SOWETO
>
> These murdered flowers
> blossoming
> will fruit in freedom
> These rising shoots
> will tree into free spaces
> beyond tomorrow.
> (p. 48)

Most of the poems in the volume, however, assert and reinforce Osundare's connection with his rural roots and nature. This connection occurs in poems throughout the volume and specifically in the nine poems in the section titled "Songs of Dawn and Seasons," in which he presents nature as a guiding principle and metaphor for human life. Osundare's willingness to return to and even embrace agrarian tradition suggests that education did not alienate him from his people and their concerns. Rather he uses his literary background and skills as a writer to enhance his connection with and commitment to the downtrodden, oppressed, and dispossessed. In the process of asserting this allegiance in his writing, he consistently repudiates those in power who effect these conditions and the ramifications of their actions.

Village Voices

In his second volume of poems, *Village Voices* (1984), Osundare portrays the activities, concerns, and attitudes of peasants. For example in "Eating Tomorrow's Yam," he details the concerns of a farmer; in "The Prisoner's Song," he convincingly portrays the bluster of a prisoner; and in "Alarinka," he captures the listlessness of a wanderer. Although Osundare sympathetically enters the lives and minds of his characters, he avoids naïveté and sentimentality in his characterizations.

For the first time in his poetry, he projects a clear revolutionary proletarian consciousness. His abhorrence for the duplicity of the political establishment comes through in such poems as "The New Farmers Bank" and "A Farmer on Seeing Cocoa House, Ibadan." "The Politician's Two Mouths" ends with a warning to the reader:

> The politician's mouth has two edges
> like Esimuda's sword
> it is murder both ways
> . . .
> When the man of power
> tells you his tale
> ask him to wait till
> you bring a sieve
> (p. 57)

In affirming his understanding of his sources, Osundare castigates other poets whose claims to connections with the common people are spurious:

> You singer of royal songs
> Your drum, dumb in the marketplace,
> Only talks in the palace of gold
> Your songs extol those whose words
> behead the world.
> (p. 2)

A Nib in the Pond

In his third volume of poems, *A Nib in the Pond* (1986), Osundare repeats and elaborates the thematic materials of *Songs of the Marketplace.* In "Calling a Spade," he declares:

> No need hiding
> in the tabernacle of words
> so easily swept off
> by the storm of anger
>
> No need camouflaging
> behind a flimsy jungle
> of occult id-ioms
> the metaphor of protest
> flips every leaf
> in the book of change
> . . .

There is no petname for
injustice
Poverty
  has no bank for nicknames.
(p. 9)

He again affirms his political purposes, as in "Art for Ass Sake":

but how can we shut the closet on
plebeian skulls cracking
under patrician heels
on kings and queens, gorged on
our earth's wealth,
belching bullets on tattered masses

...

Art shorn of the human touch
is art for ass sake.
(p. 6)

The Eye of the Earth

In his preface to *The Eye of the Earth* (1986), Osundare establishes the origins in rural-oral societies of his poetic material: "Farmer-born, peasant-bred, I encountered dawn in the enchanted corridors of the forest, suckled on the delicate aroma of healing herbs, and the pearly drops of generous moons. Living in those early days was rugged, but barns brimmed with yams fattened by merciful rains and the tempering fire of the upland sun. ... Earth was ours, and we earth's" (p. ix).

The affirmation in this passage proceeds not solely from "passionate nostalgia" (p. x), but from the determination that "looking back becomes one of the weapons against a looming monster. ... For in the intricate dialectics of human living, looking back is looking forward; the visionary artist is not only a rememberer, he is also a reminder" (p. x). The nineteen poems in the volume, which is divided into a prefatory poem—"Earth"—and four subsections—"back to earth," "eyeful glances," "rainsongs," and "homecall"—trace the history of humanity's association with the land. Osundare writes of the structure of the book:

> The "Forest" in the first movement ... is ... echoes of an Eden long departed when the rainforest was terrifyingly green though each tree, each vine, each herb, each beast, each insect, had its name in the baffling baptism of Nature. ...
>
> "Rainsongs" is a logical continuation of "forest echoes," it being a celebration of the giver and sustainer of life. ..."
>
> "Homecall" ... raises vital queries, amplifies crucial fears about the state of earth, our home.
> (pp. x, xi, xii)

In this volume, Osundare depicts the collusion of native farmers with "the virulent advent of Europe's merchants" in betraying the land for the sake of a "cancerous god called MONEY" (p. ix); he continues by adumbrating the wider implications of this betrayal. Treatment of the land, which Osundare considers the most important natural resource, becomes a marker of human myopia, venality, and treachery, which will in the end, he warns, destroy the earth. The poems present a vision of a dying earth proceeding from the acts of the "rich and ruthless [who] squander earth's wealth on the invention of increasingly accomplished weapons of death, while millions of people perish daily from avoidable hunger" (p. xii).

The poems in this volume and in the next, *Moonsongs*, are more carefully articulated and precisely focused in their concern with nature, landscape, and rural life than the poems in earlier volumes, which makes these collections more unified in approach and sustained in achievement. The poems in *The Eye of the Earth* and *Moonsongs* also present Osundare's revolutionary agenda with greater precision, clarity, and force than in the earlier volumes by showing what nature has been, has become, and might become again, through language that is at once simple and highly allusive.

The agent of Osundare's meditations in *The Eye of the Earth* is memory, which allows him to traverse both past and present in his reflections and meditation. The order of the poems reflects the chronology of his life, and a poem titled "Farmer-Born" captures the movement through time that organizes the volume. He returns to his childhood and moves forward to the present. He recalls the past without sentimentalizing it, specifying that its essentially pristine quality contains within it "loric fear" and "leaves wounded / by the fists of time," an environment where one treads "soft-soled, the compost carpet / of darkling jungles" (in "Forest Echoes," p. 3). Poems in the volume move through the forest and describe encounters with natural phenomena, animate and inanimate; with the divinities and near divinities of the Yoruba pantheon, including Ogéèré Amókòyerí, Agbègilodós, and Ogbese, Osun's rebel daughter; and with a modern deification in the form of NEPA (National Electric Power Authority) as it has come to humanize and caution nature.

The volume's closing poems, "They Too Are the Earth," "What the Earth Said," "Ours to Plough, Not to Plunder," and "Our Earth Will Not Die," are apostrophes to earth and to its potential for restoration. The final poem is intended to be read "to a solemn, almost elegiac tune" (p. 50). The volume's last words are assertions: "Our earth will not die" (p. 50); "Our earth will see again / this earth, OUR EARTH" (p. 51). Given Osundare's concerns throughout most of the volume, one can only hope that his optimism and faith in the links he sees between his poetry and such international movements as "The Green Peace, The Women of Greenham Common, Operation Stop the Desert, and The Save the Amazon Committee" are not misplaced (p. xii).

LATER POEMS

Osundare told Ajibade in 1991 that he believed "the source of artistic excellence is variety and progress. . . . There is no way you can read without being influenced by what you read one way or another. I myself have discovered that I am getting rather philosophical" (p. 45). He was responding to a comment that his later poetry was moving toward an obscurity of language that contrasts with the directness and simplicity of his first three volumes and leaves *The Eye of the Earth* and *Moonsongs* open to the same charges that he leveled at Soyinka's poems and Okigbo's early works.

The poems of *The Eye of the Earth* and *Moonsongs* are structurally and linguistically more complicated and make a greater demand on the reader. To be fully understood and appreciated, the volumes probably require a thorough grounding in Yoruba cosmology. Osundare's increasing poetic complexity seems inevitable: as a poet finds an authentic strophe, he or she discovers how to make the craft sustain the vision. This understanding in Osundare's case results in the creation of a more comprehensive and complex cosmology. To the elemental physical landscape—earth, forest, rocks, and rivers—he adds the animate universe, to which he attends in the minutest detail—animals, birds, and even insects. The earth becomes a microcosm within the celestial macrocosm that includes the sky, stars, sun, and, especially, the moon.

Osundare places this extended inanimate and animate universe in a traditional—or imagined traditional—community. As he envisons this community, it retains its traditional assumptions and values, and therefore allows him to stage its encounter with and modification by extraneous forces. Drawing on his foundations in oral traditions, he stages these later poems as communal performances. In his early volumes, Osundare indicates that his poetry should be understood as an "oral aural" experience and performed to the accompaniment of traditional African instruments. In *Moonsongs* the communal and participatory element in the poetry is more insistent. He includes enjoinders to some poems: "To the accompaniment of lively *wọ́rọ̀* drumming, the following song, in call-and-response" (p. 1); "To the accompaniment of the song: *Ọ̀ṣùpá o i yuwá mi o, òṣùpá o, i yẹ̀yìn mi*" (p. 8); "In the background throughout, a persistent sound of pestle in mortar, supplying a rhythm to the poem and the accompanying song" (p. 29).

Moonsongs

Moonsongs (1988) is organized in three parts: "Phases 1–14"; "Further Phases 15–24"; and "Moonechoes: Shadows Across the Path," a final section of twelve poems. (The twelve poems in the final section, as its title suggests, are adjunct to rather than integrated into the main text.) The moon, as the containing metaphor of the volume, is a reflection of the life-giving force of the sun, and Osundare uses it to reflect on the uses to which humankind puts the sun's creative and restorative energy. The phrase "the moon is a mask dancing" resonates throughout the volume and helps to create a connection between the real and the quasicorporeal:

> The world is a mask dancing
> mask dancing
> mask dancing
> (p. 34)

Osundare takes the phrase from Achebe's novel *Arrow of God* (1964), in which a character reflects that "the world is like a mask dancing" (p. 72), which implies that to perceive the illusiveness of human experience as embodied in the mask, one has to view it from different positions and perspectives. Osundare equates his discoveries about human experiences to the phases of the moon. He also imagines how the moon perceives human activity. The temporal and universal, which he conveys in the moon's songs in "Phases" and "Further Phases," are contained by time:

> Time
> Time never runs its race
> Like a straight, uncluttered road
>
> . . .
>
> Time the seasons
> Season the times;
> The forest sprouts, blooms
> And rots into seed
> The seed mothers the mountain
> The mountain mothers the river
> And the river springs green flowers
> In Edens of unsinning apples
>
> I heard moonsteps in the corridors of seasons
> The sky is aflame with dusts of hurrying dials
> ("Shadows of Time," p. 72)

The behavior of personified time reflects Osundare's own apprehension and, in turn, accounts for the ordering of the poems in the volume.

Osundare establishes the moon as his muse in the opening poem of the first section, "Phases":

> Spread the sky like a generous mat
> Tell dozing rivers to stir their tongues
> Unhinge the hills
> Unwind the winds
> The moon and I will sing tonight
> (p. 1)

The volume then goes on to explore and communicate the reflections on human experience that the contemplation of the moon can evoke in the poet. *Moonsong* is concerned not only with conditions in Nigeria and not only with the opulence of Ikoyi, where the moon

> is a laundered lawn
> its grass the softness of infant fluff;
>
> . . .
>
> the ceiling is a sky
>
> . . .
>
> of pampered stars

Ikoyi contrasts with Ajegunle, where

> . . . the moon
> is a jungle,
> sad like a forgotten beard
>
> . . .
>
> and undergrowths of cancerous fury:
> cobras of anger spit in every brook
> and nights are one long prowl
> of swindled leopards
> (p. 42)

The disenfranchised and despised are found everywhere by the moon:

> With its ears the moon sees the Soweto of our skin
> and painfields so soggy with the sweat of a thousand seasons
>
> . . .
>
> In Grenada where Sunset nurtures freedom
> with bayonets and cackling cannon
>
> In Managua where reddening flares
> brave the breath of Twilight storms
>
> In the sorrows of our South deep, so deep
> like scars of millenial [*sic*] lesions.
>
> (p. 40)

Through all of the pain, the spirit of humankind, Osundare says, will endure:

> No, not yet a knell
>
> We shall not go till we have eaten the elephant of the moon
> We shall not go
> till our scrupulous eyes have stitched the broken tendons
> of the sky
> We shall not go
> till our green dreams spawn golden suns
> in the chronicle of stubborn trees.
>
> (p. 52)

Osundare understands the contending ideologies that shape the lives of ordinary people in his society; therefore, the range of tones in *Moonsongs* moves from the exuberant through the humorous, the absurd, and the grotesque. He castigates and caricatures members of the ruling class while enjoining his readers to embrace his sympathetic portrayal of the people.

Waiting Laughters

Waiting Laughters (1990) is, as Osundare says in the subtitle, "a long song in many voices." The song has four movements that all relate to the themes implied in the title—waiting and humor. The poems have the experimental character of those in the earlier volumes and call for accompaniment by musical instruments: "flute and/or Clarinet; medley of human voices" (p. 1); "kora and/or goje; medley of voices" (p. 28); "gangan, bata, ibembe in varying accents; medley of voices" (p. 44); "flute, kora, gangan, sekere; voices in final flourish" (p. 76).

Osundare draws his subject matter for the most part from Nigeria, specifically from his Yoruba inheritance, but there are poems that relate to events in other parts of Africa and throughout the black world, references to the Niger, the Nile, the Limpopo, and the Atlantic of the middle passage. Some poems celebrate agents and martyrs in the cause of African and black freedom—such as Thomas Sankara, Nelson Mandela, Steve Biko, and Walter Rodney; while others recall apostates to the cause of freedom—such as Adolf Hitler, Marcos, and Idi Amin. A poem begins:

> The innocence of the Niger
> waiting, waiting
> fourhundredseasons
> for the proof of the prow
> waiting
> for the irreverent probing of pale paddles
> waiting
> for the dispossessing twang of alien accents
> waiting
> for scrolls of serfdom, hieroglyphs of calculated treacheries
>
> (p. 37)

References to Sharpeville, Langa, and Soweto suggest that these isolated experiences encompass the history of black peoples.

These poems contain an excitement, an exuberance, that propels them forward, often as a string of images, and suggests the impatience inherent in waiting. With a playfulness in the use of language, Osundare extrapolates extended meanings from familiar words and phrases, such as "Robbing Island" and "passports are pass ports" (p. 38). Whatever the subject matter, personal reference, mood, or tone, each poem as a whole moves toward providing answers to the series of rhetorical questions posed at the end of the poem in light of the ambiguous implications of "waiting":

> What happens to the song which waits too long
> In the labyrinth of the throat
>
> What happens to the prayer which waits too long
> Without an amen
>
> What happens to the face which waits too long
> Without the memory of a mask
>
> What happens to LAUGHTER which waits too long
> In the compost of anguished seasons?
>
> What.....?
>
> (p. 94)

Songs of the Season

Songs of the Season (1990) is the product of a project Osundare launched in the Nigerian newspaper *Sunday Tribune* in 1985. In the preface, Osundare explains that the project

> has been empowered by a definable style and purpose: to capture the significant happenings of our time in a tune that is simple, accessible, topical, relevant and artistically pleasing; to remind kings about the corpses which line their way to the throne, to show the rich the slums which fester behind their castles, to praise virtue, denounce vice, to mirror the triumphs and travails of the downtrodden who ever so often the big books forget; to celebrate the green glory of the rainy season and the brown accent of the dry, to distil poetry from the dust and clay of our vast, prodigious land.
>
> (p. v)

Osundare notes that "written poetry has remained . . . an alienated and alienating enterprise in Nigeria—a painful irony in a country where every significant event is celebrated in song, drum and dance, where living still has a fluid rhythm and the proverb is one huge tome of uncountable wisdom" (pp. v–vi).

Osundare's success in this project may be measured by the fifty-seven poems in the volume under five general categories: "songs," which includes "not for the poor," "song of the street-sweeper," and "shout of the people"; "dialogue," which includes "at the senior service club" and "retiring into farming"; "tributes," such as "for the women of Greenham Common" and "for Chief Obafemi Awolowo"; "parables," such as "slaves who adore their chains" and "the king and the poet"; and "sundry strivings," with poems entitled "song for children's day" and "song for all seasons." The volume begins with an invocation to *isihun* (voice-opener) and "a song for my land," in which the poet celebrates his central experience of connection with the land, the sources of the poems in this volume.

CONCLUSION

Osundare returns to the tradition of African poetry that uses poetry as song, in order to chastise wrongdoers and create a fair and just society. His poetry is distinguished by its lyricism together with an insistently dramatic manner, derived from the African oral tradition. The banter of the African marketplace, the volubility and animation of the people of the city, and the spontaneous wit and work tunes of farmers and workers are incorporated into Osundare's poetry. His poetry is best appreciated in performance and within the larger context of oral poetry.

Selected Bibliography

SELECTED WORKS

Songs of the Marketplace. Ibadan, Nigeria: New Horn Press, 1983.

Village Voices. Ibadan, Nigeria: Evans Bros., 1984.

The Eye of the Earth. Ibadan, Nigeria: Heinemann, 1986.

A Nib in the Pond. Ife, Nigeria: University of Ife, 1986.

The Writer as Righter. Ife, Nigeria: University of Ife, 1986.

Moonsongs. Ibadan, Nigeria: Spectrum Books, 1988.

Waiting Laughters: A Long Song in Many Voices. Lagos, Nigeria: Malthouse Press, 1990.

Songs of the Season. Ibadan, Nigeria: Heinemann Educational Books, 1990.

Selected Poems. Oxford, U.K.: Heinemann, 1992.

INTERVIEW

Ajibade, Kunle. "My Visions, My Styles." In *African Concord* (9 September 1991).

CRITICAL STUDIES

Adejuwon, Femi. "Singing for the Oppressed." Review of *Song of the Marketplace.* In *Nigerian Tribune* (Ibadan) (5 March 1986).

Arnold, Stephen. "The Praxis of Niyi Osundare, Popular Scholar-Poet." In *World Literature Written in English* 29 (1989).

Bryce, Jane. "Dreams and Bullets: Nigerian Poetry." In *West Africa* (21 July 1986).

Folajike, Sanni. "Osundare's Songs of Sorrow and Hope." In *Punch* (Lagos) (1 November 1984).

Jeyifo, Biodun. "Niyi Osundare." In Yemi Ogunbiyi, ed., *Perspectives on Nigerian Literature: 1700 to the Present.* Vol. 2. Lagos, Nigeria: Guardian Books, 1988.

Nwahunanya, Chinyere. "Osundare's New Esotericism: The Genesis of Poetic Disintegration." In E. U. Ohaegbu, ed., *Language, Literature and Social Change.* Acts of the 7th annual conference of the Modern Languages Association of Nigeria, 8–11 February 1989. Nsukka: University of Nigeria, 1989.

Oni, Sanya. "Osundare: The Poet of the Market Place." *National Concord* (Lagos) (24 June 1988).

Ferdinand Oyono

1929–

CHRIS DUNTON

FERDINAND OYONO'S reputation as a writer rests on just three works published between 1956 and 1960. Since then, Oyono has occupied a succession of posts as a career diplomat and government minister, publishing nothing further. His slim output as novelist contrasts with that of his prolific fellow Cameroonian novelist Mongo Beti. Indeed, comparison with Beti's work has long served as a marker in discussing the nature—and especially the political orientation—of Oyono's fiction. Nevertheless, historical significance and intrinsic merit of Oyono's first two novels, *Une Vie de boy* (*Houseboy*) and *Le Vieux Nègre et la médaille* (*The Old Man and the Medal*), both of which appeared in 1956, have secured his reputation as one of the most striking African writers of his generation.

In discussing the African novel written in French or English, it is helpful to bear in mind that the European-style novel emerged in a context in which African-language narrative art had been thriving for centuries. Having said that, it is also significant that the African novel in French has a slightly longer history than does its English-language counterpart. Whereas Chinua Achebe's landmark Nigerian novel *Things Fall Apart* appeared only in 1958, West African writers had begun to produce novels in French some thirty years earlier.

The tenor of this early francophone African writing was essentially assimilationist—that is, sympathetic to the westernization of African cultural, social, and political life. *L'Esclave* (1929; The slave), by the Dahomean (Beninois) Félix Couchoro, is a massive morality tale that deals with adultery in a traditional setting. Through criticism of the indigenous slave system and the introduction of a group of white characters at the end of the novel, Couchoro suggests that the continuing presence of the colonial regime is essentially a benevolent influence in his society. In *Force bonté* (1926; Benevolent power) the Senegalese novelist Bakary Diallo goes further, asserting his belief in the great goodness of white people. Paul Hazoumé in *Doguicimi* (Benin, formerly Dahomey, 1938) and Ousmane Socé in *Karim* (Senegal, 1935) concentrate on asserting the integrity of African traditions, virtually ignoring the colonial presence. As Dorothy S. Blair has pointed out: "This is a period when an African intellectual who has had some success in France would be prepared to whitewash the image of the colonists and present them as having brought a measure of salvation to a primitive people" (p. 77). Even Camara Laye's masterly autobiographical work *L'Enfant noir* (Guinea, 1953; *The Dark Child*) eschews any discussion of the colonial regime, restricting itself to a tenderly nostalgic evocation of a village childhood.

In the mid 1950s, however, the tenor of the French African novel underwent a dramatic shift. Beginning in 1954 with *Ville cruelle* (Cruel City) by Eza Boto (pseudonym of Mongo Beti), a rapid succession of novels turned to address French colonial practice, dissecting it through a critique that was frequently uncompromising. In 1956—a remarkable year for French African writing—five such novels appeared: Sembène Ousmane's *Le Docker noir* (*Black Docker*), Bernard Dadié's *Climbié* (*Climbié*), Beti's fiercely controversial *Le Pauvre Christ de Bomba* (*The Poor Christ of Bomba*), and Oyono's first two novels.

These novels appeared as France edged toward granting independence to its African colonies. Yet one has to guard against casual assumptions about their impact on an African readership. Whereas Couchoro, a Beninois living in Togo, wrote for a local readership through the Togolese press, novelists such as Beti and Oyono were, initially at least, primarily addressing a European audience. What one can say is that in metropolitan France in the 1950s, the novels of Beti and Oyono, especially, contributed to the bitterly contested recognition that some form of independence for the African colonies was inevitable. The impact of their writing was considerable. These were novelists, after all, who rejected the assimilationist assumptions of earlier African writers as deeply insulting and as false to the historical consciousness of their people.

LIFE AND THE COLONIAL EXPERIENCE

Ferdinand Léopold Oyono was born on 14 September 1929 in the village of N'Goul'emakong, near Ebolowa (south of Yaoundé), in Cameroon. His father, Etoa Jean Oyono, was a secretary-interpreter for the French colonial regime; his mother, Mvodo Belinga Agnès, the daughter of a chief, worked as a seamstress after the breakup of the marriage.

Richard Bjornson has demonstrated how the colonial secretary-interpreters formed the "nucleus of an intellectual elite" (p. 23) whose children had enhanced educational opportunities and often occupied significant positions in the postcolonial regime. The record of Oyono's career bears this out. Having completed primary school in the regional administrative center, Ebolowa, in 1946, he went on to the *école supérieure* in Yaoundé and then the lycée at Ebolowa. In 1950 he was sent to France, first to a lycée in Provins (Seine-et-Marne), then to Paris at the Sorbonne, where he read politics and law. He received the *licence* in law in 1959. Much of his spare time in Paris was devoted to acting: his theatrical flair is apparent in the often sparklingly funny dialogue sections of his novels. All three of his published works had been completed by the time he returned to Cameroon in 1959. The first two, at least, received exceptionally wide publicity in the French press, given pride of place in the review sections of *Le Figaro littéraire* and *Les Lettres françaises*, two prominent literary journals based in Paris. Some papers greeted their anticolonial critique with virulent hostility, but most had only praise for their brilliant construction and for the density and sharpness of their attack.

Like that of Beti, Oyono's critique of European rule should be read in the light of his country's particularly harsh colonial experience. Invaded first in the late nineteenth century by the Germans, who instituted forced labor and a brutal penal code, the country was recolonized after 1918, this time by the British and French, between whom it was partitioned. While these two powers' authority was sanctioned by League of Nations—and later by United Nations—mandate, in reality the territory was administered as a de facto colonial possession.

In the case of the French, this involved a continuation of forced labor; the imposition of the *indigénat*, a harsh body of laws relating to "offenses" on the part of blacks; the encouragement of a quasi-settler regime, with thousands of French, Greeks, and Lebanese entering the country in every capacity from colonial administrator to petty trader; and the institution—in theory, at least—of the code of assimilation, under which black subjects were able to gain privilege and even the status of French citizens on evidence of adoption of French cultural and political values. All of these features are depicted in Oyono's fiction. What does not find mention there is the anticolonial struggle mounted by the Union des Populations du Cameroun (UPC) in the 1950s; the movement was defeated by the French with the imposition of the neocolonial regime of Ahmadou Ahidjo upon independence in 1960. This significant absence in Oyono's writing will be considered later.

HOUSEBOY

Each of Oyono's novels has a protagonist who is wrapped in the assimilationist dream, who is driven by the desire to become a "somebody" under the colonial regime. Joseph Toundi Ondoua, the young hero of *Houseboy*, leaves home the day before he is due to undergo the rite of circumcision, lured by the glamour of employment by a white priest. Father Gilbert treats him with a benign species of racism, as a kind of pet animal. After the priest's death, Toundi is employed as houseboy by the local commandant (equivalent to a district officer in the British colonial system). Despite Commandant Decazy's overt brutality, Toundi now believes himself well on the way to arrival, a privileged black, maintaining that "the dog of the King is the King of dogs" (p. 20). His position becomes endangered, however, when he witnesses Madame Decazy's adultery with another colonial official, the civil engineer Moreau.

Discovering the affair, Decazy negotiates a kind of frigid reconciliation with his wife. Toundi is now in greater danger. Unable from the outset to conceal his absorption in the whites' affairs—to turn a knowing blind eye as the other servants do—he now appears to the Decazys the chief articulator of their sexual guilt before themselves. As Madame's maid, Kalisia, warns him: "At the Residence you are something like . . . the representative of the rest of us. . . . while you are still here, they can never forget about it altogether" (p. 116). Worse, Toundi's knowledge endangers the hegemony of the whites by exposing the lie behind their projection of themselves as the blacks' moral superiors. In Carroll Yoder's words, "A society that justifies its presence by the superiority of its own culture cannot afford to be judged by those it oppresses" (p. 147).

Oyono treats with great skill the psychological crux in which the three now find themselves: the Decazys locked into a part masochistic, part sadistic reception of their shame, and Toundi unable to free himself from identification with their status and their emotions. Finally the whites decide Toundi must be excised from their lives. He is imprisoned on a trumped-up theft charge and savagely beaten. Managing to escape from jail, he makes his way to neighboring Spanish (now Equatorial) Guinea, where he dies in the presence of one of his compatriots.

Houseboy is a masterly novel on a number of counts. Part of its continuing impact lies in Oyono's satirical depiction of the racism, snobbery, and sexual immorality of the whites. This is a merciless satire but—given the actual French colonial practice in Cameroon—hardly exaggerated. Long sections of dialogue between the whites are beautifully perceptive and telling, ruthlessly delineating their shallowness and venality.

Equally impressive is Oyono's handling of point of view and of the psychology of his central character. Toundi's flight to Spanish Guinea provides a convenient framing device. The novel begins with an account by an anonymous Cameroonian of the boy's death and of the discovery of notebooks in which Toundi has recorded his story. The effect of the framing narration is to universalize Toundi's experience: whatever his individual failings—his naïveté and his internalization of the whites' racism—it is important that his exploitation and maltreatment be seen as characteristic of the colonial regime. The decision to present the bulk of the novel as a first-person account, through the medium of Toundi's diaries, allows Oyono to depict in detail the state of consciousness of the would-be *assimilé* who abandons his own culture in the hope of being privileged by the whites.

From the beginning Toundi is given ample evidence that to the whites he is irremediably inferior, an assessment vital to their continuing economic exploitation of the colony. He notes that in the first moments of his meeting with Decazy, "After [the commandant] had looked at me a long while, he asked me point-blank if I were a thief" (p. 24). Throughout, the colonialists' racist conceptualization of the colonized and their responses to the latter are depicted with a satire that is simultaneously fierce, deft, and economical (the commandant's first interview with Toundi is a brillant example of this). The other servants try their best to persuade Toundi to see his situation objectively. The commandant's cook warns him, "When will you grasp that for the whites, you are only alive to do their work and for no other reason" (p. 100). Yet Toundi remains besotted with his employers, his empathic identification with them unbroken until too late.

The arrival of Madame Decazy intensifies his infatuation; he vows not to sully the hand she has briefly held on meeting him: "My hand is sacred and must not know the lower regions of my body." When he discovers Madame's infidelity, his sympathy transfers to her husband. Only toward the latter part of the story does Oyono show Toundi gradually arriving at an understanding of his actual situation. Yet even now he is still unable to take dynamic action to free himself from his persecutors. His single act of rebellion is a trivial and private one—spitting discreetly in the commandant's drinking water. It is only when he is committed to prison that the whites have no more mysteries for him to reflect upon. His language now is direct and unelaborated, notating the bare facts of his existence:

> Water-party.
> Water, sweat. Whip, blood.
> Up the slope, killing. All in.
> (p. 134)

It is, significantly, not part of Oyono's program to show Toundi learning to engage in active struggle against the colonialists. Isolated from his fellow blacks, abandoning his family, and sexually inhibited, he remains a passive victim. *Houseboy* proposes no action, even though the book was written during the years of a fierce political struggle for independence in Cameroon. What it does do is ask with anguish the questions "What kind of people are we?" (p. 133) and "Where is it all leading to?" (p. 133)—questions summarized especially in Toundi's words to the compatriot who discovers him on his deathbed: "What are we blackmen who are called French?" (p. 7).

THE OLD MAN AND THE MEDAL

According to Oyono, his second published novel, *The Old Man and the Medal*, was written simultaneously with *Houseboy*. Coming to a halt on one manuscript, he would turn to the other, until both were finished. Like *Houseboy*, Old Man uses satire to expose the gulf between colonialist rhetoric and the harsh realities of the regime; as in *Houseboy*, Oyono achieves a gradual darkening of tone as the novel's central character comes to understand the degradation implicit in his position as a colonial subject.

The plot is somewhat more streamlined. Laurent Meka, an old Mvema villager, is informed by the authorities that he will be awarded a medal in recognition of his long-standing acquiescence to the whites: he has previously given his ancestral land to the Catholic church, and both his sons died in service in World War II. A telling contrast exists between Meka and his ancestors, who fiercely resisted German colonial rule.

This medal for servitude is to be awarded, ironically, on the French national holiday, 14 July—a day that commemorates liberation in the storming of the Bastille. Much of the novel deals with Meka's preparations for the ceremony and the event itself. At the reception afterward, Meka becomes drunk, falls asleep, and is left alone in the community center. Waking during a massive rainstorm, he panics and wanders into the European residential area. Under the *indigénat* it is an offense for any black to be there at night without a permit; unrecognized by the police and having lost his medal, Meka is arrested and verbally and physically abused. Freed the next day by the somewhat embarrassed authorities, he returns to the village and recounts his story. He and the villagers now recognize their true status under the colonial regime.

Despite Oyono's continuing preoccupation with the harshness and hypocrisy of colonial rule, the whites feature far less prominently as characters here than in *Houseboy*. They are almost entirely absent from the first part of the book, as well as from its final section. Oyono's focus is trained, rather, on the mental processes of the colonial subject, on the way Meka and his community conceptualize their role under colonial rule.

Unlike Toundi, Meka is a mature man, yet he has lived his whole life under a commanding fixed idea—his deluded belief that the domination of his land by the colonial power is to his advantage. In the first section of the novel, Oyono (relatively gently) deflates that belief by satirizing Meka's preoccupation with making himself smart for the ceremony: spending a small fortune on European shoes he cannot comfortably wear and on a ludicrous jacket made by a charlatan tailor. Oyonò's satire here is aimed both at Meka's inexperience of the modern world and at the system that exploits this; but ultimately its target is that naïveté of Meka's, which renders him unable to see that he is being exploited. Chapters in this section alternate between Meka's preparations in his village and preparations made by his brother-in-law Engamba, in a neighboring village, to pay a congratulatory call on the old man. In this way Oyono shows that the assimilationist delusion is not held by Meka alone: upon learning about the award, Engamba gleefully observes, "I am the brother-in-law of a man with a medal!" and "Isn't the friend of a chief something of a chief himself?" (p. 39).

The middle section of the novel, dealing with the medal-giving ceremony and the reception, is a tour de force of satirical observation. From the beginning, when Meka is placed in the center of a whitewash circle like a stage prop, waiting for the arrival of the colonial governor, Oyono precisely delineates both the whites' exploitation of the old man as symbolic function (demonstrating the rewards of acquiescence) and Meka's misapprehension of his true position.

It is not that the medal has no value: theoretically it may release Meka from the restrictions of the *indigénat* and of the forced-labor levy. But Meka grossly misjudges its deeper significance as a token of his complicity in his own subjugation. Oyono marks this misjudgment by tracing Meka's reflexes and thoughts during the ceremony: believing himself rising to the clouds when the medal is pinned on his chest and despising the traditional chiefs over whom he believes he now takes precedence. The reception scene is dominated by official speeches, which cruelly reveal the limits the whites place on their "friendship" with Meka and the old man's persistent delusion of grandeur. In between these two satirical scenes, however, Oyono has introduced a brief episode that cuts harshly across the wry comedy. Watching the ceremony, Meka's wife, Kelara, hears a young man criticize the medal as an inadequate reward for the loss of Meka's land and his two sons. A short chapter then focuses exclusively on Kelara's revelatory assessment of her husband: "Is any wife or mother more wretched than I am? I thought I had married a man, a real man . . . instead I married an arse-full of shit. My children, my poor children—sold like the Lord who was sold by Judas . . . He at least did it for money" (p. 99).

In this carefully engineered narrative, much of the first two-thirds of the novel in fact provides ironic preparation for what follows. References to the prospect of rain, for instance, are placed throughout, so that when the storm breaks and traps Meka, the rain registers as poetic justice. In the prison scene Oyono abandons satire; as in the last pages of *Houseboy*, here he directly demonstrates the brutality of the regime. The satirical approach reemerges only when he returns Meka to his village and dramatizes the old man's highly embroidered account of his ordeal and the villagers' response.

The nature of this response provides perhaps the best measure of the novel's orientation. Oyono's dissection of the colonial regime, of its procedures and its rhetoric, is certainly uncompromising. The publication of *Houseboy* and *Old Man* caused sufficient offense to the colonial authorities for Oyono's father to lose his job. Yet Oyono here demonstrates only a very qualified sympathy for the victims of colonial rule. Or, to reposition these terms, the problem is that he depicts them, at the best, as victims and never as agents in potential command of their own affairs.

The question has to do with the all-inclusive ambit of the novel's satire. For Oyono the most positive aspect of the Mvemas' life appears to be their sociability: a genuine accord and affectionate interdependence are stressed throughout the novel. There is also an astringent pathos in the villagers' recognition of their actual status as Meka recounts his humiliation. All this, though, is offset by Oyono's satirical delineation of the community's limitations. Frantz Fanon, analyzing colonialist vocabulary in his *The Wretched of the Earth* (1967), notes that "the terms the settler uses when he mentions the native are zoological terms. . . . The native knows this, and laughs to himself every time he spots an allusion to the animal world in the other's words" (pp. 32–33). Grimly ironic, then, is the demeaning effect of Oyono's constant reference to the Mvemas—to Meka and his wife especially—through animal metaphors: they are likened to baboons, chimps, dogs, and camels in a plethora of comparison that runs through the entire novel.

More significant is the emphasis Oyono places on stagnation, on the community's terminal inability to contest colonial rule. The novel's ponderous opening sentence sets the tone as Meka wakes, as he does every morning, with a beam of sunlight falling on his left nostril. The novel closes with Meka insisting, "We can't do anything about what has happened. The whites will always be the whites" and with his recognition—the book's final line—"I'm just an old man now. . . ." (p. 167). This fact is significant, too: with the exception of the youth who criticizes Meka at the ceremony, *The Old Man and the Medal* is populated entirely with old men and women, whose ability to transform their environment appears negligible.

ROAD TO EUROPE

Oyono's third novel, *Chemin d'Europe* (*Road to Europe*), was published in 1960. It has received far less attention than his earlier novels and was not translated into English until 1989. (Translations of *Houseboy* and *The Old Man and the Medal* had appeared in 1966 and 1967, respectively.) Its relative lack of appeal can probably be attributed to its narrow range and experimental nature: a first-person narrative, it yields its ultimate meaning in the texture of the narrator's voice, a voice that is laborious, ponderous, pretentious, and obscene.

Attending by chance a revivalist meeting at which Africans are encouraged to confess their life stories, the young protagonist, Aki Barnabas, delivers an autobiographical account of himself that is designed to fulfill his one ambition — to persuade the church authorities to send him to France. His narrative, which forms the substance of the novel, is saturated with the sentiment that dominates his life — the desire to assimilate, to become a black Frenchman.

His story covers his early years at a seminary, where he embarks on a lifelong love-hate relationship with the whites who rule his country, resenting (and describing in painful, often scatological, detail) their hypocrisy and cruelty, yet desiring all the time to identify with them, to occupy their role. Barnabas goes on to describe his employment by a succession of whites, each more ludicrous than the last. Throughout there is a powerful sense of his affective predicament, despising each individual white, recognizing how they exploit him, yet yearning to be identified with them. He reveals his lack of sympathy for his father (depicted as a ridiculous figure) and his passionate attachment to his mother, whose affection he is, however, entirely prepared to exploit.

An element of homoeroticism, combined with Barnabas' failure to sustain a relationship with the prostitute Anatatchia, helps to build the impression of a self-absorbed, culturally fragmented social isolate. This impression is carried powerfully as well by Barnabas' invariably scathing assessments of his own people and by the extremely elaborate, highly adjectival language and complex syntax he invents to tell his story. If the whites are presented as monsters, some of the most spectacularly unpleasant descriptions in the book are applied by Barnabas to his compatriots: to his father and to his village chief (in places the texture of his account recalls the French novelist Louis-Ferdinand Céline). Oyono's purpose is to project the thought processes of a victim of the Eurocentric fixation. Though Barnabas succeeds, according to his own terms, in the end *Road to Europe* is a more pessimistic novel than its predecessors. Compared with Meka and Toundi, Barnabas is relatively well educated and, in a sense, highly articulate, yet his subservience to a fixed image of his role as black Frenchman is so deeply entrenched that his personality appears far more drastically subverted than that of the old man or the houseboy.

OYONO'S DIPLOMATIC CAREER

Oyono returned to Cameroon from France in 1959, on the eve of his country's independence, and immediately allied himself with the conservative regime of Ahmadou Ahidjo. His first appointment was as director of the Bureau d'Etudes in Yaoundé; barely a year later he was appointed ambassador to France, an extremely prestigious posting. He was later ambassador to Guinea, Ghana, and Morocco; to Liberia; and to the Benelux countries and the European Union (then called the European Economic Community). As Cameroon's ambassador to the United States, he chaired the African group of delegations and in that capacity spoke persuasively against the apartheid regime in South Africa. Oyono also served as the director general of UNICEF for a brief period beginning in 1977. After Ahidjo suddenly retired from the presidency in 1982 and was succeeded by Paul Biya, Oyono continued his diplomatic career. In August 1985 he was appointed secretary-general of the presidency, a rough equivalent to the post of prime minister, for which there was no provision under the Cameroonian constitution. A year later, he seemed to be less in favor with Biya, having been relegated to the post of housing and town planning minister. A succession of other ministerial postings followed.

During this period Oyono published no further work: *Road to Europe* remained, apparently, his final contribution to African literature. His publishers in Paris, Julliard, had long since announced a fourth novel, *Le Pandémonium.* In an interview given in 1976, Oyono described it as being very long and complex, and still awaiting a final revision. Twenty years later, this work still had not appeared.

The reasons for Oyono's protracted silence after his return to Cameroon attracted considerable speculation. Was this a direct reflection of his inability to write on conditions under the postcolonial regime, given his indebtedness to that regime for a diplomatic and ministerial career, and perhaps given his unwillingness—as an incisive social critic—to paint a portrait that was merely anodyne? The realities of the Ahidjo regime—nondevelopmental exploitation of natural resources; unequal distribution of wealth; the rapid development of a massive, Eurocentric, kleptocratic civil service; and the brutal suppression of political opposition—could hardly be glossed over without that error of omission being glaringly obvious. Was it less damaging to Oyono's reputation as a writer for him to remain silent?

This is pure speculation. It is worthwhile, though, to contrast Oyono's career as writer with that of Mongo Beti. The two novelists were of the same generation and from the same region of Cameroon, and they made their reputations simultaneously as the authors of fierce critiques of colonial rule. Beti, a member of the rigorously anticolonial UPC, remained in self-imposed exile in France after Cameroon's independence; and although he, like Oyono, published nothing for many years after 1960, from the mid 1970s on, he brought out a series of new novels and essays strongly critical of the Ahidjo and Biya regimes. The contrast between Oyono's and Beti's chosen options is most clearly shown in a 1972 incident, when under pressure from the Cameroonian government, the French authorities seized all copies of Beti's *Main basse sur Cameroun* (The plundering of Cameroon), a documentary and polemic account of civil-rights abuses and economic corruption under Ahidjo, and threatened to deport Beti to Cameroon. The Cameroonian ambassador to France at that time, who voiced his government's objections to the book, was none other than Oyono. Oyono's career also contrasted with that of other "senior" Cameroonian writers, such as René Philombe and Benjamin Matip, who developed an increasingly radical critique of the neocolonial regime in Cameroon through the 1960s and 1970s. Furthermore, the period produced dozens of younger writers, many of whom were forced to write from outside the country, whose work was often proscribed in Cameroon.

CONCLUSION

Several intrinsic features of Oyono's writing suggest a fundamental conservatism in his thinking that may be obscured by the rigorousness of his critique of colonial rule. In a sense, Oyono's depiction of the colonial situation is incomplete. From very shortly after World War II, Cameroonian political life was dominated by contesting arguments as to what species of independence and what form of government the territory should seek: retaining close association with the former colonial powers or not, socialist or otherwise. This debate consolidated in the formation of political parties, then the armed struggle waged by the UPC, and the eventual violent suppression of that organization. The earlier part of this history coincides with the period covered by Oyono's three novels, yet, with the exception of one oblique reference in *Road to Europe*, the events of Cameroon's turbulent pre-independence years are unmentioned by Oyono. Colonial rule is strongly critiqued, but the controversy over forms of self-government is something he clearly did not wish to touch upon. It is a glaring and significant absence in his work.

Beyond this, one has to note the insistent foregrounding in Oyono's work of conditions of passivity, delusion, and despair—an emphasis that deepens as one moves from the first two novels to the third. *Houseboy* ends with the death of its passive, virtually helpless central character. Yet the fact of Toundi's youth and the sense of waste his death provokes have an impact that has no equivalent in *The Old Man and the Medal.* In this novel populated by the aged and the ineffectual, the central character's recognition that his life has been a tragic waste is not liberating but debilitating. There appear to be no prospects for a different future. In *Road to Europe* the impasse is total: the confined perspective of the novel (restricted to Barnabas' point of view) cynically implies that the young man's eagerness to sell himself and his own people is an irremediable state of affairs. Oyono's reputation remains centered on the perceptiveness of his critique of colonial rule. It is worth bearing in mind, however, the intensity and subjectiveness of his imaginative involvement with states of despair, passivity, and capitulation.

Selected Bibliography

NOVELS

Une Vie de boy. Paris: Julliard, 1956, 1969; Benin City, Nigeria: Ethiope, 1975. The 1975 ed. has an introduction by Kwabena Britwum.

Le Vieux Nègre et la médaille. Paris: Union Générale d'Editions, 1956, 1972, 1979.

Chemin d'Europe. Paris: Julliard, 1960, 1973.

TRANSLATIONS

Houseboy. Trans. by John Reed. London: Heinemann, 1966, 1975. Also published as *Boy!* New York: Collier Books, 1970. The latter ed. has an intro. by Edris Makward.

The Old Man and the Medal. Trans. by John Reed. London: Heinemann, 1967.

Road to Europe. Trans. and with an intro. by Richard Bjornson. Washington, D.C.: Three Continents Press, 1989.

INTERVIEW

"Entretien avec Ferdinand Oyono." In *Cameroon Tribune* (23 February 1976).

CRITICAL STUDIES

Awoonor, Kofi. *The Breast of the Earth: A Survey of the History, Culture and Literature of Africa South of the Sahara.* Garden City, N.Y.: Anchor, 1975.

Bjornson, Richard. *The African Quest for Freedom and Identity: Cameroonian Writing and the National Experience.* Bloomington: Indiana University Press, 1991.

Blair, Dorothy S. *African Literature in French: A History of Creative Writing in French from West and Equatorial Africa.* Cambridge, U.K.: Cambridge University Press, 1976.

Boafo, Y. S. Kantanka. "Portraits dans *Le Vieux Nègre et la médaille.*" In *Présence francophone,* no. 19 (fall 1979).

Britwum, Kwabena. "Regard, mémoire, témoignage: Ou l'Oeil du sorcier dans *Une Vie de boy* de Ferdinand Oyono." In *Présence francophone, no.* 14 (spring 1977).

Chevrier, Jacques. Une Vie de boy: *Oyono.* Paris: Hatier, 1977.

Dunton, Chris. "Ferdinand Oyono's *Houseboy* and *The Old Man and the Medal.*" In Samuel O. Asein and Albert Olu Ashaolu, eds., *Studies in the African Novel.* Ibadan, Nigeria: Ibadan University Press, 1986.

Fanon, Frantz. *The Wretched of the Earth.* Trans. by Constance Farrington. Harmondsworth, U.K.: Penguin, 1967; New York: Grove Press, 1968.

Kibera, Leonard. "Colonial Context and Language in Ferdinand Oyono's *Houseboy.*" In *African Literature Today,* no. 13 (1983).

Mercier, Roger, Monique Battestini, and Simon Battestini. *Ferdinand Oyono: Écrivain camerounais.* Paris: Nathan, 1964.

Minyono-Nkodo, Mathieu-François. *Comprendre* Le Vieux Nègre et la *médaille.* Issy-les-Moulineaux, France: Les Classiques Africains, 1978.

Wauthier, Claude. *The Literature and Thought of Modern Africa.* Trans. by Shirley Kayl. London: Heinemann, 1966; Washington, D.C.: Three Continents Press, 1979.

Yoder, Carroll. *White Shadows: A Dialectical View of the French African Novel.* Washington, D.C.: Three Continents Press, 1991.

Alan Paton

1903–1988

PETER F. ALEXANDER

ALAN STEWART PATON was born on 11 January 1903 in Pietermaritzburg in Natal, which was then a British colony and in 1910 became one of South Africa's provinces. He was the oldest of four children, two boys and two girls. His parents were Eunice Warder James Paton, born in South Africa to British parents, and James Paton, a Scot who had emigrated to South Africa in 1895 and was a shorthand writer in Pietermaritzburg all his working life.

A FATHER'S INFLUENCE

James Paton was a tormented soul who influenced his children for good and ill far more than their mother did. A great deal of his famous son's character was formed under his influence. Much of this influence was malign, for James Paton was domineering and violent. He regularly beat his children and also, it seems, his wife. In public he was an unimpressive figure, short and quiet spoken, but in the Paton home, a small house on Pine Street, he was a bullying tyrant. He made rules covering the behavior of every member of his family and embracing almost any activity in the home; floggings with a cane followed any disobedience.

There were rules about who could eat what; James Paton and his mother, whom he had brought out from Scotland some years after he emigrated, got most of what little food was consumed in the frugal household. There were rules, too, about which friends his children could have, what might be done on which day, who might go into which room, and so on. No child was allowed to go about unsupervised at any time, presents could not be taken to children's birthday parties, not even the mildest expletive could be used in conversation, warm undershirts were to be worn in the subtropical summer, playing tennis and dancing were forbidden, Saturday was a holy day when almost all activities were banned. The list seemed unending.

Alan Paton later described this regime as authoritarianism maintained by the use of violence. Looking back when he was old, he remarked of James Paton, "His use of physical force never achieved anything but a useless obedience. But it had two important consequences. One was that my feelings towards him were almost those of hate. The other was that I grew up with an abhorrence of authoritarianism. . . ." (*Towards the Mountain*, p. 14). Alan Paton retained this detestation of authoritarianism, and his unwavering determination to fight authoritarians, all his life. It is not too much to say that his life was largely formed by it.

However, in fairness it has to be added that James Paton's influence was not entirely negative. Although his own education had been cut short by the poverty of his parents in Scotland, he had a love of literature and managed to impart it to his children, particularly to his elder son. In addition he delighted in music and organized musical evenings, to which he invited students from the local university. At these soirees his wife played the piano and his whole family, including the children, sang parts. James Paton was also a keen debater: he took his children to hear him speak, and as they grew, he encouraged them to take part in debates. In addition, he was a poet who published regularly in the local newspapers and in the annual Natal *Eisteddfod Book*, an activity that spurred his elder son to emulation.

James Paton had two other enthusiasms that he communicated to his children. The first was a love of nature and of walking in the countryside; his elder son's delight in nature shows in almost everything he wrote. The second was a passionate religious belief. James had been brought up a Christadelphian but had left the Christadelphian ecclesia (assembly) in Pietermaritzburg when he married Eunice James, who had been raised a Methodist and was therefore a nonbeliever in the eyes of the Christadelphians.

By way of compensation James Paton constructed a religion all his own. Religious activity took up most of Sunday. In the morning his family walked to the Christadelphian service, leaving James behind with one child to keep him company. When they returned from the long service and had had lunch, a further service was held in James's bedroom; the children took turns preaching to him on a text assigned the previous week. Alan's sermons were thoroughly prepared and carefully researched with the aid of concordances and commentaries. He preached before his father from the age of five, so it is not surprising that his use of English in later life was deeply imbued with biblical cadences and a love of the language of the King James Bible.

But this religious study did more than form Alan Paton's style. His view of life was based upon biblical morality. He very gradually came to be able to shrug off his father's humiliating and petty rules as "the lesser moralities," but to the greater moralities that he had learned from the Bible, he held until the end of his long life.

EARLY EDUCATION

Paton's mother, who had been a teacher, taught him to read and write before he went to school. His academic career was precocious and extraordinarily swift. At the age of six he entered school, and rapidly advanced from the first grade to a class three levels above it. As a result he was very small compared with other boys in his group until the end of his school career.

Because his father's training had made Paton unusually docile and timid, the other children inspired terror on the playground. In the classroom, however, he excelled. Competing against children two or three years older than himself, he headed the class without apparent effort throughout his school career. Paton gradually got used to being both the smallest and the brightest boy. However, this did not make him the most popular. In the classroom he was triumphant; on the playground, one humiliation succeeded another.

Paton's younger brother, Atholl, could (and did) beat him in their regular quarrels; Alan, who knew he was small and easily bullied, tried to escape attention. Camouflage was his best defense. His most painful memories were of occasions on which he failed to avoid being noticed. One of these occurred when one of his schoolmates spotted his shoes:

> I wore a pair of shoes that did not lace up, but had a strap that went over the instep and was

fastened by a button. These shoes were pronounced by one of the older boys to be girls' shoes, but I denied it, I am sure not hotly and angrily, but no doubt quietly and gently. I had no idea that such a small matter could attract such great attention, but soon there was a crowd of boys around me, and there was general agreement that I was wearing girls' shoes.

(*Towards the Mountain*, p. 22)

Another incident also involved being brought to the attention of bigger boys, but the emotion it produced in Paton was not humiliation, but shame. In essence it was a simple enough event, and most other boys would have forgotten it at once. Paton never put it from his mind, and the memory grew in importance to him until it became in retrospect a life-changing event. What happened was this: on a winter day his mother sent to school a basket containing scones and a drink for him. When the black servant asked for him on the playground, Paton, mortified to find himself singled out in this way, denied that the food was for him and allowed some of his schoolmates to eat it. And when the servant saluted him on leaving, he ignored the salutation.

Paton recorded this incident many years later, in his moving story "The Gift," and he told it again in his autobiography *Towards the Mountain* (1980). But there is an earlier account, in an unpublished novel titled "John Henry Dane":

One cold biting day I had an experience of which even the philosopher of twenty-eight [the protagonist's age at the time he tells the story] is a little ashamed. My mother was in the village, staying with her bachelor brother, Mr Thompson. And at the short-break, which we country bumpkins called "little play-time," a native boy approached with a basket of warm buttered toast & a jug of hot tea. It was the very day for such a gift, & I looked longingly at it, not knowing it was mine.

"Dane, you lucky devil, here's some grub for you," one of the bigger boys told me.

"It's not mine," I said.

"But the nigger says it's for you."

"It's not mine," I said vehemently.

Some obscure motive—fear of eating something that would single me out from the shouting personless crowd where I was content to lose myself—perhaps fear of owning to a mother & the fact of being loved—who knows?

"You can't waste it, you fool."

"You can have it. It's not mine," I said doggedly.

"Here goes," said the lucky one, & I tried to watch carelessly the sharing of my mother's gift. But the feeling of cowardice, the knowledge of my own strangeness, set me drifting to a place where I was hidden from the scene of this incomprehensible treachery.

I told my mother the story years afterwards, & felt even then the shame & the need for forgiveness. Of all my queer actions it still remains the most incomprehensible.

(Alexander, pp. 18–19)

Paton gradually came to understand that "incomprehensible" action. It became for him a story of the betrayal of a dearly held principle in the face of social disapproval. His brooding on the shame of this betrayal made him ever more determined not to slip into treachery of this sort again, on a bigger scale. He gained strength from the view that he had something to expiate. Significantly, in the later versions of this story, particularly the one in his autobiography, the betrayal focuses not on the mother's gift but on the black boy who brings it:

I went further along the wall so as not to be seen by the boy. I had not been standing there long when some of the schoolboys came to me and said, your boy's here with a basket. But I, though inexperienced in lying, denied that such a boy could be there. So they brought the boy, and of course it was our boy, and he smiled at me uncertainly because of the strangeness of the place, and I denied all knowledge of him. But he told them he was certainly our boy, and that I was the son of the house, and that my mother had sent me something warm to eat and drink. I denied him the second time.

(*Towards the Mountain*, p. 23)

Childhood embarrassment at being singled out in public has, in the mind of the mature writer, assumed the significance of Peter's denial of Christ. Such moments as these formed Paton's character, and moral scrupulousness and honesty became two of his most prominent traits.

COLLEGE EDUCATION

Paton finished school with excellent results at the end of 1918. Because his father declined to support him through medical school, he was forced to seek a scholarship from the Natal Education Department, which meant becoming a teacher. He studied for a science degree at Natal University College, Pietermaritzburg.

Though Paton lived at home during his four years at University College, his father was obliged to allow him much more freedom; this he enjoyed to the full, joining in many of the activities of his university and distinguishing himself at acting, debating, and the affairs of the Students Representative Council (a students' union) and of the Student Christian Association (SCA). Through the SCA, Paton met a group of idealistic young men and women, of whom Railton Dent and Reg Pearse most strongly influenced him. From Dent in particular he learned a lesson he never forgot, as he recorded years later in *Towards the Mountain*:

> Dent was the son of a Methodist missionary, and he was a committed Christian. Committed Christians have faults just as commonly as other people, but I could see no fault in him. He was I think the most upright person I ever was to know, and his influence on me was profound. He did not make me into a good man, that would have been too much. But he taught me one thing... that life must be used in the service of a cause greater than oneself. This can be done by a Christian for two reasons: one is obedience to his Lord, the other is purely pragmatic, namely that one is going to miss the meaning of life if one doesn't.
>
> How Railton Dent *taught* me this, I don't quite know. I suppose that my reverence and affection for him was so great that I caught it from him. And I must have caught it thoroughly, because in the course of a life which I have not considered conspicuously good, I have never given up *trying to be obedient.*
>
> (*Towards the Mountain*, p. 24)

With the examples of Dent and Pearse before him, Paton began to seek ways of dedicating his life to helping others. He helped organize an annual SCA holiday camp for boys and girls on the south coast of Natal, a missionary activity that he continued for many years. At these camps he met like-minded men and women; notable among them was Jan Hofmeyr, a brilliant Cape Afrikaner (one of Dutch-settler descent) who during the 1930s rose to cabinet rank in the South African government. Paton also began to seek political influence among his fellow students, being elected president of the Students' Representative Council in 1923. In 1924 the students sent him to England as their representative to the Imperial Conference of Students at London and Cambridge, his first trip out of South Africa and a great widening of horizons for him.

Paton's other extracurricular activity at University College was writing verse. At first the poems were collaborative efforts with two of his friends—they met at night in the Pietermaritzburg cemetery to read poetry by candlelight—but soon he began to publish on his own, in the student magazine and the annual Natal *Eisteddfod Poetry Book*. The earliest of these original poems, signed "Ubi," is a fair example of his juvenile verse:

> To a Picture
>
> He gazes on me with his long-dead eyes,
> And dumbly strives to tell me how he died,
> And shows the hilt-stabbed dagger in his side;
> I see mad terror there; the murd'rous cries
> Draw near—more near—half-tottering he tries
> To reach the door—one step!—"unbar, 'tis I."

But none unbar — I hear the broken cry,
I see the mirrored anguish in his eyes.
So conjure I the tale; the faded print
Hangs on the bedroom wall, and there I see
Those wild eyes ever gazing on my bed.
They lead me to strange wondering; what hint,
What sign, what tragic muteness will there be
In mine own eyes, when they do find me dead?
(Alexander, pp. 47–48)

TEACHING CAREER

In 1925, having taken a bachelor of science degree and a teaching diploma, Paton was sent to the small farming town of Ixopo, as a house master at the high school there. At first he found the work daunting, and he was not a success with his pupils. Although the school was small and pupils were few, several of the older boys were only a few years younger than Paton, and they were physically larger than he. As their house master he had to live with them, which meant he was on the job twenty-four hours a day. The strain gradually told.

Paton thought his pupils undisciplined. He was particularly shocked to find that the older boys and girls were allowed to be friendly with one another, touching and even kissing. His father's teaching had shown him only one way of dealing with this state of potential immorality: he used the cane with energy, and was soon feared and hated by the boys. The girls disliked him almost as much, for he turned on them his father's weapons of ridicule and humiliation. As a result, when he tried to persuade them to attend the annual SCA camp that year, none accepted. He remained a master more feared than liked throughout his teaching career.

In Ixopo, which lies in beautiful rolling countryside, Paton continued his practice, begun under his father's influence, of taking long walks over the hills. On the weekends he commonly walked twenty miles a day, and on many occasions covered thirty or even forty. These walks gave him the intimate knowledge of Ixopo's surroundings that he used to such effect in *Cry, the Beloved Country* (1948). His love of the landscape spoke in the very first paragraph of that novel:

> There is a lovely road that runs from Ixopo into the hills. These hills are grass-covered and rolling, and they are lovely beyond any singing of it. The road climbs seven miles into them, to Carisbrooke; and from there, if there is no mist, you look down on one of the fairest valleys of Africa. About you there is grass and bracken and you may hear the forlorn crying of the titihoya, one of the birds of the veld. Below you is the valley of the Umzimkulu, on its journey from the Drakensberg to the sea; and beyond and behind the river, great hill after great hill; and beyond and behind them, the mountains of Ingeli and East Griqualand.
>
> (p. 3)

It was at Ixopo that Paton met and fell in love with Doris (Dorrie) Lusted. She was five years his senior, and she was married, to a man who was dying of tuberculosis. Paton wooed her assiduously; her husband died on 25 May 1925, and they were married on 2 July 1928. The relationship was not always easy, for Dorrie remained deeply attached to the memory of her first husband for a number of years, an attachment of which Paton was very jealous. The relationship was a source of both joy and pain.

Very shortly after his marriage, Paton took a teaching post at the high school from which he had graduated, Maritzburg College. His strong sense of the need to do something practical about the sufferings of the poor in South Africa showed itself in his active social work in Pietermaritzburg, and in such poems as "The Hermit," which he published in 1931:

I have barred the doors
Of the place where I bide,
I am old and afraid
Of the world outside.

How the poor souls cry
In the cold and the rain,
I have blocked my ears,
They shall call me in vain.

If I peer through the cracks
Hardly daring draw breath,
They are waiting there still
Patient as death.

The maimed and the sick
The tortured of soul,
Arms outstretched as if
I could help them be whole.

No shaft of the sun
My hiding shall find,
Go tell them outside
I am deaf, I am blind.

Who will drive them away,
Who will ease me my dread,
Who will shout to the fools
"He is dead! he is dead!"?

Sometimes they knock
At the place where I hide,
I am old, and afraid
Of the world outside.

Do they think, do they dream
I will open the door?
Let the world in
And know peace no more?
(*Knocking on the Door*,
pp. 8–9)

It was also while teaching in Pietermaritzburg that Paton experimented with literary forms other than poetry. In 1930 he began a novel "Brother Death," which includes characters who later reappeared in *Cry, the Beloved Country*, and in 1934 he wrote several chapters of a largely autobiographical novel, "John Henry Dane"; neither has been published. Paton also produced a series of fragmentary stories set in Ixopo; one of them, "Secret for Seven," focuses on the cultural clash between whites and blacks that was to be one of his major themes. He also continued to produce poetry, and between 1932 and 1935 he wrote a play, *Louis Botha*, that showed his growing sympathies with the Afrikaners, whose language he was learning.

DIEPKLOOF

In 1934 Paton suffered a severe attack of typhoid, from which he nearly died. The effects of this experience, combined with a renewed crisis in his marriage that prompted him to have an extramarital affair, made him determine on a change of course. He applied for the job of warden at three of South Africa's borstals (juvenile reformatories), hoping to be appointed to the one for whites in Cape Town; to his dismay, and to the horror of his wife, he was appointed to South Africa's only reformatory for black Africans, Diepkloof, near Johannesburg. Paton's friend Jan Hofmeyr, who had been appointed minister of education and thus had the final responsibility for reformatories, wrote to him that it was hard to know what could be done with the place. When Paton traveled there to take charge, in July 1935, it must have been with a sinking heart.

Diepkloof had been built as a prison for adults and looked the part, with heavy bars on the windows and grim, dilapidated buildings enclosed by a high, barbed-wire fence. Uniformed guards, black and white, patrolled ceaselessly, armed with heavy sticks they used to administer beatings at will. The 360 inmates ranged from boys of nine who had been confined for misdemeanors as trivial as stealing a pot of jam, to young men in their early twenties who had committed rape or murder and were prone to violence. The prisoners were crammed into overcrowded cells for twelve hours each day, with one latrine bucket for twenty-two of them; they slept on the damp earth floors, with only two or three thin blankets to ward off the bitter cold of the high veld winter; they were allowed neither warm clothing nor shoes. Predictably, there was a steady trickle of deaths from respiratory infections and from highly contagious diseases such as typhoid, since there was no place to isolate such patients.

Paton came to think of Diepkloof as a microcosm of South African society. That such a comparison could be drawn in 1935 is a terrible indictment of South Africa fully thirteen years before the National Party came to power, and shows that apartheid did not start in 1948. It was a comparison he drew in the poem "To a Small Boy Who Died at Diepkloof Reformatory" (1949), which ends thus:

Here is the warrant of committal,
For this offence, oh small and lonely one,
For this offence in whose commission
Millions of men are in complicity
You are committed. So do I commit you,
Your frail body to the waiting ground,
Your dust to the dust of the veld,—
Fly home-bound soul to the great Judge-President
Who unencumbered by the pressing need
To give society protection, may pass on you
The sentence of the indeterminate compassion.
(*Knocking on the Door*, pp. 68–69)

Paton began to believe that Diepkloof's reform could serve as a pattern for the reform of South Africa as a whole. Diepkloof's reform, though it took several years to effect, can be readily described. A semantic change, significantly enough, came first. Some months after Paton's arrival, the warden's title was changed to "principal," the inmates were referred to as "pupils," the black head warder was the "head teacher," and the other warders became "supervisors." And the official name of the institution, in Afrikaans, became *Verbeteringskool* (reformatory school). Behind the semantic changes lay a conceptual alteration; Diepkloof had been transferred from the Department of Prisons to the Department of Education, and Paton was expected to transform the place. It was, like South Africa in the 1990s, on the verge of dramatic practical change that no one had any clear idea of how to effect without violent unrest.

Paton's answer was to introduce a series of rapid incremental changes, all designed to increase the freedom and the responsibility of the pupils. He saw it as vital that freedom and responsibility go hand in hand. He began by relaxing what seemed unnecessary prohibitions on the smoking of tobacco; he had bucket latrines built; he revolutionized the diet by introducing fresh fruit, vegetables, and more meat; he built a laundry; he introduced the wearing of jerseys and sandals in winter; he hired new staff who had not been trained for prison work and therefore were open to new and liberal ideas; he enlarged the school; and he provided helpers for the head teacher.

Above all, Paton began to break down the punitive discipline and replace it with something approaching a contract system. If the inmates would cooperate, for instance, in keeping silence after the nine o'clock bell rang, he would give them previously unheard-of privileges, such as leaving their dormitories open from the 5 P.M. rollcall until 9 P.M. He began with the dormitory for the smallest boys and then, step by cautious step, opened the others. Soon he left them open all night.

Over the next months Paton gave more freedom: he began marching the entire body of pupils outside the wire fence for parades; subsequently he had the main gates removed, then the wire from the front of the building, then the entire fence came down. A fine bed of geraniums was planted where the fence had been. As news of what he was doing spread, Paton became known, not always approvingly, as the man who had torn down the barbed wire and planted geraniums. Next, boys who had served nine months with good behavior were given the freedom of the entire large farm on Sunday afternoons, after promising not to run away. The widespread beatings were curbed, and the principal reserved to himself alone the right to cane or whip the pupils.

Above all, Paton worked to reintegrate the Diepkloof inmates into the society of South Africa, by building free hostels into which they could move after a time and live permanently outside the main block. And he planned, as a final step, to send them to a school in the nearby black township, thereby linking them back into the society that had cast them out.

His aim was nothing less than the healing of a riven society, and it was an aim that clearly had ramifications in the country as a whole.

The effect of these reforms was remarkable. Before Paton's arrival, escapes from the institution were frequent. Boys working on the farm would make a sudden dash for freedom, and many of them got away, at least for a time; in 1935, with 360 inmates, there were 13 runaways per month, on average. Once the reforms began, the numbers of runaways began to decline; by 1948, with 600 inmates, many more of whom were in a position to escape easily than formerly, there were only 3 runaways per month.

CRY, THE BELOVED COUNTRY

Paton had not merely reformed Diepkloof, he himself had undergone a conversion from the harsh disciplinarian he had been at Ixopo to a man who believed firmly in the superiority of love, or at any rate of care, as an instrument of reformation and discipline. And he believed, increasingly, that it was a lesson the whole of South African society needed to learn. He tried hard to convert Minister of Education Hofmeyr to his point of view, hoping that Hofmeyr would offer him a job at his side in politics, but he was disappointed. In consequence Paton began to publicize his work at Diepkloof through speeches and lectures, and after 1942 he published articles on the theory of prison reform and the value of liberal ideas. In several of these articles he put forward a comprehensive program for reforming South African society by bringing blacks into the mainstream of the nation's economic and political life.

Paton's calls for action were on the whole ignored, however, although there was one furious attack on him in 1945 by the editor of the influential Afrikaans paper *Die Transvaler*, Hendrik F. Verwoerd, who, when the Nationalists came to power in 1948, became the chief architect of apartheid. Paton recognized that he was losing the war of ideas in South Africa; he needed to find a means of reaching the hearts of a wider audience.

Paton found that audience during a tour in 1946–1947 of reformatories in Europe and North America. Traveling alone for months, inspecting reformatories by day and spending nights in cheap hotels, he became intensely homesick and found himself thinking continuously of South Africa and his family. These longings, together with his reading of John Steinbeck and Knut Hamsun, crystallized on 25 September 1946 in Norway, while he was sitting in the Nidaros Cathedral at Trondheim; he went back to his hotel room and began writing the novel he titled *Cry, the Beloved Country*. Paton wrote it in hotels and on board ships, in Scandinavia, England, the United States, and Canada, finishing it in a hotel in San Francisco on 29 December 1946. The book was published by Scribners early in 1948. It was an immediate success, and by the time of Paton's death in 1988 it had sold more than 15 million copies. Since then its sales have continued to climb steadily, year by year: in 1991 it sold just under 100,000 copies worldwide. It was filmed in 1951 by Zoltan Korda and again in 1995 by Darrell James Roodt.

The reasons for this astonishingly sustained success are not hard to find. The novel is a deeply moving account of the search of a humble black Anglican priest, the Reverend Stephen Kumalo, for his son, Absalom, and sister, Gertrude, who have gone to work in Johannesburg and have not returned. In the course of his search, Kumalo leaves his impoverished rural parish near Ixopo and travels to Johannesburg, where he finds that his sister has turned to prostitution and Absalom has murdered Arthur Jarvis, the son of a white Ixopo farmer, James Jarvis. Absalom is convicted and sentenced to death, and Kumalo returns home with Gertrude's son and Absalom's pregnant wife. The novel ends with the reconciliation of Kumalo and Jarvis, and Jarvis' determination to rise above tragedy by helping the impoverished black community.

No summary can convey the extraordinary beauty of the language or the deeply moving nature of the novel, with its plea for understanding and cooperation between the races. Its emotional drive is striking, and it is the chief element the modern reader, particularly the non–South African reader, notices. But its first readers saw it as a novel not primarily of emotion but of ideas, and they did not always like the ideas. Paton's university friend Railton Dent, who was one of the models for Jarvis, wrote to him:

> Perhaps my main critical reaction is that your book would have been a finer work of art had you refrained from attempting to show so many facets of our so-called Native Problem. It seems to me that you have tried to bring in something of everything. Not only the frightening conditions of Johannesburg, and the appeal to Oppenheimer [the chief mining magnate] to do all in his power not to allow these conditions to be repeated at Odendaalsrust [where new mines were being opened up], or anywhere else, not only the political aspirations and agitations of the Natives, but also the equally, though not so obviously terrifying conditions in the country reserves.
>
> (Alexander, p. 226)

It is plain that to Dent the novel seemed to be made up of a series of political ideas derived from close observation of social conditions in South Africa, and flowing directly into action to relieve the distress among blacks. Paton essentially agreed with this view of the novel.

Cry, the Beloved Country focuses on the interaction between blacks and whites, in particular on what western influence was doing in 1946, when the book was written, to the old tribal cultures. The contrast between Ndotsheni, in rural Natal, and Johannesburg, the big city, is a strongly drawn contrast designed to show that the tribal order is being destroyed and nothing put in its place. "Deep down," Paton writes early on of Kumalo, "the fear of a man who lives in a world not made for him, whose own world is slipping away, dying, being destroyed, beyond any recall" (p. 14). And Kumalo's friend Msimangu says somberly:

> The white man has broken the tribe. And it is my belief... that it cannot be mended again. But the house that is broken, and the man that falls apart when the house is broken, these are the tragic things. That is why children break the law, and old white people are robbed and beaten.
>
> (pp. 25–26)

It is plain, then, that *Cry, the Beloved Country* is as much a didactic novel as anything Dickens wrote. However, it is not just a didactic novel, and certainly it cannot be summed up as being "about" black-white conflicts; Paton was not a Marxist, and this book is not socialist realism. But it is a politically aware novel, and it has a clear political agenda behind it, a political agenda that had gradually become clear to Paton through his contact with young, delinquent blacks in his work as a reformatory warden. He believed that the system of separation of the races, by locking blacks out of any real possibility of advancement, was storing up disaster for his country, and he feared that by the time whites came to recognize the wrong they were committing, it might be too late. "I have one great fear in my heart," says a black character in the most widely quoted passage from *Cry, the Beloved Country*, "that one day when they are turned to loving, they will find we are turned to hating" (pp. 40–41).

OPPOSING APARTHEID

The great success of *Cry, the Beloved Country*, which was accelerated by the coming to power of the Nationalists within months of the book's publication, freed Paton from his work at Diepkloof; he resigned on 30 June 1948 and devoted himself to writing full-time. He rented a house at Anerley, a village on the south coast of Natal, where he had spent childhood holidays and where the SCA camps were still held. He commemorated this return to childhood scenes in one of the many poems he wrote at this time, "Only the Child Is No More" (1948):

The sea roars as ever it did
The great green walls travel landwards
Rearing up with magnificence
Their wind-blown manes.

His wonderment I recapture here
I remember his eyes shining
I remember his ears hearing
Unbelievable music.

I hear it now, but the high notes
Of excitement are gone
I hear now deeper
More sorrowful notes.

All is the same as ever it was
The river, the reed lagoon
The white birds, the rocks on the shore
Only the child is no more.
(*Knocking on the Door*, p. 64)

The "deeper / More sorrowful notes" of this poem reflect a depression that came over Paton at intervals during the years immediately following the success of *Cry, the Beloved Country*, a depression caused by his vain attempts to write a book he could consider a worthy successor to his first novel. Through 1948 and 1949 he tried, and failed, to write prose. Another poem he wrote during this period, "I Have Approached," begins thus:

I have approached a moment of sterility
I shall not write any more awhile
For there is nothing more meretricious
Than to play with words.
(*Knocking on the Door*, p. 74)

In an effort to reproduce the circumstances of solitude in a foreign land under which he had written *Cry, the Beloved Country*, Paton traveled to the United States in 1949; he spent some months living alone in a cabin in northern California and trying to write. Again disappointed, he destroyed the novel he produced, but it was here that he wrote the best of his poems. After being told by telegram that his younger son had been confirmed in Johannesburg, he wrote "Meditation for a Young Boy Confirmed" (1950), the first stanza of which is

I rise from my dream, and take suddenly this
 pen and this paper
For I have seen with my eyes a certain
 beloved person, who lives in a
 distant country,
I have seen hands laid upon him, I have heard the
 Lord asked to defend him,
I have seen him kneel with trust and
 reverence, and the innocence of him smote
 me in the inward parts.
I remembered him with most deep affection,
 I regarded him with fear and
 with trembling,
For life is waiting for him, to wrest the
 innocence from his young boy's eyes,
So I write urgently for this beloved person,
 and indeed for all beloved persons.
I write indeed for any person, whoever may
 find something in these words.
(*Knocking on the Doors*, p. 86)

Upon returning to South Africa in 1951, Paton involved himself in the making of Zoltan Korda's film of *Cry, the Beloved Country*, and started to participate directly in South African politics. Hendrik Verwoerd had become minister of native affairs in 1950, and apartheid was now rapidly taking shape as a unified legal system of racial separation; by 1951 the African National Congress' Defiance Campaign had begun. Paton, who increasingly spoke and wrote against apartheid and its underlying ideology, found himself torn between his dream of being a full-time writer and the compulsion to involve himself in politics.

TOO LATE THE PHALAROPE

Late in 1951 he wrote another novel, working mostly in a London hotel; titled *Too Late the Phalarope* (1953), it was the second of his novels to be published. Whereas *Cry, the Beloved Country* had focused on the impact of

South African society on blacks, *Too Late the Phalarope* places the Afrikaner at center stage, and in particular examines the effect on Afrikaner life of the laws against interracial relationships—the Immorality Act and the Mixed Marriages Act—that the Nationalist government had enacted.

The novel focuses on Pieter van Vlaanderen, a heroic figure who is brought down and destroyed by the very system of which he is a part. A widely admired war hero, rugby player, and scholar, he is a lieutenant of police in a small town in the eastern Transvaal and in his position should uphold and enforce the Immorality Act. Instead he sleeps with a black girl, Stephanie, is found out, arrested, and tried. The shame leads to the destruction of his family.

Too Late the Phalarope is an elaborately and consciously constructed novel that moves to its tragic conclusion with all the ineluctability of a Greek tragedy. And in fact it has a number of links to Greek tragedy, from the heroic protagonist who is brought down by a tragic flaw, to the use of a narrator who, like the chorus, comments on the action and predicts what is to come. Yet though it is a more polished piece of work than *Cry*, it lacks the power of the earlier novel and has generally been judged inferior to it. This is partly because the details of the tragedy are less obviously universal than those of *Cry, the Beloved Country*, partly because the tension is reduced by the repetitive predictions of the chorus, and partly because van Vlaanderen is a little too good to be true. Although the novel sold well initially and had generally good reviews, Paton was not entirely satisfied with it. He embarked on a political career with a will, having convinced himself that for him, writing was a by-product of other activities.

1950s AND 1960s

In May 1953, Paton helped to found the South African Liberal Party, becoming one of its two vice presidents. He became its president in 1956, and retained that position until the party was forced to disband in 1968 by a law making multiracial groups illegal. The Liberal Party, though it never succeeded in getting any of its candidates elected to Parliament, had influence well beyond its numbers, chiefly because of Paton's fame and the fact that his was a voice that could not be silenced. During the 1960s and 1970s, when his colleagues were banned or imprisoned, one after another, or chose to leave the country, Paton continued to speak out powerfully, in hundreds of articles and speeches, against the injustice and folly of apartheid.

Apart from articles, which he poured out in a ceaseless stream, Paton produced a number of factual and political books designed to increase awareness of what was happening in his country: *The Land and People of South Africa* (1955); *South Africa in Transition* (1956), a volume with photographs by Dan Weiner; *Hope for South Africa* (1958); *The People Wept* (1959); and *The Charlestown Story* (1959). These books, because they were factual and not polemical, could scarcely be objected to by the Nationalists. The very objectivity of their descriptions of what apartheid was doing made them devastatingly effective.

Throughout this period, Paton continued to spend time on more creative writing as well. During 1959 he wrote the libretto for a musical set in a black township near Durban, with music by a black composer, Todd Matshikiza. The result, *Mkhumbane*, opened in Durban to great success just after the Sharpeville massacre in March 1960, in which sixty-nine black protesters at a demonstration were killed by police. Encouraged by the success of *Mkhumbane*, Paton took on another dramatic collaboration. *Sponono*, written with Krishna Shah, is based on three of Paton's short stories drawing on his Diepkloof years. It was such a success in South Africa in 1962 that it opened on Broadway in 1964 and has been revived several times.

Paton also found time to write what he considered one of his best books, a meticulously researched biography of his friend Jan Hofmeyr, who had died in 1948. Paton had been devoted to Hofmeyr, whom he always considered to be the best potential Liberal leader in South Africa, and he was devastated by his early death. He had saluted Hofmeyr at the time with the moving poem "On the Death of J. H. Hofmeyr":

Toll iron bell toll extolling bell
The toll is taken from the brave and the broken
Consoling bell toll
But toll the brave soul
Where no brave words are spoken

...

Clap iron bell clap iron clapper
And drown the clapping of the million million
Who clap the great batsman returning
To his Captain's pavilion

(*Knocking on the Door*, p. 67)

Yet Hofmeyr had been a disappointment to Paton, for the potential leader had chosen never to found and lead a Liberal party. Paton's biography, *Hofmeyr* (1964), is intended as more than a tribute to a politician; it is a history of the Liberal movement in South Africa and an examination of the triumph of Afrikaner nationalism—an examination, in other words, of how South Africa came to be in its desperate state.

The study of recent South African history fascinated Paton all the more as the present grew more threatening and the South African government moved ruthlessly against its opponents. The withdrawal of Paton's passport in 1960 was followed by the banning of publication and travel for many Liberals and the arrest of others; many fled abroad, and others turned to violence, calling themselves the African Resistance Movement (ARM) and blowing up high-tension-line towers during 1964. When the ARM members were arrested that same year, having been betrayed by one of their number, Paton, who had not known of their plans, felt profoundly wounded by their action.

Paton himself became the focus of police harassment. He continued to be deprived of his passport for a decade; he was threatened with house arrest, and harassed and followed by police wherever he went; his phone calls and mail were intercepted; his house was searched; his car was first damaged and then destroyed—but he continued to warn and to protest. Paton's worldwide fame prevented the government from imprisoning him. The eventual outcome of this campaign was the passing of the 1968 law that outlawed multiracial groups. Rather than submit to it, the Liberal Party disbanded, a bitter blow to South African moderates.

LATER LIFE

To add to the pressure on Paton at this time, his wife, a lifelong smoker, developed emphysema and was slowly asphyxiating through the second half of the 1960s. When she died, on 23 October 1967, Paton himself wanted to die and went through a long period of depression in which he left his mail unanswered, drank heavily, and got a great deal of adverse publicity when he was accused of trying to procure the sexual services of a black woman, in a curious echo of *Too Late the Phalarope*. This accusation was never proven, but neither was it refuted.

Paton was saved from this dark period by his secretary, Anne Hopkins: they fell in love during 1968 and married on 30 January 1969. There were strains in the marriage, however, for Anne Hopkins was more than twenty years younger than Paton and she had teenage children from a previous marriage; a good deal of adjustment was required on both sides. But Anne proved effective at protecting Paton from the multitude of demands on his time that frittered away his energies, and under her influence he began writing again.

Paton's first major book to be published after his remarriage was *Kontakion for You Departed* (1969), published in North America as *For You Departed.* It is a deeply moving account of Paton's first marriage, half memoir, half religious meditation on the meanings of life and death. In it he makes the first attempt to review his life, a review that continues with distinction in his volumes of autobiography. Several of his friends disliked *Kontakion*, considering that it revealed too many intimate details of his relationship with his first wife. In fact, though, there is much about Paton's first marriage that he continued to conceal, including his wife's physical coldness toward him and a long extramarital affair he had during the 1950s. What is striking about the book is the chronological fragmentation (achieved by repeated movements from past to present and back again) through which Paton convincingly conveys the dislocation and psychological confusion suffered by the recently bereaved.

Paton also returned to biography. During the early 1970s he wrote his lively account of the life of Archbishop Geoffrey Clayton of Cape Town and began planning a life of the South African poet Roy Campbell. *Apartheid and the Archbishop: The Life and Times of Geoffrey Clayton, Archbishop of Cape Town* (1973) is, like *Hofmeyr*, much more than a biography. It goes over much the same ground as the Hofmeyr volume, but this time from the perspective of the slow growth of organized Christian opposition to apartheid. Although it was an examination of the roots of apartheid, and a vindication and encouragement of opposition to it, the volume attracted only a small and specialized audience. The projected book on Roy Campbell, on the other hand, did not lend itself to such treatment, since Campbell in his later years was more interested in fighting communism than apartheid. Paton abandoned the project in 1974.

Paton's passport was returned to him in 1970, when Harvard offered him an honorary doctorate. Paton had loved the United States since his first trip there in 1946, and once he was able to travel again, he visited North America as often as he could, making thirteen trips in all. He admired and envied the strength of the U.S. Constitution, believing that if South Africa had had the same separation of powers, and a similar system of checks and balances, the Nationalist government would not have been able to suppress black and white opposition as it had.

Paton refused to acknowledge the triumph of apartheid or the defeat of Liberal ideas. To the end of his life he turned out a constant stream of political articles—warning, persuading, protesting—that were extraordinary in both number and power. Some of them were collected by Edward Callan in *The Long View* (1968); further collections appeared in *Knocking on the Door* (1975), edited by Colin Gardner, and in *Save the Beloved Country* (1987), edited by Jans Strydom and David Jones. But these volumes represent only a small portion of Paton's extraordinary output. Besides writing, Paton put an immense amount of energy into charitable work, helping, for instance, to run the Phoenix Trust, a Gandhian settlement for Indians in Natal; educating large numbers of young blacks out of his own financial resources; and speaking tirelessly for whatever groups he thought his influence might help.

In 1977, at the age of seventy-four, Paton began summing up his life as a whole in a first volume of autobiography, *Towards the Mountain*. The title refers to that holy mountain of the Lord mentioned by Isaiah, where none shall hurt or destroy; the volume was as much a vision of the ideal society as an account of Paton's life. It takes his life from birth up to the time he published *Cry, the Beloved Country*; every detail is chosen not just for the light it sheds on Alan Paton the individual, but also for the light it sheds on the society in which he grew up, and for the indication it gives of the kind of society South Africa could become. This is the theme that gives the book its remarkable unity; Paton looks before and after, and the book is as much a prophecy as a memoir.

In 1980, at the age of seventy-seven, he embarked on the second volume of his autobiography, and found himself dealing with the period, during the 1950s and 1960s, of his greatest political involvement. At this point he conceived the plan of writing the story not as a memoir but as a novel—or, rather, a trilogy of novels. The first of the projected series, *Ah, but Your Land Is Beautiful*, written with great rapidity, was published in 1981.

The novel mingles real events with fictional ones, and real with fictional characters, to describe the Defiance Campaign (in which Indians and blacks used facilities reserved for whites, and white sympathizers entered black townships without the requisite permits) and to trace the political events that followed the Defiance Campaign: the increasing repression by the Nationalists and the increasing polarization among their opponents. Central to the novel are the events surrounding the foundation of the Liberal Party; it ends with the election of Hendrik Verwoerd as the leader of the Nationalist Party (and therefore as the South African prime minister). It is a most vivid picture of the increasing repression suffered by members of the Liberal Party in the 1950s and 1960s.

Ah, but Your Land Is Beautiful was received politely but without real enthusiasm by the critics. This was partly because of the complexity of its plot and the number of its characters, a reflection of the difficulty Paton had experienced in trying to turn history into art. But it was also because the simple, solemn power of *Cry, the Beloved Country* and even of *Too Late the Phalarope* was lacking; the humane vision was obscured by a busy involvement in the details of South African politics, and even Paton's character sketches seemed constrained by his determination to do justice to the originals on whom he was drawing. He admitted as much in his correspondence when he said he quailed at the difficulty of drawing just portraits of people in the Liberal movement by whom he had felt betrayed.

This difficulty, combined with the lukewarm critical reception of the book, persuaded Paton to abandon the planned trilogy and instead return to the autobiography to deal with his personal history in the Liberal Party. He began writing the second volume of his autobiography, *Journey Continued* (1988), in 1984, and finished it just before his death. It is a less appealing volume than *Towards the Mountain*, for much of it consists of detailed history, the result of research rather than of memory transmuted through art. And there is in its second half a sense of flaccidity and tiredness, which perhaps results from the fact that Paton was in his eightieth year when he began it.

Paton continued his wide range of activities until just before his death: traveling; serving on the editorial board of the Liberal journal *Contact*; taking an active part in such political gatherings as the Indaba (discussions between leaders of Natal and the KwaZulus in October 1986); and turning out newspaper articles. He died on 12 April 1988 after a short struggle with cancer of the esophagus. His ashes were scattered in the garden of his Botha's Hill home, in the cool hills not far from Pietermaritzburg, where his journey had begun eighty-five years before.

CONCLUSION

The enormous success of *Cry, the Beloved Country* always overshadowed Paton's other work, and tempted some critics to label him a one-book man. He was not. His two other novels are both remarkable works of art, and though neither had the enduring and almost universal appeal of *Cry, the Beloved Country*, Paton remarked that they were better-constructed books. They succeed, too, in showing the extraordinary breadth of his interests and his sympathies with all the major ethnic groups in South Africa, not excluding the Afrikaners. But they, and all his books, also reveal the extent to which Paton saw his writing as fitting into the wider framework of his political and religious activities. He refused to live the life of the dedicated writer—dedicated, that is, to writing above all else. He believed firmly that a life lived for oneself and not for others is a life not worth living. All his writings, therefore—his three novels included—are not just works of art but acts of urgent communication, demanding from their readers not merely comprehension and appreciation but also action.

Paton's talent was multifaceted, showing itself not just in novels, but also in fine poetry, in two pioneering biographies, in his autobiographies, in his devotional volume *Instrument of Thy Peace* (1968), and in *Kontakion for You Departed*, which is a combination of the biographical and the devotional. Because the unparalleled success of *Cry, the Beloved Country* obscured the richness of Paton's other achievements, it is likely that a mature assessment of his full value in the context of South African literature has yet to be made. His was a profoundly humane and civilized vision, and the apparent triumph, in South Africa in the 1990s, of the values for which he strove and wrote throughout his life would have given him deep satisfaction had he lived to see it.

Paton maintained with all his power the Judeo-Christian affirmation of the worth and dignity of the individual. Running through the richly varied fabric of his life is the unbroken thread of his commitment to what he saw as the moral course: he sought out (and believed he had found) the right way to live, which was to live for others. He pursued that way to the end.

Paton's Christian creed was probably best summed up in practical essentials: to uphold human rights and dignity, to lift the downtrodden, and to promote a common society in opposition to the polarization of apartheid. He glorified God in loving his fellow humans. He hated the power-hungry, exercised intelligence and independence, and had faith in the decency, tolerance, and humanity of the common person. He liked to quote the epitaph on the tombstone of Sir Robert Shirley, who "did the best of things in the worst of times, and hoped them in the most calamitous"—words that applied to himself. Paton showed immense courage, not least in never abandoning hope of a better world.

Selected Bibliography

BIBLIOGRAPHIES

Bentel, Lea. "Alan Paton: A Bibliography." M.A. thesis, School of Librarianship, Witwatersrand University, 1969.

Callan, Edward. *Alan Paton.* Hamburg, Germany: Hans Christians Verlag, 1970. Intro. by Rolf Italiaander.

COLLECTED WORKS

Songs of Africa: Collected Poems of Alan Paton. Durban, South Africa: Gecko Books, 1995.

NOVELS

Cry, the Beloved Country: A Story of Comfort in Desolation. New York: Scribners, 1948; London: Jonathan Cape, 1948; Toronto: Saunders, 1948; London: Penguin, 1958; New York: Collier Books, 1987.

Too Late the Phalarope. New York: Scribners, 1953; London: Jonathan Cape, 1953; Cape Town, South Africa: Frederick L. Cannon, 1953.

Ah, but Your Land Is Beautiful. Cape Town, South Africa: David Philip, 1981; New York: Scribners, 1981; London: Jonathan Cape, 1981.

SHORT STORIES

Tales from a Troubled Land. New York: Scribners, 1961. Repr. as *Debbie Go Home.* London: Jonathan Cape, 1961.

PLAYS

Lost in the Stars. With Maxwell Anderson. New York: Sloane Associates, 1950.

Sponono. With Krishna Shah. New York: Scribners, 1965. Repr. Cape Town, South Africa: David Philip, 1983.

BIOGRAPHIES

Hofmeyr. London: Oxford University Press, 1964. Abridged by Dudley C. Lunt as *South African Tragedy: The Life and Times of Jan Hofmeyr.* New York: Scribners, 1965. Abridgement repr. as *Hofmeyr.* Cape Town, South Africa: Oxford University Press, 1971.

Apartheid and the Archbishop: The Life and Times of Geoffrey Clayton, Archbishop of Cape Town. Cape Town, South Africa: David Philip, 1973; New York: Scribners, 1973; London: Jonathan Cape, 1973.

AUTOBIOGRAPHICAL WORKS

Kontakion for You Departed. London: Jonathan Cape, 1969. Repr. as *For You Departed.* New York: Scribners, 1969.

Towards the Mountain. New York: Scribners, 1980; London: Oxford University Press, 1980; Cape Town, South Africa: David Philip, 1980.

Journey Continued. London: Oxford University Press, 1988; New York: Scribners, 1988; Cape Town, South Africa: David Philip, 1988.

MISCELLANEOUS VOLUMES

The Land and People of South Africa. Philadelphia: Lippincott, 1955, 1964; Toronto: Longman, 1955. Repr. as *South Africa and Her People.* London: Lutterworth Press, 1957; rev. ed. 1970.

South Africa in Transition. New York: Scribners, 1956. With photographs by Dan Weiner.

Hope for South Africa. London: Pall Mall Press, 1958; New York: Praeger, 1959.

Instrument of Thy Peace: Meditations Prompted by the Prayer of St. Francis. New York: Seabury Press, 1968; London: Collins, 1970.

The Long View. Ed. by Edward Callan. New York: Praeger, 1968; London: Pall Mall Press, 1969.

Knocking on the Door: Shorter Writings. Ed. by Colin Gardner. Cape Town, South Africa: David Philip, 1975; New York: Scribners, 1975; London: Rex Collings, 1975.

Diepkloof: Reflections of Diepkloof Reformatory. Comp. and ed. by Clyde Broster. Cape Town, South Africa: David Philip, 1986.

Save the Beloved Country. Ed. by Jans Strydom and David Jones. Johannesburg, South Africa: Hans Strydom, 1987; New York: Scribners, 1989.

PAMPHLETS, CONTRIBUTIONS TO BOOKS, MISCELLANEOUS WORKS

Freedom as a Reformatory Instrument. Penal Reform Pamphlet 2. Pretoria: Penal Reform League of South Africa, 1948.

The Negro in America Today: A Firsthand Report. Washington, D.C.: Civil Rights Committee and Education and Research Department, Congress of Industrial Organizations, 1954.

Salute to My Great Grandchildren. Johannesburg, South Africa: St. Benedict's Press, 1954.

The Charlestown Story. Johannesburg, South Africa: The Liberal Party, 1959.

The People Wept. Kloof, South Africa: Alan Paton, 1959.

Federation or Desolation. Alfred and Winifred Hoernlé Memorial Lecture. Johannesburg: South African Institute of Race Relations, 1985.

ARTICLES IN PERIODICALS

"Real Way to Cure Crime: Our Society Must Reform Itself." In *Forum* 6, no. 44 (1944).

"Who Is Really to Blame for the Crime Wave in South Africa?" In *Forum* 8 (December 1945).

"The Novelist and Christ." In *Saturday Review* 37 (December 1954). Written with Liston Pope.

"The Narrowing Gap." In *Africa Today* (November/December 1957).

"The Attitude of the Church and the Christian Towards the State." In *Background Information to Church and Society* 19 (March 1958).

"Liberals and the Nationalist Party." In *Contact* 1 (April 1958).

"The Days of White Supremacy Are Over." In *Contact* 2 (January 1959).

"South African Treason Trial." In *Atlantic* 205 (January 1960).

"The Hofmeyr Biography." In *Contrast* 3 (October 1964).

"Alan Paton Reports on South Africa." In *Commonweal* 82 (May 1965).

INTRODUCTIONS

Grant, George C. *The Liquidation of Adams College.* N.p., n.d. [1957].
Kuper, Leo, Hilstan Watts, and Ronald Davies. *Durban: A Study in Racial Ecology.* London: Jonathan Cape, 1958; New York: Columbia University Press, 1958.
Rubin, Leslie. *This Is Apartheid.* London: Christian Action Pamphlets, 1959.
Hooper, Charles. *Brief Authority.* London: Collins, 1960.
Non-Racial Democracy: The Policies of the Liberal Party of South Africa. Pietermaritzburg, South Africa: The Liberal Party, 1962.
Brookes, Edgar H. *Three Letters from Africa.* Pendle Hill Pamphlet 139. Wallingford, Pa.: Pendle Hill, 1965.

CRITICAL AND BIOGRAPHICAL STUDIES

Alexander, Peter F. *Alan Paton: A Biography.* Oxford, U.K., and New York: Oxford University Press, 1994. Includes an exhaustive bibliography.
Black, Michael. "Alan Paton and the Rule of Law." In *African Affairs* 91 (January 1992).
Brown, R. M. "Alan Paton, Warrior and Man of Grace." In *Christianity and Crisis* 48 (June 1988).
Callan, Edward. *Alan Paton.* New York: Twayne, 1968; rev. ed. 1982.
———. "Alan Paton and the Liberal Party." In Callan, ed., *The Long View.* New York: Praeger, 1968.
———. Cry, the Beloved Country: *A Novel of South Africa.* Boston: Twayne, 1991.
Chisholm, Linda. "Education, Punishment and the Contradictions of Penal Reform: Alan Paton and the Diepkloof Reformatory, 1934–1948." In *Journal of Southern African Studies* 17 (March 1991).
Duncan, Ronald M. "The Suffering Servant in Novels by Paton, Bernanos, and Schwarz-Bart." In *Christian Scholar's Review* 16 (January 1987).
Gardner, Colin. "Alan Paton: Often Admired, Sometimes Criticized, Usually Misunderstood." In *Natalia* 18 (December 1988).
———. "Paton's Literary Achievement." In *Reality* 20, no. 4 (1988).
Linnemann, Robert J. "Alan Paton: Anachronism or Visionary." In *Commonwealth Novel in English* 3 (spring/summer 1984).
Monye, A. A. "*Cry, the Beloved Country:* Should We Merely Cry?" In *Nigeria Magazine*, no. 144 (1983).
Morphet, Tony. "Alan Paton: The Honour of Meditation." In *English in Africa* 10 (October 1983).
Moss, Richard. "Alan Paton: Bringing a Sense of the Sacred." In *World Literature Today* 57 (spring 1983).
Nash, Alan. "The Way to the Beloved Country: History and the Individual in Alan Paton's *Towards the Mountain.*" In *English in Africa* 10 (October 1983).
Paton, Anne. *Some Sort of Job: My Life with Alan Paton.* London: Viking Penguin, 1992.
Rive, Richard. "The Liberal Tradition in South African Literature." In *Contrast* 14 (July 1983).
Rutherford, Andrew. "Stone People in a Stone Country: Alan Paton's *Too Late the Phalarope.*" In Richard Welsh, ed., *Literature and the Art of Creation.* Totowa, N.J.: Barnes & Noble, 1988.
Stevens, Ian N. "Paton's Narrator Sophie: Justice and Mercy in *Too Late the Phalarope.*" In *International Fiction Review* 8 (winter 1981).
Thompson, James B. "Poetic Truth in *Too Late the Phalarope.*" In *English Studies in Africa* 24 (March 1981).
Watson, Stephen. "*Cry, the Beloved Country* and the Failure of Liberal Vision." In *English in Africa* 9 (May 1982).
Watts, Neil H. Z. "A Study of Alan Paton's *Too Late the Phalarope.*" In *Durham University Journal* 76 (June 1984).

Okot p'Bitek

1931–1982

J. P. ODOCH PIDO

OKOT p'BITEK was born in 1931 in Gulu, the only town of any size in Acholiland in northern Uganda. His mother, Cerina Lacwaa, was a composer and singer, and his father, Jebedayo Opii, a teacher. His writings are influenced by oral literature, his mother's songs, and the stories his father performed around the evening fire.

Jebedayo Opii and Cerina Lacwaa left their ancestral home at Ladwong and went to the town of Gulu in search of religion and education, which they found through the Christian Missionary Society. Leaving Ladwong was stressful. Jebedayo found and used the expression *bibedo tek* (will be famous) to ease the stress and leap into a new life. *Bitek*, derived from *bibedo tek*, became Jebedayo's nickname. Okot hid his Christian name, Jekeri, and adopted his father's nickname, Bitek. Though he never made public why he hid his Christian name, several explanations are possible. One may be that he disliked Christian religion and another might be that he sought to fulfill his father's wish of becoming famous. Or he may have been following the custom of British gentlemen who identified themselves by their family names: some school-educated Acholi emulated British culture since it was fashionable and the symbol of civilization. Okot's first name is derived from *kot*, which means "rain" in Acholi. Lakot or Akot is the name given to a female child who is born when rain is falling, while the name Okot is given to a male child who is born when rain is falling.

Okot attended Gulu High School and Kings College Budo, and then from 1952 to 1954 the Government Training College, Mbarara, for teacher training. He created a literary reputation at an early age with publication of the novel, *Lak tar* (*White Teeth*) in the Acholi language in 1953. Soon afterward he completed an early version of *Wer pa Lawino* (*Song of Lawino*), which was rejected by publishers presumably because of its explicit treatment of sex. He taught for three years at Sir Samuel Baker's School near Gulu and achieved fame as a soccer player; he was chosen to play for the Ugandan national team. He began studies in England in 1958 and received a certificate in education from Bristol University and a law degree from the University College of Wales, Aberystwyth. In the early 1960s he studied in the Institute of Social Anthropology at Oxford University, where he wrote a thesis titled "Oral Literature and Its Social Background Among the Acholi and Lango"; he received a bachelor of literature degree in 1964.

Back in Gulu, he joined the staff of the Department of Sociology at Makerere University College, then in 1966 became a tutor in the Extra-Mural Department, where he organized a Gulu festival of Acholi culture, at which he sang and danced. He also expanded and translated *Wer pa Lawino* (1969), which had been published as *Song of Lawino* in 1966. In 1966 he was appointed director of Uganda's National Theatre and Cultural Centre, where he developed songs, dances, puppet shows, and theatrical performances to create a national Ugandan culture out of the diverse and vibrant local traditions. In 1967 he was dismissed from his post for his criticism of politicians, and in 1968 he continued his academic career at Nairobi University College, where he was director of the Western Kenya section of the Extra-Mural Department. In the 1970s he published *Song of Ocol* (1970), *Song of a Prisoner* (1971), and *Song of Malaya* (1971). For the latter two volumes he received the 1972 Kenyatta Prize for Literature. Acholi oral literature continued to influence his writings, such as *The Horn of My Love* (1974) and his collection of oral narratives, *Hare and Hornbill* (1978). He died of a liver infection on 20 July 1982.

Many scholars, especially western literary historians and critics, have examined and commented on Okot and his work, often using the input of East African writers, scholars, and laymen. It is important to understand this crucial East African writer from an African point of view. For Africans, it is equally important to learn something of the Acholi perspective on Okot and to delve into the cultural roots of his inspiration and artistic direction. As the Acholi say, "No one live alone," and Okot did not live alone; his biography includes his contemporaries—whom Okot would refer to as his age-mates—family, clan, ethnic group, and regional group.

The author of the East African classics *Song of Lawino*, *Song of Ocol*, *White Teeth*, and other works did not write in isolation. He was a drinker at a well who shared its depths with his own people by capturing the oral culture in writing and with outsiders by broadcasting Acholi culture and history in print. He lived and died in times of uncertainty and change in Uganda and Acholi culture. Okot was the product of changes that he disliked and longed to purify but did not tackle head-on. Rather, he stated his opinions through his characters and commentaries on everyday life.

THE CWAA HERITAGE

An Acholi saying effectively suggests why Okot's background and early years in this culture are so central to an understanding of his life and works. The Acholi say "a man's first wife is his mother" because his first wife teaches him the lessons his father and other men cannot teach. In a culture where a man spends most of his time growing up with other males, he learns very little from women. He often marries before he is ready to be the man, husband, and father his community expects. His first wife becomes the teacher who polishes and prepares him to be the individual that she and the community want. Since she contributes significantly to the making of her husband, she is said to be his mother, one who gently and patiently teaches him the finer details of how to live his life.

Cwaa is a subgroup of the Acholi, and PaCwaa, a subclan of Cwaa, is Okot's native home and people. Okot's cultural background is like his first wife in that it taught him a few lessons his family could not teach him. It provided him with his first impressions of life and was the reservoir of knowledge from which he drew. Okot is a person of Cwaa origin; yet many scholars who examine and write about his work tend to ignore this important biographical fact. Consequently, we all miss one of the cultures that provided Okot with the raw materials for many of his books. *White Teeth*, *Song of Lawino*, *The Horn of My Love*, *Religion of the Central Luo* (1971), *Acholi Proverbs* (1985), and other volumes are as much products of Cwaa culture as of Okot.

There are two theories of how the Cwaa arrived in northern Uganda: they were either part of the Luo migration, or they came from Didinga in Sudan and went to Anuak (Anywak) in southwest Ethiopia before migrating to and settling in Uganda. The latter version is more popular in Mucwini, the largest Cwaa community, which is commonly referred to as *pen* (navel of) Cwaa—the essence of Cwaa country, people, and life. The people of Mucwini trace their migration route from Anuak through Moru Ikokoro (present-day Lukoro Hill in southern Sudan) to Agoro Hill at the Uganda-Sudan border and then to Ladwong Hill in Patiko in the Gulu District of northern Uganda. After losing a major war and fearing for their lives, the majority of the Cwaa people returned to live near their cousin clan Agoro, after whom Agoro Hill is named. Okot's PaCwaa is the group of the Cwaa people who remained behind at Ladwong.

However one explains the presence of the PaCwaa subclan in Patiko, neighboring clans have viewed the PaCwaa people as outsiders rather than full members of the Patiko clan, which is made up of Lukal, Lugaya, and Lugwiyi subclans. As a squatter subclan, PaCwaa has experienced a level of persecution and harassment that forced it to create a closely woven community with one *mwoc*—an utterance that unifies members of the community and works very much like a national anthem. As a member of PaCwaa subclan, Okeca, the main character in *White Teeth*, introduces himself with his *mwoc*,

> I come from Patiko:
> We are lions
> We are an okra dish
> A little dish of okra
> Finishes a big lump of *kwon*.
> (p. 1)

Kwon is Acholi bread made by boiling and kneading millet flour. Patiko is Okeca's place of physical belonging; but his more intimate identity resides in animals and plants, lions and okra, as expressed through his *mwoc*. The PaCwaa people like to identify with the strength and power of a lion, which is disguised in things as simple and ordinary as a dish of okra that may look small but produces big results (symbolized by a big lump of millet bread).

THE CWAA CULTURAL PRACTICE

The PaCwaa people's cultural home is Cwaa, not Patiko, and they display typically Cwaa behaviors. They are fond of *poro tino*, which means to behave like a young person. Imitating youth is one of the means through which adults learn from the junior members of the community, keep pace with their youth, and control the events in their society. It gives elderly people a sense of self-worth by enabling them to feel young and sexually productive; to be barren is the greatest misfortune that can befall an Acholi. In line with the cultural practice of imitating youth, Okot was famous for saying "my wife" to every young woman he met. The phrase "my wife" did not bother the Acholi, who understood and appreciated its role in preparing girls to be wives. However, it greatly offended non-Acholi people who did not understand the cultural connotations and mistook it for a strange display of an oversized sexual appetite. Okot's connection to the youth culture in Acholi is evident in the jocular spirit of *White Teeth*. It also made him aware of the tension experienced by young people as a result of the confrontation between the forces of modernity and traditional Acholi values and customs, a tension captured in *Song of Lawino*.

PaCwaa people enjoy *arony*, torturous and greatly humiliating jokes. The Acholi sometimes employ *arony* as a form of negative commentary or protest against political leaders and their governments. In *Artist the Ruler* (1986), Okot describes the effects of these jokes on leaders and observes that most leaders find the indirect jokes difficult to tolerate. In *Artist the Ruler* it is clear that this sort of joke made Okot flee Uganda in 1968 and take refuge in Kisumu, Kenya. In a conversation with Milton Obote, the president of Uganda and a Lango, Okot made reference to "burning in the grass like the Omiru," an intentionally derogatory remark. Milton Obote could not tolerate this kind of joke. According to oral history on the Aconya period, the Acholi and Langi once went to war against each other. During the war, the Langi hid in the bush and the Acholi set the bush on fire, burning the Langi warriors and giving victory to the Acholi. *Omiru* has its origin in the word *merok*, meaning perpetual hostility or belligerence. *Lamerok* means a perpetual enemy; in essence, *omiru*, *lango*, and *merok* all refer to traditional enemies. While in Kisumu, Okot found solace in *omin*, the way the Luo of Kenya show a sense of brotherhood with Lwo-speaking Ugandans. Kisumu not only provided a safe place for Okot, it also gave him the emotional comfort and peace of mind he required to write *Song of Ocol*, *Song of a Prisoner*, and more.

PaCwaa are known for *tek wic*, which means being shameless or overly bold, and Okot was no exception. Those who were close to him know that he was quick to grab the buttocks or touch the breasts of women in public. Although this aggressive behavior embarrassed and angered many, especially the educated women in Nairobi, Okot saw it as a culturally acceptable way to tease respectable women. His students at University College in Nairobi knew that he was shameless in performing sexual gestures in the lecture halls. Most of his students were so astonished and embarrassed that they missed the messages intended in his acts. Cwaa elders are known for disguising the more serious aspects of their lessons in humorous or shameful jokes. In this case Okot was actually telling his students that they were young and in order to grow up they needed to remove prejudices, control wasteful preoccupations, listen carefully, and learn the lessons of life from elders.

In their migration to their present home in Acholiland, northern Uganda, the Cwaa people passed through the land of hostile people and could not have survived the journey without evasive techniques. Cwaa are well known for never informing outsiders of what they are about to do, especially regarding travel and raid plans. When they are obliged to give information, they preserve secrecy by telling lies. Thus, people of Cwaa origin are said to like "speaking the back of words," that is, saying the opposite of what is meant. Apart from hiding information, Cwaa like speaking tangentially, and this is seen in their poems, songs, and other artistic forms of expression. Subtlety is a way of avoiding political punishment and indirectly, cautiously, and wisely approaching any hazardous or valuable goal in life. As any member of his community would have done, Okot often stated his opinions on issues obliquely. In this respect he used characters—such as Okeca in *White Teeth*, Lawino in *Song of Lawino*, Prisoner in *Song of a Prisoner*, and Adok Too in *Artist the Ruler*—to say the things he himself wanted to say.

The Personal *Mwoc*

Among the Cwaa people, the most discreet yet public commentary on everyday life is a personal *mwoc*, a short poem used as a nickname that individuals give themselves. This becomes their personal identification, independent of the community *mwoc*. Individuals often use *mwoc* to enforce approved behaviors or to punish and correct those who make mistakes. Okeca's *mwoc*, Atuk, draws attention to one event he witnessed and found odd because it broke the rules of good conduct:

> You disturbed *ten*
> In your mother-in-law's hut.
> . . .
> Your eyelids are dark
> Because you do not want to share
> The carcass of the cow
> That had died of dysentery.
> (*White Teeth*, p. 1)

As this example suggests, it is unthinkable for anyone to disturb *ten*, or a column of pots, in his mother-in-law's hut. A Cwaa mother-in-law is respected and feared like a god; her house is the last place to make a mess. It is also embarrassing to eat alone, especially when the food is of as little value as the carcass of a cow that has died of dysentery. As Okeca tries to do, through his nickname, Okot, through his writing, undertook to correct wrongdoers and preserve Acholi cultural values.

Sometimes *mwoc* is an insight into an aspect of life stated philosophically, a realization of a truth that comes after a long period of experience, observation, and questioning. Okeca's father's *mwoc*—*Lak tar miyo ki nyero ii lobo* ("It is white teeth / That make us laugh in this world," *White Teeth*, p. 1) becomes a philosophical statement on life. Okot used the spirit in Okeca's father's *mwoc* to gain insight into everyday life and to guide the writing of his first novel, *White Teeth*, published in the Acholi language in 1952 and in English in 1989. The intellectually stimulating quality of such a *mwoc* is evident in the many equally correct but also contradicting answers to the question of why we laugh. Okeca said he laughs because

> the whiteness of my teeth, not happiness, not pleasures, not the softness of my inside, my white teeth force me to laugh, for fear that girls might think my teeth are rotten and rusty like those of the bull edible rat.... I am not cheerful, not odd, not funny, nor am I special. It is the white of my teeth that makes me laugh.
>
> (*White Teeth*, p. 2)

By using his Ladwong roots, Okot intended to invoke the wisdom of his ancestors and through this to elevate himself to the position of a great scholar, teacher, and philosopher. After all, *ladwong* literally means a wise old man, and Okot's adoption of his father's nickname, Bitek, was an outward signal of his respect for his father. The patriarchal inheritance, male chauvinism, and the wish to be an elder and philosopher all played a part in Okot's literary efforts.

Much has been said on how Okot, through his work and behavior, revealed many Cwaa cultural attitudes. The Cwaa, on the other hand, might say Okot spoke "as if his mouth were struck by the scrotum of a billy goat," meaning that he talked without holding anything back; he made public what should have remained secret. He also qualified as *latunege ki remo* (one with a bloody horn), meaning one who draws people into a fistfight because he reminded the world of its unpleasant past. Okot was *latung twe* (one who darts about) because he missed nothing, spoke about what he saw, was famous, and appeared to be in many places and heading in many directions. Considering how he treats Ocol, the husband of Lawino in *Song of Lawino* and *Song of Ocol*, and Taban lo Liyong, the controversial Ugandan writer, in the preface to *The Horn of My Love*, the Cwaa might also say that Okot was *lebe kec* (tongue was bitter), that he liked to say nasty things.

ROLES OF HISTORY AND EDUCATION IN OKOT'S LIFE

Many of Okot's admirers feel that history favored him. His native home was within reach of the Christian mission and school, so he received a formal education. Therefore, he was prepared when African countries were gaining political independence from colonial Europe but were uncertain about the nature of African identity. He wrote and published when the demand for knowledge about Africa was on the rise. Most of all Okot was blessed with the ability to see, remember, and reconstruct the events of the times.

Okot witnessed children being taught to use *itwanyo*, carbolic soap, the beginning of western-style hygiene in his native home, Ladwong; in *White Teeth*, Okeca's uncle, Sergeant Otto Bwangamoi, is a soldier who teaches children to wash and smear their bodies with carbolic soap. Sergeant Otto's captivating war stories entice many young men to join the military and eventually become agents of social and cultural change in Acholiland. The second chapter of *White Teeth* dramatizes the influence of the military on courtship. Scholars see Okot's vivid descriptions of Acholi courtship as influenced by the military and by those who have worked in urban centers as a commentary on social changes.

Okot also witnessed the transformation of the Acholi belief system at close range, since his home was near the Christian Missionary Society premises in Gulu. He was at hand when the clergy and church elders were struggling to translate the Bible from English to Acholi. In translating the Bible, the church had to consider the Acholi concepts of religion, God, life after death, and so on. Some of these issues became centerpieces of Okot's *African Religions in Western Scholarship* (1970) and *Religion of the Central Luo* (1971).

To speak the Acholi language in the school compound was a punishable offense in the 1950s, when Okot was in school. Every pupil in grades four to six was required to speak English in school. Students who did not speak English had to carry a bell; the last pupil to carry the bell on Friday received four strokes of the cane the following Monday. Yet many of the students found English difficult to learn. To speak like native speakers was the goal all tried to achieve but none fully realized; even such rigorous methods as force, insult, and shame failed to make Acholi children speak English as desired by the school authorities. After many years of suffering and surviving at school, the children spoke what was termed Acholi-English, which derived from translating Acholi into English. Okot was a part of this experience and derived his style of writing from Acholi-English, which sometimes makes his work opaque to non-Acholi speakers.

As a schoolteacher, Okot himself employed unconventional methods. While he and Taban lo Liyong were teachers in Gulu High School, a junior secondary school, they spearheaded a campaign to harass *abaja* (freshmen or newcomers). The two instituted bullying because they said it was necessary to toughen the boys and make them men, but did not teach the men what to do with their toughness. Such intimidation hurt and traumatized many children; it forced some out of school and made others think that brute force would take them far in life. Okot and lo Liyong likened bullying in the school to similar practices in the grazing ground, which they knew of in theory but not in practice. Although bullying is common to the grazing ground, in that context it teaches endurance as a means to survive such disasters as drought, famine, epidemic, and raids rather than toughness for its own sake. Bullying in the grazing ground was done to ensure food for one's goats and to gain territory, not to enjoy the suffering of the young and helpless.

WHITE TEETH

White Teeth is the story of Okeca, an Acholi boy who is very young when his father dies. His father leaves behind thirty-five Karamoja goats and a daughter, Aciro, who is expected to fetch a bride-price when she marries. However, upon the father's death, Acholi tradition requires that Okeca, his sister, and his mother be taken care of by Okeca's father's brother, who resents the financial obligation this duty entails. So, years later, when Okeca requires cash for a bride-wealth to marry Cecilia Laliya, his uncle refuses, aware of Okeca's ability to use the bride-wealth that the family will receive when Aciro marries. But Aciro is only seven years old; furthermore, she is a sickly child. If she is asked to marry at all, she does not promise to bring in a large sum of money, or she may die before marrying. So Okeca goes to Kampala to try to earn a living and save some of his monthly wages to raise a bride-wealth to marry Cecilia Laliya. After working on a sugar plantation in Kakira,

Okeca is pick-pocketed on his way home to Gulu and loses all his savings. Okeca returns home on foot and penniless.

The difficulties of one poor Acholi youth in *White Teeth* reflect the Acholi culture during the 1950s. It is a story of cultural change hidden in complex native idioms and expressions. The novel paints the Acholi as naive villagers who were driven to urban centers in search of riches and found themselves chasing mirages. Instead of finding fortunes, the Acholi found themselves embracing western culture. Okot observed that the villagers struggled in ignorance to adapt to western culture, an effort that would adversely and unnecessarily change Acholi culture. Okot chose Okeca to represent his feelings and indirectly speak out about the ignorance of the Acholi and the cultural changes he considered unfortunate.

Okeca is the short form of *kom-an-kec* (my body is bitter)—that is, I am unlucky. Acholi who are confronted with a misfortune say "*koma kec.*" When parents have only one male child they often name him Komakec because they fear that death will take away their only son and end the family line. The name is in a sense the parents' plea with death to spare their only son and keep alive their hope of familial continuity that can only be provided by a son. Given the cultural significance of the name, it is possible that Okeca's place at the center of *White Teeth* was an appeal to the Acholi audience.

Okot himself qualified to be named Okeca as an only son and then an only child after the death of his sister in childhood. Okot's view of himself as an only child in *White Teeth* seems to be reflected in Okeca's loneliness in Kampala, where he is surrounded by thousands of the non-Acholi. Okot's experiences of life after his sister died could be likened to Okeca's experiences in the city; he is confined by the horizon of tall buildings, oppressed by the landscape of concrete walls, daunted by the exaggerated scale of the wide streets, and forced to perform difficult tasks with high penalties for errors. Moreover, Okeca's relatives behave as if they were not related to him at all.

In Okeca's story, Okot examines why Acholi youth leave their homes for the urban wilderness, and he warns of the hopelessness and frustration of urban migration. Okot's messages are camouflaged by the emphasis placed on producing children in Acholi culture. Familial continuity is the ultimate goal in the mind of every Acholi; marriage promises continuity, and bride-wealth is the legal means by which an Acholi may marry. Any relative who ignores an appeal for bride-wealth is seen as one who refuses to provide for the continuity of the family line. If relatives cannot provide bride-wealth for a young man, he is then free to do what he can to provide for himself. Many young men in the 1950s used to say "to marry without a sister [who is a source of bride-wealth] needs joining the army or going to Kampala"; the saying became the theme of songs (*White Teeth*, p. 21). Although these songs were ostensibly laments for the lack of bride-wealth, they were, in fact, either appeals to elders for bride-wealth or a means of accusing and embarrassing those who failed to provide their sons with the wealth to marry.

Young men like Okeca knew their relatives would permit them to do anything, including going to work in urban areas, if they did so in the name of marriage. Young men found a lack of bride-wealth to be the most effective excuse for leaving home. The absence of opportunities for upward mobility, the oppressive Acholi culture, and the desire to experience city life may have been the real reason many young men left their villages for urban centers.

Some of the rural Acholi young men perceived urban migration as a traditional hunting expedition. Acholi hunters, in the 1950s and before, frequently went on solo hunting expeditions, some of which took as long as a month. The hunter's absence did not worry his family because an expedition that lasted up to one month meant the hunter had struck something as valuable as an elephant, providing plenty of smoked meat and tusks which could be bartered for such valuable goods as guns. The song *Ladwar orii itim, pud yango* (The hunter has taken long in the bush, he is still skinning) is a testimony to the peace of mind the hunter's family enjoyed. Young men like Okeca mistook one year of a jobless or wage-earning life in an urban center for a great achievement because their absence was much longer than any traditional hunting expedition, even though one year of urban occupation proved far less profitable than a one-week hunting expedition.

In *White Teeth,* Okot also related how the Acholi people reacted to their initiation into a cash economy during the 1950s. Many Acholi saw urban life as an opportunity to earn cash, which had become known by various names (*rubia, agwiling, peca, otongolo*). However, it seems some of the people who went to urban centers to look for jobs and earn wages did not have a clear understanding of a cash economy. People imagined they would earn money but not spend it and become rich. As happened to Okeca, some people worked for a long time but returned to their rural homes without any savings. The trend of working in urban centers and returning home without much financial benefit has continued since the 1950s.

SONG OF LAWINO AND *SONG OF OCOL*

Song of Lawino is frequently seen as the publication that brought Okot to literary fame because it openly stood for Africanness at a time when the forces of progress, development, and new religions scared most people away from asserting their African identities. Lawino, the main character in the poem, not only makes social and cultural comments but also speaks for the voiceless majority who helplessly stand between modern and traditional cultures. (However, some critics argue that Lawino failed the silent majority; they believe that only Okot and *Song of Lawino* became famous while westerners learn little about the Acholi population and culture that inspired the poem. This argument suggests that individualized creativity and achievement, which characterize artistic endeavor in the west, also motivated Okot to write *Song of Lawino.*)

Lawino's reaction to Clementina, her husband's westernized lover, creates the impression that Lawino is a newly married woman, for a woman seasoned in marriage would not be bothered by the likes of Clementina. Perhaps Lawino is quarreling more than singing; young women quarrel with their rivals as a means of protecting their territory. Acholi culture is full of songs that are often accompanied by instruments or dances, for different purposes and occasions. Women compose and use songs to address situations they cannot fight physically, to enliven work they find tedious, to praise themselves and give themselves a sense of self-worth in a society that assigns them a peripheral role. Some women sing in praise of their husbands and other members of the society, to show love and a sense of glory. A young woman sings to remember the vibrant days when she danced to hit tunes of *larakaraka* (the teenage "get-stuck" dance) and to try to recapture vividly the mood that enticed her to dance provocatively before her lover. To Okot the Acholi songs were entertaining and educating, and as records of history they fit his intellectual interest in anthropology.

Song of Lawino is entertaining and teaches a sense of self-worth that resists the effects of western cultural domination. However, many Acholi would find it less a song than a *ceko lok* (boiling words), a colorful dramatization of everyday events and a style of popular expression. Furthermore, songs that are as public as *Song of Lawino* form part of dances, yet even an experienced Acholi dancer would find it difficult to dance to *Song of Lawino*. The Acholi dancer would think that *Song of Lawino* was also inspired by non-Acholi influences, especially Okot's contact with songs written and published in the United States during the 1950s.

In the dedication to *Song of Ocol*, Okot says that his mother taught him songs and was the chief inspiration behind *Song of Lawino*. The inspiration, one which George Heron in *The Poetry of Okot p'Bitek* supports, reflects the roles Cwaa women have played in the history of their people. The women of this region performed tasks traditionally assigned to men, and there are many examples of their unconventional deeds. First, they successfully defended their home at the foot of Ladwong Hill against an attack that claimed the lives of their strongest men. The successful defense of Ladwong Hill paved the way for the Cwaa people's return to Agoro. (The journey to Agoro never materialized, however; the European colonialists found the Cwaa while they were in transit, thought they were merely roaming, and so fixed them in their present home in Kitgum District.) Second, according to oral history, at one time the people of Padibe killed almost all Cwaa men in a clan raid. Cwaa women took time, courage, and wisdom to construct life out of the wreckage of war and groomed their sons into warriors to avenge the death of their husbands. Arising from the second achievement, women became the chief architects of the sayings "Cwaa people speak with grass in their mouth" (that is, they hide their true intentions) and "forever the chase between Padibe and Cwaa" (a never-ending process). These two historical incidents and the place of women in Acholi life, especially in music, reinforce Okot's claim that his mother's music inspired *Song of Lawino*.

While many Acholi songs are composed by women, men also compose and use songs to whip up the courage required to perform extraordinary tasks, express emotions or opinions, and inform and educate members of the community. Some of the men's songs are answers to demands made by women; *Song of Ocol* is a typical male song because it is a response to the accusations in *Song of Lawino*. The expression *nyuka ka oton ii cip pe nange* (it is impossible to lick porridge from a fibrous skirt)—that is, some events are impossible to reverse—aptly summarizes the text in *Song of Ocol*. The Acholi use the expression when it is expedient to accept an unexpected and unpleasant end. *Song of Ocol* is Okot's way of agreeing with Lawino and her resistance to westernization, while also accepting the social and cultural changes taking place in Africa.

In *Song of Ocol*, Lawino meets her match. She is silenced because her song is viewed as "the confused noise made by the ram after the butcher's knife has sunk past the wind pipe" (*Song of Ocol*, p. 10). Some scholars agree with *Song of Ocol*'s answer to *Song of Lawino*, primarily because Lawino is seen as a menace who insisted on telling her husband the truth, a truth that he hated but was unable to avoid. She put her husband on the spot and defeated him. Lawino also upset those who thought leaving African traditions for a western way of life was fashionable and progressive. They thought they had come a long way and were upset when Lawino kept telling them that they were misguided.

On the other hand there were those who cheered and encouraged Lawino because she spoke for those who were intimidated into silence. Advocates of Africanness and blackness may be upset to find Ocol challenging their hero, Lawino. *Song of Ocol* is an answer to *Song of Lawino* and a continuation of the debate between traditional African culture and a western way of life.

Okot himself did not live a traditional Acholi life; for example, around 1977, he drove a British-made Jaguar car and lived in Hurlingham, a posh Nairobi neighborhood. Okot was a member of the academic community and regularly met with his colleagues in the Senior Common Room of the Nairobi

University College, where he challenged senior professors to academic duels by calling them headless, bush poets, and *jarwas* (savage tribalist). Okot, despite his own somewhat western lifestyle, provoked intellectual debates on *ocol* (blacks). The word *ocol* is derived from *col* (black, the color) or *acol* (I am black) and was, at one time, a name children gave to their age-mates who were uniquely and beautifully black. In the postcolonial era, *ocol* came to refer to the Acholi who pretentiously imitated Europeans. It was intended to raise the level of "black" consciousness among the Acholi. It is probable that the works of other writers on "being black" inspired Okot in the writing of *Song of Lawino* and *Song of Ocol.*

The debate over the role of formal education is another factor that may have influenced *Song of Ocol.* In general, Okot's generation saw education as a gateway to the benefits of independence and felt they were entitled to wealth and power. The promise of attaining a better life, that is, a western lifestyle, through education seemed feasible and was so attractive that students overlooked the bumps in the road leading to the fruits of independence. There was no method for distributing the spoils of independence, which resulted in general dissatisfaction. Many educated people, including Okot, questioned and continue to question the point of expensive formal education that does not lead to a better life. In the absence of adequate answers, they declare—as Okot does in *Song of Ocol*—that formal education is useless and should be forgotten.

While Okot doubted the usefulness of formal education, he was a meticulous researcher. He traveled to many parts of Kenya to learn more about Kenyans, including the Kalenjin, whom the Kavirondo Luo refer to as *JoLango* (a perpetual enemy). Intending to remind the Luo never to forget their traditional enemy, Okot implies in *Song of Ocol* that the Luo were cowards who ran a thousand miles—until Lake Victoria stopped them—to escape Kalenjin warriors.

SONG OF A PRISONER AND *SONG OF MALAYA*

When Uganda became independent in 1962, the country was short on the educated population required to run the civil service and economy of the country; Okot found a teaching job at Sir Samuel Baker's School near Gulu. He enjoyed his job; teachers had influence, respect, and hope for advancement to positions of national leadership. Yet Ugandan politics forced him to flee the country. His exit was a disappointment, but Okot was ready; engagement in cultural activities gave him the much-needed experience, information, and inspiration to research and write on culture and change that he had played a part in shaping.

Around 1962, in the midst of the struggle for independence, Okot joined Uganda People's Congress (U.P.C.), which enabled him to see inside party politics and set him on a course to write about political issues. While it is not certain why Okot joined the U.P.C. rather than the Democratic Party (D.P.), the only other rival party at that time, it is likely that he joined the U.P.C. because of his religious affiliation. He grew up a Protestant, and the U.P.C. was considered the Protestant party while the D.P. was primarily Catholic. Okot attended Protestant school; religious rivalry with the Catholic school was tense enough to cause fistfights during or after soccer matches, and students sang derogatory songs about religious differences. However, Okot, as a member of the U.P.C., was not happy with some of the party practices and began writing about his concerns.

One political practice he disliked was that while the senior members of the U.P.C. enjoyed the fruits of "Uhuru," political freedom from Britain, Okot and many other Ugandans *ogik ki ngwece* (stopped at its smell), meaning they did not fully benefit from such freedom. Okot told Milton Obote that inequality and class stratification had begun and needed to be checked as it was likely to destroy the very essence of independence—national unity, peace, progress, and freedom. But Obote did not believe there was any threat to Uhuru and thought Okot was a nuisance and forced him out of Uganda. Okot began his life of exile in Kisumu, Kenya, where he felt excluded from his Acholi community. *Song of a Prisoner*, which Okot wrote while he was in exile, may have been influenced by his feeling of abandonment, and it depicts what he saw as Africa's struggle with the evils of Uhuru—confusion, unpleasant experiences, doubt, and regret.

Okot was not alone in questioning the meaning of Uhuru; Ajuma Oginga Odinga felt there was independence without Uhuru while Phares Mukasa Mutibwa suggested that independence has yielded unfulfilled hopes. Education gave students the hope that they would become leaders and wealthy if they worked hard and did well in the classroom. However, the vast majority of those who excelled in the classroom did not become leaders or rich. Consequently, educated people have tended to blame independence for failing to fulfill their hopes. *Song of a Prisoner* joined a chorus of voices that said national leaders had used Uhuru for personal gain. While government leaders benefited from Uhuru the poor were beaten, jailed, and even killed without cause.

Song of a Prisoner is generally understood to be Okot's examination of the unfulfilled expectations of Uhuru, but it may also reflect his community's struggle to understand the meaning of independence. Tiberio Okeny, Elisa Latim, Peter Oola, Peter Abe, Eginio Obonyo, and other prominent Acholi political leaders of the 1950s failed to communicate the essence of independence to their people. These leaders interpreted independence as political freedom, but in practice Uganda, as a British protectorate, heard of but did not directly experience colonial oppression. Individual freedom could not make much sense to Acholi people since they live with and for each other. As a community the Acholi always felt independent from outsiders and did not like outsiders to depend on them. Independence, with the resulting dependency on other nations for financial, technological, and food assistance, was difficult to understand. Centralized government was also unfamiliar because the Acholi governed through elders. Elders agreed by consensus what their community did, how their people behaved, and who enforced the law. The Acholi struggle to understand Uhuru may have provided the initial frame around which Okot constructed *Song of a Prisoner*.

Song of a Prisoner and *Song of Malaya* are often published together because they are considered too small as separate works, yet they are not necessarily a logical pairing in terms of subject matter. *Song of Malaya* could more readily be seen as a companion to *White Teeth* if Okeca's story was viewed as the beginning of urban migration. This migration intensified in the 1960s when the desire for formal education and white-collar jobs increased. While Okeca went to town to save up money to marry the girl he loved, most Acholi young men in the 1960s went to town in search of education and white-collar jobs. And, unlike Okeca, who returned to his rural home after he felt he had achieved his goal, most of these young men became acclimated to urban life and came to view the city as their home. *Song of Malaya* is primarily the story of urban dwellers.

In addition to employment and education, other engagements found space in many of the young men's hearts and initiated them into urban life. They came to the city expecting alcohol, music, dancing, vehicles, paved streets, tall buildings, and consumer goods as well as prostitution and casual sex. Prostitution and casual sex were exotic compared to the traditional Acholi view of sex as a serious business to ensure the continuity of the family. Traditionally sex also symbolized a lifelong commitment to the body and soul of one's partner rather than *kwany ikati* (pay, take, and leave), the estranged spirit of commerce. Okot may have found *malaya* (prostitution) intriguing, especially its power to transcend sexual taboos and draw two strangers into a quick partnership. Like many of his Acholi contemporaries, Okot may have feared the consequences of *malaya* on the established Acholi sexual practice.

Intoxicated by the exotic possibility of *malaya* and free from the conservative traditional culture, Acholi young men with little sexual experience came to town and bought and consumed sex. For many this was their first sexual encounter with a non-Acholi woman. The experience of prostitution, combined with the crossing of ethnic boundaries, was enticing. If the sex partner was Baganda (the majority community in Uganda)—as Okot describes in *Song of Malaya*—the experience was puzzling because Baganda women scream during sex as a way of cheering on their male partners, unlike Acholi women, who enjoy sex in silence. Okot not only writes about colorful moments of *malaya* but also articulates its damaging consequences such as teenage pregnancy, unfaithful marriages, the spread of sexually transmitted diseases, and the decay of sexual morals.

ACHOLI PROVERBS

Apart from songs and dances, Acholiland is full of proverbs, many of which appear in Okot's *Acholi Proverbs* (1985), published posthumously. As Lubwa p'Chong suggests, Acholi proverbs are statements of wisdom that unmistakably express the likes and dislikes of Acholi people. Although the origin of some of the proverbs and the fine points of interpretation vary from one part of Acholiland to another, Okot had started to record Acholi wisdom as it appears in proverbs. Of course, Okot used Acholi proverbs to enliven his expressions discreetly in many of his works.

Reading some of Okot's works is like listening to folktales. In the Acholi community, every child, teenager, and adult tells and listens to folktales in the evenings, around the fire; folktales are a major form of entertainment and a way to teach children how to live when they grow up: what to believe, how to behave, and what to wear. Folktales also train young people to use words accurately and vividly. Okot's cultural background helped make him an accomplished oral artist who communicated messages and meanings with a great sense of humor, accuracy, and color. To this background in oral communication he added the techniques of perspective and image making that he learned in school and painted his experience of a world at a crossroads between two cultures. In this painting of his world, Okot put Acholi culture in the foreground, while the rest of the world, though still visible, receded to the background.

CONCLUSION

Okot's works have been translated from Acholi to English and from English to other languages. His *Song of Lawino* has become a classic of East African literature. For those few Acholi who were literate in the 1950s, *White Teeth* was a welcome change from the Bible and literature written for English speakers. *White Teeth* is a history of the Acholi in the 1950s and a reasonably accurate vision of what was to happen to urban Acholi from the 1960s to the 1990s. Like Okeca, many Acholi left their rural homes and traveled to urban centers in order to become wealthy but returned to their homes poor.

In *Song of Lawino* and *Song of Ocol*, Okot spoke out on the cultural changes taking place in Acholiland and beyond. But changes continued to occur. Starting in the 1960s, Acholi women attended school, used cosmetics, wore high heels and tights, and engaged in casual sex. In the 1990s, those who were westernized like Clementina drove cars; spoke Swahili, English, Italian, Russian, Chinese, and Arabic; wore combat uniforms and led an army of soldiers as Alice Abongowat, popularly known as Lakwena, did in the 1980s. Men like Ocol in the 1990s are no longer sons of chiefs; they expect their parents to buy them clothes, build them houses, and find bride-wealth for their prospective wives. Like Ocol, these young men speak many foreign languages; but unlike Ocol, they are uncertain of their African identity. They straighten their hair, buy finger rings instead of accepting them from their girlfriends, and shake hands with their mothers-in-law in public.

Some aspects of Acholi culture described in *White Teeth* and *Song of Lawino* remained distinctively Acholi but also underwent change. For instance, *larakaraka*, the "get-stuck" teenage dance continued with the drums and drumming essentially unaltered. But the songs and performers are new, and the threat of sexually transmitted diseases has relocated the spiritual center of the dance since "getting stuck" (freely enjoying making love) has become potentially deadly. A new dance, *dingidingi*, emerged after *White Teeth* was published in 1952. It is a dance that the teenagers of Palabek in northwestern Acholiland derived from one of the Baganda dances. Although *dingidingi* started in the small corner of Acholiland, by the mid 1960s it was popular throughout the land. *Dingidingi* is seldom mentioned in Okot's works, yet the dance was the centerpiece of Ugandan political rallies and was the nerve of the Heart Beat of Africa, a dance troupe Okot (himself a gifted performance artist) directed and took on a tour of Europe and other parts of the world. Western-style dance, which Lawino considers foreign, absorbed *lukemu* (a kind of hand piano) and *adungu* (harp) and was greatly influenced by the beat of Zairian music.

The Horn of My Love is a beautiful collection of Acholi songs that offers a glimpse of Acholi thoughts and philosophy of everyday life, which need further analysis if they are to be understood by non-Acholi speakers. It is unfortunate that Okot did not like analysis; in *The Horn of My Love* he says that "missionaries, anthropologists, musicologists and folklorists . . . have plucked songs, stories, proverbs, riddles etc. from their social backgrounds and, after killing them by analysis, have buried them in inaccessible and learned journals and in expensive technical books" (p. ix). This lack of analysis puts Okot's collection out of the reach of those who have not experienced the conditions that gave birth to the songs. Okot's treatment of abstract aspects of the Acholi culture points to the need to analyze this collection of songs since they are likely to form important historical and anthropological records.

The Cwaa are known for behavior that can be construed as arrogant, obstinate, and shameless; Okot exhibited many of these Cwaa traits. Yet as a Cwaa junior elder, he was also knowledgeable, a philosopher, artist, and orator.

Selected Bibliography

BIBLIOGRAPHIES

Lindfors, Bernth. "A Checklist of Works by and About Okot p'Bitek." In *World Literature Written in English* 16 (1977).

Ofuani, Ojo A. "Okot p'Bitek: A Checklist of Works and Criticism." In *Research in African Literatures* 16 (fall 1985).

SELECTED WORKS

Lak Tar. Nairobi, Kenya: East African Literature Bureau, 1953.

"Oral Literature and Its Social Background Among the Acholi and Lang'o." Bachelor of literature thesis, University of Oxford, 1964.

Wer pa Lawino. Nairobi, Kenya: East African Publishing House, 1969.

African Religions in Western Scholarship. Kampala, Uganda: East African Literature Bureau, 1970; Totowa, N.J.: Rowman and Littlefield, 1972.

Song of Ocol. Nairobi, Kenya: East African Publishing House, 1970.

Religion of the Central Luo. Nairobi, Kenya: East African Literature Bureau, 1971; Kampala, Uganda: Uganda Literature Bureau, 1980.

Song of a Prisoner. New York: Third Press, 1971.

Two Songs: Song of a Prisoner, Song of Malaya. Nairobi, Kenya: East African Publishing House, 1971; Nairobi, Kenya: Heinemann, 1988.

Africa's Cultural Revolution. With an intro. by Ngũgĩ wa Thiong'o. Nairobi, Kenya: Macmillan Books for Africa, 1973.

The Horn of My Love. London: Heinemann, 1974; New York: Humanities Press, 1974.

Hare and Hornbill. London: Heinemann, 1978.

Acholi Proverbs. Nairobi, Kenya: Heinemann, 1985.

Artist the Ruler: Essays on Art, Culture, and Values. Nairobi, Kenya: Heinemann, 1986.

ARTICLES

"Culture and the Community." In *African Adult Education* (Lusaka) 1, no. 2 (1968).

"The Poet in Politics." In *Black Orpheus* 2, no. 3 (1968).

"What Is Literature?" In *Busara* (Nairobi) 4, no. 1 (1972).

"The Crisis in the Teaching of Literature in East African Universities." In Andrew Gurr and Angus Calder, eds., *Writers in East Africa.* Nairobi, Kenya: East African Literature Bureau, 1974.

"African Culture in the Era of Foreign Rule." In *Thought and Practice* (Nairobi) 2, no. 1 (1975).

"The Future of Vernacular Literature." In Arne Zettersten, ed., *East African Literature: An Anthology.* New York: Longman, 1983.

TRANSLATIONS

Song of Lawino: An African Lament. Nairobi, Kenya: East African Publishing House, 1966; New York: Meridian Books, 1969.

White Teeth. Nairobi, Kenya: Heinemann, 1989.

INTERVIEWS

Lahui, J. "Okot p'Bitek . . . to Sing *Song of Lawino.*" In *Papua New Guinea Writing* 23 (1976).

Lindfors, Bernth. "An Interview with Okot p'Bitek." In *World Literature Written in English* 16 (1977).

Petersen, Kirsten Holst. "Okot p'Bitek: Interview." In *Kunapipi* 1, no. 1 (1979).

Zettersten, Arne. "Okot p'Bitek and the East African Literary Situation." In *Commonwealth Newsletter* (Århus, Denmark) 10 (1976).

CRITICAL STUDIES

Asein, Samuel Omo. "Okot p'Bitek, Literature, and the Cultural Revolution in East Africa." In *World Literature Written in English* 16 (1977).

Gathungu, Maina. "Okot p'Bitek: Writer, Singer, or Culturizer?" In Chris L. Wanjala, ed., *Standpoints on African Literature: A Critical Anthology.* Nairobi, Kenya: East African Literature Bureau, 1973.

Heron, George. *Notes on Okot p'Bitek's* Song of Lawino *and* Song of Ocol. Nairobi, Kenya: Heinemann, 1975.

———. *The Poetry of Okot p'Bitek.* London: Heinemann, 1976.

———. "Okot p'Bitek and the Elite in African Writing." In *Literary Half-Yearly* 19, no. 1 (1978).

Heywood, Annemarie. "Modes of Freedom: The Songs of Okot p'Bitek." In *Journal of Commonwealth Literature* 15, no. 1 (1980).

Igwe, Bernard Ezuma. "Form and Value in the Poetry of Okot p'Bitek." Master's thesis, University of British Columbia, 1975.

Jonaid-Sharif, Lutfurahman. "Okot p'Bitek's *Song of Lawino*: The Dynamics of a Voice." In *Griot* 3 (winter 1984).

Lindfors, Bernth. "The Songs of Okot p'Bitek." In G. D. Killam, ed., *The Writing of East and Central Africa.* London: Heinemann, 1984.

Mutibwa, Phares Mukasa. Foreword in Alex Mukula, *Thirty Years of Bananas.* Kampala, Uganda, and Nairobi, Kenya: Oxford University Press, 1993.

Nwachukwu-Agbada, J. O. J. "Okot p'Bitek and the Story of a Paradox." In *Commonwealth Essays and Studies* 12 (fall 1989).

Odinga, Ajuma Oginga. *Not Yet Uhuru: The Autobiography of Oginga Odinga.* London: Heinemann, 1967; New York: Hill and Wang, 1967.

Ofuani, Ogo A. "The Traditional and Modern Influence in Okot p'Bitek's Poetry." In *African Studies Review* 28 (December 1985).

———. "Digression as Discourse Strategy in Okot p'Bitek's Dramatic Monologue Texts." In *Research in African Literatures* 19 (fall 1988).

Ogunyemi, Chikwenye Okonjo. "The Song of the Caged Bird: Contemporary African Prison Poetry." In *ARIEL* 13 (October 1982).

Ojaide, Tanure. "Poetic Viewpoint: Okot p'Bitek and His Personae." In *Callaloo* 9 (spring 1986).

Ojwang, Humphrey. *Okot p'Bitek on Trial.* Nairobi, Kenya: Lifelong Educational Materials, 1993.

Okoh, Nkem. "Writing African Oral Literature: A Reading of Okot p'Bitek's *Song of Lawino.*" In *Bridges* (Dakar, Senegal) 5, no. 2 (1993).

Okumu, Charles. "The Form of Okot p'Bitek's Poetry: Literary Borrowing from Acoli Oral Traditions." In *Research in African Literatures* 23 (fall 1992).

Wanambisi, Monica Nalyaka. *Thought and Technique in the Poetry of Okot p'Bitek.* New York: Vantage, 1984.

Ward, Michael R. "Okot p'Bitek and the Rise of East African Writing." In Bruce King, Kolawole Ogungbesan, and Iya Abubakar, eds., *A Celebration of Black and African Writing.* Oxford, U.K.: Oxford University Press, 1975.

Weinstein, Mark. "The Song of Solomon and *Song of Lawino.*" In *World Literature Written in English* 26 (fall 1986).

Pepetela

1941–

CLIVE WILLIS

ARTUR CARLOS Maurício Pestana Dos Santos was born on 29 October 1941 in the Angolan coastal city of Benguela of white Portuguese colonial parents. He studied in Lisbon and Paris and finally graduated in sociology in Algiers in 1966. The name Pepetela (the Umbundu word for "eyelash") is a translation of his Portuguese surname, Pestana, and was adopted by him as a literal nom de guerre while fighting in a Marxist guerrilla group, the Movimento Popular para a Libertação de Angola (Popular Movement for the Liberation of Angola, or MPLA), for the colony's independence from Portugal. Angola became independent in 1975.

There is a factor that unifies the writers of fiction—the Brazilians José Lins do Rego, Graciliano Ramos, João Guimarães Rosa, and Jorge Amado; the Americans John Steinbeck, John Dos Passos, and Ernest Hemingway; and the Frenchman Roger Vailland—who Pepetela claims were the strongest influences on him in the 1950s and 1960s. They share an interest in social and economic forces that would appeal to a young man drawn to the politics of Marx and Lenin.

Pepetela's first short stories appeared in the 1960s in magazines and anthologies in Portugal, Brazil, Angola, and Belgium. His real literary career, however, did not begin until 1976, with the first edition of *As aventuras de Ngunga* (*Ngunga's Adventures: A Story of Angola*). His works had major appeal on three counts: their scrutiny of Marxism; their tendency toward mythopoeia, or the creation of myths; and their focus on the concept of *angolanidade*, that is, Angolan cultural awareness with strong emphasis on the historical heritage. Taking his works by order of composition, one begins with the remarkable *Muana Puó* (the title is a girl's name), which was written in 1969 but not published until 1978.

MUANA PUÓ

Muana Puó is an elegant fable, an allegory of the Angolan war of independence from Portugal and of the uneasy world that Pepetela predicted would follow freedom from colonialism. It is a deliberate enigma, as Pepetela openly confirms, the keys to which in some cases fit neatly, while others fit ambiguously. Much of the emblematic fable, however, remains as inscrutable as the Chokwe girl's mask that dominates the work and appears pictorially on almost half the pages of the text.

This fable deserves close reading, especially since Pepetela claimed, in a 1990 interview with Margret Ammann and José Carlos Venâncio, that "every idea that I later develop is to be found there" (p. 7). In this fable, Pepetela describes the development of a relationship between two nameless characters, referred to only as "she" and "he," who are prefigured by the right and left sides, respectively, of the mask. She and he live apart, under the illusion that they, like their fellows, are bats (Angolans) producing honey in a limited oval world for the oppressive ravens (Portuguese) who control their lives. Despite the mountain that separates them, the pair become aware of each other in their quest to move from the darkness into light, a quest myth that also involves finding Calpe, "the city of one's dreams" (p. 114). Calpe represents both the Marxist-Leninist utopia and the idyll of the couple's love. This utopia is a classless society in which capitalism has no role; in such a society the bourgeoisie (middle-class capitalists) ceases to exist and all citizens belong to the proletariat (those who earn wages by selling their labor). Encouraged, the couple and other bats struggle up the mountain toward the light at the top: "The bats then realized that God was a mere invention, with which the ravens had always held them in subjection, so as to get the honey without working for it."

Pepetela allegorically portrays the attacks on the colonial estates of northern Angola of 1961, the seizing of Portuguese armaments, the increased Portuguese military presence, and the anguish of the ideological debates on both sides. The fable is divided into two parts, the past and the future. In the first part the mask symbolizes the joy of hope as expressed in dance, but in the second part the future brings tears of disillusion. The underlying incompatibility of the couple is fully established when his love for her is answered only by tenderness. Meanwhile, the bats, having ousted the ravens, realize that they are human. They start to build their new world, but it remains stubbornly oval, as it was during the raven's reign, falling short of the ideal—and implicitly, round—world. Skepticism creeps in as the couple revisits Calpe. Despite the surface perfection, the male protagonist feels like an anachronistic misfit in a collectivist new world that has outstripped his dreams.

She responds to this dissident view by accusing him of being still partly a bat and provoking his jealousy by an unsatisfying promiscuity. Their idyll is at an end and utopia unattained. He goes back to his desert and commits suicide. Group ideals have been fulfilled but not those of the individual, though Pepetela hints that one day they may be. The mask with its two incompatible sides is a metaphor for discordant political ideals; this is its mythic property. The clash between individualism and collectivism is an obsessional element in Pepetela's work, and there is a clearly discernible track, as he works through this issue, from *Muana Puó* to the novel *Mayombe* (1980), which was written in 1971. The world of myth is still present in *Mayombe*, but it is attenuated by the needs of an essentially neorealist composition.

MAYOMBE

In the late 1960s, Pepetela joined the Marxist guerrillas who were fighting in the oil-rich Cabinda enclave during the liberation struggle against the Portuguese colonialists (1961–1974). He incorporated his experience into the novel *Mayombe* to describe the activities of a combat group at large in the forest of Mayombe, which stretches from Cabinda into the Congo People's Republic. In *Mayombe*, Pepetela focuses on three forms of liberation: political, cultural, and sexual. The last of these gets too close to male hedonism to have any durable message, but in his concern for cultural liberation Pepetela launches such a virulent Marxist attack on the negative aspects of tribalism that he portrays it as a form of racism. He is mainly interested, however, in stressing the scant opportunities afforded to the individual by collectivist society. In this work, as he develops ideas that are only suggested in *Muana Puó*, he distances himself from those in the mainstream of Marxist-Leninist orthodoxy, whom he accuses of betraying the Marxist ideal at every turn, as in their adherence to tribalism. Pepetela has come to view the Marxist ideal as unrealizable.

The combat group of sixteen is led by the protagonist, Commander Fearless. Yet, within this small group, there is a variety of opinions. Fearless knows that he has no future in politics. Pepetela must have known, even in 1971, that as an advocate of the individualist position—and as a white man—there could be no long-term political career for him. Fearless, his Bakongo alter ego, is variously criticized for his leadership: by João, his political commissar and second in command, for liberalism and anarchism; by the deeply embittered Miracle for being an inexperienced intellectual; and by the young New World for being a vain, petty bourgeois. The commissar and New World are keenly orthodox Marxists, yet their contrastive shortcomings are not lost on Fearless: his commissar becomes wildly emotional under stress, while New World's youthful and inflexible dogmatism, though impressive, is not to Fearless' taste.

Fearless' first concern rests with the individual and not with political ideals; as a former seminarian and lapsed Catholic, he regrets what he sees as the religious zeal in Marxism, although he claims that his views broadly conform with general Marxist thinking. For Fearless, there can be no Marxist-Leninist millennium, no 100 percent collectivist utopia, just as there can be no Christian paradise: both are mere abstractions. If Marxism could fulfill 50 percent of its objectives, it would do well. Slow progress in an underdeveloped independent Angola would generate critical reactions, purges, counterrevolutionary elements, and opportunities for the ambitious and unscrupulous. Fearless has no illusions about his self-confessed "anarchist nature." Human factors, in his view, will always modify political aspirations.

The most radical utterance that Pepetela places in the mouth of Fearless refers to formerly proletarian intellectuals, among whom the first president of an independent Angola, António Agostinho Neto, and other revolutionary and postrevolutionary leaders might well have seen themselves targeted:

> It is demagogy to say that the proletariat will take power. Who takes power is a small group of men, on the best of hypotheses representing the proletariat or seeking to represent it. The lie begins with saying that the proletariat has taken power. To belong to the leadership team, it is necessary to have a reasonable political and cultural training.
>
> (p. 80)

In tackling the commissar and New World, Fearless rejects references to humble origins. For him the notion of the intellectual as proletarian is the "first lie" and populist demagogy at its most deceitful: "Are you, Commissar, a peasant? Because your father was a peasant, are you a peasant? You have studied a little, read much, for years engaged in political work, are you a peasant? No, you are an intellectual! To deny it is demagogy, populism" (p. 80). The paradoxical outcome will be totalitarianism, a denial of democracy, individualism, and freedom, despite such socialist structures as agrarian reform and public ownership.

Along with political idealism, Fearless dismisses the whole gamut of corrupt practices that he sees as being imposed in the name of Marxism. In particular he points to the abuses of family connections in the MPLA and to the nature of so-called democratic decisions: "So do not say that you would submit to the view of the mass, when you know perfectly well that you can influence that mass" (p. 93). Fearless, like the male protagonist of *Muana Puó*, sees no role for himself in an independent Angola.

It is clear why the work was unpublished for so long: publishers feared it would be banned. To the credit of President Neto, a poet himself, he authorized the publication of *Mayombe*, though he did not live to see the event. In the end it won the Prémio Nacional de Literatura (National Prize for Literature) in 1980.

Although Pepetela destroys the myth of a Marxist utopia in this novel, he also presents positive mythopoeia. In the epigraph, he asserts that his narrative is "the tale of Ogun, the African Prometheus"; the guerrillas of the novel "dared challenge the gods by opening a path through the dark forest." By championing the individual human spirit, Fearless comes nearest to incorporating the concept of Ogun-Prometheus. Significantly, Pepetela chose Ogun, a Yoruba-Nigerian deity, to join with the Titan Prometheus. As blacksmith, Ogun overlaps with that role of Prometheus; as warrior and hunter, he portrays the struggle for independence; and, in assuming the mantle of Prometheus in defiance of the malevolent colonialist Zeus, Fearless' challenge constitutes a ready corollary. This time, however, the prize is not fire, intelligence, or technology, but the liberation of the African. Rather than choose a Bantu-Angolan deity, Pepetela internationalizes his hero principle.

The challenge for Fearless involves discovering "*the frontier between truth and lies*"; it is "*a track in the desert*," and the final answer does not lie in the "*green of Mayombe*" (p. 184). The mythic coding is enigmatic, but plainly Fearless must die. He was born "*out of his time, like any tragic hero*" (p. 184). His deep desire for the liberty of the individual is out of phase with the future independent Marxist state. As the guerrillas conduct a successful assault on a Portuguese base, Fearless falls, mortally wounded, and experiences one last vision of individual freedom as his spirit is absorbed by the "forest's syncretism" (p. 182) and is finally at one with the green giant, the "Mayombe-god" (p. 51).

NGUNGA'S ADVENTURES

While *Mayombe* was held back from publication until 1980, Pepetela wrote more orthodox works as befit his status in the MPLA. The sequence is significant: in 1972 he was transferred from Cabinda to the Eastern Front, where he wrote the didactic novella *Ngunga's Adventures*. In the year of its mimeographed publication, 1973, he became the MPLA's permanent secretary for education and culture. He moved to Luanda, Angola's capital, and in 1974 became a member of the MPLA delegation and, in 1975, director of political orientation. He fought in the liberation struggle of 1975–1976, against the invading South Africans, assorted international mercenaries backed by the United States, and the two other Angolan liberation movements, the Frente Nacional de Libertação de Angola (National Front for the Liberation of Angola, or FNLA) and the União Nacional para a Independência Total de Angola (National Union for the Total Independence of Angola, or UNITA). The MPLA, strongly aided by Cuban troops and Soviet weaponry, expelled the invading forces. Pepetela then held the post of deputy minister of education from 1976 to 1982. In this period, he published the two Marxist plays, *A corda* (1978; The rope) and *A revolta da casa dos ídolos* (1980; The revolt of the house of idols), the cryptic *Muana Puó*, and, only after much anxiety and soul-searching in high places, *Mayombe*. Considering that novel's criticism of Marxism as practiced in Angola, it is hardly surprising that then he stepped down from political office.

Ngunga's Adventures, in which each of the twenty-eight brief chapters demonstrates a moral, is based on the experiences of a thirteen-year-old orphan boy, Ngunga, who learns of the weaknesses that Angolans must struggle to overcome. He apprehends the prejudices that fracture society: the differences of race and class, the gulf between the sexes, between the old and the young, between traditional practices and the needs of an egalitarian society. The struggle is not solely against colonial oppression, though Ngunga fights this too and kills three Portuguese. He then settles into a school in the liberated zone to seek an education in order to equip himself to argue against such practices as the traditional purchase of women via the payment of the bride-price. Stylistically, the work owes much to oral tradition. As the epilogue reveals, Ngunga disappears in the guerrilla conflict and ends as a figure of mythic proportions. Unlike the much criticized Fearless, Ngunga is an exemplar.

THE DIDACTIC PLAYS

The Manichaean emphases of *Muana Puó*—the sharp contrast between light and darkness, between whites and blacks, presented as eternally irreconcilable adversaries—returned in the didactic plays *A corda* and *A revolta da casa dos ídolos*. The former is a slight twelve-scene play in which two teams of teenagers, led by a male dancer, vie to reenact contemporary demonology by vilifying Holden Roberto (the FNLA leader), Jonas Savimbi (the UNITA leader), "the Racist," "the American," and so on.

A revolta da casa dos ídolos is set in 1514 in the Kingdom of the Kongo in what is now northern Angola. Here, Pepetela condemns historical demons. In this three-act play, the Portuguese colonialists are condemned for invoking patrilineal succession to install Afonso I as head of state, thus jettisoning the democratic elective principle. Pepetela's anticlericalism is as vehement as in *Mayombe*, but his focus on whoring and boozing missionaries cheapens the real argument. The parasitic chieftains (the feudal *manis*) survive on skulduggery and the proceeds of slavery and taxation. The main vehicle for the onslaught is the youthful Nanga, who is treacherously murdered by the *manis* at the height of the revolt when the house of idols is torched by Portuguese soldiers. Nanga's resonant argument is that victory depends on the "people, united," and although he does not reject outright the reliance on amulets and ancestor spirits, he plainly regards them as less effective. In the final scene, Nanga's beloved, Kuntuala, mythicizes him: she predicts that one day the shadows that have descended on the Kongo will be torn aside and that "Nanga's light will glow like the sun over all this land" (p. 157).

YAKA

When *Yaka* was published in 1984, Pepetela was no longer part of the political machine, having taken up a post in sociology at the University of Angola (now Universidade Agostinho Neto) and become a committee member of the Angolan Writers Union. *Yaka*, a saga about a colonialist family, once again won him the National Prize for Literature, in 1985. The novel spans the life of Alexandre Semedo, from his birth in the bush in 1890 until his death in the garden of his house in Benguela in 1975 amid shelling from the invading South African forces. *Yaka* reaches back not only into nineteenth-century colonial history, but also into precolonial Angolan culture. European myth is also present in terms of both Portuguese dreams of empire and the lore of ancient Greece. These symbols of white colonialist prejudice are progressively overwhelmed by Angolan symbols.

Yet Pepetela teases us. His principal myth-bearing emblem is an ancient, wooden one-meter-high statue called Yaka, which was acquired by Alexandre's father. It has always had a strange effect on Alexandre, and he vainly seeks to enter into dialogue with it because he suspects it enshrines some great power. But Yaka only talks to the reader, thus doubly mocking Alexandre's incomprehension. But we too are faced with a paradox. We are told in the foreword that "the statue is pure fiction . . . but its myth needed to be created. Because only myths have reality" (p. 6).

Pepetela is tempting us to argue with him. But the assertion is plain: the statue, like the mask of *Muana Puó*, represents a mythic force that has a base in reality, a base he has elsewhere increasingly referred to as *angolanidade*, a concept with cultural, anthropological, even political resonances. Alexandre is the novel's main representative of white colonialism, though he often despises its shortcomings, which are represented by the members of his family, to whom he has steadfastly refused to speak for over ten years. He has always lived with an inexplicable fear that is compounded whenever he contemplates the statue's bulging eyes. But there is another emblem, a dagger that belonged to a chieftain who was murdered by members of Alexandre's family. Alexandre has always refused to touch it, dreading its animist and fetishist associations.

Among his large family, there are only two relatives for whom he has any regard: Chico, the son of his illegitimate mulatto daughter; and Joel, a white great-grandson. They are the only ones who stay in Angola after independence and become Alexandre's heirs, though there is a hint that they, like Ngunga in *Ngunga's Adventures*, might soon meet their deaths in the liberation struggle of 1975–1976. For Alexandre, Chico represents the breakdown of the ancient Manichaean polarities of black and white. Because of Joel's incipient *angolanidade*, Alexandre, in an anagnorisis, a moment of recognition, breaks his long silence and speaks again. Joel represents for him a sensitive blending of European background and the Angolan culture portrayed in the dagger. Joel emblematically adopts the name Ulysses as his nom de guerre and accepts the gift of the dagger, thus uniting the two cultures.

Joel, in the novel's second anagnorisis, recognizes that the statue is a satirical caricature of a white colonialist. The statue has been a metaphor for both Alexandre's conscience and Angolan history, which is so richly present in this work. But the stronger myth is personified by Joel as he takes his place alongside Ngunga and Fearless, the other mythic heroes of the final independence struggle.

Marxism-Leninism in this novel is satirically represented by Alexandre's white granddaughter Olívia. In her early twenties, she switches from flagellant would-be novice nun to ardent apostle of the proletarian revolution. Posters of Lenin and Che Guevara, the Latin American revolutionary leader, oust pictures of Jesus on her bedroom wall; she reaches a level of such orthodoxy as to leave behind even the political commissar and New World of *Mayombe*. Olívia condemns the conflict as a "bourgeois war" and the Angolan proletariat for having no "class consciousness" (p. 279). Rather, she emigrates in haste with her bourgeois colonialist father, announcing that she is off to Portugal to participate in an authentic socialist revolution, for there the working class possesses a "solid proletarian ideology" (p. 289). Joel and Chico scorn her addiction to theory and stress that she has no true empathy with the ordinary people of Angola, who are too busy fighting for freedom and material benefits to be concerned about socialist niceties.

O CÃO E OS CALUANDAS

Pepetela's distancing himself from the Marxist theoreticians and from Marxism's more enthusiastic practical exponents truly finds expression in *O cão e os Caluandas* (The dog and the people of Luanda). Written and published in 1985, this episodic novel is a collage of short stories, dramatic scripts, reports, interviews, and so forth. Its linking element is a wandering Alsatian dog with an apparent social conscience and a capacity for being in more than one place at the same time. Although seemingly a stray with temporary owners, the dog also knows a separate existence on a rural estate, where it belongs to a nouveau riche family.

The events of the novel are enacted in the year 1980, but purport to be set down by an author writing from the vantage point of the year 2002. The view of the first five years of the Marxist experiment is not encouraging, although Pepetela presents it lightheartedly. The catalog of problems is long: vice, unemployment, and people surviving off odd jobs; black markets, food shortages, orchestrated factory pilfering, and special shops for people in certain privileged categories; filthy streets, stinking buildings, rats everywhere, and frequent power failures; bureaucratic snarls, "backhanders," and illegal loans of public property; squatters, machismo, incessant calling of trivial political meetings, and a tendency to bury money in the ground rather than trust it to banks; prejudice-linked disadvantages for mulattoes and local whites; and inevitably the purists who are the only ones marching in step and to whom everyone else is a petty bourgeois.

The anonymous author claims to be baffled by the sequence of events and invites his readers to help him to understand it and to interpret certain mysteries surrounding the Alsatian. When on the estate, the dog loathes a tentacular bougainvillea, a vine covered with sharp thorns that is closely identified with the corrupt owner of the estate, who is rapidly earning a dishonest fortune. Significantly, the plant—a metaphor for the unscrupulous excesses to which capitalism can be prone—has already destroyed a climbing plant covered in attractive red berries, a metaphor for communism. Finally, the Alsatian triumphs in a duel with the bougainvillea and walks away, battered and bleeding, but his victory is a victory for a middle way between two extremes; he represents the common sense of the Angolan people.

This use of symbols and emblems, be they animals, statues, daggers, or masks, is a conscious and deliberate attempt to foreground the values of traditional Angolan culture and to use the forces of nature and mythic symbolism to reinforce *angolanidade*. Hand in hand with this effort goes social criticism that debunks obsessive quests for utopias. Pepetela, despite his anticlericalism, manifestly and unwittingly aligned himself with Cardinal John Henry Newman, England's most illustrious nineteenth-century cleric, in espousing the view that society cannot truly change until individuals change (and never vice versa). This view stood in sharp contrast to the argument of the Soviet geneticist Trofim Denisovich Lysenko, who proposed that the Marxist utopia would effect a change in human nature. Pepetela came to believe that Marxism was spiritually bankrupt.

LUEJI

To reemphasize the foundations of *angolanidade*. Pepetela next turned to oral tradition to re-create the stories surrounding the establishment of the Lunda Empire in *Lueji* (1990). His main focus in this novel is on the Lunda expansion in the last decade of the sixteenth century. The Lunda area is essentially the present-day northeastern Angola, but also extends into Zaire to the north and Zambia to the east. The novel focuses on the accession of the renowned Lunda queen, Lueji, who defeats the military challenge of her powerful half brother and, through dynastic marriage, lays the foundations of a great empire of interrelated kingdoms in the savannah of central Africa. Significant, however, is how Pepetela skillfully interlaces the story of Lueji with that of a twentieth-century *mestiça* (mulatto woman), a ballerina named Lu. By this interweaving, he suggests that Lu is in some sense a reincarnation of Lueji or, at least, a descendant of Lueji's, and therefore a potential recipient of the animist force of her ancestor's spirit.

Pepetela portrays Queen Lueji's accession as a remarkable event in Lunda prehistory that belongs to a mythical past about which anthropologists have found a cat's cradle of oral traditions. Sovereignty over Lunda in the late sixteenth century was decided electively by the council of chiefs with the proviso that the elected monarch belong to the extensive royal family, which in the Lunda creation myth directly descends from the great mother serpent that created the world. Lueji had two half brothers, Tchinguri, who was violent, irascible, and courageous, and Chinyama, who was hedonistic and cowardly. When Tchinguri killed his father, King Kondi, in a quarrel, the chief of the council took the uprecedented step of passing the sovereignty to a woman, Lueji. This was a break with tradition in that, although Lunda lineages descend matrilineally, authority rests with the males.

In Pepetela's version, the eighteen-year-old Lueji shows wisdom and skill in holding the Lunda capital, Mussumba, against a siege mounted by Tchinguri with his superior army. Instrumental in this victory is another unprecedented occurrence: her marriage outside the Lunda ethnic group to King Ilunga, who brings with him vital new technology in iron smelting that provides Lueji with superior weaponry. Subsequently, members of Lueji's family and of her husband's emigrate to establish Lunda sway over an ever-expanding area. Lueji then breaks with tradition again. In order to counterbalance the principle of matrilineal succession generally, she establishes the principle of "positional succession" (p. 463). According to this, a male successor acquires not only the goods or political status of his predecessor, but also his social identity. In other words, he becomes the predecessor.

In presenting Lueji as the origin of these two principles, Pepetela introduced a contradiction of the oral tradition, according to which matrilineal succession was the result of Lueji's greatness and "positional succession" was a previous norm. At all events, the generic title for Lunda kingship, Mwatiamvwa, has lasted down the years from the time of Lueji's successor to the twentieth century. Moreover, Pepetela's novel wholly fits Northrop Frye's criteria in *Fables of Identity* (1963) with its creation myth, survival myth, Artemis myth (complete with idyllic lake and "canonical" roses), its marriage and divinization of royal figures, the new city, and the quest myths of the Lunda diaspora.

Lu lives in a fairly cosmopolitan, if not particularly booming, Luanda in the year 1999. Society is loosely socialist, and there is distaste for bourgeois profiteers; conversely, there is clear scope for individual expression, especially in the arts. A struggling ballet group, of which Lu is the principal ballerina, resolves its crisis by writing and choreographing a ballet that is entirely based on Angolan traditions. She researches oral traditions about Lueji, who was purportedly an exultant dancer, to the point where she feels that the spirit of Lueji is taking over. The successful end product is fashioned out of music and rhythms played on Angolan instruments, and the choreography allows for the individualist elements in Angolan dancing. *Lueji* offers a rich broth of anthropological and ethnographic referentiality: family spirits, holy relics, ancient oral tales, ethnic rituals and practices, and amulets of every kind. Presented in an ample lexical framework, these factors combine to produce a beguiling and heady potion.

Pepetela's quest to reveal the underlying mechanics of African cultural values lies at the heart of his *angolanidade*. The anonymous Bantu narrator of *Lueji* fiercely deplores the previous suppression of such factors. He believes that Angolan writers must be prepared to work away from the powerful European norms and develop their own versions of the truth. Such a breakaway inevitably involves the reformulation and reinvention of myth. Lu argues that in plotting her ballet she is less concerned with the historical truth than with the underlying truth. This interest permits the insertion of elements, for example, modes of dancing, that are not demonstrably Lunda, though doubtless they are similar. However, since there are conflicting versions in oral tradition of the story of Lueji, all serving differing ethnic ideologies, Lu believes she has the right to devise her own version, especially because scholarly research seems incapable of further penetration of the objective truth. Pepetela emphasizes that Angolans need heroes, whether they be royalty like Lueji or commoners like Nanga, Ngunga, Fearless, or Joel; once they become heroes they are transfigured. Art aggrandizes its very subject matter.

A GERAÇÃO DA UTOPIA

In 1990, Pepetela wrote *Luandando*, a whimsical guide to Luanda, and was also planning *A geração da utopia* (The utopia generation), a novel that once again won acclaim for its frankness about broken illusions. Pepetela's international stature was evident from the fact that *Luandando* was published by ICANEF, a French oil company, while a German agency, Deutsche Akademische Austauschdienst, gave him a scholarship in 1991 to spend a year in Berlin writing *A geração da utopia* (1992). This novel covers thirty years of Angolan history (1961–1991), and Pepetela did not hide the fact that the protagonist Aníbal is his alter ego. Significant years are selected for each of the work's four parts. The first part opens in Lisbon in 1961 and highlights the lives of students from the Portuguese colonies, in particular four from Angola: Sara, a white medical student; Vítor, who is politically ambitious but idle; Malongo, who spends most of his time loafing in bars or playing on the second team of Benfica, Lisbon's and Portugal's leading soccer club; and Aníbal, the dreamer-intellectual. All live in an atmosphere of tension as the liberation struggle of 1961–1974 breaks out. Although shadowed by the political police, they escape from Portugal, zealous to work for an independent Angola.

In the second part, Pepetela focuses on Aníbal, who leads a combat group on the eastern front in 1972 and becomes disillusioned by the internal regionalist conflicts that threaten prosecution of the war. In Part Three, Sara finds Aníbal ten years later, surviving as a near recluse and underwater harpoonist, in an isolated bay near Benguela, sickened by the way so many of his former comrades have evolved into self-seeking bureaucrats in Luanda. Sara, whose dedication to the MPLA had once been optimistic and unswerving, is able, through their discovery of latent love for each other, to give him a reason to live. In the final part, which takes place in the Luanda of 1991 and beyond, Pepetela paints a depressing picture of social reality. Vítor, now a government minister, is involved in shady deals with Malongo, now a black marketer. Aníbal comments that the three estates have become the bureaucratic establishment, the racketeers, and the people; he dreads the possibility of an Angola dominated by "the most barbarous capitalism the world has ever seen" (p. 233).

Pepetela concludes the novel with the idea that Aníbal and Sara are members of a failed generation; utopian dreams are cast aside, leaving only the hope that the next generation will do better. He returned to Angola from Berlin in 1992 to resume his teaching post in sociology at the Universidade Agostinho Neto. One of the grounds for his return had been the guarded hope of the negotiated peace in the long civil war between the MPLA government and the rebel forces of UNITA. Pepetela's worst fears were confirmed by the outbreak of even fiercer hostilities after UNITA's refusal to accept the results of the September 1992 elections.

CONCLUSION

In 1995 Pepetela published the short novel *O desejo de Kianda* (The desire of Kianda), a modern parable in which a series of buildings collapse in Luanda; their site is a former saltmarsh, whose spirit, Kianda, symbolizes ancient cultural values that have been jeopardized by high-rise buildings, acquisitiveness, political corruption, and computer-obsessed society.

From *Muana Puó* to *O desejo de Kianda*, the trajectory of Pepetela's work reveals a sensitive development from a concern for Angolan independence from Portugal, through an increasing disillusionment with the Marxist dream, to the quest for a middle path between capitalist excess and communist dogma, and for the restoration and, in some measure, the fashioning of an Angolan cultural heritage.

Selected Bibliography

SELECTED WORKS

As aventuras de Ngunga. Lisbon, Portugal: Edições 70, 1976.

Muana Puó. Lisbon, Portugal: Edições 70, 1978.

A corda. Luanda, Angola: União dos Escritores Angolanos, 1978.

Mayombe. Lisbon, Portugal: Edições 70, 1980.

A revolta da casa dos ídolos. Lisbon, Portugal: Edições 70, 1980.

Yaka. São Paulo, Brazil: Ática, 1984.

O cão e os Caluandas. Lisbon, Portugal: Publicações Dom Quixote, 1985. Publ. as *O cão e os Calus.* São Paulo, Brazil: União dos Escritores Angolanos, 1985.

Lueji. Lisbon, Portugal: Publicações Dom Quixote, 1990.

Luandando. Paris and Luanda, Angola: ICANEF, 1990.

A geração da utopia. Lisbon, Portugal: Publicações Dom Quixote, 1992.

O desejo de Kianda. Lisbon, Portugal: Publicações Dom Quixote, 1995.

TRANSLATIONS

Ngunga's Adventures: A Story of Angola. Trans. by Chris Searle. London: Young World Books, 1980.

Mayombe. Trans. by Michael Wolfers. London: Heinemann; Harare: Zimbabwe Publishing House, 1983.

INTERVIEWS

Ammann, Margret, and José Carlos Venâncio. "Pepetela, um construtor da angolanidade." In *Jornal de letras, artes e ideias* 10 (2–8 October 1990).

"Colóquio sobre *Mayombe.*" In *Lavra e oficina,* no. 25/26/27 (October/November/December 1980).

Correia, Rosa. "Conversa com Pepetela." In *Letras e letras,* no. 52 (7 August 1991).

Guardão, Maria João. "Pepetela e a guerrilha da ecrita. In *Jornal de letras, artes e ideias* 8 (4–10 October 1988).

Guterres, Maria. "*Lueji — O nascimento dum império:* A procura da angolanidade." In *Bulletin of Hispanic Studies* 71 (1994).

"Inquérito aos escritores: Pepetela." In *Lavra e oficina,* no. 5 (February 1979).

Jones, Isabel. "Concretizar lusofonias: Pepetela, Angola." In *Letras e letras,* no. 16 (5 April 1989).

Múrias, Manuel Beça. "Angola assumiu mais depressa a história sem complexos." In *O jornal,* no. 437 (8 July 1983).

Neves, Loja. "Pepetela." In *Expresso* (17 November 1990).

Silva, Rodrigues da. "De utópico a profeta." In *Jornal de letras, artes e ideias* 12 (11–17 August 1992).

CRITICAL STUDIES

António. Mário. "Pepetela: *Mayombe.*" In *Colóquio-Letras,* no. 64 (November 1981).

Billingham, Rosemary. "A mulher na obra de Pepetela." In *Angolê,* no. 11 (October/December 1988).

———. "Pepetela: A Profile." In *Wasafiri,* no. 10 (summer 1989).

Bueti, Rui. "*Mayombe*: Ar fresco na literatura angolana." In *Expressinternacional* supplement of *Expresso* (7 November 1981).

———. "Pepetela: *Yaka.*" In *África* (December 1985/February 1986).

Carneiro, João. "Pepetela: *A revolta da casa dos ídolos.*" In *Colóquio-Letras,* no. 70 (November 1982).

"Cinema: *Mayombe.*" In *AfricAsia* (February 1984).

Conrado, Júlio. "A rainha da Lunda." In *Jornal de letras, artes e ideias* 10 (30 October–5 November 1990).

Desti, Rita. "Pepetela: *As aventuras de Ngunga.*" In *Colóquio-Letras*, no. 41 (January 1978).

———. "Pepetela: *A corda.*" In *Colóquio-Letras*, no. 54 (March 1980).

Lepecki, Maria Lúcia. "Pepetela: *Mayombe.*" In *Expresso* (9 April 1982).

Martinho, Fernando J. B. "*Muana puó*—Enigma e metamorfose." In *África* (April/June 1979).

———. "*O cão e os Caluandas,* de Pepetela." In *Revista ICALP*, no. 12/13 (June/September 1988).

Melo, João de. "Pepetela: *Mayombe.*" In *África* (January/June 1981).

Mestre, David. "Um livro exemplar (*Lueji*)." In *Jornal de letras, artes e ideias* 8 (4–10 October 1988).

Rodrigues, Filomena. "Pepetela: Um encontro no presente." In *Letras e letras,* no. 40 (February 1991).

Secco, Carmem Lúcia Tindo Ribeiro. "De utopias, crises e desencantos." In *Letras e letras,* no. 102 (November 1993).

Silva, Rodrigues da. "Do sonho à amargura." In *O jornal* (7 August 1992).

Vasconcelos, Adriano Botelho de. "Dialogando." In *Angolê*, n.s., no. 4 (June 1990).

Willis, Clive. "*Mayombe* and the Liberation of the Angolan." In *Portuguese Studies* 3 (1987).

———. "Colonialism and After in Angola: Myths and Marxism in the Works of Pepetela." In *Journal of the Institute of Romance Studies* 1 (1992).

You, Jong Hwi. "A peste em *Mayombe.*" In *Angolê*, no. 7 (October/December 1987).

William Plomer

1903–1973

NEIL POWELL

WILLIAM PLOMER was one of the twentieth century's all-around men of letters, but his work has been undervalued precisely because he cannot be pigeonholed as novelist, poet, biographer, editor, or librettist—though he was all of these—and instead deserves the simple epithet "writer." Not only was he alarmingly versatile, he was also compulsively nomadic. Living in Africa, Japan, and England, as well as spending time in Greece, Plomer, who in 1949 published a collection of stories set in these places as *Four Countries*, was no mere tourist. His preference for traveling light included an intense loathing of almost all possessions: he refused to have a car or a telephone, and his only property was a modest bungalow in Sussex, England. Yet his stance of a willfully deracinated outsider enabled him to become an exceptionally shrewd and skillful observer of the societies on whose edges he teasingly hovered.

NOMADIC YOUTH

Because of his gambling debts and an affair with a gamekeeper's daughter, Plomer's father, Charles Campbell Plomer, had been sent in disgrace to South Africa from England in 1889. In South Africa he proved restlessly unsuccessful in a variety of occupations, including soldier, policeman, and journalist, before working for the Department of Native Affairs in Pietersburg, where William Charles Franklyn Plomer was born on 10 December 1903. His mother, Edythe Mary Waite-Browne, was a sensitive though ill-educated and impractical woman, a childhood friend of the man she married in London on 1 June 1901, who never really took to Africa. In his parents' irreconcilable clash of temperament lay the seeds of Plomer's rootlessness.

In 1908, devastated by the death of her second son, John, from malaria, Edythe returned to England with William, whose grandfather insisted that he be educated there. Edythe's sister Hilda had married the headmaster of a preparatory school at Spondon, then a quiet country village in Derbyshire, where, between 1909 and 1911, William spent the happiest years of his childhood. "As I was only five years old," he recalls in *Double Lives* (1943), "I seldom went to lessons or games with the other boys, and being parted from my parents and without brothers and sisters I found myself in one of those isolated and somewhat anomalous situations which were often to recur . . . in my later life" (p. 73). Meanwhile, their financial circumstances much improved by legacies, his parents had moved to Johannesburg. In 1911 Edythe returned again to England, where in August she gave birth to her third son, Peter. Accompanying them back to South Africa, William became a pupil at St. John's College, Johannesburg, in 1912. For two years, the Plomers uncharacteristically prospered, until the civil unrest of 1913–1914 persuaded them to set sail once more for England.

It was "an eventful voyage" on which Plomer said he "got into various kinds of boyish mischief" (*Double Lives*, p. 92), including a precocious homosexual relationship with a young steward. He then spent three miserable years at Beechmont, a boarding school in Kent, before going on to Rugby; but the family's sudden wealth had almost as swiftly diminished, and in 1918 he was on his way back to Johannesburg for two more years at St. John's College. Although Plomer's education was extraordinarily fragmented, it left him with a quirky resilience and an unshakable determination to be a writer: by 1920 he had already written poems set in both England and Africa, some of which he would shortly send to Harold Monro in London. His father, however, decided that the strong, tall, yet reserved and myopic, seventeen-year-old should be a farmer, and in June 1921 Plomer was packed off to Molteno in the Eastern Cape and apprenticed to a sheep farmer named Fred Pope. As a career it made no sense at all, but Plomer, as he would so often do, set about transporting some of the experience into fiction.

Late in 1922, Charles Plomer retired from his civil service job and sought his son's help in running the trading station at Entumeni—which, aptly, means "the place of thorns"—in Zululand. A vastly unpromising enterprise, it nevertheless suited Plomer well enough: he admired the Zulus, enjoyed the social isolation, and completed his first novel, *Turbott Wolfe*, which he submitted to Leonard Woolf at the Hogarth Press in London in December 1924, just after his twenty-first birthday. His work for the trading station included trips to Durban, where he met the poet Roy Campbell and a journalist with the *Natal Advertiser*, Laurens van der Post. With these literary friends, the publication of his novel (which appeared, after some delays, in February 1926), and the imminent launch of Campbell's magazine, *Voorslag* (Whiplash), his days as a trading-station assistant were drawing to an end. From the start, *Voorslag* was threatened by the gulf between the antiracist radicalism of its editors and the businesslike caution of its proprietors, yet it inspired Plomer to feverish creative activity, including poems, polemics, and the stories "Portraits in the Nude" and "Ula Masondo." Nevertheless, his surprising and decisive next move was prompted not by Campbell but by van der Post, who had been invited to Japan and suggested that Plomer accompany him.

For van der Post, it was a brief trip; for Plomer, it lasted three years. He found work teaching English, which he enjoyed, and embarked on a huge autobiographical novel, of which only the Japanese section survived as *Sado* (1931). Alienated from white South African society, he was more at ease in a culture that seemed both to tolerate his homosexuality and to mirror his introspective reserve: visitors to his house in Kami Nerima were impressed by its wholly un-English, oriental austerity. By 1928, however, he was troubled by Japanese "nationalistic paranoia," and he had begun to turn his satirical eye on the country in the stories collected as *Paper Houses* (1929); it was time to leave, so in March 1929 he set off, via the Trans-Siberian Railway, for England. "You've come back with a golden face," his mother told him, when he arrived; and indeed he felt like a foreigner (*At Home: Memoirs*, 1958, p. 30).

LITERARY LONDON

Although he was widely traveled and successfully published at the age of twenty-five, Plomer had no experience of English literary life because, upon returning to England, he at first lived with his parents, who had rather unpromisingly settled at Pinner in Middlesex. Through Leonard and Virginia Woolf, however, he was soon mixing shyly with "many persons of literary distinction or unusual character," as he coyly put it in *At Home* (p. 44), and receiving offers to review books. Virginia Woolf approved of him: although "thickly coated with a universal manner," he possessed "the wild eyes" that she thought "the true index of what goes on within" (*The Diary of Virginia Woolf*, vol. 4, p. 85). E. M. Forster wrote admiringly to him, leading to a lifelong friendship; an earlier admirer, the painter and playwright Anthony Butts, who had written to him in Japan and whom he met for the first time in May 1929, would become a closer, if more complicated, friend and the model for the character Toby d'Arfey in *Museum Pieces* (1952). By September 1929, Plomer felt sufficiently confident in his freelance literary life to leave Pinner and take a room in Bayswater, West London. In November, his landlady was murdered in the house by her jealous husband, but the place's sudden notoriety did not dissuade him from holding a birthday party there a fortnight later or from using the incident in his next novel, *The Case Is Altered* (1932).

The following May, Plomer and Butts set off, at Butts's expense, for a three-month tour of Europe, which became a six-month stay in Greece. Plomer incautiously fell in love with a sailor named Nicky, who left him financially impoverished, ill with gonorrhea, and above all emotionally wounded; subsequently he would do his best to keep his sexual encounters and his deep friendships separate. Returning to England in November, he resumed work on his autobiographical novel, eventually jettisoning all but the Japanese section, and assembled a third collection of poems, *The Fivefold Screen* (1932). By the end of 1931 his spirits and Butts's finances had recovered sufficiently for them to take a house in Palace Gate; the arrangement lasted less than a year, and Plomer moved to a flat off the Fulham Road.

Meanwhile, he had met Hugh Walpole, who was chairman of the selection committee for the Book Society (which chose *The Case Is Altered* as the book of the month for August 1932), and Rupert Hart-Davis, its young manager. When Hart-Davis became a director of the publishing house of Jonathan Cape in 1933, Plomer quickly joined him there, first as an author and, beginning in 1937, as publisher's reader; his association with Cape continued until his death. His transition from author to reader is significant: during the latter part of the 1930s, the balance of Plomer's literary activity shifted decisively from writing his own books to evaluating the work of others, either in manuscript for Cape or in reviews for periodicals such as the *Spectator*, the *Listener*, where his friend Joe Ackerley became literary editor in 1935, and *New Writing*, which had recently been founded by John Lehmann. By a happy chance, at this low point of his own creative energy, in September 1937 he found, among manuscripts waiting for him to read at Cape, two manuscript notebooks (with the promise of twenty more to follow) of a Victorian clergyman's journal. He had stumbled upon the work that would make him better known than any of his own books, *Kilvert's Diary, 1870–1879*, which was published in three separate volumes from 1938 to 1940 and in abridged form in 1944.

Editing Kilvert, writing reviews, and broadcasting for the British Broadcasting Corporation helped to sustain him through the outbreak of World War II in September 1939 and his mother's death a month later; he had also begun work on the grotesque satirical ballads that became his most famous poems. In July 1940, his friend Ian Fleming, who was later to become famous for his James Bond novels, recruited him into Naval Intelligence, which provided him with a fairly comfortable desk job at the Admiralty, alongside which he could conveniently sustain his literary life: toward the end of the war, for instance, he lunched regularly with the English poet and novelist Roy Fuller, who worked in the same building, and Ackerley. The suicides of Virginia Woolf and Anthony Butts within two months of each other in 1941 shook him deeply, prompting the self-examination that informs his first and best book of memoirs, *Double Lives*.

Under Ackerley's tutelage he had become accomplished in the pursuit of casual sex, but in 1943 he mistakenly approached a heterosexual sailor, who became outraged and summoned a military policeman. The potential scandal was hushed up, but Plomer, after destroying hundreds of letters, retreated still further into his shell of self-contained reticence. Fortunately, in June 1944 he met Charles Erdmann, then working in a restaurant in London's Soho district; Erdmann remained his companion for the rest of his life. *The Dorking Thigh and Other Satires*, which takes its name from his most popular and widely anthologized ballad, appeared in 1945.

Soon after the war, he began his fifth novel—an English anecdotal tragicomedy that became *Museum Pieces*—but an invitation from the composer Benjamin Britten to deliver a talk at the first Aldeburgh Festival of Music and the Arts in 1948 heralded an unexpected development in Plomer's career. He became a regular visitor to Aldeburgh and, after two abortive collaborations with Britten on operas for children, was commissioned to write the libretto for *Gloriana* (1953), which was planned to celebrate the coronation of Queen Elizabeth II and premiered at Covent Garden in London in June 1953. Undeterred by the work's initially lukewarm reception, Britten invited Plomer's collaboration on another project, which was to have a Japanese theme and was referred to as "the Noh libretto." After modifications that would have exhausted the patience of most writers, this libretto became the thoroughly anglicized *Curlew River* (1964). Two other "church parables," *The Burning Fiery Furnace* (1966) and *The Prodigal Son* (1968), followed.

RETREAT TO RUSTINGTON

Depressed by the noisy intrusiveness of the city and feeling he should live closer to his elderly father in Hove, Plomer moved with Erdmann to a bungalow at Rustington in Sussex in July 1953. He soon managed to telescope his London commitments into a single weekly visit centered on his Wednesday meetings at Cape, but he did not become entirely reclusive. In July 1956, he revisited Johannesburg and addressed a conference on "South African Writers and English Readers." His interest in the literature and politics of South Africa was rekindled, and on his return to England he persuaded John Lehmann, who had become editor of *London Magazine*, to devote the January 1957 issue to South African writing. The visit also prompted another retrospective journey in the shape of his second autobiography, *At Home*.

The publication of his *Collected Poems* in 1960 completed Plomer's major literary output. Although he produced two more volumes of poetry and, just before his death, an expanded *Collected Poems* (1973), his final decade was relatively leisurely. He read, reviewed, served as judge at literary competitions; made regular visits to the Aldeburgh Festival and to Kilvert celebrations in Clyro, Wales; and maintained relaxed social contacts with old friends, such as van der Post and Hart-Davis, whom he appointed his literary executor. He received honors, including the Queen's Gold Medal for Poetry in 1963 and the CBE (Commander of the Order of the British Empire) in 1968. In August 1966, he and Erdmann moved a few miles inland to an even less distinguished bungalow in Adastra Avenue, Hassocks; the anonymity of the place and its mildly ludicrous address delighted him.

Plomer suffered two coronary thromboses during the night of 15 September 1973, and in the early hours of the following Friday Erdmann heard a choking cry for help from Plomer's room. There was, of course, no telephone and no car at the bungalow and the nearest public telephone was out of order; by the time the doctor summoned by Erdmann's efforts arrived, it was too late. Plomer died at 4:30 A.M. on 20 September 1973; he was cremated in Brighton, and a memorial service was held at St. Martin-in-the-Fields on 7 November 1973.

NOVELS

Plomer, like E. M. Forster, published five novels during his lifetime, and there are other striking similarities between the two writers: both produced most of their fiction relatively early in their careers, covered a variety of countries and cultures, treated large themes with ironic restraint, and used female characters to mask their homosexuality.

Turbott Wolfe

The weaknesses of *Turbott Wolfe* (1925) are those of a book begun when its author is not even twenty: the fidgety insistence of its repeated parenthetical "said Turbott Wolfe"; the archness of a narrator who addresses his author as "My good William Plomer" (p. 92); the sense of exuberant ventriloquism. There are also astonishingly abrupt shifts of tone. Within a single page of text, the snappily epigrammatic style so typical of his later prose—"She was barefaced by day and barebacked by night," he writes of a circus wife—gives way to the authentic voice of youthful discovery: "It came upon me suddenly in that harsh polyglot gaiety that I was living in Africa; that there is a question of colour" (p. 62). This "question of colour," the novel's central theme, is treated with a passionate frankness that amazed its early readers. For Turbott Wolfe, the English painter who runs the trading station at Ovuzane in Lembuland, which is closely modeled on Entumeni in Zululand, the theoretical position is clear: he knows that "this is going to be a black man's country" (p. 113), and he supports the political tenets of young Africa, including the belief that "*miscegenation is the only way for Africa to be secured to the Africans*" (p. 144). Yet, when a white woman friend proposes to marry an African, Wolfe is conventionally alarmed: "Do you honestly mean to tell me that it's your intention to marry a black man—that nigger?" (p. 183).

Plomer explores Wolfe's self-contradictions with considerable subtlety, but the minor characters, from detestable white farmers to the admirable Lembu people, almost inevitably tend toward well-drawn stereotypes. More interesting are the two figures, other than Wolfe, who embody elements of Plomer: the overheated missionary Friston, who knows that "the white man's day is over" (p. 123) but mysteriously vanishes, and Mabel van der Horst, the mannishly outspoken Desdemona, who in marrying her Othello precipitates the book's denouement. In the end, Wolfe is given notice to quit the trading station, which is sold to a racist aptly named Bloodfield. The concluding note of ideals and desires that are simultaneously thwarted exactly parallels that of E. M. Forster's *A Passage to India* (1924) with its "No, not yet" and "No, not there."

Sado

Sado (1931), too, bears an odd resemblance to *A Passage to India*: its emotional fulcrum is a highly charged, obliquely disastrous picnic outing. Virginia Woolf complained that *Sado* was not really a novel but an episode, and it might be called a chamber novel: like a string quartet, the book is carried by four people, who are only occasionally augmented by others. The Plomer figure is Vincent Lucas, a young painter who arrives almost accidentally in Japan, is befriended by an engineer named Komatsu and his English wife, Iris, and in turn befriends the student Sado. When he moves with Sado into Komatsu's garden house, Lucas "begins to learn how much there is that is admirable in the Japanese way of living" (p. 70), but he also confronts a racial and cultural gulf that is more profound than anything in *Turbott Wolfe.* On one level, Plomer presents a thinly veiled story of homosexual love, treated with a delicacy that is both touching and absurd: "Sado looked at him and smiled. And Lucas trembled, as if, under the midday glare, he were cold" (p. 179). More insistently, however, he addresses the threat of resurgent Japanese nationalism, which is represented by Komatsu, and the irreconcilability of cultures. Plomer suggests four responses to the "present chaos of transition in East and West": the reactionary, the revolutionary, the indifferent, and his own liberal humanist position in which "one can strive to think, to keep one's balance, to treat past and future with equal respect" (p. 163). His stance has softened from the more strident radicalism of *Turbott Wolfe*, but in the end the cultural gap remains unbridgeable: "There they were, representing respectively West and East, the reformer and the resigned" (p. 194). For all its thoughtfulness and eloquence, *Sado* is a book frustrated by its own theme.

The two novels that Plomer wrote rapidly in the early 1930s are more conventionally commercial, the work of a young freelance writer trying to earn his living as a novelist. Nevertheless, *The Case Is Altered* (1932) is interesting both as Plomer's attempt to expiate his guilty sense of having been an unwitting and improbable cause of his landlady's death and for its grotesque fascination with the murder of the character Mrs. Fernandez. The writing comes uncannily close to the rhythm and mock-rhapsodic tone of his later ballads: "And now Natalie's door was in sight. If only that door had been open, that trapdoor into peace!" (p. 292). *The Invaders* (1934), which is about a girl from the country who comes to London, is Plomer's least autobiographical novel and his least satisfactory.

Museum Pieces

His distinctive strength as a novelist lay less in imaginative originality than in transmuting his experiences, spiced with memorable and, when possible, ludicrous anecdotes, into fiction: his fifth novel, *Museum Pieces* (1952) does precisely this. It is his most accomplished book, the only one that succeeds completely on its own terms, though some readers might argue that the terms are less ambitious than those of *Turbott Wolfe* or *Sado.* It is essentially the story of Anthony Butts and his mother, Mrs. Colville-Hyde, who are transformed as Toby d'Arfey and Mrs. Mountfaucon into the "museum pieces" of the title: "'The trouble with us, my dear mother,' [Toby d'Arfey] was saying, 'is that we're museum pieces'" (p. 83). Many of the book's apparently preposterous scenes, such as when Mrs. Mountfaucon takes a lobster to the pharmacy to be chloroformed so that her son can paint it, are drawn from their eccentric lives. But the real triumph of *Museum Pieces* is Plomer's ingenious solution to the problem of narrative tone, which afflicts so much of his earlier fiction.

The book is narrated in the first person by Jane Valance, a recently widowed archivist living in modest, indeed writerly, circumstances in Tregunter Road, Earl's Court, London: "Am I," she asks herself with wicked irony, "setting out to write a memoir in the form of a novel, or a novel in the form of a memoir?" (p. 7). The answer is that Plomer is doing the former and Valance the latter. While her gender enables her to fall in love with Toby, her occupation and independence account for the enthusiastic curiosity that informs her dealings with the d'Arfey family. Although Forster's influence remains detectable, there is a new note of genially acidic satire in the writing that is strongly reminiscent of Barbara Pym, whose novels Plomer was reading for Cape. Epithets and cadences are detonated with lethal precision: "In came Mildred Purbind, in a reddish beige coat and skirt, with a regrettable fur collar to the coat, and on her head a miscarried-looking hat, obviously quite new. In her arms she carried a domed glass case of stuffed humming-birds, at which I caught the Countess casting the kind of glance that is equivalent to a shrug" (p. 73).

This impeccably sustained comic surface counterbalances the more somber underlying themes of family and fortune in terminal decline. Mrs. Mountfaucon, her house sold and her best possessions destroyed in the Blitz during World War II, ends up in a tiny flat, where she tends her balcony window boxes with a toy watering can, and dies after a fall; by this time Toby, who was confined by his illness to a bizarre nursing home, has already killed himself. Yet, despite its inescapably pessimistic conclusion, *Museum Pieces* is above all a celebration of civilized if eccentric values, of a life that "seemed to have been the expression of an insatiable appetite for something unattainable, something that included peace and power and order" (p. 255). For once, the moral peroration rings absolutely true, for Valance's voice is Plomer's, and the sentiment is earned by Plomer's life. In the postwar world, he knew he was becoming something of a museum piece himself, and he wrote no more novels.

OTHER PROSE

Plomer used the short story in two distinct ways. His early stories are essentially pendants to his first two novels and deal with matters of cultural, racial, and national identity. The best are those set in Africa, including the substantial "Ula Masondo" (in *I Speak of Africa*, 1927), which shares a setting with *Turbott Wolfe* and concerns a young African who leaves Lembuland, is corrupted by urban life in Johannesburg, and on his return home refuses to recognize his mother, who hangs herself; and "The Child of Queen Victoria" (in *The Child of Queen Victoria and Other Stories*, 1933), a steadier yet still more haunting narrative about an innocent former schoolboy's discoveries and self-discoveries while working as a station assistant. The later stories tend to be neatly turned ironic miniatures: in "No Ghosts" (in *Four Countries*), for instance, a lady novelist who visits a stately home in search of "local colour" finds it only by sitting on a freshly painted bench. This sort of anecdote also characterizes Plomer's ballads.

During the 1930s Plomer published two biographies. The first, *Cecil Rhodes* (1933), is a potboiler, though notable for the author's surprisingly frank dislike of his subject, the British administrator in South Africa; but the second, *Ali the Lion: Ali of Tebeleni, Pasha of Jannina, 1741–1822* (1936), a study of the eighteenth-century Albanian warlord Ali Pasha, is another matter altogether. Plomer relishes Ali's energetic, hedonistic violence and comments cheerfully after a particularly brutal episode: "Revenge, filial piety, despotic vanity, and lustful cruelty were all satisfied, and Ali returned to Jannina in the best of tempers" (p. 173). The book is splendidly readable and, as with all Plomer's finest work, in its most grotesque moments often irresistibly funny. His autobiographies, *Double Lives* and *At Home*, which were revised and combined as *The Autobiography of William Plomer* (1975), are also entertaining, but his reticence about his adult private life brings an odd, chilly emptiness to the later chapters.

POETRY

Plomer began his literary career as a poet and sent work to the poet and publisher Harold Monro as early as 1921, for which he received fulsome encouragement that abruptly and dismayingly dried up. It might be said that he began as a poet with more subject than form and became a poet with more form than subject. Many of the first poems he wrote in Africa are close to heightened, fragmented prose, in the manner of D. H. Lawrence, while others, such as "Ula Masondo's Dream," provide faint intimations of his later ballad style. Subsequent poems on African subjects, including most of those in his substantially revised 1973 edition of *Collected Poems*, are full of well-observed details yet flatly expressed. Japan, however, brought a welcome degree of lightness and transparency to Plomer's poetry—notably in pieces with short suspended lines, such as "White Azaleas" and "The Gingko Tree"—though it was not until his sojourn in Greece that he allowed his acute sensitivity to place to be informed by emotional directness, as it is in "Three Pinks":

> See, in the exsiccate light of Attica
> The pepper-tree garden where last night by full moon
> An old woman disturbed our intimacy
> To sell us three pinks with long stems.
>
> See now, the Acropolis is still unsunned.
> Forestall dawn with yet one more kiss,
> Last of the night or first of the day—
> Whichever way one may chance to choose to regard it.
>
> (*Collected Poems*, 1973, p. 66)

His elegy in memory of Anthony Butts, *In a Bombed House*, which was privately published in 1942, is a moving tribute to "a true eccentric" (in *Collected Poems*, 1973, p. 90), but his main poetic reputation was established by the ballads, beginning with *The Dorking Thigh* in 1945. Their tone is distinctive and instantly recognizable. They have less in common with the English poet John Betjeman—Plomer has neither his gentility nor his prosodic refinement—than with the tradition of music-hall humor typified by Max Miller. Sometimes their appeal is simply that of seaside-postcard naughtiness:

> You can safely bet that it's French Lisette,
> The pearl of Portsdown Square,
> On the game she has made her name
> And rather more than her share.
> ("French Lisette: A Ballad of Maida Vale,"
> in *Collected Poems*, 1973, p. 110)

At best they achieve an irresistible if excruciating camp knowingness, as in the opening stanza of "The Playboy of the Demi-World: 1938":

> Aloft in Heavenly Mansions, Doubleyou One—
> Just Mayfair flats, but certainly sublime—
> You'll find the abode of D'Arcy Honeybunn,
> A rose-red sissy half as old as time.
>
> (*Collected Poems*, 1973, p. 119)

By comparison, such antics as the discovery of a severed limb in a house called "Ye Kumfi Nooklet" in "The Dorking Thigh" seem schoolboyish, though that poem's popularity is indisputable. A more amusing variant on this theme is "The Flying Bum: 1944," which is based on an actual incident in which a flying bomb caused "a lightly roasted rump of horse" to land among the diners in the Tottenham Court Road vegetarian restaurant frequented by Plomer, Ackerley, and Fuller (in *Collected Poems*, 1973, p. 129).

For Plomer, the ballads were an almost perfect solution to his poetic dilemma: they enabled him to deploy his brilliant social observation and his wry satirical wit without compromising his shield for personal life. For his readers, the gain is perhaps less clear-cut: we may, after all, suspect that finer poems might have resulted if he had put more of his vulnerable self into them. There is more than a hint of Plomer's eventually feeling this too, for in his last two collections—*Taste and Remember* (1966) and *Celebrations* (1972)—he included poems of greater intimacy and frankness, such as "A Casual Encounter," which is dedicated to the memory of Constantine Cavafy, a friend of Forster's, and deals with the kind of sexual life led by Plomer thirty years earlier. In "No Identity," he takes a wry glance at his bungalow life and provides an explanation, and self-estimation, that seems both honest and accurate:

> My need
> As a poet (not every poet's) is this—
> To be immersed in a neutral solution, which

Alone provides an interim, until through the grey
Expectant film invisible writing comes clean.
(*Collected Poems*, 1973, p. 270)

CONCLUSION

William Plomer's literary career seems almost designed to resist summary. His two finest novels, the first and last, are profoundly different: one a passionate South African polemic, the other a quintessentially English tragicomedy. His development as a serious poet was diverted by an addiction to satirical ballads, yet these turned out to be among his most celebrated works. He was an eighteenth-century warlord's biographer and a nineteenth-century parson's editor. His achievement seems a procession of paradoxes.

But the truth is perhaps simpler than that: Plomer was a man whose attention was continually engaged by whatever seemed interesting or quirky, and he had the good fortune to live—at least until his retreat to Sussex—a suitably eccentric and varied life. What he wrote about was what was there. He may not have possessed great creative originality, and he was certainly inhibited by his reticence about his private life, but he was an outstanding observer and a literary professional of the best and rarest sort.

Selected Bibliography

COLLECTED WORK

Collected Poems. London: Jonathan Cape, 1960; rev. and expanded ed. London: Jonathan Cape, 1973.

SELECTED WORKS

Turbott Wolfe. London: Hogarth Press, 1925; new ed. with intro. by Laurens van der Post, London: Hogarth Press, 1965. Novel.

I Speak of Africa. London: Hogarth Press, 1927. Stories.

Notes for Poems. London: Hogarth Press, 1927. Poetry.

The Family Tree. London: Hogarth Press, 1929. Poetry.

Paper Houses. London: Hogarth Press, 1929. Stories.

Sado. London: Hogarth Press, 1931; New York: Oxford University Press, 1990. Novel.

The Case Is Altered. London: Hogarth Press, 1932. Novel.

Fivefold Screen. London: Hogarth Press, 1932. Poetry.

Cecil Rhodes. London: Peter Davies, 1933. Biography.

The Child of Queen Victoria and Other Stories. London: Jonathan Cape, 1933.

The Invaders. London: Jonathan Cape, 1934. Novel.

Ali the Lion: Ali of Tebeleni, Pasha of Jannina, 1741–1822. London: Jonathan Cape, 1936. Biography.

Visiting the Caves. London: Jonathan Cape, 1936. Poetry.

Selected Poems: London: Hogarth Press, 1940; 2d ed., 1946.

In a Bombed House, 1941: An Elegy in Memory of Anthony Butts. London: W. Plomer, 1942. Poetry.

Double Lives. London: Jonathan Cape, 1943. Autobiography.

Curious Relations, with Anthony Butts. London: Jonathan Cape, 1945. Stories.

The Dorking Thigh and Other Satires. London: Jonathan Cape, 1945. Poetry.

Four Countries. London: Jonathan Cape, 1949. Stories.

Museum Pieces. London: Jonathan Cape, 1952. Novel.

A Shot in the Park. London: Jonathan Cape, 1955. Poetry.

At Home: Memoirs. London: Jonathan Cape, 1958.

A Choice of Ballads. London: Jonathan Cape, 1960. Poetry.

Taste and Remember. London: Jonathan Cape, 1966. Poetry.

Celebrations. London: Jonathan Cape, 1972. Poetry.

The Butterfly Ball and the Grasshopper's Feast. With Alan Aldridge and Richard Fitter. London: Jonathan Cape and Times Newspapers, 1973. Poetry.

The Autobiography of William Plomer. London: Jonathan Cape, 1975.

LIBRETTOS

Gloriana, with Benjamin Britten. London: Boosey and Hawkes, 1953.

Curlew River, with Benjamin Britten. London: Faber and Faber, 1964.

The Burning Fiery Furnace, with Benjamin Britten. London: Faber Music, 1966.

The Prodigal Son, with Benjamin Britten. London: Faber Music, 1968.

EDITIONS AND TRANSLATIONS

A Japanese Lady in Europe, by Haruko Ichikawa. New York: E. P. Dutton and Company, 1937.

Kilvert's Diary, 1870–1879, by Francis Kilvert. London: Jonathan Cape, 1944.

A Message in Code, by Richard Rumbold. London: Weindenfeld and Nicolson, 1964.

Selected Poems, by Ingrid Jonker. London: Jonathan Cape, 1968.

INTRODUCTIONS

Gold Fever, by Lewis Mariano Nesbitt. New York: Harcourt, Brace and Company, 1936.

To the Mountain, by Bradford Smith. London: Hamish Hamilton, 1936.

Redburn, by Herman Melville. London: Jonathan Cape, 1937.

Selected Poems, by Herman Melville. London: Hogarth Press, 1943.

Billy Budd, by Herman Melville. London: John Lehmann, 1947.

In the Year of Jubilee, by George Gissing. London: Watergate Classics, 1947.

A Life's Morning, by George Gissing. London: Home and Van Thal, 1947.

Saturday Night at the Greyhound, by John Hampson. London: Eyre and Spottiswoode, 1950.

White Jacket, by Herman Melville. London: John Lehmann, 1952.

The Dark Child, by Camara Laye. Trans. by James Kirkup. London: Collins, 1955.

Victory, by Joseph Conrad. London: Oxford University Press, 1957.

South Africa, by Hanns Reich. New York: Hill and Wang, 1961.

Unto Dust, by Herman Charles Bosman. Cape Town, South Africa: Human and Rousseau, 1963.

The Last Tribal War, by Richard Freislich. Cape Town, South Africa: Struik, 1964.

South of the Zambesi: Poems from South Africa, by Guy Butler. London: Abelard-Schuman, 1966.

Friedlander, Zelda, ed. *Until the Heart Changes: A Garland for Olive Schreiner.* Cape Town, South Africa: Tafelberg-Uitgewers, 1967.

The World My Wilderness, by Rose Macaulay. London: Collins, 1968.

CRITICAL STUDIES

Alexander, Peter F. *William Plomer: A Biography.* Oxford, U.K.: Oxford University Press, 1989.

Atkinson, Michael. "Three Approaches to the Study of English: Milton's *Samson Agonistes*; Plomer's *A Shot in the Park*; Ken Kesey's Fiction." Master's thesis, Pennsylvania State University, 1967.

Doyle, John Robert. *William Plomer.* New York: Twayne, 1969.

Oxley, William. *Areopagus; or, A View of the Acropolis of Poetry: Two Gentlemen of Voorslag, Roy Campbell and William Plomer.* Salzburg, Austria: Institut für Anglistik und Amerikanistik, Universität Salzburg, 1982.

Ross, Alan, ed. "About William Plomer." In *London Magazine* 13 (December 1973/January 1974); special issue devoted to Plomer on the seventieth anniversary of his birth.

Toerien, Barend J. "Selected Poems." In *World Literature Today* 63 (summer 1989).

Touhy, Frank. Review of *Sado.* In *Times Literary Supplement* (27 September 1991).

Ola Rotimi

1938–

MARTIN BANHAM

OLA ROTIMI (Emmanuel Gladstone Olawale Rotimi), a Nigerian playwright, was born on 13 April 1938 in Sapele, a town in what is now Delta State. His mother, Dorcas Oruene Addo Rotimi, was a Nembe, an Ijọ people, from the Rivers State of Eastern Nigeria, and his father, Samuel Enitan Rotimi was an Egba, one of the Yoruba people. The ethnicity of Rotimi's parents is worth noting because marriage between people from different cultural and linguistic backgrounds within Nigeria has never been commonplace, and the bane of Nigeria since independence has been the creation of political camps based primarily, and aggressively, on ethnic loyalties. Rotimi's work consistently highlights the need to forge political and cultural unity out of diversity. In his plays, he brings together languages and performance traditions from all over Nigeria to create a unified expression. The critic Reuben Abati emphasizes the nationalist scope of Rotimi's work:

> Rotimi's nationalism derives from [a] concern with truth and justice and is observable in the structures he presses to dramatic service. Many national dramatists are handicapped by their almost literal adherence, perhaps by accident, to the notion that all national literatures are local before being national. In other words the national dramatist works within the confines of a native culture; he then transcends the given boundaries to espouse a vision that is national and universal, informed by the survival of a larger race. In Rotimi, the very fact of nationality is in-built in his drama . . . the whole of Nigeria is Rotimi's laboratory.
>
> (*Guardian*, Lagos, 15 May 1993, p. 7)

The radicalism in Rotimi's work may also owe something to his father's role as an active trade-union organizer in Lagos, the former Nigerian capital. His plays also reflect his formal training in playwriting: from 1959 to 1963, he was a student of fine arts at Boston University, as a Nigerian federal government scholar in theater arts; and from 1963 to 1966, he was a Rockefeller Foundation scholar in playwriting at Yale University, where he earned a master's degree in fine arts. He returned to Nigeria in 1966 as a research fellow in drama at the University of Ife, which later became Obafemi Awolowo University, where he coined the title for the university acting company, the Ori Olokun Players, and was acting head of the Department of Dramatic Arts from 1975 to 1977. In 1977 he moved to the University of Port Harcourt in Rivers State, Nigeria. In 1991 he returned to Obafemi Awolowo University and started a professional theater group called the African Cradle Theatre (ACT), which staged three widely acclaimed productions before funding problems caused it to close. As defined by

Rotimi, the mission of ACT was "to animate both the traditional and modern cultures of our African people" (Abati, p. 7). He remained at Obafemi Awolowo University until 1994, when he moved to the United States.

EARLY PLAYS

Our Husband Has Gone Mad Again

His first two plays, *Our Husband Has Gone Mad Again* (1977) and *To Stir the God of Iron* (unpublished), were written when Rotimi was a student in the United States. The first is a lighthearted satire that centers on the political ambitions of a former military officer, Lejoka-Brown, who is vain and self-seeking. Although the play's action is farcical, it gained an increasing and awful relevance as Nigeria moved from one military government to the next. Not surprisingly, the play remained popular and was staged in 1993 to contribute to the thirty-second UNESCO (United Nations Educational, Scientific, and Cultural Organization) International Theater Day in Nigeria's new capital, Abuja. Lejoka-Brown's problems begin when his new wife arrives from the United States, a development that takes his political ally, Okonkwo, by surprise:

OKONKWO: You... have a third wife?
LEJOKA-BROWN: Hunh? No no, no—this woman who is arriving from America is not my *third* wife.
OKONKWO: Oh, I thought you said...
LEJOKA-BROWN: She is my *second* wife...
OKONKWO: Hunh?
LEJOKA-BROWN: Although she thinks she's the *first*, but that's beside the point.

(I, i, p. 8)

In this play, Rotimi effectively contrasts the ridiculous postures of men—particularly the preposterous Lejoka-Brown—with the determination of women to unite against exploitation. Rotimi won the award for the best student drama at Yale in 1966 for this play, which shows a considerable ingenuity, confidence in stagecraft, and an ability to control multiple locations without the loss of theatrical pace. Rotimi's ear for the nuances of language and his appreciation for a range of physical and vocal action, qualities that become more sophisticated in his later work, are also evident.

To Stir the God of Iron

To Stir the God of Iron, which he wrote in Boston in 1962–1963, is loosely based on the story in the biblical Gospel of John of the woman taken in adultery (and possibly also on the medieval play of that title). There are three versions of the play, which was refashioned in Nigerian terms as *Cast the First Stone* (1968) and *When Criminals Turn Judges*, which was broadcast by the British Broadcasting Corporation (BBC) in 1990. The "Nigerianization" of the two later versions is slight and mainly a matter of updating events to reflect the changes in Nigeria. In the original play the rich adulterer is the proud owner of a Raleigh bicycle; in the radio play his wealth is expressed through his motorcycle, "Kawasaki 125—double silencer"! In the first version the wronged husband has been crippled fighting the Germans in World War II; in the radio version he is a victim of the Nigerian civil war (1967–1970), which he angrily refers to when addressing those who taunt his wife as "your civil war." In a typically Nigerian fashion, the linguistic images respond to the changing world: one character in the play tells another that "like the engine of the Volkswagen, your brain is housed in your buttocks!" As in the biblical tale, those who would cast the stones (literally, in the action of the play) are seen to be full of sin themselves; for instance, the Pharisee figure is "Bar Jesus," a drunken evangelist. The play is an attempt to fuse protest and satire with religious hypocrisy. The protest is most evident in the radio version, in which criminals and rich exploiters are depicted as the despoilers of society, but its basic success is in the flexible adaptation of a traditional moral tale to the Nigerian context.

MAJOR DRAMA, 1966–1970

Rotimi's reputation was established with three major dramas that he wrote and staged after returning to Nigeria in 1966: *The Gods Are Not to Blame* (1971), *Kurunmi* (1971), and *Ovonramwen Nogbaisi* (1974). These plays were first staged at the Ori Olokun Cultural Centre of the Institute of African Studies, University of Ife, for the occasion of the annual Ife Festival of the Arts in 1968, 1969, and 1971, respectively.

The Gods Are Not to Blame

In *The Gods Are Not to Blame*, Rotimi reworks Sophocles' *Oedipus Rex* in Yoruba terms. Talking to the Nigerian critic Dapo Adelugba, Rotimi said: "The decision to write on the *Oedipus Rex* saga posed no problem at all. . . . Nigeria was in the throes of a civil war flared by ethnic distrust. A shattering tragedy like Oedipus's calamity should bring out the warning against this cancerous foible, I thought" (in Dapo Adelugba, ed., *LACE Occasional Publications* 1, 23 June 1984, University of Ibadan, pp. 26–27). Rotimi also refers to the cultural similarities between the Greek and Yoruba worldviews, which he felt would make Nigerian audiences sympathetic to the play. The Oedipus figure is King Odewale, who is led with appropriate dramatic irony to his awful fate. The title of the play, however, makes an important statement: Rotimi suggests that the king—and perhaps leaders in general—finds it too convenient to blame disaster on external forces rather than accept responsibility. The plague that settles on the people through their leader's vanity and transgressions works as a metaphor for the evils of civil war.

While powerfully revising Sophocles' drama, Rotimi created a work that succeeds in its own right. The play gave the first evidence of his taste and flair for large-scale productions as he exploits a wide range of indigenous theatrical means, such as music, musical instruments, song, dance, and ritual chants, in an effort to create a trans-Nigerian theatrical idiom. Rotimi described in his lecture delivered at the University of Benin on 4 May 1987, "The Trials of African Literature," the language of the play as English "domesticated," a term he uses to convey a traditional linguistic identity that enables him to "catch the mode of traditional African parlance." (Rotimi's interest in the debate over the appropriate language for African authors to use is central to his 1991 inaugural lecture as a professor at the University of Port Harcourt, "African Dramatic Literature: To Be or to Become.") The 1968 Ife Festival production of *The Gods Are Not to Blame* established him as a director of extraordinary skill, capable of a dynamic use of large casts, epic themes, and innovative performance spaces.

Kurunmi

Kurunmi is set during the Ijaiye (a group of Yoruba people) wars of the late nineteenth century. The conservative Kurunmi, "Generalissimo of the Yoruba Empire and Lord of Ijaiye," resists a change in the traditional rights of succession of the Alafin, or King of the Oyo (a Yoruba state) Empire. His resistance precipitates a bloody civil war among the constituent Yoruba camps within the empire. Kurunmi's position is ambiguous. He fights for what he believes to be right, but he is stubborn and inflexible. He loses his sons in the bloodshed and dies by his own hand, bewildered and destroyed. But he is presented with dignity, wit, and compassion; particularly in his exchanges with the Christian missionary, the Reverend Adolphus Mann, he emerges as a man of wisdom. At the heart of the play is a world of intriguing and double-dealing politics, where changes in the practice of government may be interpreted as either advancing with the times or maneuvering for advantage. The play carries a dedication to "The Palm Trees of Ijaiye," which is complemented by the verse:

> The palm trees will
> grimly
> show you, if you care,
> the scars from bullets
> shot over a hundred years ago
> but
> they will say
> *nothing.*

This poem reinforces the parallels between the historical events that Rotimi examines and the destructive split in the political ranks of the Yoruba people: the conflict in the 1960s between the Action Group of Chief Obafemi Awolowo and the rival Nigerian National Democratic Party of his erstwhile deputy leader, Chief Samuel Ladoke Akintola, led to a breakdown of law and order in Western Nigeria and indirectly to the civil war. The Nigerian actor-playwright Hubert Ogunde responded to this same split with his play *Yoruba ronu* (1964; Yoruba think), which led to his company being banned from performing in Western Nigeria. Rotimi's reference is more oblique than Ogunde's but nonetheless exact.

Ovonramwen Nogbaisi

Ovonramwen Nogbaisi also takes its title from a historical figure, the king of the Benin Empire from 1888 to 1897 and the man attacked, along with his people, by the British punitive expedition of 1897. Rotimi, in a note to the play, observes that Oba Ovonramwen Nogbaisi was a man "long portrayed by the biases of Colonial History in the mien of the most abominable sadist" (p. xi). In the play, Rotimi challenges that viewpoint and shows how the ignorance and blundering prejudice of the colonial authorities caused the horrific bloodshed during the sacking of Benin. Once again he portrays a traditional ruler attempting to hold his people together in a rapidly changing world, but he is mostly concerned with rehabilitating the memory of a man who was humiliated and misrepresented by the colonial power in order to justify its own expansionary ambitions. Rotimi expresses how underneath the pretense of a civilizing mission there was explicit acceptance that the purpose of colonial conquest was economic. When a British officer in the military column asks, "Why the insistence on entering Benin in spite of the Oba's objections?" the vice-consul of the Niger Coast Protectorate answers, "Commerce, Mr Campbell! That is your answer!" (p. 31). In his play *Death and the King's Horseman* (1975), the Nigerian dramatist Wole Soyinka offers another view of the tragic human consequences of the insensitive and ignorant action of a colonial power, but Rotimi's play emphatically identifies the hypocrisy of so much colonial action.

Ovonramwen Nogbaisi remained popular and pertinent decades after it was published. A production in Lagos in May 1992 brought warm critical appreciation:

> The personality of Oba Ovonramwen Nogbaisi is no longer conceived as the "bloodthirsty king" as depicted by Europeans. Rather, the king is upheld...as a courageous leader who was provoked to the defence of a rich cultural heritage entrusted to him by his ancestors.
>
> (Muyiwa Awodiya, in *Daily Times*, Lagos, 6 June 1992, p. 12)

> It presents a lasting touchstone on which the relationship between Africa and the metropolitan west is evaluated.
>
> (Ben Iwala-Tomoloju, in *Guardian*, Lagos, 16 May 1992)

In a preview of the 1992 production published in the *Guardian*, Lagos, of 18 April 1992, Jahman Anikulapo wrote that Rotimi's message in the play "is that African nations would remain in economic and cultural bondage until they break away from the control of Europe and the West."

There have been more cautious and critical responses to the play, which point, perhaps, to the hazards of treating historical subject matter. Chris Dunton, in a careful and detailed analysis, suggests that its limitation "stems from Rotimi's refusal to undertake a more radical inquiry into the political structures of (in this case) an absolutist regime" (p. 21) and that "the dominant image is of a figure trapped by his own increasingly aghast realization of the dangers of making wrong decisions, whose vision of power leads him deeper and deeper into a helpless sclerosis" (p. 23). Brian Crow has suggested, in interesting relationship to the quoted comments of the newspaper critics, that the play might, in fact, be seen entirely as sympathetic to Ovonramwen Nogbaisi—an African leader beleaguered by colonial or neocolonial forces—and "arouse in the audience a regretful nostalgia" that could be used as an excuse for present-day failings (p. 23). As Crow suggests, there is the risk in writing a history play of having one's contemporary meaning trapped in the seductive fascination of the subject.

Akassa Youmi

Another historical play, *Akassa youmi* (*Part One*) (Akassa war), which was unpublished as of 1996, was produced by Rotimi in 1977. The play is set among the people of the Niger Delta, in particular the Nembe area, and concerns the Akassa raid of 1895 when Koko, King of Brass, led a bloody revolt against the Royal Niger Company. Under the leadership of the adventurer Sir George Goldie, the company was establishing a trading stranglehold on the area and destroying the livelihood of the local people. Koko had been converted to Christianity and Europeanized in dress and manner, but, provoked by the behavior of Goldie's men, he threw aside his new religion and, invoking the charms of his people's traditional deities, set out to war. Thomas Packenham in *The Scramble for Africa 1876–1912* (1991) details the consequences:

> The Brassmen wreaked vengeance on the Company's boatyard and engineering workshops, and massacred the Kru-boys who worked for the Company. About seventy-five natives were shot or hacked to death in their shanties; others were trussed up and taken off in the war canoes. Later that morning the defenceless British Vice-Consul at Brass was astounded to see canoe-loads of prisoners brought back to the town, with drums beating and flags flying. The majority were then cooked and eaten during an orgy of human sacrifice.
>
> (p. 463)

Part One of Rotimi's drama ends with the victorious Brassmen returning to their lands before the incident described by Packenham. The essence of the play to this point is the conversion of Koko from docile Christian to war leader. Throughout the first part, Rotimi stresses how the company and its agents provoked the Brass. In the opening scene, a young Nembe woman is humiliated by "the Whitemen and their black Krooboys! Who else?" which alludes to a rape committed by a company clerk that caused outrage at the time. Koko changes from the man taught to turn the other cheek into the leader "Shark-That-Knows-No-Rest!" who outmaneuvers the fainthearted and the Christians among the other leaders of the community and joins with the guerrilla leader "Crocodile-Without-Shame" to launch the attack on the company.

Despite the horrors of the actual historical incident, the colonial government saw enough fault in the company's position not to launch a punitive strike against Koko. However, the company itself was politically too strong to be moved, and the Brassmen were, in Packenham's words, "left to starve" (p. 465).

A number of interesting features in the play parallel the issues and methodology of *Kurunmi* and *Ovonramwen Nogbaisi*. The way that factionalism allows people to be exploited is again highlighted with contemporary relevance. A historical figure is re-examined more sympathetically from a Nigerian point of view. The scale of the play is daunting as it moves rapidly from one location to another with a potential cast of hundreds. Rotimi's use of proverb often makes for witty and authentic dialogue, as in the following exchange between Koko and Crocodile-Without-Shame:

CHIEF KOKO:	You will be patient with me till tomorrow.
C-W-S:	Patience! Patience is plantain and fish in a pot—quick to finish.
CHIEF KOKO:	Crocodile, you talk too boldly—don't forget I am the shark himself.
C-W-S:	The boasting shark is meat for the crocodile in water!
CHIEF KOKO:	The boasting of the crocodile ends in the water—when it drifts to land it becomes meat, as you are now in my pot!
C-W-S:	The boasting pot must take care lest it crack on the fire.
CHIEF KOKO:	The boasting of Fire ends in the face of water from the cracked pot!
C-W-S:	The boasting of Water vanishes in the face of hot ground.
CHIEF KOKO:	The boasting of hot ground means nothing to the hoe!
C-W-S:	The boasting of the Hoe is useless to the ground with rocks.

In personal correspondence Rotimi has said he plans to write Part Two of *Akassa youmi,* which he describes as a "metaphor for contemporary politico-economic striving of the African peoples." With this extraordinary story of his mother's Nembe people only partially told, Rotimi plans to apply the violent ending of the events of 1895 to Nigeria a century later. In an interview with Dunton, Rotimi explained that in Part Two he will look at Koko "in isolation, in the village where he was exiled, ruminating on the problems of leadership, on the mistakes he might have made" (p. 153).

Holding Talks

In 1979 Rotimi published *Holding Talks,* which was first staged in 1970, and staged *If: A Tragedy of the Ruled* (published in 1983). Both plays take him away from the past and firmly into the present. *Holding Talks* is subtitled *An Absurdist Drama,* though it might more accurately be described as witty satire. It is a short play, set in a poverty-stricken barber shop. The play begins with the almost immediate death of the barber, and the action consists of endless talk between a customer referred to only as Man and the barber's apprentice, with occasional set-piece intrusions from the outside world represented by a blind beggar, his boy-guide, a press photographer, and an outwitted policewoman. As Rotimi says in a note to the play, "In this play, nothing really gets done. Things get close to being done; but nothing gets really done because there is always some justifiable rationalization for that which really needs to be done not to be done." The comment on Nigerian life is self-evident. The play has in situation, language, and action a macabre humor and a strong theatrical framework. Moments of inaction are endlessly and comically extended, and meaningless routines of dialogue are played with for their own enjoyment, which partly explains why Rotimi described this play as absurdist. For instance, as soon as Man is seated in the barber's "rusty swivel chair," an elaborate farce is played out with a fan:

APPRENTICE:	Music, sir?
	[*Without interrupting his humming, Man shakes his head.*]
MAN:	No.
	[*He points at the standing fan.*]
APPRENTICE:	Yes sir.
	[*He crosses over to the location of the fan. He turns the knob to activate the fan. Naturally, everybody looks in that direction, expecting results. The vanes begin to revolve, slowly, very slowly.*]

MAN: High, put it on high.
APPRENTICE: Yes sir.
[*Clicks knob farther, clockwise. Again, everybody stares in anticipation. Fan refuses to pick up speed.*]
MAN: Is that maximum?
APPRENTICE: No, sir, this is high, sir. Do you want maximum, sir?
MAN: Maximum, yes, try maximum.
APPRENTICE: Yes sir.
[*Fumbles with knob again, turning it as far as it can go. Suddenly—an effect! A funny clanking rattle of rusty metal in harsh friction with rusty cogs issues forth from the axle of the fan. But the revolution remains at the same rate: slow, defiant, indolent.*]
MAN: Is that maximum?
APPRENTICE: Maximum, sir. Yes sir.
BARBER: That is maximum, sir.
MAN: I see. Let him try high again, then.
BARBER: Go back to high.
APPRENTICE: Yes, sir.
[*Turns. Noises vanish, but the speed of revolution is unchanged.*]
MAN: Good, now put it down to low, very low.
APPRENTICE: Yes, sir.
[*Turns. No difference.*]
MAN: Better... very good. Leave it like that. Very good.
[*Resumes humming.*]

(pp. 2–3)

In a production of the play staged by ACT in December 1992, Rotimi played Man and the decrepit barbershop bore the slogan "Kalamazoo Barbaring Corner; A Tryal Will Convict You." Critic Oji Onoko, reviewing the production in the *African Concord* of 21 December 1992, saw the play as "a scathing satire on those whose lot it is to get things done but rather choose to do nothing in the name of 'conferences, symposia, lectures, meetings'" ("Rooting for Excellence," p. 48). The latter point is made explicit in the opening moment of the play, when the Apprentice with "nothing to do... is leafing through the pages of some tattered newspapers, stopping now and again to read out, in an unfeeling, idle drawl, the captions on some of the pages—all of which report on TALKS—all species of TALKS: national, international, continental, intercontinental—you name it" (p. 1). In *Holding Talks* Rotimi employs comedy—albeit dark comedy—to explore his theme, but in *If* the tone is angrier and more somber.

If: A Tragedy of the Ruled

In a personal note to the present writer at the time of the publication of *If*, Rotimi wrote, "*If* marks a departure from my earlier creative directions, and the beginning of a new phase both in style and concerns." While in the earlier plays he had obliquely concerned himself with political crises, his new plan, despite the essentially indirect and metaphorical approach of much African art to its subject, was to be more explicit. The dedication of the play, after a personal consecration, is "to the New Generation of the Ruled, menaced by the incubus of an eternal drift" (p. v). The action is arranged in a series of "Happenings." The setting is the courtyard or compound of a one-level apartment building, which works perfectly with the open-air courtyard theater that Rotimi prefers. His concern for the way the play should work in action is conveyed by "A Note on the Dynamics of This Production": "This... is a drama of juxtaposed, variegated actions: a further exploration of theatrical 'naturalness' in the evocation of African atmosphere and rhythms through time, space, sound and matter" (p. viii).

As this note implies, and the structure of the play reinforces, the varied life of the characters of this compound is presented with a naturalness that subordinates the development of a single story line to the cumulative development of a picture of persecution, poverty, prejudice, and corruption in the face of which the residents either fight or succumb. Often this fullness is effected with considerable technical skill as concurrent scenes are controlled by a shifting focus. The residents of the compound are a microcosm of Nigerian society in terms of class, occupation, religion, and linguistic origin. Dominating them at the outset is the landlord, who abuses his control of their mean accommodations and seeks political power through blackmail. As the action develops, the residents find ways of working together to assert their rights and dignity, though the end of the play remains pessimistic.

A major thread running through the action is education. The honored senior person in the compound is a retired teacher, Papa; a gifted young boy, Onyema, represents the hopes and aspirations of youth that may be achieved through education. Onyema's death toward the end of the play works as a comment on the violence of the world around him and a gesture of despair. Banji (alias "Di Law"), a fellow resident, gives his obituary:

> That's Onyema's response, his own answer to a Society rife with contradictions. He saw what happened at the party. A rich man brandishing his loathsome power so much so... it provoked even the deaf and dumb....
>
> Later he again was witness to the consequences of Affluence disgraced by the deaf and dumb. The arrest and brutal manhandling of the common man proved too revolting for his young mind to bear. He must have asked himself one question: does a boy like him, honest and sensitive—does he stand a chance in a nation with no value for the dignity of man? A nation where Money and Position mean everything? What is the future of our *children*? Indeed *where* is the future of Africa herself?
>
> (pp. 79–80)

The play incorporates many similar moments where the political message is forefronted. Hamidu, a young medical doctor (alias "Ernesto Che Guevara") doing his national youth service idealistically in a town distant from his home, gives a powerful oration that centers on the play's title: "*IF* the masses, the oppressed masses—...for a change will use their votes as tools for their own freedom. *IF* that fails, then mass-struggle becomes imperative....The day one poor man starts loving another poor man, is the day the oppressors start shitting in their pants (pp. 16–17). Various panacea—Christianity, Marxism, education—are advocated for the relief of oppression. Rotimi portrays Christians as decent and well-intentioned, but essentially passive and accepting, looking for ultimate relief in heaven; Marxism as frustrated by the lack of any coherent sense of class solidarity within the community and offering no solution to society's problems; and education as tantalizingly beyond the reach of the needy. Individuals and families struggle to survive with "*IF* only" their common refrain.

Like *The Gods Are Not to Blame*, *If* demands attention to the issue of language, which Rotimi implicitly identifies as the essential tool at the heart of matters of unity and progress. The play uses standard English, variants of English, pidgin, and indigenous languages. In many cases, these languages indicate the educational background of the speaker, but pidgin, for instance, is also used to give a witty and effective dynamic to specific characters. Adiagha (alias "Mama Ukot"), wife of Akpan (alias "Ten Trouble, One God"), storms out on her husband, accusing him of putting his pursuit of academic and professional qualifications before the provision of food for the family and of being misled by the political debates within the compound:

> Money no dey, money no dey, but the crazeman dey buy book.... Everyday a return work; e eat; open book; e go come butu, dey talk grammar with Che Guevara and Banji. Den e go begin sing: "Tio lele, tio lele...Nigeria will be great!" Nigeria go great, Nigeria go great: na by sing nahim country dey take great? Ehn? No be inside belle nahim person dey take know country wey great?...Dis Che Guevara, abi na Che

Guava, weder na Che Paw-paw abi na che Banana him say him be sef—di man be doctor. Banji get degree for lawyer. My man yon na Njakiri: suffer-head! Money no know him face; chop no know my belle."

(pp. 38–39)

Adiagha's punning on Che Guevara (Guava/Paw-paw/Banana) provides rich comedy, but the pidgin also allows Adiagha to voice her frustration powerfully. Other less formally educated characters use proverbs to explain their position, as does Betty, the landlord's sometime girlfriend who is accused by other women in the compound of being a prostitute (a "bamboat" in pidgin). She offers a proverb to say that things may not be as they seem on the surface: "Na who say fowl no dey sweat for body, because feder no gree person see sweat?" (p. 15). Such devices are not only verbally engaging, but also extremely effective in the theatrical context in which Rotimi is working. Audiences familiar with the proverbs immediately understand them, invest them with further dimensions of meaning, and often respond with approving comments. A more remarkable instance of Rotimi's exploration of innovative uses of language comes in an extended dialogue in which a Kalabari fisherman is introduced into the action for one scene, seeking help for the plight of the fishermen of the rivers. In this scene, Rotimi uses translation as a dramatic device and underlines the way in which language can be used to divide and rule. Rosa, an occupant of the compound, who has the fisherman with her, addresses Banji, the lawyer:

MAMA ROSA: [*Introducing Fisherman*] Dis na my broder wey I go bail now-now for Police Station, sah. Dem catch am for fishing-port say e no pay tax. Monday na court. Broder, I no know anybody for dis country. I beg, make you help me.

BANJI: I see. What really happened?

MAMA ROSA: [*to Fisherman, in Kalabari language*] Mioku, duko o pirii. Ye goyegoye duko o pirii. [*Meaning: Now tell him. Tell him everything*]

FISHERMAN: Duko o pirii, yeri njibabo.

MAMA ROSA: He say him be Fisherman.

FISHERMAN: Tari i da so njibaboo.

MAMA ROSA: Him papa na fisherman.

FISHERMAN: Ida da so tari njibaboo.

MAMA ROSA: Him papa-papa, na fisherman.

FISHERMAN: Toru me anie wamina dumo doki yee.

MAMA ROSA: Na river be dem life.

FISHERMAN: Mioku torume dikibujiri ofori bara ke fi korotee.

MAMA ROSA: Now di river done spoil finish.

FISHERMAN: Pulo-ida ogbome pulo ke toru memgba wasama famatee!

MAMA ROSA: Oil Company dem done pour oil for all di river.

FISHERMAN: Wamina pembe kurukuru apu so benki bu sote pulo. Ke wamina njiba toruma buu sara famatee.

MAMA ROSA: Our Black people dem done join white people, take oil spoil di river.

FISHERMAN: Mioku wamini njibapuma gbosibi fikorotee. Deri nji so bari oforii, pei be ye so. Mioku wa eri bari ye pulo sukume minji torume wasamate gba wa dikiari!

MAMA ROSA: Fisherman dem no get anytin again. Fish for sell no dey; fish to eat sef, no dey. So-so black oil full up for river, dey look dem for face!

FISHERMAN: Tombo namakoriba, te ani buu igbigi nyanaba tereme anie mbo inete komsini oso-igbigi gbeba ani bara oko-a?

MAMA ROSA: a nim... [*meaning: that's right*] Person go work, get money before he pay tax, no be so?

FISHERMAN: A biim o gboru ye mie wa pirii. O mie bari munoso o mie bia-a?

MAMA ROSA: He wan to beg you to do one ting for am. He say: you go fit?

BANJI: What is it?
MAMA ROSA: Anie tie?
FISHERMAN: Wa alagba biari.
MAMA ROSA: E say make you give dem gun.
BANJI: Give them what?
MAMA ROSA: Gun, gun!
FISHERMAN: O duko ke Komsini pirii mine ini alagba ke wa pirii miete wa inote Pulo-ida-ogbome na owuso bari bara.
MAMA ROSA: He say tell Gov'ment make Gov'ment give dem gun to fight di Oil Company dem.

...

FISHERMAN: Pulo-ida-ogbome na owusome mweni Komsinime balafamari bebe wamini njibapuma wa balafa-aa. Kuma yee Komsinime pa anie mie ke wa pirii. Alagba ke wa pirii. Fatee.
MAMA ROSA: If Gov'ment dey fear di oil people, di fisherman dem no dey fear. So, tell Gov'ment to give dem gun. Das all.
BANJI: I see... Tell him that that won't work.
MAMA ROSA: Ori mee anie sarasara-aaa.
FISHERMAN: Tie gote?
MAMA ROSA: Why?
BANJI: Tell him it is the same Government that has given power to the Oilmen to look for oil in the river.
MAMA ROSA: Ori mee paa gbori Komsini anie koro ke pulo-ida piriye mine n pulo idaa toruma bio.
FISHERMAN: [*incredulously*] Komsini, I-ya-h! [*meaning: Our Government? Impossible!*]
BANJI: And that Government will arrest anybody who dares to disturb the Oilmen!
MAMA ROSA: Ani saki Komsini mbo oloba ani boo te pulo-ida dasema boo.
FISHERMAN: Kura pulome ani wa bari.
MAMA ROSA: But di oil dey kill dem.
BANJI: It's the oil that gives life to the nation.
MAMA ROSA: Ori mee pulome anie dumo ke se me piriari ye.

Fisherman lowers to a squat, unnerved, confused.

(pp. 25–27)

The constant need for translation in this scene authenticates both the characters and the situation and is a device Rotimi explores more fully in *Hopes of the Living Dead* (1988). The scene is also interesting in terms of the structure of the play. The fisherman has no further role in the action but is brought in to show another face of exploitation. His dilemma was familiar to the audience at Port Harcourt for which this play was originally created, since this is the part of Nigeria, in the delta of the river Niger, where the major impact of exploration and drilling for oil has been felt, with the consequent distortion of the economy and ecology of the area.

In *If*, Rotimi fully engages the contemporary political debate within Nigeria. At times, however, his point of view is presented without subtlety and in language and form that verge on agitprop. The New Nigerian Youths' Brigade, for instance, sings a song proclaiming:

> Self-reliance self-help
> This is the only way
> The only way, the only way
> To build a great nation.
>
> (pp. 58–59)

The play's achievement, however, is in creating a rich, diverse, and truthful picture of life in the compound and to make it relevant to the life of the nation. It does so not only through the power of the central message but also through its wit, humor, and humanity.

Reviewing in *Newswatch* a 1993 Ibadan production of *If*, the Nigerian critic and poet Niyi Osundare wrote:

> the rulers are the dream-killers. This play invites us to a comparison between the ruler who takes without giving, who commands everyone without obeying anyone, an emperor separated from the people by distances littered with decrees and edicts, by centuries of medieval *shogunism*. In full contrast to this is the leader who is also the best follower, who is always with the led, sharing their pains and their pleasures, shrewd; empowered by foresight... Nigeria, Rotimi seems to be telling us, is a country

> waiting for the right person at the helm... who through honesty, persistence, consistency and visionary intelligence will be able to transform our millennial handicap into revolutionary advantage.
>
> ("Endless Search," 21 June 1993, p. 38)

Osundare relates the debate directly to the struggle to return Nigeria (and much of Africa) to stable democratic rule and to free it from military dictatorships. His reference to the shogun points to Rotimi's direct confrontation with immediate and potentially dangerous issues in this play.

Hopes of the Living Dead

Hopes of the Living Dead returns to one feature of the earlier plays in that it takes a historical incident as its inspiration, but with a firm allegorical intent and a sophistication of the dramaturgical experiments that Rotimi began in *If*. The play is based on the life of Ikoli Harcourt Whyte (1905–1977). Harcourt Whyte has an enduring reputation as a composer of choral music, but the play is about him as someone afflicted with leprosy. Together with forty other lepers, Harcourt Whyte was, in 1924, treated in Port Harcourt General Hospital in an experimental program initiated by Dr. Fergusson, a Scot. On Fergusson's departure, the experiment was discontinued and the colonial authorities attempted to disperse the lepers without the prospect of further treatment. The lepers were led in their resistance to this move by Harcourt Whyte, who rejected attempts by the authorities to bribe him away from their struggle with the offer of special privileges. He demanded from his fellow patients self-reliance and self-help, and the triumphant finale of the play records the establishment of the Uzuakoli Leper Settlement where the people could live in security, work for themselves, and receive appropriate treatment. The vulnerability among the patients that the authorities hoped to exploit was the diversity in their backgrounds and languages. The unity that Harcourt Whyte demanded meant surmounting the ignorance and prejudice created by these divisions. The parallel with the political unity of present-day Nigeria is clear.

Hopes of the Living Dead is a genuinely exciting and moving story that is all the more effective because it is essentially true; it also is relevant to the ills of contemporary society. Theatrically the play is energized by the suspenseful action, Rotimi's skill at creating characters, splendid moments of physical farce and verbal comedy, and Harcourt Whyte's songs and music. This play requires a cast of about thirty performers plus singers and includes more than fifteen languages. Rotimi takes the linguistic experiments in *If* to their logical conclusion: in a multilingual nation all languages can be and are used simultaneously, and "translation" is effected with a surprising degree of ease and fluency.

These experiments with language are the political heart of the work. In a review of a production of the play at Ibadan University, Osundare describes language as

> a vehicle for [the play's] thematic thrust. So many times the stage turns into a cacophony of tribes as each character shouts his desperation in his own language. At such moments, tension takes possession and communal unity receives a savage punch. It is part of the abiding optimism of the play, however, that "though tribe and tongue may differ," a common problem steers the people towards a unified goal.
>
> ("Parables of Hope," in *West Africa*, 28 October 1985, p. 2268)

Osundare also points out that in *Hopes of the Living Dead* Rotimi, for the first time, creates a woman character, Harcourt Whyte's co-leader Hannah, who holds a dominant position of community leadership. The optimism that Osundare notes in *Hopes of the Living Dead* contrasts strongly with the pessimism of *If*, but in other ways the plays work within a similar form. The single setting this time is the hospital, from which the lepers refuse to move and where they fight their battles, verbal and physical, internal and external. The play divides into three parts entitled "Crisis," "Strain of Leadership," and "Solidarity and Movement." Each part is subdivided into "Happenings." Again, Rotimi aims to avoid the limitations of linear plotting and to create an environment where the passing of time is less relevant than the building of communal will. As with *If*, small self-contained incidents contribute to this total picture. In a typical incident, one of the patients, known by his alias, "Catechist," returns from an unexplained absence from the hospital, bringing with him a family of beggars, man, woman, and child. His action suggests that even the poorest and most afflicted can see someone who is worse off than they. The refrain "each one tell one" punctuates the action and sets off a chain of simultaneous translation in which English is translated to Hausa, Hausa to Yoruba, Yoruba to Igbo, Igbo to Tiv, and so on through the range of languages shared by the patients. The exchange between the fisherman, Mama Rosa, and Banji in *If* is here infinitely extended in its possibilities.

The following example shows how the "each one tell one" refrain is both made explicit in terms of one recorded act of translation and implicit in terms of the imagined (and required) stage action, where murmured simultaneous translations complement and animate the action. It should be remembered in this context that some members of the play's various audiences in Nigeria will be knowledgeable in one or more of the specific languages used; thus the audience to varying degrees will be in the know or need to be told what is being said.

> *In the Hospital Ward. A general state of listlessness pervades the setting: inmates in intimate clusters. The gathering is mixed—men and women.*
>
> Editor *is distinctly apart, bent over his bed, writing. Presently,* Hannah *and* Harcourt Whyte *enter.*
>
> HANNAH: Some people have started gathering into groups with people of their own kind. That too must stop.
>
> HW: (*surveys the group glumly*) Sister Hannah has just told me that some of you again refused to eat today. Well, we can't go on like this. Each one tell one. We simply can't starve ourselves to death—which is what they want. Now everybody must try and eat something.
>
> INMATE: (*to whom* Nweke *has been interpreting; retorts in Ibibio*) Idehe ke nnyin iyomke ndi idu uwem.
>
> NWEKE: He says it's not that we don't want to be alive.
>
> INMATE: Akpa, mpo se idiah mi idhi se ekool ndi idia.
>
> NWEKE: To begin with, what we get to eat these days, is not worth calling food.
>
> HW: I know—but—
>
> INMATE: Idihi ade ede mfana.
>
> NWEKE: He says even that is not the complaint.
>
> INMATE: Ke ntak nnyin idi idionke idia ke ndik iyun imani ntak ideme ke ndik.
>
> NWEKE: It is the fear of not knowing. We go to sleep in fear, and wake up still in fear.
>
> INMATE: Owo idia mkpo mfin, nyene nson nda, ke uwen odude ke ida idia mkpon—ade ede ndia ndi idia.
>
> NWEKE: To eat today, and be confident that so long as there is life, one will also eat tomorrow—that *is* eating.
>
> HW: I know. Each one tell one, it's six weeks now since the doctor left us. The question in the minds of all is: what are we doing? Well, we are asking the authorities to tell us what they plan for us. It's from their reply that we'll know exactly what will happen to us. And knowing, we shall decide on what to do. Our brother will now read the letter we're writing to the Government. Each one tell one as he reads.
>
> (pp. 20–21)

One of the intriguing dimensions of this approach is the way in which it keeps the audience on its toes. Although members of an audience in Nigeria might have a familiarity with some of the languages, those audience members who do not understand these languages will share the frustration of the characters on stage. They will also invest the action with an urgency to know what is going on and an impatience with those who will not fight to overcome the barriers to understanding that allow for exploitation.

The play is a lesson in resourcefulness, accepting no obstacle as too great to be overcome. For instance, in one scene an inmate, a former army corporal, repulses efforts by the police to eject the patients from their ward. Frustrated at not being able to pick up a police rifle that he has knocked from its owner's grasp because he has no fingers on his hands with which to grip it, he sees his leprous mutilation as a weapon and advances upon the police with his arms extended, causing them to flee in panic. The scene is moving, triumphant, and farcical all at the same time. A similar image of self-help emerges in the final scenes when the patients are preparing to move to their settlement at Uzuakoli. They refuse free food, determining to grow their own, and adapt tools and create teams of workers to allow them to overcome the ravages of their disease. The play ends with a graphic exhortation by Harcourt Whyte:

> Now we've won our freedom. But this is only the beginning of a new struggle, my people. From this day on, things will happen to us. Perhaps, rough things: things without gladness. But... together. To tackle them, we must stand together, children of our fathers. Not apart. The day children of the porcupine made bond to drift apart: one, going this way, a mouse; the other going that way, a bush rat, is the day both mouse and bush rat became food for cats. Together, then, we move. If not for our own gains, then for the gains of our saplings to come.
> *(pause)*
> To this day, together we have braved the rough waters. Is it not so? Must the people already on dry land laugh at us now, turning back?
> *(crowd responds variously in the negative)*
> Must our saplings, yet to be born, curse our spirits, lacking in strength? Tell me. If the river stops the arm of the paddler going backwards, must it stop him going forward also? Forward then—together. Wisdom of the crab: it says "forward"!
> *(sidling first to the right, then left)*
> This way—forward... that way, it is forward. Rather than go backwards, the crab breaks off its legs!
> *(slight pause)*
> Forward then. Together, to turn our troubles into blessing. To wrestle our troubles of today, we draw strength from our hopes of tomorrow. Where there is no hope in our gaze into tomorrow, is when we perish in the darkness of today. To ourselves then, let us turn for strength in our struggle. Children of our fathers—to our new struggle!
>
> *Instantly, they all pick up their tattered belongings, foodstuffs, farming implements, fishing nets etc. and hurry out purposefully. There is singing (no dancing).*
>
> (pp. 111–112)

Rotimi dedicates *Hopes of the Living Dead* to Harcourt Whyte and three radical leaders among the older generation of Nigerians: Michael Imoudu, a trade-union leader prominent in the struggle against colonial rule; Aminu Kano, a northern politician who struggled to promote a radical democratic agenda against feudal opposition; and Tai Solarin, an outspoken educational and social reformer.

Everyone His Own Problem

The short radio play *Everyone His Own Problem* (*Everyone His/Her Own Problem* in Rotimi's records) was broadcast on the BBC African Theatre program in 1986. The play centers on a young banker, Oginni, and a prostitute, Philomena, who face charges in court the following day. Oginni is accused of stealing from his bank, and Philomena protests that she has been framed by a soldier who tried to rob her. They consider themselves victims rather than villains, but they know that the system will not be interested in "background" details, only in accusations, and that they cannot escape conviction. As Philomena expresses it: "Did money lose, or money not lose? Nigeria doesn't like background. We like 'tory.' Money lost. That's 'tory.' If money lost, that means someone stole it. Finish."

They find in each other a truthfulness and decency, which creates a bond that the play implies may carry them through their present tribulations. Although this is a slight piece, it is a sensitive portrayal of good people in a corrupt environment, and as such touches on issues explored more fundamentally in Rotimi's major dramas.

CONCLUSION

Rotimi argued in his 1987 lecture at the University of Benin that committed literature is not limited to any single formula: "It is committed to the extent that it demonstrates the imperative for ameliorating the condition of man." His experiments in theater have made a forceful contribution to the public debate within Nigeria and have on occasion been regarded by the authorities as unsuitable for public celebrations. The strength of his work lies not in the propagation of a simple ideological dogma, but in its powerful advocacy of political and social action, an advocacy that is based on thoughtful and concerned analysis.

Selected Bibliography

BIBLIOGRAPHY

Lalude, O. O. *Theatre Arts: Ola Rotimi and His Works. An Annotated Bibliography.* Unipolib Bibliographic Series. Port Harcourt, Nigeria: University of Port Harcourt Library, 1984.

PLAYS

The Gods Are Not to Blame. London: Oxford University Press, 1971.

Kurunmi. Ibadan, Nigeria: Oxford University Press, 1971.

Ovonramwen Nogbaisi. Benin City, Nigeria, and Ibadan, Nigeria: Oxford University Press, 1974.

Our Husband Has Gone Mad Again. Ibadan, Nigeria: Oxford University Press, 1977.

Holding Talks: An Absurdist Drama. Ibadan, Nigeria: University Press Limited, 1979.

If: A Tragedy of the Ruled. Ibadan, Nigeria: Heinemann Educational Books, 1983.

Hopes of the Living Dead. Ibadan, Nigeria: Spectrum Books, 1988.

CRITICAL STUDIES

Abati, Reuben. "Ola Rotimi: The Writer as Nationalist." In *Guardian* (Lagos) (15 May 1993).

Adelugba, Dapo. "Wale Ogunyemi, 'Zulu Sofola and Ola Rotimi': Three Dramatists in Search of a Language." In Oyin Ogunba and Abiola Irele, eds., *Theatre in Africa.* Ibadan, Nigeria: University of Ibadan Press, 1978.

Banham, Martin. "Ola Rotimi: 'Humanity as My Tribesman.'" In *Modern Drama* 33 (March 1990).

Crow, Brian. "Melodrama and the 'Political Unconscious' in Two African Plays." In *ARIEL* 14 (July 1983).

Dunton, Chris. *Make Man Talk True: Nigerian Drama in English Since 1970.* Oxford, U.K.: Zell, 1992.

Folarin, M. "Ola Rotimi Interviewed." In *New Theatre Magazine* 12, no. 2 (1972).

Johnson, Alex C. "Ola Rotimi: How Significant?" In *African Literature Today* 12 (1982).

———. "Two Historical Plays from West Africa." In *Komparatistische Hefte 8* (1983).

Nawāl al-Saʿadāwī

1931–

DINAH MANISTY

A LEADING EGYPTIAN FEMINIST, writer, psychiatrist, and political activist and president of the Arab Women Solidarity Association (AWSA), Nawāl al-Saʿadāwī (Nawal El Saadawi) is known above all for her sincere and courageous struggle against the oppression, both mental and physical, of women. As a result of her literary and scientific writings against the oppression of women in the Arab world, she has faced enormous difficulties and even dangers. In 1981 her outspoken views led to her imprisonment under former Egyptian president Anwar al-Sādāt, and she was released one month after his assassination in October 1981. Under President Husni Mubārak the Egyptian government banned her from appearing on radio and television and shut down the AWSA magazine *Nūn*, of which al-Saʿadāwī was editor in chief. Six months following the demise of *Nūn*, on 15 June 1991, the government issued a decree that closed down AWSA, handing over its funds to an apolitical association called Women in Islam.

While al-Saʿadāwī has criticized the government for being only nominally democratic and for playing into the hands of western capitalist interests, she has also accused militant fundamentalists of invoking the name of God for political ends and for misinterpreting Islam in order to reinforce the patriarchal system. This criticism has resulted in her name appearing on a death list issued by extremist Islamic organizations. This list has been publicized in a neighboring Arab country and is recorded on cassettes that are widely distributed throughout the country. The Egyptian government placed al-Saʿadāwī under around-the-clock protection in Egypt, and the death threat was also one of the factors that led her to accept visiting professorships during 1993 and 1994 at Duke University in North Carolina and at the University of Seattle in Washington.

FEMINIST BELIEFS

As Egypt's leading feminist, al-Saʿadāwī believes that women's rights and human rights are one and the same: "You cannot separate the liberation of women from the liberation of the land and the economy and the culture and the language," she says (interview by Winokur, p. D-7). Al-Saʿadāwī believes that the Arab world has answered to foreign interests for too long and that, until it rediscovers its independence, Arab women cannot be wholly free. In her view, it is the legacy of years of western colonialism, and not Islam, that is the main obstacle to progress in the Arab world: western influence has hindered rather than benefited the liberation of women in Arab countries because, in the west, female sexuality is portrayed in a prostituted form. This, in turn, has played into the hands of the fundamentalists, who justify the veiling of women as a necessary protection against such corrupting influences.

Her views against what she calls the patriarchal class system have been formed since early childhood, during which she saw injustice and particularly discrimination against women. Although al-Saʿadāwī's mother perpetuated traditional practices toward daughters, the freedom and education her parents did allow her enabled her to think about and articulate what caused injustice and what could be done about it. The views she formed led her to challenge conventional values and institutions of her society, including male authority, religion, and capitalism. The lingering memory of her own clitoridectomy, which was supervised by her mother, led al-Saʿadāwī to campaign actively against the practice of female circumcision and try to force society to change and abolish the structures that she argues maintain women as "victims of the crudest, most cruel and sometimes most sophisticated forms of oppresson and exploitation" ("Women and Islam," 1982, p. 206). As an adult her views crystallized into leftist feminism; she became convinced that the problem of injustice and male domination of society was created not by religion but by capitalism:

> I firmly believe that the reasons for the lower status of women in our societies, and the lack of opportunities for progress afforded to them, are not due to Islam, but rather to certain economic and political forces, namely those of foreign imperialism operating mainly from the outside, and of the reactionary classes operating from the inside. These two forces cooperate closely and are making a concentrated attempt to misinterpret religion and to utilize it as an instrument of fear, oppression and exploitation.
>
> (*The Hidden Face of Eve*, 1980, p. 41)

Al-Saʿadāwī's declared aim, which she has tried to promote through the motto of AWSA, is "unveiling the mind," because she believes that "a veil over the mind is more dangerous than a veil on the face" ("Contemporary Thought and Women," [1988?], p. 10). The former allows static thought to spread and produces a social order perpetuated by rules that impose only one authority and allow only one opinion. "Absolute authority and dictatorship" thus prevail in both the state and the family: a veil over the mind does not permit dialogue, discussion, or differences of opinion but allows only obedience and the fear of punishment by authority or by God. Releasing the constraints on thought and mind is a prerequisite for any positive social, economic, or political change, writes al-Saʿadāwī. "Arab feminism tries to link politics, economics, history, religion, morals, art, literature, psychology, sexology and education as well as other fields of knowledge that have been separated, partitioned ever since the birth of the patriarchal class system. This separation led to ... the absence of an overall view of the human being and life and to the imposition of the contradiction between mind and body or between thought and matter" ("Contemporary Thought and Women," p. 5).

Al-Saʿadāwī believes that freedom of the mind and freedom of the body cannot be separated, since their separation would lead to mental and psychological deformation in both men and women. The mental and physical suppression imposed on women has led to limitation of their minds and to flabbiness in their bodies.

> Women very often imagine that their happiness is to be found only in submission to a man. This is the false consciousness which most women are living with today and which is characteristic of all oppressed beings.... The democratic essence of the feminist movement aims essentially at freeing woman's mind from this false consciousness and overcoming the mental, psycho-

logical and bodily distortion with which her nature has been afflicted.

("Contemporary Thought and Women," pp. 34–35)

In the same article, al-Saʿadāwī talks about the need to confront the moral dualism—a reflection of the duality in contemporary Arab thought worldwide—that considers honor to be concentrated in a woman's body and determined by her sexual behavior while the sexual behavior of men is regarded as irrelevant. She deplores the fact that political figures in Arab countries attempt to use Islam as a basis for this duality (p. 7).

Al-Saʿadāwī played an important part in the passage of Egypt's personal-status laws, which were intended to give women new divorce and voting rights, in March and July 1979. These laws were revoked in 1985 because of pressure from the Islamic fundamentalist lobby. This setback focused her attention on the need for women to gain political power—she believes that a wide network of women's groups is a prerequisite to the creation of an effective Arab feminist movement—while at the same time women need to attract as many men to the movement as possible to reverse a situation in which marriage and divorce are still regulated by Islamic law.

LIFE

One of nine children, al-Saʿadāwī was born in the small village of Kafr Tahla in Qalubiyya Province in the Egyptian Delta, north of Cairo, on 27 October 1931. She attended an English school in Minuf, followed by an Egyptian primary school for two years; she then became a boarder in a secondary school in Helwan. She began her medical career in rural Egypt in 1955 after graduating from the medical school at Cairo University. She has reflected on her experiences at the university in the novel *Al-Bāḥithah ʿan al-ḥubb* (1974; published in 1983 as *Imraʾatān fī imraʾah* and translated into English in 1985 as *Two Women in One*). She wrote her first piece of creative writing, *Mudhakkirāt ṭiflah ismuha Suʿād* (Memoirs of a child named Suʿād), in 1944, although it was not published until 1990. Her first published work was a collection of short stories, *Taʿallamtu al-ḥubb* (1958; I learned to love). In 1970 she published her first nonfiction work, *Al-Marʾah waʾl-jins* (Women and sex), while serving as director of health education in the Ministry of Health and editor of *Health* magazine. The book was censored because of its frank and scientific discussion of the customs and taboos surrounding Arab women and their sexuality, and she lost both posts. To avoid Egyptian censorship, she started publishing in Lebanon. In 1978 she took a position with the United Nations in Addis Ababa, Ethiopia, as an adviser on women's programs. In 1979 she moved to the Lebanese office of the United Nations, where she became responsible for women's programs in the Arab region. In 1980 she resigned her UN post and returned to Egypt to devote her time to writing. She wrote about her 1981 imprisonment in *Mudhakkirāti fī sijn al-nisāʾ* (1983; *Memoirs from the Women's Prison*); also inspired by her prison experience is her play *Al-Insān: Ithnā ʿashara imraʾah fī zinzānah* (1983; Mankind: Twelve women in a cell).

Her courageous position about women's autonomy was applied equally in her private life; she left two oppressive husbands, the first a physician and the second a lawyer. She is now married to Sherif Hetata, who is a medical doctor and a novelist and who has translated many of her books. She has two children: Mona Helmi, a writer, and Atef Hetata, a film director and writer.

Prizes awarded to al-Saʿadāwī include the Literary Award of the Supreme Council for Arts and Social Science, Cairo (1975), which was given to her at a time when al-Sādāt's regime supported a so-called liberalization program to restore democracy; the Literary France-Arab Friendship Award from the Franco-Arab Association, Paris, France (1982); the Gibran Literary Prize, Australia (1988); and the medal of the Libyan People's Republic, First Grade (1989). Her books have been translated into English, French, German, Dutch, Danish, Swedish, Norwegian, Italian, Portuguese, and Persian, among other languages.

NONFICTIONAL WORKS

In her first work of nonfiction, *Women and Sex* (1970), al-Saʿadāwī raises many of the controversial issues that she develops further in later works, including honor and virginity; work and education for women; marriage, polygamy, divorce, and *bayt al-taʿa* (the house of obedience, a system in the religious law that gives the husband the right to force his wife to live with him, even against her will); and finally the subject of genital mutilation, the importance of sex, and the right of women to orgasm.

In *Al-Wajh al-ʿārī lī ʾl-marʾah al-ʿarabiyyah* (1977; *The Hidden Face of Eve: Women in the Arab World*), al-Saʿadāwī covers a range of topics from prostitution and sexual relationships to marriage and divorce; she relates the personal and disturbing account of her own circumcision at the age of six. Other nonfictional works include *Al-Rajul waʾl-jins* (1973; Men and sex) and *Al-Marʾah waʾl-ṣirāʾ al-nafsi* (1976; Woman and neurosis), which deal with problems of sexuality and the necessity to address these problems in order to achieve the well-being of the individual and of society as a whole.

Al-Saʿadāwī believes (like the French writer Simone de Beauvoir) that the differences between men and women are not inherent in their nature but are learned within society. The social institutions and laws regulating Arab women's lives in marriage and divorce must be changed if the Arab world is to progress. Cultural and media organizations, as well as mass communication—television, radio, magazines, newspapers, the publishing industry—must all take responsibility for bringing about the necessary social changes. They must, among other things, represent women in roles other than cooks, dishwashers, fashion models, or consumers of beauty aids.

In her theoretical works, al-Saʿadāwī asserts that the condition of Arab women can only be improved by structural means, by bringing about changes in the existing politico-economic system of the Arab world and by reforming the laws and regulations that oppress women in these societies.

THEMES IN AL-SAʿADĀWĪ'S FICTION

Al-Saʿadāwī is a writer who, we sense, has lived through the issues about which she writes. Writing becomes indivisible from her own reality, which has led to the criticism that her works are autobiographical and in some way reduced as a result. She has been accused by some critics of blatant identification with her heroines and of venting her personal narcissistic obsession through their sexual traumas.

Al-Saʿadāwī has talked about the conflict in her life between science and art, that is, between her role as a doctor and her role as an artist/writer. In an interview with Allen Douglas and Fedwa Malti-Douglas, she has said:

> I didn't have many problems as a physician, but I did as a writer. I could work in a hospital and have equal pay. . . . But once I opened the door and entered my home I faced problems as a wife. In Egypt, under Nasser, women were encouraged to work. It's not like that now. Now, in the public sector, women like my daughter suffer, women are being discouraged from working, because of unemployment, because of the veil. This is the regression in our society.
>
> (p. 399)

Al-Saʿadāwī is part of a generation of Egyptian women writers concerned with articulating woman's voice and challenging the male monopoly on discourse. The strongly patriarchal nature of both Arabic society and its traditional literary establishment has made the emergence of women's discourse extremely difficult. As the Egyptian critic Sabry Hafez has noted, patriarchy in general is a social order that structures norms of behaviors, patterns of expectations, and modes of expression, but in Arabic culture it has acquired a divine dimension through the religious ratification of male supremacy enshrined in the Qurʾān. The divine is a masculine-singular voice and enforces the structural order that permeates all forms of social interaction. The divinity bestowed on men also encompasses the masculine classical language of the Qurʾān and slights the feminine spoken language of everyday life.

Al-Saʿadāwī has deliberately chosen to break with the traditions of Arabic letters and adopt a simple yet powerful style to make her work accessible to a wider Arabic-language readership. Many critics angrily deny literary importance to her considerable and varied literary corpus. Yet this criticism often seems to be a tribute of sorts.

In one of her later novels, *Suqūt al-imām* (1987; *The Fall of the Imam*), she experiments with language so that it might reflect more of what she feels: "As you know the Arabic language, like the English language, is very male-oriented. And the language of the Quran is very male.... We are still using a language that is alienating us.... In my new novel... I am really trying to change the language. Because when you change the content, you have to change the form" (interview by Douglas and Malti-Douglas, pp. 402–403). She wants her writing to be more unrestrained because, even though she is relatively freer than other women writers, she still suffers from internal censorship, which is a response to repressions and oppressions imposed from outside:

> Of course, I can't write with all the courage I want. For many reasons: because I live in the Arab world, because I am limited by the publishers.... I want to write freely about... religion, sex, God, authority, the State. But the publishers also censor me. Even in Beirut... There are concepts that cannot be accepted at all in the Arab countries. Therefore no one would read my books. So, while my books are read because of this compromise, and I want to be read rather than be totally isolated, I pay a price for this.
>
> (p. 403)

The most striking feature of al-Saʿadāwī's works is the central narrative role she gives to her heroines, strategically positing a woman's voice as a direct challenge to the patriarchal thought that seeks to suppress that voice. In her introduction to *Imraʾah ʿinda nuqtat al-ṣifr* (1976; *Woman at Point Zero*), the Algerian writer Assia Djebar says, "We [women] from the Maghreb... have rolled about in the Arabic language as though in a grotto of fear, of memories and of ancestors' whisperings." In al-Saʿadāwī's work, says Djebar,

> A new, fresh discursive field is imperceptibly traced for other Arab women. A point for take-off. A combat zone. A restoration of body. Bodies of new women in spite of new barriers which in the internal, interior language at once retracted and proclaimed, public and no longer secret find roots before rushing forth ... a loud voice that gives body.
>
> This book is dealing with birth—birth of a word.
>
> (Badran and Cooke, pp. 387–388)

More than any other contemporary Egyptian writer, al-Saʿadāwī concerns herself with the body. Her novels display the need for her heroines to transcend the body—to go beyond its social and physical constraints—in order to gain control of their voice. The female body of al-Saʿadāwī's heroines is wounded, bleeding, chained, and shackled. She must retrieve it before she can articulate her new discourse—an alternative truth and a narrative instrument that permits her to vie with the male writer in the process of textual creation.

Al-Saʿadāwī's fictional works vary widely in form, content, style, and as narrative intent. The four novels discussed in this essay focus on the range of themes that concern her most; they display the diversity in her style and have been the subjects of critical debate and literary exchange.

MEMOIRS OF A WOMAN DOCTOR

Mudhakkirāt ṭabībah (1958; *Memoirs of a Woman Doctor*) was al-Saʿadāwī's first published novel, written in her twenties when she had just graduated from medical school. In the introduction to the book's English edition, al-Saʿadāwī described it as a "simple spontaneous novel" in which there is much anger against the oppression of women in her country but also "a great deal of hope for change, for wider horizons and a better future" (p. 8). The novel charts the journey of a young Egyptian woman as she rebels against family and social limitations to search for her identity through becoming a doctor. Neither her experiences in medicine nor her personal relationships resolve the search for selfhood; after an unhappy marriage she immerses herself in her work, becoming a successful doctor while simultaneously becoming aware of societal injustice and hypocrisy. The novel ends somewhat abruptly with her "finding herself" through love.

In this early work, al-Saʿadāwī raises many of the issues that appear in her nonfiction and introduces a theme that recurs in later fiction—the negative influence of the mother and her role in perpetuating social and moral taboos that place women in an unequal role. "It was my mother who controlled my life, my future and my body right down to every strand of my hair. . . . How could she possibly love me when she put chains on my arms and legs and round my neck everyday?" (pp. 16–17). "I'd prove to nature that I could overcome the disadvantages the frail body she'd clothed me in, with its shameful parts both in and out" (p. 23).

The autobiographical aspect of her works, which is particularly relevant to *Memoirs*, has raised much controversy, notably among male critics such as Georges Tarabishi and Sabry Hafez. In *Women Against Her Sex* (1988), Tarabishi argues that al-Saʿadāwī's struggle against femininity is not socially focused but is instead biological and that by spurning her own sex she is internalizing oppression. He quotes from al-Saʿadāwī to support his argument: "The conflict between me and my femininity began very early on, before my female characteristics had become pronounced and before I knew anything about myself, my sex and my origins, indeed before I knew the nature of the cavity which had housed me before I was expelled into the wide world." He argues, "Femininity for someone who struggles against it even before she is aware of its existence can hardly be seen as positive" (p. 35–36), and adds, "The woman who sees members of her own sex as nothing but a common herd will, body and soul, stamp out both femininity and sex. . . . She will internalize oppression and end up becoming her own oppressor" (p. 38).

Al-Saʿadāwī's reply to Tarabishi, which makes up a chapter in *Woman Against Her Sex,* expresses sentiments felt by many female authors and feminist critics both in the Arab world and the west: "I fully believe that had the novels been written by a man, Tarabishi would not have found the same need to identify the author with his heroes. This is one of the problems facing women writers" (p. 190). The main struggle in her novels, she argues further, revolves around "unjust laws and social conditions which oppress women intellectually, ideologically and sexually. It is a moral, political and social struggle and not a biological struggle against the organs of the body, whether masculine or feminine" (p. 206).

By denying the autobiographical foundation of the novel, however, al-Saʿadāwī is in danger of denying it the very basis on which it can best be judged. Little evidence exists of the author's attempt to equip her protagonist with independent, ideological concepts, which means the protagonist cannot effectively relate to the social world and becomes a vehicle of the author's intentions. The strong authorial intrusion in her work—a recurring accusation, by al-Saʿadāwī's own admission—too often results in a monophonic narrative and overtly subjective view of the world.

WOMAN AT POINT ZERO

Woman at Point Zero is a story told to al-Saʿadāwī, in her capacity as a psychiatrist, by Firdaus, a prostitute, on the eve of her execution for murdering her pimp. It is a story of a woman's attempt to escape male domination: by her father, uncle, husband, employer, pimp. The only choice she is given in life is death.

Firdaus' body, which has been violated throughout her young life, is reclaimed symbolically beyond death through her words and voice. Her voice can only be transmitted to another woman in an enclosed prison cell and will release itself only when her imminent death allows her symbolically to transcend the boundaries of society to a world beyond, without limitations. The "dangerous and wild truth" she transmits is a challenge to male discourse and rises higher and higher—a voice described by Assia Djebar as one "that does not sigh, that does not complain, that accuses" (Badran and Cooke, p. 386). Behind the voice of the righteous prostitute in Cairo is the strong voice of al-Saʿadāwī, the contemporary Arab writer who is addressing every woman in a society in which sexual oppression is only just beginning to be recognized:

> I have triumphed over both life and death because I no longer desire to live nor do I any longer fear to die. I want nothing. I fear nothing. Therefore I am free.... This freedom I enjoy fills them with anger. They would like to discover that there is after all something which I desire, fear, or hope for. Then they can enslave me once more.
>
> (*Woman at Point Zero*, pp. 100–101)

GOD DIES BY THE NILE

Mawt al-rajul al-waḥīd ʿalā al-arḍ (1976; *God Dies by the Nile*) is one of al-Saʿadāwī's boldest statements against Islam and official religious discourse. She considers it her most significant novel, one that contains a metaphor for the regime of Anwar al-Sādāt and explores the class dimension of the oppression of women as well as men.

At the center of this story is Zakeya, an illiterate peasant woman, whose two nieces are sexually exploited and victimized by the mayor in a game of desire and power that he can win only through the support of the other three important men of the village: Sheikh Hamzawi of the mosque, who symbolizes Islam; Sheikh Zahran, chief of the village guard, who symbolizes law enforcement; and Hajj Ismail, the village barber and mediator, who knows all the village secrets. All three power bases operate through a system of corruption in which peasants are systematically exploited and duped into submission.

Zayeka is a formerly religious woman who, with the realization that—for her—Allah is dead, frees herself from the painful ignorance of her life as a poor woman. She understands the source of her oppression and misery and in her mind has destroyed it. In prison she says: "I know it's Allah my child.... He's over there, my child. I buried him over there on the bank of the Nile" (p. 138).

THE FALL OF THE IMAM

In the feminist tale and political allegory *Suqūt al-imām* (1987; *The Fall of the Imam*), al-Saʿadāwī again exposes the suffering of women under patriarchal rule and the hypocritical exploitation of religion by an oppressive state machine. The novel's heroine is the illegitimate daughter of the imam, a corrupt, despotic character who uses his power to exploit religion for his own ends. The balance of power that preserves the social order is maintained at the expense of women: the heroine's mother, a prostitute, is stoned to death for the threat that her connection to the imam poses; her daughter is shot for avenging her mother's death and for her refusal to keep silent about her identity.

This tale is presented as a female version of the story of Christ: the heroine names herself Bint Allah (daughter of God) and sets herself against the imam (and by implication against religious patriarchy). Like Christ, she is condemned to death for speaking in a way that challenges the prevailing discourse of authority. As political allegory, the novel, like *God Dies by the Nile*, is based on the sociopolitical life of Egypt under Sādāt, on whom the character of the imam is based.

As in al-Saʿadāwī's earlier novels, male desire is paired with power and corruption, and—like male power—is satisfied at the expense of women. Woman's body—Bint Allah's body—is symbolically offered up as sacrificial evidence at her trial, and she is denied a voice. The judge—the imam—shouts down her oral testimony: "Silence. May your tongue be cut out of your mouth. Remove your clothes so that I can examine you, for I am the one to know whether anyone has touched you, be it man or spirit, for there are evil spirits that go with women in the dark of night" (p. 141). Women's desire is dangerous or challenging, particularly if it is voiced. Voicelessness is a metaphor for women's lack of power. As the imam breaks her hymen with his hand, Bint Allah lies tied to a table with a deep wound in her body. Her individual sacrifice is located in the body.

Like the voice of Firdaus in *Woman at Point Zero*, Bint Allah's voice accuses and challenges: "If my body dies my heart will live on the barest minimum and everything in me dies before my mind. No one of you has ever possessed my mind" (p. 175). Her rational mind is a danger to the authorities and must be suppressed. The novel closes with the announcement of the official censorship of her trial and the burial of her file deep down in the earth forever.

Al-Saʿadāwī has adopted a modernist style in this work (as opposed to the realism of *God Dies by the Nile*); its timeless, spaceless, balladlike structure is expressed through a confessional form. The majority of characters—the imam/judge (speaking in different voices and appearing in different guises), the chief of security, the legal wife, the great writer, the philosopher, and the heroine—are allowed to speak in turn, suggesting a potential for ideological debate within the novel. This dimension is not exploited beyond an episodic level, however; invariably the individual narrations are preempted by authorial intervention in the third-person narrative, thereby reintroducing the problem between intention and realization of *Memoirs of a Woman Doctor*. Al-Saʿadāwī's protagonists are not prepared for active political roles; their experiences do not sharpen their intellects but frequently result in the reinstatement of oppression in a new form. In this case mother and sister and countless mothers and sisters (all "children of God") suffer the same fate—and the cycle of female limitations continues, unimpeded.

CONCLUSION

Al-Saʿadāwī's stark descriptions of the life of an Egyptian woman have doubtless shocked many people. She does not believe fate is in the hands of God; her two female protagonists in *God Dies by the Nile* and *Woman at Point Zero* take actions that directly determine their final destiny and that would seem to challenge their oppressors. More significant, the protagonists continue to challenge authority by refusing to comply with attempts to alter their fates. Firdaus, after murdering her pimp, refuses to repent, then refuses to appeal for a pardon from the death sentence. Bint Allah's final statement to the chief of security in *The Fall of the Imam* subverts the official discourse of the imam, the nation, and God by questioning their logic and sanity. Bint Allah's rationality becomes "more dangerous than any of her madness" (p. 175) and others can silence her truth only by death. Thus, while the actions of her heroines do not offer means of escape except through death or imprisonment, their voices represent a challenge to the official truth and raise the fundamental question of the relation between language and power. Men are seen to manipulate the language of the official media and religious dogma. By giving her heroines a voice, al-Saᶜadāwī suggests the potential for undermining the solidarity between logocentrism and patriarchy and suggests how the question of language is linked to both gender and identity. The plight of her heroines reflects a reality in both Arabic society and its traditional literary establishment, which are also predominantly male controlled and oriented, making the emergence of women's discourse extremely difficult.

The problem with al-Saᶜadāwī's work is that the potential for subverting the status quo through textual strategies is not realized, and the gap between her intention and narrative realization is something she will have to be judged by. She aspires to create justice for women—civil liberties, equality, and self-determination—but her one-dimensional approach impoverishes her narrative. Her novels contain fragmentary characters who are objects of authorial discourse and not, despite the first-person narrative, subjects of their own directly signifying discourse. As a result, the reader gains no insight into the dynamics of the process that generates political conditions and ideological thinking or understanding of the contradictions inherent in the mechanics of oppression and exploitation of religious dogma.

The gap between al-Saᶜadāwī's standing in the west and her reputation in her own culture, within the context of Arab culture at large and Arabic literature in particular, is also problematic. Many other competent Arab women novelists (for example, the Egyptian writers Raḍwa ᶜĀshūr, Salwā Bakr, Latīfah al-Zayyāt) who share al-Saᶜadāwī's political views and her position on the struggle for women's rights are neither widely translated nor known in the west, even though they address the same issues more profoundly. If something in her writing appeals more to western than to Arab readers, it might be that al-Saᶜadāwī tells the western reader what he or she wants to hear about the nature of treatment of women in a Muslim culture. In so doing she runs the risk of vindicating the main tenets of the traditional orientalist discourse on the position of women in Arab society and confirming many of the prevalent stereotypes about Arab women and men. It is easy to see how the lack of hope and possibility of survival as a woman that emerges in these works has angered those Arab women who look for a different heroine, less a victim but someone who can transform her destiny through her own action. For although the Arab reality is a grim one on the political and sociological levels, other Arab women writers—for example, the Lebanese writers Ḥanān al-Shaykh and Hudā Barakāt, the Palestinian Liyānah Badr, and the Syrian Ghādah al-Sammān—have developed narrative strategies in which their heroines are able to voice their oppression with a conviction that suggests that the status quo is amenable to change.

Selected Bibliography

NONFICTION

Al-Marʾah waʾl-jins. Cairo: Dār al-Shaᶜb, 1970; Beirut, Lebanon: al-Muʾassasah al-ᶜArabiyyah lī ʾl-Dirāsāt waʾl-Nashr, 1971.

Al-Rajul waʾl-jins. Beirut, Lebanon: al-Muʾassasah al-ᶜArabiyyah lī ʾl-Dirāsāt waʾl-Nashr, 1973.

Al-Unthā hiya al-aṣl. Beirut, Lebanon: al-Muʾassasah al-ᶜArabiyyah līʾl-Dirāsāt waʾl-Nashr, 1974.

Al-Mar'ah wa'l-ṣirā' al-nafsī. Beirut, Lebanon: al-Mu'assasah al-'Arabiyyah lī'-l-Dirāsāt wa'l-Nashr, 1976.
Qaḍiyyat al-mar'ah al-miṣriyyah al-siyāsiyyah wa'l-jinsiyyah. Cairo: Dār al-Thaqāfah al-Jadīdah, 1977.
Al-Wajh al-'ārī lī'l-mar'ah al-'arabiyyah. Beirut, Lebanon: al-Mu'assasah al-'Arabiyyah lī'l-Dirāsāt wa'l-Nashr, 1977.
'An al-mar'ah. Cairo: Dār al-Mustaqbal al-'Arabī, 1986.
Ma'rakah jadīdah fī qaḍiyyat al-mar'ah. Cairo: Dār Sīnā, 1992.

MEMOIRS AND AUTOBIOGRAPHIES

Mudhakkirātī fī sijn al-nisā'. Cairo: Dār al-Mustaqbal al-'Arabī, 1983.
Riḥlatī hawla al-'ālam. Cairo: Kutub al-Hilāl, 1986.
Mudhakkirāt ṭiflah ismuha Su'ād. Cairo: Dār Nashr Taḍāmun al-Mar'ah, 1990.
"An Overview of My Life." In *Contemporary Authors,* autobiography series, 1990 ed. Detroit: Gale Research.

NOVELS

Mudhakkirāt ṭabībah. Cairo: Maktabat al-Nahḍah al-Miṣriyyah, 1958.
Al-Ghā'ib. Cairo: al-Hay'ah al-'Āmmah lī'l-Kitāb, 1967.
Al-Bāḥithah 'an al-ḥubb. Cairo: al-Hay'ah al-'Āmmah lī'l-Kitāb, 1974. Later published as *Imra'atān fī imra'ah.* Cairo: Maktabat Madbūlī, 1983.
Imra'ah 'inda nuqtat al-ṣifr. Beirut, Lebanon: Dār al-Ādāb, 1976.
Mawt al-rajul al-waḥīd 'alā al-arḍ. Beirut, Lebanon: Dār al-Ādāb, 1976; Cairo: Maktabat Madbūlī, 1978, 1983.
Ughniyyat al-atfāl al-Dā'iriyyah. Beirut, Lebanon: Dār al-Ādāb, 1978.
Riḥlatī fī al-'ālam. Cairo: Dār Nashr Tadāmun al-Mar'ah al-'Arabiyyah, 1987.
Suqūt al-imām. Cairo: Dār al-Mustaqbal al-'Arabī, 1987.
Al-Ḥubb fī zaman al-nafṭ. Cairo: Maktabat Madbūlī, 1993.
Jinnāt—wa iblīs. Beirut, Lebanon: Dār al-Ādāb, 1992.

SHORT-STORY COLLECTIONS

Ta'allamtu al-ḥubb. Cairo: Maktabat al-Nahḍa al-Miṣriyyah, 1958.
Ḥanān qalīl. Cairo: Mu'assasāt Rūz al-Yūsuf, 1962.
Laḥẓat ṣidq. Cairo: Al-Kitāb al-Dhahabī, 1965.
Al-Khayṭ wa al-jidār. Beirut, Lebanon: Dār al-Ādāb, 1972; Cairo: Dār al-Sha'b, 1972.
Kānat hiya al-aḍ'af. Beirut, Lebanon: Dār al-Ādāb, 1977; Cairo: Maktabat Madbūlī, 1983.
Al-Khayṭ wa'ayn al-ḥayāt. Cairo: Maktabat al-Madbūlī, 1979.
Mawt ma'ālī al-wazīr sābiqā. Beirut, Lebanon: Dār al-Ādāb, 1979.

PLAYS

Al-Insān: Ithnā 'ashara imra'ah fī zinzānah. Cairo: Maktabat al-Madbūlī, 1983.
Isīs. Cairo: Dār al-Mustaqbal al-'Arabī, 1986.

TRANSLATIONS

The Hidden Face of Eve: Women in the Arab World. Trans. and ed. by Sherif Hetata. London: Zed, 1980. Nonfiction.
Woman at Point Zero. Trans. by Sherif Hetata. London: Zed, 1983. Nonfiction.
God Dies by the Nile. Trans. by Sherif Hetata. London: Zed, 1985. Novel.
Two Women in One. Trans. by Osman Nusairi and Jana Gough. London: Saqi Books, 1985; Seattle, Wash.: Seal Press, 1986. Novel.
Memoirs from the Women's Prison. Trans. by Marilyn Booth. London: Women's Press, 1986. Memoirs.
Death of an Ex-Minister. Trans. by Shirley Eber. London: Methuen, 1987. Short stories.
She Has No Place in Paradise. Trans. by Shirley Eber. London: Methuen, 1987. Contains the short stories collected in *Kānat hiya al-aḍ'af* and also includes three stories ("She Has No Place in Paradise," "Two Women Friends," and "'Beautiful'") not in the Arabic edition.
The Fall of the Imam. Trans. by Sherif Hetata. London: Methuen, 1988. Novel.
Memoirs of a Woman Doctor. Trans. by Catherine Cobham. London: Saqi Books, 1988. Novel.
The Circling Song. Trans. by Marilyn Booth. London: Zed, 1989. Novel.
My Travels Around the World. Trans. by Shirley Eber. London: Methuen, 1990. Memoirs.

Searching. Trans. by Shirley Eber. London: Zed, 1991. Novel.

The Well of Life; and, The Thread: Two Short Novels. Trans. by Sherif Hetata. London: Lime Tree, 1993.

The Innocence of the Devil. Trans. by Sherif Hetata. London: Methuen, 1994. Novel.

INTERVIEWS

Douglas, Allen, and Fedwa Malti-Douglas. "Reflections of a Feminist: Conversation with Nawal al-Saadawi." In Margot Badran and Miriam Cooke, eds., *Opening the Gates: A Century of Arab Feminist Writing*. London: Virago, 1990.

"Interview with an Angry Woman" (in Arabic). In *Zahrat al-khalīj* 609 (24 November 1990).

Winokur, Julie. "Speaking Her Mind, Angering Her Nation." In *San Francisco Examiner* (26 September 1993).

ARTICLES

"Women and Islam." In *Women's Studies International Forum* 5, no. 2 (1982).

"Contemporary Thought and Women." In *Papers of the Arab Women Solidarity Association*. Cairo: AWSA, [1988?].

"Feminism and Fundamentalism." In *Islamic Fundamentalism: A Debate on the Role of Islam Today*. London: Institute for African Alternatives, 1989.

CRITICAL STUDIES

Accad, Evelyne. "Rebellion, Maturity, and the Social Context: Arab Women's Special Contribution to Literature." In Judith E. Tucker, ed., *Arab Women: Old Boundaries, New Frontiers*. Bloomington: Indiana University Press, 1993.

Badran, Margot, and Miriam Cooke, eds. *Opening the Gates: A Century of Arab Feminist Writing*. London: Virago, 1990.

"El-Saadawi, Nawal." In *Contemporary Authors*, 1986 ed. Detroit: Gale Research.

Hafez, Sabry. "Intentions and Realization in the Narratives of Nawal El-Saʿadāwī." In *Third World Quarterly* 11 (July 1989).

———. *The Genesis of Modern Arabic Discourse*. London: Saqi Books, 1993.

Hall, Marjorie Joan. "The Position of Women in Egypt and Sudan as Reflected in Feminist Writings Since 1900." Ph.D. diss., University of London 1977.

Horsey, Glynis Ann. "An Introduction to the Written Works of Nawal al-Saʿadāwī." Ph.D. diss., University of London, 1988.

Kabbani, Rana. "Fatal Passivity: Women in Arabic Fiction." In *Third World Quarterly* 10 (January 1988).

Kilpatrick, Hilary. "Women and Literature in the Arab World: The Arab East." In Mineke Schipper, ed., *Unheard Words: Women and Literature in Africa, the Arab World, Asia, the Caribbean, and Latin America*. Trans. from the Dutch by Barbara Potter Fasting. New York: Allison & Busby, 1985.

Malti-Douglas, Fedwa. *Woman's Body, Woman's Word: Gender and Discourse in Arabo-Islamic Writing*. Princeton, N.J.: Princeton University Press, 1991.

Manisty, Dinah. "Changing Limitations: A Study of the Woman's Novel in Egypt (1960–1991)." Ph.D. diss., University of London, 1993.

Park, Heong-Dug. "Nawal al-Saʿadāwī and Modern Egyptian Feminist Writings." Ph.D. diss., University of Michigan, 1988.

Ramadan, Sumayya. "Reply to *Woman Against Her Sex*" (in Arabic). In *Al-Fikr al-ʿarabī al-muʿāsir waʾl-marʾah*. Cairo: Dār Tadamun al-Marʾah al-ʿArabiyyah, 1988.

Saiti, Ramzi. "Paradise, Heaven, and Other Oppressive Spaces: A Critical Examination of the Life and Works of Nawal El-Saʿadāwī." In *Journal of Arabic Literature* 25 (1994).

Sullivan, Earl L. *Women in Egyptian Public Life*. Syracuse, N.Y.: Syracuse University Press, 1986.

Tarabashi, Georges. "Nawal al-Saʿadāwī's Female and the Myth of Self-Sufficiency" (in Arabic). In *Al-Adab min al-dākhil*. Beirut, Lebanon: Dār al-Ṭāliʿah, 1978.

———. *Woman Against Her Sex: A Critique of Nawal El-Saadawi*. London: Saqi Books, 1988.

Zeidan, Joseph T. *Arab Women Novelists: The Formative Years and Beyond*. Albany: State University of New York Press, 1995.

Al-Ṭayyib Ṣāliḥ

1929–

PHILIP SADGROVE

THE SUDANESE WRITER al-Ṭayyib Ṣāliḥ has been described as the "genius of the modern Arabic novel." He has lived abroad for most of his life, yet his fiction is firmly rooted in the village in which he spent his early years. His most well-known work is the modern classic *Mawsim al-hijra ilāʾl-shamāl* (1967; *Season of Migration to the North*), which received great critical attention and brought new vitality to the Arab novel.

Ṣāliḥ has not been a prolific writer; his early work, including *Season of Migration to the North*, remains the best of his oeuvre. He has received critical acclaim in both the west and the east. In Sudan he is without rival, and his writing has played a considerable part in drawing attention to Sudanese literature. Arabic literature has been dominated by social criticism, social realism, and committed literature depicting the bitter realities of life; Ṣāliḥ managed to break with this trend and return to the roots of his culture, capturing the mystery, magic, humor, sorrows, and celebrations of rural life and popular religion.

LIFE

Born to Muḥammad and ʿAʾisha Ṣāliḥ in 1929, Ṣāliḥ grew up in the large, main village of the Merowe district, al-Dabba, in the northern province of Sudan. Ṣāliḥ regards this area, midway between the border town of Wadi Halfa and the Sudanese capital, Khartoum—between the land of the Shaigīya Arabs and that of the Nubians—as one of the country's centers of civilization. His father's family were small-scale farmers and merchants with a tradition of religious scholarship. As a child he worked in the fields with his family. He had a traditional Islamic upbringing, attending a *khalwa* (religious school), where he studied the Qurʾān. His attachment to his village has remained strong; although he has not lived there since age ten, he has returned regularly and writes about it as though he had never left.

Ṣāliḥ attended Wādī Sayyidinā School in Omdurman for his secondary studies. He planned to become an agricultural expert. He studied sciences at Khartoum University and then went on to study economics and political science at the University of London and education at the University of Exeter. He describes his studies abroad as a period that enabled him to discover anew the fundamentals of his own culture. After a short period teaching in Sudan, he joined the British Broadcasting Corporation as a scriptwriter and later became head of drama in the BBC television's Arabic-language service. He then worked for the Sudan Broadcasting Service.

After some years as director of information with the government of Qatar, he became an adviser to UNESCO (United Nations Educational, Scientific, and Cultural Organization). He has been a regular contributor to the Arabic press, with a column in *Al-Majalla* magazine.

Like several characters in his fiction, Ṣāliḥ married a British woman of Scottish descent. They have three daughters, Zeinab, Sara, and Samira. Ṣāliḥ describes himself as a religious person; he regularly reads the Qurʾān and considers it one of the greatest influences on his life and literature. He has also described himself as a socialist, believing that social injustice works against social harmony. This is reflected in his fictional village, where there is a sense of fraternity and egalitarianism. He shares with many of his contemporaries a belief in Arab unity.

Ṣāliḥ mentions Charles Dickens and William Faulkner among those whom he greatly admires. He has also acknowledged the influence of the Egyptian writers Muṣṭafā Ṣādiq al-Rāfiʿī, Aḥmad Zakī, and Ibrāhīm ʿAbd al-Qādir al-Māzinī, Sudanese writers Jamāl Muḥammad Aḥmad (his friend and teacher) and Aḥmad al-Ṭayyib, the Lebanese writer Mārūn ʿAbbūd, and, among western writers, Shakespeare, Jonathan Swift, and Joseph Conrad. He regards the writings of the Egyptian Yaḥyā Ḥaqqī as closest to his own. He has expressed his admiration for such seminal Arabic works as Ṭāhā Ḥusayn's *Al-Ayyām* (*The Days*), Tawfīq al-Ḥakīm's *Ahl al-kahf* (*The People of the Cave*), Maḥmūd Abbās al-ʿAqqād's *Al-ʿAbqarīyāt* (*The Geniuses*), Najīb Maḥfūẓ's trilogy (al-Thulāthiyya) and *Mīrāmār* (*Miramar*), Yaḥyā Ḥaqqī's *Khalīhā ʿalā Allāh* (*Leave It to God*) and *ʿAntar wa-Jūlyīt* (*Antar and Juliette*), Yūsuf Idrīs' *Ākhir al-dunyā* (*The End of the World*) and *Lughat al-āy āy* (The language of pain), Maḥmūd al-Masʿadī's play *Al-Sudd* (*The Dam*), and Yūsuf al-Sibāʿī's *Innī Rāḥila* (I am leaving). In Ṣāliḥ's youth, al-Sibāʿī was his favorite writer.

Ṣāliḥ began writing his short stories in the 1950s. The summer of 1960, when he was on holiday in a small village near Cannes, France, was his most fertile period; in a month's time he finished *ʿUrs al-Zayn* (1966; *The Wedding of Zein*) and wrote about a third of *Season of Migration to the North*, after which he stopped writing for four years. He became a writer almost against his will: Ṣāliḥ believes, like his character Muṣṭafa Saʿīd in *Season of Migration to the North*, that a writer is somehow superfluous in a country that needs agricultural experts, engineers, and doctors. The late Palestinian poet Tawfīq Ṣāyigh, his friend and mentor, helped him accept this commitment. In the 1960s Ṣāyigh would patiently wait until Ṣāliḥ had finished whatever he was writing and immediately publish it in *Ḥiwār*, the journal he edited in Beirut. Ṣāliḥ published *The Wedding of Zein* and *Season of Migration to the North* in *Ḥiwār* in 1964 and 1966, respectively; he brought out two parts of the unfinished trilogy, *Bandar Shāh, Ḍaw al-Bayt*, in 1971, and *Bandar Shāh, Maryūd*, in 1977. *The Wedding of Zein* was adapted into a play in Libya sometime in the late 1960s and was made into a film by the Kuwaiti director Khalīd Ṣiddīq, who won an award for it at the Cannes Film Festival in 1976. *Season of Migration to the North* was performed on stage in Beirut in the early 1970s.

THEMES

Ṣāliḥ shares the belief, prevalent in classical Arabic literature, that writing is in essence a moral act. For him the literary person is, in some way, a historian and a thinker who should shed light on social problems. He has tried, like an archaeologist, artistically to uncover some of the fundamental beliefs, history, myths, and legends of his people. Most of his stories have the flavor of the popular and fabulous tales of the traditional Arab storyteller, the *ḥakawātī*. In his fiction he has chosen to describe the fictional village of Wad

Ḥāmid, a symbolic representation of his own village on the banks of the Nile, but he could be writing about any one of a thousand villages in Sudan. (He chose this name before he realized that a village so named actually existed.) When he depicts the religious beliefs of the villagers, he is describing not an ideological or fanatical Islam but a mystical and spiritual religion. He believes that, in his literature, the village life he portrays amounts to a plea for toleration, historically in line with the Sudanese character. He depicts a society with room for all, one in which some people drink and some pray.

While his work is not autobiographical, many elements of his own experiences and observations enter his fiction. Everything he has written shows his attachment to, and respect and admiration for, his native society. He has focused on rural communities, for he believes they have retained most of the essential aspects of traditional, precolonial culture. His ambition, partially fulfilled, has been to transform ordinary Sudanese characters into mythical characters, similar to those in the *Iliad.* Many of his characters, their ancestors, and their offspring resurface throughout his writing.

Alienation and integration are the two poles of much of Ṣāliḥ's work. The soul of the intellectual, the narrator in his stories, is constantly nurtured by memories and dreams, often sentimental, of the simple life and values of his grandfather in the village. When Ṣāliḥ's intellectuals fail to adjust to Europe, they seek refuge in the bosom of the village, yet they are inevitably incapable of adjusting to village life and traditional culture. Alienation results from the intellectual's being unable to choose sides in the confrontation of North and South, the confrontation between the Arab Muslim and the western European worlds. Two powerful forces, modernity and tradition, perpetually collide.

Ṣāliḥ was criticized for his frank treatment of sex in *Season of Migration.* For Ṣāliḥ, sex functions in the novel as a way of expressing in fiction the awkward situation in which the hero, Muṣṭafā, finds himself, requiring him to respond to a dominant civilization. Although scarce reference to sex appears elsewhere in Ṣāliḥ's oeuvre, his use of the erotic represents a mild rebellion against the somewhat prudish and restrained approach to sex in most Arab writing.

In Ṣāliḥ's writing, specific time and place are not important. Rather, he relies on flashbacks, reminiscences, forward projections, dreams, nightmares, and the retelling of the same event in different ways and with different words. Truth and lies, dream and reality, are constantly juxtaposed. With the exception of *Season of Migration,* his fiction skillfully weaves the classical Arabic language and the dialect of northern Sudan. He is careful to ensure that every colloquial word he employs has a classical Arabic root and is thus intelligible to other Arabs. Despite claims that the literary use of the colloquial language poses a threat to standard Arabic, Ṣāliḥ, like the Egyptian short-story writer Yūsuf Idrīs and others, has used colloquial Arabic for dialogue because it is the language that characters speak in their day-to-day lives.

EARLY STORIES

In the *Ḥiwār* magazine of March–April 1966, Ṣāliḥ published seven short stories in which he introduced the people of the village of Wad Ḥāmid. The stories, which became part of a 1966 volume titled *ʿUrs al-Zayn: Riwāya wa-sabʿ qiṣaṣ* (translated in part in *The Wedding of Zein and Other Stories*) and which were later collected in *Dawmat Wad Ḥāmid, sabʿ qiṣaṣ* (1969; The doum tree of Wad Ḥāmid, seven stories) are notable for the sympathy and humor with which Ṣāliḥ treats the people of his fictional village. Ṣāliḥ describes the story "Dawmat Wad Ḥāmid" ("The Doum Tree of Wad Hamid"), written in 1960, as the beginning of his commitment to literature and one of the most sincere stories he has written. It is a tale of the confrontation between traditional beliefs and the modern world told as a monologue by an old man to a young man about the village of Wad Ḥāmid, its life, its river, its irritating sand flies and horseflies, and in particular its holiest spot, the doum tree over the tomb of the village holy man, Wad Ḥāmid. A symbol of protective mystical forces, the tree casts "its shadow . . . across the cultivated land and houses right up to the cemetery" (*The Wedding of Zein and Other Stories*, p. 4). The villagers seek protection from illness and other worldly troubles at the tomb under the tree. The authorities make various attempts to cut down the tree, to make way for a stopping place for a steamer or to build a water pump for an agricultural scheme, but the villagers resist all these with force, and rather than the tree it is the government that falls. Although the villagers lead a difficult life, they are happy, and under the saint's protection they survive. The story concludes that progress and tradition can coexist; "what all these people have overlooked is that there's plenty of room for all these things: the doum tree, the tomb, the water-pump, and the steamer's stopping place" (*Wedding*, p. 19).

"Nakhla ʿalāʾl-jadwal" ("A Date Palm by the Stream") is the earliest story in the collection, written in 1953. The principal character is Maḥjūb, a farmer ruined by successive droughts who is forced to sell his beloved date palm to meet the costs of the coming religious festival. He and the tree, which had seemed to bring him brief good fortune, were kindred spirits that had grown, prospered, and suffered together. His only son had forgotten his family, going to Egypt to earn a living. The father mocks the modern world that is enticing the youth and destroying the old social values. His oft-repeated pious prayer, *yaftaḥ Allāh* (God help us), is answered when this absent son, Ḥasan, sends money, enabling the family to pay its debts and save the tree.

"Ḥafnat tamr" ("A Handful of Dates"), written in 1957, introduces as a child the narrator featured in several of Ṣāliḥ's stories. The story concerns Masʿūd, who has mortgaged his property to meet the expense of his many marriages. The narrator's grandfather and others are slowly taking over all of Masʿūd's possessions; on this occasion they have come to seize his date harvest. The narrator thinks their treatment of Masʿūd is unjust and cruel; he vomits the handful of dates given to him as a sign of his rejection of their values. For the narrator's generation, the individual, such as Masʿūd, has the right to follow his or her own path to happiness. For all his misfortunes, however, Masʿūd is cheerful and sings, whereas the narrator's grandfather never laughs.

In "Risāla ilā Īylīn" ("A Letter to Aileen"), written in 1960, a Sudanese writes to his beloved English wife during his first trip back to Sudan for a brief holiday since their wedding a year earlier. She is worried he may not return. She has married "a lost stranger, who carries in his heart the worries of a whole generation? . . . You married a troubled East at the crossroads. You married a cruel sun, a chaotic mind and hopes that are as thirsty as the deserts of my people" (pp. 27–28). Back in his native village, Aileen's husband comes to realize he is also a stranger among his own people.

In "Hākadhā yā sādatī" (Thus it is, dear sirs), written in 1961, a foreigner meets his future wife at a party in Europe. His hosts expect him to abide by their social customs; although he does not like to drink, they ply him with whiskey. He is repeatedly asked whether he likes their country and whether he thinks it is the most beautiful in the world. At last he plucks up courage to say what he really thinks. Two years before he had been in a relationship with a woman who left him because he was a liar and a hypocrite; now he tells a woman who has attracted his attention at the party that in fact he does not like her country, and he points out all its faults. Charmed by his honesty, she responds to his advances. He has at last asserted his identity in this alien land.

"Idhā jā'at" (If she comes), also written in 1961, follows the various thoughts that run through the minds of three young friends—two men and a woman—as they sit waiting for business at their newly opened travel agency. One of the men, Amīn, thinks about how he tried and failed to establish a relationship with the young woman. The second man, Bahā', looks forward to his rendezvous that evening with an attractive Swedish woman, "if she comes."

"Muqaddimāt" (Premises) is a series of five very short pieces that Ṣāliḥ wrote in 1962: "Ughnīyat ḥubb" (The song of love), "Khuṭwa li'l-Amām" (A step forward), "Laka ḥattā 'l-mamāt" (For you until death), "Al-Ikhtibār (The experiment), "Sawzān wa-ʿAlī" (Susan and ʿAlī). These stories, each just one or two pages long, describe liaisons in London between English women and foreign men, presumably Sudanese. Ṣāliḥ shows that such cultural fusions can work and that many who hesitate to develop such relationships will regret it.

THE WEDDING OF ZEIN

The novella *ʿUrs al-Zayn* (*The Wedding of Zein*), one of Ṣāliḥ's most popular works, was first published in part in *Ḥiwār* in May–June 1964 and in its entirety in *Al-Khartūm* in December 1966; it first appeared in book form in 1966 with the seven stories of *Dawmat Wad Ḥāmid.* In this novella we enter, as in the work of the Colombian writer Gabriel García Márquez, a world that joins the supernatural and the miracles of progress and science. Zein's humanity and his friendship with the village holy man, al-Ḥanīn, lead people to believe that Zein is one of God's saints. At the end of the story, at his wedding, Zein's life-enhancing spirituality brings everyone together, breaking all political, religious, and ethnic barriers in the village. Zein, the village idiot, is like most of Ṣāliḥ's favored characters, all laughter, compassion, love, and life. He has no fixed home, is poor and ugly, with only two teeth in his mouth, yet he is rewarded for his love of humanity when he marries Niʿma, the most beautiful woman in the village. The only person Zein despises is the imam, the representative of orthodox religious authority. The imam is utterly contemptuous of the concerns of the local people; for them, his sermons evoke only hellfire and death. At the wedding Zein and the imam are finally reconciled, showing that popular religion and orthodox Islam can coexist.

Zein is seriously wounded in a fight with Sayf al-Dīn, a wastrel, drunkard, womanizer, and former prisoner. Zein returns from two weeks of treatment at the modern hospital transformed with new pearly dentures, a modern miracle. When Zein and Sayf fight again, al-Ḥanīn intervenes to save Sayf, and as a result Sayf turns to the path of virtue. Thanks to the blessings of al-Ḥanīn the villagers prosper materially and spiritually. The village sees miracle after miracle. The government, which they liken to a refractory donkey, builds a secondary school and a large hospital, organizes an agricultural scheme, and introduces water pumps. As in "The Doum Tree of Wad Hamid," modernization comes with the blessings of popular Islam. *The Wedding of Zein* represents Ṣāliḥ's hopes and dreams of what could be achieved in a society that is calm and stable, harmonious and happy, in which all problems are resolved peacefully.

SEASON OF MIGRATION TO THE NORTH

Season of Migration to the North was the work that made Ṣāliḥ's reputation; critics greeted it enthusiastically when it first appeared in *Ḥiwār* in December 1966. Ṣāliḥ had intended to write a straightforward thriller about a crime of passion, but his final work proved to be so multifaceted that it has provoked endless speculation. Ṣāliḥ admits that he fell under the influence of Sigmund Freud, reading more than once his *Civilization and Its Discontents* and becoming fascinated by Freud's theory of man divided between Eros (love) and death. In structuring his novel, Ṣāliḥ was influenced by Shakespeare's *King Lear* and *Richard III* and by Joseph Conrad's *Heart of Darkness* and *Nostromo*; *King Lear* is full of counterpoised characters and events, a process that Ṣāliḥ mirrors in *Season of Migration.*

The protagonist of the story, the narrator, celebrates his return to the "warmth of the tribe" in his native village, having left the coldness of Europe after seven years of work on a doctorate in literature at a British university. On his return he "felt not like a storm-swept feather but like that palm tree, a being with a background, with roots, with a purpose" (*Season*, the 1970 edition, p. 2). The narrator has no name, but we learn in *Bandar Shāh, Daw al-Bayt* that he is called Muḥaymīd and he was the child in the short story "A Handful of Dates." The narrator discovers that there is a newcomer in the village named Muṣṭafā Saᶜīd. His curiosity is aroused when he hears the newcomer reciting English poetry. Slowly Muṣṭafā's story is unraveled. He is an outsider; he belongs nowhere. His father was from the ᶜAbābda tribespeople, who lived in the border region of Sudan and Egypt and worked as guides for Horatio Kitchener's army during the British reconquest of Sudan after the Mahdi's revolt. His mother was a slave from southern tribes. In other words, Muṣṭafā is not part of the stable, mystic society that the village represents. Although, like the narrator, he has been exposed to the west, Muṣṭafā is immune to cultural influences, and this in the end prevents him from adapting to life in the Sudanese village: "I was like something rounded, made of rubber: you throw it in the water and it doesn't get wet, you throw it on the ground and it bounces back" (p. 20). Ṣāliḥ has explained that it would be difficult to find a person like Muṣṭafā in real life; he is an amalgam of dreams, myth, illusion, and speculation.

Muṣṭafā had been the first Sudanese to be sent on a scholarship abroad and subsequently the first to marry a British woman. He had arrived in a London emerging from World War I and the oppressive atmosphere of the Victorian age and had spent some thirty years there. His sharp intellect had enabled him to be appointed professor of economics at the University of London. Both the narrator and Muṣṭafā Saᶜīd, as intellectuals who have left their home environment, face the existential dilemma of finding a supportable role in life. A generation separates them; Muṣṭafā is in his early fifties. Both the narrator's and Muṣṭafā's stories are told in the first person. Thus, Ṣāliḥ creates a world of conflict in which nothing is certain. The reader is not sure which of the two figures really exist or whether they are doppelgängers, different aspects of one and the same person. For instance, at one point the narrator enters Muṣṭafā's secret room in his house in the village:

> Out of the darkness there emerged a frowning face . . . that I knew but could not place. I moved towards it with hate in my heart. It was my adversary Muṣṭafā Saʾeed. The face grew a neck, the neck two shoulders and a chest, then a trunk and two legs, and I found myself standing face to face with myself. This is not Muṣṭafā Saʾeed—it's a picture of me frowning at my face from a mirror.
>
> (p. 135)

To prepare for writing the novel Ṣāliḥ researched crimes of passion; he also became interested in figures like Lawrence of Arabia and Sir Richard Burton who had shown a strange fascination with the Arab world. In the relationship between the Arabs and the west, both sides have had misconceptions of one another. The Arabs have regarded Europeans as sexually promiscuous, while Europeans imagine that the Arabs are an oversexed but repressed people. Arab writers have for some time been intrigued by the perils, personified by European woman, that await the young "oriental" who spends years in the alien environment of the west. Notable tales of Arabs abroad facing such perils have been written by the Egyptians Ṭāhā Ḥusayn in the novel *Adīb*, Tawfīq al-Ḥakīm in *ʿUṣfūr min al-sharq* (*Bird of the East*), and Yaḥyā Ḥaqqī in *Qindīl Umm Hāshim* (*The Saint's Lamp*) and by the Lebanese Suhayl Idrīs in *Al-Ḥayy al-Latīnī* (*The Latin Quarter*).

In an interview, Ṣāliḥ explained his character's reaction to Europe:

> In Europe there is the idea of dominating us. That domination is associated with sex. Figuratively speaking, Europe raped Africa in a violent fashion. Muṣṭafā Saʿīd, the hero of the novel, used to react to that domination with an opposite reaction, which had an element of revenge seeking. In his violent female conquests he wants to inflict on Europe the degradation which it had imposed upon his people. He wants to rape Europe in a metaphorical fashion.
> (Berkley and Ahmed, pp. 15–16)

Muṣṭafā, born in 1898, is a child of the British occupation of Sudan (1898–1956). In London he sees himself as a new Tarek ibn Ziyad, the Moorish conqueror of Spain; "I'll liberate Africa with my penis" (*Season*, p. 120). His sexual exploits precipitate the suicides of three British women in love with him: Ann Hammond, a student, who acts like his slave and who "yearned for tropical climes, cruel suns, purple horizons" (p. 30); Sheila Greenwood, a waitress in a Soho restaurant, who is attracted by his black skin, "the colour of magic and mystery and obscenities" (p. 139); and Isabella Seymour, the wife of a successful surgeon.

He finally meets his match in Jean Morris. He pursues her for three years until, tired of the chase, she asks him to marry her. In the sexual war between them she destroys his possessions—tearing up an important book, burning a piece of research on which he had worked for weeks. She boasts to him of her infidelity. She eggs him on to kill her and submits to her own murder with pleasure. As he is killing her they both realize they are for the first time truly in love. This is the only meaningful point in his life; the rest was a lie. Muṣṭafā is not entirely to blame for all that happens; he merely stirs the "still pool in the depths" (p. 31) of others. He is sentenced to seven years in prison; on his release he wanders aimlessly around the world until the late 1940s. Muṣṭafā comes to Wād Ḥāmid, an "obscure" village where he is unknown. He blocks out his past and tries to become a useful member of the community, to lead a normal life. He attends Friday prayers regularly, buys a farm, marries Ḥusnā bint Maḥmūd, and they have two sons. It is at this point that the narrator first meets Muṣṭafā.

The narrator and Muṣṭafā struggle to determine their futures by coming to terms with their real selves. Perhaps prompted by the narrator's probings, Muṣṭafā realizes that the life he is leading in Sudan is as much a lie as the life he had spent in England. He disappears one day from the village in the flood season, either drowning by accident or committing suicide. He leaves behind a letter that places his wife, sons, and private papers in the care of the narrator, thus dragging the narrator further into Muṣṭafā's personal hell. Although the narrator has none of Muṣṭafā's vices, his actions also lead to the destruction of another's life: Muṣṭafā's widow, Ḥusnā, begs to be married to the narrator rather than be forced by her family to marry Wad al-Rayyis—forty years her senior and notorious for his many marriages and divorces—but the narrator allows the forced marriage to go forward. When Wad al-Rayyis attempts to claim his conjugal rights, Ḥusnā kills him and then herself. Too late, the narrator sides with her, realizing he was in love with her. He has come to believe that in this modern world it is not appropriate to force a woman into a marriage against her will. He realizes that he too is an outsider and that he cannot accept the mentality of the villagers: "There is no room for me here. Why don't I pack up and go?" (p. 130).

After Ḥusnā's death, the narrator decides to enter the secret room Muṣṭafā had built by his house, a copy of an English room with a fireplace, Persian rugs, and shelf after shelf of books. Here Muṣṭafā kept photographs of his mistresses, personal papers, and notes that he wanted to be discovered after his death. Exploring the room, which no one had been permitted to enter while Muṣṭafā was alive, the narrator finds a notebook titled "My Life Story." All it contains is a dedication: "To those who see with one eye, speak with one tongue and see things as either black or white, either Eastern or Western" (pp. 150–151). In the final chapter the narrator leaves the secret room and the legacy of Muṣṭafā to complete his story. To dispel the rage he felt at Muṣṭafā's treatment of his victims, the last of whom was Ḥusnā, the narrator undertakes to swim across the river from the village to the northern shore. Halfway across, unable to go any farther, and about to drown, he summons the strength to scream out for help. Unlike Muṣṭafā, he chooses life, because he feels ties with others and because he has duties to perform. Torn between Europe, represented by the northern bank of the river, and his native land, represented by the village in the south, he chooses the latter. The narrator is prepared to face the world unperturbed about the meaninglessness of life.

The skillful narrative techniques, interweaving the narrator's experiences and Muṣṭafā's story with an often poetic density of descriptive style, hold the reader in suspense to the very end. The fragmented chronology is complex; there are continuous shifts of time and space, constant flashbacks from Sudan to Muṣṭafā's earlier life in London. Dark events hinted at are gradually revealed. The murder of Jean Morris and Muṣṭafā's trial are alluded to in the second chapter, yet the full details of the relationship are not revealed until the penultimate chapter. The story of the narrator's return to Sudan and his quest for the truth about Muṣṭafā are covered chronologically; the actual time covered in the village is just a few years. The work is written in a simple and often colloquial style. The special tone was superbly translated into English by Denys Johnson-Davies.

BANDAR SHĀH, ḌAW AL-BAYT

The modern fable, *Bandar Shāh, Ḍaw al-Bayt* (1971) is set some twenty to thirty years after *Season of Migration* and *The Wedding of Zein.* The narrator of *Season of Migration*, the sixty-year-old Muḥaymīd, returns to his village to become a farmer, having retired from his post in education. His life away from the village was not of his own choosing; it had been dictated to him by others, in particular his grandfather. In a bizarre way he still idolizes his village, which the villagers themselves more realistically view as a place where life is barely supportable. He meets his old friends and catches up on the stories of the village.

Several villagers have had the same dream about the novel's eponymous hero, Bandar Shāh, who belongs to the generation of the narrator's grandfather. Bandar Shāh has one grandson called Maryūd, who bears a striking resemblance to the narrator; Maryūd is also the narrator's pet name. Bandar Shāh and his grandson have become mythical figures. In their common dream, the villagers witness the sons of Bandar Shāh being driven in chains before him in his palace near the village. Maryūd whips them, and soldiers carry their bodies outside. The struggle of the generations depicted in this portentous dream is echoed in the village.

For Ṣāliḥ, both Bandar Shāh and Muṣṭafā before him are Faustian characters who arrogantly want to assert their presence in the world. Ṣāliḥ has explained that he chose the title, *Bandar Shāh*, because the problem facing his people is the search for the modern city (*bandar*) and the need to create an adequate means of governing themselves, a need expressed by "ruler" (*shāh*). The older generation, represented by Bandar Shāh and the narrator's grandfather, feels that only it can control the general chaos, and this perception easily turns to tyranny. But a new generation of leaders, led by al-Ṭurayfī, defeat Maḥjūb, the narrator's close friend, in the elections for the presidency of the agricultural cooperative; it is al-Ṭurayfī who now "wants to play Bandar Shāh" (p. 42). Al-Ṭurayfī believes he stands for the march of civilization, the age of science and technology. Maryam, mother of al-Ṭurayfī, sides with her brother, Maḥjūb, in the dispute and consequently leaves her husband's house for good.

Ḍaw al-Bayt is introduced in the telling of the local tradition about Bandar Shāh's father's arrival in the village. A stranger, a wounded white soldier in Turkish uniform, is carried by the flooding river to the village. He has completely forgotten his past. He is fed and cured and later converts to Islam, being given the name Ḍaw al-Bayt. Ḍaw al-Bayt soon settles into his new home and teaches the peasants how to grow new crops. The story of Ḍaw al-Bayt's appearance in the village in some ways echoes the story of Muṣṭafā. Both have mysterious pasts, marry girls from the village, become farmers and valuable members of the community, and then suddenly depart as if they had never existed.

They both disappear in the Nile during the flood season. Ḍaw al-Bayt's death is supernatural as described by the men who were repairing a waterwheel when they were swept away with him and who were miraculously saved with his help. He is last seen by one of them hovering like an angel; the man "glanced at Ḍaw al-Bayt as if he was suspended between sky and earth surrounded by a green glow" (p. 135). He is endowed with supernatural qualities; "perhaps the man was sent to us in this way bringing goodness and blessing" (p. 113). Ḍaw al-Bayt leaves behind a son, ʿĪsā, later known as Bandar Shāh.

BANDAR SHĀH, MARYŪD

The short volume *Bandar Shāh, Maryūd* (1977) continues Muḥaymīd's reminiscences. Maryūd, meaning "beloved" in the dialect, is the name that Maryam, the sister of Maḥjūb, had given Muḥaymīd when he was a youth; Maryam had been his first love. The tale unfolds during the course of Muḥaymīd's journeys around the village alone, or in the company of friends, or as he visits the tomb of Maryam. There are frequent flashbacks to his childhood, to his relations with his grandfather and with Maryam, to Maryam's death and to the story of Bilāl, the father of his friend Ṭāhir Wad Rawwāsī. The story of Bilāl and his slavelike attachment to the imam, Shaykh Naṣr Allāh Wad Ḥabīb, replicates the relationship between Zein and al-Ḥanīn in *The Wedding of Zein.* Like Zein, Bilāl is blessed and good-natured; his call to prayer—the shaykh had chosen him to be the muezzin—has a supernatural effect on all who hear it. Tradition relates that Bilāl is the twelfth son of Bandar Shāh, from a female slave. History repeats itself, and the reader concludes that no matter what happens the village will never change completely because it has its own immutable identity.

On the last page of the book, we are reminded of the clash of generations of the first volume of the trilogy: the beloved grandfather in *Season of Migration* turns out to be highly manipulative; it was he who had prevented Muḥaymīd from marrying Maryam. When Maryam dies, her last words condemn the two generations of grandfather and grandson:

> You two are of greater weight in the balance of men. But your father is worth more than you and your grandfather in the balance of justice. He loved untiringly, and gave without expecta-

> tion. He drank like a bird, kept on travelling and left in a hurry. He dreamt the dreams of the weak and was nourished with the sustenance of the poor. His soul had been tempted by glory, but he restrained it and when life called him . . . when life called him.
>
> (p. 88)

In this remark Ṣāliḥ is reiterating that the past and the future are in a perpetual conspiracy against the present. He rejects the calculating joyless grandfather and the cold-blooded intellectual and reminds his reader once more of the simple values in life, personified by such innocents as Zein, Bilāl, and Muḥaymīd's father.

"THE CYPRIOT MAN"

The story "Al-Rajul al-qubruṣī" first appeared in 1976 and was translated as "The Cypriot Man" in 1980. This is perhaps Ṣāliḥ's most complex story; there are two differing texts. The narrator, another villager with a clear place in the schema, is sitting by the swimming pool in a hotel in Nicosia, when a stranger, the Cypriot Man—in fact, the angel of death—begins talking to him, reappearing throughout the story in various guises. While sitting there, the narrator mentally travels back to Wad Ḥāmid to talk to his friend Ṭāhir Wad Rawwāsī. The narrator has a heart attack in his hotel bed but survives; the same night his father dies in his Sudanese village. The simple soul of the father had been accepted as ransom for that of the narrator; he may not be so lucky next time. The father had died peacefully in his bed after having visited friends and relatives, drinking some coffee, and performing the evening prayer. The narrator is warned by the Cypriot Man that death will assume various guises to bring about his eventual downfall: rank, money, the flattery of a beautiful woman who wants to interview him, or just the empty applause of a huge crowd. Death is near; "beware, for you are now ascending towards the mountain peak" (p. 7). A reader may hope that this ominous note was not the swan song of Ṣāliḥ's fiction.

CONCLUSION

Although his published work spans a twenty-year period up through the 1970s, Ṣāliḥ, through the clever manipulation of time, has written a chronicle of the mythical, supernatural, and real history of a Sudanese village covering a period of about 150 years, from the early nineteenth century in the time of the Turks to the age of the empty revolutionary jargon of the postindependence era. Ṣāliḥ himself is perhaps the narrator, Muḥaymīd; like the narrator on his return to the village, he is always asking questions; "you might say that he wants to write a chronicle" (*Maryūd*, p. 27). The bulk of his oeuvre is a complex interconnected puzzle, a single opus, with numerous counterparts and parallels in the stories that slowly reveal more about the village of Wad Ḥāmid. Although the physical misery of agricultural life is always in the background, the story of Wad Ḥāmid chiefly provides a nostalgic description of the intangible human and spiritual values, and the myths and legends, that give the village its special enduring identity, which Ṣāliḥ clearly hopes will be preserved from corrupting forces, whatever form they may take. With his double culture, Ṣāliḥ remains attached to Sudan's folklore, popular mysticism, and traditional ways of life, but he aspires to renewal, progress, and evolution.

Selected Bibliography

COLLECTED WORKS

Al-Aʿmāl al-kāmila. Beirut, Lebanon: Dār al-ʿAwda, 1971–1986. Includes *Mawsim; ʿUrs; Dawmat; Bandar Shāh, Ḍaw al-Bayt;* and *Bandar Shāh, Maryūd.*

SELECTED WORKS

ʿUrs al-Zayn: Riwāya wa-sabʿ qiṣaṣ. Beirut, Lebanon: al-Dār al-Sharqiyya, 1966.

Mawsim al-hijra ilāʾl-shamāl. Beirut, Lebanon: Dār al-ʿAwda, 1967.

Dawmat Wad Ḥāmid, sabʿ qiṣaṣ Beirut, Lebanon: Dār al-ʿAwda, 1969.

Bandar Shāh, Ḍaw al-Bayt: Uḥdūtha ʿan kawn al-ab ḍaḥīya lī abīh wa ʾbnih wa ʾbnih. Beirut, Lebanon: Dār al-ʿAwda, 1971.

Bandar Shāh, Maryūd. Beirut, Lebanon: Dār al-ʿAwda, 1977.

"Al-Rajul al-qubruṣī." In *Majallat al-dawḥa* (January 1976).

TRANSLATIONS

"The Doum Tree of Wad Hamid," "A Handful of Dates," and *The Wedding of Zein*. In *The Wedding of Zein and Other Stories*. Trans. by Denys Johnson-Davies. London: Heinemann, 1968.

Season of Migration to the North. Trans. by Denys Johnson-Davies. London: Heinemann, 1969, 1970.

"The Cypriot Man." Trans by Denys Johnson-Davies. In *Encounter* (April 1980).

"A Letter to Aileen." Trans. by Nakdimon Shabbethay Doniach. In *Journal of Arabic Literature* 11 (1980).

"A Date Palm by the Stream." Trans. by Denys Johnson-Davies. In *Azure: The Review of Arabic Literature, Arts, and Culture* 8 (1981).

Bandarshah. Trans. by Denys Johnson-Davies. London: Kegan Paul International, 1996.

INTERVIEWS

Berkley, Constance E., and Osman Hassan Ahmed. *Tayeb Salih Speaks: Four Interviews with the Sudanese Novelist*. Washington, D.C.: Embassy of the Democratic Republic of the Sudan, 1982.

CRITICAL STUDIES

Abbas, Ali Abdallah. "Notes on Tayeb Salih: *Season of Migration to the North* and *The Wedding of Zein*." In *Sudan Notes and Records* 55 (1974).

———. "The Strangled Impulse: The Role of the Narrator in Tayeb Salih's *Season of Migration to the North*." In *Sudan Notes and Records* 60 (1979).

Abu Deeb, Kamal. "Sālih, al-Tayyib." In Tracy Chevalier, ed., *Contemporary World Writers*. Detroit: St. James Press, 1993.

Alrawi, Karim. "The Village and the World: Tayeb Salih." In *Afkar Inquiry* 2, no. 3 (1985).

Amyuni, Mona Takieddine. "Tayeb Salih's *Season of Migration to the North*: An Interpretation." In *Arab Studies Quarterly* 2 (winter 1980).

———, ed. Season of Migration to the North *by Tayeb Salih: A Casebook*. Beirut, Lebanon: American University of Beirut, 1985.

Berkley, Constance E. "The Roots of Consciousness Moulding the Art of al-Tayeb Salih: A Contemporary Sudanese Writer." Ph.D. diss., New York University, 1979.

———. Review of *The Wedding of Zein*. In *Journal of Arabic Literature* 11 (1980).

———. "El Tayyeb Salih: An Introductory Essay in Appreciation." *Pacific Moana Quarterly* 6, nos. 3–4 (July–October 1981).

———. "Systems of Thought in el Tayeb Salih's ʿAl-Rajul al-Qubrosi' ('The Cypriot Man')." In *The Search: Journal of Arab and Islamic Studies* 4, nos. 1–3 (1983).

Davidson, John E. "In Search of a Middle Point: The Origins of Oppression in Tayeb Salih's *Season of Migration to the North*." In *Research in African Literatures* 20 (fall 1989).

Harb, Ahmad Musa. "Half-way Between North and South: An Archetypal Analysis of the Fiction of Tayeb Salih." Ph.D. diss., University of Iowa, 1986.

Harrow, Kenneth W. "The Power and the Word: *L'Aventure ambiguë* and *The Wedding of Zein*." In *African Studies Review* 30, no. 1 (March 1987).

Ḥijāb, Nadia. "Meet the Maker of Modern Arab Mythology." In *Middle East* (June 1979).

John, Joseph, and Yosif Tarawneh. "Quest for Identity: The I-Thou Imbroglio in Tayeb Salih's *Season of Migration to the North*." In *Arab Studies Quarterly* 8 (spring 1986).

Johnson-Davies, Denys. "The World of Tayeb Salih." In *Azure: The Review of Arab Literature, Arts and Culture* 8 (1981).

Kambal, Z. el-D. S. "The Thematic Concerns of al-Tayyib Salih: A Study of His Short Stories and Novels." Ph.D. diss., University of Exeter, 1984.

Makdisi, Saree S. "The Empire Renarrated: *Season of Migration to the North* and the Reinvention of the Present." In *Critical Inquiry 18* (summer 1992).

Matar, Nabil. "Encounter with the Snake God." In *Middle East* (June 1979).

Nasr, Ahmad A. "Popular Islam in al-Ṭayyib Ṣāliḥ." In *Journal of Arabic Literature* 11 (1980).

Neville, Jill. "Much Earthier, More Truthful and More Vivid than *Coronation Street*." In *Sunday Times* (London) (2 May 1967).

Peled, Mattityahu. "Portrait of an Individual." In *Middle Eastern Studies* 13, no. 2 (1977).

Peters, Barbara-Diane. "Power Relations and Conflict in Selected Works of Tayeb Salih: Implications for a New History." Ph.D. diss., University of Wisconsin—Madison, 1989.

Shaneen, Mohammed. "Tayeb Salih and Conrad." In *Comparative Literature Studies* 22, no. 1 (1985).

Siddiq, Muḥammad. "The Process of Individuation in al-Tayyeb Salih's Novel *Season of Migration to the North.*" In *Journal of Arabic Literature* 9 (1978).

Tube, Henry. "New Novels." In *Spectator* (20 September 1969).

Wielandt, Rotraud. "The Problem of Cultural Identity in the Writings of al-Ṭayyib Ṣāliḥ." In Wadad al-Qāḍī, ed., *Studia Arabica and Islamica: Festschrift for Ihsan Abbas on His Sixtieth Birthday.* Beirut, Lebanon: Imprimerie Catholique, 1981.

Olive Schreiner
1855–1920

CHERRY CLAYTON

OLIVE SCHREINER holds a special place in the hearts of most South Africans, and her name has become synonymous with an embattled, visionary feminism. She is viewed as a founder and foremother in many respects. Her acclaimed landmark novel, *The Story of an African Farm* (1883), is generally seen as the first remarkable imaginative achievement by a white South African writer; her allegory "Three Dreams in a Desert" (published in *Dreams*, 1891) and her feminist study of women's work, *Woman and Labour* (1911), gave passionate expression to feminist issues and inspired many sympathetic readers. Her eloquent political pamphlets published at key moments of South African history, such as during the Anglo-Boer War (1899–1902) and the establishment of the Union of South Africa (1910), marked her as a concerned English South African who tried to marry the best of English liberal traditions to indigenous social and political structures. She was loyal to both South Africa and England. This fact divided her emotionally and practically; she spent her life alternating between the two countries, finding in England a stimulating intellectual environment and cultural richness, while South Africa offered her the deep stability and peace she had found in her childhood attachment to certain landscapes. All of her writing, both fiction and nonfiction, reflects this dual allegiance.

CHILDHOOD AND ADOLESCENCE

Olive Schreiner spent her childhood and adolescence in isolated areas of the Cape Colony, to which her parents, Gottlob Schreiner, a German missionary, and his refined English wife, Rebecca Lyndall, had emigrated in 1838. Olive Emily Albertina, their ninth child (there were twelve children, of whom seven reached adulthood), was born at the isolated Wittenbergen mission station on 24 March 1855 and named after three brothers who had died in childhood. A certain morbidity in Schreiner's temperament may be traced to these circumstances, as well as to the effect of a grieving mother. Her intense reactions to her parents' evangelical religion and to the landscapes within which she found her own identity are key elements in her fiction. A setting forth into spaces within nature, a private fantasizing and storytelling, and a sense of personal freedom and integrity within African landscapes are found in the three novels conceived and written almost entirely during her youth in South Africa, before she left for England at the age of twenty-six.

Schreiner needed to escape the philosophical and social prisons built around her by the doctrine of predestination and her mother's conventional sense of propriety, especially where her daughters were concerned. Schreiner's young protagonists, such as Undine (in her first completed novel, *Undine*, published posthumously in 1928) and Waldo (of *The Story of an African Farm*) agonize over their rejection of God, conduct solitary rituals in the African veld to test divine power, and strive to retain some connectedness with divine benevolence while rejecting social hypocrisy as well as the creeds that seem to damn human beings to hellfire without giving them a fighting chance. Schreiner's fiction is grounded in a resistance of the human spirit, a strong impulse toward freedom and justice.

VICTORIAN WOMEN

The Victorian emphasis on duty, obedience to God and parents, and preordained roles for women within domestic spheres fired Schreiner's rebellions and her writing. All of her writing turns on these struggles against fixed authority and on her need to work out, from her own perceptions, principles, and experience, a just and rational basis for human existence, education, and work, especially the relationship between the sexes. As an adolescent she refused to go to church with her family after she had decided to be a freethinker, and thus endured punitive treatment from her family and a degree of ostracism for her independent stand. She would often find herself in this position during her lifetime, and she identified strongly with dissidents, lonely forerunners, and social prophets. She was a rebel by nature and on principle.

One of the most sustained forms of Schreiner's rebellion was against conventional marriage, which she saw as the exchange of sexual services for economic support. Her most famous heroine, Lyndall of *The Story of an African Farm*, refuses to marry the man who has made her pregnant because he satisfies only one part of her nature: "there is a higher part that you know nothing of," she tells him (Part Two, Chapter 9). While Schreiner's female protagonists seem to engage in tortuous maneuvers around men, love, and marriage, and alternate between fiery speeches and childlike pathos, these fictional situations point to a real difficulty that intelligent Victorian women had in trying to reconcile marriage, which was regarded as the only respectable and worthwhile aim for women, with an independent intellectual life. In Schreiner's third novel about women's lives, *From Man to Man* (begun before she left South Africa but published posthumously as an incomplete novel in 1926), the topic of marriage is given much fuller and more sustained attention. This is achieved by having two sisters as protagonists. One of them, Bertie, destroys her chances of conventional happiness by being seduced by her tutor and telling her suitor about the relationship. The other, Rebekah, marries her first sweetheart, only to have her life made intolerable by her husband's infidelity, her own economic dependence, and the lack of any fulfillment except domesticity and motherhood. The contrasted lives of the sisters offer a very full picture of the constricted opportunities for white colonial women at the time.

Education was not often given to women on the same basis as men, and Schreiner felt the injustice of this within her own family. Her elder brothers, Fred and Theo, were both given the best schooling available and were sent to London University; Will, her younger brother, was a brilliant scholar and Cambridge graduate who rose to be prime minister of the Cape Colony and later high commissioner for South Africa in England. Olive, who clearly had an outstanding intellect and a hunger for knowledge, was taught by her mother at home and given very little formal schooling. The results of this situation were her fragmented attempts to acquire enough professional training to be a nurse or doctor, which was her first dream, and a tendency to live vicariously through the work of her male friends. On the other hand, her deprivation caused her to read voraciously; Havelock Ellis, her closest confidant during her London years, thought that her prose style gained by being a spontaneous expression of her deepest thoughts and feelings and that a formal education might have destroyed this spontaneity. Here is one of her typical long sentences, which is also a statement of her artistic vision of variety and human interconnectedness, from *The Story of an African Farm*:

> She drew a long breath. "When my own life feels small, and I am oppressed with it, I like to crush together, and see it in a picture, in an instant, a multitude of disconnected unlike phases of human life—a mediaeval monk with his string of beads pacing the quiet orchard, and looking up from the grass at his feet to the heavy fruit-trees; little Malay boys playing naked on a shining sea-beach; a Hindoo philosopher alone under his banyan-tree, thinking, thinking, thinking, so that in the thought of God he may lose himself; a troop of Bacchanalians dressed in white, with crowns of vine-leaves, dancing along the Roman streets; a martyr on the night of his death looking through the narrow window to the sky, and feeling that already he has the wings that shall bear him up" (she moved her hand dreamily over her face); "an epicurean discoursing at a Roman bath to a knot of his disciples on the nature of happiness; a Kaffir witch-doctor seeking for herbs by moonlight, while from the huts on the hillside come the sounds of dogs barking, and the voices of women and children; a mother giving bread and milk to her children in little wooden basins and singing the evening song. I like to see it all; I feel it run through me—that life belongs to me; it makes my little life larger; it breaks down the narrow walls that shut me in."
>
> (Part Two, Chapter 6)

For Schreiner, writing was an act of empathy that connected her with a wider life and allowed her to escape the condition of solitude.

INFLUENCE OF CHILDHOOD

Schreiner's first three novels, written between 1873 and 1881 (she wrote only one other, *Trooper Peter Halket of Mashonaland*, 1897)—*Undine*, *The Story of an African Farm*, and *From Man to Man*—all have a strong focus on childhood experience, on the suffering and pleasure of childhood, on children's sense of wickedness and the intensity of their desire to make sense of the world around them. The epigraph to *The Story of an African Farm*, from the nineteenth-century French writer and politician Alexis de Tocqueville, points to the shaping power of early influences and impressions; the last sentence reads, "The entire man is, so to speak, to be found in the cradle of the child." All three novels show a wonderful skill in depicting a continuity of character and temperament in the central figures as they move from childhood into young adulthood. As children they are intense and striving, opposed by harsh, intolerant, or punitive adults, living in their dreams and inner conflicts. As they grow, they find their movement into the wider world, outside an isolated farm setting, checked by loss, conflict, and disillusionment. There is no worthwhile work for men and women, and women are offered a parody of education at "finishing schools": Lyndall says they "finish everything but imbecility and weakness, and that they cultivate" (Part Two, Chapter 4). Staying on the farm leads to stagnation, but the outside world offers no real fulfillment. The motto of Part Two of *African Farm* reads: "And it was all play, and no one could tell what it had lived and worked for. A striving, and a striving, and an ending in nothing."

This motto is borne out by the plots of Schreiner's novels. The two most talented characters in *African Farm*, Lyndall and Waldo, both die young. Undine dies at the end of her story. Bertie, the younger sister in *From Man to Man*, would have died from a "loathsome and terrible disease" in a brothel if Schreiner had finished the book. While Schreiner throws off the constriction of theological predestination in her fiction, her characters seem to be doomed to destruction in their struggles against material odds and socially sanctioned roles. Schreiner dramatized very bleakly the materialism, rigid belief systems, and unthinking conformity of the society she lived in, and showed how sensitive young adults could be crushed by such values and systems.

SOUTH AFRICAN CONTEXT

If Schreiner's view of life's possibilities appears pessimistic, it should be seen against the frontier culture in which she grew up. She recorded her earliest impressions of a brutal and militaristic society in "The Dawn of Civilization," a pacifist article written toward the end of her life and published in 1921. She records there her early impressions of violence and injustice everywhere:

> I had grown up in a land where wars were common. From my earliest years I had heard of bloodshed and battles and hair-breadth escapes; I had heard them told of by those who had seen and taken part in them. In my native country dark men were killed and their lands taken from them by white men armed with superior weapons. . . . I knew also how white men fought white men; the stronger even hanging the weaker on gallows when they did not submit; and I had seen how white men used the dark as beasts of labor, often without any thought for their good or happiness.
>
> (p. 913)

This violence, one of the constant features of life in South Africa, created a strong and lasting impression. It gave rise to her pacifist beliefs and shaped her depiction of life on a South African farm in the karoo (a semidesert plateau marked by low ironstone hills called "kopjes" or "koppies" and sparse vegetation) in her most famous novel.

Though adults often behave brutally toward one another and toward children and animals, the landscape itself—the terrain, sky, vegetation, and small creatures of southern Africa, both in the bush world of the eastern Cape, where the Schreiners' early mission stations were located, and on the karoo farms where Schreiner was a governess as a young woman—could offer solace, familiarity, peace, and a sense of wholeness. Such mystical moments of self-affirmation are apparent even in Schreiner's apprentice novel, *Undine*. Undine, on an unpleasant journey toward the diamond fields with her harsh employers, walks away from the wagons and finds an empty riverbed, with "great dark boulders" lying "quiet and unmovable" on a bed of white sand. A little higher up there is a stream:

> The silver band of water as it crept through the sand made no sound, and the long low tremulous bank of maiden-hair fern, though it heaved and swayed to and fro in the stillness, made no sound. High on the western bank of the stream against the white dreamy evening sky, the branches of the oliven trees were visible, with pale, quivering, up-pointed leaves.
>
> (1928 edition, pp. 278–279)

Such moments in African landscapes, always solitary and silent, seem to offer the characters a reaffirmation of self and a sense of coherence within the natural world that is lacking in jarring social encounters or aggressive human relationships. They are always key moments in the evolution of her characters' consciousness and lives.

UNDINE

In *Undine*, which Schreiner did not think worth publishing, a hesitation is evident between South Africa and England as the setting for the action. The novel begins on a rather vague South African farm, then quickly moves to an even more ethereal England. Only at the end of the novel is there a recognizable setting, in a journey by ox wagon and in the tent camps of the diamond fields at Kimberley (called New Rush when Schreiner was there, briefly, in 1872). It is here that Undine has a glimpse of an independent working life for women, but only working-class women are shown with a degree of independence. The plot of the novel is extremely improbable, and the motives and relationships often obscure, but in *Undine*, Schreiner was working out her own adaptation of the form of the novel, trying out characters, settings, and scenes; experimenting with melodrama and sensationalism; and mingling realism, allegory, and fairy tale. She was finding ways of telling her own story, which is essentially the story of the conflicted desires and potentialities of talented young white colonial women, though it subtends the wider story of Victorians in spiritual crisis and Victorian women in subjection to patriarchal norms.

Though the settings in *Undine* are not realized in any detail, the events are often autobiographical, and the frustrated emotions that seethe about the cardboard male figures are the result of an unhappy love affair in Schreiner's adolescence. Her adolescence and young womanhood were spent in conditions of dependence within English South African or Boer (Cape Dutch) families in the karoo, working as a governess. Her father's bankruptcy after an unsuccessful career as missionary and trader created great economic stress within the family, and at fifteen Olive was sent off to family and connected friends as household help and a teacher of children. Complex emotional stresses led to a lifelong vulnerability and restlessness, as well as an asthmatic condition that undermined her health, happiness, and productivity. Conflicted feelings about family relationships and lovers are very evident in *Undine*, and the male characters are aloof, supercilious, and callous or, if they are kind and devoted, effeminate. Although Undine has the makings of an independent life at the end of the story, the novel has a conventionally melodramatic ending with Undine prostrating herself before the corpse of her long-sought and worthless lover, Albert Blair, before she herself dies.

There is excessive martyrdom in *Undine*, and self-prostration before worthless men remained a thread in the other novels. Such elements, reflecting an overwhelming need for love and emotional reassurance, coexist in Schreiner's fiction with discursive and didactic feminist speeches, of which the most famous is Lyndall's passionate declaration to Waldo of woman's condition, "to be born a woman [is] to be born branded," in *African Farm* (Part Two, Chapter 4). Men are made for work; women, for appearances, passivity, and the marriage market. Their true potential atrophies under such social restrictions and distorting roles. Women cannot travel freely or participate in professional training and real work in the world. Men have power; women are encouraged to spend their energies on men. This is a powerful exposition, and a full statement of women's distorting socialization in the Victorian age. It is a rhetorically constructed and energetic speech, anchored from time to time in the fictional situation. Such "interpolations" reveal how Schreiner was using the novel as a vehicle for social criticism of a more direct kind, making space for her feminist indignation at injustice and inequality. There are similar discursive and expository sections in *From Man to Man*, on the double standard for sexual behavior within marriage, and on racial prejudice and social evolution. This combination of the novel of ideas and intellectual critique with a colonial, South African farm setting is the hallmark of Schreiner's fiction.

THE STORY OF AN AFRICAN FARM

The Story of an African Farm, first published under the conventional male pseudonym Ralph Iron, surpasses *Undine* in its commitment to the realities of a colonial time and place. As Schreiner wrote in her preface to the second edition, her apparently aimless action would follow the pattern of "the life we all lead," which is not that of a neatly packaged play. She was not trying, either, to write a story of "wild adventure" for armchair readers in Piccadilly. She had seen that the writer, like a painter, has a duty to the environment he or she knows: "Sadly he must squeeze the colour from his brush, and dip it into the grey pigments around him. He must paint what lies before him" (preface to the second edition). *The Story of an African Farm* succeeds in the task of presenting the daily struggles for survival on a farm in the karoo. Though the struggles are the inner ones of thoughtful and talented youth, they are always anchored in the red sand of the farm, the ostrich camps, the koppie, the dam and the kraals, the spaces within and outside the farmhouse: roof, loft, outhouse, low stone walls. At the same time the power of the shaping imagination is registered at once in the opening of the novel:

> The full African moon poured down its light from the blue sky into the wide, lonely plain. The dry, sandy earth, with its coating of stunted "karroo" bushes a few inches high, the low hills that skirted the plain, the milk-bushes with their long, finger-like leaves, all were touched by a weird and almost oppressive beauty as they lay in the white light.
>
> (Part One, Chapter 1)

In the next section of the chapter ("The Sacrifice"), we are given a view of the farm in the blazing sunlight: "The plain was a weary flat of loose red sand, sparsely covered by dry karroo bushes, that cracked beneath the tread like tinder, and showed the red earth everywhere."

These contrasting views on reality, the economy of presentation, and the ability to anchor visionary rhetorical flights and didactic speeches in the concrete details of South African spaces contribute to the finished effect of the novel, a sense that it has said what it wants to say, and that what it wants to say is inevitably enigmatic. Waldo's stranger points to the evocative nature of art: it "says more than it says, and takes you away from itself. It is a little door that opens into an infinite hall where you may find what you please" (Part Two, Chapter 2).

The Story of an African Farm is divided into two parts with two abstract, generalizing, bridging passages in the middle of the novel: "Times and Seasons" (Part Two, Chapter 1) and the Hunter allegory, which is told by a stranger ("Waldo's stranger") as an interpretation of Waldo's carving (Part Two, Chapter 2). Part One tells a story of colonial invasion and attempted usurpation of the farm in semicomic, parodic fashion, the rise and fall of Bonaparte Blenkins on a farm ruled over by a fat and ignorant Boer woman, Tant' Sannie. These two figures, having ousted the gentle German missionary father of Waldo, the young, dreamy herdsman, tyrannize over the three children: Lyndall, who follows the beautiful, intelligent orphan model laid down by Undine; Em, the Boer woman's plain and domestic stepdaughter; and Waldo, who endures the religious crisis of faith that was Schreiner's own. Though these characters could be said to represent aspects of Schreiner herself, they are also aspects of everyone (intellect, body, and soul) and characters who have their own vivid reality as they interact with one another and with the outside world. The style of Part One is farcical and external, quoting and misapplying biblical texts to show how hypocrisy and greed can operate under the cloak of religious piety in Bonaparte Blenkins and Tant' Sannie. It has elements of pastoral comedy and culminates in the downfall of Blenkins when his plans to marry Tant' Sannie become too sly and ambitious.

The two bridging sections of the novel broaden the implications of the individual characters' lives and deepen the mood of the novel to embrace philosophy, vision, and dream. They prepare us for the more somber unfolding of the characters' lives as young adults. The Hunter allegory tells of a man's journey to capture the white bird of truth. He has to overcome many temptations and endure many forms of suffering, and he dies realizing that his quest is unfulfilled after much arduous searching and labor. His consolation is that he has carved out a stair on which others will climb. This allegory reveals

Schreiner's self-consciousness about her position within history as a pioneer; it counts the cost of being an isolated and oppositional thinker and rejoices in a vision of a better future. Her reading of Herbert Spencer's *First Principles* (1862) had given her a belief in the moral evolution of humanity that helped her out of her youthful atheism. Her own idealism always rises out of the ashes of bleak disappointments and crushed aspirations. The Hunter allegory, with its central motif of a painful quest, ties together the life journeys of the characters, and its mood of stubborn aspiration suffuses Part Two.

Part Two of the novel shows the children as young adults and defines each in relation to a particular "stranger." Waldo's stranger is his opposite: a cultivated traveler who has eloquence but little warmth or interest in his own life or in Waldo's. Em's stranger is Gregory Rose, an effeminate English colonial who rents half of Tant' Sannie's farm and becomes engaged to Em. When Lyndall returns from school, Gregory Rose transfers his attentions to her; thus Em learns of the disillusionments and compromises of love through her stranger. Lyndall's stranger is her lover and the father of her expected child. Like Undine, she tries to bargain with the men who love her in order to establish some element of power and choice in the process of mating and marriage. She first asks Gregory Rose for his name and the status of his wife; then she agrees to go away with her stranger but will not marry him. Finally she is found alone, abandoned in an upcountry hotel after the death of her child. Gregory Rose, disguised as a woman, nurses her as she dies. They travel in a covered wagon toward a "blue mountain" that becomes, when they reach it, "low and brown, covered with long waving grasses and rough stones" (Part Two, Chapter 12).

The story of Lyndall's death is not told by the impersonal narrating voice but by Gregory himself, after he has returned to the farm. The novel is marked by such complex and shifting narrative forms and points of view, but the farm is the ground and anchor of all the stories that the novel tells. Waldo, too, narrates his adventures beyond the home farm only after his return, in a long letter written to Lyndall (who is already dead). He describes how his search for meaningful work in the world led to brutalizing labor and demeaning company. As a nineteenth-century freethinker, he comes to terms with Lyndall's death without the promise of an afterlife. *African Farm* shows us how the struggle between religious belief and evolutionary science was a lived reality, not a dead letter, for Victorians struggling with the problem of meaning in the world.

Waldo dies on a perfect day, after the drought has broken and the worlds of nature, culture, and humanity seem reconciled in a deep peace: when "great men blossom into books," when

> life is delicious; well to live long, and see the darkness breaking, and the day coming! The day when soul shall not thrust back soul that would come to it; when men shall not be driven to seek solitude, because of the crying-out of their hearts for love and sympathy.
>
> (Part Two, Chapter 14)

This vision of a harmonious future is central to South African fiction, which records a history of contention and violent racial and factional confrontations. Though Schreiner approaches the racial issue only through her evolutionary idealism and certain key symbols, such as the beating of a black ox that Waldo witnesses, the novel is rife with a sense of a struggle for survival, an aggressive self-assertion. Its ending seems to arise organically from previous events and scenes. The closing mood is one that temporarily reconciles the ceaseless dialectic of form and events.

FROM MAN TO MAN

From Man to Man was the third novel that Schreiner had completed in an early form before she left for England in 1881. She tried to recast it completely after it had been rejected by a publisher, and she later added chapters and the wonderful "Prelude" to the main story, which offers a lyrical encapsulation of the life of the main figure in the novel, Rebekah. (Rebekah, like Lyndall, was named after Schreiner's mother.) The "Prelude" describes a day in the life of a five-year-old girl as she wanders about the farm on the day her younger sister is born. Schreiner herself had been very affected by the death in 1865 of her younger sister Ellie (Helen) at the age of eighteen months. This event, as Karl Schoeman suggests, may have been an important source of the image of the dead child that prevails in Schreiner's fiction. *From Man to Man* was dedicated to this little sister, as well as to Schreiner's own daughter, who died during the first night after she was born. Later, Schreiner felt that Ellie's life and death were a turning point in her own faith, as she was able to reconcile herself to death and to see Ellie as taken up by an impersonal and pantheistic principle. The process is similar to the one Schreiner has Waldo go through after Lyndall's death in *African Farm.*

The "Prelude" establishes the idea of affectionate sisterhood, of jealousy and rivalry, and of storytelling and fantasy as consolatory activities. Sibling jealousy in the "Prelude" prefigures the rivalries between women that permeate the novel, and shows that they can be overcome. It also establishes the beauty and security of the farm, a much more protected and cultivated space than the farm in the two earlier novels. The main story is that of Rebekah, the older, intellectual sister, and Bertie, the sensual and domestic younger sister. Their narratives interweave, with the home farm and the mimosa flowers on the plain as a bedrock of memory that unites them. The novel concentrates on the lives of fairly cultivated English South Africans and on the fates of colonial women. It unfolds with great charm and a greater sense of social interaction, of town life as well as of life in rural isolation. It also moves the setting to England, when Bertie, after her seduction and broken engagement, goes to England with a Jewish diamond buyer. The link with mineral exploitation establishes one of Schreiner's constant themes: of sexual relations as an economic exchange or trade.

Rebekah's marriage starts off promisingly, with love between two young cousins, and it shows the pleasures of domesticity and motherhood. It then depicts Rebekah's growing disillusionment at the infidelity of her husband, his assumptions of her total dependence, and her attempt, this time more successfully, to establish an independent space for herself as the owner of a small farm. The later chapters, which tail off, develop a more promising relationship between Rebekah and a man who is attractive to her as well as an intelligent companion. Her projected ending, however, would have shown Rebekah renouncing this man and relationship. Schreiner never outgrew her desire for self-renunciation.

From Man to Man has a rich lyricism to it, an ability to depict mood, and an evocative use of the imagery of the home farm. It is a novel that understands homesicknesses and exile, which Schreiner, by the time of her revisions, had experienced in England. It does not have the bare integrity of place, or the abrupt treatment of character and event, of *African Farm.* It is a richer work, and a more strongly feminist work in that it insistently reveals that whether women married or not, their options were extremely limited, their fates were generally controlled, and their intellectual lives were stunted by role expectations.

LONDON YEARS: 1881–1889

Schreiner spent the years from 1881 to 1889 in England, with excursions to the Continent. She used Eastbourne, in Sussex, where her elder brother, Fred, was a schoolmaster, as a base during the first year of her stay, but tried to remain independent of his family as much as she could. (He did in fact give her an annual allowance without which she would not have survived.) She was homesick in London, and these years served as the basis for her depiction, in *From Man to Man*, of Bertie's growing depression and lack of self-identity while imprisoned in a gray and gloomy London climate. The publication and successful reception of *The Story of an African Farm* made Schreiner a celebrity, bringing her new friends and new problems. She did not cope well with social interaction and sophisticated social pressures. Many anecdotes describe her hiding under the table to avoid visitors. Though she met and was lionized by George Moore, Frank Harris, and Arthur Symons and she was overjoyed by the sympathetic reviews given to *The Story of an African Farm*, especially by Henry Norman and Havelock Ellis, she did not do much creative work during this period of her life.

Schreiner's chief relationships during this period were with Havelock Ellis, then a struggling medical student with literary ambitions, and the mathematician Karl Pearson, with whom she at one time planned to write a historical study of the lives of women. She was looking for a mate yet was terrified of marriage, seeing it as a form of death to her ambitions and creativity as a writer. Though she and Ellis soon realized they would never be compatible lovers, they settled into an intimate confessional relationship and corresponded voluminously. Ellis was also her informal guide to contemporary English fiction; they discussed the books of the day, the plays of Henrik Ibsen, artistic methods, and the intimate problems of Victorian men and women in marriage or in relationships outside marriage. Schreiner was passionately attracted to Karl Pearson, but also tried to set up a working collaboration with him that would be more comradely. When she felt that Pearson's friend Elizabeth Cobb was growing destructively jealous, her relationship with Pearson broke down and she fled to the Continent to recover. She tried to create a fictional bridge over these painful love relationships, in which it seemed impossible to reconcile passion and friendship between men and women or to create trust between women.

DREAMS

At this time Schreiner created short "dreams" attuned to the symbolist mode being ushered into England by the enthusiasm of the critic Arthur Symons, who called her brief allegories "poems in prose" which expressed "that passion for abstract ideas which in her lies deeper than any other" (Clayton, 1983, p. 78). She had always written allegories and included them in her novels, but during the 1880s these visionary prose poems became a way of transcending personal pain and loss, by dramatizing the principle of renunciation of personal love. The allegories work through the conflicts of actual relationships by invoking the future of humanity or showing an evolutionary ascent to a realm where sex no longer exists and all can be forgiven. There is something lacerated and extreme in the vision of the allegories collected in *Dreams*, yet the tone is calm and contemplative.

Most of the dreams anchor a visionary flight in a particular but briefly sketched place, either a desertlike African setting or favorite places on the Italian Riviera, such as Alassio, where a ruined chapel, Santa Croce, offered her a point of tranquillity and a landscape closer to what she had known in the Cape Colony. The mood of the allegories is reverie, and the internal vision of exploitation, struggle, or emotional pain is reconciled by a brief, codalike ending that repeats and varies the opening setting. The dreamer goes back, refreshed, into the stream of daily life, in an encouraged and transformed state.

One of the strongest dreams, "Three Dreams in a Desert," allegorizes the stages of female struggle out of historical subjection and through evolutionary stages. It ends with a vision of "brave women and brave men, hand in hand. And they looked into each other's eyes, and they were not afraid" (p. 84). This ideal state is projected into the future. Constance Lytton, recalling the impact of a reading of this allegory organized by Freedom League suffragettes in Holloway Prison, London, said: "It fell on our ears more like an ABC railway guide to our journey than a figurative parable" (First and Scott, p. 185). Another allegory, "The Sunlight Lay Across My Bed," cast Schreiner's "socialistic strivings" into visionary form. Oscar Wilde published one of her allegories in *Woman's World*, of which he was editor, and the volume was extremely successful, being reprinted more than twenty times in England, selling 80,000 copies, and appearing in translation in Austria, Germany, France, Italy, Finland, Sweden, Norway, and Holland. Schreiner was hailed as a seer, but by that time she was back in South Africa, growing excited about the vision of the imperialist dreamer Cecil Rhodes: a united South Africa under the British flag.

SOUTH AFRICA: 1890–1913

In the years between 1890 and 1913—those of Schreiner's maturity, marriage, and political involvement in the key events that took the country through a devastating war (the Anglo-Boer War, 1899–1902) and toward the formation of the Union of South Africa in 1910—Schreiner's writing was put in the service of more immediate polemical ends. During this period she wrote out of a direct concern with immediate political events and a desire to use what influence she had as a spokeswoman for South Africa in England to shape the course of history.

Schreiner's political hopes and her growing antipathy to the expansionist ambitions of Cecil Rhodes, who was appointed prime minister of the Cape Colony in 1890, became entangled with her relationship with the man she married on 24 February 1894, Samuel Cron Cronwright, a young farmer with intellectual interests who was an ardent admirer of *The Story of an African Farm* and revered its creator. They set out to oppose Rhodes's imperialistic ambitions for British control of southern Africa. His "organization of diamond mining as a highly capitalized and concentrated mining industry" (First and Scott, p. 201) and his creation of the Chartered Company (later the British–South Africa Company) to annex territory and make war in the hinterland made Schreiner increasingly hostile to the man and his aims, and she followed his career with a close interest and an uncanny instinct for what he would do next. Schreiner had been writing patriotic articles on South Africa, its landscapes, and its inhabitants, and rejoicing in the renewed vigor she felt after returning to familiar terrain. These essays on South Africa, later collected in *Thoughts on South Africa* (1923), contain her clearest expository prose and a firm statement of her attitudes toward the country and its peoples, as well as thoughts on the "woman question" in South Africa.

TROOPER PETER HALKET OF MASHONALAND

Schreiner's antipathy to Rhodes culminated in her satirical, polemical novel, *Trooper Peter Halket of Mashonaland*, designed as a liberal reprimand to Rhodes and a message to an international audience about the activities of the Chartered Company in Matabeleland and Mashonaland. The novel continues the mode of allegory but puts it to more extended socially reformist uses, and it captures the revealing speech habits of a young member of the Chartered Company and his associates in Mashonaland in order to reveal the rapacity and greed of Rhodes and his Chartered Company.

The story concerns young Trooper Peter Halket, who comes to Africa as a mother's boy, very naive in his admiration of Rhodes and in his unthinking imperialism. One night, while he is keeping vigil on an isolated koppie, a "stranger" appears who is, unknown to him, Jesus Christ. Christ questions him about his activities and makes it clear that there is a nobler basis for action than the organized pillage of the Chartered Company. Peter is converted to a vision of future harmony when black and white will stand "shoulder to shoulder" as "brethren and the sons of one Father" (1974 edition, p. 79). The next night he frees a black prisoner tied to a tree. The wounded prisoner escapes, but Peter is himself shot by the Captain. Peter's blood mingles with the prisoner's blood at the foot of the tree.

Trooper Peter was a direct intervention in the relationship between South Africa and England at a crucial historical juncture; the Jameson Raid (1896) had revealed that Rhodes's aggression had turned against the Transvaal and its mineral wealth, and that he was trying to stir up war. It was the point at which British imperialism became directly exploitative and revealed a new aggression in southern Africa. The novel is about the solitary conscience and about the need for a ringing moral denunciation of imperialism disguised as moral improvement and "civilization." It links the exploitation of women with that of the land and its resources. Schreiner had written a piece called "Our Waste Land in Mashonaland" (collected in *Thoughts on South Africa*, 1923), in which she raised the issue of a national park. This region of southern Africa (first Mashonaland, then Rhodesia, and still later Zimbabwe), with its spectacular Victoria Falls, had always occupied a place in her imagination. In *Trooper Peter* she tried to write another demythologizing of the African adventure story, one satirizing imperialism. The novel also proposes that liberalism and martyrdom are inescapably connected and that moral denunciations have symbolic weight but do not deflect the flow of destructive events. At the end of the novel, when the troops are about to move on after Peter's death, one Englishman comments, "There is no God in Mashonaland" (p. 121).

Schreiner was proud of having written the novel, though its publication alienated many members of her own family as well as those who saw it only as a bitter attack on Rhodes. The novel became notorious for a frontispiece showing black figures suspended from a "hanging tree" and white men standing about as spectators. Schreiner had letters from knowledgeable people confirming that the crimes she had depicted were a mild version of what actually happened in Matabeleland and Mashonaland.

POLITICAL PAMPHLETS AND SHORT STORIES

During the 1890s the great mineral wealth that had been opened up in the Orange Free State and the Transvaal had made those two republics an arena of conflicting interests. Cecil Rhodes was a key figure in this struggle, but the Schreiners (including Schreiner's husband, now called Cronwright-Schreiner) were also key players. Schreiner's younger brother, Will (W. P.), was attorney-general to Rhodes until the Jameson Raid (an attempted British coup to capture Johannesburg from the Boers in 1895–1896) discredited Rhodes and Leander Starr Jameson. Schreiner and her husband had attempted public discrediting of Rhodes and his corrupt methods of gaining power; *Trooper Peter* was another blow in that struggle. As the tension between England and South Africa built toward war, Schreiner tried more direct forms of spokesmanship to rouse the British people to an understanding of the dimensions and gravity of the situation in the Transvaal.

Her pamphlet *An English South African's View of the Situation: Words in Season* (1899) was a graphic outline of the dual allegiance of first-generation English-speaking South Africans, those who "learnt to love this land in which we first saw light" but were also "bound to England not only by ties of blood, but that much more intense passion which springs from personal contact alone" (pp. 4–5). Recalling her own intense experiences in the 1880s, she describes how "the memory of fog-smitten London is inextricably blended with all the profoundest emotions, the most passionate endeavours, the noblest relations our hearts will ever know" (p. 10). She proceeds to sketch the different allegiances of the descendants of the Cape Dutch and French Huguenots, who display "a certain dogged persistence, and an inalienable, indestructible air of personal freedom" (p. 14), but she also points out their harsh treatment of the indigenous races.

It is a well-argued, comparative assessment of the different kinds of allegiance and assimilation that various groups experienced in South Africa. Schreiner's explanations are intended to help an English audience understand the question of the franchise in the Transvaal, which became the ostensible flash point of war. Vivid African parables and analogies dramatize her polemic:

> I have seen a little meer-kat attacked by a mastiff, the first joint of whose leg it did not reach. I have seen it taken into the dog's mouth, so that hardly any part of it was visible, and thought the creature was dead. But it fastened its tiny teeth inside the dog's throat, and the mastiff dropped it, and mauled and wounded and covered with gore and saliva, I saw it creep back into its hole in the red African earth.
> (pp. 83–84)

This passionate but rationally argued work is one of Schreiner's most eloquent pieces of political writing.

The Anglo-Boer War, which drew English South Africans much closer to the Boer cause as the struggle continued, inspired what may be Schreiner's finest short story, "Eighteen-Ninety-Nine," published in *Stories, Dreams, and Allegories* (1923). The story depicts the historical phases of settler life in South Africa, with a sympathetic female perspective on the suffering and sacrifice of the Cape Dutch families. Schreiner's other short stories are variations on the themes of the need for renunciation of fulfillment in love and marriage, and the victim figure of childhood. She wrote very few short stories; her more characteristic short prose piece was the "dream" or allegory. Here she was partly influenced by her friend Edward Carpenter, the Sheffield socialist whose prose poems such as *Towards Democracy* (1883) and *England's Ideal* (1887) she greatly admired.

Schreiner's other significant pamphlet was *Closer Union* (1909), first published in 1908 as a letter to the *Transvaal Leader.* She wrote it in response to the discussions on the possible future structure of the Union of South Africa. She was an impassioned federalist and believed in the rights of small groups, minorities, and disenfranchised majorities. She wrote prophetically at this time, when native rights were being crushed and overlooked, of the future dangers of an oppressed proletariat. In these years the formation of the Union laid the groundwork of a racist state and exclusive white power. In the women's suffrage struggle the same process occurred: white women were enfranchised in 1930, but black women were not. Schreiner herself had opposed the racial exclusivity of the Women's Enfranchisement League.

WOMAN AND LABOUR

After the loss of their home in Johannesburg, which had been looted during the war, the Cronwright-Schreiners lived in the area of Hanover and De Aar in the northern Cape. Schreiner's husband became an insurance agent, auctioneer, and justice of the peace, and his business gradually expanded. Ironically, these years were a period of growing isolation and disappointment for Schreiner, who seemed unable to do much creative work and whose marriage was being eroded by mistrust and separate spheres of conventional activity. Her increasing feeling of detachment from her husband and her marriage made possible the completion of a work close to her heart, but one that she regarded as a fragment of an earlier work on the history and situation of women. *Woman and Labour* (1911) has some of her old passion but seems anchored in an earlier time, in the predicaments of Victorian women who, once married, were confined within the home and were not admitted into meaningful work or professions. The work was dedicated to the British suffragette Lady Constance Lytton (1869–1923), who embodied an ideal for Schreiner, "in which intellectual power and strength of will are combined with an infinite tenderness and wide human sympathy" (1978 edition, p. 29).

Woman and Labour combines a materialist analysis of women's subordination with a spirit of visionary optimism, a hope that the book might work toward "a clearer perception of the sex relation between man and woman as the basis of human society, on whose integrity, beauty, and healthfulness depend the health and beauty of human life, as a whole" (pp. 25–26). She defines the modern "Woman's Labour Problem" as a loss of "her ancient domain of productive and social labour." A decline in childbearing and the size of the family, as well as the large number of women excluded from marriage and motherhood, had exacerbated the problem of women's idleness. Women desperately needed "new forms of labour and new fields for the exercise of their powers" (p. 67), in order to achieve a sense of "dignity and value." Schreiner resists the assimilation of the female labor problem to the system of male labor, and points out distinctions. Nevertheless, the arrest in the development of women is "an arrest in both, and in the upward march of the entire human family" (p. 132). The woman's movement is described as a powerful involuntary surge: "Our woman's movement resembles strongly, in this matter, the gigantic religious and intellectual movement which for centuries convulsed the life of Europe; and had, as its ultimate outcome, the final emancipation of the human spirit" (p. 136).

The work is full of Schreiner's ardent spirit; it is a call to arms and a celebration of the strength and centrality of women historically even as it points out their subordination in a male-dominated world. The chapter "Woman and War" suggests that the difference in reproductive function between man and woman may place male and female at a slightly different angle with regard to war, and that "war will pass when intellectual culture and activity have made possible to the female an equal share in the control and governance of modern national life" (p. 178). Schreiner's argument is that "no step in the reproductive journey" is quite identical for the man and the woman, but there is no dividing wall, except artificially erected ones, in the field of labor. She also answers recurrent objections: that women will lose their "womanliness" or that the race will die out. Her reply is that sexual love gains when it is part of an equal partnership between unconstrained human beings with equal functions in the world. Her ideal remains lifelong monogamous love, and she sees a role for the "New Man."

Woman and Labour may have its roots in a turn-of-the-century movement to recognize women's rights to education and work, but many of its core problems—the need for economic independence, pay for household labor, the link between pacifism and feminism, and arguments about the relative weighting of biological and sociocultural factors in determining women's history—are extremely modern and still relevant. The work is copiously illustrated with African analogies or examples. It has a great onward sweep in style and feeling, and yet a rational and logical structure, following the rational feminist model of John Stuart Mill, one of the writers she most admired. The work also provides an intellectual justification for the kind of fiction

Schreiner kept trying to write, the "problem" novel:

> The art of our age tends persistently to deal with subtle social problems, religious, political, and sexual, to which the art of the past holds no parallel; and it is so inevitably, because the artist who would obey the artistic instinct to portray faithfully the world about him, must portray that which lies at the core of its life.
>
> (p. 270)

This sentence validates Schreiner's project as a novelist: fidelity to the world around her meant portraying the core problems of her contemporaries, as well as the "grey pigment" of a particular landscape. *Woman and Labour* explains, too, why prostitution became such a key issue for writers like Schreiner and Thomas Hardy: it was one of the more obvious evils springing from an imbalance in power and wealth, and yet one that attracted the moral condemnation of a society losing its grip on religious certitude.

CONCLUSION

In 1913 Schreiner separated from her husband and went to live in England. She had become increasingly preoccupied with her health: asthma had been a lifelong problem, and heart disease ran in the family. From 1914 to 1919 she lived a lonely life, though her loneliness was alleviated by the presence of her brother Will and his family in London when he was high commissioner for South Africa. World War I intensified her personal gloom and her pacifism: she was once more in an embattled minority with the conscientious objectors. Her last piece of writing, "The Dawn of Civilisation," drew together her pacifism and her very earliest responses to the country in which she had been born and with which she had had such a rich, embattled, creative relationship.

In this piece Schreiner recalls the destructive conflicts all around her as a child: "the man with the gun was always there" (p. 913). She recalls the anguished questions to which this violence and aggression gave rise: "Why did the strong always crush the weak? Why did we hate and kill and torture?" (p. 913). As she meditates on these questions while walking along the mountaintops, an answer is given to her in a visionary moment. She looks at a dark island in the stream as the sun rises:

> It shot its light across the long, grassy slopes of the mountains and struck the little mound of earth in the water. All the leaves and flowers and grasses on it turned bright gold, and the dewdrops hanging from them were like diamonds; and the water in the stream glinted as it ran.... I seemed to *see* a world in which creatures no more hated and crushed, in which the strong helped the weak, and men understood each other, and forgave each other, and did not try to crush others, but to help. I did not think of it as something to be in a distant picture; it was there, about me, and I was in it, and a part of it. And there came to me, as I sat there, a joy such as never besides have I experienced, except perhaps once, a joy without limit.
>
> (p. 913)

This vision, Schreiner concludes, can be made a reality only if every individual strives to do so. Though she had tried to confront cruelty and injustice, she never lost sight of that visionary moment "even as a man who clings with one hand to a rock, though the waves pass over his head, yet knows what his hand touches" (p. 914). One of the qualities that make Schreiner a memorable writer and widespread influence on others is this tension between a clear view of human aggression and the violence of history, and a visionary hope, located in an illuminated African landscape, that such violence might come to an end. As a writer, a woman, and a "citizen of the world" (a title she wanted to earn), she constantly put her writing at the service of this broad, humanitarian view and tried to make it a reality to herself and others.

In August 1920, Schreiner returned to South Africa. She died soon afterward at Wynberg, on the night of 10 December 1920, of heart failure. She was buried temporarily at Maitland, and later was ceremoniously reinterred on a karoo mountain peak called Buffels Kop, overlooking the farm where she had been a young governess and writer, and where she had been courted by her husband. She was a brave founding figure, always attentive to the central questions of women's lives and their wider relationship with society. In following her own impulses and sense of justice to the end, she became a model of pioneering feminist struggle while illustrating the high price often paid by such foremothers within history. The division of her talent into fiction and polemical nonfiction underlines the way in which South African writing has never been able to dissociate itself from the immediate challenges of political and social questions. Some recent critics have stressed the responses of Schreiner's healing imagination to a wounded society, finding in her fiction resonant symbols of an imaginative wholeness. Others have pointed out the ways in which her writing participated in the general blindness of imperialism to questions of racial oppression and how she rewrote Europe in Africa. Many of her attitudes to indigenous people now seem patronizing and stereotypical, framed within a facile evolutionism. Her own childhood, in a society that marginalized black women and yet made them powerful mother-surrogates and illicit lovers, made her attitudes to African women ambivalent. For the impact of her feminist writings on Englishwomen struggling for the right to vote, one has to read the moving accounts of her contemporaries, such as Constance Lytton, who saw her as an inspiration in their historic struggle.

Although Schreiner's writing now seems to be almost wholly concerned with the problems of white colonial women's lives, she embedded those lives in a memorably detailed environment that includes racial and social issues as part of an organic fictional web and as part of an evolving female consciousness. Thus her novels are historical evidence of the interconnections of all forms of injustice and power in South Africa and prove that liberty is ultimately indivisible.

Selected Bibliography

BIBLIOGRAPHIES

Davis, Roslyn. *Olive Schreiner, 1920–1971.* Johannesburg, South Africa: Witwatersrand University Press, 1972.

Verster, Evelyn. *Olive Emilie Albertine Schreiner (1855–1920): A Bibliography.* Cape Town, South Africa: University of Cape Town Press, 1946.

FICTION

[Ralph Iron]. *The Story of an African Farm: A Novel.* 2 vols. London: Chapman and Hall, 1883; Boston: Little, Brown, 1924. With intro. by Samuel Cron Cronwright-Schreiner, London: Unwin, 1924. With intro. by Francis Brett Young, New York: Modern Library, 1927. With intro. by Isak Dinesen, New York: Printed for the members of the Limited Editions Club at Westerham Press, U.K., 1961. With afterword by Doris Lessing, Greenwich, Conn.: Fawcett, 1968. With intro. by Dan Jacobson, Harmondsworth, U.K.: Penguin, 1971. With intro. by Richard Rive, Johannesburg, South Africa: Ad. Donker, 1975. With intro. by Cherry Clayton, Johannesburg, South Africa: Ad. Donker, 1986. Ed. with an intro. by Joseph Bristow, Oxford, U.K., and New York: Oxford University Press, 1992.

Dreams. London: Unwin, 1891; Boston: Roberts Brothers, 1891; Boston: Little, Brown, 1916.

[Ralph Iron]. *Dream Life and Real Life.* London: Unwin, 1893; Boston: Roberts Brothers, 1893.

Trooper Peter Halket of Mashonaland. London: Unwin, 1897; Boston: Roberts Brothers, 1897. With intro. by Trevor Huddleston, London: Benn, 1959. With intro. by Marion Friedmann, Johannesburg, South Africa: Ad. Donker, 1974. With intro. by Sally-Ann Murray, Johannesburg, South Africa: Ad. Donker, 1992.

Stories, Dreams, and Allegories. With intro. by Samuel Cron Cronwright-Schreiner, London: Unwin, 1923; New York: Stokes, 1923.

From Man to Man; or, Perhaps Only. With intro. by Samuel Cron Cronwright-Schreiner, London: Unwin, 1926; New York: Harper and Bros., 1927. With intro. by Paul Foot, London: Virago, 1982.

Undine. With intro. by Samuel Cron Cronwright-Schreiner, New York: Harper and Bros., 1928; London: Benn, 1929.

NONFICTION

The Political Situation. Written with Samuel Cron Cronwright-Schreiner. London: Unwin, 1896.

An English South African's View of the Situation: Words in Season. London: Hodder and Stoughton, 1899. Also publ. as *The South African Question.* Chicago: Charles H. Sergel, 1899.

A Letter on the Jew. Cape Town, South Africa: H. Liberman, 1906.

Closer Union. London: Fifield, 1909. Repr. with foreword by Donald Molteno, Cape Town, South Africa: Constitutional Reform Association, [1924?].

Woman and Labour. London: Unwin, 1911; New York: Frederick A. Stokes, 1911. Facs. repr. with preface by Jane Graves, London: Virago, 1978.

"The Dawn of Civilisation: Stray Thoughts on Peace and War—The Homely Personal Confession of a Believer in Human Unity." In *The Nation and the Athenaeum* (26 March 1921).

Thoughts on South Africa. London: Unwin, 1923. With foreword by Richard Rive, Johannesburg, South Africa: Africana Book Society, 1976.

ANTHOLOGIES

Olive Schreiner's Thoughts About Women. Ed. by A. Purcell. Cape Town: South African News, 1909.

The Silver Plume: A Selection from the Writings of Olive Schreiner. Ed. by Neville Nuttall. Johannesburg, South Africa: Afrikaanse Pers Beperk, 1957.

Olive Schreiner: A Selection. Ed. by Uys Krige. Cape Town, South Africa: Oxford University Press, 1968.

A Track to the Water's Edge: The Olive Schreiner Reader. Ed. by Howard Thurman. New York: Harper and Row, 1973.

An Olive Schreiner Reader. Ed. by Carol Barash. London and New York: Pandora, 1987.

CORRESPONDENCE

The Letters of Olive Schreiner, 1876–1920. Ed. by Samuel Cron Cronwright-Schreiner. London: Fisher Unwin, 1924; Boston: Little, Brown, 1924.

Olive Schreiner: Letters 1871–99. Ed. by Richard Rive. Cape Town, South Africa: David Philip, 1987; Oxford, U.K., and New York: Oxford University Press, 1988.

The Missionary Letters of Gottlob Schreiner 1837–1846. Ed. by Karel Schoeman. Cape Town, South Africa: Human and Rousseau, 1991,

My Other Self: The Letters of Olive Schreiner and Havelock Ellis, 1884–1920. Ed. by Yaffa C. Draznin. New York: Peter Lang Publishers, 1993.

BIOGRAPHICAL STUDIES

Buchanan-Gould, Vera. *Not Without Honour: The Life and Writings of Olive Schreiner.* London: Hutchinson, 1948.

Cronwright-Schreiner, Samuel Cron. *The Life of Olive Schreiner.* London: Fisher Unwin, 1924; Boston: Little, Brown, 1924.

First, Ruth, and Ann Scott. *Olive Schreiner.* London: Andre Deutsch, 1980; New York: Schocken, 1980.

Fradkin, Betty M. "Olive Schreiner and Karl Pearson." In *Quarterly Bulletin of the South African Library* 31, no. 4 (1977).

Friedmann, Marion V. *Olive Schreiner: A Study in Latent Meaning.* Johannesburg, South Africa: Witwatersrand University Press, 1954.

Hobman, Daisy Lucie. *Olive Schreiner: Her Friends and Times.* London: Watts, 1955.

Meintjes, Johannes. *Olive Schreiner: Portrait of a South African Woman.* Johannesburg, South Africa: Hugh Keartland, 1965.

Schoeman, Karel. *Olive Schreiner: A Woman in South Africa, 1855–1881.* Trans. by Henri Snijders. Johannesburg, South Africa: Jonathan Ball, 1991.

———. *Only an Anguish to Live Here: Olive Schreiner and the Anglo-Boer War 1899–1902.* Cape Town, South Africa: Human and Rousseau, 1992.

CRITICAL STUDIES

Ayling, Ronald. "Literature of the Eastern Cape from Schreiner to Fugard." In *ARIEL* 16, no. 2 (April 1985).

Barash, Carol. "Virile Womanhood: Olive Schreiner's Narratives of a Master Race." In Elaine Showalter, ed., *Speaking of Gender.* London: Routledge, 1989.

Barsby, Christine. "Olive Schreiner: Towards a Redefinition of Culture." In *Pretexts* 1, no. 1 (winter 1989).

Beeton, Ridley. *Olive Schreiner: A Short Guide to Her Writings.* Cape Town, South Africa: H. Timmins, 1974.

———. *Facets of Olive Schreiner: A Manuscript Source Book.* Johannesburg, South Africa: Ad. Donker, 1987.

Berkman, Joyce Avrech. *Olive Schreiner: Feminism on the Frontier.* St. Albans, Vt., and Montreal: Eden Press Women's Publications, 1979.

———. *The Healing Imagination of Olive Schreiner: Beyond South African Colonialism.* Amherst: University of Massachusetts Press, 1989.

Blake, Kathleen. *Love and the Woman Question in Victorian Literature: The Art of Self-Postponement.* Brighton, U.K.: Harvester Press, 1983; Totowa, N.J.: Barnes and Noble, 1983.

Bolin, Bill. "Olive Schreiner and the Status Quo." In *UNISA English Studies* 31, no. 1 (April 1993).

Bradford, Helen. "Introducing Palinsky Smith." In *English in Africa* 21, nos. 1/2 (July 1994).

Casey, Janet Galligari. "Power, Agency, Desire: Olive Schreiner and the Pre-Modern Narrative Moment." In *Narrative* 4, no. 2 (May 1996).

Chrisman, Laura. "Colonialism and Feminism in Olive Schreiner's 1890s Fiction." In *English in Africa* 20, no. 1 (May 1993).

Clayton, Cherry. "Olive Schreiner and Katherine Mansfield: Artistic Transformations of the Outcast Figure by Two Colonial Women Writers." In J. Bardolph, ed., *Short Fiction in the New Literatures in English.* Nice, France: Faculté des Lettres et Sciences Humaines, 1989.

———. "Olive Schreiner: Paradoxical Pioneer." In her *Women and Writing in South Africa: A Critical Anthology.* Johannesburg, South Africa: Heinemann, 1989.

———. "Women Writers and the Law of the Father: Race and Gender in the Fiction of Olive Schreiner, Pauline Smith and Sarah Gertrude Millin." In *English Academy Review* 7 (1990).

———, ed. *Olive Schreiner.* Johannesburg, South Africa: McGraw-Hill, 1983.

Coetzee, J. M. "Farm Novel and Plaasroman in South Africa." In *English in Africa* 13, no. 2 (October 1986). Repr. in his *White Writing: On the Culture of Letters in South Africa.* New Haven, Conn.: Yale University Press, 1988.

Donaldson, Laura E. "(ex)Changing (wo)Man: Toward a Materialist-Feminist Semiotics." Chapter 6 in her *Decolonizing Feminisms: Race, Gender, and Empire Building.* Chapel Hill: University of North Carolina Press, 1992.

Driver, Dorothy. "Women as Sign in the South African Colonial Enterprise." In *Journal of Literary Studies* 4, no. 1 (March 1988).

DuPlessis, Rachel Blau. "The Rupture of Story and *The Story of an African Farm.*" Chapter 2 in her *Writing Beyond the Ending: Narrative Strategies of Twentieth Century Women Writers.* Bloomington: Indiana University Press, 1985.

Gorak, Irene E. "Olive Schreiner's Colonial Allegory: *The Story of an African Farm.*" In *ARIEL* 23, no. 4 (October 1992).

Gray, Stephen. "Schreiner and the Novel Tradition." In his *Southern African Literature: An Introduction.* Cape Town, South Africa: David Phillip, 1979.

Heywood, Christopher. "Olive Schreiner's Influence on George Moore and D. H. Lawrence." In Christopher Heywood, ed., *Aspects of South African Literature.* London: Heinemann, 1976.

Horton, Susan. *Difficult Women, Artful Lives: Olive Schreiner and Isak Dinesen, in and out of Africa.* Baltimore, Md.: Johns Hopkins University Press, 1994.

Jacob, Susan. "Sharers in a Common Hell: The Colonial Text in Schreiner, Conrad and Lessing." In *The Literary Criterion* 23, no. 4 (1988).

Kaarsholm, Preben. "The Significance of Evolutionism in Olive Schreiner's *African Farm.*" In Britta Olinder, ed., *A Sense of Place: Essays in Post-Colonial Literatures.* Götenborg, Sweden: Gothenburg University Press, 1984.

Lenta, Margaret. "Independence as the Creative Choice in Two South African Fictions." In *ARIEL* 17, no. 1 (January 1986).

———. "Racism, Sexism, and Olive Schreiner's Fiction." In *Theoria* 70 (October 1987).

Lewis, Simon. "Graves with a View: Atavism and the European History of Africa." In *ARIEL* 27, no. 1 (January 1996).

Marquard, Jean. "Hagar's Child: A Reading of *The Story of an African Farm.*" In *Standpunte* 29, no. 1 (February 1976).

———. "Olive Schreiner's 'Prelude': The Child as Artist." In *English Studies in Africa* 22 (March 1979).

McClintock, Anne. "Olive Schreiner: The Limits of Colonial Feminism." In her *Imperial Leather:*

Race, Gender and Sexuality in the Colonial Contest. New York: Routledge, 1995.

McMurry, Andrew. "Figures in a Ground: An Ecofeminist Study of Olive Schreiner's *The Story of an African Farm.*" In *English Studies in Canada* 20, no. 4 (December 1994).

Middleton, Victoria. "Doris Lessing's Debt to Olive Schreiner." In Carey Kaplan and Ellen Cronan Rose, eds. *Doris Lessing: The Alchemy of Survival.* Athens: Ohio University Press, 1988.

Monsman, Gerald. *Olive Schreiner's Fiction: Landscape and Power.* New Brunswick, N.J.: Rutgers University Press, 1991.

———. "Olive Schreiner's Allegorical Vision." In *Victorian Review* 18, no. 2 (winter 1992).

———. "Writing the Self on the Imperial Frontier: Olive Schreiner and the Stories of Africa." In *Bucknell Review* 37, no. 1 (1993).

Paxton, Nancy L. "*The Story of an African Farm* and the Dynamics of Woman-to-Woman Influence." In *Texas Studies in Literature and Language* 30, no. 4 (1988).

Pechey, Graham. "*The Story of an African Farm:* Colonial History and the Discontinuous Text." In *Critical Arts: A Journal of Media Studies* 3, no. 1 (1983).

Ross, Robert. "A New Time for the Fiction of Sarah Gertrude Millin and Olive Schreiner." In *World Literature Written in English* 24, no. 2 (1984).

Sarvan, C. P. "Olive Schreiner's *Trooper Peter Halket*: An Altered Awareness." In *International Fiction Review* 11, no. 1 (winter 1984).

Scherzinger, Karen. "The Problem of the Pure Woman: South African Pastoralism and Female Rites of Passage." In *UNISA English Studies* 29, no. 2 (September 1991).

Showalter, Elaine. *Gender and Culture at the Fin de Siecle.* London: Bloomsbury, 1991.

Smith, Malvern Van Wyck, and Don Maclennan, eds. *Olive Schreiner and After: Essays on Southern African Literature in Honour of Guy Butler.* Cape Town, South Africa: David Phillip, 1983.

Stanley, Liz. "Olive Schreiner: New Women, Free Women, All Women (1855–1920)." In Dale Spender, ed., *Feminist Theorists: Three Centuries of Women's Intellectual Traditions.* London: Women's Press, 1983; New York: Pantheon, 1984.

Visel, Robin. "'We Bear the World and We Make It': Bessie Head and Olive Schreiner." In *Research in African Literatures* 21, no. 3 (fall 1990).

Vivan, Itala, ed. *The Flawed Diamond: Essays on Olive Schreiner.* Sydney, Australia, and Mundelstrup, Denmark: Dangaroo Press, 1989.

Voss, Anthony E. "A Generic Approach to the South African Novel in English." In *UCT Studies in English*, no. 7 (September 1977).

Voss, Tony. "Avatars of Waldo." In *Alternation* 1, no. 2 (1994).

Wade, Michael. *Black on White in South Africa: A Study of English-Language Inscriptions of Skin Colour.* London: Macmillan, 1993.

Walkowitz, Judith R. "Science, Feminism and Romance: The Men and Women's Club, 1885–1889." In *History Workshop*, no. 21 (1986).

———. *City of Dreadful Delight: Narratives of Sexual Danger in Late-Victorian London.* Chicago: University of Chicago Press, 1992.

Wilkinson, Jane. "Dust and Dew. Moonlight and Utopia. Natural Imagery in the First South African Novel." In *Commonwealth Essays and Studies* 14, no. 2 (spring 1992).

Winkler, Barbara Scott. "Victorian Daughters: The Lives and Feminism of Charlotte Perkins Gilman and Olive Schreiner." In Joanne B. Karpinski, ed. *Critical Essays on Charlotte Perkins Gilman.* New York: G. K. Hall, 1992.

MANUSCRIPTS

The most substantial collections of Schreiner's manuscripts are at the Harry Ransom Humanities Research Center, University of Texas at Austin (its collections include the voluminous correspondence between Havelock Ellis and Olive Schreiner); the Karl Pearson Collection at University College Library, London; the Edward Carpenter Collection at the Archives Division of Sheffield City Libraries, Sheffield, U.K.; the South African Library, Cape Town; the Cullen Library of the University of the Witwatersrand, Johannesburg; and the National English Literary Museum and Documentation Centre, Grahamstown, South Africa. Smaller collections are housed at the J. W. Jagger Library, University of Cape Town; the Strange Africana Library at the Johannesburg Public Library; Albany Museum, 1820 Settlers Memorial Division, Grahamstown; the Cory Library, Rhodes University, Grahamstown; the Brenthurst Library (Private Africana Collection of Mr. H. F. Oppenheimer), Johannesburg; and the Cradock Public Library,

South Africa. Joyce Berkman lists some other relevant sources of archival material in her study of Schreiner *The Healing Imagination.* Yaffa C. Draznin has edited some of the Schreiner-Ellis correspondence in the Harry Ransom Humanities Research Center in her *My Other Self: The Letters of Olive Schreiner and Havelock Ellis* (see under Correspondence). Ridley Beeton has offered commentary on some of her manuscripts located in the same collection at Austin, Texas. Karel Schoeman's two intensively researched biographical publications (see under Biographical Studies) list many relevant archival resources.

Sembène Ousmane

1923–

KHALID AL MUBARAK

SEMBÈNE OUSMANE, born 8 January 1923 at Ziguinchor, in the Casamance region of southern Senegal, is unique among African writers because he made his mark as a pioneering novelist during the colonial period and continued to write in the postcolonial era. He then changed track, studied cinema, and went on to make an equally important contribution as a film director who wrote his own screenplays and made brief appearances as an actor. The films addressed the same themes that informed his novels and short stories, and most had the same titles as the published works of fiction (for example, *Xala* and *The Money-Order*).

Sembène has distinguished himself as an original writer. Despite living abroad for many years, he has looked to African traditions for inspiration and has considered himself to be an extension of the griots, "the story-tellers, clowns, heralds, genealogists, musicians, oral reporters, or paid flatterers or insulters" found at the courts of chiefs or established on their own in towns and villages (Pfaff, p. 29). This—needless to say—is the antithesis of the approach of accomplished francophone figures like Sembène's most celebrated countryman, the poet and former president, Léopold Sédar Senghor.

Sembène's achievement is all the more remarkable because, apart from one year of cinema studies at the Gorki Studios in Moscow in 1962, he had very little formal western education, having left school at the age of fourteen and held various jobs. Sembène worked as a plumber, bricklayer, and apprentice mechanic. Like his Wolof father, Sembène also worked as a fisherman. He was drafted into the French colonial army when World War II broke out. His unit served in both Italy and Germany. When the war ended, he was demobilized in Baden-Baden, Germany, and returned to Dakar, where he again engaged in manual labor. He was there when the workers of the Dakar-Niger Railway went on strike in 1947–1948.

The search for work took Sembène to Marseilles, France, where he worked as a docker for ten years. The French Left was on a high wave following the collapse of fascism and enjoying the prestige of resistance to the German occupation and to Francisco Franco's dictatorship in neighboring Spain. Sembène, radicalized by the atmosphere, became a trade-union leader; joined the French Communist Party, remaining a member until Senegal's independence in 1960; and educated himself in the "university of life," as he put it.

Sembène wrote poetry before concentrating on short stories and novels. Recognition was slow but sure. He won many prizes and honors, including the prestigious literature prize at the first Festival of Negro Arts in Dakar (1966), for *Véhi-Ciosane; ou, Blanche-Genèse, suivi du Mandat* (1965; *The Money-Order; with White Genesis*) and the best foreign film award at the 1970 Atlanta Film Festival, for *Le Mandat* (*The Money-Order*).

After 1962, the cinema took more and more of Sembène's time. He set up his own film studio in Dakar (Films Domirev) and led—against formidable odds—a confrontation with the giant French and international distribution networks. One "confrontation" that he seems to have lost with most critics was over his name. His given name, Ousmane, is confused with his patronymic, Sembène—as is the case with the Guinean novelist Camara Laye. Ousmane is often used as his "surname."

COLONIAL VERSUS AFRICAN

The theme that pervades much of Sembène's work is the conflict between Africa and colonialism. In his portrayal of this conflict, Sembène leaves his readers in no doubt about his sympathies and commitment and draws upon his direct personal experience to give his writing an unmistakable documentary or semi-autobiographical focus.

Between 1956 and 1960, Sembène published three novels: *Le Docker noir* (1956; *The Black Docker*), *Ô pays, mon beau peuple!* (1957; Oh my country, my good people!), and his masterpiece, *Les Bouts de bois de Dieu* (1960; *God's Bits of Wood*). In *God's Bits of Wood*, Sembène treats the 1947–1948 Dakar-Niger Railway workers' strike. One of the strike leaders, Mamadou Keïta, summarizes the workers' grievances in demanding the same rights as the French workers in Senegal: "Why should they be paid more? ... And when they are sick, why should they be taken care of while we and our families are left to starve?" (Doubleday edition, p. 21). As the strike drags on, the strikers' case is both Africanized (they receive solidarity funds from Dahomey, now Benin) and internationalized (they receive donations from left-wing trade unions in France). They even receive money from a maverick member of the colonial administration, Leblanc, who is foolish enough to disclose his action while under the influence of alcohol, thus ensuring his death at the hands of his own people. The conflict is by no means white versus black, but exploiter versus exploited. The strike leader, Lahbib, says to the representative of the railway company and colonial administration, "You do not represent a nation or a people here, but simply a class. We represent another class whose interests are not the same as yours" (p. 250).

The Marxist terminology should come as no surprise, in view of Sembène's political ideas. The novel was hailed by some critics as an example of socialist realism. Although the strikers win their struggle in the best tradition of didactic writing, Sembène's talent shines through the straitjacket, especially in the allegorical episodes of Ramatoulaye's killing of her brother's ram in order to feed the strikers' families and the women's clash with the police. Both symbolize the wider struggle between the strikers and the colonial administration. The building of the Dakar-Niger Railway itself is an analogy to the linkage between different parts of Africa (and the broad theme of African unity) and the terms under which it is to be constructed—through fairness and justice or under tutelage.

Any racist overtones to the struggle are negated by inserting lines from the folktale "Legend of Goumba N'Diaye," which conclude the novel: "*Happy is the man who does battle without hatred*" (p. 333). Thus, African heritage, not Marxism, provides the moral, because Goumba N'Diaye is the historical (and mythological) founder of the Wolof empire, which was established between the late twelfth and mid fourteenth centuries. He is also the progenitor of a dynasty that ruled most of Senegal until the French conquest in the 1890s. Oral tradition has it that he emerged from water to settle disputes. This made him a symbol of order and justice.

Confrontation with France takes another form in the short stories "Lettres de France" ("Letters from France") and "La Noire de ..." ("The Promised Land") in *Voltaïque* (1962; *Tribal Scars and Other Stories*). Both were the basis for the film *La Noire de ...* (1966; *Black Girl*). A poor Senegalese girl is overjoyed when she lands the job of maid for a French family and sails to the "promised land" amid the great expectations of family and friends. She finds herself isolated and trapped in prejudice and merciless work. She ends up committing suicide.

In "Letters from France," an old black docker who went to France as a young man has lost his job and survives on food provided by the welfare committee and what he earns by selling kola nuts. He marries a Senegalese girl by proxy, after sending her family an "improved" photograph of himself. The young wife writes to a friend about her misery, trapped in a matchbox of a room with a man old enough to be her father. Pessimism and optimism are interwoven as the old man dies and his young widow returns to Africa with her baby daughter, making a choice for the future that is the opposite of her husband's. Fine touches highlight a radical interpretation of the plot, mainly through the exploration of characters. Both Arona, a young Senegalese leader of the Association of Black Workers in France, and Madame Barone, a French Communist, are portrayed sympathetically as supportive radicals. Madame Barone tells the young woman that there are two kinds of morals, one for the rich and the other for the workers. Arona comments on African cloth made in France: "African material stamped Boussac," a reference to the biggest French textile manufacturer.

Diouana, the girl who takes her life in "The Promised Land," exemplifies the chasm between reality and expectation. It is a hard-hitting and heartrending portrayal of an injustice that began during the slave trade and continued in different forms. The poem at the end is explicit (perhaps too explicit) about the message the writer is trying to convey:

> Diouana,
> Our sister,
> The slave-ships no longer ride the bar.

and

> Diouana,
> ...
> Image of our Mother Africa,
> We lament over your sold body,
> Your are our
> Mother, Diouana.
> (pp. 100–101)

Diouana represents Africa, which continues to suffer after the end of slavery.

LANGUAGE

An aspect of the rape of Africa about which Sembène feels very strongly is the question of language. In *African Writers on African Writing*, edited by G. D. Killam, he explains the two strands of his approach, the theoretical and the pragmatic. Rejecting Négritude because it entails "shutting ourselves up completely in a black world," he declares that "until we have made the African language part of our educational system, in the primary school and elsewhere, our literature will still be subject to the control of other powers, or other people's good intentions." On the other hand, he goes on, "I could have written *Le Docker noir* in Wolof. But then who would have read it? How many people know how to read the language?" Sembène was astute enough to realize that whatever the language of publication, a book's African readership will be limited. He preempts criticism by stating: "Very well then. Even written in French, how many Africans have read *Le Docker noir*? 85% of people here are illiterate.... That means that our public is in Europe.... Unfortunately, I think I have no readers in Africa" (pp. 150–152).

Sembène puts his finger on the solution to the problem but realizes that until there are enough literate Africans to form a reading public that makes writing, publishing, and distributing in African languages economically viable and financially rewarding, writing in a European language is the only realistic option. His preoccupation with the question of language is evident in several novels.

In *God's Bits of Wood*, the old woman Niakoro says to her granddaughter:

> Among my people, who are your father's people, too, no one speaks the white man's language, and no one has died of it! Ever since I was born . . . I have never heard of a white man who had learned to speak Bambara, or any other language of this country. But you rootless people think only of learning his while our language dies.
>
> (p. 16)

In *Xala* (1973; *Xala*), Adja Awa Astou, El Hadji Abdou Kader Beye's first wife, is a member of a Wolof language group. His eldest daughter, Rama, a university student, joins a Wolof-language association. Reversing the rules, prevalent in schools, that are designed to restrict Wolof and other African languages, the association makes its members pay a fine whenever they speak in French. She says to her fiancé, who apologizes for arriving late: "You'll have to pay a fine! You spoke in French" (p. 48). Soon afterward, Rama refuses to speak in French to a traffic policeman who stops her.

El Hadji, while visiting his first wife, looks over Rama's shoulder and asks:

> "What's that?"
>
> "Wolof."
>
> "You write in Wolof?"
>
> "Yes. We have a newspaper called *Kaddu* and we teach anyone who wants to learn how to write in Wolof."
>
> "Do you think it will be adopted as the language of the country?"
>
> "Eighty-five per cent of the people speak it. They only need to know how to write it."
>
> "What about French?"
>
> "An historical accident. Wolof is our national language."
>
> (pp. 94–95)

It is noteworthy that a Wolof-language magazine called *Kaddu* did exist, established by Sembène himself in 1972. His preoccupation with the question of language was the main reason behind his decision to become a filmmaker. He was eager to cross the barrier of illiteracy and reach out to the whole population.

Sembène's first films, like his novels, were in French; financing for the films came mainly from French sources. The turning point came with the screenplay of *The Money-Order* (1968), which Sembène wrote in Wolof (a French version also was made). After that, Wolof became the norm, although versions with French (and English) subtitles or dubbing also were made. This radical attitude is comparable to that of Ngũgĩ wa Thiong'o, who started to write only in his mother tongue, Gĩkũyũ (or Kikuyu). Sembène's use of Wolof placed him on a par with novelists of other nationalities who reached a wider national, regional, and international reading public by having their work translated into English or French immediately after the publication of the original.

CORRUPTION AND COLLAPSE

In *Xala*, African language is introduced with the intention of underscoring the other major theme that permeates Sembène's novels: disappointment at the failure of many African states to make significant progress after attaining independence. Many of those who took over from the colonialists proved incapable of dealing with the problems attendant on managing their countries and bringing about progress and development. They spoke the colonial languages, upheld colonial (European) values, and generally modeled themselves on the departing rulers, for whom they became conduits and middlemen in a neocolonial relationship. The loser was the common citizen who hoped to reap the benefits of the anticolonial struggle.

In *Xala* the inability of African rulers to translate dreams into reality is represented by a physical malaise. El Hadji decides to marry a third wife who is young enough to be his daughter. On the wedding night, the father of eleven discovers that he is unable to consummate the union. Embarrassment turns into a crisis of confidence that causes the decline of his business. This *xala*, or curse of impotence, is the focus of the novel (and the 1974 film based on it). In contrast to the often predictable, one dimensional flow of Sembène's "socialist realism" in several novels (for example, *God's Bits of Wood*), the portrayal of impotence as a social metaphor in *Xala* reflects Sembène's developing craftsmanship. The Businessmen's Group to which El Hadji belongs is shown riding a wave of success, celebrating the appointment of one of their number as president of the Chamber of Commerce and Industry. This coincides with El Hadji's third marriage.

The lifestyle of the businessmen is not a sign of wisdom or accountable leadership of the economy. In a fit of rage, El Hadji himself spells out the truth: "What are we? Mere agents, less than petty traders! We merely re-distribute. Re-distribute the remains the big men deign to leave us. Are we businessmen? I say no! Just clodhoppers!" (p. 92). Later in the same speech he asks: "Who owns the banks? The insurance companies? The factories? The businesses? The wholesale trade? The cinemas? The bookshops? The hotels? All these and more besides are out of our control.... The colonialist is stronger, more powerful than ever before.... He promises us the left-overs of the feast if we behave ourselves" (pp. 92–93).

Under the facade of independence, the new African establishment is deep in corruption and nepotism. The beggar who claims to have brought about El Hadji's *xala* explains the grave injustice he and his clan have suffered:

> Do you remember selling a large piece of land at Jeko belonging to our clan? After falsifying the clan names with the complicity of people in high places, you took our land from us. In spite of our protests, our proof of ownership, we lost our case in the courts. Not satisfied with taking our land you had me thrown into prison.... People like you live on theft.... You and your colleagues build on the misfortunes of honest, ordinary people. To give yourself clean consciences, you found charities, or you give alms at street corners to people reduced to poverty.
> (pp. 110–111)

El Hadji eventually loses his wealth and, in the hope of regaining his virility, is subjected to a humiliating ritual during which he is stripped naked and spat on by a horde of beggars—Sembène's ultimate comment on the performance and deserved fate of the rapacious African bourgeoisie.

The failure of the bourgeoisie to deliver the fruits of independence is taken up in *The Money-Order* (in *The Money-Order; with White Genesis*). It portrays the web of bureaucracy that enmeshes a simple illiterate citizen, Ibrahima Dieng, when he receives a money order of twenty-five thousand francs from his nephew in Paris. The ostensibly simple act of cashing the order turns into a series of riddles that baffle Dieng. He is asked for an identity card. His lack of one leads him to the photographer and several offices for a birth certificate and a fifty-franc stamp. His wives take provisions on credit from the local shopkeeper. Many neighbors and friends hope to cash in on the money order. Dieng's sister comes from the countryside for her share of the money.

In the end, Dieng signs a power of attorney for Mbaye, who belongs to the "New Africa" generation and is described as "a businessman, always ready to do a deal, asking a percentage on each commission according to its value. It was said of him that there was no difficulty he could not resolve" (p. 127).

Mbaye cashes the money and pretends that his wallet was stolen. This is the culmination of bureaucratic misfortunes that prove a Dakar saying: "Never upset a civil servant. He has great power" (p. 88). On a bus Dieng overhears a conversation between a father and son that summarizes the way of the world:

> "You did give it to him?"
> "He wants too much."
> "Everyone has his price. The main thing is to get what you want."
> "Where is the country going to? Every time you want something, you have to pay."
> (p. 101)

The answer to the question "Where is the country going to?" is provided in *Le Dernier de l'empire* (1981; *The Last of the Empire*), which tackles the ultimate postindependence African disease, the military coup. This novel is so scathing that Sembène took the exceptional step of writing a foreword designed to ward off potential litigation. After stating that Senegal has "borne and bred only men and women worthy of our esteem and entire trust, worthy of the position they occupy even fleetingly," he goes on to praise them as "far superior to the mediocre types portrayed in this book." He then declares that he will not hesitate to take legal action against anyone who makes any comparison or connection between the Senegalese leaders and the fictional characters of the novel. Since no coup has ever succeeded in Senegal, it is evident that the novel's inspiration was drawn from general African, Asian, and Latin American examples. Indeed, the power struggle that takes place behind the scenes to succeed an ailing president of a republic (or any ruler) is a fact both of history and of contemporary practical politics all over the world.

Sembène imagines the mysterious disappearance of the president of the republic. The dead body of his driver is found in his car; he himself has disappeared. Fearful of repercussions, members of the ruling establishment close ranks and agree to keep the matter a secret while engaging in a vicious competition, primarily between the prime minister and the minister of finance and economy. Each does his best to undermine the other's position in a way that reveals the real cracks in the edifice, which collapses when the military takes over.

The plot to discredit the prime minister, Daouda, involves distributing leaflets that include damaging secret information about members of the government. Only Mam Lat Soukabé, the minister of finance and economy, could have supplied such details: "The names cited, the bank account numbers revealed, the descriptions of villas could only have been supplied by him" (p. 158). In the riot that ensues, the demonstrators pull passengers out of government cars:

> "Why are you driving [an] SO [Service Officiel] car?"
> "I'm the wife of ... the father of ... the uncle of ... the mother of ... the son of ... the daughter of ..."
> "What about us, who are we?"
> "Yes, are we the bastards of Independence?" thundered a voice.
> (p. 161)

The seemingly inevitable "revolutionary takeover" by the army results from the failure of the system to deliver. In an echo of the "First Declarations" heard in many African capitals, its leaders state: "Faced with a deteriorating social climate, the rule of anarchy, prevarication and corruption, the embezzlement of public funds, the systematic plundering of the national economy, the committee of High Ranking Officers under the direction of Colonel Mame, has been compelled to take control of the country's affairs" (p. 169). Faithful to the script, the military prohibits political parties, suspends the constitution, dissolves the National Assembly, and assuages fears by promising to start preparations for returning power to civilians.

The European military adviser to the general divulges the secret of the president's disappearance to him, then adds: "The position is vacant. Now is the time to occupy it . . . General" (p. 179). This disclosure is a hint at the involvement of the former colonial power in destabilizing the corrupt system. The general himself does not act, but others do.

Sembène uses *The Last of the Empire* to sum up earlier comments and works. The corrupt businessman says, "Ever since Sembène's film *Xala*, we businessmen have started calling ourselves economic operators" (p. 143). He makes fun of African leaders' overeagerness to introduce new "theories" of government. The president is the initiator of "Authenegrafianitus," the pompousness of the very name suggesting the chasm between the European-educated elite and the simple peasants of Africa.

TO TOUCH THE UNTOUCHABLE

A remarkable aspect of Sembène's achievement is the way he addresses "untouchable" themes in his novels. In *The Last of the Empire* he draws attention to the nonrecognition of forbidden intellectual and artistic themes by making Daouda, the prime minister, a man marked by his low-caste origins. Madjiguène says to her journalist partner when they discuss the options of successors to the president: "Surely you know about Daouda's caste origins"; "Do you think I would be living with you if you were of casted birth?"; "I know that Mam Lat Soukabé and his gang, as well as my ex-husband, are opposed to Daouda because of his origins" (p. 122).

The innuendo and confrontation reach their sharpest climax when the coup leaders arrest Daouda and take him to the place where they are keeping the president. The latter proceeds to needle his protégé:

> ". . . Don't forget who you are."
>
> "What do you mean?" asked Daouda, his fury mounting to a peak.
>
> "You know what I mean," answered Léon Mignane, shrugging his shoulders contemptuously. (p. 203)

Another untouchable theme avoided by most African writers is the role of Africans in the slave trade. It is considered unbecoming to acknowledge or mention it, and many practice self-censorship and pretend that such a role never existed. In *Tribal Scars and Other Stories*, Sembène portrays the brutality of the white slave traders. He underlines the dignity and the determination of those who resisted enslavement. But he also depicts the active participation and the trickery of Africans in hunting and handing over fellow Africans to the main overseas dealers. In "Le Voltaïque" ("Tribal Scars"), Momutu says:

> This is our work. We scour the grasslands, take prisoners and sell them to the whites. Some captains know me, but I entice others to this bay and some of my men lure the crew off the ship. Then we loot the ship and get the prisoners back again. We kill any whites left on board. It's easy work and we win all round. (p. 107)

Yet another untouchable theme consistently broached by this iconoclastic novelist and filmmaker is that of religion, which is invariably depicted as a negative influence. The imam is used by the colonial administration in *God's Bits of Wood* to break the spirit of the strikers. He tells the womenfolk: "It is not up to us to rebel against the will of god, even when the reasons for that will are a mystery to us" (p. 172). A well-orchestrated plan that includes both Muslim and Christian religious leaders is under way. A campaign to demoralize and undermine the unity of the strikers—particularly of their wives—is undertaken by the men who are their "spiritual guides," the imams and the clergy of other groups. After the prayers and religious services all over the city, there is a sermon whose theme is always the same: "By ourselves we are incapable of creating any sort of useful object, not even a needle; and yet you want to strike against the *toubabs* who have brought us all of these things? It is madness" (p. 204).

In "Souleymane" ("The Bilal's Fourth Wife"), another story in *Tribal Scars and Other Stories*, the muezzin of the mosque is a master of dissimulation. Regarded as pious by the members of the congregation and well respected, he has a soft spot for young girls, although he already has three wives whom he bullies regularly. He asks the young girls to sweep the courtyard of the mosque or fetch water for ablutions. "Sometimes, while pretending to help them, he fumbled at their clothing and pawed them" (p. 10). He eventually takes a young girl as a fourth wife; but she ends up having an affair with his nephew, who is of her generation. The disapproving references to polygamy (which also recur in *Xala* and *God's Bits of Wood*) criticize a practice that is sanctioned not only by Islam, but also by indigenous culture and religions, which had approved widespread polygamy before Islam made inroads in West Africa.

Even the celebrated indigenous tradition of the griot is not safe in Sembène's novels. In *The Money-Order*, he shows how the tradition can be abused and reduced to a means of fleecing people with money by pretense and deceit. Gorgui Maïssa gets a one-hundred-franc note from a young man by extolling his noble lineage:

> "You know him?" Dieng asked, when calm had returned.
>
> "Know him? You *are* simple. I heard someone mention his santa, his family name, and I embroidered on it. . . . You know nothing about life today."
>
> (p. 91)

Sembène's readiness to take on and challenge deeply ingrained beliefs and attitudes has often aroused strong opposition. His film *Ceddo* (1976; *Common People*) was banned in Senegal (which has a Muslim majority) for eight years because it criticizes the conversion of Africans to Islam.

The overlapping, contradiction, or coexistence of different religions and cultures provides rich material for Sembène's *White Genesis* (in *The Money-Order; with White Genesis*). In this novella of incest set in colonial times, a pillar of village society impregnates his daughter. Unlike the prime minister in *The Last of the Empire*, both parents are of noble birth and high caste lineage. The father, Guibril Guedj Diob, is the chief of the clan. The mother, Ngone War Thiadum, commits suicide after learning of her husband's guilt. What punishment to impose on Diob puzzles the elders of the community, who owe allegiance to three laws: the *adda*, or custom; the religious (Islamic) laws; and the laws introduced by the French. Massar poses the question thus: "According to Koranic law, Guibril Guedj Diob deserves to die. This is what the scriptures say. But have the penalties demanded by the scriptures for infringement of the law ever been applied here?" (p. 42). According to the imam, the *adda* stipulates either death or expulsion from the community for incest. The griot thinks that the case is crystal clear — but with an unexpected twist. He opposes punishing Diob because he suspects that Diob's younger brother is not solely after justice; he wants to replace his discredited brother. "Medoune Diob has something else at the back of his mind." He "is more concerned about the succession of the Ndiobene than about punishment" (p. 46).

The chief's deranged son kills him — urged on, as the griot believes, by Medoune Diob, who takes over as chief. Banished, Medoune Diob's niece, with her baby, leaves for Dakar. The hope is — in Ghanga Guisse's words — that the baby daughter, despite the shameful circumstances of her conception and birth, "may acquire nobility and nobility of conduct. Out of them, the future will be born" (p. 69). The griot, too, leaves the village, disappointed and hoping to find a place where "the truth will be the concern of honest minds and not a privilege of birth" (p. 65) because "the blood of truth is always noble" (p. 66).

JOURNEYS

The two journeys in *White Genesis* illustrate a pattern of noble and ignoble departures that can be traced in most of Sembène's fiction. The physical and geographical journey is used to examine concealed layers of sociopolitical ideas. In *Ô pays, mon beau peuple!*, the young man returns home with a white wife and new ideas. He is out of place and is ultimately murdered. In "Letters from France," the young girl undertakes two journeys, one arranged for her to Paris to marry the old man, and the other decided upon by herself, taking her daughter back to Africa. In his search for a cure of his *xala*, El Hadji embarks on a long drive, deep into the countryside, in order to see a famous marabout (holy man). He is forced to abandon his Mercedes and take a cart, and then to continue on foot. He leaves the city with its bright lights and amenities, seeking an answer in traditional medicine.

Apart from the symbolic march of the women in *God's Bits of Wood*, the most articulate leader of the strike, Ibrahim Bakayoko, also undertakes a journey. "The fisherman put relays of boats at his disposal, and with them he went up the Sénégal and Bakoy rivers as far as Kati" (p. 308). After that, he travels on dirt paths and little-used roads in order to avoid arrest following the sabotage of the railroad (for which he was not responsible). He finds safety and shelter among the people until the moment of triumph.

A different journey, away from the people, is recounted in "Mahmoud Fall" ("The False Prophet") in *Tribal Scars*. In this short story, Aidra (whose real name is Mahmoud Fall) decides "to journey towards the sunset," where he installs himself as an imam. He collects a great deal of money, then absconds. The escape demonstrates that he is a crook who uses religion to deceive innocent believers.

A similar journey of revelation is in *The Last of the Empire* when Professor Fall decides to return to France, declaring: "I never renounced my [French] nationality. We were French before we were Senegalese. . . . Blacks are all crazy. . . . Incapable of governing themselves" (p. 219). The overthrown president of the republic, too, returns to Paris, saying to his longtime colleague Cheikh Tidiane:

> "Do you remember, Cheikh? ... It was you who wrote to me then ... asking me to come back here."
>
> "Yes, Léon! That was when we still had dreams."
>
> (p. 228)

Where have all the African dreams gone? Can they be recaptured? What sort of exploratory journeys are needed for that? Sembène poses fundamental questions in a most acute manner. In the process, he has secured for himself a prominent place among those who are after the "blood of truth," a search that transcends what is geographically Senegalese or African.

Selected Bibliography

SELECTED WORKS

Le Docker noir. Paris: Nouvelles Éditions Debresse, 1956.

Ô pays, mon beau peuple! Paris: Amiot-Dumont, 1957. Ed. by Patrick Corcoran. London: Methuen Educational, 1986.

Les Bouts de bois de Dieu. Paris: Livre Contemporain, 1960.

Voltaïque. Paris: Présence Africaine, 1962.

L'Harmattan. Paris: Présence Africaine, 1963.

Véhi-Ciosane; ou, Blanche-Genèse, suivi du Mandat. Paris: Présence Africaine, 1965.

Xala. Paris: Présence Africaine, 1973.

Le Dernier de l'empire. Paris: L'Harmattan, 1981.

Niiwam, suivi de Taaw. Paris: Présence Africaine, 1987. Two novellas.

TRANSLATIONS

God's Bits of Wood. Trans. by Francis Price. Garden City, N.Y.: Doubleday, 1962; London: Heinemann, 1976.

The Money-Order; with White Genesis. Trans. by Clive Wake. London: Heinemann, 1972.

Tribal Scars and Other Stories. Trans. by Len Ortzen. London: Heinemann, 1974.

Xala. Trans. by Clive Wake. London: Heinemann, 1976; Westport, Conn.: Lawrence Hill, 1976.

The Last of the Empire: A Senegalese Novel. Trans. by Adrian Adams. London: Heinemann, 1983.

The Black Docker. Trans. by Ros Schwartz. London and Portsmouth, N.H.: Heinemann, 1987.

Niiwam and Taww. Oxford, U.K., and Portsmouth, N.H.: Heinemann, 1992.

FILMS

L'Empire Sonhrai. 1963. In French.

Borom Sarret. 1963. In French.

Niaye. 1964. In French. Based on *White Genesis.*

La Noire de ... (Black Girl). 1966. In French. English version, 1969.

Le Mandat (The Money-Order). 1968. In Wolof and French. English version, 1969.

Taw. 1970. In Wolof.

Emitai. 1971. In Diola and French.

Xala. 1974. In French and Wolof.

Ceddo. 1976. In Wolof.

Camp de Thiaroye. 1988. With Thiero Faty Sow.

CRITICAL STUDIES

Amuta, Chidi. *The Theory of African Literature: Implications for Practical Criticism.* London: Zed Books, 1989.

Bachy, Victor. *To Have a History of African Cinema.* Trans. by Dalice A. Woodford from *Pour une histoire du cinéma africain.* Brussels, Belgium: QCIC, 1987.

Blair, Dorothy S. *African Literature in French: A History of Creative Writing in French from West and Equatorial Africa.* Cambridge, U.K.: Cambridge University Press, 1976.

Carter, Donald. "Sympathy and Art: Novels and Short Stories." In *African Literature Today*, no. 5 (1971). Includes a review of *God's Bits of Wood.*

Chinweizu, Onwuchekwa Jemie, and Madubuike Ihechukwu. *Toward the Decolonization of African Literature.* Enugu, Nigeria: Fourth Dimension, 1980; Washington, D.C.: Howard University Press, 1983.

Conde, Maryse. "Sembène Ousmane—*Xala.*" In *African Literature Today*, no. 9 (1978). A review.

Diawara, Manthia. *African Cinema.* Bloomington: Indiana University Press, 1992.

———. "New York and Oagadougou: The Home of African Cinema." In *Sight and Sound* n.s. 3, no. 11 (1993).

Gellar, Sheldon. *Senegal: An African Nation Between Islam and the West.* Boulder, Colo.: Westview Press, 1982; 2nd ed., 1995.

Gordon, David C. *The French Language and National Identity (1930–1975).* The Hague, Netherlands: Mouton, 1978.

Irele, Abiola. *The African Experience in Literature and Ideology.* London and Exeter, N.H.: Heinemann, 1981.

Killam, G. D., ed. *African Writers on African Writing.* Evanston, Ill.: Northwestern University Press, 1973.

King, Bruce, and Kolawale Ogungbesan. *A Celebration of Black and African Writing.* Zaria, Nigeria: Ahmadou Bello University Press, 1975; New York: Oxford University Press, 1975.

Klein, Leonard, ed. *African Literatures in the Twentieth Century.* Harpenden, U.K.: Oldcastle Books, 1988.

Malkum, Lizbeth, and Roy Armes. *Arab and African Film Making.* London: Zed Books, 1991.

Ngara, Emmanuel. *Art and Ideology in the African Novel: A Study of the Influence of Marxism on African Writing.* London: Heinemann, 1985.

Ngũgĩ wa Thiong'o. *Decolonising the Mind: The Politics of Language in African Literature.* London: James Currey, 1986; Portsmouth, N.H.: Heinemann, 1986.

Peters, Jonathan A. "Sembène Ousmane as Griot: *The Money-Order with White Genesis.*" In *African Literature Today*, no. 12 (1982).

Pfaff, Françoise. *The Cinema of Ousmane Sembène, a Pioneer of African Film.* Westport, Conn.: Greenwood, 1984.

Stam, R., and L. Spence. "Colonialism, Racism and Representation: An Introduction." In *Screen* 24 (March/April 1983).

Zell, Hans M., and Helene Silver, eds. *A Reader's Guide to African Literature.* New York: Africana, 1971; London: Heinemann, 1972.

Léopold Sédar Senghor

1906–

ABIOLA IRELE

IT IS INDICATIVE of the thematic and formal development of the poetry of Léopold Sédar Senghor that *Chants d'ombre* (1945; *Shadow Songs*), his first published volume, begins with an elegy, "In Memoriam." In the poem, the Christian celebration of All Souls' Day becomes an occasion not so much for a meditation on the dead as for a reflection on the poet's personal situation in a hostile environment. The elegiac mode serves to give voice to his acute sense of exile, marked concretely by his physical separation from his homeland. In his solitude, his thoughts turn to his native land, and although the poem's dominant mood is one of mournful loss, this mood is related less to the fact of death—either as a universal factor of human awareness or as a specific circumstance of its manifestation—than to the drama of his divided consciousness. His recital of his anxieties, in nightmarish imagery, leads insistently to the compensatory move implied in these lines of rededication:

> O Forefathers! You who have always refused to die,
> Who knew how to resist Death from the Sine to the Seine,
> And now in the fragile veins of my indomitable blood,
> Guard my dreams as you did your thin-legged migrant sons!
>
> (*The Collected Poetry* [*CP*], p. 3)

The solace the poet derives from this invocation to his ancestors enables him, at the end of the poem, to confront his "brothers who have blue eyes and hard hands," representing the white world into which he has been thrust and to which he is placed in an ambiguous relationship. The recalling of his African antecedents, with all the affective charge they come to carry for him in his predicament, thus serves as a mode of defense against the vicissitudes of a problematic existence.

This conjunction of an introspective and a celebratory tone in the work that inaugurated Senghor's published poetry registers at once the two principal themes around which all the subsequent poetry is organized: the elegiac recall of a revalued past and the lyrical evocation of an ideal of renewal. Senghor infuses his work with a collective black consciousness, which is central to the concept of Négritude.

The declamatory style of so much of Senghor's poetry, already apparent in the poem "In Memoriam," has fostered a view of his work as mere self-dramatization, the expression of a gesture unrelated to the urgent pressures of real experience. For instance, Wole Soyinka, in an astringent criticism, has described Négritude as "this magnitude of unfelt abstractions" (in "And After the Narcissist?" in *African Forum* 1, spring 1966), a judgment whose negative import is also specifically addressed to the meaning of Senghor's poetry, so closely bound up as it is with Négritude, both as literary movement and as concept. It is therefore essential for a proper appraisal of Senghor's achievement not only to place his poetry in the historical context of its inspiration—to consider it, in its primary discursive nature, as a form of testimony—but also to insist on its true character and direction as an expressive mode.

The cultural and spiritual dilemma that provides the point of departure of Senghor's poetry was an urgent one for a whole generation of black intellectuals confronted with the psychological pressures of the colonial situation. Senghor's poetry is not only representative of a general response, but it also gives a peculiarly intense voice to a widely felt sentiment:

> And this other exile, much harder on my heart,
> Is the tearing apart of one self from the other,
> From my mother's tongue, from the Ancestral
> skull,
> From the tom-tom of my soul.
>
> ("Letters to the Princess,"
> *Éthiopiques*, 1956; *CP*, p. 105)

Given this background, it was inevitable that the quest for identity should have become central to the thematic development of Senghor's poetry. However, although this theme often lends his expression an affecting pathos, its significance is not limited to its relation to his individual psychological states as conditioned by his personal experience. It also provides the thematic foundation for an original poetry that reflects the poet's deepest inclinations. In the circumstances of Senghor's poetic vocation, a reclamation of his African inheritance was essential to exploring poetically what he felt to be his authentic universe of being. The progression of Senghor's poetry has thus followed a course from the exploration in the early volumes of the condition of exile and a corresponding reaffirmation of his identity to the elaboration in the later volumes of a personal vision of the world, expressed in a tone and register native to his sensibility and consciousness:

> But if I have to choose at the eleventh hour,
> I would choose the poetry of the rivers, the winds,
> the forests,
> The assonance of the plains and streams, choose
> The rhythm of my naked body's blood,
> Choose the vibrating balaphons and the harmony
> of the chords
>
> ("To the Music of Koras and Balaphon,"
> *Shadow Songs*; *CP*, pp. 18–19)

As the quotation suggests, the whole bent of Senghor's expression has been to invest his native continent with poetic significance so that Africa becomes for him nothing less than symbol and embodiment of the entire realm of nature. Thus, in reasserting African values, Senghor has also found a framework within which to create an imaginative world appropriate to his personal background, one that not only affords him the basis in image and symbol for his poetic vision but also represents a source of poetic knowledge.

LIFE AND CAREER

Léopold Sédar Senghor was born on 15 August 1906 (according to some sources) in Joal, a coastal village in the Sine-Saloum basin of Senegal. His father was a Serer, the dominant ethnic group in the region, and his mother was a Peul, an ethnic group related to the Fulani of the Fouta Jallon at the source of the river Niger in Guinea. Senghor's double ancestry, reflecting the long interaction of peoples and cultures in the West African savanna, has not only contributed to the vivid sense of history that informs his poetry but has assumed a special importance for him as a sign of his universal vocation. As he says in "Prière des tirailleurs sénégalais" ("Prayer of the Senegalese Soldiers"), which was first published in *Hosties noires* (1948; *Black Hosts*):

> I grew up in the heartland of Africa, at the
> crossroads
> Of castes, of races and roads.
>
> (*CP*, p. 50)

Senghor's childhood seems to have been a sheltered one in which he was the focus of devoted attention within a large household. He has often recalled the two most important influences stemming from his childhood: his maternal uncle, "Tokor" Waly, who introduced him to the traditional culture of his people, and the poet Marône Ndiaye, who awakened his young sensibility to the singular tonalities of their oral poetry. His reminiscences of his early years have understandably been colored by nostalgia, so that he has endowed his natal village with the aura of an earthly paradise, in his phrase the "kingdom of childhood" ("le royaume d'enfance").

At the age of seven, Senghor was sent by his father to the Catholic missionary school at the nearby village of Ngasobil, where he began his formal education and came for the first time into sustained contact with the French language. (Senghor's native language was Serer, and he also spoke Wolof.) On completion of his elementary education in 1922, he entered the Collège Libermann in Dakar, a junior seminary, with the intention of studying for the priesthood, but he left a few years later after a disagreement with the father superior. He then enrolled at the Lycée van Vollenhoven, the state secondary school in Dakar, where he became a star pupil, winning the prize in French every year. He obtained his *baccalauréat* (secondary-school diploma) in 1928 and was awarded a scholarship to continue his studies in France, entering the Lycée Louis-le-Grand in Paris the following year to prepare for the entrance examination to the prestigious École Normale Supérieure. In the course of his literary studies at the lycée, he encountered modern French literature, in particular French poetry, exemplified by the work of Charles Baudelaire and his symbolist successors, and sustained in its evocative and mystic orientation by Paul Claudel, Charles Péguy, and St.-John Perse, and, in an even more intense register, by André Breton and his surrealist cohorts. Apart from these literary influences, he also discovered the writings of Maurice Barrès, whose organic nationalism has shaped French conservative thought, and the vitalist, anti-intellectual philosophy of Henri Bergson, the most highly regarded philosopher in France in the years between the two world wars. The influence of these and other French writers, such as Arthur Gobineau and Pierre Teilhard de Chardin, has remained pervasive in Senghor's poetry and intellectual writings.

Senghor soon became a central figure among the group of French-speaking African and West Indian students and intellectuals living in Paris during the interwar years. In the autumn of 1932, he met Aimé Césaire, who had just arrived in Paris from Martinique to begin his studies at the Lycée Louis-le-Grand. A close friendship developed between them that had important consequences for modern literature, for it was out of their relationship that what came to be known as Négritude developed. Together, they read and discussed the writings of the "new anthropology," notably the work of the Frenchman Maurice Delafosse and the German ethnographer Leo Frobenius, whose revision of the conventional image of Africa as a continent devoid of cultural attainments lent Senghor and Césaire renewed confidence in their own effort for the revaluation of the black race. They also became acquainted with the literature of the Harlem Renaissance, which, in its strong articulation of the new black consciousness in the United States, gave form to their preoccupations as colonized subjects.

The pervasive malaise in Europe during these years, marked by political unrest and social agitation as well as a questioning of traditional values in the wake of the carnage of World War I, also favored the growth of a strong self-awareness among French-speaking black intellectuals. The awarding in 1921 of the Prix Goncourt (the leading French literary prize) to René Maran, a West Indian, for his novel *Batouala* drew attention to the colonial problem; the *Revue du monde noir*, run by the Nardal sisters, originally from Martinique, fulfilled an important role as an organ of black solidarity. The appearance in 1932 of the journal *Légitime Défense*, the sole issue of which contained an indictment of French colonialism as well as a manifesto for a committed black literature in French modeled on the Harlem Renaissance, signaled the emergence of a new militancy among the French-speaking black elite. It was in these circumstances that, with the collaboration principally of Césaire, Léon Damas from French Guiana, and Birago Diop from Senegal, Senghor founded *L'Étudiant noir* as a forum for the examination of the colonial situation and the cultural problems posed to the black elite by the French policy of assimilation. His first essays on the African renaissance date from this period, reflecting the growing self-assurance with which black intellectuals in Paris began to challenge the cultural premises of French colonialism and to assert their racial and cultural identity. These developments culminated with the 1939 publication of Césaire's long poem *Cahier d'un retour au pays natal* (1947; "Notes on a Return to the Native Land"), with its passionate celebration of Négritude, the term he had coined to express the collective consciousness of the black race and its new affirmative posture in relation to the historical moment.

Senghor failed to gain admission to the École Normale Supérieure and continued his studies at the Sorbonne. By 1932, he had obtained his *diplôme d'études supérieures* (equivalent to the master's degree) with a thesis on Baudelaire, and three years later he passed the highly competitive examination for the *agrégation* degree (roughly equivalent to a doctor of philosophy), the first African to do so and for which he was required to become a French citizen. He was appointed to teaching positions in lycées, first in Tours and later in the suburbs of Paris, and began to write the poems later collected in his first volume, *Shadow Songs*. At the outbreak of World War II in 1939, he was drafted into the army and saw action on the northern front, where he was taken prisoner by the Germans in 1940 during the collapse of France. He spent the next two years in various prisoner-of-war camps, where he wrote most of the poems of *Black Hosts*. Released on health grounds and confined to Paris, Senghor resumed his teaching and was appointed in 1944 to the chair of African languages at the École Nationale de la France d'Outre-Mer.

Elected at the end of the war in 1945 to the French Constituent Assembly as one of the deputies for Senegal, Senghor embarked on a political career alongside his literary and intellectual activities. The same year saw the publication of *Shadow Songs*. In 1947, he participated in the founding of *Présence africaine* by Alioune Diop, a journal devoted to the promotion of African civilization and dialogue with other cultures. In 1948, *Black Hosts* was published, as well as his historic *Anthologie de la nouvelle poésie nègre et malgache de langue française* (Anthology of new Negro and Malagasy poets), which brought together poems by writers of French expression from Africa, the West Indies, and Madagascar and may be said to have launched Négritude as a movement, largely through the contribution of Jean-Paul Sartre, whose prefatory essay, "Orphée noir" ("Black Orpheus"), contained the first systematic elucidation of the term.

Sartre's definition of Négritude in his preface as "l'être-dans-le-monde-du-Noir" (the-being-in-the-world-of-the-Negro) assimilated the movement to the existentialist philosophy of which he was at the time the foremost exponent in France. Examining the work of the black poets in Senghor's anthology with reference to the specific social and political situation of the black race and in the historical context of colonialism, he saw Négritude as "an affective attitude to the world," a passing phase of black existence and awareness that would be superseded by the advent of a new world without racial and class divisions. However, in Senghor's later formulations, the term designates an original disposition of black people as shaped by the African environment and the constitutive elements of African civilization—hence his definition of Négritude as "l'ensemble des valeurs de la civilisation africaine" (the sum total of African values). For him, this totality stands as the "objective correlative" of a collective ethos distinguished by modes of feeling and doing and, above all, by a unique manner of relating to the world, of an essentially mystical quality.

Because he seemingly "essentializes" black identity, Senghor's theory of Négritude has elicited strong reactions and provoked a lively debate that had hardly abated by the 1990s. Négritude, however, should be viewed more properly as a concept of culture, one that not only fulfilled an imperative psychological need—to restore balance to the lacerated consciousness of the assimilated black intellectual—but also served to redefine the terms of the relationship between peoples and cultures within a comprehensive understanding of the world. Although Senghor's formulations are immediately applicable to Africa and black people elsewhere, they have a wider compass, resting as they do on a strong valuation of difference and a wholehearted recognition of the variety of human experience. Nonetheless, despite his insistence on the singular endowments of black people, Senghor does not posit the incommensurability of the varied cultures of the world but, on the contrary, makes allowance for their convergence in what he calls a "civilization of the universal." Négritude represents an imaginative ideal in his poetry with suggestive possibilities for the life of the spirit that Senghor has sought to communicate.

The 1949 publication of *Chants pour Naëtt* (Songs for Naëtt), a volume of love poems dedicated to his first wife, Ginette, confirmed Senghor's status as one of the leading French-language poets. Reelected in 1951 to the French National Assembly (formerly Constituent Assembly), Senghor found himself engaged in intense parliamentary activity, serving on various commissions dealing with the colonies and as junior minister in successive cabinets of the Fourth Republic. During this period, he produced a stream of essays on various aspects of African culture that established his reputation as perhaps the leading contemporary African intellectual. In this respect, his keynote addresses at the First Congress of Negro Artists and Writers, organized in Paris in 1956 by the Société de Culture Africaine (Society for African Culture), affiliated with *Présence africaine*, and at the Second Congress, held in Rome in 1959, may be said to constitute the core of his theory of Négritude and his contribution to contemporary African thought.

After an interval of seven years during which Senghor published only a few occasional poems in periodicals, another volume of poetry, *Éthiopiques*, appeared in 1956. Charles de Gaulle's dramatic return to power in France two years later gave a new direction to Senghor's political career. With the dissolution in 1960 of the French Community (a union of France and its former colonies that De Gaulle had established as an institutional complement to the Fifth Republic), the French colonies in Africa attained formal independence. Senghor became president of the Mali Federation (a union of Senegal and French Sudan) and, after its breakup a few months later, of the Republic of Senegal. As head of state, Senghor became preoccupied over the next twenty years with the problems of nation building, and his concern with questions of social and economic development led him to evolve in the early 1960s a theory of African socialism, as an extension of Négritude. He continued however to publish poetry steadily, and *Nocturnes* appeared in 1961, followed by *Elégie des Alizés* (*Elegy of the Trade Winds*), published in a limited edition in 1969, and *Lettres d'hivernage* (*Letters in the Season of Hivernage*) in 1972. Senghor relinquished office in 1980 after a carefully prepared transition of power. His election in 1983 to the Académie Française consecrated his eminence on the French literary and intellectual landscape.

POETRY

The relation between the poetic vocation and political activity is central to Senghor's imaginative expression, one to which he devoted special attention in the dramatic poems "Chaka" ("Shaka") and "Le Kaya-Magan" ("The Kaya-Magan"), as well as in his book of interviews, *La Poésie de l'action: Conversations avec Mohamed Aziza* (1980; The poetry of action). This relation is, however, more complex than is suggested by the limited view of commitment often urged against him by his critics, for if his poetry does not always evince an intransigent militant tone, it assumes a polemical character as much by design as by implication; its ideological thrust emerges from an earnest and consistent refusal of assent to the racial and cultural postulates of western imperialism.

Shadow Songs

The title of Senghor's first volume is doubly significant in this regard. The epithet *ombre* (shadow), which qualifies *chants* (songs), denotes the state of marginality in relation to a dominant presence and takes on its full meaning in its representation of a climate of ambiguities and uncertainties in which the poet exists. The *chants*, developed in the volume both as laments and odes, work insistently toward a reversal of this meaning, investing it with a new connotation, that of an area of quiet repose, of a private realm from which the poet reaches out to a fuller and healthier sense of himself.

Although tending constantly toward celebration, the imagery in Senghor's first volume develops essentially as a function of the poet's meditation on the state of alienation, formulated in specific historical and cultural terms. The poems dramatize, in the first instance, Senghor's crisis of identity as a man of two worlds and chart the course of his mind from an unsettling indeterminacy to a state of inner coherence. This movement toward self-integration begins with a retreat into memory, associated with childhood and his distant origins:

I have chosen to live near the rebuilt walls of my
  memory
And from the top of the high ramparts
I remember Joal-of-the-Shades,
The face of the land of my blood

("Porte dorée"; *CP*, p. 3)

The return to origins is developed at length in "Que m'accompagnent kôras et balaphong" ("To the Music of Koras and Balaphon"), an ode that gravely retraces the poet's spiritual biography. The dialectic of the poem is determined by the conflict between the two worlds of the poet's experience, with Africa seen in terms of its past nobility and present distress and Europe as the embodiment of a moment of historical tension. This and other poems in Senghor's first volume, such as "Le Retour de l'enfant prodigue" ("Return of the Prodigal Son"), bear witness to Senghor's sense of cultural deprivation and to his conscious effort to repossess his African inheritance. The mystical exploration of this inheritance in "Nuit de Sine" ("Night in Sine") expands the theme of the ancestors of "In Memoriam" into a statement of renewal:

Let me breathe the odor of our Dead, let me
  gather
And speak with their living voices, let me learn to
  live
Before plunging deeper than the diver
Into the great depths of sleep.

(*CP*, p. 7)

Apart from the poet's personal investment in his theme, it is evident from the poems in *Shadow Songs* that Senghor is already giving a new dimension to French poetry by taking it beyond exoticism, with all that the term implies of the decorative use of and largely impersonal stance toward an unfamiliar world. What is at work here is a process of internalization along with a gathering of moral and spiritual strength in the African poet's confrontation with an unacceptable historical situation:

They call us men of cotton, coffee, and oil
They call us men of death.
But we are men of dance, whose feet get stronger
As we pound upon firm ground.
("Prayer to the Masks"; *CP*, p. 14)

In *Shadow Songs*, Senghor elaborates through poetry rehabilitation of his African background, in a subtle but calculated contestation of the ideological discourse of European colonialism regarding his continent. In the volume, he is visibly staking out a claim to an alternative world of values, fully aware of the counterdiscursive implications of his act. It is instructive to observe his reversal of the western convention of the love poem in favor of his personal background in the rhapsodic fervor of the litany of praises that constitute "Femme noire" ("Black Woman"), one of his best-known poems. In the poem, Senghor appropriates classical western and biblical references and turns them to his account in his conflation of the female figure addressed in the poem with the African landscape, evoked as a symbolic presence and represented as the incarnation of the enduring qualities of the black race in its organic bond with the life of the universe. In this fundamental sense Africa receives a form of consecration in Senghor's poetry:

Naked woman, black woman
I sing your passing beauty and fix it for all Eternity
before jealous Fate reduces you to ashes to
nourish the roots of life.
("Black Woman"; *CP*, p. 9)

This, then, is poetry of self-reconstruction, the re-creation of a stable sense of identity, brought into active consciousness in a new relation to a designated community of beings and souls. The personal note merges with the collective, subserving a conception of the poet as guardian of the collective memory. Senghor's reconnection to his origins thus finds expression in terms of a strongly articulated historical consciousness:

Elephant of Mbissel, hear my reverent prayer.
Give me the skilled knowledge of the great
Timbuktu doctors,
Give me Soni Ali's strong will, born of the Lion's
slobber—
A tidal wave to the conquest of a continent.
Blow upon me the Keïta's wisdom.
Give me the Guelwâr's courage, gird my loins with
the strength of a *tyedo.*
Give me the chance to die for the struggles of my
people,
And if necessary in the odor of gunpowder and
cannon.
("Return of the Prodigal Son"; *CP*, p. 34)

The radical stance of the concluding lines, even when their political force has been discounted, represents a forthright statement of the realignment of Senghor's personal allegiances that propels the unfolding of his ideological project in *Shadow Songs.* More significant, however, is his imaginative recreation of a world that offers him both respite from the tensions of his lived situation and, in broader spiritual terms, the prospect of regeneration. This correlation of the public voice and a renovated awareness of the self implicit in *Shadow Songs* comes to the fore in his second volume, *Black Hosts.*

Black Hosts

As the title indicates, *Black Hosts* is a memorial to the unsung heroes of World War II: its black victims—African as well as American—who were hosts of death, their supreme sacrifice unappreciated by the white people for whom they served merely as cannon fodder. The composition of the volume thus represents an act of racial solidarity, stated unambiguously in its introductory poem:

Who can praise you, if not your brother-in-arms,
your brother in blood,
You, Senegalese soldiers, my brothers with warm
hands,
Lying under ice and death?
("Liminary Poem"; *CP*, p. 40)

Black Hosts registers the critical response of the colonized black poet to the contradictions of the west, and the poet's indictment of this civilization is fully conveyed in "Au Guélowâr" ("To the *Guélowâr*"), with its ironic reference to the "cruelty of civilized men." The catalog of grievances that accompanies his "Prière de paix" ("Prayer for Peace") is sufficient testimony to the connection the poet makes between the savagery of the European war and the violations of colonialism. A common thread of bitter recrimination runs through the volume, manifested as much in the private melancholy of "Ndessé" as in the sharp public rancor of "Tyraoye" ("Thiaroye"). This note of bitterness, which lends its particular tonality to the poet's expression in the volume, is contained with obvious moral strain in these lines from the pointedly titled "Assassinats" ("Assassinations").

There they lie stretched out by the captive roads along the routes of disaster
Thin poplar trees, statues of dark gods draped with their long, gold coats
Senegalese prisoners lying gloomily on French soil...

O black Martyrs, immortal race, let me say the words
That forgive.

(*CP*, pp. 57–58)

The grim reality of the European war provides Senghor the occasion for giving vent to his pent-up resentments. However, the pronounced ambivalence of many of the poems, highlighted in "Prayer for Peace," has tended to obscure the theme of protest that dominates the volume and that makes it the most "committed," in the usual sense of the word, of all of Senghor's work. The ambivalence, however, is a function of the immense disillusionment of the poet as he considers the discrepancy between humanist ideals of western civilization, which he has internalized, and the objective historical manifestations of that civilization. Moreover, a strong element of commiseration moderates the indignation underlying the poems of *Black Hosts,* for if the spectacle of death and desolation indicates a dehumanization that demonstrates the destructive impact of western civilization, it also inspires pity for its victims, regardless of their race or nationality. As had been the case for Wilfred Owen and the English poets of World War I, this eminently human emotion was for Senghor a legitimate subject of poetry. It must be recalled that Senghor writes from direct experience of the war, so the volume is partly a chronicle of events; the elegiac nature of the poems is thus very much in keeping with the subject. The moral reflection on the events, intensified by the theme, is directly related to the quest for sustaining values. This quest finds expression in "Chant de printemps" ("Song of Spring"), in which, in a predictably partisan move, Africa is presented as the providential source of the values necessary for universal renewal.

Thus, we find in both *Shadow Songs* and *Black Hosts* the attachment of Senghor's feeling to external circumstances. The poems invoke a concreteness of experience that testifies to the way in which Senghor finds himself situated in history. The thematic progression in both volumes is posited on the affirmation of Africa as a distinctive physical environment and cultural and spiritual universe and on the interaction of the poet's memory and sensibility with the human values proposed by this universe. This reality, apprehended poetically, affords Senghor the individual perspective on the world that governs his expression in subsequent works.

Éthiopiques

Explaining in the 1956 postface to *Éthiopiques* the motivation for his constant recourse to African references in his earlier volumes, Senghor ascribes a visionary purpose to his poetry: "All I had to do was name the elements of my childhood universe in order to prophesy the city of tomorrow, which will be reborn from the ashes of the old; this is the mission of the Poet." The nationalist overtones of this statement, though muted, are insistent, inasmuch as Senghor invokes a transformed political order as the justification of his poetry, an order sanctioned by those he calls "the legitimate princes" in his "Épîtres à la princesse" ("Letters to the Princess"). The statement can be read nonetheless as the championing of the source of art that has nothing to do, however, with aestheticism—that is, with a conception of art as pure realm separated from concrete life—but derives its force from a live sense that pervades traditional societies, of art as profoundly implicated in vital processes.

Senghor endeavors to actualize this fundamental insight in *Éthiopiques*. The eight poems that constitute the first part of the volume present a series of evocations animated by an essential vitalism. He gives an enhanced dimension to nature poetry in "Congo," in which the African river is evoked not just as the heart of the black continent but, further, as the manifestation of natural energies. "L'Absente" ("The Absent Woman") enunciates a hieratic conception of poetry even in its immersion in the daily realities of social and material life. The "absent woman" of the poem is at once the spirit of Africa and the poetic ideal, to which Senghor aims to give sensuous meaning. The multiple associations in the poem are developed through concrete evocations, culminating in the affirmation of the visionary role of the poet who is at the core of human experience and the mediator of the ideal life. This privileged function is adumbrated in "L'Homme et la bête" ("Man and Beast"), in which Senghor draws on Dogon myth to affirm the sovereignty of the poetic consciousness within the realm of nature:

> The golden brow harnesses the clouds
> Where icy eagles soar, and thoughts circle his brow
> His cardinal eye is the serpent's head.
>
> (*CP*, p. 75)

The antithetical structure of "À New York" ("To New York"), with its opposition of two realms of life and expression along the racial divide, offers a poetic demonstration of the values of Négritude to which these evocations tend. Senghor's identification of Harlem and its black community with the elemental forces is not, however, altogether partisan. Although the black race is celebrated as bearer of vital values, these are not so much counterpoised to the technical civilization associated with the white race as presented as complementary to the instrumental reason whose triumphal progress threatens the world with spiritual dessication and the denial of profound human needs. The mythology of the poem thus moves toward an ideal of reconciliation:

> New York! I say New York, let black blood flow into your blood.
> Let it wash the rust from your steel joints, like an oil of life
> Let it give your bridges the curve of hips and supple vines.
>
> (*CP*, p. 88)

The poem attests to Senghor's catholic temperament, his inclination toward conciliation, and his refusal of simple antinomies. It also reflects the conviction about the real possibility of the unity of head and heart that he advocates in his intellectual writings. The dialectic entailed in this view is addressed in both heroic and personal terms in "The Kaya-Magan," a monologue evoking the emperor of the ancient empire of Ghana. The mystical conception of kingship attributed to the Kaya-Magan of the poem approximates Senghor's ideal of politics as a mission informed by spiritual values. The Kaya-Magan is thus both the epitome of ancient Africa and the image of the ideal poet-politician, in whom the tension between political commitment and the poetic vocation is resolved. More fundamentally, he emerges at the end of the poem as the unifying symbol of a new, integrated consciousness:

For I am both sides of a double door, the binary rhythm of space
And the third beat, I am the movement of drums,
The strength of future Africa.
(*CP*, p. 79)

The obvious personal reference of this declaration connects directly with Shaka's celebration of the creative potential of art in the dramatic poem of his name:

I am the drumstick that beats and furrows the drum.
Who called it monotony? Joy is monotonous,
Beauty monotonous
Eternity is a cloudless sky, a blue noiseless forest,
A solitary voice that is true....

Let the drums raise up the sun of the New World.
("Shaka"; *CP*, p. 100)

The view of human experience summoned up in these lines conditions even the intimate tone of the poems addressed to his French wife and her family circle in the sequence that constitutes the second part of *Éthiopiques.* The juxtaposition of the African world with the European society revolves around the contrast of their respective histories, material conditions, social manners, and mores; the poet and his French wife thus function largely as embodiments of these contrasts. The correlation of the love theme with his habitual preoccupation with race in "Princesse, ton épître" ("Princess, Your Letter") foregrounds the involvement of the poet's African background, experience, and immediate interests, public and private, with his individual relationship to the foreign woman. The personal reference thus serves primarily to delineate the texture of a settled way of life that has formed his sensibility and whose coherence speaks to the commonality of human forms of sociability, even in the variety of their expressions.

Nocturnes

Senghor is at his most personal and lyrical in *Nocturnes,* the first part of which contains poems published under the title *Chants pour Naëtt* and revised as *Chants pour Sigare.* He does not always avoid the pitfalls of sentimentality in his treatment of the love theme that drives the volume. The obvious derivativeness (from Baudelaire) of the verse "And we will be bathed my love" illustrates the affected tone of many of the poems in the volume. But there can be no doubt of the sustained lyricism Senghor achieves in other poems that resonate with a more heartfelt engagement with his theme. In particular, "Une main de lumière" ("A Hand of Light"), by bringing together the western and African convention of the pastoral, strikes a note of spontaneous feeling that is enforced by the direct impact of the imagery drawn from the African landscape.

Letters in the Season of Hivernage

Letters in the Season of Hivernage continues the tenor of *Nocturnes* but considerably expands its scope. The volume takes the form of an intimate diary of the poet's activities and his emotional states during a period of separation from his second wife. The word *hivernage* refers to the dry hot season in Senegal, corresponding to the summer months in Europe when the French colonists returned to France for their annual holiday; Senghor's wife continued this practice during her sojourn in Senegal as the president's wife. The diary is thus not only a record of the practical routine of life during her absence but a means of communication that makes her present to his mind. The poems formulate the quality of a relationship that unites two souls within an order of the imagination. Of particular interest is the way the image of woman as reference of poetic feeling is complicated by the relationship between the black poet and the object of his devotion, who is both a white woman and his life companion. This determines the series of polarities developed in the volume as a means of rendering the rhythm and harmonies of experience, a series that extends its significance to a statement of dualism as principle of life. The perception of earth and sky as the primordial couple dictates other derivations of this principle: man and woman, white and black, absence and presence, joy and sadness, light and darkness, and day and night are run together to establish the leitmotif of the volume. The sharply contrasted moods of the opening and closing poems, "Je me suis réveillé" ("I Awoke") and "Le salut du jeune soleil" ("The New Sun Greets Me"), define the outer frames of the volume, which moves from the note of distress:

I awoke this evening beneath the warm rain,
And in the night of my anguish I saw winged
  panthers,
Amphibious sharks, and yellow crabs eating clear
  to my brain.
("I Awoke"; *CP*, p. 167)

to final exultation:

At the end of the test and the season, at the bottom
Of the gulf, God! may I find again your voice
And your fragrance of vibrating light.
("The New Sun Greets Me"; *CP*, p. 188)

Within this comprehensive frame Senghor expresses his attachment to the loved one:

But in the heart of the cold season, when the purer
  curves
Of your face shall appear, your cheeks more
  hollow, your look
More distant, my Lady, when your skin, your
  neck,
Your weary body, your thin hands will be streaked
With furrows like winter fields, I will find the
  treasure
Of my rhythmic quest and the sun behind the long
  anguished night,
The waterfall and the same chant murmuring from
  your soul
("You Speak"; *CP*, p. 183)

In the sublimated eroticism of these lines, the fundamental categories of time and space provide the framework for the elemental images with which Senghor celebrates what, in another poem of *Letters*, he calls "the wedding of flesh and blood."

Elegies

The elegies unite the themes and figures of Senghor's poetry and afford a sharp relief to the two currents of his expression. (Although the first poems specifically designated as "Elegies" appear in *Nocturnes*, the other elegies are brought together in a section of *Poèmes* under the title "Élégies majeures," which is also discussed here.) The public voice related to the objective world of historical events, with its corresponding style of demonstration, sets the background for the private tone of self-examination and subjective feelings, with its style of evocation. The concern in both with the dramatization of the issues of existence gives Senghor's elegiac form a somewhat wider definition than is implied by its conventional theme of death. For Senghor, the form functions as a mode for the contemplation of the human condition. "Élégie des Alizés" ("Elegy of the Trade Winds") demonstrates this orientation in its relation to a critical point in his own life. With the onset of old age, "the autumn of my life" as he called it in a speech in Dakar on his seventieth birthday, the poet begins to reckon with the prospect of death. His awareness of the irresistible flow of time registered here provides the central theme of "Élégie de minuit" ("Elegy of Midnight"), which develops around a series of antithetical values: youth/age, dream/action, poetry/politics, repose/agitation—all expressive of an aspiration to harmony with the world. In "Élégie des circonis" ("Elegy of the Circumcised"), from *Nocturnes*, Senghor revisits the theme of childhood and the opposition of innocence and experience in general human terms, detached from the contextual frame of its earlier expression. Regret over the loss of spontaneous self-expression associated with childhood ("to die to the beauty of the song") is combined with renewed appreciation of the singular fact of existence so that a poetic meditation develops into a celebration of the poet's presence in the world:

> The poem is a snake-bird, the dawn marriage of
>   shadow and light
> It soars like the Phoenix! It sings with wings
>   spread
> Over the slaughter of words.
>
> (*CP*, p. 143)

"Élégie des eaux" ("Elegy of the Waters") turns on the theme of mortification and purification, as in "Neige sur Paris" ("Snow on Paris"); its apocalyptic imagery, recalling the biblical flood, leads however to a note of serenity: water emerges at the end as the image of an original essence, with a sacramental import. The Christian associations suggested by Senghor come together to furnish the controlling idea in the two elegies to his old schoolmate and president of France, Georges Pompidou, and to Martin Luther King, Jr., pastor and hero of the U.S. civil rights movement. Both elegies proceed in dirgelike fashion, toward a confident affirmation of faith in the afterlife that draws directly on Christian iconology and conceptions, as in the elegy to Pompidou: "Of bliss, tell me friend, is that what heaven is like / Are there brooks of serene milk, of radiant honey among cedar trees?" ("Elegy for Georges Pompidou," *Major Elegies*; CP, p. 225). The anguish of death is thus displaced by a stoic resignation to its inevitability and compensated for by the poet's contemplation of the profound mystery of life. In their general tone, Senghor's elegies are, therefore, far removed from the dark brooding associated with the form. They proclaim the metaphysical triumph of an original life of creation over apparent decay, of the eternal over the transient.

The elegies offer a summation of the themes of Senghor's poetry. They compose a narrative of his encounter with history, his responses to its solicitations, and his knowledge of the world as derived from the contemplation of lived experience. It is this experience in its concrete aspects that stands behind his achievement as poet of the African renaissance.

LANGUAGE AND IMAGERY

While the force of this achievement is widely recognized, its nature and significance in literary terms have been matters of divergent opinions. It is therefore important to consider, if only briefly, the language and imagery of his poetry, which ultimately depend on both its texture as verbal art and its appeal as expressive mode.

In an early poem, "Lettre à un poète" ("Letter to a Poet") from *Shadow Songs*, addressed as homage to Aimé Césaire, Senghor salutes the innovative significance of his friend's poetry:

> Your bed presses the earth, easing the toil of
>   wetland drums
> Beating the rhythm of your song, and your verse
> Is the breath of the night and the distant sea.
> You praised the Ancestors and the legitimate
>   princes.
> For your rhyme and counterpoint you scooped a
>   star from the heavens.
>
> (*CP*, p. 5)

The nature of the passage is a manifesto, for it indicates Senghor was also conscious of moving in his own poetry toward a new aesthetic. Of necessity, the novel experience he brought to the language of the colonizer dictated a new mode and accent to convey its particularity in full. Senghor's poetry thus provides an early illustration of the tension in the new African literature between the frame of reference of the African imagination and its adopted European language of expression. Senghor himself has clarified the deliberate syncretism that presides in his own poetry and whose significance he has generalized with reference to the poets of his 1948 anthology: "Our ambition is modest: to be precursors, to open the way to an authentic black poetry, one that does not, for all that, decline to be French" (*Poèmes*, p. 165).

We get an idea of the character of the syncretism in question by attending to the salient features of his poetic language, which infuse the movement of his verse with the quality of African orality. His frequent recourse to the apostrophe (or direct address), his use of parallelism, enumeration, repetition, and, above all, his reliance on sound effects, such as alliteration, assonance, onomatopoeia, and ideophones, point to procedures intended to endow his expression with a distinctive tonality. These procedures, integrated into the verse form known as *verset*, with its ample, respiratory movement, have enabled Senghor to exploit the structure of the French language itself to express his African sensibility.

This observation prompts a final consideration of the nature and quality of Senghor's imagery. The fact that his diction owes so much to the rhetorical manner of French Romanticism creates an impression of a simplicity of texture, but this is only apparent, belied by the complex associations of his imagery. Senghor is a highly self-conscious artist, and the reflections on poetry scattered throughout his theoretical writings are fully exemplified in his own work. Thus, his images do not merely erect a structure of allegories, as in Romantic poetry, but correspond to the movement of the poet's emotional life and beyond, to imaginative awareness of the inner movement of things. It is this quality of the image that he has described as its "analogical" function, one that predominates in his own deployment of imagery, especially when it incorporates aspects of African cultural practices:

May a thousand stars be lit each night on the
 Great Square
May twelve thousand bowls ringed with sea
 serpents be warmed
For my pious subjects, for the fawns of my womb,
The residents of my house and their dependents.
("The Kaya-Magan," *Éthiopiques*; *CP*, p. 78)

It is of course not essential to look for a point-by-point correspondence between the African references and his own thought, as elaborated in his theory of Négritude. What is important is to see how Senghor reclaims for himself the essential spirit of African systems of belief and how this determines a hyper-Romanticism that aligns his poetry with the modernist quest for a new transcendental reference not underwritten by the orthodoxies of established religions. There is a negative aspect to this quest, which sometimes leads to a mindless primitivism in modern literature. In Senghor's case, however, this quest reflects a deliberate effort to validate the structure of the traditional thought of his own African world, its allusive immediacy, and the symbolic mode for which poetry provides the ideal medium of expression. Through the constellation of his images, he has evolved a poetic cosmology derived from a personal understanding of African animism, grounding his poetic thought in a vision attuned to his background: "I saw the festival of Night begin at retreat of day / And I proclaim Night more truthful than the day" ("To New York," *Éthiopiques*; *CP*, p. 88).

Africa functions, then, not only as the prime mediator of Senghor's self-awareness but also, and more fundamentally, as the anchor of his poetic consciousness:

I know that the arrogance of these hills calls to my
 pride.
Standing on the jagged summits crowned with
 fragrant gum trees,
I seize the navel's echo beating the rhythm of their
 song
—A lake of deep waters sleeps in its watchful
 crater.

I know that only this rich black-skinned plain
Is worthy of the plowshare and the deep flow of
my virility.
("Beyond Eros," *Shadow Songs*; *CP*, p. 29)

The particular energies of Senghor's poetry are tensed against the historical determinations of its inspiration. The essential impulse of his poetic expression, as indeed of his entire intellectual work, has been the need to confront the pressures of the peculiar historical experience of black people in their relationship to the western world. As is evident, however, from a consideration of its development, the range of reference and significance of his poetry have been extended beyond the limits defined by this imperative. This progression begins to be felt in *Éthiopiques* and *Nocturnes*, which expand on the theme of conflict and antithesis dominant in the earlier volumes to reflect the poet's intuition of the structure of dualities in the universe. This later development is even more marked in *Letters in the Season of Hivernage* and the elegies, which represent a sustained poetic meditation on the ultimate dichotomy of the human condition: the gift and mystery of life and the ineluctable fact of death. If, then, Senghor's poetry has served as the medium of response to the tensions of his existential situation, it has also enabled him to transcend a negative experience in an ideal of reconciliation with the self and in a unified vision of humanity and of the world. The poetry thus stands beyond the individual reference and its historical determinations to explore, in properly imaginative terms, the drama of a universal human condition.

Selected Bibliography

POETRY

Chants d'ombre. Paris: Seuil, 1945.
Hosties noires. Paris: Seuil, 1948.
Chants pour Naëtt. Paris: Pierre Seghers, 1949.
Éthiopiques. Paris: Seuil, 1956.
Nocturnes. Paris: Seuil, 1961.
Élégie des Alizés. Paris: Seuil, 1969.
Lettres d'hivernage. Paris: Seuil, 1973.
Élégies majeures. Geneva: Regard, 1978. Repr. with "Dialogue sur la poésie francophone." Paris: Seuil, 1979.
Poèmes. Paris: Seuil, 1982. Consists of *Chants d'ombre, Hosties noires, Éthiopiques, Nocturnes, Poèmes divers, Lettres d'hivernage, Élégies majeures, Poèmes perdus,* and "Élégie pour Phillipe-Maguilen."

PROSE

Liberté I: Négritude et humanisme. Paris: Seuil, 1964.
Liberté II: Nation et voie africaine du socialisme. Paris: Seuil, 1971.
Liberté III: Négritude et civilisation de l'universal. Paris: Seuil, 1977.
Liberté IV: Socialisme et planification. Paris: Seuil, 1983.
Ce que je crois: Négritude, francité, et civilisation de l'universel. Paris: Bernard Grasset, 1988.
Liberté V: Le Dialogue des cultures. Paris: Seuil, 1993.

TRANSLATIONS

Selected Poems. Selected and trans. by John Reed and Clive Wake. Oxford, U.K.: Oxford University Press, 1964; New York: Atheneum, 1964.
On African Socialism. Trans. by Mercer Cook. New York: Praeger, 1964.
Selected Poems/Poésies choisies. Trans. by Craig Williamson. London: Rex Collings, 1976.
Selected Poetry and Prose. Trans. by John Reed and Clive Wake. London: Heinemann Educational Books, 1976.
The Collected Poetry. Trans. by Melvin Dixon. Charlottesville: University Press of Virginia, 1991.

INTERVIEW

La Poésie de l'action: Conversations avec Mohamed Aziza. Paris: Stock, 1980.

CRITICAL STUDIES

Adotevi, Stanislas. *Négritude et négrologues.* Paris: Union Générale d'Éditions, 1972.

Bâ, Sylvia Washington. *The Concept of Negritude in the Poetry of Léopold Sédar Senghor*. Princeton, N.J.: Princeton University Press, 1973.

Blair, Dorothy S. *African Literature in French*. Cambridge, U.K.: Cambridge University Press, 1976.

Guibert Armand. *Léopold Sédar Senghor*. Paris: Seghers, 1961. Collection Poètes d'aujourd'hui.

———. *Léopold Sédar Senghor: L'Homme et l'oeuvre*. Paris: Présence Africaine, 1962. Collection Approche.

Hausser, Michèle. *Pour une poétique de la Négritude*. 2 vols. Paris: Silex, 1988; Éditions Nouvelles du Sud, 1991.

Irele, Abiola, ed. *Selected Poems of Léopold Sédar Senghor*. Cambridge, U.K.: Cambridge University Press, 1977.

Kennedy, Ellen Conroy, ed. *The Négritude Poets*. New York: Viking, 1975.

Kesteloot, Lilyan. *Les Écrivains noirs de langue française: Naissance d'une littérature*. Brussels, Belgium: Institut Solvay, Université Libre de Bruxelles, 1963.

———. *Comprendre les poèmes de L. S. Senghor*. Issy-les-Molineaux, France: Éditions Saint Paul, 1986. Collection Les Classiques africains.

Lagneaux-Kesteloot, Lilyan. *Black Writers in French*. Trans. by Ellen Conroy Kennedy. Philadelphia: Temple University Press, 1974. Repr. Washington, D.C.: Howard University Press, 1991. (Translation of Kesteloot, *Les Écrivains noirs de langue française*.)

Lebaud, Geneviève. *Léopold Sédar Senghor ou la poésie de l'enfance*. Dakar, Senegal: Nouvelles Éditions Africaines, 1976.

Leusse, Hubert de. *Léopold Sédar Senghor, l'Africain*. Paris: Hatier, 1967.

———. *De* Poèmes *aux* Lettres d'hivernage. Paris: Hatier, 1975. Collection Profil d'une oeuvre.

Melady, Margaret Badun. *Leopold Sedar Senghor: Rhythm and Reconciliation*. South Orange, N.J.: Seton Hall University Press, 1971.

Mezu, S. Okechukwu. *Léopold Sédar Senghor et la défense et illustration de la civilisation noire*. Paris: Didier, 1968.

———. *The Poetry of Léopold Sédar Senghor*. London: Heinemann Educational Books, 1973.

Moore, Gerald. *Twelve African Writers*. London: Hutchinson, 1980.

Ndiaye, Papa Gueye. *Éthiopiques: Édition critique et commentée*. Dakar, Senegal: Nouvelles Éditions Africaines, 1974.

Nespoulis-Neuville, Josiane. *Léopold Sédar Senghor: De la tradition à l'universalisme*. Paris: Seuil, 1988.

Osman, Gusine Gawdat. *L'Afrique dans l'univers poétique de Léopold Sédar Senghor*. Dakar, Senegal: Nouvelles Éditions Africaines, 1978.

Peters, Jonathan. *A Dance of Masks: Senghor, Achebe, Soyinka*. Washington, D.C.: Three Continents Press, 1978.

Spleth, Janice. *Léopold Sédar Senghor*. Boston: Twayne, 1985. Twayne World Author's Series.

———, ed. *Critical Perspectives on Léopold Sédar Senghor*. Washington, D.C.: Three Continents Press, 1993.

Towa, Marcien. *Léopold Sédar Senghor: Négritude ou servitude?* Yaoundé, Cameroon: Éditions CLE, 1971.

Van Niekerk, Barend van Dyk. *The African Image (Négritude) in the Work of Léopold Sédar Senghor.* Cape Town, South Africa: A. A. Balkema, 1970.

BIOGRAPHICAL AND GENERAL STUDIES

Crowder, Michael. *Senegal: A Study of French Assimilation Policy*. London: Oxford University Press, 1967.

Hymans, Jack. *Léopold Sédar Senghor: An Intellectual Biography*. Edinburgh, U.K.: Edinburgh University Press, 1971.

July, Robert William. *The Origins of Modern African Thought*. New York: Praeger, 1968.

Markowitz, Irving Leonard. *Léopold Sédar Senghor and the Politics of Négritude*. New York: Atheneum, 1969.

Mortimer, Edward. *France and the Africans, 1944–60*. New York: Walker, 1969.

Vaillant, Janet G. *Black, French, and African: A Life of Léopold Sédar Senghor*. Cambridge, Mass.: Harvard University Press, 1990.

Abū al-Qāsim al-Shābbī

1909–1934

ROBIN OSTLE

ABŪ AL-QĀSIM AL-SHĀBBĪ was born in 1909 in the al-Shābbiyya district of Tozeur, an oasis town in the Jarīd (Djerid) area of southwestern Tunisia. His father, a graduate of Al-Azhar Mosque University in Cairo, was a *qāḍī*, or Islamic law judge. Al-Shābbī was educated in a highly traditional *kuttāb* school, which concentrated on Arabic grammar and learning the Qur'ān by rote. From there he went on to the Tunisian equivalent of Al-Azhar, Zaytouna University in the capital, Tunis. Here he developed his knowledge of the traditional Islamic sciences, the Arabic language, and classical Arabic literature, before moving on to the law college, from which he graduated in 1930.

Although biographies have been written, the details of his personal life are somewhat sketchy: his father's death in 1929 made it necessary for him to leave Tunis in order to look after his family in Tozeur; that same year he began to experience symptoms of the heart disease from which he died at the age of twenty-five. His biographers make veiled references to an unhappy marriage and also to an unrequited love affair that ended with the death of his beloved. Al-Shābbī has only one *dīwān* (collection of poetry), *Aghānī al-ḥayāt* (*Songs of Life*), which he was preparing for publication at the time of his death. The book was not published until 1955.

Al-Shābbī occupies an unusual place in the history of modern Arabic literature for a number of reasons: he is the only Arab poet from North Africa (Libya, Tunisia, Algeria, Morocco) to have achieved a genuinely international reputation, in spite of the fact that he died before he could develop his talents beyond their exciting and promising beginnings. He is one of the foremost figures in the Romantic movement of Arabic literature, which had its heyday in the period between the two world wars in Egypt and the Levant (countries bordering on the eastern shore of the Mediterranean Sea, including Turkey and Syria). Most of the other members of the movement were inspired directly by the Romantic poets of England and France in the eighteenth and nineteenth centuries. Al-Shābbī, however, knew no foreign language; his only contact with other literatures was through irregular access to translated material. He is also unusual in that his attitudes to literature and society can properly be described as revolutionary. Although this was one of the hallmarks of Romanticism in its European context, such qualities are much less obvious in the Romantic literature produced in the Arab world between 1910 and 1940.

LINKS WITH EGYPT AND THE *MAHJAR*

In order to assimilate the most modern trends in Arabic poetry at the time, al-Shābbī depended on his contacts with writers in the Arab world beyond the relative isolation of Tunisia under the French protectorate. In Egypt, very much the center of the Arabic Romantic movement, a leading role was played by the poet and academic Aḥmad Zakī Abū Shādī (1892–1955) and the periodical he edited, *Apollo* (1932–1934). One of Abū Shādī's most notable achievements was to make *Apollo* a focal point for the encouragement of young writers both within Egypt and beyond, and his call for cooperation between Arab writers in different countries meant much more than paying lip service to a principle. Al-Shābbī was one of the most important contributors to *Apollo* from outside Egypt: the first direct reference to him appears in the March 1933 issue, and in the number of April 1933 two of his poems, "Prayers in the Temple of Love" and "Happiness," were printed for the first time. One of Abū Shādī's own collections of verse, whose title translates as "The fountain" (1934), contains a brief foreword written by al-Shābbī in which the young poet expresses his admiration for the editor of *Apollo.*

Another highly significant external influence detectable in al-Shābbī's work is that of the *mahjar* (émigré) poets who formed the other most important school of Romantic writers in modern Arabic. They were a group of Syro-Lebanese poets who established themselves in New York during the first two decades of the twentieth century and whose writings, although published in the United States, had an important catalytic effect in the Arab world. By the time that al-Shābbī was at the height of his literary activities in the 1920s, the names of Jubrān Khalīl Jubrān and Mīkhāʾil Nuʿayma were increasingly familiar in Arab literary circles. There are significant echoes of typical *mahjar* themes in the work of the precocious Tunisian poet.

THE YOUTHFUL REBEL

Al-Shābbī expressed his powerful opposition to tradition both in literature and in life amid political circumstances that were depressing in the extreme. In the 1920s and the 1930s, the grip of the French protectorate must have seemed an immovable obstacle to the visions and aspirations of the young people of his generation. There was no question of political independence, not even of the ambiguous and circumscribed kind that Egypt had attained in 1922. The Destour (Constitutional) Party in the 1920s had not yet been recognized as a formidable nationalist group, although this changed in the 1930s, when nationalist stirrings acquired greater vigor and momentum.

In 1934, the year of al-Shābbī's death, there emerged the Neo-Destour Party, which over the next twenty years maneuvered independence for Tunisia. (France recognized Tunisia's independence in 1956.) For al-Shābbī and his closest colleagues, life was a constant struggle between aspiration and harsh reality. He belonged to a small group of writers and journalists who met regularly in a café in the old city of Tunis; among them were the Islamic modernist and social reformer Tāhir al-Haddād (who died in 1935) and the prose writer ʿAlī al-Dūʿājī (who died 1949). The times in which they lived gave constant drama to their existence, a drama frequently tragic in tone as the tenacity of their literary and journalistic activities in difficult circumstances took a heavy toll on their careers and, in some cases, their lives. Probably the most destructive factor of all was the strain of living with visions that found substance in literary form but were denied a more concrete embodiment.

A dramatic illustration of al-Shābbī's radical commitment to change came in 1927, when he swept into the Khaldūniyya Institute in Tunis and delivered a lecture entitled "The Poetic Imagination and the Arabs." It was published in book form in 1929 and achieved notoriety far beyond Tunisia. It represents a bitter and extreme attack on certain aspects of traditional Arab-Islamic culture:

> Arabic literature no longer suits our present spirit, temperament, inclinations or aspirations in life. . . . It was not created for us, children of

these times, but for hearts that are now silenced by death.... We must never look upon Arabic literature as an ideal which we have to follow or whose spirit, style and ideas we have to imitate, but we consider it simply as one of those ancient literatures which we must admire and respect and no more.

(Von Grunebaum, p. 196; Badawi, 1975, p. 159)

The lecture is extreme in its views and quite unscholarly in many instances. It should be seen as an emotional reaction of frustration, but valuable as a flamboyant rhetorical protest against the travesties of Islamic values and civilization as they existed in the unhappy state of al-Shābbī's own society or as they had been distorted in the ossified, irrelevant education that he had received in the archaic system of the Zaytouna University. The same lecture contains a revealing passage on one of the most sensitive subjects of debate between traditionalists and progressives in al-Shābbī's time. He objects vehemently to the manner in which much of classical Arabic literature had portrayed women:

> The attitude of Arabic literature to woman is base and ignoble, and sinks to the lowest depths of materialism. It only sees in woman a body to be desired and one of the basest pleasures in life to be enjoyed....
>
> Have you ever heard of anyone among [the Arab poets] talk about woman, who is the altar of love in this universe, in the way a devout worshipper talks about the house of God?
>
> (Ostle, 1991, p. 108, and 1992, p. 128)

Here al-Shābbī is displaying his rather imperfect knowledge of the rich variety of the classical Arabic literary tradition, for while it is true that much of old Arabic poetry did indeed celebrate the physical attributes of women, it is less than just to suggest that psychological and spiritual subtleties were neglected by the classical authors. Nevertheless, this partial view of the literary heritage was widely shared by many Arab Romantic poets in the 1920s and 1930s, not least by Abū Shādī and a number of the *Apollo* poets in Egypt. They took as their models and their inspiration the highly idealized, spiritual representation of love and women that had been characteristic of European literature in its more intensely Romantic phases, and none was more single-minded than al-Shābbī in writing love poetry that was ethereal and platonic in theme and in language. For him, the classical Arabic literary imagination was a symbol of the mentality that had reduced women to a subordinate and degraded status and was largely responsible for the weakness of Arab states and societies.

An excellent example of the manner in which al-Shābbī celebrates the female ideal is his famous poem "Prayers in the Temple of Love," in which he elevates woman to a plane of adoration in order to compensate for centuries of degradation at the hands of Arab-Islamic tradition. The opening lines are typical of the manner in which he strings together images and associations with great economy in a seamless flow:

> You are as delightful as childhood, as dreams,
> as melody, as the new morning,
> As the laughing heavens, as the moonlit night,
> as the rose, as the smile of the newborn child.
>
> (1966, p. 183)

Through the extraordinary musicality of his language and the skillful repetition of syntactic structure and vocabulary, the poet creates a strong sense of liturgical incantation and divine mystery appropriate to the scene of worship in which he invites the reader to participate. Although these qualities are difficult to render in translation, the following lines should give some suggestion of the magical qualities of the original:

> You ... What are you? A beautiful sketch of
> genius from the art of this creation.
> You contain what it contains of mystery, depth
> and holy reverend beauty.
> You ... What are you? You are a dawn of
> enchantment revealed to my enamored
> heart....
> You ... You are life in its heavenly holiness, in
> its unique pleasant enchantment.

You ... You are life in the delicacy of the dawn,
in the splendor of the new-born spring.
You ... You are life at all times in a new
freshness of youth.
You ... You are life. In you and in your eyes are
signs of its spreading magic.
(1966, p. 185; Ostle, 1992, p. 129)

Such celebrations of the female ideal are typical of al-Shābbī's amatory verse. They are mostly devoid of elements of psychological or physical realism; rather, they are holy, almost statuesque, representations. The issue of women's emancipation had been a subject of hot debate among Arab intellectuals since the nineteenth century, and it remained a focus of the greatest controversy in the 1920s and 1930s. However, in the societies of Egypt and the Levant where the debate was pursued, the controversy was in no sense accompanied by rapid social change on a wide scale that might have contributed to radically changing the position of women in society. The poetry of al-Shābbī and a number of other Romantic poets in Egypt seems to have responded to a relatively static situation by replacing one set of symbols with another that, ironically, in some respects were even further removed from reality than their equivalents in classical Arabic poetry.

Two of the criticisms leveled at classical poetry by modern Arab authors are a lack of concern for overall structure and an undue emphasis on the individual line as the unit of composition. This is an exaggeration by the modern critics, for it is misguided to suggest that much of classical poetry lacks an integral structure or unity; however, this was an aspect of composition that modern authors increasingly began to take seriously, and most of al-Shābbī's work illustrates a careful concern for the structure and organic unity of individual poems.

This is demonstrated to excellent effect in al-Shābbī's "The Stream of Love," where the metaphor for the course of a love affair is the path of a stream. The poem opens with impressions of vigor, energy, and unadulterated happiness. This strong, intoxicating stream represents the beginnings of love and passion, which the poet likens to the swift and varied movements and noises of a river in the early stages of its long course. But just as a stream inevitably flows toward a stage that is darker, more sluggish, and devoid of vitality, so the progress of the poet's love goes through the same debilitating process. The latter part of the poem is a profusion of tears, pain, and darkness equal in intensity to the joy and happiness of the first sections. Now the stream flows with bitterness and anguish through silence, darkness, and flowers that wilt and droop (in contrast to the previous smiling scenes). The doleful climax is filled with long, mournful sounds surrounded by thick, impenetrable mists. The difference from the original energy and optimism could not be more overwhelming, and the structure of the poem is a wonderful demonstration of the al-Shābbī's overall care for the unity of his composition.

THE POLITICAL POET?

Al-Shābbī is one of the few Arab Romantics who has a deserved reputation for political engagement and a radical commitment to change, even though he did not write a significant number of poems with overt political themes. Pieces such as "The Cry," "Oh Defenders of the Faith," and "To the People" are few in number, and they tend to be sarcastic and disillusioned comments about the lethargy and weakness of the Tunisian people, rather than rousing inspirational verses for the nationalist cause. In fact, they are reminiscent of the frustrated tone of his famous lecture "The Poetic Imagination and the Arabs." What has gripped the imagination of subsequent generations of Arab readers is the fact that the sum total of al-Shābbī's brief life relates allusively and symbolically to the state of his nation. The body politic of his time was in a palsied state, just as his own body suffered from fatal heart disease, yet small groups of

Tunisian nationalists possessed visions and faith that transcended the depressing contemporary reality. Similarly, throughout his work there is a constant alternation between mimesis and symbol.

The dominant theme pervading al-Shābbī's work is the antithesis of light and shade, usually expressed through the image of the pure, joyful dawn that succeeds the dark, melancholic night. The constant implication is that of a new start of resurrection after the sufferings of life. His poem "The New Morning" is the clearest statement of his glowing vision of this dawn of life after death. The fact that this poem was written in 1933, when al-Shābbī was already in the grip of his final illness, adds to the poignancy of the vision in relation to his situation. The first stanza of three lines has a tone of gentle reconciliation as the poet comes to terms with life's burdens:

> Wounds be calm, and sorrows be silent
> The time of lament and the age of madness are dead.
> Morning has peered out beyond the peaks.
> (Ostle, 1991, p. 109)

This opening stanza is repeated twice in the body of the poem as a calming refrain. The reader is left in no doubt that the "new morning" is a resurrection, as the poet tells how he has buried pain in the valleys of death and has scattered his tears to the winds of nonexistence. The early verses between the refrains tell quietly and without regret how his life has been: the events of his experience have been transformed into the music of his verse; his heart has become a shrine for beauty that has been constructed from visions and imagination. At this stage he prefers to soothe his wounds and grief and to forget the periods of darkness, in order to concentrate on the certainty of redemption. Again one has to admire the meticulous development of the poem, which begins in a gentle, restrained voice as the dawn first appears over the peaks. It moves inevitably to a final joyous crescendo in the full, glorious arrival of the morning. The sun breaks through the clouds and leaves behind the mountains of toil and trouble, dispelling the mists of grief:

> From behind the clouds and the surge of waters
> I am called by the morning and the Spring of life . . .
> Farewell! Farewell! Oh mountains of trouble.
> Oh Mists of grief. Oh valleys of hell.
> (Ostle, 1992, p. 127)

LIFE AND DEATH

During the last two years of his life, the painful mystery of death looms large in a number of al-Shābbī's finest poems that stand in poignant relation to his physical deterioration. The central character of "Story of the Cemetery" (1932) is the spirit of a philosopher encountered by the poet as the latter wanders among the tombs. He explains to the poet that the point of suffering in life is to attain purity of spirit:

> We were created to attain the summit of perfection, so becoming worthy of the glory of immortality.
> (1966, p. 205)

Through the fires of grief and anguish, explains the philosopher, a person is purified and prepared for the life hereafter. The poet remains consumed by doubt and curiosity: What is the nature of the philosopher's "perfection," and will it not lead to further strivings and discontent once it has been attained? The poet's skepticism banishes the spirit of the philosopher from the scene, and he is left among the tombs, alone in his doubt and uncertainty.

"In the Shadow of the Valley of Death" is a piece strongly reminiscent of some of the work of the North American *mahjar* poets. Its main objective is to express the poet's intense, pained perplexity. No answers are offered to the questions posed by the great mystery of death, and the poem is devoid of any complex thought or philosophical dimension. However, the poet is not content merely to catalog his sufferings, isolation, and disappointed loves. Although death remains an unresolved mystery, his frustration with life is such that any new experience is to be preferred.

> The enchantment of life has dried up, weeping heart.
> So come on! Let us try death! Come on!
> (1966, p. 209)

Henceforth al-Shābbī seems to adopt a consciously Promethean reaction to death. Thus in "Song of the Colossus," written some months before he died, death holds no fear for him; in what remains of life, he will concentrate on the realms of the spirit and the emotions, which are the proper concerns of the poet. Although his body is hastening toward physical destruction, disease can never fetter his proud spirit:

> Despite the disease and my enemies, I shall live on like the eagle above the lofty summit,
> Looking at the illuminating sun, mocking the clouds, the rains and the hurricanes,
> Not beholding the despairing shadow, and not seeing what lies in the bottom of the black abyss.
> (Ostle, 1992, p. 129)

Thus he mocks fate and death. He persists in looking toward the dawn, which has sustained him for so long, and continues to produce his own enchanting form of music, rising above all suffering and tribulation through the fiery strength of his spirit. He looks for an ultimate consummation between his spirit and the ideal realm of beauty to which he has constantly aspired. The context for this search is supplied by the dawn, the recurrent dominant image throughout his work:

> That I may melt in the everlasting dawn of beauty, and drink from the spring of lights.
> (1966, p. 257)

DESIRE FOR LIFE

Al-Shābbī was not widely known in the Arab world until the 1950s, when his single collection of verse was first published. By this time Romanticism had lost its credibility as a mode of artistic expression in the region, so it is hardly surprising that one of his best-loved pieces is a poem that has an overtly political theme: "Desire for Life," dated 16 December 1933. It was set to music, and its opening lines became familiar in many Arab countries in the 1950s, the period of the definitive end of colonialism in its various forms:

> If the People one day desires to live, then Fate must needs respond.
> The darkness must give way to light, and bonds must also break.
> (1966, p. 240; Ostle, 1991, p. 109)

The first section of the poem expresses one of the recurrent themes in al-Shābbī's verse: the poet's desires and aspirations for life are so intense that they will overcome even Destiny, the traditional all-powerful arbiter in Arabic poetry. In the subsequent sections the tension rises as the poet begins a dialogue with some of the elemental forces of nature: the wind, the darkness, the forest, and the earth itself. The use of onomatopoeic vocabulary—words whose sounds suggest their meanings—of a harsh solidity adds to the sense of massive force as al-Shābbī creates a world very different from his usual one of delicate light, shade, quiet sounds, and gentle, evanescent effects. After the onset of winter, only the seeds remain beneath layers of fog, ice, and clay, desperately clinging to dreams and memories of life. The dreams locked within the dormant seeds have a dramatic awakening as the earth is riven by the life, power, and light of spring. In a typical feature of al-Shābbī's style, the language takes on a tone of devotional incantation as the awakening seeds are blessed for their constant faith and are rewarded with the earth and the heavens and everything in them.

Such a powerful vision of resurrection creates a bridge between al-Shābbī and the generation of Arab poets in the 1950s and 1960s. Although the later generation had assimilated a variety of myth and legend that had more in common with T. S. Eliot than with the traditional Arab heritage, those poets' use of the myths of fertility rites as symbols of death and resurrection would have been keenly appreciated by al-Shābbī. This is particularly so when these myths are related to the destinies of societies in the throes of dramatic, if not violent, transformation.

CONCLUSION

Al-Shābbī's poetry is intensely personal and subjective, but it is not a poetry of withdrawn escapism. It has a strong foundation of external validity rooted in the condition of Tunisian society at a particularly difficult moment in its history. The career of this gifted individual, wracked by physical and spiritual crises, can be seen as a metaphor for the tribulations experienced by the majority of his contemporaries—an idea explored in books such as *Abū al-Qāsim al-Shābbī, shā'ir al-hubb wa'l-thawra* (1962; Abū al-Qāsim al-Shābbī, poet of love and revolution), by Rajā al-Naqqāsh, and *Kifāh al-Shābbī* (1957; Al-Shābbī's struggle), by Muḥammad Karrū, the Tunisian scholar who has been the most indefatigable exponent of al-Shābbī's work. Later generations of writers have tended to forget or to undervalue the extent to which the work of the best of the Arab Romantics crystallizes the painful dilemmas that gripped both individuals and societies between the two world wars.

Selected Bibliography

SELECTED WORKS

Aghānī al-ḥayāt. Cairo: Dār al-Kutub al-Sharqiyyah, 1955; Tunis, Tunisia: al-Dār al-Tunisiyyah lī 'l-Nashr, 1966.

Al-Khayāl al-shiʿrī ʿinda al-ʿarab (The poetic spirit of the Arabs). Tunis, Tunisia: n.p., 1961.

TRANSLATION

Songs of Life: Selections from the Poetry of Abū al-Qāsim al-Shābbī, 1909–1934. Carthage, Tunisia: National Foundation for Translation, Establishment of Manuscripts and Studies, 1987.

CRITICAL STUDIES

Badawi, Muhammad Mustafa. *Critical Introduction to Modern Arabic Poetry*. Cambridge, U.K., and New York: Cambridge University Press, 1975.

———, ed. *The Cambridge History of Arabic Literature: Modern Arabic Literature*. Cambridge, U.K., and New York: Cambridge University Press, 1992.

al-Hilaiwī, Muḥammad. *Rasa'il al-Shābbī*. Tunis, Tunisia: n.p., 1966.

al-Jayyusi, Salma al-Khadra'. *Trends and Movements in Modern Arabic Poetry*. Leiden, Netherlands: Brill, 1977.

Karrū, Abū al-Qāsim Muḥammad. *Kifāh al-Shābbī*. Tunis, Tunisia: al-Sharikah al-Tunisiyyah lī 'l-Tawzi, 1957.

———. *Āthār al-Shābbī wa sadāhu fī 'l-sharq*. Beirut, Lebanon: n.p., 1961.

———. *Al-Shābbī: Ḥayatūh, shiʿruh*. Beirut, Lebanon: 1964.

Moreh, Shmuel. *Modern Arabic Poetry 1800–1970*. Leiden, Netherlands: Brill, 1976.

al-Naqqāsh, Rajā. *Abū al-Qāsim al-Shābbī, shā'ir al-hubb wa'l-thawra*. Cairo: Dār al-Maʿārif, 1962.

Ostle, Robin C. "Mahmūd al-Mas'adī and Tunisia's 'Lost Generation.'" In *Journal of Arabic Literature* 8 (1977).

———. "The Romantic Poets." In Muhammad Mustafa Badawi, ed., *The Cambridge History of Arabic Literature: Modern Arabic Literature*. Cambridge, U.K., and New York: Cambridge University Press, 1992.

———, ed. *Modern Literature in the Near and Middle East 1850–1970*. London: Routledge, 1991.

Von Grunebaum, Gustave Edmund, ed. *Arabic Poetry: Theory and Development*. Wiesbaden, Germany: Harrassowitz, 1973.

Bode Sowande

1948–

OSITA OKAGBUE

BODE SOWANDE was born in Kaduna, Nigeria, on 2 May 1948. He attended Government College, Ibadan, and later the University of Ife (now Obafemi Awolowo University), at Ile-Ife, graduating with a degree in French in 1971. From 1973 to 1977 he was at Sheffield University, England, studying for a doctorate in dramatic literature. He taught theater at the University of Ibadan after leaving Sheffield. Sowande was a resident playwright for the Orisun Theatre, Lagos, from 1968 to 1971, and in 1972 he founded Odu Themes in Ibadan. In late 1990 he retired from university teaching to manage his professional company, Odu Themes Meridian. Sowande has won numerous awards, including the T. M. Aluko Prize for creative writing in 1966; the University of Ife creative writing award in 1968; the University of Sheffield Edgar Allen Award in 1975; and the Association of Nigerian Authors drama award in 1987 and 1989.

Little has been written about Sowande, except for Chris Dunton's study *Make Man Talk True* (1992), which examines Nigerian drama in English since 1970. This critical neglect is unfortunate, because Sowande deserves more than the occasional mention; he has been prolific, with seven plays and two novels published between 1979 and 1986. Between 1987 and 1993, Sowande wrote and produced plays that include *Arede Owo* (1990), a Yoruba play (Yoruba is one of the three major ethnolinguistic groups in Nigeria); *My Life in the Bush of Ghosts* (1990), a stage adaptation of Amos Tutuola's famous 1954 novel; a Yoruba adaptation of Molière's play *L'Avare* (1669); and *Tornadoes Full of Dreams* (1990). In addition to these full-length plays, Sowande has written for television, his best effort being the acclaimed *Acada Campus* series (1980–1982). He has much unpublished work, notably "Abiku's Fancies," "A Child of the Soil," "Bar Beach Prelude," "Caught in the Web," "Paint Me Blacker," and the very ambitious "African Trances," which encompasses the history of black oppression.

TOWARD A NEW THEATER AESTHETIC

Sowande's drama is informed by an essentially humanist vision. He belongs to the new breed of Nigerian dramatists who espouse a new theater aesthetic different from the "traditionalist" aesthetics of Wole Soyinka, J. P. Clark-Bekederemo (John Pepper Clark), and Ola Rotimi. Sowande's group is concerned with utilizing the revolutionary potential of the theater in the quest for a more humane social order. For them, "the theater when skilfully employed can become a powerful weapon for the regulation of communal values or, conversely, for radical change" (Kimberly W. Benstein, "The Aesthetics of Modern Black Drama: From Mimesis to Methexis," in Errol Hill, ed., *The Theatre of Black Americans*, vol. 1, Englewood Cliffs, N.J.: Prentice-Hall, 1980, p. 63). Two things set this group apart: their dialectical view of the human race and history, and a desire to develop a revolutionary aesthetic for the theater. They see the individual as the subject-object of history, not the passive creature of the traditionalists who struggles hopelessly against a fate he or she can hardly influence, let alone change. This philosophy of the person in a universe where he or she is maker and product of history is central to Sowande's Babylon trilogy, published in the collections *A Farewell to Babylon and Other Plays* (1979) and *Flamingo and Other Plays* (1986).

Having neither the verbal pyrotechnics of Soyinka nor the creative audacity of Femi Osofisan, Sowande relies on a consistently progressive humanism to give his drama a simplicity and focus that the work of the other two sometimes lacks. The best example of his humanism is the trilogy in which every action represents a step in the movement away from a Babylon that has to be destroyed so Utopia can be established. The three plays explore the dialectics between Babylon and Utopia, but what is most impressive is Sowande's use of metaphors of and dialectics between Babylon and Utopia for cross-criticism. Utopia, he suggests, denounces Babylon while announcing a freer society that all good people should aspire to build.

THE BABYLON TRILOGY

The Night Before (first published in 1972) is, according to Sowande, a compulsive response to "the recent flashpoints in students' agitations for an alternative society" that "were still freshly branded in my memory" (author's note to *The Night Before*, in *A Farewell to Babylon and Other Plays*, p. 7). After the Nigerian civil war ended in 1970, university students stepped up their demonstrations to demand better government from both the civilians and the military. The demonstrations, which continued throughout the 1970s and 1980s, sometimes led to riots, tear-gas confrontations, and tragic deaths; the first casualty was Jasper Koyo, shot by the police at the University of Ibadan in 1971.

A sense of anguish and disillusionment pervades *The Night Before*, but also present are the hope and innocence of youth on the verge of entry into the world of work and responsibility. The dream of the young undergraduates—Moniran, Onita, Moye, Dabira, Nibidi, and Ibilola—on the eve of graduation is to smash Babylon and in its place establish an alternative society in which all can find happiness. But the night before graduation is a night of initiation filled with the temptations and betrayals that the graduates are going to encounter once they leave the safe walls of the university; their friendships are tested and soured by a new awareness of evil in their new world. The night ends with the symbolic burning of Dabira's academic gown while the others helplessly gaze through the flames at the terrifying future into which they are being born as the new architects of a better society. Despite its bleary-eyed innocence and posturing, *The Night Before* is redeemed by a compact structure and sharp focus. That, combined with a creative exuberance, makes it the most successful play in the trilogy.

A Farewell to Babylon (first produced in 1978), the second play in the trilogy, explores the ironic situation of Moniran and Onita, who pursue the same dream of an alternative society from different perspectives. Moniran attacks Babylon from the inside by becoming one of its most powerful civil servants: the head of Octopus (the state secret police) and a trusted lieutenant to the head of the state. His plan is to overthrow the Eagle of the Realm by a coup d'état. Onita attacks from the outside through his lectures and writings and finally by joining the farmers who are revolting against the government. But the consequences are tragic: Moniran's mistake in putting Onita in the same prison cell with the drug addict Cookie leads to Onita's strangulation by Cookie. The play promises much but delivers little. Sowande displays a disappointing inability to let his drama come alive; most of the characters, including Moniran, seem to lack an inner fire to energize the action, and Sowande creates events simply to make social commentaries rather than relying on the events to generate the comments. The idea of social change is overwhelmingly blunt because Sowande's desire to articulate a social vision makes him forget that his medium is the theater, where events and characters, not the ideas or views they represent, should be dominant. This is often reflected in the language, where sometimes the lofty poetry fails woefully and the ideological statements are stilted and overdone. However, Sowande is aware of and willing to mine his rich Yoruba theatrical tradition. The abundant and effective songs, the regular dance sequences, and the mimes combine to produce the rare theatrical high points of *A Farewell to Babylon*, when characters, situations, and theme merge and most of the weaknesses disappear.

The author's note to *Flamingo* (first produced in 1982) states the utopian dream central to the Babylon trilogy:

> The major characters set out to master fate individually and collectively. . . . The circle began during their student days . . . was traced along the pathways of social conflict in *A Farewell to Babylon*, and . . . finally closes in this play *Flamingo*. Onita, Moniran, Nibidi, Kasa ascend the steps of this trilogy, and each man either masters fate or is destroyed by it. The villains, it seems, understand the spirit of their time, a *mal de siècle* whose inherent decadence becomes a prosperous sub culture.
>
> (*Flamingo and Other Plays*, p. 2)

In *Flamingo*, Moniran refuses to participate further in a "revolution" that has gone astray, and he withdraws totally from society. In self-exile, a disenchanted Moniran laments the betrayal of Utopia by his coconspirators; yet even in exile he represents a threat to the regime, so Nibidi—one of his college friends—and Kasa have him poisoned.

Flamingo displays all the weaknesses of *A Farewell to Babylon*, especially a shallowness of characters, including Moniran, whose acquaintance the reader makes for the third time but who dies as enigmatic a character as he is in *The Night Before*. He remains the undeveloped undergraduate whose greatest fear is that "someone may soon tell the truth about me. Something I don't want to know" (*The Night Before*, in *A Farewell to Babylon and Other Plays*, p. 14). *Flamingo* seems to be Sowande's attempt to provide final answers to the questions arising from the confrontation between the forces of social change and those of an implacable and corrupt social order. Unfortunately, the play's answers remain inconclusive; there is yet another coup d'état, with no guarantee that the "new brooms" will be different from those they have swept away.

In spite of the weaknesses of character, language, and events, the trilogy succeeds as a clear condemnation of the incessant and inexcusable coups that have become the usual in African politics. Sowande shows how the coups rarely touch the endemic corruption because in time the new leaders become exactly like, or sometimes worse than, those they replace. Kasa, installed at the end of *A Farewell to Babylon* as the new head of state following the coup that ousted Field Marshal, becomes another Field Marshal. And who is to say Teriba, the leader of the second coup in *Flamingo*, which removes Kasa, will not turn out to be the same? The optimism of the trilogy lies in the fact that the notion of Utopia is kept alive to move society on the journey toward the ideal for which Onita and Moniran die. In these plays Sowande seems to be suggesting that although Utopia may be an unrealizable dream, it is still worthwhile because in aspiring to it, society is propelled toward increasingly better states. This progressive optimism also is present in Sowande's subsequent plays.

CLASS CONSCIOUSNESS AND PATTERNS OF SOCIAL INEQUALITY

First produced in 1978, *Afamako* (the word meaning "workhorse" in Yoruba), the second play in *Flamingo and Other Plays*, re-creates the inhuman face of capitalist exploitation. Kadiri, the workhorse of the title, already has five children to support; when his wife drops the bombshell of a sixth being on the way, he suggests abortion, which she will not consider. The issue of whether this child will be born becomes the unspoken conflict that threatens the peace at home. Forced by family responsibilities, Kadiri decides to break a strike in exchange for assurance of job security from the manager. Ironically, he is the first to be let go—as he learns while celebrating his success in having negotiated his future. The news proves too much for his wife, who goes into premature labor that ends in a miscarriage.

Structurally, this play successfully juxtaposes images and scenes in Kadiri's home, the office, and the factory floor. The squalor of Kadiri's home is set in counterpoint to the scandalous opulence of his boss's office, and the realistic activities of the home stand in dramatic contrast to the melodramatic vacuity of the office. However, Sowande's attempt at stylization in the factory floor scenes occasionally betrays his inability to conceptualize the true dimension of capitalist intrigue in the office and its resultant exploitation of labor. Thus, these scenes are not convincing and lack the energy of the home scenes. Nevertheless, this is technically one of Sowande's best plays because it benefits from an uncomplicated dramatic structure and simple story line.

Chris Dunton calls *The Master and the Frauds* (first produced in 1979), also included in *Flamingo and Other Plays*, Sowande's most "consistently successful play" for achieving a vividly concrete language and a cohesive dramatic structuring. It is a didactic play that examines the problem of corruption in society; more specifically, he attacks the hypocrisy of a society that punishes petty criminals more severely than their crimes merit while allowing real felons to get away with their loot.

Pa Seyidi is an intellectual and teacher who undertakes to live among the oppressed masses in order to awaken in them a consciousness of their oppression and the possibility of initiating change. He teaches his students not to climb on the bandwagon of looters; unfortunately, his pupils, especially Gambo and Suberu, have experienced so much suffering and seen so much corruption around them that his teaching seems a betrayal and an attempt to keep them forever at the bottom of the social ladder. Seyidi gives marked money to Gambo to offer as a bribe to the testing officer in order to catch the officer as the big thief; but when the officer is arrested and the tests are called off, Gambo blames Seyidi for the failure to secure a test certificate that was to have helped the boy escape from his poverty. Consequently, Gambo and Suberu set upon Seyidi and kill him.

Again there is an apparent failure in the attempt by a self-appointed individual to bring about change; Seyidi's attempt to bring about social change fails like that of Moniran in the Babylon trilogy. In a way he is portrayed as a Christ who dies at the hands of the people he had come to save. The tragic irony of his choice is reflected in this scene with Gambo:

> SEYIDI: I chose you and the others. Suberu and Raliatu. I said to myself. Teach them their rights. Show them their rights. Gambo have I wasted my time with you?
>
> GAMBO: All I know is that you came with ideas that make the head swell. But what we want is something to fill our bellies.
>
> (*Flamingo and Other Plays*, p. 103)

Circus of Freedom Square (first produced in 1985), the last play in *Flamingo and Other Plays*, looks at the dichotomy between right-wing and left-wing politics and ideologies.

Sowande, it seems, believes that both are necessary for a balanced polity. His main argument is that the real problem is not the ideologies but their exponents. The play also attacks the technocrats, the middlemen of politics, who stand between rulers and the ruled, grossly misrepresenting each to the other. It is not until the ruler, Kabiyesi, disguises himself in order to get out of the palace and into the streets to find out for himself what the people really feel and think that he is able to expose Boba (the "official middleman between the throne and the people") and Taofik (a security guard) for the oppressors they are. Sowande's preoccupation as a radical writer is always to expose the deeper structures of society in order to help the oppressed masses attain true self- and class awareness.

RADICALIZING MYTH AND HISTORY

Both *A Sanctus for Women* and *Tornadoes Full of Dreams* reveal an exciting dimension to Sowande's drama: in them he plumbs his rich Yoruba folk culture, and he radically and creatively appropriates its myth and history. *A Sanctus for Women* (first produced as *The Angry Bridegroom* in 1976), the final play in *A Farewell to Babylon and Other Plays*, retells the legend of Olurombi, a woman who is reduced to poverty and forced to offer her only daughter, Simbi, to the god Iroko in exchange for wealth. The story of Olurombi is a tragedy of ignorance: Olurombi at the time of the pact does not seem to realize that later the god will actually claim her daughter.

In keeping with an avowed materialist philosophy, Sowande rejects the "religious content of the myth," and presents instead a view of the gods as "symbolising an entrenched system of exploitation or at least symbolising a religious view of existence that maintains or sustains a system of exploitation" (Bamikunle, p. 124). The play creatively interrogates the myth by subverting its basic assumption of the sanctity of the gods and the power of those who minister to them.

A Sanctus for Women powerfully demonstrates that Olurombi is reduced to poverty by the schemes of the malevolent Sala and the unforgivable indifference of society. She agrees to the pact with Iroko because she has no alternative and, as Eustace Palmer concludes, "If there is any lesson to be learnt from this play it is about the harshness and complacency of a society that connives with the wicked to reduce the good to misery" (p. 191). *A Sanctus for Women* subverts the framework of a familiar myth so as to expose the underlying structure of exploitation in a village system. Those who are economically weak, like Olurombi, are helpless before an implacable deity and his equally self-seeking allies, Sala and Old Man, who hide behind a suspect religiosity that enables them to deprive Olurombi of her most valuable possession. Old Man's injunction to his son—"To be one with the gods all that is needed is submission" (p. 171)—reveals itself as the excuse of an interested priesthood for not intervening to stop the destruction of a cornered victim.

Tornadoes Full of Dreams (first produced in 1989 and published in 1990) takes a dialectical look at history—specifically at the French Revolution of 1789 and its reverberations around the world. Sowande celebrates the fortuitous irony of the revolution as it affected the lives of the African slaves in the French Caribbean. The revolution—for liberty, equality, and fraternity as well as a just social order—did not include in its thinking the freedom of the African slaves. But the great irony was that it gave the slaves the inspiration and moral justification for their successful revolt against their masters.

Tornadoes Full of Dreams opens in Africa and describes how a sturdy and beautiful young woman is sold to the European trader Sydney, who names her Magdalena. The play then details the horrors of the "Middle Passage"—the tortuous journey across the Atlantic Ocean—and the scars that it leaves on the minds of the slaves. On reaching San Domingo, Sydney sells Magdalena to Talbot, a French planter who, like Sydney, makes her his mistress. In San Domingo the play presents glimpses of the politics of the French Revolution and the racial tensions of the French Caribbean society, where the whites know their place at the top, the blacks drudge and squirm through hellish mills of plantation slavery, and the mulattos ambivalently inhabit the middle ground. At the climax of the play, the blacks, invoking the ideals of the revolution, insist on freedom and make the colony extremely dangerous and unprofitable. Talbot tries to sell Magdalena and their three illegitimate children, but she poisons him before the trade can go through. The climax is followed by a carnivalesque scene in which most of the characters are reincarnated as contemporary types—for example, Sydney as a multinational businessman and Talbot as a banker. Thus Sowande skillfully turns this slave narrative into a powerful parable of contemporary Africa's debt-ridden predicament.

Conceptually, the play is a journey through history as well as a journey of history itself. History is the Imp, or Esu, the trickster god of Yoruba mythology, who delights in causing mischief and confusion among human beings. The theme of the play, as Sowande points out in "History as an Imp" (1990), is the "conflict between light and dark" and the character of the Imp/History embodies "the complementarity between light and dark" (p. 24). The play examines the issue of standpoints in analyzing history. History, represented in the play by the slave trade, the French Revolution, and the slave revolts in the Caribbean, can be anything to anyone, depending on the perspective from which it is viewed. The play keeps all the perspectives visible all the time through the creative symbolism of the Imp, who is history and at the same time a commentator on history.

Structurally, at the play's denouement, all the old characters return in new roles, an indication that nothing has changed, that history is an endless repetition of events and roles. However, the play ends on a note of optimism; the Africans are not fooled this time. Instead of merely waiting and wailing for reparation and justice, they take their fate into their own hands and rout their tormentors. For Sowande, then, it is not the oppression of the past or the present that matters, but the possibilities of the future. As he says in "History as an Imp," *Tornadoes* is "the passage of the Imp in two centuries of history with the future acting out our resolution in one global village" (pp. 24–25).

THE NOVELS

Our Man the President (1981) is a fictionalized presentation of the thesis that the problem of Nigeria is a problem of leadership. This is not an unusual theme for Sowande; most of his dramatic works, especially the Babylon trilogy, have been concerned with the inexcusable failure of leaders and the resulting disillusionment. Chinua Achebe presents this thesis, prevalent among Nigerian intellectuals, very well in his book *The Trouble with Nigeria* (1983); Sowande's novel, by comparison, is at best a technically flawed, inept political thriller.

The central character is Emanuel Adamu, a radical journalist who belongs to a group of young idealists determined to change the sociopolitical landscape of their country and, especially, determined to stop the election of a corrupt millionaire businessman, Chief Aloba, as president of the country. Adamu hopes to defeat Aloba through the might of his pen but discovers that money is more powerful. Adamu is compiling a dossier on Chief Aloba and his activities aimed at subverting the democratic process. But Aloba, quick to realize the threat, promptly buys the newspaper and has Adamu fired. A rival newspaper takes Adamu on and allows him the freedom to write whatever he likes. In order to dig up as much dirt as he can on his subject, Adamu has to go to Geneva, Switzerland, where he discovers that Chief Aloba's tentacles are long indeed. He is abducted from his hotel in Geneva and tortured to the point of delirium.

Eventually he is rescued and flown back to Lagos by a sympathetic secret organization. His sorry state galvanizes others into plotting the assassination of Chief Aloba. Jaiye, one of the four plotters, undertakes to kill Aloba during the opening of Hotel Father Christmas, at which the chief, as owner of the hotel, will be the guest of honor. Jaiye is successful, but dies in the ensuing gunfire.

The novel leaves many disturbing questions, and one in the end wonders whether the naive idealism of the plotters is that of Sowande himself. One can argue that he is concerned with showing that revolutionary violence can be ennobling and liberating. However, the novel fails to establish any moral framework within which Chief Aloba's murder can be justified. In the end, it boils down to the simple fact that a group of young men, however well-intentioned they may claim to be, take the law into their hands in the name of social change.

Our Man the President can be seen as evidence of Sowande's lack of a well-thought-out political and moral vision, which is why the novel hardly rises above the political-thriller genre. Sowande is still preoccupied with the group of idealists in *The Night Before*, who seem not to have matured, either in their political thinking or in their methods of achieving the sociopolitical transformation they dream of bringing about. One key problem with the novel is Sowande's failure to create any realistic ideological framework within which his characters can pursue their dreams of social change. The thoughts and situations of his characters are as rarefied as his technique and language as a novelist are inept. It is difficult to say which is more disappointing: when Sowande allows the characters to speak in their thriller banality or when he launches into his often stilted attempts at descriptive prose, like this one:

> A fine flourish of brassy Afro-beat music animated the night club.... In and out, the trumpets, the tenor and alto saxophones wove into each other as the rhythm, bass and lead guitars pulsated harmoniously. It was night in a Lagos club, where human minds were projected on ecstatic waves of delight.... Bodies closed on each other, as sweat flowed and Club Barika bubbled with the sensuality of a flesh-pot.
>
> (p. 59)

On the whole, one wonders if Sowande would not be better off concentrating his efforts on playwriting. *Our Man the President* is a technical failure, and so is *Without a Home* (1982), which repeats all the mistakes of the first novel and further exposes what was merely hinted at in *Our Man the President*: Sowande's inability to create realistic human relationships, especially between men and women. Sowande never succeeds in creating memorable female characters. This failure is more obvious in the novels, especially in *Without a Home*, which deals with the traumatic struggle of a young boy, Bafemi, to come to terms with the breakdown of his parents' marriage. Tunji, his father, ditches his mother within months of arriving in England to study and finds himself an English girlfriend, Fay, whom he proceeds to treat as badly as Mary, Bafemi's mother. For Bafemi the nightmare of being without a home of his own is made worse by his mother's suggestion of the possibility that she will marry again. The central argument of the novel seems to be Bafemi's realization (quite advanced for one of his age) of "how important it was to build a home before an establishment."

CONCLUSION

Despite his many weaknesses as a writer, Sowande has contributed to the development of a new and "revolutionary" aesthetics for African theater. He is a socially committed writer who sees his art as a viable means of contributing to the creation of a more egalitarian social order. His metaphor of Babylon and its opposition to Utopia provide a framework within which to articulate his social vision. And flawed and oftentimes rarefied as his analysis of social issues and their solutions may be, it is still a reflection of his conviction and willingness to act as a sensitive and refractive point in the psychic landscape of Nigeria. He thus merits recognition and credit for the way in which he consistently tries to articulate a humanist vision of how to improve the circumstances of all people, not just the common people of his Nigerian homeland. His vision is broad enough to include all oppressed members of the human race, as is demonstrated by the huge canvas and universal scope of *Tornadoes Full of Dreams.*

This all-embracing vision may well explain the popularity of some of Sowande's plays. *The Night Before* and *A Farewell to Babylon* are popular with university students, who see in the characters images of themselves as the heroes of tomorrow. *A Sanctus for Women* is very powerful in performance, dealing as it does with an age-old myth about poverty and the dilemmas and choices the poor have to make in their efforts to improve the circumstances of their difficult lives. The present writer put on this play twice, in 1994 and 1996, and it remained popular with an all-white cast and a predominantly white audience. This is a testimony to the universal nature and canvas of Sowande's theater, a theater that comes alive most often in performance.

Selected Bibliography

COLLECTED WORKS

A Farewell to Babylon and Other Plays. Harlow, U.K.: Longmans Drumbeat, 1979. Contains *The Night Before, A Farewell to Babylon,* and *A Sanctus for Women.*

Flamingo and Other Plays. Harlow, U.K.: Longmans, 1986. Contains *Flamingo, Afamako, The Master and the Frauds,* and *Circus of Freedom Square.*

SEPARATE WORKS

Our Man the President. Ibadan, Nigeria: Spectrum Books, 1981. Novel.

Without a Home. Harlow, U.K.: Longmans, 1982. Novel.

The Missing Bridesmaid. Ibadan, Nigeria: A.B.M., 1988. Novel.

"History as an Imp: A Playwright's Notes on the Employment of His Most Recent Play, *Tornadoes Full of Dreams.*" In *Nigerian Stage* 1 (March 1990).

Tornadoes Full of Dreams. Lagos, Nigeria: Malthouse Press, 1990. Play.

CRITICAL STUDIES

Bamikunle, Aderemi. "Nigerian Playwrights and Nigerian Myths: A Look at Soyinka, Osofisan and Sowande's Plays." In Ernest N. Emenyonu et al., eds., *Critical Theory and African Literature.* Ibadan, Nigeria: Heinemann Educational Books, 1987.

Dunton, Chris. *Make Man Talk True: Nigerian Drama in English Since 1970.* London: Hans Zell, 1992.

Maja-Pearce, Adewale. *A Mask Dancing: Nigerian Novelists of the Eighties.* London and New York: Hans Zell, 1992.

Obafemi, Olu. "Sowande, Bode." In *Contemporary Dramatists.* 5th ed. London: St. James's Press, 1993; New York: St. Martin's Press, 1993.

Osundare, Niyi. "Playhouse of History." Review of *Tornadoes Full of Dreams.* In *Nigerian Stage* 1 (March 1990).

Palmer, Eustace. "Bode Sowande's *Farewell to Babylon.*" In *African Literature Today,* no. 12 (1982).

Wole Soyinka

1934–

DEREK WRIGHT

WOLE SOYINKA is the first black African to win international fame as a dramatist and the first black African to win the Nobel Prize in literature (1986). He is a protean figure of bewildering versatility. In addition to being Nigeria's most successful playwright, he is also an innovative poet, novelist, and autobiographer, a demanding critic and editor, and a translator. His creative work ranges over many modes and genres, his criticism crosses many disciplinary and cultural boundaries, and he has experimented with new media, using film, radio, television, and records to reach a wider audience. Soyinka's multiple literary vocations have, in fact, been matched by an equal number of extraliterary talents, including working as a theater manager, actor and director on stage and in film, academic, recording artist, political activist, and dress designer. He has also been a public figure, holding the offices of secretary-general of the Union of Writers of African Peoples (1975), administrator of the International Festival of Negro Arts and Culture (1977), chair of the Council of the Oyo State Road Safety Corps (1979), and president of the Paris-based International Theatre Institute (1986).

Soyinka's multifarious identities are, however, tributaries of a single stream, fed by distinctive currents of his Yoruba culture. (Yoruba is one of the three major ethnolinguistic groups in Nigeria.) "One must never try to rigidify the divisions between one experience and another," he has insisted, for in the Yoruba view of things "all experiences flow into one another" (interview by Agetua, p. 42). Thus, Soyinka has never been afraid to utilize one of his many vocations to advance causes in another: he used the launching of his autobiography *Aké* in 1981 to attack the power abuses of Nigeria's second republican government (1979–1983) and his Nobel Prize acceptance speech for an assault on apartheid. Soyinka is, as he explained in a 1973 lecture at the University of Washington, a humanist and a human being above all else. He has been drawn into the theaters of both entertainment and politics by the same fundamental commitment to human freedom and justice—which has led him to resist all regimes that deny them—and a belief that the exemplary individual can and must influence the course of public events: the belief that "the man dies in all who keep silent in the face of tyranny" (*The Man Died*, p. 13).

BIOGRAPHY

Akinwande Oluwole ('Wole) Soyinka was born to Yoruba parents—Samuel Ayodele, a teacher, and Grace Eniola Soyinka, a teacher, trader, and shopkeeper—on 13 July 1934 in Ijebu-Isara, Western Nigeria, and grew up in the nearby city of Abeokuta. He received his primary education at the local Christian mission school where his father was headmaster and his secondary schooling at the Abeokuta Grammar School and at Government College, Ibadan. He subsequently went on to the recently opened University College at Ibadan (now University of Ibadan) and from there to the University of Leeds in Great Britain, where his studies included a course on world drama taught by the eminent Shakespearean critic G. Wilson Knight. Soyinka graduated with a degree in English in 1957 and then spent eighteen months as a play reader at the Royal Court Theatre in London, where he had close contact with the English dramatic revival of the late 1950s. Two of his early plays, *The Swamp Dwellers* and *The Lion and the Jewel*, were performed in London at this time.

Soyinka returned to Nigeria in 1960, the year of independence, and immediately launched himself into the dramatic, cultural, and political life of the new nation. During the next seven years, while holding various academic appointments at the Universities of Ife, Ibadan, and Lagos, he established two theater companies, the 1960 Masks and Orisun Theatre, which he used to achieve two important theatrical goals. First Soyinka, along with John Pepper Clark, revitalized the Nigerian English-language theater, which had lacked a writer of great imaginative power (the earlier plays of James Ene Henshaw had been remote and stilted in their form and style). Second, by working closely with traveling theater groups like that of Duro Ladipo, he forged important links between the performance idioms of festival masquerade-dramaturgy and traveling folk theater, on the one hand, and the more sophisticated literary, dialogic drama of the European tradition on the other. The period of 1960–1967 was marked by frantic and prodigious production. Soyinka published seven plays, a novel, and a volume of poems, coedited the literary magazine *Black Orpheus* (1961–1964), ran a weekly radio series called *Broke-Time Bar*, broadcast two radio plays, and conducted research into ritual dramaturgy and folk opera. He also wrote, produced, directed, and acted in *A Dance of the Forests* at the October 1960 independence celebrations. In the same year he directed *The Trials of Brother Jero* and, in 1965 and 1966, productions of his satiric revue *Before the Blackout* and his play *Kongi's Harvest*. In 1963 he married Olayide Idowu; they had three daughters and a son.

But the seven years between independence to the Nigerian civil war were also a time of deepening political crisis, during which Soyinka waged a fierce campaign in the Nigerian press against the political intimidation, repression, censorship, and corruption that prevailed under the civilian administration of the first Nigerian republic. He used his theater group to produce satiric political revues, often in buildings barricaded against armed thugs hired by local electioneering chiefs, and he was even arrested (and later acquitted) on a charge of holding up a radio station and substituting his own tape for Chief S. L. Akintola's victory speech after the rigged Western Nigeria elections of 1966. At the outbreak of civil war in 1967 between Nigeria's federal government and the breakaway republic of Biafra, Soyinka, along with other Nigerian intellectuals, attempted to form a bipartisan "Third Force" to dissuade the European powers from selling arms to either side of the bloody conflict. As part of this mission, Soyinka visited the Biafran leader Colonel Chukwuemeka Odumegwu Ojukwu in Enugu in August, which led to his arrest and detention by the federal government forces until the war ended with Biafra's defeat in 1970. Soyinka spent twenty-six months in prison, fifteen of them in solitary confinement, and, according to his prison notebook, survived two attempts on his life. A quartet of writings—the play *Madmen and Specialists* (1971), the poems in *A Shuttle in the Crypt* (1972), the novel *Season of Anomy* (1973), and the prison notes *The Man Died* (1972)—was the bitter fruit of this experience.

The cease-fire in 1970 left General Yakubu Gowon's victorious federal regime entrenched in power. Soyinka was released from prison in October, but he announced he could not live under a "genocide-consolidated dictatorship" (*The Man Died*, p. 19) and remain an unpoliticized individual. He therefore chose to spend the troubled years of Nigeria's postwar period in Ghana, England, and the United States, returning only after Gowon's fall in 1975. During his exile and following his return to Nigeria, his political involvement remained overt and intense. While in Ghana he used his editorship of the journal *Transition* (1974–1976) to attack Africa's military dictatorships. In 1978, after the latest Nigerian military government had refused permission for the staging of his *Opera Wonyosi* (published 1981) in Lagos, he used his newly formed University of Ife Guerrilla Theatre Unit to improvise revue performances in marketplaces and parking lots for trucks, exposing and excoriating the racketeering, political murders, and army outrages that were the hallmarks of the second Nigerian republic under President Alhaji Shehu Shagari. From 1976 until his retirement in 1985 Soyinka was professor of comparative literature and dramatic arts at the University of Ife. In 1986 his long literary career—including more than twenty stage and radio plays and revues, four volumes of poetry and three of autobiography, two novels, and many critical essays—was crowned with the Nobel Prize in literature.

YORUBA AND EUROPEAN INFLUENCES

Soyinka is an eclectic and syncretic writer who refuses to "preach the cutting off of any source of knowledge: Oriental, European, African, Polynesian, or whatever" (interview by Jeyifo, 1984, p. 1730). His works are artistic hybrids of mixed Yoruba and European parentage, subtly blending African themes, imagery, and performance idioms with western techniques and stylistic influences. *The Road* (1965) combines dialogue inspired by the theater of the absurd with the spectacle and atmospherics of festival masquerade and the slapstick satire of the Yoruba folk theater. In *The Lion and the Jewel* (1963), conventional motifs taken from English Jacobean and Restoration comedy—of young love foiled by ancient deceit—rub shoulders with the idioms of the Yoruba masque (a short allegorical play with masked actors), while in *The Swamp Dwellers* (1963) the poetic naturalism of the Irish playwrights John Millington Synge and Sean O'Casey is applied to an African peasant society.

In *The Strong Breed* (1963), an annual purification rite of the Niger Delta is elusively cross-referenced with the Christian Passion. Soyinka's novel *Season of Anomy* and his adaptation of *The Bacchae of Euripides* (1973) mix Greek and Yoruba mythology; in the latter the Yoruba god Ogun is fused with Dionysius and, in the mini-epic poem *Ogun Abibiman* (1976), with the Zulu leader Shaka. Soyinka's *Opera Wonyosi* transposes John Gay's *The Beggar's Opera* (1728) and Bertolt Brecht's *Die Dreigroschenoper* (1928; *The Threepenny Opera*) to Jean-Bidel Bokassa's Central African Empire. Satiric ideas borrowed from Jonathan Swift are clothed in Yoruba songs and incantatory chants in *Madmen and Specialists* and underpin the lampoon on the Nigerian craze for astrology in *Requiem for a Futurologist* (1985).

Soyinka has written: "I cannot claim a transparency of communication even from the sculpture, music and poetry of my own people the Yoruba, but the aesthetic matrix is the fount of my own creative inspiration; it influences my critical response to the creation of other cultures and validates selective eclecticism as the right of every productive being" (*Art, Dialogue and Outrage*, 1988, p. 329). The essence of his art is not pure Yoruba but a Yoruba-based eclecticism. Indeed, Soyinka came late to Yoruba religion and it was not until his mid twenties, and after a western academic education, that he undertook any firsthand study of indigenous ritual and dramatic forms. Nevertheless, his plays are permeated by the atmosphere and moral symbolism of the celebrative festivals that punctuate the Yoruba agricultural year, and the Yoruba language's treasure house of images, proverbs, and folkloric motifs survives the transplantation to foreign forms in his work. In his essay "The Fourth Stage" (1968; reprinted in *Myth, Literature and the African World*, 1976), he extrapolates a theory of tragic drama from the cultic mysteries of Ogun rites, an exercise that was clearly influenced by Friedrich Nietzsche and by the ideas of Wilson Knight, which emphasized the deep ceremonial and mythological properties of dramatic symbolism. But the ritual metaphysics of this difficult essay are informed by concepts of being that are familiar and essential to the Yoruba worldview.

At the core of these religious and philosophical concepts is a belief in the fundamental unity or "integrated essentiality" of all being, the interpenetration or "animist interfusion of all matter and consciousness" (*Myth, Literature and the African World*, pp. 51, 145). The Yoruba order of reality is an indivisible whole in which society, nature and supernature, and living, dead, and unborn all exist along a single continuum. Truths are variable emanations from a single irreducible essence; power, whether creative or political, derives from the same undifferentiated primal energy source. In this holistic order, in which everything is an aspect of something else, the mystical and the mundane are never far apart (for example, the nuts of the oil palm, which are the mainstay of Yoruba economic life, are also used in religious divination), and ritual is especially important because it serves as the meeting point of divine and human, numinous and profane, earthly and cosmic essences.

The immediate, eclectic instinct in Soyinka's dramatic thought is to celebrate individual variety and particularity—expressed in Baroka's distrust of "the spotted wolf of sameness" in *The Lion and the Jewel* (*Collected Plays*, vol. 2, p. 48)—but this is resisted in his mythopoetic writings by an opposing tendency to unify the whole of reality through essentialist concepts that seize upon the perennial and immutable in human experience, gathering the most heterogeneous phenomena into an all-embracing oneness. In the Yoruba worldview superficial differences and oppositions are bound at a deeper level by a structure of complementarities in which even extreme elements are implicit in and generated by their opposites, so that conflict is contained and harmony achieved through balance and release instead of by repression.

This principle of antinomy, of warring complementary dualities, runs through Soyinka's thought, whether he is discussing the "masochistic-hedonistic cycle" of African cuisine (in his 1962 essay "Salutations to the Gut") or the violently destructive acts of creation that release the seed of being and ensure the regeneration of nature in cosmogonic myths. The principle is equally in evidence in the bifocal vision of *egungun* festival dramaturgy, with its combination of cultic and ludic, hermetic and popular; and in the life-purchasing power of Yoruba ritual sacrifice, in which death leads to birth and in which blood, signifying the energy of new life, is a condition for the restoration of communal prosperity, the earth's fertility, and the whole continuum of existence.

In Soyinka's private metaphysics the Yoruba dynamic of complementarity and mutually determinative opposites is epitomized by his adopted personal deity, the daring pathfinder god Ogun. Ogun, says Soyinka, represents "the complete cycle of destruction and creativity" (interview included in Morell, ed., *In Person*, p. 121), a cycle in which dissolution and decay are accompanied by fertility and even slaughter may be conducive to growth. Soyinka's elastic, eclectic Ogun is a rather abstract embodiment of humanity's warring impulses and is a matrix or crucible of creative and destructive essences rather than a closely realized character. He is perpetually shifting between identities, by turns peaceful and violent, reclusive and gregarious. He is the god of iron and the road, of war and healing; patron of blacksmiths, hunters, sculptors, and mechanics; and protector of orphans. He ransacks the earth for ore and harvests it for food; as god of the road, he is a force for technological progress but is also a greedy scavenger preying on the daily wrecks it provides. Ogun's ambivalence pervades Soyinka's thought, though his presence is more evident in Soyinka's metaphysical and theoretical writings than in his well-known plays.

The areas of apparent contradiction or doubleness in human experience are represented in Soyinka's thought by what he calls, in his essay of that name, "the fourth stage" or, alternatively, the "chthonic realm" or "transitional gulf." In the tripartite Yoruba metaphysic of living, dead, and unborn, the fourth stage constitutes, collectively, the gaps in the continuum, the spaces between worlds and existences. This gulf of transition between humans and spirits (which Ogun bridges in Yoruba mythology) is inhabited by those whom the Yoruba regard as unfinished, imperfect beings because they exist halfway between states: albinos, the physically disabled, retarded people, and *abiku* spirit children who constantly cross from the unborn to the living and from the living to the dead. In Soyinka's plays these ambiguous beings partake daily of the special dangerous energy of transition that exists in the spaces between worlds and, from their liminal positions on the edge of society, are invested with abnormal vision and supernatural power. A number of the plays are set in this numinous twilight zone or fourth dimension: *The Strong Breed*, with its man-boy idiot Ifada, in the space between the old and new years; *A Dance of the Forests* (1963), which features the symbolic "Half-Child," in the turmoil between an evil past and an uncertain future; and *The Road*, in which a man-god is ritually trapped in transition, in the no-man's-land between traditional and modern cultures, Christian and Yoruba religious beliefs, and this world and the next.

EARLY DRAMA AND RITUAL PLAYS

Camwood on the Leaves

Soyinka's early plays, written in a largely naturalistic idiom accessible to western audiences, are more specifically and directly concerned with the historical transition from colonialism to independence and are explorations of cultural contrasts and confrontations in this crucial period of adjustment. The radio play *Camwood on the Leaves* (broadcast 1960, published 1973) tells the story of the sixteen-year-old Isola and how, after impregnating his childhood sweetheart, he is driven to parricide by the persecutions of his savagely repressive, puritanical father, an insecure Christian pastor who describes his own parish as "pagan." *Camwood* is a powerful psychological study of the neurotic effects of an alien repressive religion on the minds of the new African middle class—a class fearful over its exemplary status and respectability, brainwashed by Christianity into despising indigenous customs and religious beliefs, and moved to a murderous rage against all natural instinct. Behind the struggle between paternal dogmatism and youthful rebellion there is the larger conflict between Christian and African beliefs and between colonial and traditional cultures. Parricide is used to mark symbolically the departure of the new nation, on the brink of independence, from the cultural dependencies of its colonial inheritance. The play is both a national and a childhood rite of passage: with the killing of the father, the nation comes of age.

The Swamp Dwellers

In the one-act *The Swamp Dwellers* (1963), the authority challenged is traditional religion, caricatured in form by the bloated Kadiye, a corrupt profiteering village priest of the Niger Delta. The Kadiye is a self-serving opportunist who accepts sacrificial offerings to the local deity, the Swamp Serpent, but fraudulently appropriates most of the produce for his own use and uses superstition to keep the village at subsistence level. He is confronted and defiantly cross-examined about the efficacy of his sacrifices by the youth Igwezu when the latter returns from the city, where he has lost both his wife and his money to his unscrupulous brother, to find his farm ruined by flood. The play calls into question the psychology of dependency fostered by obscurantist and fatalistic religions: the Kadiye's Serpent cult helps the village to rationalize its failure and inertia, reconciles it to its sufferings, and discourages positive efforts at redress like those proposed early in the play by an enterprising wandering beggar from the Islamic north. The latter, who appears to be the play's model of self-reliance and to represent the only hope for survival, denounces the village's sluggish dependence on divine favor and resolves to reclaim land from the swamp in defiance of Serpent, priest, and community. Under his skeptical influence, Igwezu changes from a man of simple animist faith into an iconoclastic atheist, demystifying an exploitative ritual practice and revealing that there is no Serpent, only the Kadiye himself.

The play ends, however, not with a communal casting off of superstition but with a conservative community rallying to the support of its outraged priest. It is essentially a familial, domestic tragedy, and the real victims are Igwezu's parents, the eponymous swamp dwellers who occupy the stage for most of the play. Igwezu challenges the priest's authority on their behalf, directing at its proper target the resentment that they deflect off each other in futile bickerings, but he does so without their consent and support. The parents represent a moribund order, too deeply sunk in spiritual lethargy to heed the voice of dissent, and at the end of the play they side fearfully with traditional religious practice. *The Swamp Dwellers* is a somber, atmospheric drama that generates within its narrow dimensions a mood of dark foreboding and a near-tragic power.

The Trials of Brother Jero

Religious charlatanism and the psychology of dependency are again the subjects in *The Trials of Brother Jero* (1963), but here they are presented in a much lighter, comic vein. Brother Jeroboam, or "Jero," is a messianic beach prophet—a trickster who sets up a shack on Bar Beach, Lagos, prophesying golden futures in return for money—belonging to one of the revivalist Christian sects that were a marked feature of the uncertain transition from a communalist to a consumerist society at the time of independence. He is, moreover, a shameless manipulator and exploiter of his gullible disciples—notably the loyal Chume, whom he uses to advance his own material interests and to avoid paying his debts. The play, one of Soyinka's most popular and most frequently performed pieces, is a rambunctious satirical comedy with all the staple ingredients of that genre: chance encounters, confused and concealed identities, farcically piled-up incidents, the prolonging of suspense by the delayed recognition of hidden links between lives—all welded by Jero's cynical choric soliloquies. The play ends with a rather sudden and contrived stratagem: when the long-suffering Chume finally tumbles his tricks and threatens to expose him, Jero has Chume packed off to a lunatic asylum with the aid of a local member of parliament (M.P.) whom he has ensnared by prophecies of a ministry. At the close the rogue hero has escaped both the payment of his debts and the wrath of his disaffected disciple, and, with a politician among his followers, he has moved onto bigger, more dangerous game.

It is tempting, with the hindsights of the prophet's reprise in the later *Jero's Metamor-*

phosis (1973)—in which Jero is associated with the repressive post–civil war military regime of General Gowon—to make heavy weather of the moral satire in the first Jero play and to attach too sinister a significance to its predatory protagonist's criminal propensities. Jero is himself both a perfect representative of and a vehicle of satire against a society whose materialistic lusts and greeds he panders to and preys on. If societies get the prophets and the leaders they deserve, Jero's closing identification with the member of parliament reminds us that politicians also manipulate through dependency and nourish vain hopes with empty promises and ambiguously worded prophecies. With the ominous predictions of a new Ministry of War for the foolish M.P. and of "the country plunged into strife" (*Collected Plays*, vol. 2, p. 169), the satire takes a suddenly serious, darker turn. Yet, for all this, *The Trials of Brother Jero* is essentially light comedy, a picaresque trickster narrative in which the wit and ingenuity of the hero's warped genius, along with his engaging candor, are the main sources of pleasure in performance.

The Lion and the Jewel

In Soyinka's most famous early play, *The Lion and the Jewel* (1963), the theme of youthful revolt against reactionary authority is given its most subtly provocative treatment, albeit in a comedy of great wit and charm. The wily old Baroka (the Bale, or chief, and "lion" of the title) decides to entice into his harem of wives the young village beauty and "jewel" of the village, Sidi, who has been made famous by a visiting photographer for a glossy magazine and is receiving the rival attentions of an absurd, superficially westernized young schoolteacher, Lakunle. After disarming Sidi's fears by circulating a rumor that he is impotent, Baroka lures her to supper in his bedroom, where, predictably, she is seduced. The wretched Lakunle offers to take up the "fallen woman" but, in a surprising twist in the play's tail, she rejects him in favor of the more mature man.

The play, strictly speaking, is not a drama of cultural conflict between traditional and modern, or African and western, values, as has sometimes been suggested. Lakunle's half-baked, ill-assimilated values amount only to a travesty of western culture, constituted from its most tawdry trimmings—nightclubs, pinup photography, cosmetics. And if the muddle-headed schoolteacher does not represent western "progress," neither does the Bale stand for pure tradition. Traditions have no inherent value for Baroka. He simply uses them to retain power; his "traditionalism" is selective, and he is not averse to performing highly untraditional acts such as deflowering a virgin to render her ineligible for bride-price (the money the groom's family gives to the bride's family according to tradition). Baroka is modern or traditional as convenience dictates, and his selection of what is desirable from both old and new is quite erratic and capricious and is not informed by any systematic worldview or body of communal values. In the seduction scene he claims to have a traditionally discriminating view of progress, resisting it only when it "makes all roofs and faces look the same" (*Collected Plays*, vol. 2, p. 47). But the truth is that Baroka's real policy is to leave everything as it is and thus to keep intact that very sameness—"the spotted wolf of sameness"—that he claims to be resisting, and it is clear from his sophistical, salacious rhetoric that any concern he has for tradition is overridden by his enjoyment of the deception and entrapment of Sidi in his plot. The Bale, more fox than lion, is not an allegorical portrait of an ideal ancient Africa, an Africa that is deceptively weak but inwardly powerful and perpetually revitalizing itself with influxes of young blood.

The Lion and the Jewel is a slippery, controversial play, much to the despair of dogmatists: it retains a quirky, independent-minded fidelity to human experience that insists on keeping all options open, refusing to be confined in simplistic, stereotypical formulae such as stagnant traditionalism versus progressive westernization. The play is also stylistically experimental, the action punctuated with stylized comic masquerades and the illusionist idiom of the dialogue-drama woven into the presentational one of the masque pageant. The point of these masquerades is not merely to narrate events taking place offstage but also to lift the action impersonally out of the historical world of the community into the timeless realm of fable. The masquerades ritualize experience, ceremonially marking sexual milestones—bridal masque, childbirth, menopause—and compress the whole reproductive cycle into a single day: they turn the play into a comic rite of sexual passage, progressing from noontime adolescent romance to the nocturnal intrigues of adult sexuality and from there to the new dawn of childbirth prefigured by the seed in Sidi's womb.

The Strong Breed

Ritual appears in a more sinister light in *The Strong Breed* (1963), the eponymous heroes of which are the families who each year perform the hereditary duty of ceremonially carrying away from the community its accumulated pollutions. The protagonist, Eman, has absconded from his ritual heredity in his native village only to find himself pressed back into it in another village. But here strangers are forced into the role in the absence of voluntary carriers, and the year's ills are not projected into an effigy through cursing and touch, as in Eman's village, but are transferred, through real violence, to the person of the carrier himself. Eman is slow to understand these crucial differences, and the rite goes disastrously wrong when he flees from its unexpected cruelties: it ends with his pursuit through the village and his death in an animal trap.

In *The Strong Breeed*, Soyinka depicts a mechanical expiatory rite emptied of meaning to the extent that there is no moral identification of the community with the ritual vehicle. The village elders, in a spirit of cowardly expedience and self-preservation, force an innocent to expiate their sins and undertake their ordeals for them; they alienate their guilt to a scapegoat offering and then, by a logic that is paranoid in its literal-mindedness, proceed to see everything he does thereafter as evidence of his "evil" and as justification of their behavior. Soyinka's purpose is neither to ridicule nor to uphold ritual superstitions but to create the impression of a wholly self-apprehended world, viewed from an inside perspective, and to present its confusion of moral and ritual values in terms of its own customs and beliefs. In this play the available options are the rival codes of different villages, relative only to one another, and no "progressive" or "enlightened" external view, closer to the dramatist's own, is brought to bear critically upon them (as by Igwezu in *The Swamp Dwellers* or Olunde in the later *Death and the King's Horseman*, 1975).

The ending of *The Strong Breed* is ambivalent. Like Christ, Eman sacrifices himself for an ungrateful community, but because he is a coerced victim the redemptive, beneficial value of the rite is left in some doubt. It seems to be locked into a futile, self-subverting cycle, pointlessly expiating evil by an act that amasses more. And yet there is a sense in which Eman keeps faith with his heredity by infusing the debased rite with something of the communally oriented morality of the original. Eman tries to halt the ritual process because he sees, altruistically, that the performer's unwillingness and the officiants' corruption render it valueless, and this perception seems to have rubbed off on the villagers by the end of the play. The radical effect on them of the sight of the crucified Eman and their desertion of their leaders suggests that the established order has been shaken, winding back the clock on decades of corrupt malpractice, and that, as is often the case in Soyinka's work, a moribund tradition has been revitalized by an outsider's visionary apprehension.

The Bacchae of Euripides

In his adaptation (published 1973) of Euripides' Bacchae, Soyinka, in a militant mood after his civil war internment, turns his attention from the moral logic of ritual to the political logic of revolution, albeit a revolution awkwardly mixed up with Dionysian religious ecstasy. In the play's apocalyptic climax wine spurts from the severed head of King Pentheus and, in a kind of reverse transubstantiation, establishes a new fertility in flooding the fields. The rather forced and wishful symbolism transforms Euripides' tyrant from an object of divine nemesis into a sacrificial offering to the future, his blood the revolutionary energy of the new age. Once again, the action is ritualistically locked in a doomed cycle of endlessly repeated joys and horrors: out of the delirium of the wine came the spilled blood, which is now converted back to wine but may in turn become blood again. But in *The Bacchae of Euripides*, Soyinka, in a burst of revolutionary optimism, halts at the wine and the rebirth, implying a finality that takes the slaughter of Pentheus out of the fatalistic cycle of alternation. Closing the gap between ritual and reality, his adaptation questions whether societies benefit from any kind of individual sacrifice other than that in which ritual forms are strategically directed at the power centers from which evil emanates.

Soyinka's *Bacchae* is not Euripides'. His Dionysius is conceived, in Yoruba fashion, as the primal creative energy source of which the tyrant's military power taps only a fraction. In his Ogunian incarnation the god represents a harmonizing balance of extremes, not the reductive force that in the Greek original acquires disproportionate, murderous power and demands absolute submission once it has been excluded or suppressed. Though he retains the closing outrage at Dionysius' heartless justice, Soyinka's overall vision in his version is celebratory. The play ends with a disquieting acceptance of the god's alternating ecstasy and pain, his gentleness and ferocity, and even the savagery of his revenge is given a hopeful political construction, as having healing and regenerative dimensions that are not merely part of an unceasing cycle of atrocities.

Kongi's Harvest

The earlier *Kongi's Harvest* (1967), though less decisive about how to get rid of dictators, is a more complex and exciting piece of festival drama than *The Bacchae.* It is richly composite theater, dispersed over seven separate settings and combining raucous political satire with ritual choreography in a kind of ceremonial cabaret. In festival dramaturgy stylized tableaux are often substituted for action, swamping the plot in sheer spectacle, and as a result there has been some critical confusion about what actually happens in this play. Kongi, the demented dictator of the state of Isma, has imprisoned and dethroned the traditional chief, Oba Danlola. To legitimize his seizure of power, he now lays claim to the Oba's spiritual authority through his consecration of the crops at the New Yam Festival. But Danlola, a wily self-serving old rogue, refuses to surrender his sacred functions and spends most of his imprisonment elaborately posturing and playacting to keep Kongi confused about whether he will attend the ceremony at which power is to be transferred. Danlola's nephew Daodu, the head of a farming commune, and Segi, a nightclub hostess, appear to be involved in a plot against Kongi, though it is never clear whether its aim is assassination, dethronement, or mere moral confrontation. Whatever it may be, Daodu and Segi's plot evidently misfires when one of the conspirators, Segi's father, is killed in an assassination attempt of his own. Daodu and Segi then improvise: the former, replacing his uncle at the festival, denounces the dictator as he offers up the new yam while the latter, in a coup de théâtre, presents to the terrified Kongi a copper salver containing not the customary yam but the severed head of her dead father. At the end the Oba, though powerless, has survived, whereas there is some doubt about how long Kongi will last.

The pervasive presence of the New Yam ceremonials in *Kongi's Harvest* tends to polarize the play's oppositions in favor of the Oba's worldly, broad-humored, humanitarian tradition and against the warped power mania of the dictator and his made-up ideologies (Isma is the place of "isms"). The Oba is also, culturally and linguistically, the more splendid creature, his speech laced with proverbs and allusions that make Kongi's sterile verbicidal jargon sound impoverished in comparison.

And yet the parallels implicit in the cross-cutting between settings invalidate any facile oppositions, whether between modernism and native tradition or between reactionary power and revolutionary challenge. We are constantly reminded that Danlola's outmoded autocracy was also an absolutist, exploitative order, though it was enforced by magical and spiritual power instead of Kongi's brute military force. Both men identify their personalities, in cultic fashion, with the nation, the only difference being that the Oba's personality is bawdily hedonistic while Kongi's is joylessly ascetic. Both men are vain image builders and pompous poseurs insulated from reality by circles of professional flatterers. Thus, Kongi and Danlola are not opposites but mirror images, products of the same continuous king-making process in African tradition, and the play's satire is as heavily weighted against the barren ritualism of this tradition as against Kongi's empty "progressive" modernism. Once again, the traditional past is not idealized or looked to as a source of value, and the detracting satiric treatment of ritual in the play tends to regard its apparent reinstatement in the finale as problematic.

Kongi's Harvest is powerful theater, visually spectacular and rich in poetry and verbal wit, but it remains a politically vague and ritually indecisive play. Daodu is a shadowy figure, and the commune farmer and hostess cannot measure up to their mythological roles, as Spirit of the Harvest and Earth Mother, in the masque of the yam festival. Moreover, although the climax of the festival provides an apt moment for the assassination of the tyrant, just as he is about to bite hubristically into the new yam, the translation of the event into a dance overloaded with ceremonial motifs obscures the meaning and blunts the power of what should be the high point of excitement in the play. Soyinka fails to resolve the ritualism of his play within a naturalistic idiom, but he is not prepared to explode that idiom and allow the ritualistic elements to take control of the drama and refashion it according to their own autonomous design. For this, we have to turn to his two most ambitious and esoteric plays of the 1960s, *A Dance of the Forests* (written for Nigeria's independence celebrations and published in 1963) and *The Road* (1965).

A Dance of the Forests and *The Road*

In these two plays, Soyinka takes leave of the sequential, illusionist action of the European stage and plunges his drama into the very quick of the transitional zone between worlds. Here the action enters performatively into the realm of ritual, which is now not only the subject but also the structural pivot and formal determinant of the drama, so that the finished products approximate more closely the condition of rites per se. The simulated rites do not so much take place in the plays as the plays take place in the interrupted phases and scrambled time-limbos of the rites: of the *egungun* in the Drivers' Festival in *The Road* and of the tribal gathering ceremony in *A Dance of the Forests*. These plays constitute the broken ritual sequences that are merely featured in *The Strong Breed* and the later

Death and the King's Horseman, and their actions cannot end until those sequences are resumed and completed and the disturbance wrought by the interruption repaired: that is, until a propitiatory death substitutes for the omitted sacrifice in *The Road*, and until the symbolic Half-Child, in *Dance*, is returned to its mother, completing an arrested eight-hundred-year-old pregnancy. Both processes, held over from the respectively recent and historical past, have to be ritually reactivated so that the performers can be released from their suspended existences between states—into death, in the case of the *egungun* celebrant, and into birth in the case of the Half-Child.

In what appears to be the main plot action in *A Dance of the Forests*, a local deity, Forest Head, poses as a humble records clerk in order to unmask the crimes and corruptions of four people. He leads them on a spiritual quest deep into the forest where, at the masque of the court of Mata Kharibou, a barbarous twelfth-century emperor, they witness the equivalent misdeeds of their ancestral selves in earlier incarnations and are given the opportunity to make the atonements that are necessary for both personal and national new beginnings. It is not clear in this most uncentered of works, however, if this is even the seminal narrative thread of the play or, indeed, if it is a play at all rather than a pageant or festival. In addition to the random appearances of a plethora of anonymous functionaries, villagers, and courtiers, the human action is punctuated by the interventions of Yoruba gods, tutelary forest spirits, and other supernatural or allegorical beings. When the curtain falls on the splendidly theatrical masque of Mata Kharibou, the dialogue-drama is largely given over to music and mime. In the protracted tumultuous climax, balletic masquerades, divination, children's games, and all manner of allegorical presences crowd confusingly onto the stage, and a chorus of animistic spirits, using the ritually entranced human quartet as mouthpieces, proceeds to sing the earth's dismal ruined history.

Much of the play's confusion arises from its setting in the transitional zone where different orders of reality intersect. The characters metamorphose from humans into revenant spirits and from disguised to unmasked deities, and the phantasmagoric set is in a constant fury of transformation. Language, too, is in transition, shifting from an elevated Shakespearean rhetoric representing the timeless mythologized world of the forest to earthy vernacular for the humans and gnomic incantation for the climactic numinous masque. Arguably, this confusion is meaningful as a complex emanation from the new state's chaotic passage from colonialism to independence at the time of writing.

Yet there is a limit to what can be artistically justified in the name of transitional indeterminancy, and there are, by any criteria, loose ends in this sprawling work. For most of the time the humans who people the historical realm seem to be quite oblivious of and unaffected by the supernatural agencies that haunt the transitional one, resulting in an impression of two separate, parallel actions. More seriously, the elliptical, abstract mime of the Half-Child at the play's climax is too intellectually complex to be left to music alone, and the expectations raised by the play's intricate verbal elements that its oracular elements will be resolved in language are not fulfilled. The interpretive possibilities—historical, mythological, metaphysical—are so multileveled that they tend to cancel one another out and dissolve meaning, leaving only an exciting theatrical effect, as if there were some impenetrable puzzle at the core of the symbolism. Overall, the play takes on too many themes, the actors in their multiple disguises play too many parts, and there is no focal narrative or character strong enough to hold all the actions and the dense forest of symbols together. *Dance* is a magnificent, experimental theatrical hybrid, but it remains rarefied coterie drama, an occasional work written for a special event, and it has not been fully performed, outside of academic circles, since its 1960 debut.

The Road, a work of more concentrated power and accessibility, is more directly focused on explosive interruptions and resumptions of the ritual process. In the play's key event, which has already taken place when the action begins, a hurtling technological juggernaut has literally collided with a traditional religious practice: the truck driver Kotonu has run over the masked *egungun* celebrant Murano at the very moment of the latter's possession by the god Ogun in the Drivers' Festival. Kotonu has transported the body to the local "Aksident Store," where it was stolen by the proprietor, the mad Professor, a disgraced lay preacher who now earns a living as a "wrecker" and a forger of licenses. While it appears that Professor has somehow nursed Murano back to partial life and restored him to his former occupation of wine tapper, in reality Murano is dead, struck down while in transition between worlds and therefore visible only in the twilight hours; his dying has been held over in a state of mute suspension from the past, where the incompleted rite is still going on.

While the dormant but ongoing ritual process remains intact, the mask retains its inherent energy and power to possess, and in one scene it tumbles from the tailboard of the truck and reenters the action, catapulting Kotonu and his tout Samson back to the time of the accident. This is not a flashback but a sudden elision or eruption of past into present moments that dissolves the distinction between occurrence and reenactment. Within this ritual enclosure, Kotonu and Samson do not simply relive the past but literally return to it. They slip through doorways between worlds, through holes in time that lead into the other time dimension of the ritual process, where recent events, because they were interrupted in midflow, are not yet finished.

Professor's strange purpose is to "hold a god captive." A kind of spiritual voyeur, he is engaged in a futile quest to experience vicariously the mystery of death, but he fails to realize that to know what Murano knows he must be where Murano is, since "death's revelation must be total or not at all" (*Collected Plays*, vol. 1, pp. 223, 226). In the play's terrifying climax Professor sacrilegiously stages his own private *egungun* ceremony, in which he presents Murano, again wearing the ritual mask and therefore repossessed by the god, to the drivers, touts, and thugs who hang around his shop. In an ensuing scuffle Professor is fatally stabbed by one of the thugs. As Murano is released into his death in this world and the god released into the spirit world, the impeded transition is at last completed and the dancing figure vanishes, leaving behind a spinning mask.

Once again, though in a clearer and more controlled way than in *Dance*, the keynote is transitional indeterminacy, the phenomenon peculiar to the liminal phase of the rite of passage in which the celebrant is not any one thing but inhabits a plurality of identities. Thus, Murano is at once the god Ogun, the masquerader knocked down by Kotonu's truck (killed in the body but still posthumously alive in the spirit), and, in his "resurrected" form, the tapper of Ogun's favorite palm wine. At a broader symbolic level, however, he is an image of the new nation-state, suspended between worlds, the survival of the historical accident of independence uncertain. The road, representing a very doubtful kind of progress, is the historical track on which the nation, reeling from postcolonial culture shock and alienation, moves forward in its passage between a lost past and an ill-prepared future.

In this haunting play, in which the numinous touches on the material world of automobile parts and forged licenses, the road is at once the province of Ogun—its stores and bars are his shrines and tabernacles—and a manmade evil, produced by corrupt bureaucracies and reckless driving habits. Indeed, the play, in its reinterpretation of *egungun* ritual, Ogun mythology, and Christian doctrine in the light of contemporary urban experience, self-consciously concerns its own transitionality and exists in an interpretative limbo between historical and metaphysical meanings. Subsequently, there is no attempt to resolve the puzzle of Professor's death: it may be seen as an accident, a sacrifice expiating the violation of a rite, a retribution for the hubris of spying on the gods, or merely a casualty in a squalid brawl. *The Road* is brilliantly bleak drama: the dialogue piles up images of abortive waste and exudes a rich mixture of stenches but also manages to present a great deal of humor (in the conversational crossfire of the touts and thugs) and to salvage the most slender of redeeming visions from the anomic squalor and decay.

Madmen and Specialists

In the 1970s Soyinka made two further excursions into heavily ritualized drama. The first of these was his bitterly pessimistic post–civil war play *Madmen and Specialists* (1971), which takes its barbaric satiric premise of cannibalism as a remedy for famine from Jonathan Swift's pamphlet *A Modest Proposal* (1729) but goes on, using the model of the *egungun*, to present the insanities of war and genocide as a case of collective demonic possession. *Madmen and Specialists* is a play full of performances: it is scurrilously chorused by a quartet of stylized, perpetually playacting marionettes called the Mendicants and takes place in the border territory between role-playing and reality, between parody and its object.

At the play's explosive climax the insanely visionary father, who has earlier served up a feast of human flesh to army officers to illustrate to them the enormity of war, hauls one of the Mendicants, the Cripple, onto an operating table and proceeds to parody the surgical "practisings" of his son, a doctor turned sinister intelligence specialist. The madman takes on the role of the specialist to show the specialist that he is really a madman. But the father seems also to be conjuring up from within himself something of his son's quintessential evil and ritually exorcising the spirit of the offspring he has created.

The dramaturgical touchstone is the celebrant's passage from the satiric to the cultic phase of the rite and from parodic imitation to actual possession (hence the father's trance-like frenzy and the Mendicants' hieratic chanting). In this figurative *egungun* rite the father is possessed by his spiritually dead son, who then enters the room on cue and shoots the father: as the old man has warned, the father can be rid of his son, and the son of the father, only by the father's death. In this last grotesque twist, exorcist and exorcised reverse positions, and the parent is cast out by the son: by shooting the mad but humane man who fathered him, the specialist-son severs his last link with humanity, expelling its remaining vestiges in himself.

Madmen and Specialists is the ultimate in dramatized ritual chaos in Soyinka's writing, a figurative exorcism of the demons of war in which the esoteric style, pushed to its limits, finds its simultaneous apotheosis and exorcism. As theater, the play was a dead end. It did, however, in the raucous, grisly cabaret of the Mendicants, bring under the spotlight for the first time a feature of Soyinka's stagework—the freewheeling, satiric, agitprop revue style of theater—which had until then been only intermittently present and which was to dominate his dramatic writing from the mid 1970s onward.

Death and the King's Horseman

The other play in the category of extensively ritualized drama is *Death and the King's Horseman* (1975), based on an actual 1945 incident of a colonial officer's intervention to prevent the royal horseman, the Elesin, from committing ritual suicide at his king's funeral, whereupon the Elesin's son would take his father's place in the rite. This play has attracted much criticism, largely because of the liberties Soyinka took with history. Principally to highlight the different cultural values attached to individual sacrifice by the Yoruba and the British, he sets the episode in World War II, and he weakens the Elesin's will by having him succumb to a sudden deathbed desire for a beautiful young girl. Furthermore, although there is abundant evidence in the text of long-standing interactions between the colonial and indigenous cultures, the play, because of Soyinka's tendency to mythologize history, creates the dual impression that the Elesin's failure is a sudden isolated episode rather than the culmination of a gradual historical process and that Yoruba Oyo culture has been wrenched from its moorings by a single, epochal dereliction of duty.

More seriously, Soyinka turns the Elesin's son, the character Olunde, in reality a local trader still steeped in the traditional world, into a western-educated doctor and intellectual—an alteration that is essentially an exercise in cultural polemics. Olunde's action is important as a symbolic demonstration—by one who has experience of both native and colonial cultures—of the indigenous culture's ability to handle its crises through its own resources. The self-sacrifice is morally and imaginatively true insofar as it expresses faith in the essence of a culture and, specifically, in an ethic of sacrifice that has survived the influences of western education. The fact that Olunde is an outsider and therefore a force for radical change in his society is also of ritual value. Although he respects the past, he knows that history does not stand still. He expects to resume his overseas medical training afterward, for in the completion of the burial rites the old order embodied by the father is buried as well, making way for the new: the son dies in place of the father, partly to indicate that he did not intend to live like him. The Yoruba world traditionally distrusts any excessive stability; ritual is one of the key instruments for incorporating modernizing currents of change from one generation to the next, thus preventing the past from becoming fixed, a concept that is emboldened by Olunde's expatriation.

Plays Versus Rites

In addition to his prolific dramatic output, Soyinka, in his critical writings, has derived an impressive theory of drama from Ogun festival rites, but it is of limited practical application to his plays. In his discussion of the ritual and mythological archetypes of Yoruba drama in *Myth, Literature and the African World*, Soyinka conflates the different legends of Ogun, god of transition, and of Obatala, god of passive suffering and redemptive wisdom. The two become complementary rather than contradictory forces: Ogun's transitional energy is actually made to issue out of Obatala's inertia and is then reabsorbed into his harmony, a pattern repeated in the release of Dionysius' energy from Pentheus' imprisonment in *The Bacchae* and of Olunde's from Elesin's in *Death and the King's Horseman.* The ritual paradigm for Soyinka's drama and the metaphysical law of his Yoruba universe are the same: rebellious chaos and disintegration, caused by Ogun's assertive challenge, are repeatedly accommodated by the quiescent harmony and complacent wisdom represented by Obatala but are never fully resolved. In the course of this perpetual interflow of disturbance and conciliation, infraction and reparation, the Ogunian protagonist injects new strength or knowledge into the lifeblood of the community and supplies the vital conduit of transitional energy necessary to recharge the universe and keep it from settling into a stagnant harmony.

It would, however, be unwise to force Soyinka's plays into this narrow conceptual framework. Whatever the author's theoretical insistence on the sacrificial teleology of Yoruba tragedy, his own creative practice always leaves some doubt about the beneficial or redemptive carryover effect for the community. Society is not regenerated by the deaths of the parasitic Professor in *The Road* and the tyrant Pentheus in *The Bacchae* but is merely better off without them: the logic is more material and pragmatic than sacrificial. The prevailing feeling of waste and desolation at the end of *Horseman* is closer to Shakespearean tragic conventions than to the Ogunian model.

It is also unwise to attach too literal a value to Soyinka's analogy of cultic drama (the drama of the gods) with theater (the human drama), and of the stage actor with the possessed celebrant of the Ogun rite. Although Soyinka's essay "The Fourth Stage" promises in its subtitle to locate the origins of Yoruba tragedy in "The Mysteries of Ogun," it is actually not an analysis of dramaturgy or any other aspect of theater but a rather turgid piece of metaphysical lyricism on the subject of religious ecstasy.

Finally, of course, a play is about reality while a rite is its own reality, and even Soyinka's most ritual-intensive dramas are, necessarily, imitations. They are not rites proper or even naturalistic reproductions that can be pinned down to particulars but are poetic conceptions, visionary reworkings of ritual, through metaphor, into art. Soyinka's use of ritual elements is always highly idiosyncratic and reinterpretive, full of ironic barbs and twists—as, for example, in *Kongi's Harvest*, where the New Yam Festival, which usually marks renewal and new beginnings, is made to signal the end of an era. His primary interest is not in the specifics but in the *idea* of the festival and its imaginative possibilities (for communal purification and regeneration) in the troubled transitions of modern African history.

In Soyinka's stage practice, ritual is as slippery and multifaceted as its metaphysical interpretation in "The Fourth Stage" (as Ogun's drama of transition) is narrow and selective. In the individual plays traditional ceremonial practices may be beneficial or exploitative, repressive or subversive, and are defined by the uses they are put to. They may sanctify evasion, brutality, or corruption (*The Strong Breed*, *The Swamp Dwellers*); or merely endorse empty moral gestures against evil (*Kongi's Harvest*); or be transformed from tools of oppression into instruments of insurrection (*The Bacchae*). Ritual elements and devices may be overtheatrical or simply untheatrical, and when Soyinka does attempt a pristine cosmic drama of transition, in *A Dance of the Forests*, the result is a bewildering multiplicity of social and ritual identities, humans and spirits, agencies and essences, which finally collapses in total confusion.

Whatever one makes of Soyinka's metaphysics, the gains that accrue from their visionary insights to his dramaturgy are undeniable—notably, an atmospheric power of a frightening intensity and a haunting sense of the numinous that comes from belief in contiguous, parallel worlds, negotiable by transitional crossings. Nevertheless, plays are in the end enactments of human crises, not rites charting the motions of primal mythological forces. Not surprisingly, Soyinka's hostile critics, notably those on the Nigerian Left, have regarded his rendering of human lusts and follies in terms of occult essences as a retreat from the complexities of historical experience into a private metaphysical fantasy that is of dubious relevance to the contemporary Nigerian situation.

AGITPROP SATIRE

After 1975, whether in response to the pressures of this criticism or to the exigencies of the worsening political situation in Nigeria, Soyinka chose to strip the complex Yoruba ritual and mythological idiom from his drama in favor of the subversive, agitprop satiric revue, aimed at a mass audience and written for performance rather than publication. This largely unscripted, hit-and-run street theater, performed in marketplaces and parking lots, was mounted with minimal publicity, usually vanishing before the players could be rounded up by the police of the latest repressive regime. Over the next decade Soyinka's so-called shotgun satires—"you discharge and disappear" (Gibbs, p. 63)—ran a constant caustic calypso on ministerial embezzlement and racketeering, political assassinations, military atrocities, municipal breakdowns, and many other scandals and outrages. Sometimes pointedly local in reference, as in the unpublished "Rice Unlimited" (1981) and "Priority Projects" (1983), and sometimes concerned with evils on the African continent at large (*Opera Wonyosi*), the revue satires were both spontaneous and politically relevant. In their published form, however, they suffer from a limiting ephemerality, and when their virtuoso satiric techniques are allowed to interfere with the dramatic integrity of fully crafted stage plays, the results are disappointing: a linguistic flatness and satiric meanness of characterization (*A Play of Giants*, 1984), and a mechanical lining up of slight, insubstantial targets, as in the lightweight satire on astrology, *Requiem for a Futurologist*.

Opera Wonyosi

Opera Wonyosi (1981), which obliquely lampoons the 1970s oil boom through the escapades of a clique of Nigerian expatriates living in "Emperor" Jean-Bedel Bokassa's Central African Empire, is an exuberant and devastating satire on power and the criminal lengths that people go to acquire it. Although written with Soyinka's characteristic exuberance and wit, it suffers from the tying back of its action to the Gay and Brecht originals (Mackie's sexual intrigues are poorly integrated into the anti-Nigerian satire), and its extreme length draws attention to the episodic, patchwork revue structure. The merciless satire takes on too many issues for any to be focused clearly, and as the topical references to guilty parties crowd thick and fast into the speeches, the play goes into a satiric overkill that diffuses its intensity. Nevertheless, the stylized ballad opera form, with the actors assuming a variety of roles, was to prove a favorite of Soyinka's in the following years, one he repeated with more success in the twin texts of *From Zia, with Love; and, A Scourge of Hyacinths* (1992), in which his satiric rage is unleashed on power scandals and abuses in the area of drug trafficking.

A Play of Giants

A Play of Giants is a surreal fantasia of international poetic justice in which an African dictator, on a visit to the United Nations in New York, takes a group of Russian and American delegates hostage. He threatens to release the Soviet-supplied rockets from his embassy arsenal unless an international force is sent to crush the uprising in his own country. The play's ghoulish quartet of African despots are the postcolonial products of the western superpowers, but now the monsters have escaped their makers' control and the horrors have come home to roost in their backyards. *A Play of Giants* is horrifically funny, particularly in its fantastic, farcical satirization of infamous contemporary figures, such as Bokassa, the Zairean president Sese Seko Mobutu, and the Ugandan dictator Idi Amin. But history plus burlesque does not quite equal drama. The characters are mere vaudeville puppets, burbling nonsense and twitching at the behest of every passing sadistic and vainglorious whim, and the fact that their real-life models were much the same does not make them theatrically viable. As the revue play, with its deepening bitter-satiric tone, has come to constitute Soyinka's characteristic response to Africa's worsening crises, there has unfortunately been a thinning of the rich texture of his drama.

POETRY

Idanre

With the exception of his autobiographical writings, Soyinka's achievements in other genres have been less spectacular than his dramatic ones. His poetry is notorious for its clotted syntax and knotty grammar, its tortured diction and overloaded metaphors, and most especially for its tendency to subsume human emotions and experience into mythic archetypes. In the dense little lyrics that make up the "other poems" of *Idanre and Other Poems* (1967), desire and grief are imaged in terms of plant life, tides, and seasonal change ("Psalm," "Season," "Dedication"). In the more harrowingly intimate lyrics "A Cry in the Night" and "A First Deathday," which concern a stillborn child and one who dies on its first birthday, respectively, the imagery of seedtime and harvest is, however, bitterly ironic, and the same rival mythopoetic and mythoclastic impulses are in evidence in the "October '66" poems. Here the truckloads of soldiers bound for the front are a "crop of wrath," an unseasonal mock sacrifice on the false altar of civil war ("Ikeja, Friday, Four O'Clock"), and the poet's pathetic-fallacious attempt to place the slaughtered Igbos in the broader context of nonhuman nature, by transforming the broken skulls into acorns cropped as part of the seasonal process, is seen as an evasion of the horror—an "idyll sham" ("Massacre, October '66").

The twenty-five-page epic title poem is a different matter. Here the reader needs to be equipped with the full Yoruba mythological arsenal prior to an assault upon the text, and Soyinka's preface and notes are more distracting than illuminating. "Idanre," which combines a mystical overnight experience on Mount Idanre with the mythology of Ogun's descent among men, is a magnificently jumbled, furiously inspirational piece, written in a kind of cosmic delirium, and full of intellectual loose ends as a result of its crossing of different legends. Its thunderous phrases and flashing images convey a sense of tremendous scope and power, transcending its individual opacities, but the final effect is more high-sounding than meaningful, and the verses frequently collapse into incoherent esoteric verbiage. The archetypal, elemental struggles of mythic forces are not informed by any humanizing perspective, and today the poem's chief value is as a mine for images and motifs in the early plays and dramatic theory.

A Shuttle in the Crypt

A Shuttle in the Crypt (1972) is the bitter distillation of Soyinka's imprisonment, the testament of a poet driven to the brink of madness by the "mind-butchers" of military power; it is the literature of survival, more functional than meaningful. The shuttle of the title is the poet's imprisoned mind that shunts back and forth in it solitary confinement, first finding relief in the vituperative clarity of satire leveled at the federal regime ("Background and Friezes"); then liberating itself imaginatively into the world's literatures, using sheer technical execution as a discipline to hold itself together ("Four Archetypes"); and finally, as the landmarks of being subside and material reality vanishes, retreating into the remote, mystic inner reaches of consciousness ("Animystic Spells," "Chimes of Silence"). In the vacuum of utter seclusion, language, which is all the poet has to reassure him of his continuing consciousness, floats objectless and the mind begins to contemplate its own void. In the unbearably strained poems that result, the tangled, esoteric style reaches extremes in demented punning and incantatory repetition, a hermetic therapy of sheer sound without pretension to meaning. *A Shuttle in the Crypt* is the poetry of private mystic revelation in extremis, unnegotiable and often impenetrable: its searing vision cannot easily be transported back into the dimness of ordinary reality.

Ogun Abibiman

Soyinka's next excursion into verse was the twenty-two-page epic *Ogun Abibiman* (1976), in which he combines a direct call to frontline states to take action against South Africa with a mythologized manifesto for its liberation (in which Ogun, Yoruba god of war, joins forces in violent, mystical union with the legendary Zulu chieftain Shaka). *Ogun Abibiman* is poetry of the public voice, passionately committed, but curiously impersonal and unengaging, carrying no deep emotional conviction. Although refreshingly lucid after Soyinka's earlier two volumes of poetry, its forced doggerel rhetoric is sadly lacking in the inner tensions that give the earlier lyrics their personal intensity and human resonance.

Mandela's Earth

Soyinka is on more secure ground in *Mandela's Earth and Other Poems* (1988). These poems profess "a stark view of the world," but they claim to "splay its truths / In a shadow play of doubts" ("Dragonfly at My Windowpane," p. 59, ll. 20–21), refracting the public scene through personal fears and uncertainties. In "Apologia," Nelson Mandela is imaged as a rock of truth and faithful belief, holding firm against the dark warp of the poet's uncertainty and black Africa's inertia and weak self-judgment. In the "other poems" of the volume the bitter-satiric vision targets Nigeria's post–oil boom elite ("Apollodorus on the Niger") and displaced dictators who in their heyday filled their private pools with banknotes and, while their subjects starved, fed caviar to their dogs ("After the Deluge"). The best poem in the volume, however, is the magnificent closing composition, "Cremation of a Wormy Caryatid." The "caryatid" of the title is a richly decorated Yoruba doorpost. Worm-eaten, it is consigned to the funeral pyre, but the sculpted figures—the ancient warriors, regalia, and sacrificial animals—suddenly leap back to life in the incandescent flames, in the very death of the artwork that gave them life, and the poem becomes at once a haunting elegy for a lost hierarchic culture and an expression of its dynamism in decay, its resilience even in the throes of dissolution.

FICTION

Soyinka's two novels suffer from a dense overloading of language similar to that of the early poetry, usually when naturalistic scenes are charged with gratuitously poetic resonances or when there is a confusion of real and metaphoric identities. *The Interpreters* (1965) focuses on five recently returned university graduates of the generation of Nigerian independence and their corporate revolt against brazen government corruption, press dishonesty, and academic hypocrisy—a revolt, however, that is soon harmlessly deflected into so many private self-gratifying quests and elitist cults of sensibility and taste.

In the second half of the novel, the five "interpreters" abandon social action for the pursuit of their several mythical essences in the artist Kola's painting of the pantheon of Yoruba gods, and their lives become the locus of cosmic, metaphysical forces. The main difficulty in the book is in determining the status of Kola's pantheon, which at times seems to be a merely whimsical and idiosyncratic creation, full of rarefied correspondences, and as shifting and unstable as the novel's time schemes and stylistic registers. It is ultimately impossible to say exactly at what level and in whose mind, if anyone's, the meaning and value of the pantheon is constituted. And the novel is much like the pantheon—an overcrowded, undisciplined, unfocused canvas, often giving disproportionate space to minor characters whose place in the symbolic religious scheme is unclear. The book's main subject seems to be art itself—seen either as an opiate or as a dangerously desensitizing influence. The five artist-intellectuals, concerned only with registering the "significance" of a fugitive thief instead of helping him, cause his death through their collective indifference; unable to alter their society, Kola and his friends merely "interpret" it.

In *Season of Anomy* (1973), a fictional transposition of the 1966 massacres that led to the civil war, art ventures out into the public domain and assumes a more subversive role. The musician Ofeyi plans to undermine both his employer, the Cocoa Corporation, and its parent, the ruling military-industrial "Cartel," by disseminating through advertising campaigns the communalist political ideas of a village utopia called Aiyero. The Cartel's response is to arouse tribal hatreds against all Aiyero men (thus implying that the federal regime directed hatred at all Igbo, from whom many progressives and activists came). In the ensuing wave of terror and massacre Ofeyi's band is wiped out and its dancer, Iriyese, abducted. The subsequent quest for Iriyese takes Ofeyi on a nightmare trip through a landscape of genocidal slaughter and mutilation, described with graphic, horrifying realism. Ofeyi's ordeal, however—because it is underpinned by Orpheus' search for Eurydice in the underworld—finally takes refuge in the seasonal fatalism of myth and the lone private quest of the Orphic artist figure. The rescue of the standard-bearer and dubious revolutionary figurehead Iriyese is a merely symbolic salvage operation, in which the political campaign is dissipated into familiar ritual patterns.

Both novels focus on the intellectual elite, the second switching from its isolated sensibility to its tormented conscience. In neither of the books, however, is character conceived in an individuated way; rather, it is, as in Kola's painting of the godhead, a plurality of manifestations. Instead of rounded characters, we are given unevenly developed and erratically focused composite personalities that seem to embody different aspects of the author's awareness and temperament, using the devices of the pantheon in the first book and the archaic morality tradition of externalized alter egos in the second (the mystic pacifist Tailla and the anarchist assassin Demakin have no existence except as Ofeyi's "good and bad angels"). Equally, both novels are preoccupied with the dilemma of the artist and his or her proper function during seasons of corruption and catastrophe.

AUTOBIOGRAPHY

The area of prose writing in which Soyinka has made the greatest impact, particularly in his later career, is autobiography. In the acclaimed *Aké: The Years of Childhood* (1981) he recounts the first ten years of his life—a child prodigy who takes himself to school at age three, speaks English to a white colonial officer at four, enters the local grammar school at nine, and serves as a teacher and messenger in the Egba Women's Movement at ten—all in a delightfully self-mocking, tongue-in-cheek prose that marvelously evokes the child's sense of himself. Yet to reach puberty, the precocious genius muses about prospective wives, falls into fits of distraction in which he wrecks his father's rosebed and fires his father's gun, and transforms into comic human personae the mystifying abstractions "Temperature" and "Birthday."

The subtitle indicates, however, that Soyinka is also writing about the place and time of his childhood. The narrative pursues the extended self of the community and its progress in a series of outward expansions, starting with the child's rebellion against adult discipline and ending with the nation's growth to political maturity and organized protest against both internal and external oppressors. The series of inductions and boundary crossing undertaken by the young Soyinka are reenacted at a higher level by the Egba women's renegotiation of lines of class and gender to challenge the powers of local patriarchy and the white colonial administration.

Yet, except for the odd authorial intrusions and adult retrojections—such as the carefully staged, imaginatively reconstructed dialogue in the account of the women's uprising—Soyinka meticulously sustains the miniaturized, autonomous worldview of the child. Because the childhood is spent in colonial times, this worldview is inevitably a double perspective, straddling value systems and full of foreign colonial impingements that have been assimilated into and transformed by the host culture. Thus the Edenic apple becomes a pomegranate; the child imagines the mysterious supernatural companions of the *oro* (someone thought to be a reincarnated spirit, especially in forest regions) as being like the Wolf Cubs, or Boy Scouts; and he can make sense of the church's stained-glass figure of Saint Peter only in terms of the *egungun* whose strange noises occasionally penetrate the parsonage walls. His mother, though nicknamed "Wild Christian," fills her children's heads with tales of forest spirits alongside Bible stories and, adhering to a traditional faith in magical protective substances, has their hair cut by a pagan neighbor.

Aké is a treasure trove of anecdotes about the world in which Soyinka grew up and a quarry for the raw material of incidents and characters in the plays and poems (for example, the *abiku*, the child's death on its first birthday). It has quickly become a classic of childhood memoirs, nostalgic without being sentimental and never flinching from the darker side of Yoruba life (instanced in the stoning of a pregnant madwoman). It remains Soyinka's most compelling and enchanting prose work.

His next volume of memorabilia, *Isara: A Voyage Around "Essay"* (1989), lacks *Aké*'s childhood magic and charm but is perhaps a more penetrating and complex, if less animated, portrait of a society in transition. *Isara*, a more overtly fictional memoir constructed from letters, reports, and committee minutes, delves further back, ten years before Soyinka's own birth, into the life of his father and the western-educated generation that was at the forefront of the Nigerian independence movement before World War II. Soyinka re-creates with a deft comic touch the traumas, confusions, and dilemmas of the insecure provincial schoolmasters, businessmen, lawyers, and unionists who took up the white man's political and economic burdens during this epochal period and who subsequently grew uneasy with an indigenous way of life they could neither reject nor replace. In *Isara* the grandfather's syntheses of modern and traditional are opportunistic marriages of convenience: he has himself baptized for purely political reasons and sends his son to a seminary to spy on the ways of the white man. His son's generation, however, lives in an altogether more spiritually tormented, anxiety-ridden world where business tycoons and teachers guiltily consult mediums on profits and career plans, and the father, though he persists with the European treatment for his wife's mysterious malady, holds in secret reserve the last resort of fetishistic ritual medicine.

Following the pattern of *Aké*, in the last third of *Isara* the collective protagonists progress from local kingmaking to the election of state leaders and become caught up in broad public movements and events. It is the task of these men to carry the depopulated, disease-infested, backwoods wilderness of Isara out of its provincial insularity and into the modern world. Retracing their journey, the sprawling narrative in the book proliferates characters right up to the closing sequence, etching an exuberant portrait gallery of entrepreneurs, eccentrics, and rogues, hapless con artists and African cowboys, all caught comically between cultures. *Isara* is another evocative memoir done with great charm and care, a loving reimagining of things past.

CONCLUSION

Thus, in the 1980s Soyinka's multifaceted literary genius acquired yet another dimension. The "macrocosmist" and mythopoetic essentialist of metaphysics and cultural theory was joined by the miniaturist of the memoir. To the satirist of the comedies and revue plays and the ritualist of the tragic dramas was added an imaginative historian of great power and penetration. Soyinka continued to mine this rich vein in *Ibadan, the Penkelmes Years* (1994), a work of "faction" (according to the author's foreword) in which, masquerading under the alter ego of the character Maren, he deals with his secondary schooling at Government College, Ibadan, his student days in London and Paris, and the troubled years following his return to Nigeria in 1960, ending with his arrest in 1965 for holding up a radio station and making a pirate broadcast. Shortly after the publication of this work, Soyinka once more ran afoul of the Nigerian military government. After criticizing its cancellation of democratic elections he was placed under house arrest in September 1994, and his passport and United Nations papers were confiscated. He managed, however, to slip across the border into Ghana and onto a flight to Paris. He is currently living in London, where his plays are regularly performed.

Selected Bibliography

BIBLIOGRAPHIES

Gibbs, James, Ketu H. Katrak, and Henry Louis Gates, Jr. *Wole Soyinka: A Bibliography of Primary and Secondary Sources.* Westport, Conn.: Greenwood Press, 1986.

Lindfors, Bernth, and James Gibbs, eds. *Research on Wole Soyinka.* Trenton, N.J.: Africa World Press, 1993.

COLLECTED WORKS

Three Plays. Ibadan, Nigeria: Mbari, 1963. Repub. as *Three Short Plays.* London and New York: Oxford University Press, 1969. Contains *The Swamp Dwellers, The Trials of Brother Jero,* and *The Strong Breed.*

Five Plays. London: Oxford University Press, 1964. Contains *A Dance of the Forests, The Lion and the Jewel, The Swamp Dwellers, The Trials of Brother Jero,* and *The Strong Breed.*

Collected Plays. Vol. 1. London: Oxford University Press, 1973. Contains *A Dance of the Forests, The Swamp Dwellers, The Strong Breed, The Road,* and *The Bacchae of Euripides.*

The Jero Plays. London: Methuen, 1973. Contains *The Trials of Brother Jero* and *Jero's Metamorphosis.*

Collected Plays. Vol. 2. London: Oxford University Press, 1974. Contains *The Lion and the Jewel, Kongi's Harvest, The Trials of Brother Jero, Jero's Metamorphosis,* and *Madmen and Specialists.*

Six Plays. Intro. by Soyinka. London: Methuen, 1984. Contains *The Trials of Brother Jero, Jero's Metamorphosis, Camwood on the Leaves, Death and the King's Horseman, Madmen and Specialists,* and *Opera Wonyosi.*

PLAYS

A Dance of the Forests. London: Oxford University Press, 1963.

The Lion and the Jewel. London: Oxford University Press, 1963.

The Road. London: Oxford University Press, 1965.

Kongi's Harvest. London: Oxford University Press, 1967.

The Trials of Brother Jero. Nairobi, Kenya: Oxford University Press, 1969.

The Strong Breed. Ibadan, Nigeria: Orisun Acting Editions, 1970.

Before the Blackout. Ibadan, Nigeria: Orisun Acting Editions, 1971.

Madmen and Specialists. London: Methuen, 1971; New York: Farrar, Straus & Giroux, 1971.

The Bacchae of Euripides: A Communion Rite. London: Methuen, 1973; New York: Norton, 1974.

Camwood on the Leaves. London: Methuen, 1973.

Death and the King's Horseman. London: Methuen, 1975; New York: Norton, 1975.

Opera Wonyosi. London: Rex Collings, 1981; Bloomington: Indiana University Press, 1981.

A Play of Giants. London: Methuen, 1984; Portsmouth, N.H.: Heinemann, 1988.

Requiem for a Futurologist. London: Rex Collings, 1985.

Childe International. Ibadan: Fountain Publications, 1987. Originally part of *Before the Blackout.*

From Zia, with Love; and, A Scourge of Hyacinths. London: Methuen, 1992.

POETRY

Idanre and Other Poems. London: Methuen, 1967; New York: Hill & Wang, 1968.

A Shuttle in the Crypt. London: Rex Collings/Methuen, 1972; New York: Hill & Wang, 1972.

Ogun Abibiman. London: Rex Collings, 1976.

Mandela's Earth and Other Poems. New York: Random House, 1988; London: Andre Deutsch, 1989.

NOVELS

The Interpreters. London: Andre Deutsch, 1965; London: Heinemann, 1970; New York: Collier, 1970; New York: Holmes & Meier, 1972.

Season of Anomy. London: Rex Collings, 1973; New York: Third Press, 1974; London: Nelson, 1980.

AUTOBIOGRAPHIES

The Man Died: Prison Notes of Wole Soyinka. London: Rex Collings, 1972; New York: Harper & Row, 1973; London: Penguin, 1975; New York: Farrar, Straus & Giroux, 1988.

Aké: The Years of Childhood. London: Rex Collings, 1981; New York: Random House, 1982.

Isara: A Voyage Around "Essay." New York: Random House, 1989; London: Methuen, 1990.

Ibadan, the Penkelmes Years: A Memoir 1946–1965. London: Methuen, 1994. Soyinka describes this as a work of "faction."

CRITICISM

Myth, Literature and the African World. Cambridge, U.K.: Cambridge University Press, 1976.

Art, Dialogue and Outrage: Essays on Literature and Culture. Ibadan, Nigeria: New Horn Press, 1988.

The Open Sore of a Continent: A Personal Narrative of the Nigerian Crisis. New York: Oxford University Press, 1996.

ESSAYS

"Cor, Teach." In *Ibadan* 7 (November 1959).

"The Future of African Writing." In *Horn* 4 (June 1960).

"Amos Tutuola on Stage." In *Ibadan* 16 (June 1962).

"Salutations to the Gut." In Frances Ademola, ed., *Reflections: Nigerian Prose and Verse.* Lagos, Nigeria: African Universities Press, 1962. Repr. in O. R. Dathorne and Willfried Feuser, eds., *Africa in Prose.* London: Penguin, 1969.

"Nigeria's International Film Festival 1962." In *Nigeria Magazine* 79 (December 1963).

"And After the Narcissist?" In *African Forum* 1 (spring 1966).

"Of Power and Change." In *African Statesman* 1 (July–September 1966).

"The Nigerian Stage: A Study in Tyranny and Individual Survival." In *Colloquium on Negro Arts.* Paris: Présence Africaine, 1968.

"The Terrible Understanding." In *Atlas* 15 (January 1968).

"The Choice and Use of Language." In *Cultural Events in Africa* 75 (1971).

"Gbohun-Gbohun—The Nigerian Playwright Wole Soyinka in His Dealings with the BBC." In *Listener* (2 November 1972).

"Ethics, Ideology, and the Critic." In K. H. Petersen, ed., *Criticism and Ideology.* Uppsala, Sweden: Scandinavian Institute of African Studies, 1988.

"Religion and Human Rights." In *Index on Censorship* 5 (May 1988).

"Power and Creative Strategies." In *Index on Censorship* 7 (July 1988).

"This Past Must Address Its Present." In *Black American Literature Forum* 22 (fall 1988). Nobel Prize acceptance speech.

"Bangs Big and Small." In *Weekend Guardian* (21–22 October 1989).

"Twice Bitten: The Fate of Africa's Culture Producers." In *PMLA* 105, no. 1 (1990).

EDITIONS AND TRANSLATIONS

The Forest of a Thousand Daemons. trans. from Yoruba of D. O. Fagunwa, *Ògbójú Ode Nínú Igbó Irúnmalè.* London: Nelson, 1968; Atlantic Highlands, N.J.: Humanities Press, 1969; New York: Random House, 1983.

Poems of Black Africa. Ed. with intro. and biographical notes by Soyinka. London: Heinemann, 1975.

INTERVIEWS

Agretua, John. "Interview with Wole Soyinka in Accra." In Agetua, ed., *When the Man Died.* Benin City, Nigeria: Bendel Newspaper Corp., 1973.

Akarogun, Alan. "Interview with Wole Soyinka." In *Spear* (May 1966).

Borreca, Art. "Idi Amin Was the Supreme Actor: An Interview with Wole Soyinka." In *Theater* 16 (spring 1985).

"Conversations with Chinua Achebe." In *Africa Report* (July 1964). A discussion with Achebe, Lewis Nkosi, and others.

Fabre, Michel, and Jean-Pierre Durix. "Conversations with Wole Soyinka." In *Commonwealth: Essays and Studies* 15 (spring 1993).

Gates, Louis S. "An Interview with Wole Soyinka." In *Black World* 24 (August 1975).

Gibbs, James. "Soyinka in Zimbabwe: A Question and Answer Session" (29 November 1981). In *Literary Half-Yearly* 28 (July 1987).

Gulledge, Jo. "Seminar on *Aké* with Wole Soyinka." In *Southern Review* 23, no. 3 (1987).

Harding, Jeremy. "Interview: Wole Soyinka." In *New Statesman* (27 February 1987).

"Interview." In *The Militant* 2 (December 1972).

Jeyifo, Biodun. "Wole Soyinka: A *Transition* Interview." In *Transition* 42 (1973).

———. "Soyinka at Fifty." In *West Africa* (27 August 1984). Repr. in part as the introduction to *Six Plays*. London: Methuen, 1984.

Katrak, Ketu. "Question and Answer Session with Soyinka at the African Studies Association Conference, Los Angeles, November 1979" and "Interview with Soyinka at the University of Ife, November 1980." In her *Wole Soyinka and Modern Tragedy*. Westport, Conn.: Greenwood Press, 1986.

Morell, Karen L., ed. "Televised Discussion," "Penthouse Theater," and "Class Discussion." In *In Person: Achebe, Awoonor, and Soyinka at the University of Washington*. Seattle: University of Washington, Institute of Comparative and Foreign Area Studies, 1975.

Mphahlele, Ezekiel, Lewis Nkosi, and Dennis Duerden. "Wole Soyinka." In Duerden and Cosmo Pieterse, eds., *African Writers Talking*. London: Heinemann, 1972.

Stotesbury, John A. "Wole Soyinka." In *Kunapipi* 9, no. 1 (1987). Repr. as "The Reader, the Regime and the Writer." In Raoul Grandqvist and Stotesbury, eds., *African Voices: Interviews with Thirteen African Writers*. Sydney, Australia: Dangaroo Press, 1989.

Wilkinson, Jane. "Wole Soyinka." In her *Talking with African Writers*. London: James Currey; Portsmouth, N.H.: Heinemann, 1992.

"The Writer in Africa Today." In *Africa Currents* 7 (autumn 1976–winter 1977).

CRITICAL STUDIES

Adelugba, Dapo, ed. *Before Our Very Eyes: Tribute to Wole Soyinka*. Ibadan, Nigeria: Spectrum, 1987.

Agetua, John. *When the Man Died*. Benin City, Nigeria: Bendel Newspaper Corp., 1975.

Attwell, David. "Wole Soyinka's *The Interpreters*: Suggestions on Context and History." In *English in Africa* 8, no. 1 (1981).

Black American Literature Forum 22 (fall 1988). Special issue on Soyinka.

Booth, James. *Writers and Politics in Nigeria*. London: Hodder & Stoughton, 1981.

———. "Myth, Metaphor, and Syntax in Soyinka's Poetry." In *Research in African Literatures* 17 (spring 1986).

Brockbank, Philip. "Blood and Wine: Tragic Ritual from Aeschylus to Soyinka." In *Shakespeare Survey* 36, no. 1 (1983).

Crow, Brian. "Soyinka and His Radical Critics: A Review." In *Theatre Research International* 12 (spring 1987).

Dunton, Chris P. *Notes on Three Short Plays*. Harlow, U.K.: Longman/York Press, 1982.

Durix, Jean-Pierre, ed. *Commonwealth: Essays and Studies*, no. SP1 (1989). Special issue on *A Dance of the Forests*.

Fraser, Robert. *West African Poetry: A Critical History*. Cambridge, U.K.: Cambridge University Press, 1986.

Gates, Henry Louis, Jr. "Being, the Will, and the Semantics of Death." In *Harvard Educational Review* 51 (February 1981).

Gibbs, James. *Study Aid to* Kongi's Harvest. London: Rex Collings, 1973.

———. *Notes on* The Lion and the Jewel. Harlow, U.K.: Longman/York Press, 1982.

———. "The Masks Hatched Out." In *Theatre Research International* 7 (October 1982).

———. *Wole Soyinka.* London: Macmillan, 1986.

———. "Biography into Autobiography: Wole Soyinka and the Relatives Who Inhabit *Aké*." In *Journal of Modern African Studies* 26 (September 1988).

———, ed. *Critical Perspectives on Wole Soyinka.* Washington, D.C.: Three Continents, 1980; London: Heinemann, 1981.

———, ed. *Research in African Literatures* 14 (spring 1983). Special issue on Soyinka.

———, ed., *Literary Half Yearly* 28 (July 1987). Special issue on Soyinka.

Gikandi, Simon. *Wole Soyinka's* The Road. Nairobi, Kenya: Heinemann, 1985.

Goodwin, Ken. *Understanding African Poetry: A Study of Ten Poets.* London: Heinemann, 1982.

Griffiths, Gareth. *A Double Exile: African and West Indian Writing Between Two Cultures.* London: Marion Boyars, 1978.

Irele, Abiola. *The African Experience in Literature and Ideology.* London: Heinemann, 1981.

Jeyifo, Biodun. *The Truthful Lie: Essays in a Sociology of African Drama.* London: New Beacon Books, 1985.

Jones, Eldred. *The Writing of Wole Soyinka.* London: Heinemann, 1973; Boston: Twayne, 1973. Rev. eds. London: Heinemann, 1983, 1988.

Katrak, Ketu H. *Wole Soyinka and Modern Tragedy: A Study of Dramatic Theory and Practice.* Westport, Conn.: Greenwood Press, 1986.

King, Bruce. *The New English Literatures: Cultural Nationalism in a Changing World.* London: Macmillan, 1980.

Knipp, Thomas R. "Irony, Tragedy, and Myth: The Poetry of Wole Soyinka." In *World Literature Written in English* 21 (spring 1982).

Larsen, Stephen. *A Writer and His Gods: A Study of the Importance of Yoruba Myths and Religious Ideas to the Writings of Wole Soyinka.* Stockholm, Sweden: University of Stockholm, Department of History and Literature, 1983.

Lindfors, Bernth, "Wole Soyinka, When Are You Coming Home?" In *Yale French Studies* 53 (1976).

———. "Begging Questions in Wole Soyinka's *Opera Wonyosi*." In *ARIEL* 12, no. 3 (1981).

———. ed. *Critical Perspectives on Nigerian Literatures.* Washington, D.C.: Three Continents, 1975.

Maduakor, Obi. *Wole Soyinka: An Introduction to His Writing.* New York: Garland Press, 1986.

Maugham-Brown, David. "Interpreting and *The Interpreters*: Wole Soyinka and Practical Criticism." In *English in Africa* 6, no. 2 (1978).

Moore, Gerald. *Wole Soyinka.* London: Evans, 1971. Rev. ed., 1978.

———. *Twelve African Writers.* London: Hutchinson, 1980.

Ogunba, Oyin. "The Traditional Content of the Plays of Wole Soyinka." In *African Literature Today* 3 and 5 (1969 and 1971).

———. *The Movement of Transition: A Study of the Plays of Wole Soyinka.* Ibadan, Nigeria: Ibadan University Press, 1975.

Olney, James. "*Aké*: Wole Soyinka as Autobiographer." In *Yale Review* 73 (1983).

Osofisan, Femi. "Tiger on Stage: Wole Soyinka and Nigerian Theatre." In Oyin Ogunba and Abiola Irele, eds., *Theatre in Africa.* Ibadan, Nigeria: Ibadan University Press, 1978.

Osundare, Niyi. "Words of Iron, Sentences of Thunder: Soyinka's Prose Style." In *African Literature Today* 13 (1983).

Peters, Jonathan A. *A Dance of Masks: Senghor, Achebe, Soyinka.* Washington, D.C.: Three Continents, 1978.

Priebe, Richard K. "On Form and Ideology, with Specific Attention to Soyinka's *Aké*." In Stephen Arnold, ed., *African Literature Studies: The Present State.* Washington, D.C.: Three Continents, 1985.

———. *Myth, Realism and the West African Writer.* Trenton, N.J.: Africa World Press, 1988.

Probyn, Clive. *Notes on* The Road. Harlow, U.K.: Longman/York Press, 1981.

———. "Waiting for the Word: Samuel Beckett and Wole Soyinka." In *ARIEL* 12, no. 3 (1981).

Roscoe, Adrian. *Mother Is Gold: A Study in West African Literature.* Cambridge, U.K.: Cambridge University Press, 1971.

Sotto, Wiveca. *The Rounded Rite: A Study of Wole Soyinka's Play* The Bacchae of Euripides. Malmö, Sweden: CWK Gleerup/Lund, 1985.

Wright, Derek. "The Ritual Context of Two Plays by Soyinka." In *Theatre Research International* 12 (spring 1987).

———. "The Festive Year: Wole Soyinka's *Annus Mirabilis.*" In *Journal of Modern African Studies* 28, no. 3 (1990).

———. "Ritual and Revolution: Soyinka's Dramatic Theory." In *ARIEL* 23, no. 1 (1992).

———. "Soyinka Past and Present." In *Journal of Modern African Studies* 30 (December 1992).

———. "Soyinka's Smoking Shotgun: The Later Satires." In *World Literature Today* 66 (February 1992).

———. *Wole Soyinka Revisited.* New York: Twayne, 1993.

Efua Theodora Sutherland

1924–1996

JAMES GIBBS

EFUA THEODORA SUTHERLAND'S "New Life at Kyerefaso" (1960) is one of the two most frequently anthologized pieces of prose by African writers, along with "The Complete Gentleman," a story from *The Palm-Wine Drinkard and His Dead Palm-Wine Tapster in the Deads' Town* (1952) by the Nigerian writer Amos Tutuola. Both stories originate in a folktale that is told in various ways along the West African coast. Briefly, it is the story of a proud young woman who rejects all the local suitors and marries a stranger, only to discover that he is a monster.

The tale has been interpreted in different ways. Tutuola, in a magnificent display of inventiveness, reduces the "complete gentleman," who cuts a dashing figure in the market, to a skull and puts the shallow young woman who was attracted by his outward appearance into a perilous position. Sutherland's version radically departs from both the original and Tutuola's retelling: her stranger impresses not through his appearance but because "he... mingles sweat and song," because for him "toil is joy and life is full and abundant." Foruwa, the young woman, is not proud but perceptive, not scornful of local suitors but appreciative of a man who has "travelled to see how men work in other lands" and has "that knowledge and . . . strength."

The stranger's craftsmanship—his skills as a builder, farmer, and weaver of baskets and *kente* cloth—impresses first Foruwa and then the community. A true inspiration, his example is followed, and, the storyteller informs the audience, "A new spirit stirred the village.... The people themselves became more alive and a new pride possessed them. They were no longer just grabbing from the land what they desired for their stomach's present hunger and for their present comfort." The brief story ends with a procession in which the fruits of the harvest are carried to the royal house where Foruwa's mother, the Queen Mother, waits to receive them. In this retelling of the story, which provides part of the plot of Sutherland's play *Foriwa* (1967), the young woman and her mother occupy center stage for much of the time. Foruwa makes a wise choice in accepting the stranger, and the "new spirit" that stirs in the village promises an illustrious future. Rough parallels can be drawn between Sutherland—her life and work—and "New Life at Kyerefaso," her most frequently published story.

CAPE COAST

Efua Sutherland (née Morgue) was born in Cape Coast, Ghana (then the British colony of the Gold Coast), on 27 June 1924, named Nana Ama Nyankoma, and christened Theodora Olivia. The castles of Elmina, built in 1482 near where the European incursion into West Africa began, and of Cape Coast, constructed by Swedes in the 1650s, dominate the area and provide constant reminders of the centuries of contact between the coastal Fanti community into which Sutherland was born and Europe. Dungeons in which Africans had been imprisoned before being transported to the plantations of the Americas and rusting canons projecting over battlements draw attention to the inhumanity and violence of much of that contact.

Sutherland was related to those who had contributed significantly to the life of the local community. Her family included members of the royal house of Anomabu and nationalists who had joined the pioneering Aborigines' Rights Protection Society. Sutherland's mother, Olivia Morgue, was killed in a car accident at the age of eighteen. Following the accident, Sutherland's father, Harry Peter Morgue, a much respected teacher of English and other subjects, and her grandmother, Arba Mansah, became important influences.

During the first part of the twentieth century, Cape Coast developed into a major center for education, and Sutherland began her schooling at Saint Monica's School, an Anglican school founded in 1926 and staffed by Sisters of the Order of the Holy Paraclete, based in Yorkshire, England. She continued her education in Asante-Mampong, where the Sisters had a convent and primary boarding school. In 1936 the teacher training college, which the Sisters had established at Cape Coast, moved to Asante-Mampong, and in 1946 a secondary school was opened there. Sutherland became deeply involved with these institutions.

One of Sutherland's uncles was at Saint Monica's brother school, St. Nicholas Grammar School, Cape Coast, which later became Adisadel College. The school had important positions in a town that was sometimes called "the Athens of West Africa" and, in addition to academic and athletic activities, contributed to the cultural life of the community. For example, drama flourished at Adisadel, where the Athenian tradition was manifest in a series of productions of plays by classical dramatists: Sophocles' *Antigone* in 1934–1935, Aeschylus' *Agamemnon* in 1936, and Euripides' *Alcestis* in 1944–1945. In his history of the school, G. McLean Amissah reports that the choruses were spoken in Greek and that, by popular request, the production of *Antigone* was staged not only at the school but also in the town, in Sekondi, and in Kumasi.

TEACHING

From an early age, Sutherland expressed an interest in teaching, and in a sense her whole career reflects this vocation. At the age of about eighteen she started teaching at senior primary level and then joined the staff of Saint Monica's Training College. From 1947 to 1950 she was in England, first at Homerton College, Cambridge, and then, for a year, at the School of Oriental and African Studies at the University of London. On her return to the Gold Coast, she went back to Asante-Mampong and later transferred to Fijai Secondary School in Sekondi, and from there to Achimota School.

These moves are easily recorded, but the changes they involved and the experiences they afforded are more difficult to assess. First, when she left Cape Coast to continue her education in Asante-Mampong, a town beyond Kumasi, Sutherland was exposed to communities that had been comparatively little affected by European influences. Her coastal Fanti accent was distinct from the Akan spoken in the inland town. Some of the students who moved with the school from Cape Coast were frightened by the new environment and felt hemmed in by the forest and all that it contained.

On spacious premises with large playing fields, the students at Asante-Mampong could concentrate in a way that was not possible in crowded Cape Coast with all its distractions. The Sisters were making a substantial contribution to educating women in the country, drawing strength from their religious convictions and their base within the Anglican Church. Their missionary zeal was often communicated to the pupils, who were encouraged to contribute to improving the quality of life in nearby villages, in some of which Sunday schools had been started. One of the villages Sutherland visited was Kyerefaso, whose name she took for the title of her best-known story. In the villages, Sutherland developed an interest in nature and the environment, which the Sisters encouraged, and her experiences strengthened her feeling that her vocation was to be a teacher. At this stage, however, her vocation was intensely religious, and she considered becoming a nun.

In 1947, at the age of twenty-three and with five and a half years of teaching experience, Sutherland set off for England with a great sense of adventure to begin a two-year teacher-training course at Homerton College in Cambridge. She was impressed by the high standards, experimentation, and planning at the college and by the way her lecturers encouraged her desire to orient her work toward Africa. During her time at Homerton, where she specialized in education and divinity, she impressed those she worked with. They recorded their appreciation of her maturity, her personality, her care in preparing lessons, and the trouble she took to communicate clearly. Not surprisingly she conveyed to her geography classes a vivid sense of what it was like to live in Africa, and her English classes included not only textual analyses of Shakespeare's plays but also storytelling sessions.

From the beginning of her time in England, as she wrote in an August 1949 letter reproduced in an undated issue of *St. Monica Calling*, she resolved to keep her eyes and ears "wide open" and to ask many questions. The two years in Cambridge whetted her appetite for "work among students in [her] own country" (p. 26). Her exposure to the children's books and the material available to teachers in England was a revelation. What she saw made her determined to provide African children with books that reflected their own experiences and were attractively produced.

After leaving Cambridge, she went to London, where she spent a year at the University of London's School of Oriental and African Studies, specializing in English linguistics. She also took an interest in African languages and drama, which she saw as being taken seriously by academics and teachers. London in the late 1940s and early 1950s provided opportunities to meet some of those in the forefront of the struggle for African political and cultural independence.

Interviewed by Maxine Lautre in 1968, Sutherland spoke about being on "a journey of discovery" and referred to her Christian upbringing in Cape Coast, which had not exposed her to certain "hidden areas of Ghanaian life" (p. 189). She told Lee Nichols that she began taking writing seriously at Easter 1951, shortly after her return home from England, and started composing poetry. She indicated that the needs of children in the villages and of the student-teachers she was supervising stimulated her. The intense spiritual life of the Sisters of the Order of the Holy Paraclete may also have affected some of this verse and contributed a religious dimension.

In the early 1950s she married William Sutherland, an African American from Orange, New Jersey, who became involved in establishing a partly vocational school at Tsito in the Volta Region. When talking of this project, which encountered opposition from entrenched British prejudices, Sutherland gives great credit to her husband, who remained at the school from 1951 to 1957 before returning to Accra and then moving on to work with such organizations as the Non-Violent League and the World Peace Brigade. The couple's three children, Esi Reiter, Ralph Gyan, and Muriel Amowi, who have since become a university teacher, an architect, and a lawyer, respectively, helped their mother in several theatrical projects.

CREATING A NATIONAL THEATRICAL TRADITION

The task of creating a national theatrical tradition was undertaken with a new urgency during the second half of the 1950s as the Gold Coast approached and, in 1957, achieved independence as Ghana. In addition to festivals, folk narratives, and performance conventions, the relevant traditions in the Gold Coast included creative writing both in local languages, such as Twi, Ewe, and Ga, and in English. There was also a history of literary societies in which cultural and political aspirations found expression.

In 1957, a writers' society came into existence with Sutherland as the prime mover. Eleven years later she told Lautre, "I started a Writers' Society . . . to get more people interested in [writing] primarily... for children" (p. 184). The new organization, supported by such distinguished and established authors as J. B. Danquah, J. H. Kwabena Nketia, and Michael Dei-Anang, recognized the need to produce a journal, which resulted in the publication of *Okyeame.*

In 1958 Sutherland was the driving force in creating the Ghana Experimental Theatre. She told Lautre: "To give another reason why people would want to write I... develop[ed] the experimental theatre programme" (p. 184). It built on existing interest in the theater and on an awareness that festivals and rituals were frequently spectacular and, in many instances, contained ingredients of the theater. The production of plays at schools, at teacher training colleges, and for radio blossomed. Since these were dominated by naturalistic conventions and stage plays were almost always presented behind proscenium arches, there was room for experiment. With the interest in "African personality" that marked the late 1950s and changing attitudes toward folk and popular culture came a greater acceptance of the traditions of drama and theater within Akan culture and within the mixture of cultures that had long flourished in towns near the coast, such as Cape Coast, Sekondi, and Takoradi.

The writers' society and the Experimental Theatre group came into existence when Ghana was at the forefront of the independence movement in sub-Saharan Africa. Prime Minister Kwame Nkrumah, who had a high profile as a spokesman for Pan-Africanism, proclaimed the importance of the arts in society and took a personal interest in several of Sutherland's projects. The national coffers were well stocked, and new life seemed to be flowing through the country. Sutherland's eloquence and striking presence, her contacts and ability to draw the best out of others propelled her into leadership roles. She became identified with the cultural and political movement that was bringing together different generations and different disciplines and uniting Ghanaians and those from the diaspora who had "returned" to share in the adventure of the independent nation. Her contribution to the movement was complemented by the work of others, such as Philip Gbeho in music, Kofi Antubam in art, J. H. Kwabena Nketia in research, and Joe de Graft in the theater.

POETRY

Developing a literary culture and taking the national theater movement into a new phase were slow processes. Laying foundations took time, and only after several years was it possible to identify achievements. Although her published output was small and her accomplishment in the form limited, Sutherland first made an impact as a poet. She began writing verse during the 1950s that was initially published in Germany. In 1957 four poems appeared under her maiden name in *An Anthology of West African Verse*, which was edited in Ibadan, Nigeria, and during the 1970s her work was included in two other collections.

The verses she contributed to *Messages: Poems from Ghana* (1971) are representative of her strengths and weaknesses. "The Redeemed" shows her feeling for the dramatic, her preoccupation with religion, and her tendency to use obtrusive inversions of the natural word order. The Keatsian description "And the poison in me boiled / And clotted in the glare" is followed by the less ambitious but more successful pacing of the concluding lines:

> The copper neck swerved back with its load,
> And down the slope of the market road,
> She strode.
>
> (p. 159)

Confident, accomplished, and decisive women, like the one in this poem, are frequently central to Sutherland's work. There may be several reasons for this: she came from a community in which women played important political, social, and economic roles, and she went to a single-sex school run by Sisters who, by setting up educational institutions, had provided examples of what dedicated and purposeful women could achieve. But this is not to say that her presentation of women and of the position of women in society has been accepted without comment: the perspective of her more assertive fellow Fanti playwright Ama Ata Aidoo provides a striking contrast in several respects, and the profile of Sutherland by Chikwenye Okonjo Ogunyemi raises gender issues sharply and faults her work on sexual-political grounds.

The poetic control in "The Redeemed" is not evident in the metrically confused "Once Upon a Time," but it returns when she tackles another religious theme in "The Dedication." In this meditative poem, biblical echoes and images contribute to an exploration of the meaning of Christ's sacrifice and allow Sutherland to lead up to the metaphysical paradox of a "Blossoming / Cross," an image that might have appealed to the English poet and divine George Herbert.

"Song of the Fishing Ghosts" is a poem for several voices and has a distinctly dramatic quality. A blend of the lyrical and menacing, it seems to have slipped into the collection of verse from a volume of "rhythm plays" (*Vulture! Vulture!*, 1968) that Sutherland prepared for children. "A Professional Beggar's Lullaby" (p. 167), with its awkward diction ("a prodigy beggar kid") and odd descriptions ("that swanky beat"), indicates that Sutherland's touch is far from certain in this form. She left a substantial body of unpublished poetry that may occasion a reappraisal of her achievement; at present she enjoys a higher reputation as a dramatic poet than as a versifier.

OKYEAME

In 1961 the first issue of the literary journal *Okyeame* appeared. Although active in the background, Sutherland was not part of the editorial committee, which was made up of E. A. Winful, Geormbeeyi Adali-Mortty, and Cecile McHardy. They recorded their gratitude to Kofi Baako and the Arts Council of Ghana for "encouragement and assistance," which suggests that the publication benefited from the government's policy of subsidizing the arts. The format chosen, strikingly reminiscent of the Nigerian publication *Black Orpheus*, was expensive: the paper thick, the layout generous, the artwork extensive. The title of the journal was taken from the Akan word for the "linguist" or "spokesman" through whom a leader speaks to his people and formed a link with the past while clearly rooting the project in the present and looking toward the future. The first issue included fifteen poems and three works of prose fiction, one of which was a short story titled "Samantaase Village" by Sutherland.

In "Samantaase Village" Sutherland retells a familiar story in an elegant and unobtrusive style that reveals her skill as a storyteller in maintaining interest. A village plagued by nymphs, dryads, or "spirit beings associated with the forest" is saved by Afrum, whom many have regarded as a fool. Afrum meets cunning with cunning and childishness with childishness, but in a time of trouble, the despised misfit is discovered to have the skills society needs; his worth is recognized, and he is made a chief.

Sutherland's interest in a story that celebrates the spirit of playfulness and "the holy fool" recurs in *Playtime in Africa* (1960), a pictorial essay for children with text by Sutherland and illustrations by Willis Bell, a photographer with whom she worked closely for several years. An unsigned review in the first issue of *Okyeame* recommends the book as "fun" and defines "fun" as "the exercise of ingenuity, imagination and skill" (p. 44). It is clear that Sutherland gave priority to communicating—particularly with children—and identified a social role for the artist as one who both celebrates and participates in the life of the community. Showing determination and an ability to improvise, she and Bell published the book themselves in 1960. Their belief in it was confirmed when it was subsequently brought out by a Soviet publisher, and later still by Atheneum in the United States. Incidentally, this publication history reveals the cultural and political orientation of Ghana under and after Nkrumah: there were links to both the east and the west with the eventual ascendancy of American influences.

ANANSEGORO, A LOCAL DRAMATIC FORM

What an interest in folk stories and in play might mean in theatrical terms was conveyed by Sutherland's short account of a performance given by the Ghana Experimental Theatre Players in the courtyard of a teacher training college in Akropong on 27 March 1959. The occasion had been shaped to resemble the kind of storytelling session that might have been held the night before in one of the homes that stretched along the road beside the college. In such a context a storyteller recounts a familiar tale, impersonating a number of characters in the course of the narrative. There are formalized exchanges between the storyteller and the spectators and opportunities for members of the audience to interrupt the story in order to sing relevant songs. Such songs are referred to as *mboguo*, which is often translated as "interlude" or "musical interlude."

The event at the college, as described by Sutherland in "Venture into Theatre" (1961), also shared some features with productions mounted by touring companies in Europe: it had been advertised in advance, admission required a ticket, a set had been constructed, and the actors, who took on individual roles, came from out of town and had rehearsed meticulously. The combination of traditions was most apparent in the chorus of performers: they made the responses and produced a singer who led the relevant songs. Sutherland refers to this dramatic form as *anansegoro*, or spider play. In "Venture into Theatre" she explains that *anansegoro*

> was coined from Anansesem (Spider Stories) which is the traditional name for a popular class of Folk-Tales of the Akan. Ananse (The Spider) is a constant character of the Ananse Tales. The character is called Spider because of the role of cunning and ingenuity he plays. Obviously created as a vehicle for satire, the Ananse Folk-Tales are a marvellous source material for dramatic use. Recreated and contemporarised [*sic*] they offer exciting food for dramatists in this country.
>
> (p. 48)

Like others before her, Sutherland set out to develop a national theatrical tradition from existing sources. Toward the end of "Venture into Theatre," she wrote a few sentences about the group's second experiment, which was to create *asafogoro*, "big drama along the lines of Greek tragedy," based on the odes sung by the male groups that form the country's Asafo companies. Nothing seems to have come of this plan, and it is for her work in developing the *anansegoro* tradition, in creating opportunities for drama, and as a writer that Sutherland made her place.

THE DRAMA STUDIO: A BASE IN ACCRA

While the Experimental Theatre Players were preparing the *anansegoro*, Sutherland was addressing the problem of creating a suitable space for rehearsal and performance. After some time without a base, a bungalow in Accra, Ghana's capital, was secured, and then, with funding from such organizations as the Fairfield, Arthur Sloan, Rockefeller, and Ford Foundations and from the government's Arts Council, the Drama Studio was constructed. In *An African Voice: The Role of the Humanities in African Independence*, Robert W. July, an academic who worked for the Rockefeller Foundation at the time, provides an invaluable account of this project and of Sutherland's work within the national theater movement.

With an entrance inspired by the design of Asante stools, the Drama Studio was essentially an enclosed space with a raised and covered platform on one side that could be used for fairly conventional productions or as part of the auditorium. The building, intended to provide a forum for theatrical experiments, was inaugurated by a performance of Sutherland's *Odasani*, an Akan version of the English morality play *Everyman* from the late fifteenth century, in the presence of Nkrumah on 21 October 1960.

FORIWA: THE FIRST MAJOR PLAY

In the Drama Studio with twenty-eight members of the Studio Players, a new group, Sutherland's first major play, *Foriwa*, opened in March 1962. As might have been anticipated, in the light of Sutherland's interest in *anansegoro* and her emphasis on communication, the performance was in Akan. (The English text was published in 1967 by the State Publishing Corporation.) The play has much in common with the short story "New Life at Kyerefaso." The underlying situation is the same, indeed there is even a reference to the folktale on which both works are based, but the plot has been "recreated and contemporarised." Foriwa of the play is Foruwa of the story; she is a teacher visiting her hometown where her mother, a powerful woman anxiously looking out for signs of new life in the community, is the Queen Mother. The "stranger" of the story is Labaran, a university graduate and a Hausa, who has been in the village for a short while when the play opens. In that time he has worked with his hands to clear away rubbish from near the main street, and he has set in motion plans that will improve local agricultural practices. He has also taken steps to transform the postmaster's ramshackle bookstore in a dilapidated street into a center for enlightenment—a place where newspapers and books, especially well-illustrated children's books, can be bought.

The play begins at daybreak on the eve of a purification ceremony with a speech by Labaran directed to the audience and with Foriwa's rejection of a pompous and conceited suitor. In the course of the day, she learns what Labaran has been doing for the community and, predictably, agrees to marry him. The play, which also explores the Queen Mother's belief that small-mindedness and stultifying litigation should be swept away, ends with the coming together of the community in a festive mood, the presentation of gifts, a performance by an Asafo company, and the promise that new life will come to the village.

A busy, crowded play, *Foriwa* draws on various sources, is full of insights into life in Ghanaian villages, and moves to a spectacular conclusion. Gay Wilentz sees it in terms of Sutherland's concern with the "kind of values that are being passed on to the children" and has described the play as "working toward the resolution of [certain] cultural conflicts by utilizing orature and literature as vehicles for the revitalization of rural communities" (p. 194). The climax shows Sutherland working through festival theater, rather than narrative, to make an impact.

While drawing on local folk traditions, incorporating spectacular elements from traditional culture, and delighting in the comic deflation of certain social groups, the play is clearly intelligible within the European tradition and is transparently propagandist. Time and again issues close to the author's heart come to the fore, including the role of women in revitalizing communities and the need to provide books for children. There is also a deliberate attempt to contribute to nation building: Labaran is a Hausa from the north but, because he is a Ghanaian, he is not a "stranger."

The problem with Sutherland's proposed solutions to how a community's ills can be cured in this play is that they often seem inadequate. For example, Labaran is clearly anxious to provide for the physical and spiritual—or intellectual—needs of the community. In this context a bookstore has its place, but the question remains: Will this one have a high enough turnover to remain in business? In fact, one constantly feels inadequately informed about the financial implications of actions and undertakings: one inevitably asks, for example, how Labaran can afford the investments he makes. Sutherland's play neither confronts such issues nor provides a sufficiently general pattern of community development for it to be read as "a parable for the theatre." As a result, *Foriwa* is more instructive as a piece of theater that uses traditional material in a contemporary context than as a blueprint for development or a prototype of didactic drama.

EDUFA: A MIXED ANCESTRY

Eight months after the premiere of *Foriwa*, Sutherland presented Accra theatergoers with her second major dramatic text, *Edufa* (1967). We have already seen that she had been exposed to the tradition of classical theater in Cape Coast, that she aspired to create "big drama along the lines of Greek tragedy," and that she was interested in "recreating and contemporarising." With this background, it was not entirely surprising that her next play should be a reworking of Euripides' *Alcestis* set in contemporary Ghana.

Despite being caught up in the problems that adapting Greek plays to an African setting inevitably creates, *Edufa* stands on its own. Many have responded to its poignant mixture of moods and its theatrical qualities without being aware of its links with ancient Greece. Indeed the play has several strengths, including the chorus of women who help to establish the mood and become involved in the action. They fulfill some functions similar to those of a chorus in the Greek original or in *anansegoro*, but they are thoroughly integrated into the text. Senchi, the Heracles figure from *Alcestis*, is also successfully reworked: he comes across as vivid, amusing, and distinctively West African. The humor and comedy that accompany him mingle effectively with the somber mood created by the threat hanging over the household of Edufa.

In her re-creation Sutherland exploits some of the similarities between ancient Greece and contemporary Ghana, which made the productions at Adisadel compelling for Cape Coast audiences. She relishes the dramatic effectiveness of communicating through symbols and preaches a sermon against materialism. But, as with the closing moments of *Foriwa*, the confident handling of moods and of ritual action lifts the play above adaptations of European originals by other African writers.

ACADEMIC CAREER

In 1963 Sutherland moved to the Institute of African Studies at the University of Ghana, Legon. While enjoying a degree of professional security as a research associate, she remained in touch with her previous projects—indeed she took some of them with her, such as her work on *Okyeame*. Delays in publication, possibly occasioned by uncertainty about finances and printers, meant that the second volume of the journal did not appear until 1964 and that by 1969 there had been only four issues. During this period, Sutherland emerged from the shadows: she became editor, with an editorial committee that varied somewhat but frequently included Geormbeeyi Adali-Mortty, Jawa Apronti, E. Ofori Akyea, and Kojo Gyinaye Kyei. Over the same period, the involvement of the Writers' Workshop gradually diminished, and the Institute of African Studies of the University of Ghana, Legon, became the sole publisher.

After its maiden issue, the journal abandoned its lavish format and adopted a more modest appearance. It brought a series of poets to the attention of readers, printed chapters from novels and scenes from plays, fostered an awareness of literary issues, chronicled achievements, and hosted debates about the direction of Ghanaian fiction, poetry, and drama. One of the liveliest topics of debate was language, and Sutherland's commitment to Akan, the language in which she originally wrote her major plays, was indicated by the inclusion of poems in that language and by her translations from Akan to English. Poets who wrote in Akan were brought to the attention of a wider community as a result of her labor. In her role as translator, as in much else, Sutherland showed how ready she was to collaborate and cooperate, to open doors and create opportunities.

She also continued experimenting with dramatic forms. One of the productions mounted was of a play that greatly interested her for some years, *Lady Precious Stream*, an old Chinese text translated into English according to its traditional style by S. I. Hsiung. The play had made a considerable impact in London when produced in 1934 because of its complete rejection of illusionistic theater and the economical, effective, and direct convention it employed. The cast included Property Men, who, as an introductory speech by the Reader, or narrator, makes clear, "are supposed to be unseen by the audience" though they are frequently onstage assisting performers and arranging the set. The Reader then introduces the main characters, and as the play unfolds, issues of choice, framed in the context of choice of a marriage partner, come to the fore in a manner that recalls Sutherland's own writing. It seems likely that she found both the convention and the theme of the play relevant to the search that preoccupied her: the quest for a theatrical tradition accessible to ordinary Ghanaians that embodied the perceptions found in the character around which many Akan folktales were woven, Ananse the spider.

A VILLAGE THEATER PROJECT

Sutherland's contributions to *Okyeame* took many forms, and she operated simultaneously on a variety of fronts. For example, in 1968 E. Ofori Akyea wrote on the experiment in village theater that Sutherland had fostered at Atwia-Ekumfi, and the following year an extract from *The Marriage of Anansewa* (1975) was published in the journal. In Atwia, a village of five hundred inhabitants in the Ekumfi district of the Central Region, a Kodzidan—a story house, house of stories, or theater—had been constructed. Ofori Akyea wrote that it was an eleven-sided structure with a "stepped-down area . . . flanked by a higher level stage. . . . The back wall of the stage arcs gracefully, and there is a door to the dressing room at each end of the arc" (p. 82). According to the article, *kodzi* is a form of the folktale in which, as in *anansesem*, the narrator may be interrupted by those who want to sing or to provide comic relief through jokes, clowning, or wearing outlandish clothes.

In a manner that would have delighted Foruwa and Foriwa, the Kodzidan had not only added to a vigorous tradition of performance and entertainment but also brought money into the community. Ofori Akyea reported that income from performances was spent on the construction of a cooperative store, and fees from filming financed an extension of the local school. Furthermore, the Kodzidan had provided a venue for a children's drama group—a sphere of activity that Sutherland had long been interested in developing. The Atwia-Ekumfi project, which is described in some detail by July in *An African Voice*, continued to flourish and to bear unanticipated fruit late into the twentieth century. For example, sons and daughters of the village residents established a storytelling group in Accra.

Up to the time of her death, Sutherland's involvement with Atwia was consistent with her attitudes toward village communities, particularly village women, as custodians of cultural traditions and toward children as resourceful and creative elements in society. She told Nichols that "the village [communities]... have done a wonderful thing for the country. They have minded the culture. [They] are the people whom we ought to thank for what has been maintained of the culture" (1981, p. 280). She insisted that it was the "village community" that constituted the important audience: "That," she said, "is where your critics are" (p. 285).

Ofori Akyea seemed to be quoting Sutherland more or less verbatim when he wrote:

> Before the Ghanaian child goes to school he is such an imaginative and intelligent being. Before he is ten he is something else. Just what happens in the classroom must be found out.... the Ghanaian child living in an adult world develops two languages—a language for the adult world as well as a children's language. School ignores this remarkable linguistic advantage. (pp. 83–84)

Part of the experiment at Atwia was to encourage children to live vigorously in their imaginations and recognize the value of their own "language."

In 1968 Sutherland published *Vulture! Vulture!: Two Rhythm Plays*. These texts for children, *Vulture! Vulture!* and *Tahinta*, exist at one end of the spectrum of her idea of drama—at the point where drama and children's games are barely distinguishable. There is minimal authorial intervention: the plays are simple stories that have been combined with well-known children's songs or well-structured games of make-believe in order to form scripts. However, the texts, the photographs by Willis Bell, and the music arranged by Kwasi Baiden make it possible to re-create the "games" and to "produce" the plays. Sutherland wrote other plays for children, some drawing on European sources and some on African inspiration, in which she tries to preserve, share, and enrich the lives of Ghanaian children. Once again, her method was essentially based on collaboration, and, once again, it found an institutional structure: beginning in 1974 she developed some of these ideas through the Children's Drama Development Project.

THE MARRIAGE OF ANANSEWA: A FULLY FLEDGED *ANANSEGORO*

The excerpt from *The Marriage of Anansewa* that was published in *Okyeame* in 1969 provides an indication of the date by which a scripted, English version of part of the play was in existence. The full text did not appear until 1975—the kind of delay that became the norm with Sutherland's work. The text includes a foreword, in which she writes about the origin of *anansegoro*, the significance of Ananse—"a kind of Everyman, artistically exaggerated and distorted to serve society as a medium for self-examination" (p. v)—the function of the musical interludes or *mboguo*, and the problems encountered in attempting to invoke the "element of community participation" (p. vii).

The plot of the play is quickly outlined: impoverished Ananse encourages each of four chiefs to believe himself the favored suitor for the hand of his beautiful daughter, Anansewa; Ananse expects and receives gifts from each of them. When the suitors all decide to visit the young woman, Ananse extricates himself from embarrassment by announcing that she has just died. This brings a further batch of gifts; it also brings a message from Chief-Who-Is-Chief. He alone is prepared to fulfill all the obligations of a widower, and Ananse escapes from his predicament by proclaiming that this heartfelt expression of true love has been strong enough to bring Anansewa back to life. As the spectacle ends, the marriage of Anansewa and Chief-Who-Is-Chief is anticipated.

The cast for the play requires about twenty-five performers, but that number can be increased or, if necessary and by means of doubling, decreased. When not involved in the action, the performers are required by the playwright to be "grouped together as a unified pool of music-makers, dancers, actors, *and as a participating audience*" (p. ix). Props are, as in *Lady Precious Stream*, handed to the performers in full view of the audience by Property Man.

The play draws strength from Sutherland's knowledge of the aspirations and problems of her community, her ear for dialogue, her ability (partly exercised through Storyteller) to control the pace and tension, and her incorporation of various performing arts and rites of passage into the drama. It is written with verve, wit, and energy, but the playwright does not feel obliged to comment in any depth on Ananse's actions: a collaborator with the tradition, she simply presents the community's perception of the trickster hero and expects the audience to pass its own judgments. Inevitably this attitude has attracted criticism, yet the play, her most elaborate *anansegoro* text, represents a substantial contribution to the debate about the form of African drama.

KUSUM AGOROMBA: A PROFESSIONAL COMPANY

Before the Longman edition appeared, *The Marriage of Anansewa* had already been produced in Akan and English by three different groups: the Workers' Brigade Drama Group, Kusum Agoromba, and Kusum Agoromba in collaboration with the Drama Studio Players. In a statement about the group and its productions, Sutherland described Kusum Agoromba as "a full-time drama company established in 1968," based at the Drama Studio, and dedicated to performing "quality plays in Akan...in towns and villages all over the country, for the general public and for specialised audiences such as church congregations, clubs and associations" (*Kusum Agoromba Presentations*, 1968).

It was appropriate that, after the Experimental Theatre group and the Drama Studio Players, there should be a company that, like Sutherland herself, was committed to using Akan, the most widely spoken language in Ghana, as a vehicle for contemporary drama and for contributing to the national theater movement. In an interview with Nichols, she explained the company's name: "*Kusum* means the right cultural thing to do.... *Agoromba* means players" (1981, p. 284). Doing the right cultural thing clearly involved performing in Akan.

Kusum Agoromba represented Sutherland's major achievement in creating a professional theater company, and inevitably she faced problems of training, equipment, finance, organization, transportation, and communications. The brochure she wrote in 1968 shows the seriousness with which the task of assembling a repertoire was tackled and the extent of the group's success in putting shows together. The productions, all of which were in Akan and several of which had strong musical components, were *Odasani*; *Yaa Konadu*, a version of Anton Chekhov's *A Marriage Proposal* (1889); *Blood Is Mysterious*; *The Rumor-Monger's Fate*; *Love for Your Neighbor*, a musical play based on Robert Kofi Hihetah's novel *The Painful Road to Kadjebi* (published in 1966); *God's Time Is the Best*; *Foriwa*; and three Ananse plays—*The Marriage of Anansewa*, *You Swore an Oath* (published in 1964), and *Ananse and the Dwarf Brigade*.

The productions, which varied in length from forty minutes to two hours, represented a total of over fifteen hours of drama and, taken together, constitute a substantial achievement. The company required was large, though not necessarily as large as the twenty-eight-strong group used for the first production of *Foriwa*.

In a sense, Kusum Agoromba was both a product and a victim of Ghana's metaphorical and actual climate. During the 1970s and 1980s, political instability, high inflation, and drought radically affected the social and cultural aspirations and forms of expression of the community. Eventually, in 1987, the group became a victim of changing circumstances and of the demolition of the Drama Studio in Accra. The company was reorganized, though some members found openings at Legon and were able to continue acting.

THE ORIGINAL BOB

Sutherland's commitment to build up and provide for Kusum Agoromba, a burdensome task requiring immense resources of patience and tact, did not absorb all her energy. This was partly because of able and reliable assistants, such as Sandy Arkhurst and Alan Tamakloe, to whom she could delegate responsibilities with confidence. Her position at the Institute of African Studies involved an obligation to carry out research, and while much of her time was spent on practical projects, there was also writing to be done. In 1970 she published the fruits of her research into the life and work of Bob Johnson, one of the founders of the Ghanaian concert-party tradition, a form that had emerged from the fusion of local and imported traditions in the 1930s.

Titled *The Original Bob: The Story of Bob Johnson, Ghana's Ace Comedian*, the twenty-five-page booklet published by an Accra-based publisher "in association with" Ghana Drama Studio Publications, draws on interviews with Johnson and on long acquaintance with concert parties in performance. It traces the life of the man described as "the Father of the Concert Party" and outlines the development of the tradition of comic plays, which may have begun in Sekondi during the first decades of the century.

Since Johnson had founded a theater company and operated as a creator of plays, some illuminating parallels can be drawn between his career and Sutherland's. Johnson was, like Sutherland, a Fanti, the ethnic group most closely associated with drama in Ghana, and, like her, he found that political independence created both opportunities and complications. For example, after independence, Johnson became involved in the Workers' Brigade No. 1 Drama Group, which, while enjoying a considerable measure of state support, was expected to work uncomfortably closely with the Convention People's Party, which was in power. The profile, like Sutherland's other academic essays, is written in a balanced, elegant, and accessible manner. Published inexpensively as a pamphlet, it made a slice of Ghana's theater history available to a relatively large public.

CONCLUSION

In the last decades of her life Sutherland kept on pursuing and broadening the ambitious projects that were begun in the exciting days of striving for and achieving Ghana's independence. Her continued concern with the examination of the country's theatrical heritage resulted in the formation, in 1975, of the Drama Research Unit at the Institute of African Studies. During that period, and up until 1987, she stayed involved with the Drama Studio and Kusum Agoromba. Twenty-five years of theatrical experiments and achievements came to an end with an anniversary program. At about the same time, the Drama Studio was demolished to make way for a vast, Chinese-designed National Theatre, an expensive building that made no concessions to Ghanaian experience of drama. Inevitably, this was deeply wounding to Sutherland and profoundly affected her relationship with the national theater movement. The construction of a new Drama Studio on the campus at Legon and the establishment, at her suggestion, of a festival of historical drama at Cape Coast Castle cannot have provided more than minor sources of consolation. Her vision of the Ghanaian theater, a theater based on local experience, had been replaced by a totally different conception.

Sutherland also developed her interest in other areas, even though her undertakings were vulnerable to Ghana's uncertain political and economic times. Her interest in publishing found expression in the establishment, in 1974, of Afram Publications. She remained in close touch with the enterprise until her death. Also in 1974, she was involved in the foundation of the National Council for Women and Development and subsequently played a dynamic role in policy formation, particularly during the United Nations Decade for Women (1975–1985). The committee work that came to occupy much of her time and absorb some of her energy also included work on the Specialized Committee on Culture/Communication. In connection with this UNESCO (United Nations Educational, Scientific, and Cultural Organization) committee she campaigned for the establishment of the African Cultural Institute. In March 1984, Sutherland was among the original eighteen members of a government-appointed education commission charged with the task of advising on education "from the cradle to the grave." Her colleagues sometimes complained about the high standards she insisted on in the commission's reports, but they recognized the value of her contribution.

Her work with children continued in both national and international contexts. She was deeply involved with the Children's Drama Development Project; later she was a foundation member of the National Commission on Children (1979–1983) and chaired that commission for seven years (1983–1990). She was particularly involved in the setting up of a mobile technical workshop and in the creation of park-library complexes in major urban centers and in villages. She helped establish the Child Education Fund, ensured that children were engaged in conservation projects, and set up the Mmofra Foundation. On the international level, UNICEF (United Nations Children's Fund) drew her into the discussion when framing its code of human rights for the protection of children.

Recognition came in various ways. As a playwright she was hailed following the success of *The Marriage of Anansewa* at the second World Black and African Festival of Arts and Culture held in Lagos in 1977. For her services to literature and the arts she was presented in 1991 with a Noble Patron of the Arts Award by the Ghana Association of Writers. Four years later, the Arts Critics and Reviewers Association of Ghana recognized her contribution to the arts in Ghana with a Flag Star Award.

In recognition of her many and various contributions to her country the University of Ghana awarded her an honorary doctorate in 1991. In a gesture that was of a piece with the rest of her life, Sutherland moved from the degree ceremony, where she had been singled out for high honor, to one of the chapels on the campus. There a carefully prepared service was held, in the course of which she dedicated the doctorate to Almighty God, "to [her] professional community of artists, scholars, donors, administrators who [had]... shared with [her] in a spirit of goodwill the aspirations and burdens of the tasks undertaken for the development and promotion of dramatic art as an essential Medium of Communication in Ghana," and "to [her] personal family and friends whose love, trust and faith, whose beautiful concern and care [had] sustained [her]." She then paid tribute to "ancestral and other historical creators of Ghana's artistic heritage."

Sutherland created for herself a unique position in Ghanaian cultural life, and inevitably some people resented the influence she wielded and the power she enjoyed. So principled and determined a campaigner inevitably crossed swords, trod on toes, and was the topic of malicious speculation.

On 21 January 1996, after a prolonged sickness, Sutherland died. She was buried with appropriate ceremony some three weeks later after a distinguished memorial service at the W. E. B. Du Bois Memorial Centre for Pan-African Culture. From early in the morning of 9 February tributes were read, music was played, and poetry was recited. A volume of tributes was prepared, bearing abundant testimony to the wide range of friends she had made and to the great affection and high regard in which she had been held.

The service drew together many strands of Sutherland's life and work in the Christian context, which had been important to her from her youth. The fact that it was held in the Du Bois Centre was significant. Had the Accra Drama Studio been standing, it would have provided the obvious setting for the service, one that evoked many of her triumphs and embodied some of her dreams. The fact that the National Theatre had already risen on the site showed just how much had changed since a thirty-year-old schoolteacher began to talk about her ideas for a national theater movement and to gather around her musicians, dancers, and performers. The demolition of the Drama Studio should not be taken to suggest that her contribution to the Ghanaian theater has been obliterated, but it should be seen as raising questions about attitudes toward her work in the mid 1990s.

Selected Bibliography

BIBLIOGRAPHIES

Berrian, Brenda F. "Bibliographies of Nine Female African Writers." In *Research in African Literatures* 12 (summer 1981).

———. "An Update: Bibliography of Twelve African Women Writers." In *Research in African Literatures* 19 (summer 1988).

SELECTED POEMS

[Efua Morgue]. "Mumunde My Mumunde," "An Ashanti Story," "Little Wild Flowers," and "It Happened." In Olumbe Bassir, ed., *An Anthology of West African Verse.* Ibadan, Nigeria: Ibadan University Press, 1957.

"The Redeemed," "Once Upon a Time," "The Dedication," "Song of the Fishing Ghosts," and "A Professional Beggar's Lullaby." In Kofi Awoonor and G. Adali-Mortty, eds., *Messages: Poems from Ghana.* London: Heinemann, 1971. Includes three other poems by Sutherland.

"Song of the Fishing Ghosts" and "Our Songs Are About It." In A. W. Kayper-Mensah and Horst Wolff, eds., *Ghanaian Writing: As Seen by Her Own Writers as Well as by German Authors.* Tübingen, Germany: Horst Erdmann Verlag, 1972.

SHORT STORIES

"New Life at Kyerefaso." In Langston Hughes, ed., *An African Treasury.* New York: Crown, 1960. Frequently anthologized.

"Samantaase Village." In *Okyeame* (Accra) 1, no. 1 (1961).

Obaatan Kesewa. Accra, Ghana: Bureau of Ghana Languages, 1967.

ESSAYS, ARTICLES, AND BOOKLETS

Playtime in Africa. With photographs by Willis E. Bell. London: Brown, Knight, and Truscott, 1960; New York: Atheneum, 1962.

"Venture into Theatre." In *Okyeame* 1, no. 1 (1961).

The Roadmakers. With photographs by Willis E. Bell. Accra, Ghana: Ghana Information Services in association with Newman Neame, 1961. A pictorial essay for children.

The Second Phase: A Review of the National Theatre Movement in Ghana. Legon, Ghana: Institute of African Studies, 1965.

Kusum Agoromba Presentations. Legon, Ghana: Institute of African Studies, 1968. Brochure on productions.

"The Theatre in Ghana." In Janice Nebill, ed., *Ghana Welcomes You.* Accra, Ghana: Orientation to Ghana Committee, 1969.

The Original Bob: The Story of Bob Johnson, Ghana's Ace Comedian. Accra, Ghana: Anowuo, 1970.

PLAYS

You Swore an Oath. In *Présence africaine* 22 (summer 1964).

Edufa. London: Longman, 1967, 1979.

Foriwa. Tema, Ghana: State Publishing Corporation, 1967.

Vulture! Vulture!: Two Rhythm Plays. Accra, Ghana: Ghana Publishing House, 1968. Also includes *Tahinta.*

The Marriage of Anansewa. London: Longman, 1975.

TRANSLATIONS

"Poem in Praise of Osei Tutu from Traditional Apaee." With J. H. Nketia. In *Okyeame* 2, no. 1 (1964).

"Apetepirew," "The Tree-Felling Knife," and "Good-Hearted Drunk, I'm Suffering," by Kwa Mensah. In *Okyeame* 4, no. 2 (1969).

"Nyankonkra" and "Nea Ohwehwe Annya," by Patience Henaku Addo. In *Okyeame* 4, no. 1 (1986).

EDITORIAL ACTIVITIES

Talent for Tomorrow: An Anthology of Creative Writing from the Training Colleges and Secondary Schools of Ghana. Edited with Ellen Geer Sangster and others. Accra, Ghana: Ghana Publishing Corporation, 1966–1972.

INTERVIEWS

Lautre, Maxine. "A Recorded Interview with Efua Sutherland...on the Current Theatre Movement in Ghana." In *Cultural Events in Africa* 42 (1968). Repr. in Dennis Duerden and Cosmo Pieterse, eds., *African Writers Talking.* London: Heinemann, 1972.

Nichols, Lee, ed. *Conversations with African Writers.* Washington, D.C.: Voice of America, 1981.

———. *African Writers at the Microphone.* Washington, D.C.: Three Continents Press, 1984.

Woode, Kwesi. "Efua Sutherland: A Profile." In *Annual Writers' Congress 1973.* Accra, Ghana: Ghana Association of Writers, 1973.

CRITICAL STUDIES

Abarry, Abu Shardow. "The Significance of Names in Ghanaian Drama." In *Journal of Black Studies* 22 (1991).

Akyea, E. Ofori. "The Atwia-Ekumfi Kodzidan—An Experimental African Theatre." In *Okyeame* 4, no. 1 (1968).

Amankulor, James N. "An Interpretation and Analysis of *The Marriage of Anansewa.*" In *Okike Educational Supplement* 1 (1980).

Amissah, G. McLean. *Reminiscences of Adisadel: A Short Historical Sketch of Adisadel College.* Accra, Ghana: Afram Publications, 1980.

Angmor, Charles. "Drama in Ghana." In Oyin Ogunba and Abiola Irele, eds., *Theatre in Africa.* Ibadan, Nigeria: Ibadan University Press, 1978.

Armah, Ayi Kwei. *Fragments.* Boston: Houghton Mifflin, 1968; London: Heinemann, 1974. Contains a malicious portrait some have linked with Efua Sutherland.

Asgill, Edmondson J. "African Adaptations of Greek Tragedies." In *African Literature Today* 11 (1980).

Aworele, 'Yinka. *Critical Notes (with Questions and Answers) on* The Marriage of Anansewa. Ilesha, Nigeria: Fatiregun, 1979.

Baker, Donald. "African Theatre and the West." In *Comparative Drama* 11 (1977).

Banham, Martin. *African Theatre Today*. London: Pitman, 1976.

Branch, William B. *Crosswinds: An Anthology of Black Dramatists in the Diaspora*. Bloomington: Indiana University Press, 1993.

Brown, Lloyd. "The African Woman as Writer." In *Canadian Journal of African Studies* 9 (1975).

———. *Women Writers in Black Africa*. Westport, Conn.: Greenwood, 1981.

Carpenter, Peter. "Theatre in East and West Africa." In *Drama* 68 (1963).

Crane, Louise. *Ms. Africa: Profiles of Modern African Women*. Philadelphia: Lippincott, 1973.

Crow, Brian. *Studying Drama*. Harlow, Essex, U.K.: Longman, 1983.

Davies, Carole Boyce. "Wrapping One's Self in Mother's-Akatado-Cloths: Mother-Daughter Relationships in the Works of African Women Writers." In *Sage* 4, no. 2 (1987).

de Graft, J. C. "Dramatic Questions." In Andrew Gurr and Angus Calder, eds., *Writers in East Africa*. Nairobi, Kenya: East African Literature Bureau, 1974.

Dibba, Ebou. *Efua T. Sutherland,* The Marriage of Anansewa. London: Longman, 1978.

Drachler, Jacob, ed. and comp. *Black Homeland/Black Diaspora: Cross-Currents of the African Relationship*. Port Washington, N.Y.: Kennikat, 1975.

Etherton, Michael. *The Development of African Drama*. London: Hutchison University Library for Africa, 1982.

———. "Efua Sutherland." In Martin Banham, ed., *Cambridge Guide to World Theatre*. Cambridge, U.K.: Cambridge University Press, 1988. Substantially the same entry in Martin Banham, Errol Hill, and George Woodyard, eds., *The Cambridge Guide to African and Caribbean Theatre*. Cambridge, U.K.: Cambridge University Press, 1994.

Graham-White, Anthony. *The Drama of Black Africa*. New York: S. French, 1974.

Hagan, John C. "Influence of Folktale on *The Marriage of Anansewa:* A Folkloristic Approach." In *Okike*, nos. 27–28 (1988).

July, Robert W. *An African Voice: The Role of the Humanities in African Independence*. Durham, N.C.: Duke University Press, 1987.

McHardy, Cecile. "The Performing Arts in Ghana." In *African Forum* (summer 1965).

Muhindi, K. "L'Apport de Efua Theodora Sutherland a la dramaturgie contemporaine." In *Présence africaine* 133–134 (1985).

Nketia, J. H. Kwabena. *Ghana: Music, Dance, and Drama: A Review of the Performing Arts of Ghana*. Accra-Tema: Ghana Information Services, 1965.

Nwahunanya, Chinyere. "The Playwright as Preacher: Contemporary Morality in Three Ghanaian Plays." In *Literary Endeavour* (Anantapur, India) 10, nos. 1–4 (1988–1989). Material on *Edufa*.

Ogunyemi, Chikwenye Okonjo. "Efua Theodora Sutherland." In Bernth Lindfors and Reinhard Sander, eds., *Twentieth-Century Caribbean and Black African Writers*. Vol. 117 of *Dictionary of Literary Biography*. Detroit: Gale Research, 1992.

Okafor, Chinyere. "Parallelism Versus Influence in African Literature: The Case of Efua Sutherland's *Edufa*." In *Kiabara* 3, no. 1 (1980).

Onukwufor, Chika C. "*The Marriage of Anansewa:* A Modern West African Drama for the WAESC Candidate." In *Muse* 11 (1979).

Pearce, Adetokunbo. "The Didactic Essence of Efua Sutherland's Plays." In *African Literature Today* 15 (1987).

Schipper, Mineke. *Theatre and Society in Africa*. Trans. by Almpie Coetzee. Johannesburg, South Africa: Ravan, 1982.

Schmidt, Nancy J. "African Women Writers of Literature for Children." In *World Literature Written in English* 17 (April 1978).

———. "Children's Books by Well-Known African Authors." In *World Literature Written in English* 18 (April 1979).

Sutherland, Bill, et al. *Tributes to Efua Theodora Sutherland*, 1995. This sixty two-page booklet contains a biographical sketch and tributes from members of Efua Sutherland's family, Adotey Bing, K. E. Agovi, and representatives of Afram Publications, Atwaman, the Ghana National Commission on Children, and the Pan-African Writers Association.

Talbert, Linda Lee. "Alcestis and Edufa: The Transitional Individual." In *World Literature Written in English* 22 (fall 1983).

Thies-Torkornoo, Susanne. "Die Rolle der Frau in der afrikanischen Gesellschaft: Eine Betrachtung von Ama Ata Aidoos *Anowa* und Efua Sutherlands *Foriwa*." In *Matatu* 1 (1987).

Vavilov, V. N. "A Talented Poetess." In *Midwest Weekly* 2, no. 42 (1965).

Wilentz, Gay. "Writing for the Children: Orature, Tradition, and Community in Efua Sutherland's *Foriwa*." In *Research in African Literatures* 19 (summer 1988).

Zell, Hans, Carol Bundy, and Virginia Coulon, eds. *A New Reader's Guide to African Literature*. London: Heinemann, 1983.

Ṭāhā Ḥusayn

1889–1973

PIERRE CACHIA

ṬĀHĀ ḤUSAYN was a leading member of a generation of writers who played a seminal role in the cultural development of Arabic-speaking nations. These nations were heirs to a civilization of which Islam was the core and classical Arabic was revered as the medium of revelation even after it had ceased to be the means of everyday communication. For centuries, however, this civilization had lost much of its innovative energy, and its literature was accessible only to a small educated elite that perpetuated conventional themes and favored a style laden with extremely elaborate plays on words. Yet new forces began to stir in the Ottoman Empire (1342–1924) as European powers intervened more directly in its affairs and especially after General Napoléon Bonaparte landed his forces in Egypt in 1798. Almost every Arab country was eventually subjugated, and Egypt was occupied by the British in 1882. Although the might of the west was resented, the civilization that produced it became an object of curiosity and admiration. It fell to such as Ṭāhā Ḥusayn to channel the new forces into creative molds.

FORMATIVE YEARS

Ṭāhā Ḥusayn was born on 14 November 1889 and grew up in a large household consisting of Ḥusayn ʿAlī Salāma, who at the time was a weighman on a landed estate on the outskirts of Maghāgha, in Upper Egypt; his two wives, Nafīsa and Ruqayya; and their combined progeny. Ṭāhā was the seventh of his father's thirteen children, and the fifth of Ruqayya's eleven. (Most Arab men are identified by their personal name, followed by their father's, their grandfather's, and so on. So Ṭāhā Ḥusayn would be addressed as Dr. Ṭāhā, not Dr. Ḥusayn. When transcribed into Latin characters, different spellings are possible, the family itself favoring Ṭāhā-Ḥusayn.) The family was not without some modest means, but it was as yet untouched by modernism.

At the age of two, as a result of ophthalmia and the crude medication performed by the local barber, Ṭāhā Ḥusayn became totally blind. In 1902, when he had exhausted the resources of the village school, which included memorization of the Qurʾān, he was sent to the ancient University of al-Azhar (founded A.D. 970) in Cairo under the aegis of an older brother. He attended the last two lectures of its great reformist rector, Shaykh Muḥammad ʿAbduh, and relished the literature courses of one of the Shaykh's disciples, al-Sayyid al-Marṣafī. But with the majority of the professors, who were conservative, he was soon at loggerheads, and when he presented himself for the final examination in 1912, he was failed. He never made his peace with the institution, although it must have contributed to his lifelong devotion to classical Arabic and his mastery of it.

While still a student, he had been attracted to the circles of open-minded intellectuals, notably that of Aḥmad Luṭfī al-Sayyid, who owned the newspaper *Al-Jarīdah*, founded a political party, and later occupied a succession of prestigious cultural positions. For *Al-Jarīdah*, as well as for other papers, the young Ṭāhā Ḥusayn wrote a great deal—some verse, a few short narratives, but, above all, pugnacious articles on literary and social issues that showed little deference to the well-established writers of the day.

He also began attending lectures at the first modern Arab university—successively known as the Egyptian University, the Fu'ād I University, and Cairo University—on the day it opened in 1908. There he was impressed by an unfamiliar approach to Arabic literature, practiced not only by local scholars such as Ḥifnī Nāṣif but also by orientalists such as David Santillana, Enno Littmann, and especially Carlo Nallino. In 1914, on presentation of a doctoral thesis on the eleventh-century poet ʿAbū ʾl-ʿAlā al-Maʿarrī, Ṭāhā Ḥusayn became the university's first graduate.

He was subsequently sent on a scholarship to France, first to the University of Montpellier, then to Paris, where he studied at the Sorbonne under a number of distinguished scholars, including Gustave Lanson. For his doctoral dissertation, he worked on the fourteenth-century historian Ibn Khaldūn, whose universal history is especially highly prized for its *Muqaddima* (introduction, often called the Prolegomena), which is rich with observations on the workings of society, including the cyclical course of political dynasties; hence, Ṭāhā Ḥusayn titled his dissertation "La Philosophie sociale d'Ibn Khaldoun." With it he earned the university's doctorate in 1918, and the *doctorat d'état* the following year. He also acquired a boundless admiration for western culture, especially as manifested in France; Paris was to him what Athens had been to the ancient world, but, as he explains in *Min baʿīd* (1935; From afar), it had a superiority over Athens that two thousand years of progress had brought about. On 9 August 1917, he married Suzanne Bressau, the young Frenchwoman who, since their engagement in Montpellier on 12 May 1915, had been reading to him the texts he needed.

CAREER

Back in Egypt, he was hired to teach ancient history at his alma mater and soon caused controversy by the stress he laid on the Hellenistic contribution to Islamic thought. Yet in 1925 he published *Qādat al-fikr* (*Leaders of Thought*), in which he exalts the western mind as democratic and rational as against the oriental mind, which he describes as autocratic and religious, and he interprets all human progress in terms of the growing ascendancy of the former. Because he never mentioned Islam as part of the east, however, the implications of his views went unnoticed by the conservatives who were soon to rage against him, and the book was actually adopted as a reading text in state schools.

He was at the same time maintaining his interest in Arabic literature and in 1922 started a series of articles on the subject under the collective title of *Ḥadīth al-arbiʿāʾ* (1925, 1926, 1945; Wednesday talks)—the title echoes Charles-Augustin Sainte-Beuve's *Causeries du lundi* (1851–1862; Monday chats)—which eventually filled three volumes. He was also contributing to political journalism with hard-hitting articles on social and cultural issues in the newspapers and journals first of the Liberal Constitutionalist Party and later in those of the leading nationalist party, the Wafd. Along with a number of other liberals, he was engaged in fierce polemics with conservatives who contended that their heritage had no need of foreign importations, the more extreme opposing even the creation of new words and expressions in the language.

Ṭāhā Ḥusayn was to prove even more controversial after his transfer, in 1925, to the chair of Arabic literature, for in the following year he published his most daring book, *Fī al-shiʿr al-jāhilī* (On pre-Islamic poetry). In this, after proclaiming a Cartesian determination to take no traditional view for granted, he argued that the bulk of the magnificent corpus of ancient poems regarded as the mainspring and measuring stick of all Arabic literature had in fact been fabricated by early Muslims. This was met with vehement denunciations, and—mainly because he had adduced religious motives, including the need to support "Islamic myths," for the forgeries—the book was banned and he was tried for desertion of religious faith. He was not condemned, and he reissued the book in an expanded form under a slightly different title, *Fī al-adab al-jāhilī* (1927; On pre-Islamic literature). The university, now a state institution headed by Aḥmad Luṭfī al-Sayyid, stood by him, and in 1930 he was elected and confirmed as the first Egyptian dean of the Faculty of Arts. He in turn stoutly championed the university's independence. In 1932, when an antagonistic political party was in power, the controversy was revived, and he was dismissed from government service and prevented from lecturing. This, for a while, reduced him to penury and debt.

The fury roused by *Fī al-shiʿr al-jāhrlī* obscured its scholarly purport. As if they sensed it was more profitable to enlist religious fervor in the service of modernism than to attack its prejudices openly, a number of liberal writers turned to Islamic themes in the 1930s. In time, Ṭāhā Ḥusayn himself took to retelling stories of early Muslims, which were eventually collected in three volumes titled *ʿAlā hāmish al-sīra* (1933, 1937, 1938; On the margin of the prophet's life), the title recalling Jules Lemaître's *En Marge des vieux livres* (1905–1907). In these stories he makes no attempt to downplay or explain away miraculous interventions, and some have seen in them a concession to religious sentiment, although he clearly states his priorities in the introduction:

> There is a great difference between someone who presents these accounts to the mind as if they were facts sustained by science and conformable with methods of research, and someone who offers them to the heart and the emotions as capable of generating good impulses, diverting inclinations to evil, and helping to pass the time and to cope with the burdens of life.

Into the second volume he incorporated a story of his own creation about a Greek youth who is dissatisfied with the faith he has been taught, goes wandering about the earth in search of truth, and finds it when he is told of a prophet who does not dazzle people with physical miracles but wins them over by the exposition of his message. In this Ṭāhā Ḥusayn was casting into literary shape Shaykh Muḥammad ʿAbduh's central teaching that Islam is the religion of reason. The use by modernists of Islamic themes indicates not a retreat but a growing confidence that they, rather than conservatives, had the attention of the reading public.

Between 1934 and 1944, Ṭāhā Ḥusayn was back in government service, performing several functions in behalf of education. Then, from 1945 to 1948, he directed a publishing house called al-Kātib al-Miṣrī (The Egyptian scribe), which brought out some edited texts, a number of original books, an even larger number of translations, as well as a journal of the same name, which Ṭāhā Ḥusayn edited. It was, he claimed, because of interference from an authoritarian government that he was forced to wind down this enterprise, and he remained at odds with the authorities until the Wafd party, which had been the most popular between the two world wars, returned to power in January 1950.

Ṭāhā Ḥusayn was not formally a member of the Wafd party, but he was on good terms with its leadership. In the last cabinet it formed, which lasted two years, he was entrusted with the Ministry of Education. He had long argued that education was a need and a right for all, not a commodity "to be bought and sold like onions and leeks." As minister of education, he abolished all fees in the state pre-university school system and at the same time considerably extended it. He also saw through a number of initiatives in higher education not only in Egypt, where he founded a second university in Cairo, Ibrāhīm (later renamed ʿAyn Shams), but also abroad, for he created an Islamic Institute in Madrid and a chair of Arabic language and culture at the University of Athens.

Deep unrest in Egypt brought about the dismissal of the Wafdist government in January 1952 and put an end to the monarchy a few months later. Ṭāhā Ḥusayn returned to journalism and remained active in it through the 1950s and most of the 1960s, especially as editor of the newspaper *Al-Jumhūriya* (The republic) until his abrupt dismissal in 1964. Although he was no longer directly active in politics, he was as outspoken as ever on political ideologies, as well as on other cultural matters, and sharp in his denunciation of social conditions. Even after his health had broken down, he was assiduous in attending meetings of the Academy of Arabic Language, of which he became president in 1963 after the death of his longtime friend Aḥmad Luṭfī al-Sayyid.

Ṭāhā Ḥusayn died on 28 October 1973.

GUIDING PRINCIPLES

Eventful as Ṭāhā Ḥusayn public career was, it is as a writer that he has been most highly regarded. He came into prominence at a time when the literate were few and the main outlet for a would-be writer was journalism. Scarcely any of his contemporaries achieved fame unless they were both prolific and versatile, and Ṭāhā Ḥusayn was no exception. Although the widespread practice of collecting articles into books swells the numbers, his output was still prodigious by any standard: he is credited with 1,481 articles, forty-eight volumes of literary studies, six novels and an incomplete one published posthumously, five volumes of shorter narratives, and another twelve short stories published in journals, as well as translations of eleven books and thirty articles. To these may be added joint authorship of another seventeen books, collaboration in the editing of eight texts, and introductions to forty-two books by other writers. In his youth he composed at least twenty-three poems that were published in journals, but these he later held in low esteem and never authorized their collection in book form.

It would be fruitless to look for profound consideration and penetration, unfailing consistency, or stringent scholarship in all of this writing. Nevertheless, the richness of the material, the clarity of purpose, and the devotion and talent informing it all are unmistakable.

To begin with, Ṭāhā Ḥusayn's brushes with the religious establishment and with literary conservatives must not obscure the fact that he was steeped in Arab-Islamic heritage and prized it highly. He belonged firmly to a rising elite, which, from the last quarter of the nineteenth century, not only bewailed the cultural decline and loss of power that had afflicted Islamic countries in recent centuries, but also abhorred the artificiality that had pervaded their literature. But he had a consuming and abiding interest in what this culture had been in more dynamic times, its relevance to present experience, and its potential for new life. Furthermore, he believed devoutly in the inevitability of progress. His constant cry, therefore, was not for innovation but renovation.

Yet there can be no doubt about the source of his stimulation or the direction he wanted his society to take. Almost all the facets of life that he encountered in France were seductive, and the end products seemed to validate its institutions and professed values. Nowhere was this expressed more explicitly than when he trumpeted in *Mustaqbal al-thaqāfa fī Miṣr* (1938; *The Future of Culture in Egypt*):

> Believe me, dear reader: Our true patriotic duty once we have achieved independence and established democracy in Egypt is but this: We must expend all the power and effort and time and wealth at our command—and more!—to make Egyptians feel, individually and collectively, that God has created them for dignity, not for humiliation; for strength, not for weakness; for mastery, not for submission; for wakefulness, not for apathy. We must wipe out from the hearts of Egyptians the sinful, the abominable delusion that they were fashioned of a different clay from that of the European, given innate dispositions different from those of Europeans, and endowed with minds different from European minds.
>
> (pp. 38–39; translation by the present writer)

To make the wholesale acceptance of European examples more palatable, he took a leaf from the book of the Islamic reform movement, which claimed to be guided by the example of the Muslims of an earlier, more dynamic time, and argued that present-day Arabs ought to have no more compunction in learning from the Europeans than their forefathers had in absorbing Greek thought. At another time he went still further and contended—perhaps taking a cue from the French writer Georges Duhamel—that Egypt was not and never had been an oriental country, but was Mediterranean. How the rest of the Arab world fit into this classification was never spelled out. Ṭāhā Ḥusayn maintained that Egypt had a distinctive spirit that had manifested itself consistently since Pharaonic times. Yet in other contexts he addressed Arabs as members of the same family, and his extensive writings on their literature are not marked by regionalism. Presumably he thought of Arab culture, especially after it had incorporated Hellenic elements and thrived mainly in the Fertile Crescent, North Africa, and Andalusia, as largely Mediterranean, with Egypt as a preeminent center in this respect. Persia, however, despite its Aryan and Islamic connections, he considered oriental.

The practical outcome of these ideas was that virtually all the values he wanted to see developed and the standards he sought to apply were those prevalent in Europe, especially in France. Vehemently, consistently, stalwartly, and at no small cost to himself, he stood for democracy in politics, secularism and toleration in religion, justice and liberalism in society. In literature, he was a Romantic, for Romanticism was the dominant feature in the French literature he encountered.

But Egypt was not at the same stage of development as France. Not Ṭāhā Ḥusayn alone but all the modernists of his generation were aware that the illiterate majority did not yet share their perceptions. Although the modernists did not specify their targeted audience, their appeal was not to the masses but to an elite, which they trusted would go on widening its circle until the truths that seemed evident to them would be evident to all. In the meantime, imbued with idealism and a great sense of responsibility, they looked to the knowledgeable few to speak—and when in authority to act—in the interests of the entire nation (see Cachia, 1990, pp. 152–170, for a detailed study of one such idealist, Tawfīq al-Ḥakīm).

Not surprisingly, Ṭāhā Ḥusayn's view of religion was not that of the masses, among whom Islamic loyalties remained uppermost. He did assert that religion was "an instinct of the soul," therefore fulfilling a need of the individual; but he refused to make a distinction between one religion and another and declared Christianity to be as basic an element of Egyptian consciousness as Islam. Above all, he denied the religious establishment any right to regulate public affairs or intellectual pursuits. A modern state, he believed, had to be secular and concern itself solely with economic and civic issues.

Possibly relevant to his thinking in this respect is that in his thesis on Ibn Khaldūn he played down the role of religious faith in the social philosophy of his subject. Also intriguing are Ṭāhā Ḥusayn's departures from his main interests when, long after he had ceased to be a professor of history, he produced two studies dealing with the first four successors of Muhammad as temporal and spiritual heads of Islam. *Al-Shaykhān* (1960; The two elders), consists of one essay on Abū Bakr and one on ʿUmar and may have been meant to round off the earlier, more ambitious two-volume study on ʿUthmān and ʿAlī and his sons, *Al-Fitna al-kubrā* (1947, 1953; The great schism), which covers the great split between orthodox Islam and Shiʿism. *Al-Fitna al-kubrā* characterizes the form of government that came into being at the death of the Prophet as not a theocracy, democracy, or benevolent dictatorship, but as a combination of two elements: one humane, but deeply influenced by religion; the other aristocratic, based on kinship to the Prophet. The tension between these two is said to have been kept in check by ʿUmar but to have got out of hand under ʿUthmān, hence the dissension. But ʿUthmān's murder led Ṭāhā Ḥusayn into a somewhat anachronistic discourse on the procedure that ought to have been adopted for his impeachment.

In contemporary politics Ṭāhā Ḥusayn espoused the democracy and liberalism that had served western European nations well. But the parliamentary system set up in Egypt by the constitution of 1923 was ill controlled by a largely illiterate electorate. It made power accessible to authoritarian governments with which Ṭāhā Ḥusayn was frequently at odds. Increasingly, too, he became concerned with economic inequalities and the plight of the poor. Especially in the 1940s, his fulminations against social injustice laid him open to a suspicion that he was, in the parlance of the time, a pink, a fellow traveler, a leftist. He lent credence to the terminology in such epigrams as those found in *Jannat al-shawk* (1945; The garden of thorns):

> The young disciple to his aged master: "So-and-so yesterday leapt from the extreme Right to the extreme Left." The aged master to his young disciple: "He has despaired of the favor of the rulers and now seeks the favor of the people."
>
> (p. 64)

> The young disciple to his aged master: "What is the matter with So-and-So that he mouths the opinions of the extremists of the Left yet acts in accordance with the extremists of the Right?" The aged master to the young disciple: "He has the mind of a free man and the morals of a slave."
>
> (p. 36)

But it was not to the will of the masses that he would entrust the direction of society. His approach to the problem of poverty all along had been paternalistic. Now he questioned whether "the mind has yet attained the control of will and instinct" to make reform possible, and his exhortations and satires were directed at those who had it within their power to do good and did not.

Following the revolution of 1952, Egypt became a republic, and a new generation of intellectuals came to the fore, among whom one form of socialism or another was almost dogma. Insofar as their professed aims coincided with Ṭāhā Ḥusayn's dream of reform, they had his sympathy, but with their economic determinism he was out of tune. The last of the fiery polemics in which he engaged was in the mid 1950s against Arab Marxists, and several of his contemporaries supported him (see Semah, pp. 120–122). His strongest objection was to the intrusion of their dogmatism into the appreciation of literature. He maintained that in committing too narrowly to a social cause the writer was forgoing freedom and that literature needed to cater not only to material needs but also to intellectual and spiritual exaltation.

CREATIVE WRITING

At the start of Ṭāhā Ḥusayn's writing career, a major issue among Arab authors was language itself. It was by mastery of style that most reputations were made. At one extreme were the conservatives who tolerated no departure from the standards of the past. At the other were those who pleaded for the use of everyday speech as the true living language of the people, required at least for the sake of realism in the dialogue of plays and narratives. A middle course was adopted by a growing number of writers who were eager to communicate new ideas to as wide a public as possible, even though the readership remained confined to the literate minority. Its guiding principle was formulated by ʿAbd Allāh al-Nadīm, who had been a master of the old ornate style but who, when launching the journal *Al-Tankīt wa al-tabkīt* (Witticisms and rebukes) in 1881, undertook to keep his writing as close to the colloquial in diction and construction as possible without breaking the rules of classical syntax.

Ṭāhā Ḥusayn belonged to this stream. Solidly grounded in classical Arabic, he made full use of its range and morphological pliability for new purposes. Although somewhat wordy and fond of repetition, he wrote—and lectured—with elegance, power, fluidity, and an apparent simplicity that accommodated much artistry. It was, in fact, as a stylist that he first gained renown.

He was correspondingly intolerant of any literary use of the colloquial. Without considering that—like the once-ossified classical and any other language—the colloquial was capable of development, he pronounced it a debased idiom unfit for the expression of fine sentiment, and declared himself as aristocratic in this respect as he was democratic in others. By the same token, he denied the status of literature to folk compositions, even though he admitted they might be enjoyable.

NARRATIVES

His best known contribution to creative literature is a fictionalized account of his early days, *Al-Ayyām* (*An Egyptian Childhood*). He dictated the first volume in nine days while vacationing in France in 1926 at the height of the controversy over his book on pre-Islamic poetry. He hesitated to publish it because the background of poverty it revealed would violate a scruple nurtured by Arabs since pre-Islamic days: deeming not poverty but its display to be shameful. *Al-Ayyām* did appear nevertheless, first serially in the monthly cultural journal *Al-Hilāl* (The crescent) between December 1926 and July 1927, then in book form in 1929. Its touching evocation of the experiences of a blind boy, sensitive yet adventurous and self-assertive, in a rustic environment soon marked it as a masterpiece. It commanded attention even outside the Arab world, for it was the first modern Arabic literary work to be translated into a number of other languages. In 1932, still under attack for an attitude to Islam that conservatives deemed disrespectful, Ṭāhā Ḥusayn wrote a second volume (translated into English as *The Stream of Days*), following the same formula, that covered his days at al-Azhar. Much later—serially in 1955 and as a book in 1967—he recalled his student days in France in what has come to be known as the third volume of *Al-Ayyām*, though it is of a different temper from the other two books and is better described by the simple title under which it first appeared: *Mudhakkirāt* (Reminiscences; translated into English as *A Passage to France*).

Between 1935 and 1944, Ṭāhā Ḥusayn also wrote half a dozen novels, one of them, *Al-Qaṣr al-masḥūr* (1936; The enchanted castle), in collaboration with his friend Tawfīq al-Ḥakīm. A novel titled *Mā warāʾ al-nahr* (Beyond the river), which he started in 1946 but never completed, was published posthumously in 1975. He was not at his best, however, in a genre that calls for sustained and consistent invention. The pioneering nature of his efforts nevertheless deserves attention, for the novel was a recent introduction to Arabic literature. At the time of its publication, his *Aḥlām Shahrazād* (1943; *The Dreams of Scheherezade*) was a rare exploitation of the frame story of *The Arabian Nights,* which—as Ṭāhā Ḥusayn pointed out—had been held in low esteem by Arabs until its status was raised by the attention that Europeans gave it. An oddity is his *Al-Ḥubb al-ḍāʾiʿ* (1943; The lost love), which is set entirely in France and deals with French characters, without any reference to Arab life.

Ṭāhā Ḥusayn's novel *Duʿāʾ al-karawān* (1941) has been translated as *The Call of the Curlew*, although the *karawān* actually refers to a bird that, in an ancient Arab myth, calls for avenging the victim of a murder. It is one of the few attempts outside folk literature to confront the code of honor observed by the common people, which mandates that a woman who indulges in illicit sex must be slaughtered by her menfolk. In the novel, the victim is a peasant girl who, together with her sister and mother, is driven out of her village because of her father's scandalous sex life and reduced to working as a housemaid. She is seduced by her employer, so the three women head back home but are met by an uncle who kills the dishonored girl. Her sister then vows to avenge her by entering her seducer's service, making him fall in love with her, and then denying him. She succeeds in the first two parts of her subtle plan but then finds that she has fallen in love with him and that they need each other to outlive his sin and its consequences. The story strikes some false notes in that—in Egyptian as in many other societies—a man's indiscretions would not send his womenfolk into banishment, and the women would most likely not return to their village after one of them had faltered. But Ṭāhā Ḥusayn's aim is to bring out the injustice of the double standard and to heighten the poetic theme of love triumphing over vengeance.

Ṭāhā Ḥusayn also wrote a considerable number of shorter narratives. Those drawn from early Islamic sources in *ʿAlā hāmish al-sīra* have already been discussed. Set in the same period, the narratives of *Al-Waʿd al-ḥaqq* (1949; The true promise) are intended to exalt social responsibility. Yet others in a contemporary setting dwell on the tribulations of the disadvantaged, as is evidenced by their collective title, *Al-Muʿadhdhabūn fī al-arḍ* (published serially in 1946–1948, in book form 1949; *The Sufferers: Stories and Polemics*). Both fit in with his appeals for compassion toward the poor. There are also satirical portraits of human types that are clearly meant as reproaches to Egyptian society in *Jannat al-ḥayawān* (1950; The garden of beasts).

LITERARY CRITICISM

It is to literary criticism that Ṭāhā Ḥusayn devoted most of his energies and in which he made the most lasting impression. A phenomenon worth considering is that neither he nor any of his contemporaries who acquired a reputation as critics and as men of letters wrote a single book systematically setting out a literary creed. Theoretical presentations were left to others, who invariably translated a European work on the subject but used examples from Arabic writing to illustrate the generalizations made, thereby proving their universal applicability. This generation was excited by the influx of new models and ready-made ideas and eager to work them in a hurry into new experiences. The principles motivating the individuals who gained acceptance from the reading public have to be culled from their practice—their comments on individual authors or works, their discussion of problems of literary history, and even the direction taken in their creative writing—and from occasional pronouncements made in their voluminous writings.

Ṭāhā Ḥusayn's understanding of the essential character of literature is not easy to pin down. In his doctoral thesis on al-Maʿarrī, which was also the first substantial study of a literary figure by a modern Arab, he professed an all-embracing determinism according to which all phenomena, including poems, orations, and historical events, are "a tissue of social and cosmic forces subject to investigation and analysis, even as matter is subject to chemical action" (quoted in Cachia, 1956, p. 77). He made much of a "scientific" approach to literature, which he had learned from the orientalist professors at the new university and which he contrasted with the conventional, authority-ridden attitude of his former teachers at al-Azhar. Accordingly, the bulk of his dissertation consisted of studies of the poet's time, his life, his philosophy, and only a minor part was devoted to the aesthetic quality of his poetry. His book on pre-Islamic poetry not only invoked the example of the French mathematician and philosopher René Descartes—which amounted to little more than discarding transmitted lore such as the attribution of some poems to ancient, possibly mythical, persons, the stories woven round poets and the circumstances in which they composed certain poems, or anecdotes that may have been fabricated to explain obscure idioms. Moreover, *Fī al-shiʿr al-jāhilī* was set out in the form of a scientific experiment, following the sequence of observing, formulating a hypothesis, testing it, and reaching a conclusion.

In later writings, however, he was increasingly at odds with these early positions. He looked at attempts to reduce the study of literature to a science—by Sainte-Beuve with his classification of the personalities of writers, by the French philosopher and critic Hippolyte-Adolphe Taine with the supremacy given to environmental influences, by the French critic Vincent de Paul-Marie-Ferdinand Brunetière with his formulation of laws of literary evolution—and declared them failures. He was more comfortable with the French writer Jules Lemaître's emphasis on the artistic features of poetry and their effect on the reader. Genius, he perceived, was not to be explained by external factors; literature was a self-subsistent, self-authenticating phenomenon, and its appreciation impossible to divorce from personal taste. The most extreme indication of an apparent abandonment of objectivity came at the end of his book on the great tenth-century poet al-Mutanabbī, *Maʿ al-Mutanabbī* (1936; With al-Mutanabbī). He noticed that in the course of dictation his ideas about his subject had changed. He came to the conclusion that just as no writer records anything more substantial than fleeting moments of his own life, so no critic reflects anything more substantial than certain moments of his own life when his thoughts turn to certain moments of another writer's life. In a feeble attempt to reconcile this view with his once-vaunted belief in determinism, Ṭāhā Ḥusayn added that the critic was as much under compulsion to criticize as the writer was to write, and it must be left to natural selection to do the final sifting.

There is no denying that Ṭāhā Ḥusayn's voluminous writings grow out of shifting practices, make inconsistent claims, and are full of contradictory statements. At times he tied the themes chosen by a poet to the poet's way of dealing with them, and at others he spoke as if nothing mattered but the writer's ability to stir one's emotions. He even admitted to being animated by personal likes and dislikes. For example, although he disapproved of the artificial devices to which ʿAbū al-ʿAlāʾ al-Maʿarrī resorted, he felt a great affinity with the poet because he was also blind. He supplemented his rigorous doctoral study of the poet with two much more discursive books revealingly titled *Ṣawt Abī al-ʿAlāʾ* (1944; The voice of Abū al-ʿAlāʾ) and *Maʿ Abī al-ʿAlā fī sijnih* (1939; With Abū al-ʿAlāʾ in his prison); the title of the latter refers to a line in which the poet speaks of being in a threefold prison: the house to which he had restricted himself, his blindness, and the confinement of his soul in a vile body.

But the want of theoretical rigor does not invalidate the sum of Ṭāhā Ḥusayn's critical contribution. The part of his work that was concerned with literary history, editing texts, and elucidating often difficult material was not lacking in scholarship. It was in aesthetic evaluations that, with most of his contemporaries, he was swept up by a wave of popular romanticism that equated literary expression with an effusion of emotion, so that—echoing the French poet Lamartine's "Je chantais, mes amis, comme chante l'oiseau" (I sang, my friends, as a bird sings)—he could not imagine a literary artist confined to any kind of discipline: words must issue from the artist "as a song issues from a warbling bird, as perfume is diffused from a fragrant flower, as light is emitted from the brilliant sun" as he wrote in *Fī al-adab al-jāhilī* (p. 37).

Is there no firm core, then, to Ṭāhā Ḥusayn's aesthetic criteria? To judge by what he most often, if not invariably, praised a writer for, the overriding quality was the ability to stir the reader's emotion. The writer's motivation and the nature of the emotion roused scarcely mattered. But other considerations were often invoked. In a major study of the subject, Jābir ʿUṣfūr notes how often Ṭāhā Ḥusayn used the image of the mirror in his writing: the creative writer was to be a polished mirror reflecting his or her inner self, society, age, and the abiding concerns of humankind; in turn, the critic's role was to be a true mirror of the creative writer's. But to stress the absence of a theory that accounts for all literary manifestations, Jābir ʿUṣfūr titled his book *Al-Marāyā al-mutajāwira* (1983; The contiguous mirrors). Any readers of Ṭāhā Ḥusayn's work may well ask what it was that might be mirrored. Certainly not some objective truth—not in the praises or satires that were the bread and butter of many poets of the past, not in historical novels—but whatever the writer purposed and the reader could sympathetically experience. If in pursuing a goal the writer also revealed the inner self and further mirrored the concerns of the times or touched on an abiding truth, he or she would be reaching out to an entire generation or to the whole of humankind. That, we may infer, would be the measure of the writer's greatness but not necessarily the essence of his or her literary being. The critic was no less literary, but Ṭāhā Ḥusayn considered this type of work "descriptive" rather than "creative" literature.

From the start of his career Ṭāhā Ḥusayn's value judgments were the fruit of his subjective taste, which was not immune from the vagaries of circumstance or mood but reflected a man of wide erudition in Arabic and European cultures, of refined sensitivity, powerful purpose, and eloquent expression. In what he had to say, he was seldom less than stimulating and thought provoking.

From his scattered writings, one could piece together a defensible if not unchallengeable survey of the whole of Arabic literature. He dealt with the giants of the past from the pre-Islamic times to the middle of the thirteenth century—such as Abū Nuwās, al-Mutanabbī, and al-Maʿarrī—and showed how they could still speak to the modern mind. In the process, he raised a number of major questions about literary history that are well worthy of attention even if one disagrees with his conclusions.

Fī al-shiʿr al-Jāhilī, his book on the spurious authorship of much reputedly pre-Islamic poetry, roused so much heated controversy over secondary issues that its purport has virtually been missed. Written at a time when knowledge of oral composition and transmission was confined to narrow circles, it does suffer from the assumption that only the strictest textual reliability guarantees authenticity, so that variations in the wording of a poem or the attribution of the same line to different poets casts doubt on the entire record, and it pays insufficient attention to the cohesiveness of the corpus as a whole. Its conclusion that the bulk of this poetry was fabricated is scarcely tenable today (see Alan Jones, *Early Arabic Poetry*, vol. 1, 1992, for a concise summary of orientalist opinion on the subject). Yet it points out substantial incongruities in the record, such as the attribution of some lines to Adam or to Ishmael, and puts forward cogent reasons for suspecting not wholesale forgery but systematic tampering, at least in references to pagan deities, which are mentioned rarely and then only in uncomplimentary contexts. These points have been ignored by Arab scholars and Arabists alike. Besides, Ṭāhā Ḥusayn's conclusions in this book are not entirely negative. He picks out chains of poets, starting before the emergence of Islam in the early seventh century and stretching into unquestionably historic times, each poet beginning his career as a rhapsodist to the previous poet until he became a poet in his own right. Ṭāhā Ḥusayn suggests that valuable insights into the characteristics and development of the poetry of the time might be gained from studying these poets in sequence, but the challenge has never been taken up.

Ṭāhā Ḥusayn also made lively observations about the manifestations of political factionalism in the poetry during the Umayyad dynasty (A.D. 661–750) and about the prominence of schools of love poets in the same period. Regarding these, he again showed his skepticism of traditional lore when he pointed out the similarities among the lives of poets, each of whom yearned for the love of a particular woman, sometimes to the point of madness, as in the case of the poet who is so distraught by his love of Laylā that he is known as Majnūn Laylā—that is, Laylā's madman—whose story passed into other literatures. He surmised that these accounts were echoes of popular oral romances.

Ṭāhā Ḥusayn was no less challenging in his exposition of hedonistic poetry in the Abbasid age (A.D. 750–1258) and of the fusion of different cultural elements in this period. One of his theses was that translating Aristotle's *Rhetoric* into Arabic without a knowledge of the Greek literature to which it was relevant fostered the trend toward verbal embellishment. In general he had little regard for past Arabic criticism. Like most other Arab intellectuals, he dismissed the four centuries of Turkish domination, from the early sixteenth to late nineteenth century, as a period of stagnation.

Ṭāhā Ḥusayn coverage of modern Arabic literature was comparatively desultory. Except for *The Future of Culture in Egypt*, which was intended mainly as a blueprint for education, he produced not a comprehensive study but a multitude of piecemeal comments. He did, however, pronounce himself satisfied with the direction the modernist movement had taken, but not with its attainments. He was inclined to be severe with his contemporaries, and he was involved in a number of heated quarrels; his insistence on the correct use of the classical language sometimes gave his reviews a schoolmasterish tone. But he could also be discerning and generous. He was, for example, quick to perceive the talent of Najīb Maḥfūẓ, who was awarded the Nobel Prize in literature in 1988, and he was more tolerant than most of his generation of the prosodic liberties taken by the free-verse movement, which began to take shape in 1948.

Throughout his career, Ṭāhā Ḥusayn was a stout defender of Arabic literature as a whole. Taking both its past achievements and its future into account, he held that it deserved a place of honor among world literatures. In some of the broad issues affecting this valuation, his stance was rather apologetic. Thus he argued against the widely held view that the classical multitheme ode lacked organic unity, but he succeeded in demonstrating only that there were perceptible associations in the transition from theme to theme. He was also concerned that the absence of epic and dramatic literature in the Arab past should not be seen as a deficiency. He argued at one time that what had not been attempted ought not to weigh in the balance; at another that there were epic and dramatic elements in the corpus; at yet another that by the time the Arabs emerged into history, the opportunity was past, the Greeks themselves having abandoned these genres. In this he disregarded the Persian epic *Shāh Nāmeh*, composed in the eleventh century. Finally, despite his contempt for Arab folk literature, he did take note of the profusion of epic material in it. Had he searched more deeply, he might even have found traces of dramatic activity.

To compensate for the gaps he perceived in Arabic literature, Ṭāhā Ḥusayn exerted purposeful and sustained efforts to introduce Arabs to literary genres not strongly represented in their national literatures. Thus, although he did not make original contributions to the theater, he translated excerpts from Greek drama as well as the whole of French playwright Jean Racine's *Andromaque* (1667), which is itself based on classical literature; and he summarized the plots of a large number of modern French plays. He also tried his hand at epigrams, which were collected in the volume titled *Jannat al-shawk*, though his leisurely style did not accord well with the demands of the genre.

STANDING

Ṭāhā Ḥusayn's talents and energy earned him many honors. Under the Egyptian monarchy, he was given first the title of bey (1936) then that of pasha (1950), and after titles had been abolished by the republican regime he was awarded the state's highest decoration, the Order of the Nile, in 1965. Internationally, he received honorary doctorates from several European universities, distinctions from several academies, and the Légion d'Honneur from France. In 1949, with the backing of the French writer André Gide, he was nominated for the Nobel Prize in literature. The United Nations awarded him the human rights prize, which was delivered to him one day before his death.

To the reading public, he was known as the dean of Arab letters, for he was a commanding presence for over forty years, and—at least until the middle of the twentieth century—consistently at the cutting edge of Arab modernism. The intellectuals of the next generation were somewhat less appreciative because they expected greater philosophical rigor than he had maintained; his unmeasured admiration of Europe ill accorded with their self-assertiveness, and he did not square with their socialist ideology. It is not unusual for those who were pioneers in their youth to be regarded as outdated in their old age. But Ṭāhā Ḥusayn's successors owed it to him, and his like, that a path lay open for the further steps they wanted to take. Together with a handful of his peers, he had fought battles that needed to be fought, cleared the ground of deadwood that needed to be removed, and accustomed a generation to expect a once-decorative literature to widen its perceptions and feed its aspirations.

Some three thousand people were reported to have followed Ṭāhā Ḥusayn's funeral procession.

Selected Bibliography

BIBLIOGRAPHY

al-Sakkūt, Ḥamdī, and Marsden Jones. *Ṭāhā Ḥusayn*. Vol. 1 of *Aʿlām al-adab al-muʿāṣir fī Miṣr* (Leaders of contemporary literature in Egypt), 2d ed. Publ. jointly by Cairo: Dār al-Kitāb al-Miṣrī, and Beirut, Lebanon: Dār al-Kitāb al-Lubnānī, 1982.

COLLECTED WORKS

Al-Majmūʿa al-Kāmila. Beirut, Lebanon: Dār al-Kitāb al-Lubnānī, 1973–1974.

SELECTED WORKS

Al-Ayyām I. Cairo: Maṭbaʿat Amīn ʿAbd al-Raḥmān, 1929.

Al-Ayyām II. Cairo: Dār al-Maʿārif, 1940.

Duʿāʾ al-karawan. Cairo: Dār al-Maʿārif, 1941.

Aḥlām Shahrazād. Cairo: Maṭbaʿat al-Maʿārif wa Maktabatuhā, 1943.

Al-Ḥubb al-ḍāʾiʿ. Cairo: Maṭbaʿat al-Maʿārif, 1943.
ʿAlā hāmish al-sīra. 3 vols. Cairo: Dār al-Maʿārif, 1943–1946.
Al-Muʿadhdhabūn fī al-arḍ. Cairo: Dār al-Maʿārif, 1949.
Al-Waʿd al-ḥaqq. Cairo: Dār al-Maʿārif, 1949, 1981.
Mudhakkirāt. Beirut, Lebanon: Dār al-Ādāb, 1967. Repr. as *Al-Ayyām III*. Cairo: Dār al-Maʿārif, 1972.
Mā warāʾ al-nahr. Cairo: Dār al-Maʿārif, 1975.
Jannat al-ḥayawān. Cairo: Sharikat al-Tawzīʿ al-Miṣriyya, 1950.

ESSAYS AND LITERARY CRITICISM

Qādat al-fikr. Cario: Idārat al-Hilāl, 1925; Cairo: Dār al-Maʿārif, 1964.
Fī al-shiʿr al-jāhilī. Cairo: Maṭbaʿat Dār al-Kutub al-Miṣriyya, 1926. Expanded and reissued as *Fī al-adab al-jāhilī*. Cairo: Maṭbaʿat al-Iʿtimād, 1927; Cairo: Dār al-Maʿārif, 1981.
Hadīth al-arbiʿāʾ. 3 vols. Cairo: Dār al-Maʿārif, 1925, 1926, 1945.
Min baʿīd. Cairo: al-Maṭbaʿa al-Raḥmāniyya, 1935; Beirut, Lebanon: Dār al-ʿIlm li al-Malāyīn, 1982.
Mustaqbal al-thaqāfa fī Miṣr. Cairo: Maṭbaʿat al-Maʿārif wa Maktabatuhā, 1938.
Ṣawt Abī al-ʿAlāʾ. Cairo: Maṭbaʿat al-Maʿārif wa Maktabatuhā, 1944.
Jannat al-shawk. Cairo: Dār al-Maʿārif, 1945.
Al-Shaykhān. Cairo: Dār al-Maʿārif, 1960.

TRANSLATIONS

An Egyptian Childhood. Trans. by E. H. Paxton. London: Routledge, 1932; London: Heinemann, 1981.
Leaders of Thought. Trans. by Hasan A. Lutfi. Beirut, Lebanon: Imp. Khalife, 1932.
The Stream of Days: A Student at the Azhar. Trans. by Hilary Wayment. Cairo: al-Maʿarif Printing and Publishing House, 1943.
The Future of Culture in Egypt. Trans. by Sidney Glazer. Washington, D.C.: American Council of Learned Societies, 1954.
The Dreams of Scheherezade. Trans. by Magdi Wahba. Cairo: General Egyptian Book Organization, 1974.
A Passage to France. Trans. by Kenneth Cragg. Leiden, Holland: Brill, 1976.
The Call of the Curlew. Trans. by A. B. as-Safi. Leiden, Holland: Brill, 1980.
The Sufferers: Stories and Polemics. Trans. by Mona al-Zayyat. Cairo: The American University in Cairo Press, 1993.

CRITICAL STUDIES

Cachia, Pierre. *Ṭāhā Ḥusayn: His Place in the Egyptian Literary Renaissance*. London: Luzac, 1956.
———. *An Overview of Modern Arabic Literature*. Edinburgh, U.K.: Edinburgh University Press, 1990.
Semah, David. *Four Egyptian Literary Critics*. Leiden, Holland: Brill, 1974.
Tahar, Meftah. *Taha Husayn: Sa critique littéraire et ses sources françaises*. Tunis, Tunisia: Maison Arabe du Livre, 1976.
ʿUṣfūr, Jābir. *Al-Marāyā al-mutajāwira*. Cairo: al-Hayʾa al-Miṣriyya al-ʿĀmma li al-Kitāb, 1983.

Amos Tutuola

1920–

OYEKAN OWOMOYELA

AMOS TUTUOLA was born in 1920 in Abeokuta in the present-day Ogun State in the western part of Nigeria (then a British colony), to Yoruba parents: Charles Tutuola, a cocoa farmer, and Esther Aina Tutuola. According to the biography he appended to his first publication, *The Palm-Wine Drinkard and His Dead Palm-Wine Tapster in the Deads' Town* (1952), when he was seven years old a cousin of his father's took him to a Mr. F. O. Monu, an Igbo man, under an arrangement by which Monu would send young Amos to school in return for domestic service. Monu enrolled him in the Salvation Army school of Abeokuta in 1934 and later brought him to Lagos in 1936.

AN INAUSPICIOUS PRELUDE

Tutuola continued his schooling in Lagos under circumstances that were far from promising. He was subjected to privations by Monu's housekeeper, whom Tutuola describes as "a cruel-hearted woman": she virtually starved him, overworked him, and generally impeded his education. After two years he returned to Abeokuta, where he enrolled in the Anglican Central School, Ipose Ake. His father, who farmed about twenty miles away from Abeokuta, assumed responsibility for his schooling and living expenses, but Tutuola had to supplement what his father could afford by fetching and selling firewood. He also spent his weekends trekking to help on his father's farm.

In 1939 Tutuola's father died suddenly. Denied the means to continue his schooling, Tutuola resolved to try his hand at farming; but the venture failed, and he returned to Lagos to live with his half-brother and learn a trade. He soon qualified as a blacksmith, and in 1944 he joined the West African Air Corps of the Royal Air Force as a coppersmith based in the British colony. Demobilized after World War II, he failed in his attempt to establish himself as an independent metal-worker and later as a professional photographer. He was no more successful at finding other employment, for the demobilized combat soldiers from abroad who swelled the employment lines had priority in job placement. Under these difficult circumstances he married Alake Victoria in 1947. A year later he took a job in the Colonial Service as a messenger in the Labour Department.

These first three decades of Tutuola's life certainly were not an auspicious prelude to a successful writing career, and by Tutuola's own admission he became a published author by mere chance. In his employment as a messenger, his days consisted of long stretches of boredom spent at a desk awaiting the summons to run an occasional errand. He filled the long idle hours by scribbling stories on loose sheets of paper. Also employed in the Labour Department at the same time was his friend Edward Akinbiyi, who swapped stories with him.

When Tutuola sought to publish his stories, he first turned for some reason to Focal Press, a London publisher of photography books. Its director, A. Kraszna-Krausz, was kind enough to buy the material for a nominal sum, mainly to reward Tutuola's industry: he thought the material unpublishable. Later Tutuola saw an advertisement by the United Society for Christian Literature for books and sent another manuscript to Lutterworth Press, the society's publisher in Cambridge, England. It was not the sort of thing they published, but they forwarded it to Nelson and Sons, the London publisher of another Nigerian writer, D. O. Fagunwa. Nelson was uninterested, but Faber and Faber agreed to publish it. Tutuola's literary career thus began with the publication of *The Palm-Wine Drinkard* in 1952. He has proved a productive writer over the years, with several full-length works and a collection of short stories to his credit.

Tutuola continued to write, remaining in his messenger's job until he moved to Ibadan in 1957 to work as a storekeeper for the Nigerian Broadcasting Corporation. Also at Ibadan at the time was the pediatrician Robert Collis, on whom Tutuola's *Palm-Wine Drinkard* had made a great impression. In 1958 he persuaded Geoffrey Axworthy, then in charge of drama at the University College, Ibadan (now the University of Ibadan), to adapt the novel for the stage. Adapting it proved difficult, however, until Kola Ogunmola, the great actor and leader of a Yoruba opera troupe, was brought into residence at the university in 1962 to lend his talent to the task. Collaborating with the artist and stage designer Demas Nwoko, and with funding from UNESCO (United Nations Educational, Scientific, and Cultural Organization), Ogunmola and his troupe premiered *The Palmwine Drinkard* in April 1963. The production was a spectacular success, and it played a significant role in enhancing Tutuola's reputation as an author.

The adulation he enjoyed after his first book appeared in print did not blind Tutuola to his limitations as a writer. Rather, his success apparently persuaded him to take steps to hone his skills in the tools of his trade. He accordingly embarked on a course of self-improvement, enrolling in evening classes and expanding his exposure to mythology and literature. Among the works he read, and whose influences are apparent in his later works, are John Bunyan's *The Pilgrim's Progress*, *The Arabian Nights*, Aldous Huxley's *The Devils of Loudun*, Joyce Cary's *Mister Johnson*, Edith Hamilton's *Mythology*, and nonfictional works such as the Brookings Institution's *A Survey of Economic Education.*

Tremendous controversy has swirled in critical circles around Tutuola, one faction touting his powerful imagination and defending his use of substandard English, and another dismissing his materials as unoriginal and overindulgent, and wondering, in the novelist V. S. Naipaul's words, "in what other age could bad grammar have been a literary asset?" (p. 87). Despite all of that, Tutuola enjoys considerable following among students of African literature in Europe and the United States, and increasingly even in Nigeria, where his writing initially had generated considerable hostility. Yet it is ironic that his international reputation has not made him as visible on the international academic lecture circuit as his stature would indicate, nor has he enjoyed the status of a visiting professor of creative writing in a university as other African writers with comparable standing have. On the other hand, he received a significant early boost in 1962 when Gerald Moore included him in his critical study *Seven African Writers*. Also he was appointed as a visiting research fellow at the University of Ife (now

Obafemi Awolowo University) in 1979, and he was an associate of the International Writing Program at the University of Iowa in 1983. In the mid 1990s he was retired, living at Ibadan and sometimes at Ago-Odo.

THE PALM-WINE DRINKARD

The Palm-Wine Drinkard and His Dead Palm-Wine Tapster in the Deads' Town is an account of a young man's quest for the man who tapped palm wine for him after the tapster's untimely death. The eldest of his father's eighteen children, the young "drinkard" had been an incurable alcoholic from the age of ten, and his father had obligingly engaged the services of a palm-wine tapster whose sole duty was to keep the drinkard and his friends in steady supply of their favorite beverage. One day, though, while performing his duties, the tapster falls from the top of a palm tree and dies. The drinkard is unable to find another tapster, and his drinking friends desert him. "One fine morning," he says, "I took all my native juju [charm] and also my father's juju with me and I left my father's home to find out whereabouts was my tapster who had died" (p. 9).

The first person he approaches for directions to Deads' Town is an old man, who gives him three tasks, one being to capture and bring Death to him. He accomplishes the tasks, but the old man runs away when the drinkard approaches with Death in custody. His next adventure proves more fortunate: having found the lost daughter of the head of a town, he takes her as his wife, and she becomes his companion for the rest of his quest. Along the way they have an extraordinary son, a "half-bodied baby," who turns out to be a scourge and a pyromaniac, and whom they have great difficulty ridding themselves of, until Dance, Song, and Drum come to their rescue. On Wraith Island, the abode of the most beautiful creatures, they enjoy the hospitality of the kind inhabitants. From there they proceed toward Unreturnable-Heaven's Town, and after numerous encounters with sundry strange creatures they arrive there only to find it populated by most wicked and most contrary beings. These beings shave and pepper the couple's heads, bury them up to their necks, and leave them for an eagle to pluck out their eyes. Fortunately for them, the drinkard had tamed such a bird before he left his town, and the eagle leaves them unharmed.

Their most pleasant experience is their stay with the Faithful-Mother in her capacious and lavishly appointed White-Tree home. Here, life is a continuous round of dancing and drinking, and eating food cooked by 340 cooks. The tree also features a casino where the drinkard gambles away the money he had earlier earned from renting his fear to someone else. Life with Faithful-Mother is so comfortable that the drinkard forgets the object of his quest and wishes to remain there for good; eventually, though, the two resume their journey with the Faithful-Mother's gifts, including guns, ammunition, and cigarettes.

They eventually arrive at Deads' Town, after ten years and numerous other adventures, and there they find the tapster, whose name we now learn is Baity. Although he cannot return with them to live with "alives," he rewards the drinkard with a magic egg that provides anything he asks. The couple returns home to find the drinkard's town in the grips of famine resulting from a quarrel between heaven and earth. With the aid of the magic egg, the drinkard relieves the people's suffering, but the careless, satiated people accidentally break the egg. Left again without food, they resort to insulting their benefactor, who glues the egg back together only to discover that now it will produce only whips. The drinkard gets back at the ungrateful people by assembling them for one more "feast"—a feast of well-deserved whipping.

Tutuola has given interviewers various accounts about the sources of the materials he includes in his books and short stories. To Arthur Calder-Marshall, he gave credit for the palm-wine stories to a very old man he visited one Sunday morning on his father's farm. The old man reportedly served Tutuola some roasted yam and palm wine, which made him tipsy and sleepy. The host let him sleep off the wine's worst effects and woke him up after about an hour; then he told the tale of the palm-wine drinkard. Tutuola wrote his book in five days, writing for three hours each day. To Eric Larrabee he told a slightly different story. According to Larrabee, Tutuola got the material from an old man who told stories on a palm plantation that Tutuola frequented on Sundays. Tutuola told Larrabee that he had "composed" *The Palm-Wine Drinkard* in two days and wrote it in three months during 1950, "just playing with it," for lack of any better thing to do (p. 13). Yet to the Nigerian correspondent who wrote "Portrait: A Life in the Bush of Ghosts" in *West Africa* (1 May 1954), Tutuola gave a very different account: the sources were his mother and aunt with whom he lived in the township of Iporo-Ake, Abeokuta, and who told him stories they heard from their mother. The different versions credit "elder" figures as sources and are therefore consistent with common knowledge about the transmission of folktales in nonliterate societies. One is tempted to infer that Tutuola, perhaps with some urging from more sophisticated advisers, was attempting to downplay his undoubtedly heavy reliance on the work of D. O. Fagunwa.

Tutuola owes the success of the book, and eventually of his career, in large measure to the enthusiastic review Dylan Thomas gave *The Palm-Wine Drinkard.* He lauded the book as a "brief, thronged, grisly and bewildering story, or series of stories, written in young English by a West African, about the journey of an expert and devoted palm-wine drinkard through a nightmare of indescribable adventures, all simply and carefully described in the spirit-bristling bush" (p. 7). Other reviewers echoed the praise in Europe and the United States, where a Grove Press edition appeared in 1953. Some also acknowledged the paradoxes of his art. Larrabee, for example, described him as "an author who (1) probably has never met another author, (2) owns no books, (3) is not known to his daily acquaintances as an author, (4) has no personal contact with his publisher, (5) is not certain where his book is on sale, and (6) does not think of himself as an author" (p. 13). He also recorded Tutuola as telling him, "I think, when you reach there, the U.S.A., you write a letter to me"; asked why he wanted a letter, he responded, "so I know you not forget me" (p. 14).

That brief exchange, especially Larrabee's care to preserve Tutuola's flawed English, offers an explanation for the incredulity of many Africans, especially Nigerians, at the acclaim Tutuola and his work were receiving abroad. They had learned that dexterity in handling language was a necessity for a literary career, and they found Tutuola's critical reception befuddling. In addition, his plot was so offhand and its structure so haphazard that the western critics' praise for the work was to them inexplicable. In addition, Nigerian (especially Yoruba) readers familiar with Fagunwa's earlier works like *Ògbójú Ode Nínú Igbó Irúnmalè* (1938), which Wole Soyinka later translated into English as *The Forest of a Thousand Daemons: A Hunter's Saga* (1968), immediately recognized what Bernth Lindfors later described, in "Literary Syncretism and the Yoruba Folk Tradition" (1986), as "a strong kindred relationship between the texts [of Tutuola's works and Fagunwa's], possibly bordering on plagiarism" (p. 635). When the material in Tutuola's fiction is not lifted almost bodily from Fagunwa, it is borrowed from recognizable folktales and usually has suffered some deterioration in Tutuola's rendering. Critics have nevertheless been rather indulgent toward him — Lindfors, for example, has argued that in his borrowings Tutuola is "working well within the conventions governing oral storytelling" (p. 635). That argument is problematic, though, because Tutuola operates not in the context of oral storytelling but in that of literature.

The obvious weakness of Tutuola's command of English, his maladroit handling of plot and structure, and his lack of originality were not the only factors that caused his compatriots to suspect ulterior motives behind the praises non-African critics showered on him. There were also observations like that of Anthony West, who saw in *The Palm-Wine Drinkard* "a glimpse of the very beginning of literature, that moment when writing at last seizes and pins down the myths and legends of an analphabetic culture" (p. 17), and comments like Selden Rodman's that "Amos Tutuola is not a revolutionist of the word, not a mathematician, not a surrealist. He is a true primitive" (p. 15). I. Adeagbo Akinjobin voiced his misgivings in a letter to *West Africa* on 5 June 1954: he found the news that *The Palm-Wine Drinkard* had already been translated into French startling, for he believed that the lively European interest in the book resulted not from their assessment of its literary value but from Europeans' love to "believe all sorts of fantastic tales about Africa, a continent of which they are profoundly ignorant" (p. 41). After Tutuola had got his money, Akinjogbin complained, the ones who would suffer the consequences of the images of Africa he had propagated were "the unfortunate ones who have cause to come to England or Europe." Tutuola was undaunted by the controversy his first book generated, and two years after its publication he was out with another.

THE "BUSH OF GHOSTS" NOVELS

Evident in the second work is a characteristic that Tutuola's subsequent publications have confirmed: unlike other writers with a comparable output, he has not demonstrated a penchant or capability for much variation from one work to the next. He has largely repeated himself, indeed at times parodied himself, so much so that critics assert with justification that to have read one Tutuola work is to have read them all. The quest pattern reappears almost invariably from one book to the next, as do certain episodes and characters.

My Life in the Bush of Ghosts (1954) is a revision of a manuscript that predated *The Palm-Wine Drinkard* but was to be published much later as *The Wild Hunter in the Bush of Ghosts* (1982). In fact, in *The Palm-Wine Drinkard* the hero employs juju, which he says characters in the bush of ghosts had earlier given to him. The story in *My Life* is not by definition exactly a quest, for the hero's entry into the bush of ghosts is unintentional. *The Wild Hunter* differs only in some details from *My Life*, not so significantly that they cannot be considered together. In the first chapter of *The Wild Hunter*, a preface to the real adventure, the hero's father tells him the night before his death of his own adventure in the bush. The hero, who is twenty, begins his own career as a hunter three months after his father's death. He finds himself in the bush of ghosts because a small tree on which he had fallen asleep carries him there. The similarity of the opening, the title, and general plot layout to those of Fagunwa's *Ògbójú Ode* is unmistakable, although Tutuola's work is not as burdened with heavy-handed moralization as is Fagunwa's.

The teaser about the father's earlier experiences is absent in *My Life*, and here the hero is seven. His mother leaves him and his eleven-year-old brother in the care of her jealous junior co-wives, who abandon them at the approach of an invading army. The older brother tries to carry the hero to safety, but he keeps falling after every few steps; somewhat precociously, the seven-year-old tells his older brother to leave him and escape so as to be able later to look after their mother. Left alone, and being "very young to understand the meaning of 'bad' and 'good,'" he enters the bush of ghosts, which is "so dreadful that no superior earthly person ever entered it" (p. 22).

The hunters' careers in the bush of ghosts in both books exemplify Tutuola's repetitive exploitation of episodes and incidents in different works. For example, among those present at the hero's first wedding in the eighth town of *My Life*, at which the Reverend Devil officiates, are creatures from *The Palm-Wine Drinkard*, such as Give and Take and the Invincible and Invisible Pawn; furthermore, in the thirteenth town of the same work we encounter the "flash-eyed mother," the sole female resident and ruler of the town, and the mother of "the short ghosts" (p. 97). These details recall those pertaining to *The Brave African Huntress* (1958) and its heroine, Adebisi. In addition, the flash-eyed mother's army includes *Palm-Wine Drinkard* characters such as "all the soldiers of 'Wraith-Island' . . . 'Spirit of prey' . . . 'Invisible and Invincible Pawn' . . . White long creatures, Hungry creature, Shapeless-creatures, and also the 'Palm-wine tapster', who is living in Deads'-town" (p. 107).

In both bush-of-ghosts books, Tutuola's worlds replicate phenomena that reveal the author's admirations and aspirations. Typical is the tenth town, where the hero's dead cousin is the bishop of the Methodist synod, who earlier had introduced a Methodist church, converted the ghosts, and established a Methodist school and modern medical services, with the aid of a lady from Zulu country who serves as director of medical services (pp. 144–151). He has also built police stations as well as ordinary and assize courts —where he presides over the more difficult cases—and even prison yards (p. 152). The fourth town in *The Wild Hunter* boasts a Salvation Army church run by a benevolent South African, Victoria Juliana, one of whose accomplishments is the founding of a school for illiterate ghosts. The final stop in *The Wild Hunter* is Heaven, with "Glorious Technicolours" and busy orchestras, a scene reminiscent of the Faithful-Mother's luxurious White-Tree house in *The Palm-Wine Drinkard*. In both books the adventure ends with the hero's safe return home, with the assistance of a "Television-handed ghostess" in *My Life*, and with the aid of Miss Victoria Juliana in *The Wild Hunter*.

SIMBI AND THE SATYR OF THE DARK JUNGLE

Tutuola's third book to appear in print is *Simbi and the Satyr of the Dark Jungle* (1955). Another quest romance, it recounts the hardships a young and beautiful woman endures when she sets out in search of experience. Simbi is the song-loving only daughter of a wealthy woman who has pampered and sheltered her. When her close friends Rali and Sala are kidnapped, she becomes disconsolate and disaffected from her privileged life. "I am now entirely fed up with my mother's wealths," she muses. "I can no longer bear to remain in the happiness, etc., giving me by my mother's wealths. And merriments are now too much for me than what I can bear longer than this time. But the only things that I prefer most to know and experience their difficulties now are the 'Poverty' and the 'Punishment'" (p. 8). Against her mother's wishes, and with the help of an Ifa priest, she manages to get herself kidnapped by the same Dogo who had earlier abducted her friends, and she is off on her adventure.

Simbi has the distinction among Tutuola's works of being narrated in the third person rather than the customary first person, and it features far more dialogue than in his earlier works. An unnumbered introductory chapter gives the reason for Simbi's dissatisfaction with her life; each of the remaining twelve numbered chapters bears a thematic title indicative of the adventure the chapter will purvey. After he kidnaps her, Dogo takes Simbi to a town where nobody sings. There she is fattened, sold as a slave, and subjected to abuse by the character "myrmidon."

After she startles her master to death with her singing, she is sealed in a coffin and set adrift. Fortunately, some fishermen discover her downstream and take her as a slave to their king. Already enslaved to him are other captives Dogo had kidnapped earlier from Simbi's town. In circumstances that are unlikely in a characteristically Tutuolan way, just as the king is about to behead and sacrifice her to his gods along with the other slaves, she snatches his sword and beheads him and his attendants, freeing herself and her fellow captives. Later she escapes execution in the town of the "multi-coloured people" after she has been caught stealing their king's possessions; she fights the Satyr of the Dark Jungle, is abducted by an eagle, and is almost swallowed by a boa.

Rescued by a woodcutter, she becomes his wife, but runs away from him and his town after each of her two sons is sacrificed shortly after birth. She eventually returns home after vanquishing the Satyr a final time and releasing three kidnapped victims from Dogo, whom she also weans from his kidnapping career. Back in her town with her friend Rali and the recently released captives, Simbi goes from house to house in her village, "warning all the children that it was a great mistake to [*sic*] a girl who did not obey her parents" (p. 136). Yet her own disobedience has a happy issue, for she returns home with the three gods (of thunder, of famine, and of iron) she had acquired in the town of poverty, gods who prove most bountiful to the people of her village.

The jolting presence of "myrmidon" in the work, as well as that of the Satyr and his helper, the phoenix, attests to Tutuola's indebtedness to Hamilton's *Mythology*; Simbi's abduction by the eagle similarly attests to his debt to *The Arabian Nights*. Additional evidence of his reading is his occasional use of vocabulary that is conspicuously out of place in the context of his overall style, sometimes straying into malapropism. A good example is "myrmidon," which Tutuola uses (in quotation marks and without a definite article) to describe a new character; the reader later gathers that the character is a servant of some sort. Also, Fagunwa's ghostly presence is evident in exchanges like the one between Simbi and the Satyr at their initial meeting; the challenges and boasts are practically verbatim reproductions (in English translation) of Esu-kekere-ode's and Olowoaiye's when the two meet before the gate to Igbo Olodumare in Fagunwa's *Ògbójú Ode* (pp. 14–17).

THE BRAVE AFRICAN HUNTRESS

Although Simbi can hold her own against any adversary, male or female, human or nonhuman, Adebisi, the heroine of *The Brave African Huntress*, is even more fearsome and formidable. When her father retires as the head of his town's hunting fraternity, Adebisi inherits his mantle and hunting paraphernalia; her four older brothers had earlier disappeared during a hunting trip to the Jungle of the Pigmies. The jungle is immensely rich in minerals, but the Pigmies capture people who intrude into their territory. Apart from the Pigmies, adventurers also have to contend with dangerous animals and strange creatures. Adebisi undertakes to kill off all the Pigmies and a strange wild animal with "about sixteen horns on forehead ... a kind of two fearful eyes which had a kind of powerful light," as well as a boa constrictor (p. 16).

One of the great appeals that the early work of Tutuola's well-known compatriot Chinua Achebe had for Europeans was its anthropological quality, its exposure of the workings of African traditional institutions to the European reading public. Especially attractive to them was his liberal sprinkling of proverbs throughout the texts of *Things Fall Apart*, *No Longer at Ease*, and *Arrow of God*. By comparison, Tutuola is not a reliable guide to his society's institutions or cultural practices, notwithstanding his apologists' assertions to the contrary. He has, of course, always borrowed characters and episodes from Yoruba folktales, but unlike Achebe he had not taken advantage of his culture's rich stock of proverbs until *The Brave African Huntress.* In this work he employs proverbs as epigraphs at the heads of his chapters in which he goes on to develop the significance of the proverbs. Unfortunately, his use of the proverbs is sometimes forced and sometimes rather ineffective.

Episodes adapted from Yoruba folktales include Adebisi's discovery, when she becomes the barber to the king of Ibembe town, that the king has two horns; a wandering destitute woman's stumbling into an all-male town where she becomes royalty but, on entering a forbidden room, finds herself back in her poor state; and the sequence involving a talking gourd that chases Adebisi. The setup of the whole quest in this book recalls the story of Jigbo, son of Oluwo, in which a farmer's pampered son insists on becoming a hunter despite his parents' entreaties and suffers untold hardship after venturing into the forest.

Also of interest in this work is Tutuola's use of the Yoruba names (in English translation) for the days of the week: the Day of Immortality (*Ojó Àìkù*), Sunday; the Day of Riches (*Ojó Ajé*), Monday; the Day of Victory (*Ojó Ìségun*), Tuesday; the Day of Confusion (*Ojóo Rírú*), Wednesday; the Day of New Creation (*Ojó Àsèsèdáyé*), Thursday; the Day of Trouble (*Ojó Etì*), Friday; and the Day of Three Resolutions (*Ojó Àbá Méta*), Saturday. In the plot, the designation of the day invariably determines what Adebisi's fortune will be during that particular day. The only day on which nothing memorable happens to her seems to be Monday, the Day of Riches. Tutuola continues this usage, but only sparingly, in later works, such as *Ajaiyi and His Inherited Poverty* (1967).

With regard to Adebisi (more than to Simbi), readers must constantly remind themselves that they are reading about the exploits of a woman. She succeeds in all her tasks—killing off all the Pigmies and the dangerous animals, freeing thousands of people the Pigmies had kept in their custody, including her brothers—and returns home with precious metals, after selling which she "became a rich lady at once" (p. 150). In all of these tasks she is spectacularly violent and bloody. Whether she represents a victory for feminism or bad characterization is a judgment the reader must make.

FEATHER WOMAN OF THE JUNGLE

The essential sameness of Tutuola's works persists in *Feather Woman of the Jungle* (1962), with the difference that the plot consists of several forays into the world of weird creatures, rather than one. During the first trip, from which the book derives its title, the narrator and his brother Alabi venture into the bush in search of riches to relieve the penury that has plunged their father into disgrace. There they encounter the Feather Woman (Jungle Witch), who adds them to her collection of petrified images because they disobey her housekeeping instructions. Their sister Ashabi comes to liberate them, after she has had her own share of excitement.

The book is structured as a series of stories told in retrospect over the span of ten nights by the hero, now seventy-six and chief of his village. His audience is a crowd that gathers each moonlit night to listen to him, drink palm wine, and generally make merry. The work obviously derives its structure from Scheherazade's performance in *The Arabian Nights.* The first adventure, which involves the hero, his brother, and his sister, takes up the first two nights. The subsequent journeys are solo trips. Like Tutuola's other works, *Feather Woman* incorporates material from Yoruba folktales: for example, the three specialized hunter's dogs (Sweeper, Cutter, and Swallower) who rescue their owner from dangerous spots, and the tale of the bounteous object received from an Old Woman of the Sea, which first dispenses largess and later inflicts punishment. One interesting touch is the inclusion of elements of Yoruba mythology concerning Ile-Ife, the legendary site of the creation of the world and reputed original home of the Yoruba (where supposedly one may see the well from which the moon rises), and also the site of the shoe marks of the first white men to visit the Yoruba world. In this work, too, the hero ends his career a rich man, thanks to the diamonds he appropriates from the Land of Diamonds, where he also finds a wife, Sela.

AJAIYI AND HIS INHERITED POVERTY

Ajaiyi and His Inherited Poverty offers no appreciable departure from Tutuola's format or style. It is of particular interest, however, that the narrator here recalls experiences she had in an earlier incarnation two centuries before. Then a boy named Ajaiyi, now she is a girl; then a farmer, now she is a storyteller; then a wicked "gentile" (Tutuola's word for a pagan), now she is a Christian; then the poorest person in the village, she is now the richest. In the earlier life the narrator is fifteen and has a twelve-year-old sister, Aina; their parents are hunchbacks and extremely poor. After their parents' death the children are kidnapped and sold into slavery, and they escape being sacrificed in circumstances that repeat Simbi's. That is in fact only one of several instances of déjà vu in the story.

Leaving his sister behind, Ajaiyi embarks on the more spectacular part of his quest to escape poverty, a quest that takes him to the Creator from whom he receives no relief, and to the Devil whose offer he refuses because the strings attached are unacceptable. Back in his village with his poverty unmitigated, he is duped by the village witch doctor he consults for help. On the witch doctor's advice, Ajaiyi pawns himself for money to purchase rams to sacrifice to his dead father, rams that the witch doctor secretly appropriates for himself. In the end, the culprit's tricks are exposed, and he forfeits all his money, six thousand pounds, to Ajaiyi.

Having learned during his wanderings that possession of money could entail great misfortune, Ajaiyi resolves not to keep his new wealth but to build churches with it, one in his own village, and one in the village of each of three pawnbrokers who had earlier come to his aid. His preaching in his own church and the miraculous cures he effects through prayer convert the "evil worshippers and idol worshippers," whose monetary gifts make him a wealthy man.

This work is significant for the way in which Tutuola vividly demonstrates his characteristic creative strategy. When compared with the short story of the same title in the collection *The Village Witch Doctor and Other Stories* (1990), it fully vindicates Lindfors' statement that Tutuola's plots are characterized by a "loosely coordinated internal structure, the result of a concatenation of discrete fictive units strung together in an almost random order on the lifeline of a fabulous hero" (1986, pp. 634–635). The short story reveals the origin of Ajaiyi's poverty; he inherited it from his father Jaye, whose father Aro passed it down to him. The riches bequeathed Aro by his father had been stolen by Osanyin, the village witch doctor. Ajaiyi seeks help from Osanyin, who advises him to purchase rams and to sacrifice them to his dead father. The ending of the long fiction and the short story differ only in that the latter ends with Ajaiyi recovering the money Osanyin had stolen from his grandfather, and Ajaiyi is not inhibited by Christian scruples in the enjoyment of his newfound wealth.

THE WITCH-HERBALIST OF THE REMOTE TOWN

The Witch-Herbalist of the Remote Town (1981), Tutuola's seventh long fiction, is based on a Yoruba folktale about the Yoruba trickster Àjàpá (Tortoise). His search for a medicine to cure his wife's infertility takes him to an herbalist who gives him a potent medicine. The herbalist warns him not to taste any of it because it is a surefire and indiscriminate pregnancy inducer. Àjàpá ignores the advice and duly becomes pregnant. Tutuola's elaboration of the tale, which appeared after a long creative silence of fourteen years in which he published nothing, provides the hero with four companions — Mr First "Mind," Mr Second "Mind," and Mr Third "Mind" (the last being his memory), and his "Supreme Second" — in his encounters with the usual cast of weird adversaries, creatures like the Brutal Ape, the Abnormal Squatting Man of the Jungle, the Long-Breasted Mother of the Mountain, the Crazy Removable-Headed Wild Man, and the Offensive Wild People. The American writer John Updike detects in the story "a certain psychological realism in [the] subdivided hero as he keeps trying to rally his scattered inner forces and bring them, like a sulky committee, to a vote of action" (p. 123); he nonetheless locates the book "in the realm neither of dream or of legend but of indulged imagination" (p. 124).

YORUBA FOLKTALES

Yoruba Folktales (1986) is a collection of seven folktales told in language that is markedly different from the "young English" that is a Tutuola hallmark. It is practically flawless, although it preserves some of the peculiar usages of his earlier writing. The first two stories are about Ajantala, Fagunwa's memorable creation that has appeared several times in Tutuola's fiction. "Ajantala, the Noxious Guest Is Born" and "Ajantala and the Three Brothers" are reworkings of "Ajantala, the Noxious Guest" published in Langston Hughes's *An African Treasury* (1961). "Segi and the Boa Constrictor" is essentially the story of the Complete Gentleman from *The Palm-Wine Drinkard*, and for the others Tutuola turns to his usual sources, Yoruba folktales and Fagunwa. A new source, though, is Hubert Ogunde, the famous Yoruba opera artist whose *Half and Half* supplies the idea for "The Elephant Woman and the Hunter."

The book's publication by Ibadan University Press, with a subsidy from the Ford Foundation, represents a major coup for Tutuola and something of a formal endorsement of him by the premier university of his country. The flawlessness of its language is due to the editorial intervention of Robert Wren, whom the publishers credit for introducing them to the author. The book's designation as *Yoruba Folktales* is somewhat problematic, for while some suggestion of Yoruba ethos exists in some of the stories, in important respects they distort Yoruba beliefs and practices. Furthermore, the plots are often so illogical that they cannot support the moralizing that is a major function of Yoruba folktales. For these reasons, and because the tales are not even in the Yoruba language, one must judge the title a misnomer.

PAUPER, BRAWLER, AND SLANDERER

Tutuola followed *Yoruba Folktales* with *Pauper, Brawler, and Slanderer* (1987), the story of Prince Adegun (Pauper). At his birth an oracle predicts that he will grow up to be big and strong and a most indefatigable worker, but that the harder he works, "the more his poverty and wretchedness will become worse!" (p. 3). His father will expel him from his town of Laketu, and in his travels he will be crowned the king of a distant town. However, even that event will not end his poverty, for he will eventually be chased from the throne and the town. This prophecy comes to pass in all its particulars, and along the way Adegun marries Brawler, the daughter of one of his father's prominent chiefs, and a woman for whom "hotful" and "hurtful" brawling are an involuntary affliction that often prevents her from eating. Slanderer, the son of another of Laketu's chiefs, completes the trio of principals in the book. His slandering is later the cause of Pauper's expulsion from his throne and the source of much trouble for all three. They cause so much confusion in Laketu town that many of its inhabitants flee. In anger, the king curses the three, turning Pauper and Brawler into "immortals," and expels them all from the town.

The world of the book is one in which poverty is an existential condition that defies industry, birth into wealth, and inheritance of riches, but one in which humans can overpower and thwart death and a mortal king can transform offenders to "immortals" by mere word of mouth. Fagunwa's enduring influence is evident in this work also. At the end the characters find themselves at a place called the horizon and alternatively "the Land of Judgment," where land and sky meet. There they are lectured on the proper uses of wealth by the "Judge of Creator" on behalf of Creator. The closeness of the denouement to the Langbodo sequence of Fagunwa's *Ògbójú Ode* is not accidental. One feature Tutuola borrows in this work from Yoruba folklore is its explanatory ending: the Judge of Creator changes Pauper and Brawler into smoke and Slanderer into a whirlwind, and he disperses them all over the earth to plague people.

THE VILLAGE WITCH DOCTOR AND OTHER STORIES

After *Pauper, Brawler, and Slanderer* came *The Village Witch Doctor and Other Stories*, consisting of eleven short pieces in addition to the shorter version of *Ajaiyi and His Inherited Poverty*. Some of these were earlier published in magazines and some were broadcast on radio. "A Short Biography of Tortoise" and "A Short Biography of Yanribo" reintroduce the characters from "The Shell-Man and the Terror of the Bush" in *Yoruba Folktales*, "Ajao and the Active Bone" rehashes the often exploited motif of the all-providing object, and "The Rich Husbandman and His Odd-Looking Pawn" is a conflation of the "Give-and-Take" story from *Drinkard* as well as the incident in Fagunwa's *Ògbójú Ode* in which Olórí Igbó complains that a human being has preempted his participation in a ritual gathering by camping on his neck (versions of which have appeared in earlier works by Tutuola). Its different ending shows Tutuola's resourcefulness in making variants out of his own and others' stories. In this work, too, Wren provided some stylistic help, although not nearly as intrusively as in *Folktales*.

CONCLUSION

On the whole, Tutuola's career has been marked by ironies. It is certainly ironic that he emerged as a major writer in spite of his deficiencies in education and the skills usually considered essential for such a calling. The trends that critical reactions to his career have followed also have their ironies. The initially effusive approbation abroad had by the 1970s become overtaken by a palpable cooling of enthusiasm—yet, as if to make up for that reversal, Nigerian scholars began to warm toward him. Achebe probably raised some eyebrows when, delivering the first Equiano Memorial Lecture at the University of Ibadan in 1987, he described Tutuola as "the most moralistic of all Nigerian writers" (p. 68). Using episodes from *The Palm-Wine Drinkard*, he represented the author as posing profound moral questions about the consequences of choosing, for example, industry rather than indolence, and of respecting or violating others' spaces. Achebe's view was a major revision of the prevailing critical assessment of Tutuola's achievements. Other instances involve Omolara Ogundipe-Leslie, who in a 1970 article reassessing Tutuola's career praised his accurate representation of an African (and a Yoruba) consciousness, and Abiola Irele, who about the same time commended him for "the extension he has given to the traditional fantasy in Yoruba folktale, and to the mythical novel in Yoruba created by Fagunwa" (p. 17). Finally, Chinweizu and his coauthors of *Toward the Decolonization of African Literature* have pronounced Tutuola superior to writers from "the African bourgeoisie"—among whom they include Wole Soyinka, the Nigerian author who won the Nobel Prize in literature in 1986—on the question of fidelity to African cosmography.

Tutuola has been both a beneficiary and a victim of the vagaries of the short history of African writing. His original popularity can be attributed to the novelty and sparseness of Africans writing in European languages in the 1950s, but as more and more Africans with better literary ability than his began to be published, he inevitably lost his appeal. His work will perhaps continue to attract readers, but, without doubt, his anomalous career will continue to be of great interest to historians of African literature.

Selected Bibliography

NOVELS

Tutuola, Amos. *The Palm-Wine Drinkard and His Dead Palm-Wine Tapster in the Deads' Town.* London: Faber & Faber, 1952; New York: Grove, 1953.

My Life in the Bush of Ghosts. London: Faber & Faber, 1954; New York: Grove, 1954.

Simbi and the Satyr of the Dark Jungle. London: Faber & Faber, 1955; San Francisco: City Lights, 1983.

The Brave African Huntress. London: Faber & Faber, 1958; New York: Grove, 1958.

Feather Woman of the Jungle. London: Faber & Faber, 1962; San Francisco: City Lights, 1988.

Ajaiyi and His Inherited Poverty. London: Faber & Faber, 1967.

The Witch-Herbalist of the Remote Town. London: Faber & Faber, 1981.

The Wild Hunter in the Bush of Ghosts. Washington, D.C.: Three Continents, 1982. Rev. ed., 1989.

Pauper, Brawler, and Slanderer. London and Boston: Faber & Faber, 1987.

SHORT STORIES

"Ajantala, the Noxious Guest." In Langston Hughes, ed., *An African Treasury.* New York: Pyramid, 1961.

The Village Witch Doctor and Other Stories. London and Boston: Faber & Faber, 1990.

FOLKTALES

Yoruba Folktales. Ibadan, Nigeria: Ibadan University Press, 1986.

INTERVIEWS

Gargan, Edward A. "From a Nigerian Pen, Yoruba Tales." In *New York Times* (23 February 1986).

Nkosi, Lewis. "Conversation with Amos Tutuola." In *Africa Report* 9, no. 7 (1964).

Obe, Ad'Obe. "An Encounter with Amos Tutuola." In *West Africa* (14 May 1984).

Omotoso, Kole. "Interview with Amos Tutuola." In *Afriscope* 4, no. 1 (1974).

BIOGRAPHICAL AND CRITICAL STUDIES

Achebe, Chinua. "Work and Play in Tutuola's *The Palm-Wine Drinkard.*" In his *Hopes and Impediments: Selected Essays, 1965–1987.* London: Heinemann, 1988.

Afolayan, A. "Language and Sources of Amos Tutuola." In Christopher Heywood, ed., *Perspectives on African Literature.* London: Heinemann, 1971; New York: Africana, 1971.

Akinjogbin, I. Adeagbo. Letter to *West Africa* (5 June 1954). In Bernth Lindfors, ed., *Critical Perspectives on Amos Tutuola.* Washington, D.C.: Three Continents Press, 1975.

Armstrong, Robert Plant. "The Narrative and Intensive Continuity: *The Palm-Wine Drinkard.*" In *Research in African Literatures* 1, no. 1 (1970).

———. *The Affecting Presence: An Essay in Humanistic Anthropology.* Urbana: University of Illinois Press, 1971.

Calder-Marshall, Arthur. Review in *The Listener* (13 November 1952). Repr. in Bernth Lindfors, ed., *Critical Perspectives on Amos Tutuola.* Washington, D.C.: Three Continents Press, 1975.

Chinweizu, Onwuchekwa Jemie, and Ihechukwu Madubuike. *Toward the Decolonization of African Literature.* Vol. 1, *African Fiction and Poetry and Their Critics.* Washington, D.C.: Howard University Press, 1983.

Coats, John. "The Inward Journey of a Palm-Wine Drinkard." In *African Literature Today* 11 (1980).

Collins, Harold R. "Founding a New National Literature: The Ghost Novels of Amos Tutuola." In *Critique* 4, no. 1 (1960–1961).

———. *Amos Tutuola.* New York: Twayne, 1969.

———. "A Theory of Creative Mistakes and the Mistaking Style of Amos Tutuola." In *World Literature Written in English* 13 (November 1974).

Dathorne, O. R. "Amos Tutuola: The Nightmare of the Tribe." In Bruce King, ed., *Introduction to Nigerian Literature.* New York: Africana/University of Lagos, 1972. Repr. (rev.) in O. R. Dathorne, *The Black Mind: A History of African Literature.* Minneapolis: University of Minnesota Press, 1974.

Edwards, Paul. "The Farm and the Wilderness in Tutuola's *The Palm-Wine Drinkard.*" In *Journal of Commonwealth Literature* 9, no. 1 (1974).

Elder, Arlene A. "Paul Carter Harrison and Amos Tutuola: The Vitality of the African Continuum." In *World Literature Written in English* 28 (fall 1988).

Fagunwa, D. O. *Ògbójú Ode Nínú Igbó Irúnmalè.* London: C.M.S., 1938; Edinburgh, U.K.: Nelson, 1950.

Ferris, William R., Jr. "Folklore and the African Novelist: Achebe and Tutuola." In *Journal of American Folklore* 86 (January–March 1973).

Irele, Abiola. "The Criticism of Modern African Literature." In Christopher Heywood, ed., *Perspectives on African Literature.* New York: Africana, 1971.

———. *The African Experience in Literature and Ideology.* London and Exeter, N.H.: Heinemann, 1981.

Jones, Eldred. "Amos Tutuola—*The Palm-Wine Drinkard*: Fourteen Years On." In *Bulletin of the Association for African Literature in English* 4 (1966).

Larrabee, Eric. "Amos Tutuola: A Problem in Translation." In *Chicago Review* 10 (spring 1956).

———. "Palm-Wine Drinkard Searches for a Tapster." In Bernth Lindfors, ed., *Critical Perspectives on Amos Tutuola.* Washington, D.C.: Three Continents Press, 1975.

Lindfors, Bernth. "Amos Tutuola and D. O. Fagunwa." In *Journal of Commonwealth Literature* 9 (July 1970).

———. *Critical Perspectives on Amos Tutuola.* Washington, D.C.: Three Continents Press, 1975; London: Heinemann, 1980.

———. "Amos Tutuola's Earliest Long Narrative." In *Journal of Commonwealth Literature* 16, no. 1 (1981).

———. "Amos Tutuola's Search for a Publisher." In *Journal of Commonwealth Literature* 17, no. 1 (1982).

———. "Amos Tutuola: Literary Syncretism and the Yoruba Folk Tradition." In Albert S. Gérard, ed., *European-Language Writing in Sub-Saharan Africa.* Budapest, Hungary: Akadémie Kiadó, 1986.

———. "Tutuola's Latest Stories." In Jacqueline Bardolph, ed., *Short Fiction in the New Literatures in English.* Nice, France: Faculté des Lettres et Sciences Humaines de Nice, 1989.

lo Liyong, Taban. "Tutuola, Son of Zinjanthropus." In *Busara* 1, no. 1 (1968).

Moore, Gerald. "Amos Tutuola: A Nigerian Visionary." In Bernth Lindfors, ed., *Critical Perspectives on Amos Tutuola.* Washington, D.C.: Three Continents Press, 1975.

Naipaul, V. S. Note in *New Statesman* (April 1958). Repr. in Bernth Lindfors, ed., *Critical Perspectives on Amos Tutuola.* Washington, D.C.: Three Continents Press, 1975.

Obiechina, Emmanuel. "Amos Tutuola and the Oral Tradition." In *Présence africaine* 65 (1968).

Ogundipe-Leslie, Omolara. "*The Palm-Wine Drinkard*: A Reassessment of Amos Tutuola." In *Journal of Commonwealth Literature* 9 (July 1970).

———. "Ten Years of Tutuola Studies, 1966–1976." In *African Perspectives* 1 (1977).

Ogunyemi, Chikwenye Okonjo. "The Africanness of *The Conjure Woman* and *Feather Woman of the Jungle.*" In *ARIEL* 8, no. 2 (1977).

Palmer, Eustace. "Twenty-Five Years of Amos Tutuola." In *International Fiction Review* 5 (1978).

Parrinder, Geoffrey. Foreword to Tutuola's *My Life in the Bush of Ghosts.* London: Faber & Faber, 1954.

"Portrait: A Life in the Bush of Ghosts." In *West Africa* (1 May 1954). Repr. in Bernth Lindfors, ed., *Critical Perspectives on Amos Tutuola.* Washington, D.C.: Three Continents Press, 1975.

Priebe, Richard. *Myth, Realism and the West African Writer.* Trenton, N.J.: Africa World, 1988.

Rodman, Selden. Review in *New York Times Book Review* (20 September 1953). Repr. in Bernth Lindfors, ed., *Critical Perspectives on Amos Tutuola.* Washington, D.C.: Three Continents Press, 1975.

Roscoe, Adrian A. *Mother Is Gold: A Study in West African Literature.* London: Cambridge University Press, 1971.

Thomas, Dylan. "Blithe Spirits." In Bernth Lindfors, ed., *Critical Perspectives on Amos Tutuola.* Washington, D.C.: Three Continents Press, 1975.

Updike, John. "Three Tales from Nigeria." In *New Yorker* (23 April 1984).

Laurens van der Post

1906–

CHRISTOPHER SMITH

LAURENS VAN DER POST'S *Venture to the Interior* (1952) is one of his most popular travel books, and its title suggests certain keys to understanding his remarkably varied literary works. Most important, there is the idea of a journey contained in the word *venture*, or more particularly the idea of "safari." The word *safari*, which derives from Swahili, a Bantu language spoken in East Africa and in the Congo, implies going to the wilder parts of a country where conditions are generally harsh. There may be hardships, even some danger, but these are compensated for to a large extent. The party of travelers, who often come from privileged backgrounds and are well, if conventionally, educated, are wealthy enough to afford motor transport through the wilderness and to hire servants to minister to their needs. They have with them too an experienced guide who arranges the expedition and fills the role of an "old Africa hand," a white man who has grown up on the continent. He understands its challenging topography, teeming wildlife, rich past, and different peoples. His task is not only to organize every detail of the safari but also to help the travelers to make sense of their experience as they venture away from the civilization with which they are familiar and perhaps disenchanted. After leading the way in practice as he daily solves the difficulties of the journey, when the time comes to sit around the fire in the evening, the guide may figure as a modern-day prophet, drawing on all he has learned in life to address the problems of modern humanity and recall eternal verities.

Van der Post, who was born in 1906 to a family of South African Boers (that is, settlers of Dutch descent), seems to relish the role of literal and metaphorical safari leader, and many who have had the good fortune to know him personally, as well as many of his readers, have come to look to him as a guide in both practical matters and more broadly philosophical ones. His life has been adventurous as well as varied, and throughout his writing he stresses how taxing experiences have shaped his thought processes. What he tends to make far less of is that writing and contact with other writers have also been constants in his career.

AN IDEAL OF LEADERSHIP

In his fiction and travel books van der Post reveals much about his attitudes toward leadership. In every sort of social grouping, he is aware of hierarchy. There are, he implies, people who stand out and dominate, though generally without domineering, and others whose lot it is to follow. Those who follow in their turn receive their due portion of respect for fulfilling their roles without rising out of their proper places. For the most part, van der Post depicts societies that are male, sometimes exclusively so or with women briefly introduced with an embarrassing, as well as embarrassed, boyish bashfulness on his part. When he mentions his mother, he always places her on a pedestal, and when there is some love interest for the hero in his fiction or any reference to other men's wives in his accounts of travel, the women are given inner qualities that raise them high above men. Van der Post never forgets either how much he owes to the nursemaid who looked after him when he was a child and who told him stories that, in retrospect, he found full of meaning. Typically, however, his affection never leads him to forget that she had a different place in society, that she was a servant and that she was black.

Similar gradations emerge in van der Post's depictions of male societies. He was plainly impressed when in 1945 he came into contact with Lord Louis Mountbatten, the commander in chief of the Allies in Southeast Asia fighting Japan in the final years of World War II. Although van der Post was by no means the only person at the time to be susceptible to the charisma of this handsome, confident, and well-connected leader, he found in Mountbatten qualities that appealed to him and that are, moreover, reflected in both the heroes of his fiction and self-portraits in his travel books. He liked men of action who distinguished themselves by their physical as well as intellectual stature. We soon learn to recognize his heroes not just by their toughness but also by their costumes and weapons, which bespeak long acquaintance with the conditions likely to be encountered on a journey. A distinguished record of a military officer frequently rewarded with medals is always likely to fire his imagination, and he liked being addressed by the title of colonel even after the end of the war. He also tended to admire people whose names had historic resonance, hinting, if not proving, that their family had served the common good for generations.

Another kind of leadership, different in many details yet similar in essence when compared to military leadership, is found in *The Hunter and the Whale* (1967), a story of whaling in the Indian Ocean by Norwegian seamen sailing out of Port Natal on the South African coast. Toward the end of the novel, van der Post introduces one of his veld-hardened Boers, an expert hunter whose character and costume are typical of many van der Post characters. Also characteristically, the Boer's daughter provokes starry-eyed puppy love in Pieter, the young hero. The story is dominated, however, by Thor Larsen. Owing some character traits to Herman Melville's Ahab in *Moby-Dick* (1851), Larsen is the captain of the whaler *Kurt Hansen* and soon emerges as an enigmatic figure of power, fearlessness, and resolution who is racked by superstitions but also uncannily knowledgeable in the mysterious ways of the whales. To seek out and kill the largest of them is his obsessive desire. On land he is uneasy and often at odds with the agents for his vessel's owners, but at sea he is in his element. Although each member of the crew is expert at his job, Larsen stands head and shoulders above them all.

In particular he fascinates Pieter, a young Boer who has come from up-country and spends some seasons aboard the *Kurt Hansen*, using his sharp eyesight to good effect in the crow's nest spotting whales. Although the story is related by this youngster, who rarely misses an opportunity to show himself in a good light, it is tempting to suggest a connection between van der Post and the narrator, for Pieter both looks up to leaders and aspires to be one himself.

For van der Post, leadership is not simply a military matter or a question of exhibiting the pioneering spirit, though he certainly sets high store by this quality in both spheres. He also has a deep conviction that he has a message for humankind, which he presents with a fervor akin to that of the Old Testament prophets, with whose declarations he had become familiar when the Bible was read at family prayers in his youth. In the isolated households of the Boers, the attitudes of Calvinism that had been brought from Europe retained their pristine vigor, helping build a spirit of sturdy frontier independence. The Boers needed this spirit for survival and, more particularly, for the preservation of their culture and values as they stood up for themselves against both the British and the black peoples who were sharing South Africa with them. In strictly religious terms, van der Post could not remain loyal to the traditions of Calvinism, and his liberalism put him at odds with his fellow Boers on many issues. All the same, he had absorbed certain values, which are reflected in his deep sense of the importance of energetically proclaiming his personal convictions.

Whether van der Post's ideas and insights would have developed in other directions had he not come under the influence of the Swiss psychologist Carl Jung is a matter of debate. He clearly found in Jung a thinker who helped him to formulate his own insights by providing an intellectual framework that made them more coherent, persuaded him of their validity, and gave him further confidence in espousing them.

THE BOER INHERITANCE

In fiction and other writings, van der Post repeatedly refers to his personal experiences. Born on 13 December 1906 near Philippolis in the Orange Free State, Laurens lost his father, Christian van der Post, at an early age, and he was haunted by the vision of a man who, emigrating from Holland to South Africa in search of more promising opportunities, combined intellectual energy and considerable culture with a desire to use these advantages for the common good. Van der Post's father was rising to a position of some political eminence in the Orange Free State when war broke out in 1899 between the two Boer republics in southern Africa and the British. Only after an astonishingly prolonged resistance were the Boers finally defeated by greatly superior British forces with a huge industrial base. The qualities that van der Post glimpsed in his father, whom he never knew well, were also presented to him from his early years in the conduct and character not only of the upper echelons of Boer society generally but also of the family of his mother, Maria Magdalena Lubbe, in particular, whose history was a microcosm of the Boers' experience in southern Africa.

The Dutch had first founded settlements at the Cape in the mid seventeenth century, and their numbers were swollen when they were joined by Huguenots fleeing religious persecution by the Catholic authorities in France after the revocation of the Edict of Nantes in 1685. The Boers—the word means "farmers"—were sturdy and independent minded, inspired equally by a determination to survive often difficult conditions and by a fundamentalist Bible-based Calvinism that gave them an unshakable conviction in the righteousness of their cause. Like many persecuted religious groups, they saw themselves as a chosen people charged with a divine mission to advance a particular way of life, which equated hard work with virtue and inspired the sense that they should at all costs stand up against all who attacked them. As exiles from Europe, they clung to their old ways with dogged conservatism and passionately defended all that they had won and created in their new homeland.

After the British annexation of the Cape in 1806, the Boers began to move north, going up-country in search of new territory where they could create the huge farms to which they were accustomed and manage their domestic and political affairs without interference. Van der Post's maternal grandfather took part in the "Great Trek," as it was called, and died when his wagon train was attacked by the Matabele, a black African tribe fighting to protect its territory. Later in the nineteenth century, Christian van der Post immigrated to Africa, where he found outlets for his talents by participating in public affairs. The successes of van der Post's forebears and of the Boers in general, however, should not draw attention away from the struggles involved in a land where a living had to be wrested from the soil and where it was felt that European values had to be maintained. Wars were fought against the African tribes, and even in times of peace there was a great gulf between whites and blacks. Although they lived in proximity and in economic interdependence, the Boers' refusal to integrate—which was later codified into the doctrine of apartheid—was already evident. Not only were black Africans dispossessed of their lands, but the Boers stubbornly refused to recognize any positive values in African indigenous culture, which was progressively undermined by contact with Europeans. Language differences obstructed communication and symbolized mutual incomprehension.

Conscious of European roots yet to a degree cut off from them, the Boers saw themselves as separate from the black peoples whom they encountered every day and whom they fought for years in a relentless battle for ownership of the land. No less important was the Boers' unremitting conflict with the British, which had been dragging on throughout the nineteenth century. The very existence of the Boer republics was threatened by British expansionism from the south, especially after the discovery of gold and diamonds. Matters came to a head in the Boer War, which began in 1899 and was concluded only after three years of conflict. The British military machine was tested to its limits; the war provoked, in its closing stages, a series of unprecedented harsh measures against the Boer civilian population, and much of the country was left devastated.

The British government's decision to found the Union of South Africa in 1910 by joining together Cape Colony, Natal, and the former Boer republics of the Transvaal and the Orange Free State went a long way toward healing the rifts between victors and vanquished. Until then, however, there had been much bitterness, and afterward, though many of the Boers supported Britain in World War I, there remained a strong sense of separate communities, each with its own history, culture, and religion.

Differences of language were both a symptom and a cause of this particularism. In a gesture of reconciliation, the new union's constitution granted Dutch an equal status with English as an official language. Yet in practice the effect was separatist rather than unifying, and the Boers' sense of identity was further strengthened when in 1925 Afrikaans was adopted alongside English as the two official languages in South Africa; Afrikaans had evolved from Dutch over the centuries, partly because of isolation and partly because of contact with African languages and English.

Van der Post was an heir of the Boer patrimony. Even if he repudiated part of his legacy, it shaped his outlook, and though he did not share the attitudes of many of his fellow Boers, especially with regard to the black peoples of South Africa, the matters that concerned him were, in large measure, those that occupied them too.

The youngest child of a large family, van der Post lived in affluent circumstances on a large farm; after the death of his father he was raised by his mother and brothers. Although he received his secondary education at Grey College, a well-known private school in Bloemfontein, he did not go on to university. Instead, he started working as a journalist in Durban on the *Natal Advertiser*.

Van der Post spent much of his adult life outside South Africa, but he continued to maintain ties with his Boer heritage. He moved to England in 1928 and married Marjorie Wendt, whom he had met in South Africa. During World War II he served in the British army in North Africa and in Pacific

Asia until he was made a prisoner of war, for two and a half years, by the Japanese on the Indonesian island of Java. After the war he was rewarded for his meritorious service by being made a Commander of the Order of the British Empire in 1947. After divorcing his first wife, he married the writer Ingaret Giffard in 1949. For nearly two decades he managed his family farm in South Africa.

As an explorer he led a number of missions in Africa on behalf of the British government and the Colonial Development Corporation. His experiences were reflected not only in official reports but also in such literary works as *Venture to the Interior* (1952) and *The Lost World of the Kalahari* (1958). These books were well received by a wide readership who found in them a fascinating blend of stirring adventure and thought-provoking musing about humanity and its place in the world. Van der Post also had major successes when he presented similar material as film and television documentaries. An intrepid traveler, he also wrote books about his visits to the Soviet Union (*Journey to Russia*, 1964) and Japan (*A Portrait of Japan*, 1968). Van der Post has lived in Great Britain for the past several decades, with a residence in Chelsea, London, and another in Aldeburgh, Suffolk, a quiet seaside resort much favored by liberal intellectuals. The recipient of honorary doctorates from universities both in South Africa and in London, van der Post, who became a Fellow of the Royal Society of Literature in 1955, received knighthood in 1981.

AFRICAN CULTURE

Although born too late to witness the Boer War, van der Post knew much of the bitterness that followed it, and yet the attempts at reconciliation also left their mark, so that he was deeply aware of both differences and the need to reconcile them. He went further than most of his fellow Boers in his desire for a more profound reconciliation than was envisaged by the South Africa Act of 1909, which was essentially political legislation for the benefit of the white colonists with no regard for the black peoples in the territory. Although fully aware of the injustices the black peoples had suffered and not unsympathetic to their political aspirations, he was more interested in what could be learned from their culture. White settlers and colonial administrators found it convenient to assume that the native populations were mere savages who should be grateful when offered opportunities to work for a pittance on land they could not manage efficiently for themselves and who should be shot down if they ventured to protest against exploitation and expropriation. The Zulus won some grudging respect for their organization and prowess as warriors, but that did not save them from heavy defeat after some initial military successes in the Zulu War of 1879 and a number of uprisings in the next thirty years.

Increasing urbanization and industrialization contributed further to the collapse of village and tribal culture, with nothing very solid to replace it, though there were also attempts to organize black trade unions and political parties. Van der Post, like Jung before him, realized that so-called civilized people had much to learn from indigenous peoples, who were, in his view, mistakenly regarded as less advanced than the white races. Such peoples are, he felt, closer to the realities of the elements, and their vision is not blinkered by the disciplines of logic that reject everything that cannot be empirically proven. More primitive, not in any disparaging sense but because they have not departed so far from their origins, they are psychologically better integrated than many who consider themselves advanced. Disregard of primitive intuitions, needs, and urges, van der Post suggests in *The Lost World of the Kalahari* and other books, lies at the root of much of modern humanity's malaise, and until we recognize that fact we shall find no cure.

Van der Post argues that the strength of so-called primitive peoples comes not simply from their social institutions but also, and more significantly, from their intimate relationship with the environment. If they are not to starve they need to know every aspect of their territory, including its topography and climate, its flora and fauna. Living close to the land teaches them lessons in both conservation and cooperation, for all must work together if they are to find enough food and water without destroying the sources of these necessities, and human beings are constantly given salutary reminders of their proper place within the ecosystem.

An important element of van der Post's reflections on this theme is his deep regard for Africa, or, more precisely, for sub-Saharan Africa, for he tends to regard the Mediterranean coastal region as too much influenced by Europe. As he shows very strikingly in the early chapters of *Venture to the Interior*, his Africa is above all else a place where nature, not humans, reigns supreme. Like the Boers who found broad new pastures as they trekked across the veld, and like the prospectors who mined gold and dug diamonds in unimaginable quantities, he never doubts that this is a land of inexhaustible riches that do not yield to people without a struggle. Although the climate can be harsh, with droughts that wither decades of patient endeavor on the farms, and although people have to be prepared to fight against a hostile environment, he is always aware of Africa's boundless variety and pulsating vitality, especially in animal and bird life. Some readers may find it difficult to share his liking for hunting—even when he insists that he only kills what he and his companions need for food—but the portrayal of an abundance of game also works to convey the continent's fertility. Van der Post is aware of the importance of the interrelationship of every feature and creature in the natural environment and of the fine balance among all its constituent elements.

Few activities give him more pleasure than following a spoor, a word deriving from the Afrikaans that means an animal's track, and he presents his fictional heroes and himself as experts in interpreting the telltale signs of nature, from topography to meteorology. Frequently—for instance, in *Flamingo Feather* (1955)—his narratives contain detailed accounts of finding a way through the terrain, across marshes and watercourses, up mountains and across deserts. These images suggest that he feels able, through intuition, to read nature as if it were a text, a testament full of profound truths that may not be plain to the profane but are revealed to those with the patience to respond with faith and imagination.

THE INNER MEANING OF LANGUAGE

An indication of van der Post's sense of the meaningfulness of nature lies in his habit of interpreting the names of physical features, plants, and animals in Afrikaans or one of the African languages. In *The Lost World of the Kalahari*, for instance, he describes a beautiful site that bears "the evocative name of 'Boesmansfontein.'" We need only a hint and most of us can see for ourselves that this must mean the fountain or spring of the Bushman, a member of a distinctive ethnic group that has long resided in southern Africa. This example demonstrates how proper names in particular, as well as common nouns, carry a meaning that is only partially concealed from English speakers with some knowledge of philology.

The history of South Africa, with its successive settlements by African tribes from the north as well as by Boers, Huguenots, and the British pushing up from the Cape, led to the naming of the territory and its wildlife in a variety of different languages. To indifferent passersby, they might well be of no more interest than a geographical dictionary with a list of plants and animals full of strange-sounding names. For van der Post, however, they were the keys to deep secrets. Everything has meaning, and as narrator or safari guide he often interprets it specifically. As a child he was brought up to speak Afrikaans, but on the family farm he also became familiar with the languages spoken by the African servants. He started to learn English when he was about ten years old; that is, at an age when language acquisition ceases to be instinctual and becomes a conscious activity, especially for a Boer child who was well aware that he was learning a language imposed on his people. At about the same time he began to study German and French.

As is clear from the number of allusions to such authors as Shakespeare, Dante, T. S. Eliot, and many others in *A Walk with a White Bushman* (1986), van der Post profited from the access to European culture that language study offered, and he liked to refer to classical authors in his writing. These references are far less important, however, than his realization that under the multifarious forms of languages there lies a single reality that people apprehend in diverse ways when they use different words to refer to the same object. Of equal concern to him was people's inability to appreciate that the terms used by another person were more than conventional labels and might be insightful comments on reality. Possibly all linguists develop a sense of the mysterious relationship between words and what they purport to describe, but van der Post, himself a polyglot in a country that is officially bilingual and where African languages are heard every day, had this feeling to an unusual degree. For him, language was one of the spoors that regularly led to fresh discoveries, and he understood nature all the better because he knew how to interpret the names of landforms, flora, and fauna.

This tendency becomes all the stronger when he is with, or describes his heroes with, black Africans whose habit it is not to apply ready-made names, but to invent new, descriptive ones. In *Flamingo Feather*, for instance, Pierre de Beauvilliers—whose name, with its unmistakable French echoes and its "de," points to hereditary links with an old established aristocratic European family—demonstrates his understanding of his black porters when he falls in with their ways. He calls one of the camps "Tickie's Reprieve" because it was there that Tickie, one of the porters, had a lucky escape from a charging rhinoceros. Understanding several languages, van der Post translates what he reckons to be the meaning of the African scene and its peoples; he considers it his mission to tell the rest of the world what he intuits after interrogating a richly endowed, mercilessly challenging continent that demands respect and rewards those who respond to it appropriately.

RACE AND IDENTITY

The babel of tongues that van der Post heard and recorded in his fiction is symbolic of how varied the population of South Africa has become over the centuries. As a Boer, never forgetting the origins of his family in Holland to which he was tied with many cultural links, especially religion, he defined himself in his early years, before he became a writer, in contradistinction to other races, nationalities, and tribes. On the one hand, there were the African ethnic groups from which his forebears had wrested the land in desperate battles and with which he lived in proximity on the family farm without anything like a spirit of equality developing between black and white. On the other hand were the British who had defeated the Boers only a few years back and with whom relations still tended to be stiff and uneasy.

In discussing this issue it is important to resist branding van der Post a racist, even though many Afrikaners from his background and of his generation were responsible for the inhuman policies of apartheid. Where he differs from them is not simply in his lack of prejudice against African ethnic groups but also in his readiness to value what he can learn from them. Nevertheless, there is no denying that his upbringing and experience predisposed him to think in terms of racial categories. He has a sharp eye for ethnic types, whether European, African, or Asian. He notes their physical characteristics and recognizes their accents and vocabulary. He believes that just as their origins have to some degree determined their station in life, so too there is a reflection of their origins in their behavior.

Some readers are taken aback by van der Post's ready acceptance of such notions, and there is something disturbing and distasteful in repeated references to "the Bushman," for instance, or "the Russian," when closer acquaintance would perhaps have led him to lay more emphasis on individuation within each group. Yet the attitude he has toward others is also the one that he holds toward his own people, as well as toward different European nationalities. Anything simplistic and schematic in his response to African races has its counterpart in his portrayal of Germans or Norwegians. He was content, indeed proud, that the Boers—whom he portrays as individuals—are seen as a race apart, and experience strengthened his conviction that innate and inherited ethnic differences influence clan, tribe, and people, just as he is sure they influence him.

This, however, does not mean that van der Post looks down on people belonging to ethnic groups other than his own. Like the late-Victorian novelist H. Rider Haggard—who, as van der Post points out, altered British attitudes toward the black peoples of Africa by making clear, in novels such as *King Solomon's Mines* (1885), that he held in high regard Cetshwayo's bold, soldierly Zulu, who had put up a stiff resistance to the British in the third quarter of the nineteenth century—van der Post finds much to admire in the Bushmen. By emphasizing that the Bushmen, with a distinctive physique, unusual, almost Mongolian features, and yellowish skin pigmentation, must be regarded as the first race to inhabit the land that was to become South Africa, however, he seems to suggest that the black races that migrated south and took the best land were militaristic colonial imperialists with scarcely any better title to the territory than the Boers and the British. When van der Post writes about the nonwhite population of southern Africa, it is clear that his sympathy lies primarily with the Bushmen.

THE LOST WORLD OF THE KALAHARI

The Lost World of the Kalahari (1958), a travel book that tells of a safari carried out with the intention of making a television documentary about the Bushmen, details the sad decline of that people. Persecuted by both black tribes and Boers, the Bushmen had almost disappeared from the more fertile areas, leaving as their memorial just a few place-names and a reputation for cruelty, unreliability, and an unwillingness to enter what were considered more advanced circles. The journey of van der Post's group is long and arduous, and the account of the difficulties that must be overcome in the course of the search for the Bushmen gives some impression of the remoteness of their huts and hunting grounds. When at length the party reaches its destination, it discovers a people for whom time seems to have stood still. They are small and shy, and their possessions are few. Nature is harsh; procuring water and enough to eat is a constant preoccupation. Van der Post, however, provides information about the Bushmen's artistic bent, which found expression in brilliant cave paintings. Even though times have become more difficult for them as they have been expelled from the fertile regions into the wilderness, the Bushmen are depicted as living in close harmony with nature. They know every nutritious and medicinal plant and find drinking water where no one would think of looking.

In part an adventure story of an expedition by Landrovers, four-wheel-drive vehicles especially suitable for journeys over rugged terrain, *The Lost World of the Kalahari* is also a pilgrimage. In long sections at the beginning of the book, van der Post explains how he had long been haunted by memories of the Bushmen, mysterious beings who in earlier days were cunning and cruel during a long struggle for survival as they were ousted from their hereditary lands. Now they occasionally make contact with the white settlers, only to disappear again without a word of explanation. Van der Post's interest is in part anthropological, but he is disdainful of those who want to measure Bushmen's skulls when it would be more useful, in his view, to discover what is going on inside their heads. What he finds is a strong sense of community, with mutual support among its members, and their full integration with their surroundings. This discovery takes on special significance, since he knows that the way of life of the Bushmen is endangered. Indeed, even the visit to the Bushmen's camp by van der Post's expedition, for all the goodwill inspiring it, can easily be seen as one more instance of white men interfering with their ways.

The history of the Boers, his family background, and his experience of life combine to give van der Post a profound sense of alienation, which he considers part of the common experience of humankind. Urbanization has had the paradoxical effect of cutting people off from one another, as age-old social structures are shaken and destroyed, especially as industrialization and modern distribution methods cater to material needs without requiring the teamwork that used to bind members of a community together. Such views of the Bushmen are perhaps too idealistic, but van der Post is certain that he can learn many valuable lessons from them. In *The Heart of the Hunter* (1961), for instance, he conveys an impression of the complexity of their social organization, and if the word *primitive* is used to describe them, he would have us understand it in the sense of their having remained close to their origins, which is their source of strength.

THE INFLUENCE OF JUNG

From his experiences close to nature in South Africa and his contacts with communities not yet profoundly influenced by so-called civilization, van der Post learned to question the dry rationality that was once discouraged by religious establishments but, since the decline of religious faith, has become the chief tool of material advancement in the west. Contact with Jung's ideas strengthened his conviction that there was more to life and psychic well-being than the analytic methods of the post-Renaissance philosophers who established an intellectual basis to science by refusing to admit the validity of anything that could not be proved logically. Just as we have, despite obviously gaining material benefits, forfeited much in turning from the country to the city, so too we run serious risks if we develop an uncompromising insistence on rationality and ignore the promptings and riches of our subconscious. Doing so can leave us dissatisfied, at odds with ourselves, and irremediably fragment our vision of the world and our experience in it. In such views it is possible to detect a nostalgia for the strong religious convictions of the Calvinist Boers, who combined ruthless practicality with deep faith in the existence of transcendental values, but van der Post is by no means the only modern thinker to have urged that there is more to life than logic.

He hearkens to dreams, intuitions, telepathy, myths, and symbols as indicators of truths that might otherwise be overlooked. In this, as in his view that so-called primitive peoples can remind us of what has been lost by relying too heavily on rationality, van der Post shows his close affinity with Jung. In

Man and the Shadow (1971) in particular, he uses Jung's concept of man and the shadow to demonstrate the need to integrate all aspects of the personality, which is seen as both individual and communal. Van der Post does not urge a return to the bush or the desert, but his tendency to ignore individual differentiation when speaking of ethnic groups other than his own suggests that either he does not know them as well as he thinks or he perceives these less familiar selves as merging too completely in the communal. All the same, he believes strongly that urbanized people can learn much from the lifestyles and thought processes of those who live in primitive communities.

NOVELS

To express his ideas, van der Post used a number of literary forms. His first novel, *In a Province* (1934), was written after he had had a good deal of experience as a journalist working for South African newspapers and had contributed, in Afrikaans, to the progressive magazine *Voorslag* (Whiplash). A vivid account of conditions and political pressures in South Africa, the novel was written under the influence of his friend William Plomer, who, in *Turbott Wolfe* (1926) and *I Speak of Africa* (1927), had dared to question the prejudices of South Africa. *In a Province* is narrated in the first person in a way that creates an impression of authenticity. The young hero's personal development as he tries to make sense of what is happening around him is of secondary interest in a tale that is primarily concerned with exploring racial tensions with an unusual degree of sympathy for blacks.

Flamingo Feather (1955) is also told in the first person, and it is difficult to escape the impression that van der Post has put a lot of himself into the narrator. The story tells of the frustration of a Communist attempt to shake the South African government by stirring up rebellion among the black tribesmen. Mystery and adventure propel this fast-paced yarn, and a difficult journey into unexplored territory provides opportunities for van der Post to describe places and persons with an accuracy that bespeaks close observation. The attempt to piece together fragments of evidence into a coherent whole, which is gripping enough in itself, also reflects his abiding concern with discovering the underlying unity of apparently disparate experiences. But some readers may be disturbed by the wish fulfillment evident in the portrayal of the manly hero who, like John Buchan's Richard Hannay in thrillers written thirty years earlier, sets out to thwart the devious plots of ruthless foreigners who wish to subvert the status quo. The affectionate and detailed observation of the African scene is also a feature of *A Story Like the Wind* (1972) and *A Far-Off Place* (1974), and there is a mixture of adventure and idealism in these accounts of journeys undertaken by a white lad in the company of a young Bushman.

The Hunter and the Whale (1967), yet another first-person narrative, harks back to the boys' adventure stories of the Victorian era, such as William H. G. Kingston's *Peter the Whaler* (1851) and Frank T. Bullen's *Cruise of the Cachalot* (1898). They were written long before commercial whaling had become an example of man's ruthless exploitation of nature, and van der Post looks back to the 1920s as his young hero describes, not without a certain degree of self-congratulation, his experiences at sea. The excitement of the chase, the beauty of the ocean, and the disparate characters among the crew are all described graphically, and Thor Larsen dominates the narrative with the same unchallenged authority with which he commands his little ship. Once again the quest, this time across trackless waters, is one of the major elements in the tale, and much is made of the captain's uncanny ability to find his prey. To satisfy his ambition of killing the largest of animals, Larsen agrees to allow an experienced Boer hunter to sail out with him in search of a particularly great whale. Disregard of safety in a moment of triumph leads to tragedy.

Although precise and detailed in much of its physical and personal descriptions, *The Hunter and the Whale* cannot adequately be categorized as a realist novel. Perhaps it would be better to think in terms of "poetic realism," not only because van der Post's prose is generally full of images, even to the point of occasionally being too colorful, but also because he is not content with mere facts. Again and again events take on symbolic significance, and some of the characters, for good or ill, are larger than life, driven on relentlessly toward strangely irrational goals.

TRAVEL BOOKS

"Poetic realism" applies equally well to describing van der Post's more important travel books. *A Portrait of All the Russias* (1967) and *A Portrait of Japan* (1968), attractively illustrated with color photographs by Burt Glinn, are orthodox accounts of these two countries and particularly of their people. The longer *Journey into Russia* (1964), though lively, lacks the insight that comes from long and close acquaintance with a country and its people. This insightfulness made *Venture to the Interior* (1952) and *The Lost World of the Kalahari* so appealing to thousands of armchair travelers. There is plenty of factual detail to give authenticity to the tale, including maps and historical background to create context and the sense of a varied group of people setting out on a journey. It is not difficult to join imaginatively with them, sharing hopes and disappointments. The adventurous trip away from civilization soon takes on, moreover, something of a comforting return to the past; in *The Lost World of the Kalahari* this comes in part from the attempt to discover the ancient way of life of the Bushmen. But in this book, as in *Venture to the Interior*, many readers fall under the spell of a narrative that, with a structured group of frank characters out in the wilderness sharing excitements and challenges, recalls the adventure romances of Haggard.

Van der Post not only adds his serious reflections on the essential unity of all experience, but he also gives an extra dimension to the narrative by increasing its emotional impact. In *Venture to the Interior*, for instance, he recounts, with an astonishing heightening of human tension, the accidental death of one member of the party. Matter-of-fact observation has, it seems, only been used to create the context for a human tragedy that is etched with unforgettable directness. In retrospect, everything appears to have been leading up to this moment, and for a time every practical consideration is forgotten, for nothing seems to count but human emotion and sympathy. In *The Lost World of the Kalahari*, even more strikingly, the concern is not with human beings but with the great primal forces of the African land that have to be duly appeased before the expedition can reach its goal. Realism characterizes both of these books, but from amid all the factual information that is recorded, documented, and soberly vouched for, there emerges a realization of forces that are far more powerful than mere human concerns.

WARTIME STORIES

That extra dimension to the narrative is also evident in *The Seed and the Sower* (1963), a collection of three stories that reflect on van der Post's appalling experiences in World War II, and to *The Night of the New Moon* (1970), which explores, from an unexpected angle, the moral questions connected with the dropping of the first atomic bombs on Japan. As a young man in 1926 van der Post made a brief visit to Japan. He did not return to Pacific Asia for another sixteen years, by which time he had spent time farming in England—where, as his novel *The Face Beside the Fire* (1953) suggests, he had not really felt quite at home—and had then served for three years in the British forces. In 1942 he was posted to what were then the Dutch colonies of Sumatra and Java at a time when, in the aftermath of the fall of Singapore and the attack on Pearl Harbor, the Japanese army and navy were seemingly invincible as they advanced from island to island across the Pacific Ocean. Van der Post was taken prisoner and, like so many Commonwealth soldiers, suffered two and a half years of immense tribulations at the hands of Japanese guards as shortages of food and medical supplies threatened to bring on the prisoners' physical collapse.

Hatred might well have been the result of such misfortunes, and van der Post leaves his readers in no doubt of how ghastly the guards were. In the third tale of *The Seed and the Sower*, "The Sword and the Doll," he creates an indelible impression of the uncanny spread of terror as vague rumors of Japanese military operations turned inexorably into the certainty of invasion. More or less factual accounts—in which van der Post again artfully blends observation and imagination—serve primarily as a means of introducing exceptional characters who, amid the horrors of the prison camp, rise to extraordinary heights. These are not, however, simply tales of the heroism of the Allies; they show a readiness to explore the Japanese character, finding a nobility that is a product of ancestry and upbringing. As a result, in his prisoner-of-war fiction van der Post once again portrays, beneath the surface of frightening events, what he perceives as the essential unity of all experience. A one-sided approach never satisfies him. Thus, in *The Night of the New Moon* (1970), he justifies the dropping of the first atomic bombs, not by the military argument that it spared the United States the million casualties it was estimated an invasion of the Japanese mainland would have cost, but by suggesting that only the phenomenon of the explosions could serve, as if it were a cosmic event, to absolve the Japanese soldiers from the obligation to continue fighting, never besmirching honor with the disgrace of surrender.

CONCLUSION

A compelling storyteller with a fund of unusual experiences, van der Post always leads his readers along spoors, which he tries to trace through the tangle of conflicting perceptions back to their sources and to relate them to each other within the unifying pattern that underlies them all. Occasionally his imagination leads him into extravagance, and though his musings fascinate those who have ears to hear, they will not always convince the skeptical, who may yet be anxious to get on with the story. At the heart of his literary endeavor, for all its affectionate portrayal of Africa, is an attempt to delve into himself and to structure the apparently fractured and disjointed elements of his personality and experience. Van der Post's later books are explicitly autobiographical, and as such they invite us to interpret all his works to a large extent as reflections and refractions of his own nature. This does not, however, make them simply personal or anecdotal, for the individual is, to him, the microcosm of the universal.

Selected Bibliography

NOVELS

In a Province. London: Hogarth, 1934; Harmondsworth, U.K.: Penguin, 1984.

The Face Beside the Fire. London: Hogarth, 1953; London: Chatto & Windus, 1985.

A Bar of Shadow. London: Hogarth, 1954. First published in *Cornhill Magazine* (spring 1954).

Flamingo Feather. London: Hogarth, 1955.

The Seed and the Sower. London: Hogarth, 1963; London: Chatto & Windus, 1987. Contains the title story, "A Bar of Shadow," and "The Sword and the Doll."

The Hunter and the Whale. London: Hogarth, 1967; London: Chatto & Windus, 1986.
A Story Like the Wind. London: Hogarth, 1972.
A Far-Off Place. London: Hogarth, 1974; New York: Morrow, 1974.
A Mantis Carol. London: Hogarth, 1975; London: Chatto & Windus, 1989.

TRAVEL BOOKS

Venture to the Interior. London: Hogarth, 1952; London: Chatto & Windus, 1986.
The Lost World of the Kalahari. London: Hogarth, 1958; London: Chatto & Windus, 1988.
The Heart of the Hunter. London: Hogarth, 1961; London: Chatto & Windus, 1987.
Journey into Russia. London: Hogarth, 1964. Published in the United States as *A View of All the Russias.* New York: Morrow, 1964.
A Portrait of All the Russias. With photographs by Burt Glinn. London: Hogarth, 1967.
A Portrait of Japan. With photographs by Burt Glinn. London: Hogarth, 1968.
African Cooking. New York: Time-Life Books, 1970.
First Catch Your Eland: A Taste of Africa. London: Hogarth, 1977.
Testament to the Bushmen. With Jane Taylor. New York: Viking, 1984.

NONFICTION

The Dark Eye in Africa. London: Hogarth, 1955.
Race Prejudice as Self Rejection: An Inquiry into the Psychological and Spiritual Aspects of Group Conflict. New York: Workshop for Cultural Democracy, 1957.
Introduction to *Turbott Wolfe,* by William Plomer. London: Hogarth Press, 1965. Contains much autobiographical information.
The Night of the New Moon. London: Hogarth, 1970; London: Chatto & Windus, 1985. Published in the United States as *The Prisoner and the Bomb.* New York: Morrow, 1971.
Man and the Shadow. London: South Place Ethical Society, 1971.
The Creative Pattern in Primitive Africa. Dallas, Tex.: Spring, 1987.
The Voice of the Thunder. London: Chatto & Windus, 1993.

AUTOBIOGRAPHY

Jung and the Story of Our Time. New York: Pantheon, 1975.
Yet Being Someone Other. London: Hogarth, 1982.
A Walk with a White Bushman. London: Chatto & Windus, 1986. Conversations with Jean-Marc Pottiez.
About Blady: A Pattern Out of Time. London: Chatto & Windus, 1991; New York: Morrow, 1991.

BIOGRAPHICAL AND CRITICAL STUDIES

Allen, Louis. "To Be a Prisoner." In *Journal of European Studies* 16 (December 1986).
Baker, I. L. *Laurens van der Post:* Venture to the Interior. Notes on Chosen English Texts. Bath, U.K.: Brodie, 1963.
Carpenter, Frederic I. *Laurens van der Post.* New York: Twayne, 1969.
Debenham, Frank. *Kalahari Sand.* London: Bell, 1953. An account of a safari with van der Post.
Kemp, Cyril. *Notes on Van der Post's* Venture to the Interior *and* The Lost World of the Kalahari. London: Methuen, 1981.
Plomer, William. *Double Lives.* London: Cape, 1943.

José Luandino Vieira

1935–

PHYLLIS A. PERES

JOSÉ LUANDINO VIEIRA is the literary pseudonym, and the name by which he is otherwise known, of José Vieira Mateus da Graça. He was born in Lagoa do Furadouro (near Ourem in the Ribatejo Province), Portugal, on 4 May 1935 and was brought to Luanda as a child by his parents, who were settlers in the Portuguese colony of Angola. By choosing the name "Luandino," he announced his personal and literary identification with Luanda, the capital of both colonial and independent Angola.

Luandino Vieira completed secondary school in Luanda at age fifteen and worked at various jobs until 1961, when he was arrested and convicted for participating in anticolonial activities with Movimento Popular para a Libertação de Angola (Popular Movement for the Libration of Angola, or MPLA), one of the three main nationalist groups engaged in armed struggle in Angola, from 1961 to 1975. Luandino Vieira remained incarcerated until 1972, serving first in Luanda, then in a special prison for political detainees at Tarrafal in the archipelago of Cape Verde, and finally on parole in Lisbon, where his movements were restricted to the city. After Angolan independence in 1975, he held several important national cultural posts, most notably that of secretary-general of the Angolan Writers Union.

Luandino Vieira began his formal literary career in the mid 1950s as a contributor of fiction, poetry, and art to the Angolan literary-cultural journal *Cultura*, which was published between 1957 and 1961. The majority of Luandino Vieira's works were written between 1961 and 1973, while he was a political prisoner. After his release, he revised many of these works before publishing them. He is identified with the narratives written while in prison and has not published significant work since then. He was, however, at work on a new novel in the mid 1990s.

Critics of Luandino Vieira's prose fiction generally categorize its development chronologically: before and after the writing of *Luuanda* (1964). The first phase is characterized by an immediacy of representation, particularly in terms of an adamant anticolonial stance. The second phase, no less anticolonial, is more concerned with the creation of a uniquely Angolan literary form and language. *Luuanda*, which is written in the form of *estórias* and deeply influenced by the dynamics of oral storytelling, is therefore regarded as a turning point in Luandino Vieira's narrative style.

THE COLONIAL CRITIQUE

A cidade e a infância (The city and childhood), published in 1960, is both Luandino Vieira's first book of fiction and the first book-length collection of prose by a writer associated with the 1950s Angolan literary-cultural groups. (A 1957 edition with the same title was printed in Luanda but seized and destroyed by the police. It contained four stories, only one of which, "Encontro de acaso," is included in the 1960 edition.) The ten short stories of *A cidade e a infância* are arranged chronologically by date of composition (between 1954 and 1957). The city referred to in the title is Luanda prior to the massive post–World War II influx of Portuguese settlers into Angola and its capital. The childhood of the title, then, reflects pre–World War II Luanda amid established patterns of creolization, the process of syncretizing different cultures. The arrival of more and more settlers—an increase from 30,000 in 1930 to over 170,000 in 1961—disrupted Luanda's demographic patterns, as well as patterns of creolization. *A cidade e a infância* focuses on this displacement through reconstructing an often idealized and creolized past.

The story "Encontro de acaso" (Chance meeting), for example, concerns a chance encounter between two adults who as children had belonged to the same interracial neighborhood group. Their old neighborhood has been destroyed to make way for urbanization projects to accommodate the new settlers. The white narrator and his African friend have taken separate paths determined by the forces of colonialism. In "Faustino," the title character, a doorman at an apartment building for Europeans, revolts against the colonial system that treats him as if he were a dog.

A more overt critique of colonialism is evident in *A vida verdadeira de Domingos Xavier* (1974; *The Real Life of Domingos Xavier*), completed just days before Luandino Vieira's arrest in 1961. The novel was not published until 1974, although copies of the original manuscript circulated earlier. A French translation made from one of the copies appeared in 1971.

The Real Life of Domingos Xavier, which was written immediately after the outbreak of armed nationalist struggle in Angola, offers a vision of the MPLA in Luanda as a collectivity. The central narrative event is the disappearance and death of Domingos Xavier, an Angolan worker tortured by Portuguese authorities, who dies because he refuses to reveal the identities of MPLA militants. The novel follows several narrative lines, including Domingos Xavier's struggle to maintain his dignity in the face of a series of increasingly violent interrogations, his wife's efforts to ascertain his whereabouts, and the MPLA's attempts to discover the identity of the prisoner (Domingos Xavier) brought to Luanda. Although the title character dies, the novel is an affirmation of Angolan national identity and resistance and of the collective struggle that is reinforced by individual stories and sacrifices.

Collective struggle and identity are also the main themes of *Vidas novas* (New lives), which was written in 1962 while Luandino Vieira was awaiting trial in a Luanda prison. As was the case with *The Real Life of Domingos Xavier*, *Vidas novas* was not published until years later, in 1975, although clandestine editions circulated prior to that time. As the title indicates, the short stories in *Vidas novas* focus on the transformations of common people's lives and identities through their participation in the nationalist movement. Like Luandino's other texts from this first phase of his writing, these stories not only critique Portuguese colonial rule and the Portuguese refusal to negotiate independence but also affirm *angolanidade*, or collective Angolan identity. Thus, in one of the stories from this collection, "O exemplo de Job Hamukuaja" (The example of Job Hamukuaja), the title character, from the Cuanhama people, provides an example of resistance for his fellow political prisoner, Mário João, an Angolan of European descent.

Vidas novas also hints at the radical transformations of literary form that mark the second phase of Luandino Vieira's literary career. "Cardoso Kamukolo, sapateiro" (Cardoso Kamukolo, shoemaker) centers on the telling of a story that is set in an independent Angola. This story within a story begins with a narrative projection into the future in which a second storyteller relates a tale of the past, which is actually the present setting of the original narration. The grandfather, the future storyteller, begins his tale with the formulaic opening of traditional oral tales in Angola. He compares his own tale to the traditional ones, as "estórias do nosso povo" (stories of our people). In this manner, his exemplary story of Cardoso Kamukolo, a shoemaker who dies defending a child from a vigilante mob of angry Portuguese in Luanda, also pertains to the collective culture of a future and independent Angola.

LUUANDA AND *VELHAS ESTÓRIAS*: CREATING AN ANGOLAN LITERARY FORM AND LANGUAGE

Written while Luandino Vieira was imprisoned in Luanda, *Luuanda* received the Prémio Literário Angolano Mota Veiga, the highest Angolan literary prize, in 1964. The following year, a jury of Portuguese writers and critics awarded *Luuanda* the Portuguese Writers Society's grand prize for fiction. A controversy followed over the decision to bestow that honor on a work whose author was imprisoned for political activities against the totalitarian Portuguese New State. Members of the jury were interrogated by the secret police, and the Portuguese Writers Society was disbanded. The book was revised in 1972 while Luandino Vieira was in restricted residence in Lisbon and was translated into English in 1980 with the same title.

Luuanda represents a break from Luandino Vieira's earlier fiction, but it does not abandon the realistic representation of social conditions within a contested colonial regime. However, the collection of stories demonstrates a distinct change in narrative focus toward the actual process of narration, the question of how to narrate a story. *Luuanda* also represents Luandino Vieira's first explicit use of the *estória* form: two of the three stories include the word in their titles. The term *estória* specifies the literary incorporation of Angolan oral storytelling techniques and is used in contrast to Portuguese literary terms, such as *conto* (short story) and *história* (story). For Luandino Vieira, the *estória* is related to the *missosso*—traditional oral tales or allegories in Kimbundu, one of the several Bantu languages spoken in Angola—and represents a collective literary form. In this sense, the *estória* is a story that may be retold in many different ways, depending on the circumstances of narration. It is, then, an open form in which the written narrative represents but one possible recounting.

In *Luuanda* this open form of the *estória* appears most explicitly in "Estória do ladrão e do papagaio" ("Tale of the Thief and the Parrot"), in which the narrator not only relates the story but also directly addresses the question of how to "pôr a estória," how to "put the story." This phrase, used in Luandino Vieira's texts as an oral formulaic opening—"vou pôr a estória" ("I will now tell the story")—represents an Angolan literary version of the opening of the traditional Kimbundu *missosso*—"eme ngateletele"—an iterative form that means "I will tell this story several times." In "Tale of the Thief and the Parrot," the narrative questioning on how to tell the story leads to an extended analogy to a cashew tree (*cajueiro*) with an intricate network of roots that makes it indestructible. The *estória*, too, has multiple roots, or stories, that inform each narration. The narrator of "Tale of the Thief and the Parrot" must decide which story root to choose for this telling. In this case, the narrator focuses on the parrot, but the *estória* actually represents a convergence of stories, so that a different narrative approach would result in another version of the same *estória.* In this sense, Luandino Vieira's written incorporation of the traditional *missosso* emphasizes how the open and repetitive dynamics of orature allow for variation rather than duplication.

"Estória da galinha e do ovo" ("The Tale of the Hen and the Egg") also employs elements of traditional Angolan orature. This *estória* takes the form of a *maka,* which in Kimbundu culture involves a dispute, pleading by all sides, and a judgment on who is right or wrong. This story's *maka* focuses on an argument between two neighbors who both claim an egg—laid by a hen that belongs to another woman—found in each other's yard. Five characters from different sectors of society are summoned to judge the case. Since this is an *estória,* each character has his or her own story, a situation that presents possibilities for variations of the "The Tale of the Hen and the Egg." The ending of the story also is formulaic and invites the audience—in this case, the readers—to judge the *estória* for itself.

If *Luuanda* marks a turning point in Luandino Vieira's narrative style, that juncture also signals a transformation in his literary language. The texts that preceded *Luuanda* valorize the marginalized popular speech patterns of colonial Angola. *Luuanda* continues this practice but at the same time introduces new forms of language based on existing popular speech. These new forms have their roots in words or expressions used in Luanda and are derived either from popular practice or from the Kimbundu language. These neologisms, as well as words or expressions in Kimbundu and popular forms of creolized Portuguese spoken in Luanda, appeared without translation or footnotes until the eighth edition of *Luuanda,* which was published in Portugal in 1981. Luandino Vieira refused to provide even a glossary, because he was writing for people who spoke the language of his narratives, not for the Portuguese colonizers. The title of *Luuanda* suggests his intent: it is the transcription from the Kimbundu, in opposition to the Europeanized Portuguese spelling of the name of the city. In this way, even though the *estórias* in *Luuanda* move away from the overt political content of his two previous texts, a political statement of solidarity appears in the transformation of literary form and language through a subversive use of popular cultural practices.

Luandino Vieira's use of an open narrative form that focuses on the production of the *estória* itself is developed further in *Velhas estórias* (1974; Old *estórias*). Three of the four narratives in this collection were written during the same period as *Luuanda* but were revised by Luandino Vieira between 1965 and 1966, after his transfer to Tarrafal. In "Estória da Menina Santa" (Tale of Miss Santa), as in "The Tale of the Thief and the Parrot" in *Luuanda,* the narration involves an overt sorting out of the multiple stories of the *estória.* In this instance, the *estória* of Miss Santa's pregnancy assumes a complex and plural form as it incorporates the stories of the Portuguese merchant António Júlio dos Santos and how he became Julinho Kanini, the expansion of the Makutu neighborhood, and Kanini's arrest on charges of diamond trafficking. The narrative search to determine the form of the *estória* complicates other roots and other stories, so that this narration represents only one possible telling within the plural *estória* form and, again, does not preclude other potential versions.

The question of how to produce an *estória* also forms a central focus of the collection's final narrative, "O último quinzar do Makulusu" (The last *quinzar* of Makulusu). The narrator recounts how he and his childhood friends from the Luanda neighborhood of Makulusu would listen to Sá Domingas' tales that had been passed down from previous generations. The old woman does not simply repeat the stories but, rather, continually reinvents her tales so that they differ with each telling. This *estória* of the mythical half-human, half-animal *quinzar* (similar to a werewolf) opens and closes with the same formula used by the narrators in *Luuanda.*

Velhas estórias also demonstrates the new linguistic direction taken in *Luuanda* through a creative practice based on the use of popular speech patterns. The collection's first *estória*, "Muadiê Gil, o Sobral e o barril" (Master Gil, Sobral, and the barrel), concerns a dispute over a barrel of wine customarily received after the completion of a construction job. The dispute also takes the form of a linguistic confrontation between Sobral, the self-appointed spokesperson for the Angolan workers, and Muadiê Gil, their Portuguese boss. Sobral makes free use of creolized Portuguese, Kimbundu, English, French, and standard Portuguese. The workers eventually receive their wine, but the linguistic duel reflects a larger political context and underscores the links between political and cultural independence.

NÓS, OS DO MAKULUSU: QUESTIONING COLLECTIVITY

Luandino Vieira's second novel, *Nós, os do Makulusu* (1974; We, those from Makulusu) was written in 1967, while he was imprisoned in Tarrafal. Several themes from his earlier works converge in this novel, although the primary focus is on the disruption to collectivity in the early period of the Angolan nationalist struggle. In this sense, more than ten years after writing *A cidade e a infância,* Luandino Vieira returns to the theme of fragmented collectivity and, more important, rethinks the values of the idealized past and how to build a new collectivity in an independent Angola.

This narrative questioning is prefigured in the text's epigraph, which comes from the traditional Kimbundu *maka*: "Kututunda ni Kutuia" (The past and the future). In this tale, two men, Kututunda (the past) and Kutuia (the future) ask a palm-wine tapper for a drink. The tapper refuses Kututunda on the grounds that his name represents evil. The judge decides the *maka* in favor of Kutuia, who personifies the future, and his judgment opens *Nós, os do Makulusu.* The novel ends with the title phrase followed by a question mark. In the context of the narrative questioning, only the future can provide answers to the open ending, whether history will permit the survival of the title "we" of Makulusu.

The novel follows the stream-of-consciousness and nonsequential narration of Mais-Velho (literally, "the older one"; in this case, "the older brother"), the elder child of Portuguese settlers in Luanda. The death of the narrator's younger brother, Maninho ("little brother"), serves as the catalyst for a highly reflective narrative that is, above all, associative. In other words, the narrative stream of consciousness combines views of the past, present, and future in relation to a specific narrative event. For instance, Maninho's funeral and burial are recounted from the perspective of Mais-Velho, who relives the experiences and their emotional impact by re-creating them as narrative discourse. Events are recalled repeatedly, each time incorporating new elements that lead to a series of questionings and realizations that culminate in the novel's final question about the future of the "we" of the narration.

This "we" represents the four from Makulusu — Mais-Velho; Maninho; their younger, mulatto half brother Paizinho; and their African friend Kibiaka. Inseparable friends, the four choose different paths that represent the breakdown of collectivity and the explosion of armed conflict. In this sense, the stream-of-consciousness narration is informed at every stage by visions of Portuguese colonialism. As part of that larger history,

Mais-Velho's introspections, retrospections, and interrogations expose the contradictions of Portuguese domination manifest in socioeconomic, racial, and cultural inequality. Thus, the narrative reconstruction of the past world of the "we" of Makulusu reveals a collectivity always conditioned by colonial practices and ideologies.

In *A cidade e a infância,* the textualizations of the collective past give voice to the fragmentation precipitated by the influx of white settlers and the destruction of conditions that permitted a coexistence, however problematic, of different racial and cultural groups. *Nós, os do Makulusu* moves beyond displacement. The setting of the novel captures the total disruption in the past, while the cumulative introspections of the narration lay bare the contradictions inherent to the always tense collectivity. In *Nós, os do Makulusu,* the disintegration of collectivity is most vividly represented by the diverse paths of the childhood friends and brothers. Maninho becomes a junior officer in the Portuguese colonial army, and thus helps to perpetuate white domination. Mais-Velho and Paizinho pursue the course of clandestine organization and politicization, and Kibiaka becomes a guerrilla fighter in the nationalist movement.

The novel's final question incorporates Mais-Velho's realization that the diverse paths of the "we," while contesting the colonial system, also destroy the "we." Ultimately, however, that destruction becomes necessary so that a future based on relations of equality can be constructed. In this way the future remains an uncertainty, an open interrogation projected from within the fragmentation of past collectivity and of present conflict. *Nós, os do Makulusu,* like the traditional Kimbundu *maka* that opens its narrative, decides in favor of that uncertain future but does not negate the past. The physical destruction of the world of Makulusu and the breakdown of the "we" are irreparable; the novel questions whether the positive values that emerged from the contradictions of a collectivity in conflict can be reconciled in the uncertain aftermath of armed confrontation.

ELABORATION OF THE *ESTÓRIA* AND ANGOLAN LITERARY LANGUAGE

Although written as a novel, *Nós, os do Makulusu* has characteristics of the *estória.* It is informed by multiple stories, and its narration bears striking similarities to the open, plural, and nonlinear *estória.* Furthermore, the preeminent position of the storyteller in *Luuanda* and *Velhas estórias,* in which the narration follows a search to identify the *estória*'s roots amid a multiplicity of stories, finds a counterpart in Mais-Velho, whose associative narration is a search to give narrative form to the fragmented memory of the collective past. The novel may not directly involve the textualization of oral storytelling techniques, but the meanderings of Mais-Velho's stream of consciousness are not unlike those of orature.

The concern with how to produce an *estória* also determines the nonlinear narrative movement of Luandino Vieira's long *estória, João Vêncio: Os seus amores* (1979; *Loves of João Vêncio*), which was written in 1968 at Tarrafal. This *estória* uses a first-person narrator—João Vêncio—who tells his life stories to an unheard interlocutor, a narrative technique that Luandino Vieira also used in his *estória* "Kinaxixi Kiami," which was written in 1971. The dialogue-narration is not one-sided, however, for even though only one voice is reproduced in the text, João Vêncio continually addresses, answers, and questions the interlocutor.

Loves of João Vêncio, like many of Luandino Vieira's *estórias,* begins in midstream, in the middle of a conversation between the title character and the interlocutor, both of whom are in prison. The root of this *estória* is the interlocutor's question about João Vêncio's imprisonment. This one question opens the narrative to the multiplicity of stories that constitute João Vêncio's seemingly simple tale, for his imprisonment originates not only from a specific act of attempted homicide but also from his cumulative life experiences. João Vêncio is all too aware of the role that the interlocutor will play, and so he enters into a narrative pact with the latter. This pact is symbolized by the *missanga* (bead) necklace, which the two prisoners string to occupy their time. Together they construct both the necklace of colored beads and the *estória* of many stories. This multiplicity also can be perceived in João Vêncio's description of "his loves" as a star-shaped form, which he describes in stories that branch out from a center. These stories, however, are not independent of one another, since the *estória* takes its nonlinear and plural form from their convergence.

The nonlinear characteristic of the *estória* undoubtedly has its roots in oral tradition and the freedom of narration that belongs to each storyteller. Thus, the narrator-storyteller of "Pedro Caliota, sapateiro-andante" (Pedro Caliota, traveling shoemaker), which was written in 1971 and published in *Macandumba* (1978), begins the *estória* with Caliota's attempt to buy back a fish that he sold earlier in the day. In the middle of the narration, however, the story is interrupted so that the narrator can comment on the reverse movement of narration. The *estória* assumes this backward motion until it reaches its true root, the discovery of money in the belly of Caliota's last remaining fish. The plural nature of the *estória* is evident through Caliota's encounters during his wanderings in Luanda, for all the people he meets have their own stories. The plurality is also reflected in Caliota's own story as he wanders through Luanda believing in the good fortune of life's events. His violent death, however, is set in the historical context of the 1961 outbreak of armed conflict in Luanda. Moreover, his death is totally unexpected, and if the narrator-storyteller chastises the shoemaker for believing himself immortal and not being aware of the political context, the readers find themselves similarly caught off guard and rebuked for not being aware of the pluralistic text.

This attention to text and context also marks the second *estória* in *Macandumba*, "Cangundos, verdianos, santomistas, nossa gente." *Cangundos* is local slang for "whites"; *verdianos* and *santomistas* are renditions of popular forms of *caboverdianos* (Cape Verdeans) and *sãotomense* (people from São Tomé); *nossa gente* means "our people." This *estória* begins with the creolized Kimbundu-Portuguese lyrics of a song attributed to the musical group Ritmo Iaxikelela. Both the song and the band are inventions of Luandino Vieira, but the lyrics provide the key to the mystery of the counterfeit lottery ticket that is at the root of the *estória*. Only those who understand the creolized text can solve the mystery.

Thus, this *estória* constitutes a linguistic confrontation, not unlike the one in "Muadiê Gil, o Sobral e o barril." In "Cangundos, verdianos, santomistas, nossa gente," the storyteller continually interrupts the narration to question both the roots of the *estória* and the different social levels of language in the Sambizanga neighborhood of Luanda. Local forms of Portuguese mix freely with Cape Verdean creole, pretentious upper-class Portuguese, Kimbundu, legal language in Portuguese, and creolized speech adding to the confusion of the *estória*. Sorting out the confusion, though, is possible only for those who comprehend and manipulate the various social levels of language and are, by implication, part of "our people."

Language is also the key to understanding the earlier *estórias* of *No antigamente, na vida* (1974; In the past, in life), which was written in 1969. "Memória narrativa ao sol de Kinaxixi" (Narrative memory in the Kinaxixi sun) begins with the recollection of a word, the letter-by-letter reconstruction of "Urânia," the name of a girl whom Dinho, the narrator, claims to have met. Urânia supposedly is the apparition of the waters of the Kinaxixi neighborhood, and Dinho tells the story of their meeting to a group of Kinaxixi children. Although he does not belong to the group because he has not passed its initiation tests, he uses language and the telling of the story to gain control of the group. Dinho's position, therefore, is similar to that of Turito in "Lá em Tetembuatubia" (There, in Tetembuatubia), another *estória* in *No antigamente, na vida.* Turito, a sickly boy, mixes the French he hears from nuns in the hospital with Latin from his mother's prayers to transform his language and win over the other boys through the power of his words. Dinho likewise wins a victory through his language at the moment he realizes that it can transform reality.

CONCLUSION

Luandino Vieira's elaboration of the *estória* evokes the immediacy of oral performance and its reception. The incorporation of techniques of orature underscore the "popular" nature of the *estória* as a new literary form for a new Angolan literature. The various facets of this form — the use of the traditional *missosso,* the open narrative, simultaneous production and narration — have been adapted by other contemporary Angolan writers of fiction who term their works "estórias."

The pluralization of the *estória* gains further significance in relation to an experimentation with literary language. The latter also is based on popular cultural practices that are re-created in literary discourse so that experimentations with literary forms and languages retain collective roots in Angolan culture. Perhaps more than experimentation, Luandino Vieira's narratives have participated in a continuing elaboration and transformation of literary forms and languages that move beyond mere negation of acculturated practices to the creation of a new Angolan literature.

Selected Bibliography

SELECTED WORKS

A cidade e a infância. Lisbon, Portugal: Casa dos Estudantes do Império, 1960. Repr. Lisbon, Portugal: Edições 70, 1978.

"Os amores de Silva Chalado." In *Jornal de Angola* (30 September 1961).

Duas histórias de pequenos burgueses. Sá da Bandeira (Lubango), Angola: Imbondeiro, 1961.

Primeira canção do mar. Sá da Bandeira (Lubango), Angola: Imbondeiro, 1961.

"Zé Fintacai." In *Jornal de Angola* (31 December 1961).

"Os miúdos de Capitão Bento." In *Novos contos de Africa.* Sá da Bandeira (Lubango), Angola: Imbondeiro, 1962.

"Miúdo camba." In *Jornal de Angola* (Christmas/New Year supp. 1962–1963).

Luuanda. Luanda, Angola: ABC, 1964. Repr. Lisbon, Portugal: Edições 70, 1972; 8th ed., 1981.

No antigamente, na vida. Lisbon, Portugal: Edições 70, 1974.

Velhas estórias. Lisbon, Portugal: Plátano Editora, 1974.

A vida verdadeira de Domingos Xavier. Lisbon, Portugal: Edições 70, 1974.

Nós, os do Makulusu. Lisbon, Portugal: Sá da Costa, 1974.

Vidas novas. Porto, Portugal: Edições Afrontamento, 1975.

Macandumba. Lisbon, Portugal: Edições 70, 1978; Luanda, Angola: União dos Escritores Angolanos, 1978.

João Vêncio: Os seus amores. Lisbon, Portugal: Edições 70, 1979; Luanda, Angola: União dos Escritores Angolanos, 1979.

Lourentinho, Dona Antónia de Sousa Neto e eu. Lisbon, Portugal: Edições 70, 1981.

Estória de Baciazinha de Quitaba. Luanda, Angola: Cardernos Lavra e Oficina, 1986.

TRANSLATIONS

The Real Life of Domingos Xavier. Trans. by Michael Wolfers. London: Heinemann, 1978.

Luuanda. Trans. by Tamara L. Bender. London: Heinemann, 1980.

Loves of João Vêncio. Trans. by Richard Zenith. San Diego, Calif.: Harcourt Brace Jovanovich, 1991.

CRITICAL STUDIES

Burness, Donald. *Fire: Six Writers from Angola, Mozambique, and Cape Verde*. Washington, D.C.: Three Continents, 1977.

Butler, Phyllis Reisman. "Colonial Resistance and Contemporary Angolan Narrative." In *Modern Fiction Studies* 35 (spring 1989).

———. "Writing a National Literature: The Case of José Luandino Vieira." In Roberto Reis, ed., *Toward Socio-Criticism: Selected Proceedings of the Conference "Luso-Brazilian Literatures, a Socio-Critical Approach."* Tempe: Center for Latin American Studies, Arizona State University, 1991.

Hamilton, Russell. *Voices from an Empire*. Minneapolis: University of Minnesota Press, 1975.

———. "Black from White and White on Black: Contradictions of Language in the Angolan Novel." In *Ideologies and Literature* 1 (December 1976/January 1977).

———. *Literatura africana, literatura necessária*. Vol. 1, *Angola*. Lisbon, Portugal: Edições 70, 1981.

Jacinto, Tomás. "The Art of Luandino Vieira." In Donald Burness, ed., *Critical Perspectives on Lusophone African Literature*. Washington, D.C.: Three Continents, 1981.

Laban, Michel, et al. *Luandino: José Luandino Vieira e a sua obra*. Lisbon, Portugal: Edições 70, 1980.

Reisman, Phyllis. "José Luandino Vieira and the New Angolan Fiction." In *Luso-Brazilian Review* 24 (summer 1987).

Trigo, Salvato. *Luandino Vieira o logoteta*. Porto, Portugal: Brasília Editora, 1981.

About the Contributors

Funso Aiyejina. Poet, short-story writer, and critic. Lecturer in English, University of the West Indies, St. Augustine, Trinidad. Fulbright Scholar-in-Residence, Lincoln University, Jefferson City, Mo., 1995–1996. Has contributed poems, short stories, articles (on African and West Indian literature), and reviews to a variety of journals, including *Okike*, *Nigeria Magazine*, *West Africa*, *African Literature Today*, *World Literature Written in English*, *Kunapipi*, *Greenfield Review*, *Trinidad and Tobago Review*, *Literary Half-Yearly*, and *CRNLE Review Journal*. Publications also include chapters in *Black Culture and Black Consciousness in Literature*; *Nigerian Female Writers*; and *Perspectives on Nigerian Literature*, volumes I and II. Has had poems included in several anthologies of African poetry. Winner of Association of Nigerian Authors' Poetry Prize in 1989 for *A Letter to Lynda and Other Poems*. CHRISTOPHER OKIGBO

Nwamaka B. Akukwe. Freelance writer. Studied linguistics and African literature at the University of Nigeria, Nsukka. Taught English at the same university during the 1989–1990 Sandwich Programme. Completed a degree in law at the University of Leeds, United Kingdom, in June 1995. MARIAMA BÂ

Peter F. Alexander. Professor of English, University of New South Wales, United Kingdom. Author of *Roy Campbell: A Critical Biography*; *William Plomer: A Biography*; *Leonard and Virginia Woolf: A Literary Partnership*; and *Alan Paton: A Biography*. ALAN PATON

Roger Michael Ashley Allen. Professor of Arabic, University of Pennsylvania. Arabic Literatures Editor of the *Encyclopedia of World Literature of the Twentieth Century*. Editorial board member for *World Literature Today*. Managing Editor of the *Journal of Arabic Literature*. Coeditor of *The Cambridge History of Arabic Literature: The Post-Classical Period*. Author and editor of numerous books and articles on Arabic literature and Najīb Maḥfūẓ. Translator of several Arabic novels. NAJĪB MAḤFŪẒ

Uko Atai. Senior Lecturer in Drama/Theater and former Acting Head, Department of Dramatic Arts, Obafemi Awolowo University, Ile Ife, Nigeria. Author of *Saprites*, a 1989 British Council/Association of Nigerian Authors' Drama Award winner; and *Back-stage*, a 1992 British Council/Association of Nigerian Authors' Drama Award winner. Other publications include numerous critical essays in journals and chapters in books on the theory and practice of modern African, European, and American drama and theater. KOLE OMOTOSO

Ronald Ayling. Professor of English, University of Alberta, Edmonton, Canada. Lecturer in English, Rhodes University, South Africa, 1958–1964. Senior Research Fellow, Melbourne University, Australia, 1978–1979. Paschall Vacca Professor in Liberal Studies, Montevallo, Ala., 1992–1993. Author of *Sean O'Casey: A Bibliography* and *Continuity and Innovation in Sean O'Casey's Drama*. Has served as O'Casey's literary executor since O'Casey's death in 1964. Editor of several books on O'Casey and on J. M. Synge. Author of many articles on Anglo-Irish literature and on African writers such as Wole Soyinka, Chinua Achebe, Athol Fugard, and J. M. Coetzee. ANDRÉ BRINK

Martin Banham. Professor of Drama and Theatre Studies and Director of the Workshop Theatre, University of Leeds, United Kingdom. Editor of *The Cambridge Guide to Theatre*. Coeditor, with Errol Hill and George Woodyard, of *The Cambridge Guide to African and Caribbean Theatre*. OLA ROTIMI

Charles Bonn. Professeur and Directeur, Centre d'Etudes Littéraires Francophones et Comparées, Université Paris 13. Author of *Le Roman algérien de langue francaise* and *Kateb Yacine,* Nedjma. Editor of *Anthologie de la littérature algérienne.* MOHAMMED DIB and KATEB YACINE

David Brookshaw. Head of the Department of Hispanic, Portuguese, and Latin American Studies, University of Bristol, United Kingdom. Author of *Race and Color in Brazilian Literature* and *Paradise Betrayed: Brazilian Literature of the Indian.* Has a special interest in literature and national identity and has published widely on African literature in Portuguese. MIA COUTO and LUÍS BERNARDO HONWANA

Pierre Cachia. Professor Emeritus of Arabic Language and Literature, Columbia University, New York. Previously taught at American University in Cairo and University of Edinburgh, United Kingdom. Author of *Ṭāhā Ḥusayn: His Place in the Egyptian Literary Renaissance*; *Popular Narrative Ballads of Modern Egypt*; and *An Overview of Modern Arabic Literature.* Joint author of *History of Islamic Spain.* Editor and translator of various works. Contributor to journals and works of reference. Cofounder and joint editor of the *Journal of Arabic Literature.* ṬĀHĀ ḤUSAYN

Robert Cancel. Associate Professor of African and Comparative Literature, University of California, San Diego. Author of *Allegorical Speculation in an Oral Society: The Tabwa Narrative Tradition*, and numerous essays on African written and oral literatures and African cinema. Currently finishing a critical anthology of oral narratives of Bemba-speaking people of Zambia. NGŨGĨ WA THIONG'O

Shirley Chew. School of English, University of Leeds, United Kingdom. Coeditor of *Into the Nineties: Post-Colonial Women's Writing* and *Unbecoming Daughters of the Empire.* Editor of *Selected Poems* by Arthur Hugh Clough. AMA ATA AIDOO

Cherry Clayton. Writer and Lecturer in English, University of Guelph, Ontario, Canada. Editor of *Women and Writing in South Africa: A Critical Anthology.* Author of the poetry collection *Leaving Home* and numerous articles on Olive Schreiner. OLIVE SCHREINER

Rosemary Colmer. School of English and Linguistics, Macquarie University, Sydney, Australia. AYA KWEI ARMAH and ALEX LA GUMA

John D. Conteh-Morgan. Associate Professor of French and Francophone Literature, Ohio State University. Associate Editor of *Research in African Literatures.* Author of *Theater and Drama in Francophone Africa* and contributor to *The Cambridge Guide to African and Caribbean Theatre* and to *The Cambridge Guide to Theatre.* MONGO BETI and CAMARA LAYE

C. Brian Cox. Emeritus Professor, Manchester University, United Kingdom. Chair, Northwest Arts Board, England. Chair, Arvon Foundation, England. Author of *The Great Betrayal, Collected Poems, An English Curriculum for the 1990s,* and *The Battle for the English Curriculum.* Editor

Guy Dugas. Professor of Mediterranean Francophone Literature, Université Paul Valéry, Montpellier III. Faculty member, Centre International d'Études Francophones, Université Paris IV–Sorbonne. Member of the editorial boards of *L'Anée francophone internationale* and of *Les Carnets de l'exotisme.* Editor of *Bulletin de littérature générale et comparée.* Author of *Entre Djeha et Cagayous: La Littérature judéo maghrébine d'expression française*; *Bibliographie critique de la littérature judéo maghrébine d'expression française*; *Les Orients de Henry de Montherlant*; and *Maroc impérial.* Currently writing "Albert Memmi, from Jewish Native Misfortune to Writing Sephardic Happiness" and "Algeria's Go-between Novelists." ALBERT MEMMI

Chris Dunton. Associate Professor, National University of Lesotho. Author of *Make Man Talk True: Nigerian Drama in English Since 1970.* Now preparing a comprehensive bibliography of Nigerian English-language drama. FERDINAND OYONO

John Fletcher. Professor of European Literature, University of East Anglia, Norwich, United Kingdom. Author of *The Novels of Samuel Beckett, Claude Simon and Fiction Now, Novel and Reader*, and *Alain Robbe-Grillet.* ROY CAMPBELL and ALBERT CAMUS; translator of MOHAMMED DIB, KATEB YACINE, and ALBERT MEMMI

James Gibbs. Visiting Lecturer, University of the West of England, Bristol. Critic, teacher, director, and playwright. Has worked at the Universities of Ghana, Malawi, Ibadan, Liege, and Bristol. Specializes in African writing in English and within that area on work for the theater. EFUA THEODORA SUTHERLAND

Damian Grant. Department of English, University of Manchester. Author of *Tobias Smollett: A Study in Style.* CHRISTOPHER HOPE

Gareth Griffiths. Professor of English, University of Western Australia. Author of *A Double Exile: African and West Indian Writing Between Two Cultures.* Coauthor, with Bill Ashcroft and Helen Tiffin, of *The Empire Writes Back: Theory and Practice in Post-Colonial Literatures*, and coeditor, with Ashcroft and Tiffin, of *The Post-Colonial Studies Reader.* Has also written a monograph on John Osborne's *Look Back in Anger* and edited a collection of essays on the Australian radical dramatist John Romeril. Has published numerous essays on modern drama; on African, West Indian, Indian, Southeast Asian, and Australian writing in English; and on postcolonial literary theory. Is currently researching and writing a commissioned volume, *A History of African Literatures (East and West).* OBI EGBUNA and FEMI OSOFISAN

Sabry Hafez. Department of Near and Middle East, University London, United Kingdom. Author of *The Genesis of Arabic Narrative Discourse: A Study in the Sociology of Modern Arabic Literature.* Coeditor of *A Reader of Modern Arabic Short Stories.* YŪSUF IDRĪS

James Harrison. Professor Emeritus, Department of English, University of Guelph, Ontario, Canada. Publications include *Rudyard Kipling*; *Salman Rushdie*; two books of poetry; and numerous articles on the history of ideas and on Victorian and postcolonial literature. J. M. COETZEE

Abiola Irele. Professor of African, French, and Comparative Literature, Ohio State University. Author of numerous essays in journals and of *The African Experience in Literature and Ideology.* Editor of *Selected Poems of Léopold Sédar Senghor* and *Aimé Césaire: Cahier d'un retour au pays natal.* LÉOPOLD SÉDAR SENGHOR

G. D. Killam. Professor, Department of English, University of Guelph, Ontario, Canada. Author of *Africa in English Fiction, The Novels of Chinua Achebe, The Writings of Chinua Achebe*, and *An Introduction to the Writings of Ngũgĩ.* Editor of *African Writers on African Writing* and *Critical Perspectives on Ngũgĩ wa Thiong'o.* CHINUA ACHEBE, TANURE OJAIDE, and NIYI OSUNDARE

Daniel P. Kunene. Professor, Department of African Languages and Literature, University of Wisconsin at Madison. Poet. Author of *The Works of Thomas Mofolo: Summaries and Critiques*; *Heroic Poetry of the Basotho*; *The Ideophone in Southern Sotho*; *A Seed Must Seem to Die*; *Pirates Have Become Our Kings: Poems*; and *Thomas Mofolo and the Emergence of Written Sesotho Prose.* Wrote the text for Bernard van Beurden's *Soweto: For Choir, Two String Quartets, Double Bass and Percussion, 1989.* Translated Mofolo's *Chaka.* THOMAS MOKUPU MOFOLO

J. Roger Kurtz. Assistant Professor of Contemporary Literatures in English, Idaho State University. Author of articles on Francis Imbuga, Peter Nazareth, Lloyd Fernando, Joseph Conrad, and Marjorie Macgoye. Currently working on a history of Kenyan literature. MEJA MWANGI

Bernth Lindfors. Professor of English and African Literatures, University of Texas at Austin. Founding editor of *Research in African Literatures.* Has written or edited more than thirty books on African literatures, including *Early Nigerian Literature* and *Popular Literatures in Africa.* Coeditor of the *Dictionary of Literary Biography* series on *Twentieth-Century Caribbean and Black African Writers.* DENNIS BRUTUS

Robert McDowell. Publisher and Editor, Story Line Press. Author of *Quiet Money* (poems); *The Diviners* (book-length poem); *Because We Love the Night* (poems); and *Sound and Form in Modern Poetry*, with Harvey Gross. Translator, with Jindriska Badal, of Ota Pavel's *How I Came to Know Fish* (Czech short stories). Editor of *Poetry After Modernism.* NURUDDIN FARAH

Obi Maduakor. Associate Professor of English, University of Nigeria, Nsukka. Author of *Wole Soyinka: An Introduction to His Writing*, and numerous essays, reviews, and articles on African literature. FESTUS IYAYI

Dinah Manisty. Translator and critic. Translator of *The Golden Chariot*, by Egyptian writer Salwa Bakr (part of a series of four Arab women in translation). Author of articles on Arab women's autobiographical writings, the "mad heroine" in female narrative, and writing "the self" in modern Arabic literature. Research interest in contemporary poetry of the Arab world. Currently working on the translation of contemporary Arab poets. NAWĀL AL-SAʿADĀWĪ

Khalid al Mubarak. Assistant Head of Programming, MBC TV, London. Associate Professor (Research Associate), African Studies Centre, Cambridge University, United Kingdom. Author of *Arabic Drama: A Critical Introduction*; *Harf wa-nuqtah*, a work of criticism on Arabic literature; a chapter in G. W. Brandt, ed., *British Television Drama*; the collection of plays *Tilka al-nazrah*; the play *Rish al-naam*; and other prizewinning plays published in anthologies by the BBC and Deutsche Welle. SEMBÈNE OUSMANE

Osita Okagbue. Senior Lecturer in Theatre Studies, University of Plymouth, United Kingdom. Author of articles on African and Caribbean theater in *Maske und Kothurn, Contemporary Dramatists, Contemporary American Dramatists, ASSAPH, Okike Educational Supplement*, and *New Literatures Review.* JOHN PEPPER CLARK and BODE SOWANDE

Chidi Okonkwo. School of English Studies, University of Wales, United Kingdom. CYPRIAN EKWENSI

Robin Ostle. Fellow and Tutor in Modern Arabic, St. John's College, Oxford University. Editor of *Modern Literature in the Near and Middle East 1850–1970*. Author of the chapter on the Romantic poets in the modern volume of *The Cambridge History of Arabic Literature*. Executive Editor for modern Arabic literature in the *Journal of Arabic Literature*. ABŪ AL-QĀSIM AL-SHĀBBĪ

Oyekan Owomoyela. Professor of English, University of Nebraska, Lincoln. Has published several articles on African literatures. Books include *African Literatures: An Introduction* and *Visions and Revisions: Essays on African Literatures and Criticism*. Editor of *A History of Twentieth-Century African Literatures*. AMOS TUTUOLA

Andrew Peek. Senior Lecturer, Department of Humanities, University of Tasmania, Australia. Publications include articles, interviews, and book reviews. Editor of journals on postcolonial literatures, with a particular emphasis on African literature. Lectured in English at the University of Ife in Nigeria for three years. PETER ABRAHAMS and BESSIE HEAD

Phyllis A. Peres. Associate Professor, University of Maryland, College Park. Author of *Narrating Nation, Writing Angola* (forthcoming) and articles in *Callaloo*, *Luso-Brazilian Review*, *Modern Fiction Studies*, and *Dispositio*. AGOSTINHO NETO and JOSÉ LUANDINO VIEIRA

J. P. Odoch Pido. Lecturer, University of Nairobi, Kenya. Has presented papers on design, education, and African studies at conferences in India, Kenya, South Africa, and the United States. OKOT P'BITEK

Neil Powell. Freelance writer, editor, and lecturer. Publications include four collections of poetry (*At the Edge*, *A Season of Calm Weather*, *True Color*, and *The Stones on Thorpeness Beach*), a novel (*Unreal City*), a critical biography (*Roy Fuller: Writer and Society*), and a study of postwar English poetry (*Carpenters of Light*). Editor of *Selected Poems* of Fulke Greville. WILLIAM PLOMER

Ato Quayson. Faculty of English, University of Cambridge, and Fellow, Pembroke College, Cambridge, United Kingdom. Author of articles on African and postcolonial literature and author of the forthcoming *Strategic Transformations: A View of Nigerian Literary History from Rev. Samuel Johnson to Ben Okri*. Currently working on *Postcolonial Theory: A Critical Introduction*. BEN OKRI

Shelia Roberts. Professor of English, University of Wisconsin at Milwaukee. Visiting Professor, University of Tsukuba, Japan. South African novelist and short-story writer. Author of *Dan Jacobson: A Critical and Analytical Study*; three novels (*Johannesburg Requiem*, *The Weekenders*, and *Jacks in Corners*); two short-story collections (*This Time of Year* and *Coming In*); and several articles on Jacobson, Nadine Gordimer, and J. M. Coetzee. DAN JACOBSON

Sonya Rudikoff. Writer and critic on contemporary art, literature, feminism, and society. Author of numerous articles and reviews in *American Scholar*, *Hudson Review*, *Partisan Review*, and other journals. Extensive work on Virginia Woolf and other women writers. Engaged in a study of Mrs. Humphy Ward, Mrs. Oliphant, and writers and editors of the earlier feminist period. NADINE GORDIMER

Philip Sadgrove. Lecturer in Arabic Studies, University of Manchester, United Kingdom. Author of *The Egyptian Theatre in the Nineteenth Century*. Coauthor with Shmuel Moreh of *Jewish Contributions to Nineteenth-Century Arabic Theatre*. AL-ṬAYYIB ṢĀLIḤ

Lorna Sage. Professor of English Literature, University of East Anglia, Norwich, United Kingdom. Author of *Doris Lessing*; *Women in the House of Fiction*; *Angela Carter*; and numerous book reviews in the *Times Literary Supplement*, the *London Observer*, and the *London Review of Books*. Editor of *Flesh and the Mirror: Essays on the Art of Angela Carter*. Currently editing *The Cambridge Guide to Women's Writing in English*. DORIS LESSING

Christopher Smith. Reader in French, School of Modern Languages and European Studies, University of East Anglia, Norwich, United Kingdom. Has published on a wide range of French literature and modern English literature. Has additional interest in translation studies. BUCHI EMECHETA and LAURENS VAN DER POST

Paul G. Starkey. Senior Lecturer in Arabic, University of Durham, United Kingdom. Author of *From the Ivory Tower: A Critical Study of Tawfīq al-Ḥakīm* and numerous articles and reviews on modern Arabic literature. Editor of the *British Journal of Middle Eastern Studies*, 1990–1996. TAWFĪQ AL-ḤAKĪM

Peter N. Thuynsma. Executive Director, Institute for Human Rights Education. Former Associate Professor and Head of the Department of African Literature, University of the Witwatersrand, Johannesburg, South Africa. Author of *Footprints Along the Way: A Tribute to Es'kia Mphahlele* and several critical essays on oral and contemporary African writing. ES'KIA MPHAHLELE

Victor I. Ukaegbu. School of General Studies, Plateau State Polytechnic, Nigeria. Currently writing a dissertation on the aesthetics of Igbo masking in southeastern Nigeria. ATHOL FUGARD

Robert Clive Willis. Full Professor of Portuguese Studies, University of Manchester, United Kingdom. Author of *An Essential Course in Modern Portuguese.* Associate Editor of, and major contributor to, *Twentieth-Century Writing.* Major contributor to three Portuguese-English dictionaries. Author of numerous articles and book reviews on the literature, language, and history of Portugal, Brazil, and Portuguese-speaking Africa. PEPETELA

Derek Wright. Associate Professor of English, Northern Territory University, Darwin, Australia. Author of *Ayi Kwei Armah's Africa: The Sources of His Fiction*; *Wole Soyinka Revisited*; *The Novels of Nuruddin Farah*; and (recently completed) *New Directions in African Fiction 1970–1990: A Study of Twelve Novels*; plus numerous essays, articles, and reviews on world literatures in English. Editor of *Critical Perspectives on Ayi Kwei Armah* and *New African Writing and Criticism 1985–1995* (special journal issue). KOFI AWOONOR and WOLE SOYINKA

Chantal Zabus. Professor of English and Commonwealth Studies, University Louvain at Louvain-la-Neuve, Belgium. Author of *The African Palimpsest: Indigenization of Language in the West African Europhone Novel* and of essays on Joseph Conrad, Joyce Cary, and African and Canadian authors, on post-modern and postcolonial rewritings of Shakespeare's *The Tempest*, as well as on linguistics and feminism in postcolonial literature. GABRIEL OKARA

INDEX

Arabic numbers printed in boldface type refer to extended treatment of a subject. Volume I: 1–449; Volume II: 451–901.

A

B

C

D

E

F

G

H

I

J

K

L

O

Q

R

S

T

to work with such organizations as the Non-Violent League and the World Peace Brigade. The couple's three children, Esi Reiter, Ralph Gyan, and Muriel Amowi, who have since become a university teacher, an architect, and a lawyer, respectively, helped their mother in several theatrical projects.

CREATING A NATIONAL THEATRICAL TRADITION

The task of creating a national theatrical tradition was undertaken with a new urgency during the second half of the 1950s as the Gold Coast approached and, in 1957, achieved independence as Ghana. In addition to festivals, folk narratives, and performance conventions, the relevant traditions in the Gold Coast included creative writing both in local languages, such as Twi, Ewe, and Ga, and in English. There was also a history of literary societies in which cultural and political aspirations found expression.

In 1957, a writers' society came into existence with Sutherland as the prime mover. Eleven years later she told Lautre, "I started a Writers' Society . . . to get more people interested in [writing] primarily . . . for children" (p. 184). The new organization, supported by such distinguished and established authors as J. B. Danquah, J. H. Kwabena Nketia, and Michael Dei-Anang, recognized the need to produce a journal, which resulted in the publication of *Okyeame*.

In 1958 Sutherland was the driving force in creating the Ghana Experimental Theatre. She told Lautre: "To give another reason why people would want to write I . . . develop[ed] the experimental theatre programme" (p. 184). It built on existing interest in the theater and on an awareness that festivals and rituals were frequently spectacular and, in many instances, contained ingredients of the theater. The production of plays at schools, at teacher training colleges, and for radio blossomed. Since these were dominated by naturalistic conventions and stage plays were almost always presented behind proscenium arches, there was room for experiment. With the interest in "African personality" that marked the late 1950s and changing attitudes toward folk and popular culture came a greater acceptance of the traditions of drama and theater within Akan culture and within the mixture of cultures that had long flourished in towns near the coast, such as Cape Coast, Sekondi, and Takoradi.

The writers' society and the Experimental Theatre group came into existence when Ghana was at the forefront of the independence movement in sub-Saharan Africa. Prime Minister Kwame Nkrumah, who had a high profile as a spokesman for Pan-Africanism, proclaimed the importance of the arts in society and took a personal interest in several of Sutherland's projects. The national coffers were well stocked, and new life seemed to be flowing through the country. Sutherland's eloquence and striking presence, her contacts and ability to draw the best out of others propelled her into leadership roles. She became identified with the cultural and political movement that was bringing together different generations and different disciplines and uniting Ghanaians and those from the diaspora who had "returned" to share in the adventure of the independent nation. Her contribution to the movement was complemented by the work of others, such as Philip Gbeho in music, Kofi Antubam in art, J. H. Kwabena Nketia in research, and Joe de Graft in the theater.

POETRY

Developing a literary culture and taking the national theater movement into a new phase were slow processes. Laying foundations took time, and only after several years was it possible to identify achievements. Although her published output was small and her accomplishment in the form limited, Sutherland first made an impact as a poet. She began writing

On spacious premises with large playing fields, the students at Asante-Mampong could concentrate in a way that was not possible in crowded Cape Coast with all its distractions. The Sisters were making a substantial contribution to educating women in the country, drawing strength from their religious convictions and their base within the Anglican Church. Their missionary zeal was often communicated to the pupils, who were encouraged to contribute to improving the quality of life in nearby villages, in some of which Sunday schools had been started. One of the villages Sutherland visited was Kyerefaso, whose name she took for the title of her best-known story. In the villages, Sutherland developed an interest in nature and the environment, which the Sisters encouraged, and her experiences strengthened her feeling that her vocation was to be a teacher. At this stage, however, her vocation was intensely religious, and she considered becoming a nun.

In 1947, at the age of twenty-three and with five and a half years of teaching experience, Sutherland set off for England with a great sense of adventure to begin a two-year teacher-training course at Homerton College in Cambridge. She was impressed by the high standards, experimentation, and planning at the college and by the way her lecturers encouraged her desire to orient her work toward Africa. During her time at Homerton, where she specialized in education and divinity, she impressed those she worked with. They recorded their appreciation of her maturity, her personality, her care in preparing lessons, and the trouble she took to communicate clearly. Not surprisingly she conveyed to her geography classes a vivid sense of what it was like to live in Africa, and her English classes included not only textual analyses of Shakespeare's plays but also storytelling sessions.

From the beginning of her time in England, as she wrote in an August 1949 letter reproduced in an undated issue of *St. Monica Calling*, she resolved to keep her eyes and ears "wide open" and to ask many questions. The two years in Cambridge whetted her appetite for "work among students in [her] own country" (p. 26). Her exposure to the children's books and the material available to teachers in England was a revelation. What she saw made her determined to provide African children with books that reflected their own experiences and were attractively produced.

After leaving Cambridge, she went to London, where she spent a year at the University of London's School of Oriental and African Studies, specializing in English linguistics. She also took an interest in African languages and drama, which she saw as being taken seriously by academics and teachers. London in the late 1940s and early 1950s provided opportunities to meet some of those in the forefront of the struggle for African political and cultural independence.

Interviewed by Maxine Lautre in 1968, Sutherland spoke about being on "a journey of discovery" and referred to her Christian upbringing in Cape Coast, which had not exposed her to certain "hidden areas of Ghanaian life" (p. 189). She told Lee Nichols that she began taking writing seriously at Easter 1951, shortly after her return home from England, and started composing poetry. She indicated that the needs of children in the villages and of the student-teachers she was supervising stimulated her. The intense spiritual life of the Sisters of the Order of the Holy Paraclete may also have affected some of this verse and contributed a religious dimension.

In the early 1950s she married William Sutherland, an African American from Orange, New Jersey, who became involved in establishing a partly vocational school at Tsito in the Volta Region. When talking of this project, which encountered opposition from entrenched British prejudices, Sutherland gives great credit to her husband, who remained at the school from 1951 to 1957 before returning to Accra and then moving on of the Gold Coast), on 27 June 1924, named Nana Ama Nyankoma, and christened Theodora Olivia. The castles of Elmina, built in 1482 near where the European incursion into West Africa began, and of Cape Coast, constructed by Swedes in the 1650s, dominate the area and provide constant reminders of the centuries of contact between the coastal Fanti community into which Sutherland was born and Europe. Dungeons in which Africans had been imprisoned before being transported to the plantations of the Americas and rusting canons projecting over battlements draw attention to the inhumanity and violence of much of that contact.

Sutherland was related to those who had contributed significantly to the life of the local community. Her family included members of the royal house of Anomabu and nationalists who had joined the pioneering Aborigines' Rights Protection Society. Sutherland's mother, Olivia Morgue, was killed in a car accident at the age of eighteen. Following the accident, Sutherland's father, Harry Peter Morgue, a much respected teacher of English and other subjects, and her grandmother, Arba Mansah, became important influences.

During the first part of the twentieth century, Cape Coast developed into a major center for education, and Sutherland began her schooling at Saint Monica's School, an Anglican school founded in 1926 and staffed by Sisters of the Order of the Holy Paraclete, based in Yorkshire, England. She continued her education in Asante-Mampong, where the Sisters had a convent and primary boarding school. In 1936 the teacher training college, which the Sisters had established at Cape Coast, moved to Asante-Mampong, and in 1946 a secondary school was opened there. Sutherland became deeply involved with these institutions.

One of Sutherland's uncles was at Saint Monica's brother school, St. Nicholas Grammar School, Cape Coast, which later became Adisadel College. The school had important positions in a town that was sometimes called "the Athens of West Africa" and, in addition to academic and athletic activities, contributed to the cultural life of the community. For example, drama flourished at Adisadel, where the Athenian tradition was manifest in a series of productions of plays by classical dramatists: Sophocles' *Antigone* in 1934–1935, Aeschylus' *Agamemnon* in 1936, and Euripides' *Alcestis* in 1944–1945. In his history of the school, G. McLean Amissah reports that the choruses were spoken in Greek and that, by popular request, the production of *Antigone* was staged not only at the school but also in the town, in Sekondi, and in Kumasi.

TEACHING

From an early age, Sutherland expressed an interest in teaching, and in a sense her whole career reflects this vocation. At the age of about eighteen she started teaching at senior primary level and then joined the staff of Saint Monica's Training College. From 1947 to 1950 she was in England, first at Homerton College, Cambridge, and then, for a year, at the School of Oriental and African Studies at the University of London. On her return to the Gold Coast, she went back to Asante-Mampong and later transferred to Fijai Secondary School in Sekondi, and from there to Achimota School.

These moves are easily recorded, but the changes they involved and the experiences they afforded are more difficult to assess. First, when she left Cape Coast to continue her education in Asante-Mampong, a town beyond Kumasi, Sutherland was exposed to communities that had been comparatively little affected by European influences. Her coastal Fanti accent was distinct from the Akan spoken in the inland town. Some of the students who moved with the school from Cape Coast were frightened by the new environment and felt hemmed in by the forest and all that it contained.

Efua Theodora Sutherland

1924–1996

JAMES GIBBS

EFUA THEODORA SUTHERLAND'S "New Life at Kyerefaso" (1960) is one of the two most frequently anthologized pieces of prose by African writers, along with "The Complete Gentleman," a story from *The Palm-Wine Drinkard and His Dead Palm-Wine Tapster in the Deads' Town* (1952) by the Nigerian writer Amos Tutuola. Both stories originate in a folktale that is told in various ways along the West African coast. Briefly, it is the story of a proud young woman who rejects all the local suitors and marries a stranger, only to discover that he is a monster.

The tale has been interpreted in different ways. Tutuola, in a magnificent display of inventiveness, reduces the "complete gentleman," who cuts a dashing figure in the market, to a skull and puts the shallow young woman who was attracted by his outward appearance into a perilous position. Sutherland's version radically departs from both the original and Tutuola's retelling: her stranger impresses not through his appearance but because "he . . . mingles sweat and song," because for him "toil is joy and life is full and abundant." Foruwa, the young woman, is not proud but perceptive, not scornful of local suitors but appreciative of a man who has "travelled to see how men work in other lands" and has "that knowledge and . . . strength."

The stranger's craftsmanship—his skills as a builder, farmer, and weaver of baskets and *kente* cloth—impresses first Foruwa and then the community. A true inspiration, his example is followed, and, the storyteller informs the audience, "A new spirit stirred the village. . . . The people themselves became more alive and a new pride possessed them. They were no longer just grabbing from the land what they desired for their stomach's present hunger and for their present comfort." The brief story ends with a procession in which the fruits of the harvest are carried to the royal house where Foruwa's mother, the Queen Mother, waits to receive them. In this retelling of the story, which provides part of the plot of Sutherland's play *Foriwa* (1967), the young woman and her mother occupy center stage for much of the time. Foruwa makes a wise choice in accepting the stranger, and the "new spirit" that stirs in the village promises an illustrious future. Rough parallels can be drawn between Sutherland—her life and work—and "New Life at Kyerefaso," her most frequently published story.

CAPE COAST

Efua Sutherland (née Morgue) was born in Cape Coast, Ghana (then the British colony